HISTORICAL DICTIONARIES OF RELIGIONS, PHILOSOPHIES, AND MOVEMENTS
Edited by Jon Woronoff

Historical Dictionary of the Baptists

William H. Brackney

*Historical Dictionaries of Religions,
Philosophies, and Movements, No. 25*

The Scarecrow Press, Inc.
Lanham, Maryland, and London
1999

SCARECROW PRESS, INC.

Published in the United States of America
by Scarecrow Press, Inc.
4720 Boston Way, Lanham, Maryland 20706
http://www.scarecrowpress.com

4 Pleydell Gardens, Folkestone
Kent CT20 2DN, England

British Library Cataloguing in Publication Information Available

Library of Congress Cataloging-in-Publication Data

Brackney, William H.
    Historical dictionary of the Baptists / William H. Brackney.
        p.   cm. — (Historical dictionaries of religions, philosophies, and
    movements ; no. 25)
    Includes bibliographical references.
    ISBN 0-8108-3652-1 (cl. : alk. paper)
    1. Baptists Dictionaries.   I. Title.   II. Series.
BX6211.B73   1999
286'.03—dc21   99–21023
                                                                CIP

⊖™ The paper used in this publication meets the minimum requirements of
American National Standard for Information Sciences—Permanence of
Paper for Printed Library Materials, ANSI/NISO Z39.48–1992.
Manufactured in the United States of America.

Dedicated to

Gilbert R. Englerth (1915-1995) and William J. Hand

Friends, Mentors, and Bibliophiles who
have influenced me profoundly

Contents

Foreword

Although relative newcomers to the Christian community, the Baptists have left an indelible mark as a movement, denomination, and tradition. Due to their deep convictions and strong drive, this mark is bound to grow as more members join the fold. The expansion recently, at a time of relative stagnation among other groups, has been quite phenomenal. This not only concerns increased numbers of churches and members, but an ability to reach into very different cultures, far removed from the home bases of Great Britain and North America, and now including the rest of the Americas, other parts of Europe, Africa, and Asia. However, this expansion and the exceptional individualism of the members as well as the diversity of their groups make the Baptists difficult to define.

This *Historical Dictionary of the Baptists* goes to great lengths to describe and explain the Baptists to others, and to themselves as well. Few could expect as many entries on eminent Baptists, from the founders four centuries ago to those active today—to say nothing of the summaries of various groupings, conventions, and organizations or the resumes of Baptist activities around the world. There are also informative presentations of guiding principles, theological concepts, and church polity. This is rounded out with a chronology, list of abbreviations, and extensive bibliography.

It took William Brackney three decades to acquire this knowledge and the ability to present it cogently—very busy decades to judge by his curriculum vitae. He was a pastor of congregations, teacher at various colleges and universities, and is presently principal and professor of historical theology at McMaster University in Hamilton, Ontario. Along the way, Dr. Brackney has also edited several journals, written a number of books and countless articles, served as executive director of the American Baptist Historical Society and chair of the Study and Research Division of the Baptist World Alliance. This latest contribution is not the least and will certainly be appreciated by his students, colleagues, and fellow Baptists, as well as others for whom it will serve as a welcome tool.

Jon Woronoff
Series Editor

Preface

Baptists have been likened, somewhat unkindly, to "a herd of untamed mustangs in an unfenced prairie"! The allusion presumably is to their avowed "independency," their alleged "individualism," and their unwillingness to be "controlled" by either ecclesiastical or State authority.

The fascinating historical survey contained in this book gives ample evidence of the ruggedness of their convictions and the tenacity of their Christian witness, often in the face of great odds. The stand they have taken has consolidated that witness, not least in periods of great hardship and grave persecution. At other times, it must be confessed, it has led to schism within their own ranks and separation from other Christian bodies.

But that is only half the story. From earliest days, though differing greatly from one another in many respects, they have learned the need to associate together in the cause of the gospel and to express their churchmanship in terms of interdependency rather than dependency. There is no Baptist church, nationally or regionally conceived. Their ecclesiology lays stress on the voluntary associations of local Baptist churches which are autonomous in their church government, seeking to live their lives in the light of scripture and under the guidance of the Holy Spirit. They are not a "sect," but part of the "one, holy, catholic and apostolic Church," orthodox in their faith and seeking to be exemplary in their lives.

They are a product, under God, of the Protestant Reformation. They take their stand in the evangelical tradition and have been pioneers in missionary outreach to many parts of the world. They lay stress on personal commitment to Jesus Christ, not as a private individual act, but as an expression of their oneness with the "fellowship of believers." Their emphasis upon evangelism, accompanied by a strong social sense, is

Preface

paralleled by an equally strong emphasis on religious liberty, which has
been in evidence from Baptist origins right down to this present day.

The story is told here, not in the form of a continuous narrative, but
in the form of a dictionary. But dictionaries, we are told, are there to be
consulted, not read! Not so here, for this dictionary, in its own way, tells a
fascinating story, with new insights on almost every page. It is not only
informative; it is at the same time completely reliable, eminently readable,
and thoroughly enjoyable! To collect and evaluate its contents must have
been a mammoth task. The result is a comprehensive volume from the pen
of an eminent historian which will greatly enrich the reader's understanding
of the origins and growth of the people called Baptists.

D. S. Russell
Bristol, England

Acknowledgments

The idea of this project began while I was Executive Director of the American Baptist Historical Society some twenty years ago. I recognized the need for a concise, one volume reference tool which reduced the voluminous accomplishment of Edward C. Starr's *Baptist Bibliography* (26 vols.) and updated the work of William Cathcart's 19th-century *Dictionary of the Baptists*. Under the guidelines of the Scarecrow Press dictionaries, I developed entries on topics and geographical locations. In all, a search for as much accuracy and appropriate detail as I could achieve has delayed the book's release until now. There is nothing else available with many of the details I was able to recover, and it is my hope that the *Historical Dictionary* will make a useful contribution to religious studies.

Most dictionaries are the work of scores, if not hundreds of contributors. This book is different because it bears the name of one author who has indirectly depended upon the work and advice of many authorities and sources.

Among those I especially want to thank are: Denton Lotz, BWA general secretary for access to Alliance data, and Ruby Burke of the Baptist World Alliance for her many reference points; Betty Layton of the American Baptist Archives Center in Valley Forge, Pennsylvania; Dana Martin, Ashley Phelps, and Kate Seebach of the American Baptist-Samuel Colgate Library in Rochester, New York; Brian Vickers at Southern Baptist Theological Seminary; Lawrence Mullen at Houghton College on the Reformed Baptists; Ken Manley, Thorwald Lorenzen, and G. Noel Vose for details about Australian Baptists; Sydney Hudson-Reed and John M. Jonsson on South Africa; David Doherty for many details of Baptists in Great Britain, as well as Susan Mills and Jennifer Thorp at the Angus Collection,

Acknowledgments

Regent's Park College, Oxford; Breda Smith at the Baptist Missionary Society in Didcot; Peder Eidberg on Baptists in Norway; Alexander Pashko on Polish Baptists; Patricia Townshend, Michael Haykin, Fred Bullen, and Archie Goldie on Canadian Baptists; Karl-Heinz Walter of the European Baptist Federation, Janis Smits of Latvia, Reinhold Kerstan on Baptists in Germany, Alan Rimay on Baptists of the former Yugoslavia, and John Keith of Canadian Baptist Ministries for European Baptists; Nickolai Kornilov at the Moscow Baptist Seminary for data on Russian and CIS unions; Hakan Bengsson in Sweden; Cawley Bolt for the Baptists of the Caribbean; Norris Magnuson at Bethel Theological Seminary, Oscar Burdick for Seventh Day Baptist materials; Judith F. Bernicchi, Sandra Higgins, and Kathy Purks at Jenkins Research Library, and John Gilbert and Jason Carlisle, Division of Global Research, Southern Baptist International Mission Board, Richmond, Virginia; David E. Goatley and Cathy Mundale on Black Baptists in the United States. Noel Brackney translated some key Russian and CIS sources, Erin Brackney translated Spanish material, and Raphe Brackney collected numerous details about Baptist periodicals. David S. Russell has read the manuscript several times and made numerous helpful suggestions for improvement.

A large word of gratitude must be expressed to the trustees and staff of McMaster Divinity College in Hamilton, Ontario. The trustees very graciously granted me the research leave time to gather the material and compile the book. The Arts Research Board of McMaster University generously provided funds for overseas travel in 1997. My colleague, the acting principal, Dr. A. R. Goldie, has offered his support and staff time, Mrs.Terri Galan and later Mrs.Karen Gauthier, administrative secretaries to the principal, and my faculty colleague, Dr. Michael P. Knowles, have all helped with the technical details in the preparation of the manuscript according to the Press' guidelines. In the final editing process, Jon Woronoff has patiently shepherded the manuscript to fruition, and my wife, Kathryn, translated my script to usable type.

William H. Brackney
"Split Vieux,"
Baxters Harbour, Nova Scotia
Summer, 1999

Note to Readers

Geographical entries include the majority of countries in the world as of 1995 and the statistical data is stated as of 1995 for convenience and uniformity. A statistical note is made only for major Baptist groups in a country. Biographical entry selection is based upon a master list of deceased Baptist leaders of all persuasions (the only exception is William F. "Billy" Graham), and priority was given to suggestions from international leaders, and to selecting persons in roles not included in other reference works. Users of the dictionary should recognize that abbreviations have been kept to a minimum. Generally, organizational abbreviations are used only within the article where the organization appears. When the terminology "American" is used in the biographical entries, it designates generically a Baptist minister in any region of the United States prior to 1845; afterwards it denotes a minister or leader related to the American Baptist Churches or its predecessors.

Cross references are indicated by bold face type. "See also" references indicate entries of related interest.

Acronyms and Abbreviations

AABF	All Africa Baptist Fellowship
AB	Alliance of Baptists
ABA	American Baptist Association
ABCUSA	American Baptist Churches in the USA
ABE	American Baptist Evangelicals
ABF	Asian Baptist Federation
ABFMS	American Baptist Foreign Mission Society
ABFrMs	American Baptist Free Mission Society
ABHMS	American Baptist Home Mission Society
ABHS	American Baptist Historical Society
ABMU	American Baptist Missionary Union
ABPS	American Baptist Publication Society
ABWE	Association of Baptists for World Evangelism
ANBC	American National Baptist Convention
BBF	Baptist Bible Fellowship
BBFM	Baptist Board of Foreign Missions
BBUA	Baptist Bible Union of America
BC	Baptist Congress
BCWM	Baptist Council on World Mission
BFM	Baptist Faith Missions
BFMC	Baptist Foreign Missionary Convention
BGC	Baptist General Conference
BGTS	Baptist General Tract Society
BHMS	Baptist Home Mission Society
BJA	Baptist Jubilee Advance
BJCPA	Baptist Joint Committee on Public Affairs

BMA	Baptist Missionary Association of America
BMM	Baptist Mid-Missions
BMS	Baptist Missionary Society
BPFNA	Baptist Peace Fellowship of North America
BSSB	Sunday School Board, Southern Baptist Convention
BU	Baptist Union of Great Britain [and Ireland]
BWA	Baptist World Alliance
BWM	Baptist World Mission
CBA	Caribbean Baptist Fellowship
CBF	Cooperative Baptist Fellowship
CBFMS	Conservative Baptist Foreign Mission Society
EBC	European Baptist Convention
EBF	European Baptist Federation
EBM	Evangelical Baptist Mission
FBB	Fellowship of British Baptists
FBHM	Fellowship of Baptists for Home Mission
FEBC	Fellowship of Evangelical Baptist Churches
FMB	Foreign Mission Board, Southern Baptist Convention
GAGB	General Association of General Baptists
GARBC	General Association of Regular Baptist Churches
LBF	Liberty Baptist Fellowship
LBFMC	Lott Carey Baptist Foreign Mission Convention
MBMS	Massachusetts Baptist Missionary Society
NABC	North American Baptist Conference
NABF	North American Baptist Fellowship
NAFWB	National Association of Freewill Baptists
NBC	Northern Baptist Convention
NBCA	National Baptist Convention of America
NBCUSA	National Baptist Convention in the USA
NBMCA	National Baptist Missionary Convention of America
PBA	Philadelphia Baptist Association
PNBC	Progressive National Baptist Convention
RBA	Reformed Baptist Alliance
RUEBU	Russian Ukrainian Evangelical Baptist Union
RWF	Roger Williams Fellowship
SB	Strict Baptists
SBC	Southern Baptist Convention
SBF	Southwide Baptist Fellowship
SDB	Seventh Day Baptists
WBF	World Baptist Fellowship

A Chronology of Baptist History

1606   John Smyth separated from the Church of England
1612   First General Baptist congregation at Spitalfields, London
         Thomas Helwys publishes *The Mistery of Iniquity*
1614   Leonard Busher published a tract advocating religious toleration and baptism by immersion
1626   London area churches associated; correspondance with Mennonites
1633   Howell Vaughan gathered first congregation in Wales
1638/9 First Particular Baptist Church emerged in London
         First congregation in America founded at Providence, Rhode Island
1640   Dorothy Hazzard instrumental in founding Broadmead Church, Bristol
         Richard Blunt began practice among English Separatists of believer's baptism by immersion
1642   Great Debate at Southwark between Baptists and Anglicans
1644   First London Confession of Faith by Particular Baptists
         John Denne imprisoned for itinerant preaching at Cambridge
1654   General Baptist Assembly commenced
         Henry Dunster forced to resign as president of Harvard College
1660   John Bunyan imprisoned under the Conventicle Act
1661   Venner's Uprising of Fifth Monarchists
1663   John Clarke enabled the colonial charter of Rhode Island
1670   General Six Principle Baptists held association meeting in New England
1671   First Seventh Day Baptist congregation in America

Chronology

1678	John Bunyan published *A Pilgrim's Progress*
1679	Edward Terrill Trust laid foundation for Bristol Academy
1689	Act of Toleration passed
1691	Benjamin Keach introduced first Baptist hymnal
1700	First Baptist settlers noted in Virginia
1702	General Baptists supported mission in Carolina Colony
1707	First meeting of Philadelphia Baptist Association
1714	Hanover Coffeehouse ministerial society founded in London
1717	Particular Baptist Fund established in England
1719	German Baptist Brethren emigrated to Pennsylvania
1725	General Baptist Fund established in England
1728	German Seventh Day Baptist Church formed at Germantown, Pennsylvania
1738	Thomas Crosby published first Baptist history
1740	New Light movement began among New England churches
1742	Philadelphia Confession of Faith issued; published by Benjamin Franklin
1752	London Baptist Education Society founded
1756	Isaac Eaton founded academy at Hopewell, New Jersey
1764	College of Rhode Island founded by Philadelphia Baptists
1765	Ebenezer Moulton formed first congregation in Canada
1774	Isaac Backus presented case for religious liberty to U.S. Continental Congress
1776	Henry Alline began itinerant preaching in Nova Scotia
1777	Isaac Backus published history of Baptists in America
1781	Benjamin Randal organized Freewill Baptist Connection Elhanan Winchester of Philadelphia declared himself a Universalist
1785	Joseph Hughes of London proposed the Sunday School Society
1787	Virginia Baptists opposed slavery
1792	Baptist Missionary Society founded at Kettering First Baptist congregation established in Africa by David George
1797	Home Missionary Society formed in England
1798	First church in Asia organized at Serampore, India
1799	New Connexion of General Baptists (U.K.) formed
1800	Mary Webb formed first missionary society among Baptists in United States
1801	Georgia *Analytical Repository*, oldest Baptist paper in United States
1802	Founding of Massachusetts Baptist Missionary Society
1804	Baptists join in forming British and Foreign Bible Society

Northern Baptist Education Society formed in England
1808 David Barrow published first antislavery tract among Baptists
1810 Baptist Theological Institution at Stepney established
1812 William Staughton began theological school in his
        Philadelphia home
1813 Adoniram and Ann Judson commenced mission in Burma
        Baptist Union of Great Britain formed
        Baptist Irish Society founded
        David Benedict's history of Baptists appeared in United States
1814 First Meeting of the General Baptist Missionary Convention (U.S.)
1815 African Missionary Society of Richmond (Virginia) formed
1817 John Mason Peck and James Welch appointed missionaries to
        western United States
1819 First Baptist congregation in France
1820 Brethren in Christ formed in Lancaster, Pennsylvania, with baptist
        practices
1821 United States Congress chartered Columbian College in
        Washington, D.C.,a national Baptist university
        Lott Carey planted first congregation in Liberia
1823 Alexander Campbell began publication of *Christian Baptist*
1824 Baptist General Tract Society formed in Washington, D.C.
1825 First Baptist post-undergraduate theological seminary in United
        States opened at Newton, Massachusetts
1826 London University founded by Baptist advocacy
        Daniel Parker published theory of "two seeds"
1827 Antimasonic controversy divided Baptists in United States
1831 John Winebrenner organized Church of God, with Baptist
        principles
        First Baptist congregation in Australia founded
1832 American Baptist Home Mission Society formed
        William Knibb spoke against slavery in British Empire
1833 First Issue of *Gospel Herald* among English Baptists
1834 J. G. Oncken formed first congregation in Hamburg, Germany
        Providence, Ohio Association formed by Black churches
1835 Chemung (New York) disfellowshiped others who supported
        mission work
        William Dean commenced mission work among the Chinese
        First issue of the *Gospel Standard* among English Baptists
1838 Acadia University chartered in Nova Scotia
        Canada Baptist College opened in Montreal

1839   Julius Köbner formed church at Copenhagen, Denmark
1840   American Baptist Missionary Convention formed of Black churches
1842   Adventist movement coalesced around preaching of William Miller, a New York local Baptist preacher
1843   American Baptist Free Mission Society founded
1844   Final Meeting of the Triennial Convention
1845   Formation of Southern Baptist Convention
1846   Organization of the American Baptist Missionary Union
      Ruby Bixby, a Freewill Baptist, licensed to the ministry
1848   First Baptist church in Sweden formed
1851   Landmarkist Movement begins in United States with Cotton Grove Resolutions
      First Baptist congregation in New Zealand
      German Baptist Conference in America formed
1853   Jonathan Goble commenced mission work in Japan
1856   Charles Spurgeon's Pastor's College opened in London
1858   Gottfried A. Alf began first church in Poland
1861   Metropolitan Tabernacle opened in London
1863   Southern Baptist Sunday School Board formed
1864   First recorded baptism in Russia
1865   Letter from Baptist Missionary Society sparked Morant Bay Uprising in Jamaica
1870   General Association of General Baptists founded in United States
1871   Southern Baptists began missions in Italy
1877   Women's American Baptist Home Mission Societies founded in United States
1878   2,222 baptized in a single day at Ongole, India
1879   Baptist missions in Spain began
      Baptist General Conference of America (Swedish) organized
1880   Seminary at Hamburg, Germany, opened
1882   First meeting of Baptist Congress
1884   Great revival occurred in Belgian Congo
      First Baptist congregation in Mexico
1886   Pentecost on the Congo began at Banza Manteke
1887   McMaster University chartered in Canada
1888   American Baptist Education Society founded
      Women's Missionary Union founded by Southern Baptists
      Reformed Baptists in Canada adopted holiness theology
1890   University of Chicago re-opened with support of John D. Rockefeller

1891	First railroad chapel car put in service in United States
	Organization of Baptist Young People's Union of America
1894	Fortress Monroe Conference
1895	National Baptist Convention in the United States formed
	Irish Baptist Union reorganized; separated from British Baptists
1905	Baptist World Alliance formed
1907	Northern Baptist Convention (United States) organized
	Colored Primitive Baptists organized
1908	Southwestern Baptist Theological Seminary separated from Baylor University
1911	Free Baptists merged with Northern Baptist Convention
1915	National Baptist Convention of America founded
1918	First woman pastor in Baptist Union of Great Britain
1919	New World Movement began among Northern Baptists
1920	London Conference of European Baptists
	Helen Barrett Montgomery, first woman president of Northern Baptist Convention
	Baptist Seminary at Budapest, Hungary, opened
	Baptist Mid-Missions founded in United States
	Warren G. Harding of Ohio elected president of the United States, the first Baptist to hold the office
1924	American Baptist Association formed
1928	Association of Baptists for World Evangelism founded
	Evangelical Baptist Missions founded
1933	General Association of Regular Baptist Churches (United States) formed
1939	American Baptist Bill of Rights issued
1943	Conservative Baptist Foreign Mission Society founded
1944	Baptist Federation of Canada formed
	All Union Council of Evangelicals-Baptists formed in USSR
1945	Harry S. Truman, a Southern Baptist, elected president of the United States
1946	Baptist Joint Committee on Public Affairs formed in United States
1948	Baptists participate in World Council of Churches
1949	European Baptist Federation organized
	Baptist Theological Seminary opened at Rüschlikon, Switzerland
	Martyrdom of missionaries and workers in Bolivia
1950	Baptist Bible Fellowship formed in United States
1957	John Diefenbaker, a Baptist, became prime minister of Canada
1959	Baptist Jubilee Advance commenced

Chronology

1961	Progressive National Baptist Convention founded in United States
1968	Crusade of the Americas began
1971	James E. Carter, a Southern Baptist, elected president of the United States
1977	Liberty Baptist Fellowship founded in United States
1991	Cooperative Baptist Fellowship organized in United States
1992	Two Southern Baptists, William J. Clinton and Albert Gore elected president and vice president, respectively, of the United States
1993	Tadeusz Zielinski, a Baptist of Katowice, Poland, elected member of Polish National Parliament
1995	Baptists and Orthodox Churches engaged in international dialogue
1996	Baptist World Alliance published report, "Baptists Against Racism"
1997	Baptists in Belarus outlawed by government
1998	Baptists in the Republic of the Congo, Liberia, and Sierra Leone suffer persecution and displacement from homes

Introduction

One of the problems Baptist historians have faced is whether Baptists are a movement, a denomination, or a tradition. In some ways, they are all three. It takes all of Baptist history to comprehend their full meaning.

A New Religious Movement

Where did Baptists come from? The most plausible explanation is that Baptists were a religious sect or movement within the broad sweep of the English Reformation. They were part of a trend called Nonconformity, or to use a related term, "dissenters." By Michael Watt's definition of dissenters as persons of "devotion, discipline, individualists and humble people," Baptists qualified well as a movement of persons and organized groups (congregations) who adhered to a consistent set of ideas with an action program to alter the social order. That is, early Baptists created confessional statements of their principles, propagated their faith through worship and education, practised certain rites like believer's baptism, and sought to win converts to their religious ideals. In the strictest sense of the term "movement" the General Baptists, the Particular Baptists, and possibly the Seventh Day Baptists, were differentiated religious movements.

If one searches for the ultimate beginning of the Baptists as a *movement*, it must be the gradual conversion of an Anglican priest and an Anglican lawyer, named John Smyth and Thomas Helwys, respectively. Smyth began his pilgrimage as a Cambridge graduate who tried the priesthood, then moved to radical Puritanism, then Separatism and finally, searching his bible, a baptistic position. He met Helwys at some point in

Gainsborough, England, and brought him along the ideological continuum as well. From this root sprang theological conviction, flight into exile, differentiation of belief, and schism within the first congregation. When the small group under Helwys's leadership returned to England in 1611, they became the first Baptist congregation on English soil, the second in point of history. Smyth and his branch remained in Amsterdam and were slowly absorbed into the Mennonite community.

Influenced by Anabaptist communities and the Puritan Separatist tradition among a growing number of Christians in and around London, then other cities such as Bristol, the original two Baptist movements marked their pilgrimage with a consistent set of affirmations including individual accountability before God, the authority of Scripture, the Lordship of Christ, the necessity of a Christian experience, a believer's church, believer's baptism, and religious liberty. All of these traits may be found in earlier forms of dissent and among the Anabaptists, but not altogether as would be the case with the self-conscious Baptists.

The General Baptists were the first identifiable *movement* of Baptists and they appeared about 1612, so-called for their understanding of the work of Christ as it applied to all persons. Next in time a second grouping of Baptists arose from among those Separatists in the congregation first formed by Henry Jacob in 1613; by the 1630s this group began to wrestle with the nature of the church and the issue of baptism. Under the leadership of John Spilsbury they became, about 1640, the Particular Baptist *movement*, due to their belief that Christ's atonement applied to the elect of God. There were also other branches and patterns as variegated as the liberty to interpret Scripture: Seventh Day Baptists, Leg of Mutton Baptists, etc. England was their cradle, then Wales and Scotland and the American Colonies.

Baptists were, then, at their beginning a collection of English-speaking Christians who stressed Christian experience over doctrinal subtleties, who derived their beliefs and practices from the words of Scripture, and who professed a fairly universal need to share their faith. They were differentiated by their group origins, their theological perspectives on the breadth of the application of the work of Christ, and their positions on issues of polity and order.

Demographically, who were these Baptists and their descendants? Marius D'Assigny, an educated Anglican divine, in 1707 observed of the English Baptist community in his survey that they included mostly mechanics and tradesmen: "butchers, tallow-chandlers, peddlers, tinkers, taylors, tinmen," in short, "men of all trades and employments."[1]

Occasionally, there were to be found physicians, lawyers, military officers, and politicians, and in the early American experience numerous subsistence farmers. The Baptist ministry contained a surprising number of university and academy trained people in the English context, and this trend continued in the American colonial development. For the most part, Baptists were uncomfortable in the formal religious atmospheres of establishment Christianity and probably were not invited into many elite social circles. In 17th-century England and Wales, Baptists could be described by their social betters as uncouth and of the "meaner sort."

The Emerging Tradition

Baptists emigrated to the various British colonies for the same reason most other colonists did: improved economic opportunity, escape from an undesirable past, and religious freedom. They came as individuals without a congregation, as persons of another religious persuasion, and as entire immigrant congregations. In the North American context, Roger Williams went to Massachusetts Bay as a Puritan teacher and converted to Baptistic principles in exile in Rhode Island. There was the Swansea congregation of John Myles, which, determined to leave Wales intact, transplanted themselves to Rehoboth, Massachusetts Bay Colony. And there were people like Elias Keach who fled from his father's reputation and found himself in eastern Pennsylvania, and others like William Staughton, who shed youthful indiscretions to build a new life in the newly independent United States. There were three entry points to the American colonies, in order of frequency: Massachusetts, the Delaware Valley, and the southern tidewater region. Most went to New England and the heart of the fragile colonial American Baptist movement was to be found there before 1700. Baptists found in New England a Congregational intolerance in some ways more oppressive than in England. In Pennsylvania and the Jerseys there was more freedom in the latter decades of the 17th-century. Thus several individuals emigrated to the Middle Colonies and started congregations there with transplanted New England names. In the South, it was difficult for Baptists, who culturally irritated the Scotch-Irish Presbyterians and angered the solidly Anglican upper classes of colonial society. One historian's view of Baptists in New England is probably valid for the overall colonial experience: "the rank and file of the Baptists were honest, hard-working plowmen, artisans, mechanics, and day-laborers."[2] A few were chimneysweeps, fewer were elected selectmen. To their credit, some

Baptists tenaciously pioneered despite real persecution. By 1750 the foundations had been laid in each colonial region and a rudimentary associational life had grown among the congregations.

Baptists thrived in an unusual way as an identifiable religious community in the United States. Along the eastern seaboard and later on the frontier Baptist life was characterized by flexible organization and differences of opinion. It is overemphasizing the issue to indicate there was one primary schism--over the institution of slavery. There were actually multiple points of sharp difference which oriented Baptists into at least three kinds or types of groupings: regional, theological, and racial/ethnic.

The first American differentiation came with regionalization. New England Baptists were organized according to a pattern of towns and villages and their polity tended to reflect a kind of familial elitism. Calvinistic theology and democratic idealism merely buttressed the social reality of the New England way in the settled villages of Massachusetts, Connecticut, and Rhode Island. A kind of regional differentiation is evident in upcountry New England--New Hampshire, Vermont, and Maine--where the Freewill Baptists identified with a frontier sect orientation rather than as well-boundaried Calvinistic communities. In the Middle Colonies, Baptists tended to follow the New England pattern because of their roots, although a kind of ethnic diversification occurred in the early 18th century when Welsh Baptists moved into the region and had a profound influence on the polity and experience of Baptists in the Delaware Valley. In the South a distinctly regional ethos emerged, built of mostly frontier small congregations and rugged individualism, expressed in religious enthusiasm and rural culture. Later in the 18th century, Canadian Baptists as an outgrowth of New England and frontier New York American Baptists, formed a distinct regional movement.

A second type of differentiation occurred along theological lines. Historic emphases--bible, mission, church--became points of departure. Differing biblical interpretation of culture was at the base of the slavery debate, the choice of an authorized edition of the bible, and of course in the literalist/historical critical battles of the fundamentalist era. Many Baptists came to disagree sharply over what the authority of Scripture actually meant. Disagreements over missionary methods stemmed from the earliest differences over election versus freewill and inclusivity. Groups like Primitive Baptists, Freewill Baptists, Separate Baptists, and Conservative Baptists exhibit this ongoing differentiation. The doctrine of the church was the main issue in creedalism, gospel missionism, and ecumenism. Whole segments of the Baptist family have hived off into new forms of the tradition

Introduction

like *Gospel Standard* Baptists, Regular Baptists, Bible Baptists, and Fellowship Baptists, basically because they have well-defined views on who constitutes the church and what the role of the church in the world should be.

Baptists in the United States, predominantly a Caucasian movement at the beginning of the 19th century, witnessed delineation according to race/ethnicity diversity in all three sections and the Canadian provinces. Black Baptists in the Northern states comprised segregated communities and associations in the antebellum period. Because of their slave status in the South, Blacks naturally organized their own associative patterns, which after the Civil War, would become the nexus of denominations. In the Middle States, New England, and the Great Lakes region, attempts were made to blend Blacks and Whites in congregations, however, racial separatism still becoming the preferred pattern until the 1960s. This was also seen in the Canadian context where the early Baptist communities of Nova Scotia and New Brunswick, and later southwestern Ontario, virtually shut out the free Black communities in the 19th century. David George, a pioneer Baptist preacher in Canada and a Black Loyalist, ultimately found refuge of sorts in Sierra Leone, West Africa. This racial categorization continued with Asians and Latinos in both the United States and Canada.

Related to racial differentiation is the noticeable categorization according to ethnicity. In the 17th century there were the Welsh Baptists, who emigrated to America beginning in 1663 and continued in many cases to maintain Welsh communities. As non-British Christians moved into the Baptist family, either by evangelism or denominational conversion, there was a strong ethnicity which maintained its separateness from the mainstream. Ultimately what began as conferences of German, Swedish, Danish, or Norwegian churches became smaller denominations in their own rights, to use Robert Torbet's analysis. In Canada the groups include French, Ukrainian, Korean, Portuguese, and Polish Baptists, to mention a few. What happened in the Baptist family was not unlike the same ethnic experience that occurred among Methodists, Lutherans, and the Reformed churches in the United States and Canada.

Baptists were to be found in other British colonies as well. Early in the histories of Australia and New Zealand, Baptist people emigrated as mariners, farmers, miners, tradesmen, teachers, and convicts. Again, they emigrated for the hope of an improved socio-economic opportunity. Most were not self-consciously Baptist, but, because of their individual spiritual needs, they did coalesce into familiar religious communities.

Introduction

Outside the British homeland and North America, the Baptist movement grew as the result of intense and intentional evangelization and inculturation. Following the example of William Carey, the first missionary organizations set the patterns for others in commissioning full-time translators, evangelists, church planters, teachers, and special workers such as printers, doctors, nurses, women's workers, agricultural specialists, and administrators. As the fields of work matured, indigenous leaders filled the ranks and the missionary forces moved on to subdue another field in the cause of the gospel. In Asia, they began work first in India, then Siam, China, and the East Indies. In Africa, Baptist work began in Liberia, Sierra Leone, and the Congo, then in southern Africa and coastal regions. In Latin America, Brazil, Argentina, Chile, and Bolivia headed the early list, with Mexico, Venezuela, and Colombia opening missions later. Very early in Baptist missions, the West Indies witnessed evangelization in Jamaica, Haiti, the Bahamas, and Trinidad. In Europe the Baptist witness spread from Germany to eastern Europe and Scandinavia. In the later 19th century, energetic missionary efforts were produced in Russia and Italy. The pioneers of Baptist missions were the British Baptists and American Baptists; the most extensive investment and influence in Baptist world mission has been made by the Foreign Mission Board of the Southern Baptist Convention in the United States.

Beyond the transatlantic experience, ethnic divisions in the Baptist tradition mirror the experience in North America. Ethnic differentiation is found in Ireland, Poland, Russia and its successor states, the Balkan states, Africa, India, and the Far East. Entire organizations denoting the same geographical territory have grown up side by side in the Baptist world. Sometimes this has led to a modicum of cooperation, but often much adversity and competition results. Unfortunately, the mission fields have not resolved this problem, but have perpetuated it.

Wherever Baptist church life has been found outside its native cultures, there have been some identifiable characteristics. First is an advocacy of religious liberty. This has led to changes in public policy and laws, such as in Burma, Germany, Sweden, and Bolivia, to mention a few cases only. Next has been the development of a strong organizational support, generally referred to as the *association*. This pattern has allowed for support from the sending body and has served as a training laboratory for indigenous leadership. Third, Baptists have expended large efforts on the creation of enduring institutions such as schools, colleges, publishing houses, theological seminaries, hospitals, homes, camps, and retreat centers. Over the years, as leadership has evolved to local control, the institutions have passed into other administrations as well, including public and private models. This has led to a uniquely indigenized international denominational culture.

Historically speaking, then, Baptists are a **movement**, a **denomination**, and a **tradition**. In the beginning stages, whether during the 17th or 20th century, Baptists have behaved like a movement of spiritual renewal and awakening. Following evangelization and organizational development (local congregations and associations), a sense of coordinated, integrated institutional life has emerged, denoting the emergence of a *denominational* type. Ironically for those who desire the continuation of the movement in its informal stage, it is often governments which require at least some level of *denominational* recognition, as in the instance of Baptist churches in the Soviet or Chinese contexts or elsewhere who were (and are!) required to register their religious organizational status. Finally, the only adequate vehicle that seems appropriate to describe the acceptance of Baptist principles and the proliferation of so many parts of the Baptist family who are loath to recognize even their own heritage, plus those who own Baptist distinctives in the larger sense, is the term *"tradition."* The Baptist *tradition* includes such time-worn characteristics as the rule of Scripture, Christian experience, believer's baptism by immersion, the authority of the local congregation to govern its own affairs, separation of church and state, and a genuine urgency to proclaim the kingdom of God. As non-Baptist observers have noted, the "baptistification" of North American culture has been a major feature of the 20th century.

Baptists in the World Today

Taken as a denominational category of Protestants or the Free Churches, Baptists numerically constitute one of the top five religious groups, active in almost every nation. Their actual numbers, in excess of 35 million members, could be multiplied to 75 million, if families were counted as in the sacramental churches.

Generally speaking, Baptists are understood to be somewhere between Presbyterians and Pentecostals, an admixture of confessionalism and religious experience. They are less ethnically identifiable than Mennonites or Lutherans, and less theologically or historically articulated than Methodists or the Reformed Churches. Their closest kin are likely the Congregationalists. Baptists are evangelicals, despite their wide variety of theological statements and expressions.

Organizationally, the great numbers of Baptists worldwide belong to a convention or union which evidences the associational principle. For many, this leads ultimately to a connection with the Baptist World Alliance, an entirely voluntary body with regional sub-organizations in Europe, North America, Asia, Latin America, Africa, and the Caribbean. A smaller, disparate collection of Baptists associations and churches, mostly in Great Britain and North America, lies outside the mainstream, in defiance of collectives and conglomerates and illustrating the continuing need to be "dissenters."

No longer alone in most of their positions, Baptists advocate religious liberty, the authority of the bible, the Lordship of Jesus Christ, local church ecclesiology, democratic decision-making, a passion for witness, and religious experience. It is the peculiar combination of these character elements in the Baptist psyche, not any one uniquely, which gives the group its flavor. Where Baptists have engaged in ecumenical discussions, they have noticed their similarity to a wide range of other Christians, and likewise the larger Christian community has been shaped by Baptist emphases.

Baptist principles have influenced the form of governments and given birth to significant leadership. The Constitution and Bill of Rights of the United States, for instance, were influenced by Baptist principles, as were many nations by Baptist missionaries, notably Liberia and Bolivia. Baptists can count among their ranks presidents, prime ministers, industrial barons, and scientists. Countless institutions worldwide owe their origins to Baptists who possessed an educational or care-giving vision.

Sometimes a sect, broadly speaking a movement, historically now a tradition, and for convenience sake, a denomination, the Baptist tradition has earned its place in history and Christian witness. Its character has ensured that it will continue to create history.

Notes

1. Marius D'Assigny B.D., *An Antidote Against the Pernicious Errors of the Anabaptists or of the Dipping Sect* (London: W. Taylor, 1707), x, 139.

2. William G. McLoughlin, *New England Dissent, 1630-1833: The Baptists and the Separation of Church and State* (Cambridge, MA: Harvard University Press, 1971) Vol. I, 77.

The Dictionary

A

ABERHART, WILLIAM (1878-1943). Canadian Baptist minister and political leader, born at Hibbert, Ontario. He was educated at Queen's University and initially pursued a schoolteaching career in Brantford, Ontario, and later Calgary, Alberta. In 1915 he began to practice preaching at Westbourne Baptist Church in Calgary, and, owing to his prophetic and **dispensationalist** themes, he soon became the most popular **bible** teacher in the city. As an unpaid lay minister at Westbourne, Aberhart formed in 1918 the Calgary Prophetic Bible Conference, which drew hundreds to his church on Thursday evenings. Although raised a Presbyterian, Aberhart had himself baptized in 1920 and built a prairie-wide following from Westbourne Church. In a famous **bible** lesson, Aberhart compared Baptists to the Apocalyptic church at Ephesus, "the least of the problem churches." In November 1925 he began broadcasting the "Back to the Bible" programs from radio station CFCN in Calgary, reaching thousands of loyal listeners. In 1926 he launched his Radio Sunday School, enrolling over 9,000 children. Eventually, Aberhart entered the political realm in the Great Depression and formed from his religious following a new political party, Social Credit, which sought relief for the thousands of destitute western Canadians. In 1935 in a sweep of popularity, he was elected premier of Alberta, handing over to trusted associates the work at the Bible Institute and the church, although he returned to preach regularly. He was re-elected premier in 1940 and died in office.

ABERNATHY, RALPH DAVID (1926-1990). American Black Baptist minister and civil rights leader, born at Linden, Alabama. He was educated at Alabama State College and Atlanta University where he received the M.A. degree. He began his work as a college instructor in social sciences and quickly moved to the Baptist **ministry**, being ordained in 1948. He served two churches: First Baptist Church, Montgomery, Alabama (1951-1961), and West Hunter Street Baptist Church, Atlanta, Georgia (1961-1990). During the civil rights campaigns of the 1950s and 1960s, Abernathy joined **Martin Luther King, Jr**. and became a national organizer and leader. In 1955 in Alabama he led the bus boycott and organized the Montgomery Improvement Association. He was a founder of the Southern Christian Leadership Conference (SCLC) and served various offices in the organization, including president, 1968-1977. Abernathy sought national attention for the plight of the poor and in 1968 organized the Poor Peoples' Campaign, which set up "Resurrection City" on the Mall in Washington, D.C. Later in life Abernathy spoke openly of King's personal shortcomings, but he never renounced his friendship with the slain civil rights leader. Five U.S. colleges awarded him honorary degrees and he received the Peace Medal from the German Democratic Republic in 1971.

ADMONITION. See **Discipline, Church**.

ADVENTISM. An emphasis among Christian churches upon the second coming or return of Jesus Christ. In the early church it was related to chiliasm (the doctrine of the thousand-year reign of Christ) and claimed in its following leaders such as Tertullian and Cyprian. From about the 5th century, the Augustinian synthesis held that the millennial kingdom was to be understood as the present age, the time span between the first and second advents of Christ. This "amillennial" interpretation prevailed among the main body of Christians for many centuries. Throughout the Middle Ages and Reformation era, however, a small number of minor sects held to a literal advent of Christ and kingdom. In the 17th century the **Fifth Monarchy Movement** in England took up a form of adventism and made it a political movement. In the 19th century in the United States, **William Miller**, a Baptist lay preacher, discovered what he believed to be key elements in the calculation of the timing of Christ's return and he announced the date for 1843. Those who followed his teachings came to be called "Adventists" and eventually a separate church was formed. Many Baptists followed Miller's teachings with interest and supported lectures and purchased the publications produced by the movement. Later in the 19th century, the Adventist tradition was joined to the sabbatarian movement, particularly as taught by Ellen G. H. White (1827-1915) and the Seventh Day Adventist (SDA) movement was organized in 1860; smaller groups of Adventists remained aloof of the SDA. In the 20th century, most Baptists rejected the position of the Adventist tradition in its several forms and nomenclature. However, large numbers of Baptists do adhere to various eschatological positions on the details of the idea of a "rapture" of the church and the establishment of the millennial kingdom. Major North American spokesmen, such as **Elon Galusha, A. J. Gordon, Elmore Harris, Henry G. Weston**, and most leaders of the **fundamentalist** movement among Baptists, hold great interest in eschatological discussions.

ALBANIA. The first Baptist witness in what is now Albania occurred in the 1840s as missionaries of the **Baptist Board of Foreign Missions** (BBFM) attempted to plant churches in the region. Missionary work was forbidden by governments and discouraged by state churches until the 1990s when political change occurred. In 1993 Canadian and **Southern Baptist**s began work in Albania, with a congregation planted in Tirana. The Conservative Baptist Foreign Mission Society opened a mission to Albania in 1993, centered at Korce and the **Baptist Bible Fellowship** (BBF) opened a mission in Albania in 1995. As of 1995 the Baptist community was still in its early stages and dependent upon resources in the West.

ALDERSON, JOHN (1738-1821). American Baptist minister who pioneered church development in what is now the state of West Virginia. He was first **pastor** of the Lynville, Rockingham County, congregation, but moved west in 1777, settling at Jerrett's Fort on Wolf Creek. He pioneered a farm and was often described as carrying a gun while he plowed. Against opposition from Indian tribes and difficulties in supporting his family, Alderson preached in military forts and at farmsteads, eventually commencing what became the Greenbrier Church before 1780. In 1781 Alderson constituted this congregation, the first in the region, and he constructed the first Baptist meetinghouse in remote Indian country. His field of influence covered the extent of the southwestern Virginia frontier, and he was considered the apostle of mission-oriented Baptists after the turn of the 19th century.

ALGERIA. Baptist life in Algeria has been greatly inhibited by changing geo-political circumstances. The **Evangelical Baptist Mission**s (EBM) began a mission in Algeria in 1950 among the Berbers, La Mission Baptiste Evangélique, but was expelled in 1970.

ALL AFRICA BAPTIST FELLOWSHIP (AABF). One of the six regional fellowships of the **Baptist World Alliance** (BWA), founded in 1982 at Nairobi, **Kenya**. The fellowship was the result of the Africa for

Christ Campaign in 1982, supported by Baptists of the world to evangelize Africa. The purposes of the Fellowship are to promote education, Baptist faith and witness, mission, and **evangelism**, and to advance the objectives of the BWA.

ALL PEOPLES BAPTIST MISSION. An evangelical Baptist missionary agency formed in 1980 to facilitate church planting, **evangelism**, and literature distribution. The Mission has work in **El Salvador, Mexico**, and **Germany** and employs about 15 overseas personnel.

ALLIANCE OF [SOUTHERN] BAPTISTS. Following the 1986 annual meeting of the **Southern Baptist Convention** in Atlanta, Georgia, a group of moderate political activists gathered to assess the theological future of the Convention. In their opinion the Convention had come under the control of **fundamentalists** who sought to purge the boards, agencies, and seminaries of those who did not agree with their position. On February 12, 1987, they organized the Southern Baptist Alliance to pursue objectives like freedom of individuals to interpret the Scriptures, freedom of the local church to determine its mission, support for cooperation with other Christian bodies, a servant leadership model, **theological education** based upon responsible scholarship and open inquiry, and actions to proclaim the Good News of Jesus Christ. Individuals and churches were invited to join, upon contribution of $25.00 annually or $1.00 per resident member, respectively. The Alliance, renamed in 1992 the Alliance of Baptists, is led by a 30-member board and includes numerous congregations mostly from the eastern seaboard Southern Baptist constituency. A new school, the Baptist Theological Seminary in Richmond, Virginia, is associated with the Alliance. Offices are in Washington, D.C., and the full-time administrator is Stan Hastey, formerly with the **Baptist Joint Committee on Public Affairs**. Currently, the Alliance claims 125 churches and is associated with the publication, *Baptists Today* (1982-).

ALLINE, HENRY (1748-1784). American and Canadian New Light evangelist, born at Newport, Rhode Island. He emigrated to Falmouth, Nova Scotia, where he experienced a new birth spiritually. From 1776 to 1779 he preached around the Minas Basin region in the style of New Light evangelist, George Whitefield (1703-1770). In 1779 he was ordained an evangelist by three Annapolis Valley churches. Alline itinerated widely in Nova Scotia and New Brunswick, establishing congregations and holding public outdoor meetings; he embodied the essence of the **Great Awakening** in the Maritimes, stressing strong, direct, extemporaneous preaching, and hymn singing. He focused his efforts upon the rural regions around the Bay of Fundy where Yankees had settled and hardship was common, rejecting Calvinism for an emphasis upon God's love. At the time of his death, Alline had broadened his mission to northern New England and was remarkably close to the ministry of **Benjamin Randal**. Most of the churches he founded in the Maritimes collapsed or became Baptist. Many of the early Baptist leaders in the region owed their spiritual pilgrimages to Alline, if not their perspective in **mission** and **ministry**. While never formally a Baptist, he had a profound impact upon early Canadian Baptists in stressing experiential religion and linking their roots with the Great Awakening.

ALL UNION COUNCIL OF EVANGELICAL CHRISTIANS-BAPTISTS. See **Russia**.

AMAZING GRACE MISSIONS. An independent Baptist **missionary** agency founded in 1938 by three Texas Baptist pastors: R. E. White, H. T. Pultz, and Foy Mosher. The organization, which raises funds for various projects, assists over 30 missionary families in Europe, India, and Mexico. A newsletter, *Church Bulletin*, is published at Houston, Texas.

AMERICAN BAPTIST ASSOCIATION (ABA). An international fellowship of independent Baptist churches primarily located in the southern and southwestern United States. Mostly as a reaction to the organization of the **Southern Baptist Convention** (SBC) in the 1840s, **Landmark** Baptist theology swept through the churches of Texas, Arkansas, and Louisiana and focused on working through the local **associations**. In March, 1924, at Texarkana, Texas, several of the major landmarkist associations were merged, the Baptist Missionary Association of Texas, the Mississippi Baptist Association, and state associations of Arkansas, Oklahoma, Louisiana, Florida, Missouri, and the Old General Association, into the American Baptist Missionary Association. The term "missionary" was later dropped, leaving the official title, American Baptist Association. Successive internal leadership disagreements in 1934, 1937, and 1949 led to a schism in the Association which gave birth to the North American Baptist Association, later the **Baptist Missionary Association of America**. Educational institutions of the ABA include Missionary Baptist College, Sheridan, Arkansas (1919-1934); Missionary Baptist Seminary, Little Rock, Arkansas; Texas Baptist Seminary, Henderson, Texas; Oklahoma Missionary Baptist College, Marlow, Oklahoma; and Florida Baptist Schools, Lakeland, Florida. There are institutes in 16 locations in the United States plus **India, Mexico,**

Philippines, Korea, and **Peru.** Doctrinally the Association is fundamentalistic, holding to biblical inerrancy and that the only true churches are those which are local and practice believer's **baptism.** The periodical, *Missionary Baptist Searchlight* (1937-), is published at Texarkana.

The Association conducts a foreign mission program in over a dozen countries including Mexico, **Canada, Japan,** India, British Solomon Islands, **Honduras, Colombia, Costa Rica, Nicaragua, Germany,** Philippines, Korea, and **Israel.**

As of 1986 there were 1,705 churches with 250,000 members affiliated with the American Baptist Association. See also **Missionary Baptists.**

AMERICAN BAPTIST BILL OF RIGHTS. With the rise of international totalitarian government regimes which threatened **religious liberty** and the overtures of the Franklin Roosevelt Administration to recognize the Vatican diplomatically, three major groups in the United States joined forces to produce a proclamation for religious liberty. The American Baptist Bill of Rights was ratified in 1939 through the Joint Committee on Public Relations by the **Northern Baptist Convention** (NBC), the **Southern Baptist Convention** (SBC), and the **National Baptist Convention** (NBCUSA), a total of more than 10 million persons being represented. The document, with style and terminology borrowed from the United States Constitution, contained affirmations of **religious liberty,** spirituality, the competency of the human soul, and free churches in a free state. Condemned were paternalism (state interference in philanthropic efforts), any unions of church and state, special favors to ecclesiastical bodies, and the preference of coercion over persuasion. See also **Baptist Joint Committee on Public Affairs** (BJCPA).

AMERICAN BAPTIST CHURCHES (ABCUSA). The designation since 1973 of what was formerly known as the **Northern Baptist Convention** (NBC:1907-1950) and the American Baptist Convention (ABC:1950-1972).

The taproot of American Baptist life is the First Baptist Church in Providence, Rhode Island, the oldest Baptist congregation in North America. By 1900 over 9,000 congregations belonged to this family of churches. Gradually in the late 17th century, **associations** of congregations were formed, giving a broader shape to the concept of a denomination. Later, in the 19th century, state organizations, called "**conventions,**" were formed, beginning in South Carolina in 1821 and these added to the growth of a denominational consciousness. In the same era in the 19th

century, task-oriented societies emerged principally in New England to round out American Baptist organizational models.

Prior to the formation of a national convention in 1907, northern American Baptist congregations generally cooperated in supporting a cluster of interlocking national **voluntary** societies. These societies included tasks such as foreign **missions**, home missions, publication, and **women's** organizations. In 1814 the first comprehensive organization was formed, the **General Missionary Convention** of the Baptist Denomination in the United States of America for Foreign Missions (GMC), to which the majority of northern congregations related. When, however, the Convention fragmented in 1845 over the issue of **slavery**, the Baptist churches of the North reverted to a society model of organization, supplemented by the regular associational system. From 1846 to 1907 the national organization was known as the **American Baptist Missionary Union** (ABMU) and related societies.

Although various interests contended for a national organization throughout the 19th century, the closest proximity to a unified organization were the annual anniversary meetings when all of the societies met in a single location and conducted their business. Finally in May 1907 representatives of the state conventions, city societies, associations, and national societies gathered in Washington, D. C., at Calvary Baptist Church to form the **Northern Baptist Convention** (NBC). Among the prime movers were W. C. Bitting (1857-1931) (who became executive secretary of the Convention), A. J. Rowland (1840-1920), **Shailer Mathews, Henry L. Morehouse**, and Lathan A. Crandall (1850-1923).

The Convention operated through two boards and was visible in national meetings held in various cities across the northern and western United States. The boards and related societies adopted policies for themselves which influenced regional and congregational life as well. The NBC joined the Federal Council of Churches in 1913 and successfully completed a merger with the **Free Baptist** General Conference in 1911.

In June 1949 amidst a flurry of rapid expansion among U.S. Baptists, and the new design of the **Southern Baptist Convention** to enter northern fields, leaders of the Northern Baptist Convention brought a proposal to their annual meeting at San Francisco to change the name to the **American Baptist Convention**. The rationale was twofold: to recognize the historic nomenclature of most national American Baptist societies, and to "hold the name in trust" for other Baptist bodies to consider joining the Convention in a spirit of cooperative Protestantism.

Further modifications were made to the structure of the American Baptist Convention in the 1950s and after. In 1955 the two women's societies were integrated into the respective national mission organizations. In 1968 a   Study Commission on Denominational Structures (SCODS) was authorized and in 1972 it proposed that the entire denomination be revised to emphasize the local church and the interrelationships of regional and national organizations. The result was the American Baptist Churches in the United States of America (ABCUSA), officially recognized on January 1, 1973. Subsequently, a Study Commission on Relationships (SCOR) in 1976 recommended the establishment of covenants of relationships between regional organizations and national boards, and that agreements be reached on the support system for the denomination's stewardship. SCOR also defined the new national board structures. A third reorganization plan which would have reduced the number of regional organizations and redrawn geographical boundaries, the Study of Administrative Areas and Relationships (SAAR), was never formally adopted, but its driving impetus to reduce the number of regional organizations has slowly taken place, notably in the New England and Great Plains geographical areas.

Programmatically, American Baptists function through national boards for international, domestic, and educational ministries, plus a national benefit plan, men's and women's organizations, several commissions, and the oldest Baptist historical agency in North America. About three dozen regional organizations exist, covering all the United States, as do over a hundred associations. American Baptists operate fifteen colleges and eight seminaries in the United States and Puerto Rico, plus numerous hospitals and retirement homes.

The most ecumenical of Baptist bodies in the United States, ABCUSA has sought "associated" relationships with the **Progressive National Baptist Convention** (PNBC:1961), the Church of the Brethren (1973), and various ethnically diverse bodies such as the **German**, Swedish, **Danish-Norwegian**, Slavic, and **Hispanic Baptist** groups. Formal discussions toward a possible merger with the Christian Church (Disciples of Christ) were conducted from 1947 to 1952 but failed to produce anything more than a common hymnal. About 40 percent of American Baptist local congregations are dually aligned with either African American Baptist bodies, the Southern Baptist Convention, or an ethnic Baptist conference. American Baptists are full members of the **Baptist World Alliance** (BWA), the World Council of Churches, the **Baptist Joint Committee on Public Affairs** (BJCPA), and the National Council of Churches of Christ in the U.S.A.

The national headquarters of the American Baptist Churches was built in 1962 at Valley Forge, Pennsylvania, in a unique circular building designed by nationally renowned architect, Vincent Kling. The building reflects the interrelated yet autonomous nature of the denomination's organizational history. From 1802 to 1991 the denominational periodical was the *American Baptist Magazine*, discontinued due to falling subscriber interest, and succeeded by an informal periodical, *American Baptists in Mission* (1992-). The **American Baptist Publication Society**, (ABPS: after 1922-1924 known to the public as Judson Press in honor of **Adoniram Judson**) the denomination's book publisher from 1824, continues to produce a limited list of titles since 1986.

As of 1995 there were 5,711 churches and 1,527,470 members affiliated with the American Baptist Churches in the U.S.A.

AMERICAN BAPTIST CONVENTION. See **American Baptist Churches**.

AMERICAN BAPTIST EVANGELICALS (ABE). A voluntary association of individuals and congregations in the greater **American Baptist Churches** tradition who espouse conservative evangelical doctrines and ethical positions. Founded in 1992 at the Harmony Baptist Church in New Castle, Pennsylvania, the group has both national and regional manifestations. At the national level, members meet at the American Baptist Biennial Meeting for business, fellowship, and inspiration. In many of the regional bodies, chapters are organized and meet several times per year. At first mostly a northeastern U.S. phenomenon, there are about 1,000 members and 10-20,000 adherents in the **association**. Among the core elements of the group are the Lordship of Jesus Christ, biblical authority, Baptist heritage, and proclamation in love of the life-changing message of Christ to the lost world. Overall, there is a strong commitment to the implications of the authority of **Scripture**. In the ongoing debates in the denomination over the recognition of gay and lesbian lifestyles, American Baptist Evangelicals have often been understood as withholding support for alternative lifestyles from what they believe is clearly taught in the **bible**. The association publishes a quarterly newsletter, *ABE Connections* (1992-).

AMERICAN BAPTIST FOREIGN MISSION SOCIETY (ABFMS). The corporate name of the oldest Baptist national overseas mission organization in the United States. Founded in 1814 as the **General Missionary Convention** of the Baptist Denomination in the United States of America for Foreign Missions (GMC), the specific administration of missions was conducted by the **Baptist Board of Foreign Missions** (BBFM) in the United States from 1814 to 1846. It was this aspect of the overall work of the GMC which emerged as a single purpose society in 1826, to support overseas **missions** of the growing Baptist community in the United States. In 1846 following the schism with the churches of the South, from which the **Southern Baptist Convention** came, the **Baptist Board of Foreign Missions** (BBFM) became the **American Baptist Missionary Union** (1846-1905); in 1905 the name American Baptist Foreign Mission Society was adopted legally in recognition of its popular usage and congruity with other Northern Baptist societies.

The first field of the Society was in **Burma** (1814), set up by the first missionaries, **Adoniram** and **Ann Judson**. Burma was followed by **Liberia** (1821), **Siam** (1833), **China** (1836), **India** (1836), Europe (1839), **Japan** (1873), **Congo** (1884), and the **Philippines** (1900). The Latin American missions of the **American Baptist Home Mission Society** (ABHMS) were added in 1973; these included **Mexico** (1870), **Cuba** (1899), **El Salvador** (1911), and **Nicaragua** (1917). From 1817 to 1845 the Society also conducted missions among American Indian tribes, with notable appointments like **John Mason Peck**, **Isaac McCoy**, and **James E. Welch** serving amongst Shawnee, Choctaw, Cherokee, and Potawotami tribes. Missionary work over the years and contexts has included **evangelism**, church planting, **Scripture** translation, education, and health care. The first women missionaries were spouses of the early male appointments, the exception being **Charlotte White** who was appointed to Burma in 1814. Single women were later the responsibility of the Woman's American Baptist Foreign Mission Society (WABFMS), founded in 1877. This Society was integrated with the ABFMS in 1955.

With the formation of the **Northern Baptist Convention** (NBC) in 1905, the ABFMS became an official national society of the denomination and participated in its budget and planning processes. Since 1973 the ABFMS has been integrated with the **American Baptist Churches** as the Board of International Ministries. It maintains **missions** or cooperates in work in 24 nations.

AMERICAN BAPTIST FREE MISSION SOCIETY (ABFrMS). In the late 1830s increasing numbers of Baptist leaders in the northern United States became dissatisfied with the reluctance of the Baptist Triennial Convention to take a firm stand on the question of slaveholding. At Tremont Temple in Boston, Massachusetts, in May 1843 a group of ministers and writers, including Albert Post (1809-1887), John Duer (1823-1875), and **William H. Brisbane**, formed the American and Foreign Mission Society on the model of the American and Foreign Bible Society. In addition to being abolitionist, the Society was **antimasonic**, supported temperance, and opposed foreign immigration, oath-taking, and honorary degrees--in short an ultraistic social and political agenda. By 1848 it had changed its name to the American Baptist Free Mission

Society, doubtless a response to the national election platform that year of "Free Soil." Leaders ventured into broader concerns, notably the establishment of an undergraduate school– the New York Central College–and support for missionary work in **Haiti**, **Burma**, Africa, **Japan**, Upper **Canada**, and the western United States. The Free Mission Society was first to establish a Baptist mission in Japan. Among the outstanding leaders of the Society was **Nathan Brown**, a former missionary to Japan, who became corresponding secretary of the Society in 1858. In 1872 the Society merged its interests with other Baptist bodies, notably the Consolidated American Baptist Missionary Convention (CABMC) and the **American Baptist Missionary Union** (ABMU). Among several periodicals published by the Society were: *The Free Missionary* (Newton Centre, Massachusetts), *The Christian Reflector* (Worcester, Massachusetts), *The Christian Contributor* (Utica, New York), and the *American Baptist* (Utica and New York). See also **Antislavery and Baptists**.

AMERICAN BAPTIST HOME MISSION SOCIETY (ABHMS). The oldest of the national Baptist societies devoted to missionary work in the United States and its territories. The Society was founded in 1832 at Mulberry Street Baptist Church at an adjourned session of the Baptist Triennial Convention in New York City. The two most influential promoters of the idea were **Jonathan Going** of Massachusetts and **John Mason Peck** of Illinois.

Home missions in an earlier generation had been conducted by associations, notably the Shaftsbury (Vermont) and **Philadelphia** (Pennsylvania) Baptist Associations. In 1802 Baptists in Massachusetts formed a voluntary society, the Massachusetts Baptist Missionary Society (MBMS), to aid destitute churches and plant new congregations in northern New England and western New York state. Eventually with the expansion of settlements into the Ohio Valley, the task became immense and beyond the resources of these efforts. When the **General Baptist Missionary Convention** of the Baptist Denomination in the United States (GMC) was formed in 1814, home missions were added to that agenda and missionaries were appointed to work in the Old Northwest, the Mississippi Valley, and among Indian tribes. Home missions competed less than favorably with the Judson Mission in Burma, the Liberian Mission in Africa, and work in Europe. Thus, a new national society was formed to focus exclusively on home missions. Baptists followed the lead of Presbyterians and Congregationalists in this regard, as witnessed in the establishment in 1826 of the American Home Mission Society.

The Society turned its attention to planting new churches, working with immigrants, and establishing Indian missions. Regionally, emphasis was placed upon church planting in the upper South, the lower Ohio Valley, and the upper Mississippi Valley. Indians, new immigrants, and free Blacks reflected focal points of the Society's mission.

In 1844 a dispute arose in the management of ABHMS over whether a person sympathetic to **slaveholding** could be appointed by the Society. The issue, raised by the Georgia Baptist Convention, was a test case and the Board of Managers decided not to receive an application in which the question of slaveholding was at stake. The next year, southern Baptist congregations organized their own convention with a domestic mission board, which served their interests regardless of political concerns.

The next major phase of the Society's efforts centered on work among freedmen during and after the Civil War. The Society adopted the position that the greatest need of the former slave population was leadership development. Hence, large sums were spent to start schools of every level to train ministers and upgrade the general population's educational attainment. Subscriptions for buildings were raised and many educational missionaries were sent to the southern states.

The ABHMS was also involved in outreach beyond the national borders. As a natural outgrowth of missions in the deep South, beginning in 1870 the ABHMS entered **Mexico** and in 1898 **Puerto Rico**. Eventually missions were organized in **Cuba**, **El Salvador**, **Nicaragua**, and **Haiti**. In the 20th century, these fields were transferred to the **American Baptist Foreign Mission Society** (ABFMS).

When the **Northern Baptist Convention** (NBC) was formed in 1907, the Society became one of the cooperating national mission societies. It related to city **mission** societies and state **conventions**.

With denominational reorganization in 1968-1973, the ABHMS became the Board of National Ministries of the **American Baptist Churches in the U.S.A.** Presently the Board conducts work in **evangelism** among urban mission centers, and Native Americans, social concerns, and operates various contract services such as church loans and homes and hospitals coordination. With other American Baptist national agencies, the Board is administratively located at Valley Forge, Pennsylvania.

AMERICAN BAPTIST MISSIONARY UNION (ABMU). Official name given in 1846 to the successor organization to the **General Missionary Convention** (GMC) and **Baptist Board of Foreign Missions** (BBFM), following the schism with the churches which created the **Southern**

Baptist Convention (SBC) and the Baptist congregations of the northern states. At its outset, the ABMU faced the challenges of a depleted membership, a rising debt, and a new structure. A new constitution allowed for a society type membership which recognized proportional representation according to the magnitude of individual and congregational contributions. Eventually, three classes of membership evolved: life, honorary, and annual; this system characterized denominational funding in the North until the organization of the **Northern Baptist Convention** (NBC) in 1905.

Missions' policy under the ABMU changed dramatically. Indian **missions** in the United States were transferred to the **American Baptist Home Mission Society** (ABHMS) in 1854-1866. Mission stations in **India** were retrenched in favor of entering **Japan** and upgrading work in **China** after 1860. The Union competed for support and mission assignments with the **American Baptist Free Mission Society** (ABFrMS), until merger with that body in 1872. Expansion of fields occurred in 1884 with the takeover of the Livingston Inland Mission in the **Congo**, and in 1898 when the first missionaries were sent to the **Philippines**.

Because of the high interest of the churches in overseas missions, the ABMU in essence became the heart of a growing denomination and the centerpiece of annual mission and publication society meetings called "anniversaries." This structure prevailed until 1905 when the Northern Baptist Convention was organized and the ABMU became the American Baptist Foreign Mission Society, a name which the public had recognized for decades. See also **American Baptist Foreign Mission Society**.

AMERICAN BAPTIST PUBLICATION SOCIETY (ABPS). Founded originally in 1824 as the Baptist General Tract Society (BGTS), the ABPS was the second of the national Baptist **voluntary** societies. It was based on the model of the Religious Tract Society in Britain and the American Tract Society in New York, a Congregationalist and Presbyterian organization. Baptists who had entered the field of domestic and foreign missions earlier in the 1800s recognized the need for a printer and distributor of Christian literature. It was **Luther Rice** and **Noah Davis** who set up the BGTS in Washington, D.C., in proximity to the proposed national Baptist university and center of operations which Rice had envisioned for the Baptist movement in the nation's capital.

In 1840 the BGTS became the American Baptist Publication and Sunday School Society; in 1844 the words "Sunday School" were dropped with no lessening of the emphasis. Under the leadership of **John Mason Peck** and Benjamin Griffith (1821-1893) the Society adopted an aggressive **colporterage** program in conjunction with the **American**

Baptist Home Mission Society which earned for ABPS the reputation of being the leading educational agency in the Baptist family in the United States.

Another stream of activity which became part of the ABPS was the American Baptist Education Society (ABES), formed in 1888. This organization brought together institutions of higher education historically related to the northern Baptists plus the potential for funding sources and planning by the churches and other societies. In 1944 with reorganization of the **Northern Baptist Convention** (NBC), the Publication and Education societies were merged into the American Baptist Board of Education and Publication (ABBEP). This entity, a recognized national board of the Convention, remains the corporate title, although the name American Baptist Educational Ministries (BEM) was adopted in 1973 as part of the further reorganization of the **American Baptist Churches U.S.A.** Over the years of its work, the Board has asssumed administrative oversight for the Commission on the Ministry, the American Baptist Assembly in Green Lake, Wisconsin, American Baptist Men, American Baptist Women, and the American Baptist Historical Society. Headquarters of the Board of Education and Publication are at Valley Forge, Pennsylvania. The publishing arm of the Board has been known as Judson Press since 1922, honoring **Adoniram Judson**, first American Baptist missionary.

AMERICAN NATIONAL BAPTIST CONVENTION (ANBC). One of the predecessor national Black Baptist organizations in the United States, the American National Baptist Convention was formed in August 1886 in St. Louis, Missouri. Its purpose was to devise means for the creation of a Black national Baptist denomination, and its leaders sought to deliberate on great Baptist questions of the day. The Convention was largely the organizing genius of **William J. Simmons**, its first president. Among its achievements were the inclusion of Black women in its ranks for the first time, the first statistical analysis of the Black Baptist movement in the United States, and the calling together of diverse elements in the Black Baptist family. The Convention was often seen as a Black equivalent of the **Baptist Congress** (BC), its work carried out in the shadow of the foreign mission movement among Blacks (see **Lott Carey Baptist Foreign Mission Convention**), the leadership favored integration with White organizations, and finally it lost its great leader, W. J. Simmons, in 1890. In 1895 at a national gathering in Atlanta, Georgia, the American National Baptist Convention was merged to form the **National Baptist Convention in the United States** (NBCUSA).

ANABAPTIST. Beginning in the 16ᵗʰ century groups of European Christian believers recovered the importance of believers' **baptism** as a prerequisite to church membership. Because this involved the rebaptism of persons baptized in the Catholic tradition as infants, the Greek preposition "ana" (meaning "re") was added to the baptist idea, making the term "anabaptist" applicable to those who called for a rebaptism. Among the clusters of Anabaptists were the Swiss Brethren of Zurich who as of 1525 moved beyond the teachings of their mentor, Huldrych Zwingli (1484-1531), and practiced believers' baptism (Zwingli actually referred to them as "Catabaptists"). Other Anabaptists emerged in Poland, Westphalia, Bohemia, and the Netherlands to mention major evidences. Eventually the Anabaptist movement came to include the Mennonites, Brethren, Amish, and Hutterites as the principal surviving groups.

In the mid-20ᵗʰ century North American context Harold S. Bender (1897-1962), a professor at Mennonite/Biblical Seminary in the United States, proposed that what several of these groups had in common was their life of discipleship, and the term "anabaptist" came to be associated with a newly identified group in the era of the Protestant Reformation. In 1962 George H. Williams (1914-) at Harvard University coined the term "Radical Reformation" to include many of the Anabaptist types and others such as spiritualists, Waldensians, smaller churches of a Pietist kind, and some Unitarians. In a third round of nomenclature revision, Brethren historian Donald F. Durnbaugh (1927-) at Bethany Theological Seminary in the United States used the term "believer's churches" to designate a wider variety of Anabaptists, including the Baptists, who held to a collection of ideals other than believer's baptism, such as the Lordship of Christ, the authority of the Word of God, a covenant of believers, **missionary** service, proclamation, and Christian unity. See also **Believers' Church**.

ANABAPTIST KINSHIP THEORY. Several Baptist historians have advanced the hypothesis that the origins of the Baptist movement are to be found in the Anabaptist movement of the 16ᵗʰ century. The kinship of ideas such as **religious liberty**, congregational governance, believers' **baptism**, radical discipleship, and **mission**, suggests that whether there is any documentary evidence extant, the spiritual forbears of the Baptists are the Anabaptists. Some writers attempt to do literary analyses on confessional texts to demonstrate theological dependance, while others construct scenarios of possible personal relationships which connect the Dutch Anabaptists with English Separatists. The Anabaptist Kinship Theory generally produces an affinity for "sect-oriented" (to use Ernst Troeltsch's term) Christianity which eschews **ecumenism** and political engagement with other Protestant traditions and public issues. Among those writers in the Anabaptist Kinship school of interpretation are William R. Estep (1920-) of Southwestern Baptist Theological Seminary, James A. Mosteller (1915-) of Northern Baptist Theological Seminary, **Ernest Payne** of the Baptist Union, and **A. C. Underwood** of Rawdon College in Great Britain. See also **Puritan Separatist Hypothesis.**

ANDERSON, MARTIN BREWER (1815-1890). Baptist minister and educator, born at Brunswick, Maine. Anderson was educated at Waterville College and Newton Theological Institution. He secured a teaching position at Waterville College in Classics and mathematics and later rhetoric. In 1850 he became editor of the *New York Recorder*, a weekly Baptist journal. In 1853 he was elected the first president of the Baptist-related University of Rochester in upstate New York. During his long tenure in that office, he emphasized the sciences and social sciences, making Rochester a first-rate institution. A prolific writer, Anderson served as president of the Home and Foreign Mission Societies and advised **Matthew Vassar** on the establishment of the first American college for women.

ANGOLA. Four different Baptist groups established denominational presence in Angola. In 1878 missionaries of the **Baptist Missionary Society** (BMS) established a church at San Salvador and the Igreja Evangelica Baptista was the result. In 1929 Portuguese missionaries began their work in the country. Canadian Baptists in 1954 began assistance of the BMS. In 1968 **Southern Baptist** missionaries entered Angola and created the Convencão Baptista de Angola. A national organization, the Igreja Evangelica Baptista, was a result of the British Baptist mission.

As of 1995, there were 87 churches and 15,470 members in the Convencão Baptista de Angola, 55 churches and 34,558 members in the Igreja Evangelica do Sudoeste de Angola, and 33 churches and 16,390 members in the Free Baptist Convention of Angola.

ANGUS, JOSEPH (1816-1902). English Baptist minister, born in Northumberland. A prize-winning student in moral philosophy, he graduated from the University of Edinburgh and attended Stepney College in London. In 1837 he succeeded **John Rippon** as pastor at New Park Street Church in London. Two years later he became associated with the **Baptist Missionary Society** (BMS), later becoming its secretary (1839-49). In that role he urged the expansion of missionary work and visited many of the fields. In 1850 he was named principal of Stepney College and became a widely renowned educator among the Baptists and beyond.

During his 44 years as principal Angus improved the prospects of the College, in 1856 moving it from Stepney to Regent's Park where he negotiated a relationship with the University of London. He published a popular **bible** handbook in 1854 and edited several biographical works. Having noted several inaccuracies in the King James text of the bible, he was named to the panel of New Testament revisers. The library of Baptistiana at Regent's Park College is named in his honor.

ANTHONY, ALFRED WILLIAMS (1860-1939). Freewill Baptist minister and educator born at Providence, Rhode Island. Alfred was the son of a prominent Free Baptist minister and a descendant of Roger Williams. He graduated from Brown University and Cobb Divinity School, Bates College, and entered the pastoral ministry at Essex Street Freewill Baptist Church in Bangor, Maine. In 1887 he was elected to the Fullonton Professorship of New Testament Criticism and Exegesis at Cobb Divinity School, Bates College. In order to prepare himself for an academic career, he took further studies at the University of Berlin under Adolf von Harnack (1851-1930) and Bernhard Weiss (1827-1918). Anthony wrote a useful study of the life of Christ (1899) and a history of Bates College (1936). After Cobb Divinity School was closed in 1908, Anthony gave himself to consummating the merger between **Free Baptists** and **Northern Baptists**. He extolled the virtues of greater **mission** opportunities and he supported the Northern Baptist membership in the Federal Council of Churches. In 1918 he was elected secretary of the Home Missions Council, an affiliate of the Federal Council of Churches. To facilitate the merger among Baptists, Anthony served as corresponding secretary of the Free Baptist General Conference until his death in 1939.

ANTIGUA. Baptists entered Antigua only recently. The first to arrive were related to the **Baptist Missionary Association of America** (BMA); they started a congregation in 1960 at St. John's. In 1968 **Southern Baptists** as an outgrowth of **missions** in Trinidad began missionary work on both Antigua and **Barbuda** and established Central Baptist Church. The Antigua Barbuda Baptist Association was formed in 1980, with headquarters at St. John's, Antigua.

As of 1995, there were two churches and about 200 members affiliated with the Antigua Barbuda Baptist Association.

ANTIMASONRY. A movement which began in upstate New York in the 1820s and spread to the northeastern United States. In 1826 a Batavia, New York, stonemason named William Morgan (fl.1825) was accused of exposing Masonic secrets; he was abducted by persons alleged to be

Masons and supposedly killed. A propaganda crusade against the Fraternity was launched and scores of evangelical Christians rallied to the antimasonic political party and the concomitant religious crusade. Indeed, the enduring characteristics of Antimasonry were religiously motivated. Baptists participated in the movement by forming local **associations** and even disfellowshipping congregations which had Masonic members. An important epicenter of the antimasonic fervor was in Chautauqua County, New York, where in 1829 a parallel associational body was formed to oppose membership in local lodges. In many **associations**, and later the theologically **fundamentalistic** and **holiness** groups, Masonic membership was forbidden on the grounds that it was elitist, anti-democratic, promotive of infidelism, and unwholesomely blended biblical narrative with superstition and "Satanic" oaths.

ANTI-MISSIONARY BAPTISTS. See **Primitive Baptists**.

ANTISLAVERY, AMONG BAPTISTS. The antislavery movement was an important social concern among Baptists in the western hemisphere from the late 18th through the mid 19th century. While legal battles and debates raged in the legislatures of the United States and the British Parliament, actual application of antislavery principles led by Baptists occurred in **Jamaica, Liberia, Sierra Leone, Nova Scotia**, and **Haiti**.

The United States. In the late-18th century Baptists in the United States began to agitate against the institution of slavery and in Britain after the turn of the century. Early in the 1780s **Elhanan Winchester** openly opposed slaveholding. With the passage in 1787 of the (U.S.) Northwest Ordinance, slavery was forbidden in the Northwest Territory and the slave trade was abolished by 1807. In Pennsylvania, Virginia, and Kentucky Baptists were stimulated to action. In Virginia several prominent Baptist slaveholders manumitted their slaves, including **David Barrow** who would become a prominent emancipator in Kentucky. **John Leland** offered a resolution in the Virginia General Committee in 1789 which called for an end to slavery. The same year the **Philadelphia Baptist Association** supported the establishment of abolition societies and protection of the freedmen.

After 1790 the force of antislavery among Baptists shifted to Kentucky where Baptist ministers advocated a clause in the state constitution abolishing slavery. In the Elkhorn (Kentucky) Association in 1792 a resolution opposing slavery was passed and elsewhere several churches passed similar resolutions. At times the opposition was strong, as when David Barrow was expelled from the North District Association in 1806. A movement called the "Friends of Humanity Association" began in Kentucky in 1807 and spread throughout the Ohio Valley as far as Missouri in support of abolition. Much of the Friends of Humanity fervor died about 1816-1817 as the colonization movement became a more popular alternative and as the right of an associational body among Baptists to interfere in political and moral issues was questioned. When the American Antislavery Society was organized in 1830 by William Lloyd Garrison (1805-1879), a nominal Baptist himself, numerous Baptists in the northern states joined that segment of the abolitionist movement.

Still another form of antislavery expression in the United States was found in antislavery societies and missionary bodies. In New Hampshire, for instance, a state Baptist antislavery society was formed in 1838. When the debate over slaveholding in the General Missionary (Triennial) Convention proved frustrating for abolitionists, several prominent leaders formed the **American Baptist Free Mission Society** in 1843 and commissioned missionaries until after the Civil War. Among Black Baptists, **associations** and small societies fostered antislavery sentiments in the free black communities.

Great Britain. While earlier writers had opposed slavery, British Baptists first expressed their opposition to the institution in the 1820s and with renewed effort in the 1830s. The presence of slavery in Jamaica focused the issue through publications of the **Baptist Missionary Society** (BMS) and prompted **William Knibb** among others to strongly advocate abolition. This campaign in 1832-1833 was considered influential in the Reform Legislation of 1833, which abolished slavery in the British Empire. One of the early actions of the reorganized **Baptist Union** (BU) in 1836 was to authorize a delegation to visit the Baptists of the United States, to express among other objectives their antipathy to slaveholding. A similar delegation of English **General Baptists** visited in 1848 to carry the same message. Predominantly, the Baptists of the United Kingdom lent their moral support to the northern cause during the American Civil War.

ARCHITECTURE, BAPTIST CHURCH. The architectural style of Baptists reflects great variety and a sense of contextual evolution. In England in the earliest years of **General** and **Particular** Baptist development, the meeting places were often in homes, similar to the Elizabethan "conventicles" of other Nonconformists. **Seventh Day Baptists** met in homes and sometimes rented halls. As congregations grew in size and regularity of meetings, some of the houses were modified to include sufficient space for 25 to 30 to assemble. An important modification was the provision for an indoor **baptistry**, such as at

Tewksbury. Balconies were added as well as rooms to accommodate travelling preachers. The oldest-known structure designed as a Baptist meetinghouse was the Glass House on Broad Street in London, which was fitted with two tiers of galleries. Gradually at the time of toleration, separate meetinghouses of this kind were constructed, mostly of brick or native stone. The interiors were simple, with box pews enclosing family units. Often families rented the pews, a means of providing for the overall upkeep of the meetinghouse. It became fashionable for the pulpits of the 18th century to be elevated with a sounding board above to reflect the preacher's voice. Churches located in urban areas took advantage of interior space, while having rather simple unadorned exteriors, as in Broadmead, Bristol. Where there were large congregations, as in London, balconies were constructed for seating and frequent modifications were made. By the mid-18th century in Wales the meetinghouses were a characteristic feature of the village and rural landscapes, again constructed of brick and stone. Many of these survive into the present era.

A watershed event in the history of Baptist church architecture in Britain was the construction of Bloomsbury Chapel by **Samuel Morton Peto** in 1848. He used his own funds to construct an impressive urban edifice that resembled a cross between a French Church of England building and a chapel; the result was a two-spired magnificent Victorian structure. Peto helped to form the Metropolitan Chapel Building Society, which assisted in the construction of many commodious churches in Great Britain in the 1850s. His style was imitated throughout many English and Scottish cities.

Educational architecture among British Baptist schools is very varied. Stepney College housed an elaborate Greek revival building in London and similar facilities later at Regent's Park. At Oxford a plain quadrangle of late Victorian Oxford style encloses the facilities of the Regent's Park College. Manchester Baptist College's campus was transformed into a Georgian brick style enclosure when Northern Baptist College was completed in 1964. Spurgeon's College, originally housed in or near the Metropolitan Tabernacle, moved to Norwood Hill in 1923 to occupy an expanded Falklands Mansion on a bluff overlooking Croydon. Bristol Baptist College, which has moved several times, occupies a red brick building of columnar late-Victorian vintage in the style of Bristol University. South Wales Baptist College has been housed for most of the present century in a series of residences fronting a city street in Cardiff.

Early North American Baptist buildings were simple and, in contrast to their English and Welsh counterparts, were generally constructed of wood rather than stone. A simple rectangular building with pews occupying the majority of the floor space was common; the pews faced a pulpit and perhaps a choir area without adornments. Usually, there were no artistic windows and little more than a cross on the wall. The model for much of the 18th century must have been the New England Congregational meetinghouses, which also influenced the Middle Colonies, the South, and later eastern Canadian provinces. **Freewill Baptists** built frame structures in remote areas of New England which had plain, unpainted interiors with a woodstove situated in the middle of the box pews; similar church buildings were erected by the **Primitive Baptists** of the South and West. Among the Primitive and **Old Regular Baptists**, there are separate front doors for women and men and the interiors may exhibit pictures of former pastors and elders. Examples of the white-frame style have survived at Ossippee and New Durham, New Hampshire; Cross Roads, Virginia; Horse Creek, North Carolina; Burtonsville, Maryland; and as far west as West Union, Oregon. Interesting modifications of the frame meetinghouse design can be seen at Imlaystown, New Jersey, and Hopewell, New Jersey. Fine brick versions are at Pennypack (Lower Dublin), Pennsylvania, and Cohansey, New Jersey. In the Canadian Maritimes, surviving early frame meetinghouses are located in Pereaux and Billtown, Nova Scotia; and in Ontario at Peterborough, Charlotteville, and Strathaven.

The fine meetinghouse which **James Manning** constructed at Providence, Rhode Island, signalled a new era among Baptists in the American colonies. Completed in 1775, it towered above the city of Providence and carried a 185-foot steeple, which symbolized the emergence of Baptists as a social reality in the colonial/state capital. The Declaration of Independence was read from the steps of the meetinghouse on July 4, 1776. From the Providence design would emerge urban meetinghouses and church buildings in the South which demonstrated classical designs—Greek revival, romanesque, and even experimental. The First Baptist Church of Charleston, South Carolina (1887), exemplified the Greek revival style, and examples of romanesque could be found at University Baptist, Baltimore, Maryland, and the Baptist Temple in Philadelphia. Earlier in Philadelphia, **William Staughton** had constructed in 1811, at considerable expense, a meetinghouse in the round, with the baptistry located in the center of the congregational seating under a dome! Robert Mills (1781-1855), a prominent public architect and the designer of the Washington Monument, designed this futuristic structure, inspired by a similar plan he had made in 1804 for the "Circular" Congregational Church in Charleston, South Carolina; the Sansom Street sanctuary seated 4,000 people and introduced the auditorium concept to the preaching service. Later in 1817-1820 Mills designed for First Baptist in Baltimore a landmark building known as "Round Top."

In the 19th century, the national denominational bodies needed commodious rooms and prestigious locations to hold the Triennial assembly meetings, and this led to new meetinghouses constructed in the eastern seaboard cities: Boston, New York, Philadelphia, Baltimore, Richmond, and Charleston, though the latter would have to wait until a southern convention was organized in order to serve as a suitable travel venue.

As the social status of urban congregations rose, Baptists kept pace with Presbyterians, Lutherans, and Congregationalists in the construction of church buildings and educational space. Generally, the greater portion of space was devoted to worship, with the basement or ground level providing a social hall or church school area. Great stained glass windows in memory of departed leaders or war veterans or depicting scenes from **Scripture** were commonly found. Pipe organs became commonplace in urban Baptist churches as music became widely available and choirs were organized after the mid-19th century. It was not uncommon to have woodcarved communion tables with silver chalices and plates, brass clocks, and candlestick holders in prominent view in the city churches. Gradually, by the late 19th century, the term "meetinghouse" was replaced by "church" and theologians took care to explain that Baptists still understood the church to be "people" rather than buildings, despite the popular connotation.

An interesting feature of the last two decades of the 19th century were the Baptist "temples." These downtown churches, primarily in the northern states, were spectacles of great preaching and music similar to the Methodist great halls. In many cities—Boston, Philadelphia, New York, Rochester, New York, Cleveland, Ohio, and Charleston, West Virginia—temples became center city buildings of multiple programs and Sunday spectacles. **Russell Conwell** in Philadelphia and **Edward Judson** in New York personified the need for such a room to receive the preaching services.

The **fundamentalist** movement had a pronounced impact upon Baptist architecture in North America. Electrifying pulpiteers like **J. Frank Norris** concentrated their ministries on large crowds at worship services and protracted meetings, and this naturally led to architectural modifications. Eschewing the use of stained glass, organs, and comfortable pews, the new "evangelists" built rather plain buildings with plenty of aisle room for respondents to come forward at the altar call. The remaining space was dedicated to Sunday School classes. Norris actually inveighed against Gothic architecture and criticized his fellow Baptists who worshipped in such structures as elite and formalistic. His impact was felt in such groups as the **World Baptist Fellowship** (WBF) and the **Baptist Bible Fellowship** (BBF).

Following World War II, there was a fairly rapid expansion of Baptist church building in North America, mostly in the suburbs. Typically, these structures lacked the resources of classical or Gothic tastes, but instead were practical and fairly uniform. High ceiling exposed beam "sanctuaries" replicated in a small way the concept of the tent of the Old Testament tabernacle. In most instances the seating arrangement continued to consist of rows of pews facing the pulpit and communion table together with a center aisle.

Baptisteries in Baptist church buildings across the South and West frequently dominate the interior front, while in the northern United States and the Canadian provinces a simple cross on the wall behind the pulpit suffices. In the latter situations, the baptistery is hidden under the floor of the pulpit area.

Following the erection of the principal structure, which is usually used for worship, most building programs next turn to educational space. Typically designed for individual **Sunday School** classes and a common area for assemblies, this space is also used for community groups such as scouts or senior citizens and church fellowship dinners. In churches where exterior property is limited the basement area under the sanctuary serves these purposes.

In the present century as urban development has limited church-yard space, parking space for automobiles became a determinant of the suitability of location for a congregation. Still, an historic building which is cherished by the community and the congregation can outweigh the need to move for more space. Edifices of this type can be found in Philadelphia, Boston, Washington, D.C., Charleston, South Carolina, and San Francisco, California, for instance. In Canada, urban heritage buildings survive in Moncton and St. John, New Brunswick; Montreal, Quebec; Toronto, Peterborough, and Hamilton, Ontario; Calgary, Alberta; and Vancouver, British Columbia.

Related to North American Baptist church architecture is the design of educational buildings owned by Baptists. Often the benefactors of colleges and universities imitated styles which they designed for their local churches. This was seen in the eastern urban areas and later in Chicago, Toronto, and smaller cities such as Granville, Ohio, and Georgetown, Kentucky. They constituted a statement that graphically depicted the emerging social status of Baptists.

The first buildings of an educational use in the Baptist community were those constructed by the Brown family for the College of Rhode Island in Providence. University Hall and Manning Hall were imitations of Harvard College and a modified Greek revival style. The first national university, Columbian College in Washington, D.C., embodied a bold vision of national leadership in the nation's capital, whose facilities bankrupted its trustees. "College Hill" in Washington D.C. (later Meridian Hill Park) stood on a promontory of prized real estate value. Structures at Colgate University, Newton Theological Institution, and the University at Lewisburg in Pennsylvania were likewise designed to ⸌mbody the New England college tradition--conservative, brick, and permanent, dominant motifs of their local landscapes. With the coming of **John D. Rockefeller**'s munificence, Baptist colleges imitated the Gothic style; this is illustrated in the University of Chicago (Illinois), Colgate Rochester Divinity School (New York), McMaster University (Ontario), and the University of Richmond (Virginia). Smaller schools in the Midwest and West constructed more functional structures closely resembling Victorian brick combination classroom and dormitory facilities found throughout the United States. Examples of this style are found at Franklin College in Indiana, Shurtleff College in Illinois, Sioux Falls College in South Dakota, Wake Forest College in North Carolina (the original campus now occupied by Southeastern Baptist Theological Seminary), and Southern Baptist Theological Seminary in Louisville, Kentucky.

AREA MINISTER. Terminology applied to regional ministers in the American Baptist, British Baptist, and Canadian Baptist traditions of the 20th century. Following the adoption of the "area" terminology, travelling ministers were appointed to relate to congregations in a geographical region comprising several associations. Usually accountable to the **executive minister**, area ministers serve as resources in program interpretation to churches, staff to associational programs, **pastors** to pastors, and missionary agents. Sometimes personnel work is part of the task as when congregations are seeking new leadership

Historically, area ministers have similar tasks to the "messengers" of ancient English **General Baptist** tradition, and association missionaries in American and **Southern Baptist** polity. The first area or general superintendants in Britain were appointed in 1916. In the American Baptist family, persons holding specific program responsibilities, such as Christian education or rural ministry, began to assume oversight of certain regions; for instance, in 1948 the New York Baptist Convention began designating areas and ministers to care for churches in the areas. Later, state convention "field secretaries" evolved to area ministers, particularly in the Midwest. The title "area minister" was in broad usage by 1967 among American Baptists. Southern Baptists made use of "area workers" following World War II, which evolved into associational missionaries or superintendents of **missions** (the latter had been employed in some states since the early 1900s). See also **Executive Minister**.

ARGENTINA. Pablo Besson (1848-1932) was the founder of the permanent Baptist movement in Argentina, arriving in 1881 to start a church at Buenos Aires in 1883. In 1908 a national organization was organized, the Convención Evangelica Bautista de la República Argentina. U.S. **Southern Baptists**, who began their mission in 1901-1903, aware of the strategic location of Argentina, established the Seminario Internacional Teológico Bautista in Buenos Aires in 1953, to serve not only Argentina but also **Uruguay, Chile,** and **Paraguay.** The U.S. **Baptist General Conference** pioneered mission churches in 1955, resulting in Iglesias Bautistas Evangelicas del Norte America. The **Conservative Baptist** Foreign Mission Society (CBFMS) established a mission in 1947 which relates to the General Association of Baptist Churches of Northwestern Argentina (1972) and the Evangelical Baptist Seminary of Argentina (1965) at Salta (formerly Tucuman). The **Baptist Bible Fellowship** (BBF) has had a mission in Argentina since 1959 and the **Association of Baptists for World Evangelism** (ABWE) started a mission in 1978.

As of 1995, there were 420 churches and 56,450 members affiliated with the Convención Evangelica Bautista de Argentina. A theological school, Seminario Internacional Teológico Bautista, is located at Buenos Aires.

ARMENIA. At the political reorganization of the former Soviet Union in 1991, the Republic of Armenia emerged as a new state and with it the Baptist community. Formerly related to the All Union Council of Evangelical Christians-Baptists, Baptists in Armenia formed Soiuz Evangelskikh Christian-Baptistov Armenii in 1992. This body of churches cooperates with the **European Baptist Federation** and the **Baptist World Alliance**.

As of 1995 there were 10 churches with 2,180 members affiliated with Soiuz Evangelskikh Christian-Baptistov Armenii.

ARMINIANISM, AMONG BAPTISTS. Strictly speaking, the term "Arminian" applies to those in the theological tradition of Jacobus Arminius (1560-1609), a Dutch Reformed pastor and theologian in the **Netherlands**. Arminius came to oppose the Calvinistic understanding of predestination and stressed the involvement of human response to God's gracious offer of salvation. Arminian thought was formally condemned at the Synod of Dort in 1618 and the Arminians (also called Remonstrants) were silenced in the Netherlands for a generation. The themes of Arminian thought, however, found their way into the Church of England and smaller evangelical sects like the **General Baptists** and later the Methodists. While there is no evidence of direct dependance of any Baptists upon Arminius, those in the General, **Free(will)**, and **holiness** Baptist groups are frequently described as "Arminian" because of their emphases upon free grace, free response to the gospel, and a view of Christ's atonement as unlimited. Baptists with high Calvinist theological positions (e.g., **Strict Baptists**, **Primitive Baptists**, **Reformed Baptists**) often take offence at Arminian groups or overly evangelistic emphases, claiming either a diminution of the sovereignty of God or the possibility of lapsing into unitarian or universalist theologies. See also **General Baptists**; **Primitive Baptists**; **Strict Baptists**.

ARMITAGE, THOMAS (1819-1896). Baptist minister and historian, born in Pontefract, Yorkshire, England. He preached his first sermon at 15 years old. He emigrated to the United States in 1838 and became a Methodist minister at Washington Street Methodist Church in Albany, New York. Disagreeing with the Methodists on doctrinal and **polity** issues, Armitage converted to Baptist principles in 1848, under the influence of **Jabez Swan**, and was baptized at Pearl Street Baptist Church in Albany. That year he was called to the pastorate at Norfolk Street Baptist Church (later Fifth Avenue Baptist Church) in New York City, where he served until 1896. The day following his first Sunday at Norfolk Street, a fire destroyed the building and a new structure was soon erected at a cost of $30,000. Armitage also survived a vote of no confidence in 1853 which was rooted in 96 members' petition to obtain a new **pastor**. In 1865 he led in the construction of the Fifth Avenue Baptist Church, which became a city landmark. In 1886 he published a well-received history of the Baptists.

ARMSTRONG, ANNE WALKER (1850-1938). Southern Baptist denominational leader, born at Baltimore, Maryland. She was not formally educated but joined the Seventh Baptist Church in Baltimore then served by the venerable **Richard Fuller**. She was much interested in children's education and taught the infant's class in her home church for 30 years. In the 1880s Armstrong led in the establishment of the Women's Missionary Union and its auxiliary status with the **Southern Baptist Convention** (SBC). In 1899 she became corresponding secretary for the Union, eventually refusing to take a salary. In 1888 she wrote letters to hundreds of missionary supporters raising almost $3,000 to support **Charlotte Moon** in China. She was also active in missionary work among

African Americans, providing funds to produce literature for their churches. The Southern Baptist **Foreign Mission Board** (FMB) established in 1934 the Annie Armstrong Offering, an annual fundraising effort for foreign work.

ASHANTI. See Ghana.

ASHMORE, WILLIAM (1824-1909). American Baptist missionary, born at Putnam, Ohio. A graduate of Granville College and Western Baptist Theological Seminary, he first served the pastorate of First Baptist, Hamilton, Ohio. Under the appointment of the **American Baptist Missionary Union** to Bangkok, **Siam**, he conducted street preaching and mastered the Tie-chiu dialect. In 1858 Ashmore became a missionary in **Hong Kong** and later Swatow, **China,** where he spent the bulk of his career. In China he developed an extensive Chinese staff and built a strong theological seminary at Swatow plus a school to train women. He is best remembered for his advocacy of indigenous leadership. The theological school in Swatow was named in his honor. In addition to numerous translations into Swatow, Ashmore published an outline of theology for Chinese students in 1902.

ASIAN BAPTIST FEDERATION (ABF). A regional organization of the **Baptist World Alliance** (BWA) founded in 1975. The Federation was organized to promote fellowship, cooperation, and service among its member unions/conventions in Asia and Oceania. Mission planning and relief programs are also included in the agenda, as is the promotion of the overall objectives of the Baptist World Alliance. Structurally, the Federation consists of a General Council, an executive committee, and a congress which meets every five years in various cities throughout Asia. The Federation publishes the *Asian Baptist Digest* (1997-), formerly the *Asian Baptist News* (1972-1996).

ASPLAND, ROBERT (1782-1845). English Baptist, and later Unitarian minister, born at Wicken, Cambridgeshire, England. He was well educated at Bristol Baptist Academy and the University of Aberdeen, receiving the Ward Scholarship. He was baptized at the Devonshire Square Baptist Church and became pastor at the Baptist Chapel in Battersea in 1798. While a student at Bristol, Aspland developed unorthodox theological views, but was also known as the "boy preacher" for his communication skills. In 1799 he matriculated at Marischal College, but a year later was dropped from the rolls at Devonshire Square Church. In 1800 he joined a firm manufacturing artist's colors and did supply preaching in London. In 1801 he was called to the General Baptist Church at Newport, Isle of Wight, but two years later became secretary to the South Unitarian Society. In 1805 Aspland became minister at the Gravel Pit, Hackney Church, and remained there for 40 years. He became essentially a Unitarian, organizing a Minister's Fund and the Christian Tract Society, but also maintained personal relations and influence in the declining General Baptist community. His influence as a **liberal** thinker was greatly enhanced by his journal, *The Christian Reformer*, which he commenced and edited, 1815-1844.

ASPLUND, JOHN (1750-1807). American Baptist minister and editor, born in Sweden. Early in life he was involved in mercantile pursuits, without formal education. In 1775 he visited England and worked as a clerk. During the American Revolution he joined the British Navy and, while on duty near the American coast, he deserted ship. He settled in North Carolina, became a Baptist in 1782, and united with the Ballard's Bridge Church in Chowan County. Shortly thereafter he moved to Southampton, Virginia, to be a **pastor** through 1785 and again from 1791 to 1794. He returned to Europe in 1785 to make a survey of Dissenters and Baptists, visiting England, **Denmark**, **Germany**, **Finland**, Lapland, and the United States, covering about 7,000 miles. He made a second tour in 1794 and covered over 10,000 miles. Each of his tours produced an edition of *The Baptist Annual Register*. His purpose was twofold: to conduct itinerant preaching and to collect materials to assist future historians. Asplund reckoned that his experience as a clerk placed him in a unique position to calculate the statistics of over 250 Baptist churches and ministers. He relocated to Maryland in the early 19th century and died by drowning in an accident.

ASSEMBLY OF FREE GRACE GENERAL BAPTISTS. See **General Baptists**.

ASSOCIATION OF BAPTISTS FOR WORLD EVANGELISM (ABWE). A U.S.-based mission sending organization formed in reaction to policies of the **American Baptist Foreign Mission Society** (ABFMS) and the **Northern Baptist Convention** (NBC). In the 1920s amidst the **fundamentalist** controversy, the leadership of the NBC urged upon its missionary agency, the ABFMS, a more open policy of non-confessional personnel appointments. Moreover, one of the medical missionaries of the Society, Dr. Raphael C. Thomas (1873-1956), then a missionary in the **Philippines**, was reprimanded for his open advocacy of more attention to evangelism, and this ultimately led to his resignation from service. His relatives and supporters in the United States who were already coalescing around conservative evangelical issues in the NBC, such as a confession of faith and seminary education in the **evangelical** if not moderately **fundamentalist** tradition, assisted in the formation of a new missionary agency to carry forth Dr. Thomas's work and perhaps to expand to other fields. The original group of founders of ABWE included **Lucy W. Peabody** and Marguerite Treat Doane (1868-1954), daughter of **William Howard Doane.**

ABWE was founded in Philadelphia in 1927-1928, stressing historic Baptist principles and a voluntary association of supporters rather than a denominational body. The first field was in the Philippines, followed by **Peru, Brazil, Colombia,** South **China** (to 1953), **Hong Kong, Chile, Japan,** and **Pakistan,** to name the major areas. The mission, which operates as a faith mission and primarily accepts designated gifts, sponsors a theological seminary at Manila and a bible college in Iloilo in the Philippines, and **bible colleges** in South America. Currently, ABWE sponsors 1,162 missionaries in 39 countries. In addition, ABWE works with national Christians in over a dozen countries where Christian witness is restricted through the Global Access Partners (GAP). The official periodical of ABWE is *The Message* and the headquarters are in Harrisburg, Pennsylvania.

ASSOCIATIONS, BAPTIST. Based upon a principle common to most Christian organizations, Baptists have almost from their beginnings associated with other churches of like faith and order. The purposes of the association are mutual support, aid to destitute congregations, and advice on matters of order, **discipline**, expansion, and identity.

The Baptist association is not considered a superior body to the local congregation, rather, an advisory body voluntarily covenanting with local churches for specific tasks. Delegates or messengers from local churches usually include the pastor and one lay representative, according to the relative size of the church. Annual meetings of delegates consist of business sessions, worship and preaching, and reports on the status of members congregations. Actions may be taken in the name of the association, but are not binding on the local churches. Churches may be **"disfellowshipped,"** that is, dropped from associational membership by vote of the delegates. Theological consensus was important in the 17th and 18th centuries, usually becoming the basis of effective associative relations.

In terms of size and numbers of participating churches, the association has evolved considerably. In the beginning, the association usually represented the distance of one day's travel by horse and buggy between points of greatest distance. As the Baptist movement expanded, the political unit of the county corresponded roughly to an association's geography. Size has ranged from five to seven congregations in early days to 20 or 30 member churches in the 20th century.

The first associations among the English Baptists were formed in the 1620s. London Baptists, divided over relations with other Christians and the meaning of the magistracy, met informally and corresponded with the Dutch Mennonites. Later, the **Particular** Baptists of London formed an association, and they prepared and ratified the First London Confession of Faith in 1644. By the 1660s, Baptists in England and **Wales** had formed local and national associations and met regularly, at least once per year.

In the American colonies, the associational principle developed very early. **General Six Principle Baptist** congregations held yearly meetings in Rhode Island as early as the 1670s. In the Middle Colonies, Philadelphia churches met beginning in 1707. In New England, a **Five Principle** Calvinistic Baptist Association met from 1754, and in the South, the churches of Charleston formed an association in 1751. The Philadelphia (Pennsylvania), Warren (Rhode Island), and Charleston (South Carolina) associations became models for a rapidly expanding associational life in the United States.

The classic statement in an American context concerning the association was made by Benjamin Griffiths (1688-1768), a Philadelphia minister, who wrote in 1749 that the purposes of associations include the drafting of sound doctrine and the disowning of erroneous teachings, the sending of representatives for consultation, and the making of decisions to withdraw from defective or disorderly churches. Griffiths was careful to indicate that each congregation is independent in its authority and church power, the association being advisory and voluntary. Griffiths's statement has been referred to by both mainstream and **fundamentalist** Baptist groups in the United States.

Among Baptists in **Canada**, the first associations emerged in Nova Scotia and Upper Canada (the predecessor of modern Ontario). Missionaries from New York state and New England planted associations in the vicinity of Lakes Ontario and Erie. In Nova Scotia, the Danbury, Connecticut, Association was a specific model. Among churches in the Ottawa River Valley, English Baptist associational principles were witnessed in the formation of associations.

As Baptists spread forth, primarily from North America and Great Britain, the associational principle followed the establishment of congregations. In Europe, **J. G. Oncken** toured widely in the **German** states and Austria-Hungary and formed associations which frequently became national unions of Baptist churches. In Africa, missions to **Liberia**, the **Congo** and **South Africa** produced associations of churches. In South Asia, Indian Baptists formed their associations early in the 19th century, and the missionary churches in **China** and **Japan** did likewise in the 1860s and 1870s. Latin American associations were built on American models, differing only as influenced by northern or southern U. S. Baptist missionaries. Generally, the formation of associations precedes the creation of national unions or conventions.

AUSTRALIA. The first Baptists in Australia came amongst the pioneer settlers from Great Britain; one of these was a convict named Richard Boots who arrived in 1788 and listed his religious affiliation as "Baptist." In 1831 John McKaeg (fl.1818-1837) held the first Baptist service in a hotel in Sydney; two years later John Saunders, a missionary of the **Baptist Missionary Society** (BMS), planted the Bathurst Street Church in Sydney, New South Wales, considered the mother congregation of Baptists in Australia. For a time in the 1840s the BMS considered making Australia an official field, but declined in favor of unevangelized peoples. However, at the request of Australian leaders, the Society did send several church planters. Various states had differing beginning points of Baptist mission work, such as in 1835 at Hobart in Tasmania, considered the earliest constituted church in what is now Australia, although it survived only eight years; the first church in South Australia was established in Adelaide, following missionary beginnings with aboriginal peoples; about 1839 a congregation was gathered in Melbourne, Victoria; another at Moreton Bay, Queensland; in 1855; and in Western Australia a church was formed at Perth in 1895.

Much influenced by British Baptists, associational life emerged in 1858 in Victoria, South Australians organized an association in 1863, and in 1872 with the **Particular Baptist** Association of Australia (New South Wales). Cooperation for **mission** occurred quite early with the establishment of an auxiliary to the BMS in South Australia in 1863, which evolved into the Australian Baptist Missionary Society. The Society began a mission in East Bengal at its formation, in 1876 supported for four years a mission in **Japan**, and conducts work in **India**, **Pakistan**, and **Papua, New Guinea**. As of 1995, the Society supported 129 missionaries in 12 nations.

In 1926 a national organization, the Baptist Union of Australia, was founded from among the state associations. Presently, there are state unions in Victoria (1862), South Australia (1863), New South Wales (1868), Queensland (1877), Tasmania (1884), and Western Australia (1896). Each state body is independent, with the result that the national

Union is an advisory organization. There are six theological or secondary schools, which include Victoria Baptist College (later Whitley College) in Melbourne (1891), Queensland Baptist College of Ministries (1904), Morling College, New South Wales (1916), Kings College, Kensington, New South Wales (1910), Carey Baptist Grammar School at Kew, New South Wales (1923), Burleigh College in South Australia (1952), and the Baptist Theological College of Western Australia (1963).

In addition to the indigenous Baptist work in Australia, **Baptist Mid-Missions** (BMM) from the United States established a work in Melbourne in 1968 and later at Croydon. In 1973 the Victoria Baptist Bible College emerged from this effort. Also in 1968 the **Baptist Bible Fellowship** (BBF) established a mission, as did the **Association of Baptists for World Evangelism** (ABWE) in 1970. **Seventh Day Baptists** from New Zealand established a church at Bundaberg in 1975.

As of 1995, there were 883 churches and 64,129 members associated with the Baptist Union of Australia. The official periodical has been the *Australian Baptist* (1913-1991), afterward the *National Baptist* (1991-) and various state periodicals.

AUSTRIA. Baptist development in the heart of the Austro-Hungarian Empire may be traced to missionary work by **J. G. Oncken**. In 1847 the first Austrians were baptized and in 1851 Edward Millard began a long-term mission in Vienna which eventuated in the first congregation in 1869. A. Meereis was the first appointed pastor in 1879. In the 20th century Arnold Köster, the pastor at Vienna, unified the Baptist work and suffered greatly during Nazi occupation. In 1953 the Bund der Baptistengemeinden in Österreich (Union of Baptist Churches in Austria) was created, and the Austrian churches assisted in the creation of the German Baptist Confession of 1977. In addition to the regular Baptist work, **Baptist Mid-Missions** (BMM) from the United States established an independent mission in 1967, the **Conservative Baptist** Foreign Mission Society (CBFMS) began its mission in 1970, and the **Baptist Bible Fellowship** (BBF) opened a mission in 1984.

As of 1995, there were 16 churches and 1,090 members affiliated with the Bund der Baptistengemeinden in Österreich. A periodical, *Gemeindebrief* (Church Notes) (1950-) is associated with the Bund.

AUTONOMY OF THE LOCAL CHURCH. A much discussed facet of Baptistic identity which pertains to the local congregation. The terminology "autonomy of the local church" actually appeared as such first in the work of **E. Y. Mullins**, a **Southern Baptist** theologian, in 1898.

From the earliest development of English Baptist theological understanding of the church, Baptists have clearly articulated the freedom of a local congregation to determine its own affairs. A congregation is to be free from interference by government and from other ecclesiastical bodies. Early Baptists wrote of the independence of congregations, by which they meant that the gifts and authority of Christ were given to each congregation to manage its own affairs. At the same time, both the First and Second London Confessions of Faith also speak of the associational principle (see **Associations**) which relates individual congregations together.

In the United States, the associational principle prevailed among the scattered communities of Baptist churches along the eastern seaboard. However, in the backcountry a frontier individualism developed by the third decade of the 19th century which sought to protect the rights of the congregation. Referred to by some historians as "**local church protectionism**," this attitude was militantly expressed in the New Hampshire Confession of Faith (1832). A combination of New England protectionism, western frontier ethos, and theological obscurantism as illustrated in the antimission campaign, thus created an emphasis upon the prerogatives of the local church.

The **Landmarkist** movement carried forth the independence of the local church as one of its major assertions. Landmarkist writers such as **James M. Graves** and **James M. Pendleton** asserted that each local congregation was the "true church" and that nothing held power or authority over it or could interfere in its government. Churches were subject to the Lordship of **Christ** alone, making rules and exercising discipline under Christ's authority exclusively. A belligerent style of local church independence was revealed in Landmarkist literature, which caused much offence among other Baptists and within the larger paedo-Baptist Christian community. Because pastors often waged the debates over the rights of local churches, the Landmarkist position on this "doctrine" is seen as affirming a strong, authoritarian pastoral leadership which resists interference in its **ministry**.

In 1898 E. Y. Mullins in the southern United States wrote authoritatively on Baptist beliefs and described much of the theological basis of the idea of autonomy. In fact, the term "autonomy" is likely his addition to the Baptist vocabulary. He held that the government of each local church is democratic and autonomous, free and independent. But, lest his position be confused with Landmarkism, he also argued for cooperation as one of the highest privileges a church could enjoy.

In the present century, the "doctrine" of the autonomy of the local church has received much affirmation among independent Baptists and those who favor weak associational bodies. "Conventionism" is seen as an unwarranted interference in local church affairs, notably in decisions about distribution of funds, theological exclusivity, and selection of leadership. See also **Local Church Protectionism; Polity, Baptist.**

AZERBAIJAN. When the former Soviet Union collapsed in 1991-1992, Azerbaijan emerged as an independent state. Along with this political change, the Baptist community, which had been part of the All Union Council of Evangelical Christians-Baptists, formed the Soiuz Evangelskikh Christian-Baptistov Azerbaijana (Union of Evangelical Christians-Baptists of Azerbaijan) in 1992.

As of 1995 there were 10 churches with 780 members affiliated with Soiuz Evangelskikh Christian-Baptistov Azerbaijana.

B

BABCOCK, RUFUS (1798-1875). American Baptist minister and educator, born at Colebrook, Connecticut. Babcock graduated from Brown University and studied theology under **William Staughton** in Philadelphia. He was one of the first faculty members of Columbian College, Washington, D.C., and served pastorates in New York and Massachusetts. In 1833 he was elected president of Waterville College in Maine where he served for four years before becoming pastor at Spruce Street Church in Philadelphia. Babcock was an avid supporter of religious **voluntarism**, serving with the **American Baptist Publication Society**, the American and Foreign Bible Society, and the American **Sunday School** Union. From 1841-1845 he was editor of the newspaper, *The Baptist Memorial*. Babcock also edited the published journal of the pioneer domestic missionary, **John Mason Peck**.

BACKUS, ISAAC (1724-1806). American Baptist pastor and historian, born at Norwich, Connecticut. Backus was one of the best-known and highly regarded ministers of the Revolutionary and Early National periods. Converted in 1741 during the **Great Awakening,** he began his **ministry** as a Congregationalist and soon joined the **Separate** or New Light movement. He was ordained at Middleborough, Massachusetts, where he served his first pastorate. He itinerated widely as an evangelist and in 1756 he converted to Baptist principles and subsequently organized a Baptist congregation at Middleborough. Backus was a leading polemicist against taxation of **Nonconformists** and in 1774 he served as the agent of the Warren Baptist Association to the Continental Congress. His letter to the citizens of New England in 1777 moved many people to the cause of **religious liberty**. In 1789 Backus made a 3,000 mile tour of the middle and southern states, strengthening churches and gathering materials for a history of the Baptists. Using materials also supplied by **Morgan Edwards** and his own notes, Backus published a major historical treatise on Baptists (1804) in which he recounted the struggles of the 17th century and particularly the role of **Roger Williams** in achieving religious liberty. In recent historiography, Backus's diaries were edited by **William G. McLoughlin** of Brown University and Backus has survived as a major interpreter of 18th century Baptist thought. See also **Separate Baptists**.

BAHAMAS. Early Baptist history in the Bahamas stems from the presence of several former slaves who began preaching and gathered churches: Frank Spence (1780), Prince Williams (1790), and later, Thomas Rumer (1840). In 1833 missionaries appointed by the **Baptist Missionary Society** (BMS) in London arrived in the Bahamas and greatly aided the Baptist cause. In addition to **evangelism**, the BMS staff started Sabbath schools, temperance societies, and bible societies; in 1929 the BMS withdrew from the islands. In 1892 a Bahamas Baptist Union was formed, uniting several islands of the Baptist community. In 1925-1930 two representatives of the **National Baptist Convention in the U.S.A.**, the Rev. J. R. Evans and Mrs. Jannie Morris of Miami, Florida, visited the Bahamas and organized women's home mission societies and young people's unions, relating to the U.S. body. In 1937 the Bahamas Baptist Missionary and Educational Convention emerged, bringing much needed support from the National Baptists. U. S. **Southern Baptists** began vacation bible school ministries in the Bahamas in 1949, out of which grew the Bahamas Baptist Institute in 1953, which was ultimately merged into the Bahamas Baptist College in 1965. There is also an Independent Baptist work in the Bahamas, related to **fundamentalist** Baptists in the southern United States.

As of 1995, there were 211 churches and 55,000 members relating to the Bahamas National Baptist Missionary and Education Convention. A school, Bahamas Baptist Community College, is located at Nassau.

BAKER, ROBERT ANDREW (1910-1992). Southern Baptist minister and church historian, born at St. Louis, Missouri. He was educated at a business college and in 1932 was appointed to the U.S. Secret Service, where he spent four years as an operative. Beginning in 1936 he continued his education at Baylor University, Southwestern Baptist Seminary, and ultimately at Yale University, the latter where he studied with **Kenneth Scott Latourette** and Roland Bainton (1894-1984). From 1946-1952 he was pastor at Highland Baptist Church in Dallas, Texas. In 1952 he became professor of church history at Southwestern Seminary, succeeding his mentor, **William Wright Barnes**. Baker became one of the most influential scholars of his era in the **Southern Baptist** tradition. Among his published works were *Relations Between Northern and Southern Baptists* (1948), *The Southern Baptist Convention and Its People 1607-1972* (1974), and *A Summary of Christian History* (1959).

BALDWIN, THOMAS (1753-1826). Baptist pastor, born at Bozrah, Connecticut. Originally trained to practice law, Baldwin converted to Baptist principles in 1780 and was ordained an evangelist in Connecticut. Eventually he served the church at Canaan and was called to Second Baptist Church, Boston in 1790. In association with **Samuel Stillman** at First Baptist, Boston, Baldwin helped to make Boston an epicenter of New England Baptist life. He was active in promoting various **voluntary** associations, notably the Massachusetts Baptist Missionary Society, where he served as an officer and editor of their magazine, the oldest Baptist periodical in the United States in continuous circulation. In 1810 he published a series of letters on Baptist principles, considered by his contemporaries to be a preeminent statement of denominational beliefs. Baldwin was one of the chief promoters of establishing the Newton Theological Institution, based on the Andover Theological Seminary model of the Congregationalists. He was also the first president of the **Baptist Board of Foreign Missions** (BBFM). Baldwin's book, *The Baptism of Believers Only* (1806), is considered a classic treatment of its subject.

BALTIMORE COMPROMISE. Name given to an important agreement struck between Baptist churches in the United States who differed on the question of slaveholding and missionary appointments. At the Tenth Triennial meeting of the **General Missionary Convention** (GMC), held in Baltimore, Maryland, in May 1841 the delegates wrestled with the moral and political questions which their respective sections exhibited. Northerners were increasingly interested in a strong stand against slaveholding and wanted it placed in the bylaws of the GMC. Southerners, on the other hand, felt that political considerations had no place in **evangelical** work and would tolerate no such retrictions. Under the skillful leadership of GMC President **William Bullein Johnson** of South Carolina, the delegates agreed that the Convention had no right to interfere in political questions and that union was more important than sectional jealousies. The **Baptist Board of Foreign Missions** (BBFM), actually responsible for the appointment of missionaries, affirmed the "Baltimore Compromise" in holding that all churches are independent communities, and they had delegated no power to individuals or **associations** to act for them. The Baltimore Compromise, then, held that issues of appointing slaveholders or countenancing slaveholding were inappropriate to hold as a criterion in the work of missions.

Between 1843 and 1845, however, pressure mounted in the northern Baptist churches as the American and Foreign Free Missionary Society (ABFrMS) was formed as an **antislavery** body, and southerners looked for inviolable defenses against their pro-slavery position. When in 1844 the Acting Board of the Convention voted to refuse the appointment of a slaveholder to missionary work in a hypothetical question put to it by Alabama delegates, the Baltimore Compromise was broken and the steps toward a regional schism were taken. See **Southern Baptist Convention**.

BAMPFIELD, FRANCIS (1615-1683). Seventh Day Baptist minister and author, born in Poltimore, Devon, England. Bampfield was educated at Wadham College, Oxford, and ordained a priest in the Church of England. He served initially in Dorsetshire, where he organized various charitable enterprises for the poor; later he was a prebend in Exeter Cathedral. He moved to Sherborne, where he became a Puritan; in 1662 he was driven out by the Act of Uniformity. A Royalist under Charles I, he was also a Trier under Oliver Cromwell (1599-1658). With the passage of the Act of Uniformity in 1662, he was imprisoned for up to nine years. During his incarceration, he arrived at baptistic and sabbatarian positions and preached in the jail where he also gathered a congregation. Bampfield baptized himself in the River Salisbury. In 1676 he started a Seventh Day church at Bethnal Green in his home; in 1681 he hired Pinner's Hall to accommodate the crowds in attendance. He was arrested for conducting these services and sentenced to Newgate prison where he died. He published eight works, including a major study of the Sabbath and a defense of **religious liberty**.

BAND OF HOPE. In the **temperance** crusade in early Victorian England, organizations of children in support of the cause emerged, the leading one of which was the Band of Hope movement. At a Temperance Society meeting at Leeds in 1847, Baptist minister Jabez Tunnicliff met Anne Jane Carlile, a prison worker, and the two agreed to begin the Band of Hope to attract children to the temperance cause. Most of those who joined the Bands were from working class families of a great variety of dissenting congregations. See also **Temperance, Baptists and**.

BANGLADESH. Baptist work in this region is traced from **William Carey** who in 1793 began a mission in Bengal for the **Baptist Missionary**

Society (BMS). Various American Baptist missionaries have passed through Bengal as well, beginning with **Adoniram Judson**. With the partition of East and West **Pakistan** from **India** in 1947, the Bengal Baptist Union was forced to make administrative arrangements in the new geo-political situation. Temporarily, the West Dinajpur Baptist Union assumed leadership in the territory, but this proved inadequate. In 1955 the Bengal Baptist Union recognized the establishment of the Baptist Union of Pakistan, which encompassed the region of East Pakistan. In 1971 the Republic of Bangladesh was proclaimed amidst open military hostilities and Baptists within the country, as well as missionary organizations, provided aid and leadership in the crisis. Eventually the Baptist Union of Pakistan became the Bangladesh Baptist Sangha, still historically related to the BMS. A second organization of churches, the Bangladesh Baptist Union, relates to the mission work of Australia, New Zealand, and Southern Baptists. The **Association of Baptists for World Evangelism** (ABWE) began a mission in East Pakistan (Bangladesh) in 1955.

As of 1995, there were 372 churches with 10,345 members affiliated with the Bangladesh Baptist Fellowship, 321 churches with 12,100 members affiliated with the Bangladesh Baptist Sangha, and 140 churches with 9,844 members affiliated with the Garo Baptist Convention. There are two Baptist-related schools in Bangladesh: J.N.B. Memorial Baptist Training Institute at Mymensingh and the College of Christian Theology in Bangladesh at Dacca.

BAPTISM. Baptism is a primary rite among Baptists; according to the 18th century British-American historian **Morgan Edwards**, it was their denominating article.

The Meaning of Baptism. From a Baptist perspective, baptism is a profession of faith, an initiatory act, a symbolic rite of cleansing, a transition rite to a new creation, and an act of obedience. Based on Romans 6, baptism is a picture of the gospel at work in one's experience: crucifixion with Christ, burial with Christ, and resurrection to new life in Christ. Only the mode of immersion signifies this aspect so vividly. From Matthew 28:19,20, Baptists believe it is incumbent upon every able believer to be baptized in the name of the Father, Son, and Holy Spirit. Just as Jesus submitted himself to the baptism of John (Matt. 3: 13-17; John 1:26-34; Mark 1:9-13), so all believers must submit themselves to the example and command of Christ. Commonly in the **Black Baptist** community, baptism signifies the transition from a "bastard people" to a new social creation (II Cor. 5:17).

For Baptists, believer's baptism precedes admission to the church. Having professed one's faith in Christ through the act of baptism, a person is initiated through a faithful experience into, first, the universal body of Christ and, second, into the local congregation, the visible manifestation of the Body of Christ. It was common for early confessions of faith to limit the enjoyment of the benefits of the church, particularly admission to the Lord's Supper, to baptized believers only.

The Issue of Believer's versus Paedo-baptism. In the first generation of baptistic believers in England and later the **Netherlands**, believer's baptism was a key issue. Virtually the entire Christian community except the Anabaptist sects, practiced infant or "paedo" (meaning "child") baptism as a sacrament. This had the dual significance of introducing children at the beginnings of their lives to the Christian community as well as registering them in the social community, i.e., giving the child a "Christian" name. **Anabaptists** in the early 16th century recovered the ancient practice of baptizing believers only, which in reality limited the act of baptism to adults. Later, **John Smyth** and a small group of English Separatists began to practice believer's baptism to reestablish a "true church of true believers." This was seen as a radical act because it called into question the longstanding sacrament of the churches, both Catholic and Protestant, and because it dismissed the social significance of paedo-baptism. Baptists of all kinds in the English community of the 17th century held tenaciously to believer's baptism.

The Issue of Sacrament Versus Ordinance. Early Baptists recognized the value of the term "**sacrament**," but commonly did not use it with respect to baptism. Instead, the term "ordinance," meaning "teaching" was used to denote one of the two recognized scriptural rites of the church. Baptists universally have eschewed any concept of baptismal regeneration, preferring to understand baptism as a sign which pointed to deeper spiritual truths. In this regard they bore the marks of the English Reformed tradition. In the 20th century among British and American Baptist congregations, there is a renewed tendency to understand baptism as a sacrament, in part in response to the ecumenical dialogue.

The Issue of Mode. Early **General Baptists** in England doubtless followed the accepted baptismal mode of the English Separatist tradition: pouring or affusion. This changed, however, with the **Particular Baptists** in the 1640s. A congregation at Southwark, London, under the leadership of **John Spilsbury** sent deacon Richard Blunt to discover the ways and means of believer's baptism among the Dutch Mennonites. In a congregation at Rhynsburg, Blunt began fraternal relations and witnessed the practice of baptism by immersion. This he brought back to England

and before 1644 it was the common understanding of Particular Baptists. General Baptists appeared to have adopted the immersion mode by 1650 as well.

In the North American colonies immersion became the standard from the 1670s. It was common to baptize in ponds, streams, rivers, or any "living waters," the latter phrase in contrast with "still waters" like those in a pond. Accounts survive well into the 19th century of winter baptisms where the ice had to be broken for immersion to take place. Similarly in the early experiences of Canadian Baptists, New England practices were common.

The act of immersion consists of lowering the candidate into the water once while reciting the trinitarian formula. In some smaller Baptist bodies in the United States, triune immersion, or three times into the water by the trinitarian formula is used. Some early Baptists in England are reputed to have held candidates under water for several seconds, in order that a sense of new life and freedom would result. In colder climates in Great Britain and North America, stories abound of baptismal services during the winter months where the ice was broken on lakes or ponds to baptize candidates; at least one person is known to have died following a baptism in the winter, Ann Hart Reekie (d. 1863) of Tiverton, Ontario.

Global Generalizations. The practice of baptism in Europe follows the experience of British and American examples. For instance, **J. G. Oncken** was baptized by an American missionary, **Barnas Sears**. Oncken, in turn, practiced from his own experience as he preached conversion and believers baptism in the Lutheran, Reformed, and Catholic locales of his missionary work. In **Sweden**, the scene of believer's baptism by immersion has become the hallmark of Baptists, thanks to a famous 1886 painting by Baron Gustaf Cederstrom, "The Baptists," of a baptism at Lake Malaren, near Uppsala.

Extraordinary Issues. Generally, it is reserved to ministers (ordained or licensed), and less frequently **deacons**, to baptize candidates. On unusual occasions some people have baptized themselves. **John Smyth** read the new meaning of baptize in the New Testament, and finding no one acceptable, baptized himself and then his deacons. He rationalized this by arguing that he was ushering in a new order of the church, true believers, and that further baptisms would take their authority from Christ through his act. Later, under criticism from Mennonites, he regretted this move and probably accepted another believer's baptism from the Waterlander Mennonites. Similarly, the eccentric **Seventh Day Baptist**, **Francis Bampfield,** having arrived at Baptistic principles, baptized himself in the River Salisbury.

William Carey introduced baptistic baptismal practices to Asia. At Serampore he built the Lall Bazaar Chapel, which included a baptistry. Carey's son, Felix (1786-1822), expanded the practice to eastern India and Adoniram Judson introduced believer's baptism to Burma. As an outgrowth of missions in Siam, Baptist practices followed the Chinese community to China itself through William Dean, J. Lewis Shuck, and others. J. G. Oncken taught believer's baptism in his travels and reintroduced it to much of northern and eastern Europe (the Anabaptist sects doubtless practiced believer's baptism three centuries before). David George in Sierra Leone and Lott Carey were among the first to practice believer's baptism on the African continent in 1792 and 1821, respectively.

In the mission fields of North America, Latin America, Africa, and the Far East, believer's baptism by immersion is a distinguishing mark of Baptists. Often, a public spectacle of baptism signifies to the community that the candidates have in fact renounced former religious practices and embarked upon a new life. In 18th century Philadelphia Morgan Edwards regularly baptized new converts at a prominent site along the city's waterfront. In the next century, American Baptist evangelist Jacob Knapp in 1837 baptized 60 people in half an hour (probably the record), and frequently invited public officials, including the president of the United States, to his baptismal ceremonies. The missionary context has been the backdrop for some of the largest numbers of baptisms: American Baptist missionary in India John E. Clough in turn with six ordained pastors at Velumpilly near Ongole, baptized 2,222 persons in one day; Henry Richards (1851-1928), a missionary of the American Baptist Missionary Union (ABMU) at Banza Manteke in the Congo, baptized over 1,000 converts in a few weeks in 1886; later Chester J. Jump (1918-) also an American Baptist, baptized more than 10,000 candidates between 1951 and 1953 at Vanga in the Congo. Under the eye of the Marxist U.S.S.R. government of the era, Russian Baptists baptized 365 candidates in the river at Moscow in 1926.

"BAPTIST" (THE NAME.) In the 16th century, those who rebaptized adherents were called either "Catabaptists" or "Anabaptists," the former term used by Huldrych Zwingli (1484-1531), and the latter used elsewhere in Europe. In western Europe, several terms became common, particularly among Mennonite groups, to describe "baptizing people," including "Doopsgezinde" (Dutch for "baptism-minded people"), "Taufgesinnte" or "Taufer" (the German equivalent), and "Wiedertaufer" (anabaptist). At the turn of the 17th century, the Englishman John Smyth described believer's churches as "churches of the apostolical constitution," "primitive apostolique institution," and he himself was called a "se-Baptist" because he administered his own **baptism**. His close friend, **Thomas Helwys**, used the name "Church of Christ" in his confession of 1612, and others throughout the century used, "Churches which are commonly (though falsely) called Anabaptist," "Congregations gathered according to the Primitive Pattern," "Christians baptized upon profession of their faith," and "Baptized Believers." As yet, little evidence exists of a 17th century English Baptist church of any kind prior to 1680 being referred to simply as "baptist," (though the word appears in titles and for some isolated individuals beginning in the 1640s). The most common terminology appears to have been "Church of Christ," followed by a geographical identification. Among many General Baptists, the term "Baptized believers" was prevalent toward the end of the 18th century.

Two related terms were employed by disputants in the 17th century. Daniel Featley (1582-1645) called Baptists "Dippers" and John Tombes (1603-1676) referred to them as "Antipaedobaptists."

In the American colonies the derogatory terms "antipaedobaptist" and "anabaptist" were used to designate many early dissenters from the Puritan and Anglican positions. Antipaedopbaptists were those who waged the argument against the baptism of children; these folk were not always re-baptizers, as in the case of **Henry Dunster**, president of Harvard College. More likely was the catchall "**anabaptist**" which connected unfavorably with Münsterites and focused on the issue of rebaptism, perhaps the most repugnant issue the early Baptists advocated. Probably as a short, derogatory form of "anabaptist," the term "Baptist" was used to designate an array of people like Charles Chauncey (1592-1671), because they understood the biblical mode of baptism to be immersion. The term "baptist" seems to have emerged to designate the congregations at Boston, Newport, and Providence after the 1660s and perhaps under some influence from English Baptist and dissenting nomenclature.

The actual origin of the term "Baptist" is obscure. It may well have been intended as a shortened form of "anabaptist" or simply a colloquialism. The simple term had a biblical nuance to it, suggested by John the Baptist of the New Testament, though no one seems to have made that association directly. In any case, Edward Terrill (1634-1685) of Bristol referred to John Cann (fl.1640) as a "Baptist" in about 1640, in 1654 William Britten (1608-?) used the word in his title, *A Moderate Baptist*, Robert Pittiloh (fl.1650-1680) in Scotland used it in his book, *Hammer of Persecution* (1659), **John Bunyan** used the term in the 1670s, and it is found in the Orthodox Creed (1679). From these roots it made its way to North America. Clearly, from whatever source originally, the term "baptist" was in common usage at the beginning of the 18th century on both sides of the Atlantic.

BAPTIST "BIBLE." See **Bible**.

BAPTIST BIBLE FELLOWSHIP (BBF). A loose coalition of independent Baptist churches located in the United States and Canada. Founded in 1950 by pastors and laymen who were disenchanted with the World Fundamental Baptist Missionary Fellowship, led by **J. Frank Norris**. The Fellowship recognizes the basic tenets of Baptist **fundamentalism**, including biblical infallibility, substitutionary atonement, the literal resurrection of Christ and his premillennial bodily return, strong pastoral leadership, and autonomous local churches. An important facet of many Fellowship congregations is an aggressive **Sunday School** program, which is a primary evangelistic tool for the church. A newspaper, the *Baptist Bible Tribune* (1950-), is published.

In a loose association with great emphasis placed on local congregations, the national Fellowship is governed by a Committee of Forty-Five, with three functional committees: Administration, Education, and Missionary Work. Originally recognized, there was one school, the Baptist Bible College in Springfield, Missouri; now there are six approved institutions: Baptist Bible College East, Boston, Massachusetts; Pacific Coast Baptist Bible College, San Dimas, California; Baptist Christian College, Shreveport, Louisiana; Atlantic Baptist Bible College, Chester, Virginia; Spanish Baptist Bible Institute, Miami, Florida; Baptist Bible Graduate School of Theology, Springfield, Missouri. Currently, the Fellowship sponsors missionary work in 107 countries and has 853 missionaries.

As of 1995, there were 3,600 congregations with approximately 1.5 million members in the United States and 28 congregations in Canada affiliated with the Baptist Bible Fellowship.

BAPTIST BIBLE UNION OF AMERICA (BBUA). Under the influence of the World's Christian Fundamentals movement, in which some Baptists participated (1915-1920), Baptists in the northern United States, the **Southern Baptist Convention**, and central **Canada** issued a manifesto and call to action to oppose modernism; subsequently they organized themselves into the Baptist Bible Union of America in 1923. The stated purpose of the Union was "to unite all Baptists who believe the Word of God." Leaders of the Union included **T. T. Shields** of Toronto, **J. C. Massee** of Minneapolis, and **J. Frank Norris** of Ft. Worth, Texas, and the vast majority of members of the Union were pastors. In each of their respective convention relationships, they pressed an agenda to have a statement of faith adopted as a standard of orthodoxy. In 1925 the Union issued its own set of Articles of Faith, which was widely disseminated in the major conventions and beyond.

The BBUA reached its peak of effectiveness in 1928 when its annual convention in Toronto included delegates from 18 states and five Canadian provinces; a dubious count claimed 50,000 members affiliated with the BBUA. One of the perceived weaknesses of the Union was the avowed strategy not to separate from the respective denominational organizations; there were also conflicts over leadership and involvement in educational enterprises like Des Moines University in Iowa. Meetings of the BBUA were held in diverse northern cities such as Washington, D.C., Grand Rapids, Toronto, and Chicago; the last meeting was held at Chicago in 1930, with 35 delegates present. Supporters of the Union after 1930 gradually reorganized their efforts as Regular Baptists in Canada or as the **General Association of Regular Baptists** in the United States.

BAPTIST BOARD OF FOREIGN MISSIONS (BBFM). The title given to the administrative and executive body relating to the **General Baptist Missionary Convention** of Baptists in the United States. In 1814 at the organizational meetings of the Convention a constitution was written which created a "Baptist Board of Foreign Missions in the United States." Originally the Board was composed of 21 commissioners who were elected by the Convention for a term of three years. The purpose of the Board was to act for the Convention in setting policy and appointing missionaries in the name of the Convention. Officers of the Board included a president, two vice presidents, a secretary, and a treasurer. The first officers of the Board were **Thomas Baldwin**, president, Henry Holcombe (1762-1824) and **William Rogers**, vice presidents, John Cauldwell (fl. 1815), treasurer, and **William Staughton**, corresponding secretary. Staughton, in his capacity, was in essence the first national denominational executive in **American Baptist** history. The first action of the Board was to appoint **Adoniram Judson** as its first missionary and **Luther Rice** as its agent.

In 1820 the membership of the Board was increased to 28 and more vice presidents were allowed in order to increase regional representation. The Board also moved into the areas of **higher education** and domestic missions. In 1826 a reduction maneuver engineered by New England delegates led to the permanent location of the Board in Boston and a limitation of its activities to foreign missions. In 1832 the size of the Board was increased to 40 and again in 1841 to 60, with vice presidents elected from every state convention. Because there was a consistent difficulty in securing sufficient leadership for the meetings of the Board, in 1841 an "Acting Board" of 15 members was created of Boston local Baptist ministers and laymen. The Acting Board took strongly worded positions on controversial issues, notably the question of appointing slaveholders as missionaries. This caused friction among the southern Baptist members, few of whom ever made it to Board meetings or those of the Acting Board.

Eventually in 1845 the southern delegates to the General Missionary Convention withdrew to form the **Southern Baptist Convention** (SBC), and the following year the General Missionary Convention and the BBFM evolved organizationally into the **American Baptist Missionary Union** (ABMU), a simple voluntary society. See **American Baptist Foreign Mission Society; Baltimore Compromise**.

BAPTIST CONGRESS (BC). An organized forum for discussion of current issues and questions among Baptists in the United States from 1881 to 1915. Originally called the "Baptist Autumnal Conference for Discussion of Current Issues," the idea was taken from the Church of England which held church congresses beginning in 1861. Elias H. Johnson (1841-1906) of Providence, Rhode Island, called upon 13 distinguished colleagues from the northeastern United States in November 1881 to voluntarily organize themselves into a committee for planning and implementation. The first public congress was held in Brooklyn, New York, November 14-16, 1882, with **George Dana Boardman, Jr.** presiding. Subsequent meetings were held in Philadelphia, Indianapolis, Toronto, Richmond, New Haven, Providence, and Nashville. Presiding over the sessions were among the most distinguished Baptist clergy of the era, including **Henry G. Weston**, **Thomas Armitage**, **Walter Rauschenbusch**, and **Alvah Hovey**.

The purpose of the BC was not to advocate Baptist principles; rather, it was assumed that no denomination was infallible, including the Baptists, and papers were presented which carried a variety of topics and opinions. The Congress earned a reputation for being a forum for **liberal** expression at a time when doctrinal purity and **Landmarkism** were popular expressions of local churches. Its annual programs featured papers on the deity of Christ, social Christianity, free speech, ethical issues, the mystical element in Christianity, biblical criticism, and the use of non-canonical scriptures. Eventually, the larger interests of the Baptist community were drawn to the formation of the **Baptist World Alliance**, and after its first congress in 1905, the BC became less popular as a gathering of Baptist leaders. Through the years of its existence, the Congress published *Proceedings of the Baptist Congress* (1888-1912).

BAPTIST COUNCIL ON WORLD MISSION (BCWM). A consultative fellowship of those mission and national church bodies historically related to the **American Baptist Foreign Mission Society** (ABFMS). Beginning about 1957 various church organizations worldwide were invited to confer with the leaders of ABFMS and this evolved into a regular conciliar format in 1968. The purpose of the Council is to promote better understanding among mission partners, exchange leadership, consult about entering new fields, and cooperate with regional Christian bodies. Eighteen members comprise the Council, including church bodies in the Far East, **India**, Latin America, and Africa, plus the Board of International Ministries of the **American Baptist Churches in the U.S.A.** Current programs of the Council include student fellowships, third world missionaries, and regional stewardship conferences. Main offices for the BCWM are in Valley Forge, Pennsylvania.

BAPTIST FAITH AND MESSAGE. In the midst of the **fundamentalist** controversy and fears about the teaching of evolution theory in schools, the **Southern Baptist Convention** (SBC) in 1924 appointed a committee chaired by **E. Y. Mullins** to produce a statement of Baptist faith and message. The Committee studied the New Hampshire Confession of Faith (1833) and added 10 new articles. This document was adopted at the 1925 session of the Convention as "The Baptist Faith and Message" and it served to define the doctrinal understanding of the Convention at large through the 1950s. Again in response to a crisis among theological teachers, in 1962 a Committee was appointed by the Convention to update or modify appropriately the 1925 statement. Under the direction of Oklahoma Baptist pastor **Herschel H. Hobbs**, modest changes, mostly for clarification and elaboration, were made to the 1925 version and the 1963 Convention unanimously adopted the new Baptist Faith and Message Statement. Southern Baptists are careful to define the statement as a guide, which is in no way mandatory, even upon Convention institutions. Several seminaries, including Southern Baptist Theological Seminary and New Orleans Baptist Theological Seminary, have their own doctrinal statements.

BAPTIST FAITH MISSIONS (BFM). Founded in 1922 as Amazon Valley Baptist Faith Missions to support the work of an independent Baptist, Eric Nelson (1862-1939), the pioneer Baptist missionary in the Amazon Valley of **Brazil**. Boyce Taylor (1870-1932), a **Southern Baptist** pastor in Murray, Kentucky, founded the organization which eventually expanded fields to **Peru**. In 1941 H. H. Overby (1902-1994), Z. E. Clark (1887-1977), and a missionary, Joseph Brandon (d.1970), reorganized the mission, dropping the terminology "Amazon Valley." Still later, missionaries to **Korea, Kenya, Colombia, Honduras,** and primarily Brazil were added. At present, Baptist Faith Missions supports 11 missionaries, maintains offices in Ironton, Ohio, and publishes *Mission Sheets* (1941-). Mostly independent Baptist churches support the work.

BAPTIST FOREIGN MISSION CONVENTION OF THE UNITED STATES (BFMC). One of the predecessor organizations in the United States of **Black Baptists**. It was organized at Montgomery, Alabama, in December 1880 to conduct missions in West Africa. The Convention consisted mainly of southern Black leaders. In 1886 the Black convention was invited by the **American Baptist Missionary Union** (ABMU) to merge its overseas interests, but, owing to separatist feelings in the Black community, the invitation was rejected. For fifteen years, the Baptist Foreign Mission Convention represented the major organizing tendency among Black Baptists along with the parallel **American National Baptist Convention** (ANBC). In 1895, the Convention was merged with other organizations in the formation of the **National Baptist Convention in the United States** (NBCUSA) to become the foreign missionary arm of Black Baptists.

BAPTIST GENERAL CONFERENCE OF AMERICA (BGC). Formerly known as the Swedish Baptist Conference, the organization was formed in 1856 at Rock Island, Illinois. The first Swedish Baptist congregation in the United States had been organized also at Rock Island, three years earlier, the result of the preaching of emigrant/pioneer **Gustav Palmquist**. The movement grew slowly in the states of Illinois, Iowa, Minnesota, and Wisconsin, and in addition to Palmquist, **Anders Wiberg** and **Fredrik O. Nilson** were active in promoting **evangelism** and church planting.

As part of its program to reach immigrant groups in the eastern cities, the **American Baptist Home Mission Society** (ABHMS) began support of Swedish missions in New York in 1867 in association with Mariner's Temple Baptist Church. Other missionaries in western states were supported by both the ABHMS and the **American Baptist Publication Society**. Like the German Conference, the Swedish Conference became loosely affiliated with the American Baptist movement and provided numerous congregations which were cross-listed in the statistics. Also, overseas missionaries of Swedish-American culture were appointed under the auspices of the **American Baptist Missionary Union**

(ABMU) (later the American Baptist Foreign Mission Society) until 1944 when the Conference launched its own Foreign Mission Advance.

The early purposes of the Conference were missionary and cultural support. To meet the educational needs of the **ministry**, a theological school was started at Chicago in 1871, thereafter moving to St. Paul and Stromsberg, Nebraska, before being reorganized as a department of the Divinity School of the Baptist Union Theological School (later the University of Chicago) in 1888. A foreign mission society was organized in 1917 and provision was made for enlarged domestic mission work in that same year.

Following World War I, the Swedish Baptist Conference began to mature organizationally. When the **Northern Baptist Convention** (NBC) invited ethnic conferences to join a fundraising crusade in 1919-1921 and later to belong to the Convention as associate members, the Swedish leadership declined, in part because of problems inherent in the ecumenical stance of the Convention Baptists and perceived theological **liberalism**. Separate organizations for **missions**, a strong school at Chicago under the direction of stalwart **Carl Gustaf Lagergran**, and the establishment of churches in every section of the United States suggested a new and separate identity for "Conference Baptists." The foreign mission program of the Conference, organized independently in 1944 as a final break with Northern Baptists, has included work in **India**, **China**, **Russia**, **Burma**, **Argentina**, **Brazil**, **Japan**, **Philippines**, and **Ethiopia**. In 1914 an early interest in a mission to **Spain** had also been supported until it was transferred to the Southern Baptists in 1922.

In 1980 the Baptist General Conference established its headquarters at Arlington Heights, Illinois. In St. Paul, Minnesota, Bethel College and Theological Seminary were established from the foundation laid at Chicago. Another institution, Adelphia College, was established in 1905 at Seattle,Washington, but closed in 1918 due to financial losses. The periodical of the Conference is the *Standard* (1853-).

In 1946 negotiations took place between the **Conservative Baptist Association** and the Baptist General Conference; in another set of negotiations, the German Baptists also considered alignment with the Swedish Conference. Neither proved to be fruitful. Although separate organizationally, some cooperation has continued between the Conference and the American Baptist Convention (ABC). Swedish Baptists have served in American Baptist executive roles, notably Wilber Larson (1911-1991) in home missions, Reuben Nelson (1905-1960) as general secretary and Emmett Johnson (1928-) in evangelism. The Conference is also a member of the **Baptist World Alliance** (BWA) and cooperates with the **Baptist Joint Committee on Public Affairs** (BJCPA).

BAPTIST GENERAL CONVENTION. See **General Baptist Missionary Convention of the Baptist Denomination in the United States of America for Foreign Missions.**

BAPTIST GENERAL TRACT SOCIETY (BGTS). See **American Baptist Publication Society.**

BAPTIST HOME MISSION SOCIETY (BHMS). The oldest national domestic missionary organization among Baptists, founded in England in 1797. In 1796 John Saffery (1762-1825) and **William Steadman** made a preaching tour from Salisbury to Plymouth and reached audiences of several hundred hearers. This led to a concern for evangelism and church planting in the home land and the result was a second national **voluntary** society, "The Baptist Society in London for the Encouragement and Support of Itinerant Preaching." Prominent early board members were **Abraham Booth, John Rippon**, William Smith, and Timothy Thomas (1811-1887). The purpose of the Society was to provide and send out after due examination such Calvinistic ministers of the Baptist persuasion as appeared to be qualified for itinerant preaching. Each of the full-time missionaries was paid forty pounds per year, and in 1817 a plan for auxilliaries was put in place.

The Society's purposes and names changed over the course of its history: in 1817 it was called the Baptist Itinerant and Home Mission Society, and in 1822 simply the Baptist Home Mission Society. In 1834 the Baptist Irish Society was merged with BHMS and in 1841 the first full-time secretary was hired, Stephen J. Davis (1805-1866) of Salter's Hall. In 1875 the **Baptist Union** (BU) took responsibility for home missions, and less active in terms of separate personnel, the Society became the Home Mission Fund in 1890. In 1912 the Ministerial Settlement and Sustentation Scheme was adopted, effectively carrying forth the program of the Home Mission Society. In 1970 the Baptist Home Work Scheme was again renamed the Baptist Home Mission Scheme. Several other agencies gradually eclipsed the focus of the Home Mission Society, including the Baptist Union Annuity Fund (1875), the Church Extension Fund (1893), and the Twentieth Century Fund (1899).

BAPTIST INTERNATIONAL MISSIONS, INC. (BIMI). An independent U.S. Baptist missionary organization founded in 1960 by 160 independent Baptist pastors primarily from across the southern United States. The agency specializes in **evangelism**, church planting, and Christian education, with 1,025 missionaries in 80 countries. BIMI is based in Chattanooga, Tennessee, and publishes *BIMI World*.

BAPTIST JOINT COMMITTEE ON PUBLIC AFFAIRS (BJCPA). An organization of six Baptist national organizations which seeks to maintain a united witness for **religious liberty** in the United States. In the 1930s various Baptist groups were troubled at certain political and international events, including the rise of totalitarian dictatorships, the pilgrimage of Jewish people to the Middle East, plans of the government of **Romania** to close Baptist churches, the Japanese invasion of **China**, and the expressed design of the U. S. government to recognize the Vatican diplomatically. Throughout World War II, Southern, Northern, and National Baptists worked together in a structure called the Associated Committees on Public Affairs; in 1939 they issued the **American Baptist Bill of Rights**. These committees became in 1946 a permanent organization, the Baptist Joint Committee on Public Affairs.

Joseph M. Dawson (1879-1973), a social activist pastor and editor from Waco, Texas, was chosen executive director, with five Baptist groups coalescing in the Committee. Dawson advocated a variety of positions, including no U.S. ambassador for the Vatican, support for the United Nations, and consideration of human rights as a criterion in all U.S. foreign affairs. C. Emmanuel Carlson (1906-1976), dean of Bethel College in St. Paul, Minnesota, became Dawson's successor (1954-1971) and turned toward a more scholarly approach, providing resources for the Baptist community. The third director, James E. Wood, Jr. (1922-), moved in the same direction from 1971 to 1980, having been a professor at Baylor University. In 1980 James M. Dunn (1932-), the director of the Christian Life Commission of the Baptist Convention of Texas, became director of the Joint Committee and developed an activist approach, especially with respect to what was referred to as the "New Christian Right." The Committee has sponsored forums on religious liberty and separation of church and state, *amicus curae* briefs on U.S. Supreme Court cases, and a periodical, *Report From the Capital* (1946-), which provides watchdog service on concerns in the government which appear to have an impact upon **separation of church and state**. From 1959 to 1985 the Baptist Federation of **Canada** participated in various activities of the Joint Committee where appropriate.

BAPTIST JUBILEE ADVANCE (BJA). The official name given to the celebrations and activities associated with the 150th anniversary of Baptist organization in North America, 1814-1964. Representatives of several Baptist bodies first gathered in Chicago in 1955 to consider a joint celebration. A Steering Committee composed of delegates from the **American Baptist Convention** (ABC), **Southern Baptist Convention** (SBC), **National Baptist Convention, U.S.A.** (NBCUSA), **National**

Baptist Convention of America (NBCA), **North American Baptist Conference** (NABC), **Baptist General Conference** (BGC), **Seventh Day Baptist** General Conference (SDB) and the Baptist Federation of Canada adopted a plan of action in Bible teaching, Baptist witness, **evangelism**, stewardship, church extension, world mission ,and leadership training. The results of the year long celebrations in 1964 included better understanding of differences among Baptist groups, cooperation in several projects, a joint session of the American and Southern Baptist Conventions in Atlantic City, New Jersey, May 18, 1964, and the publication of a book, *Baptist Advance: The Achievements of the Baptists of North America for a Century and a Half* (1964).

BAPTIST MID-MISSIONS (BMM). An extensive Baptistic independent overseas **missionary** agency based in the United States. Formed in September 1920 as the "General Council of Cooperating Baptist Missions of North America," it was based on fundamentalistic principles and opposition to the modernism perceived to exist in the **Northern Baptist Convention**. The founders included a group of Baptist pastors from Ohio, Minnesota, and New York: A. H. Bond (fl.1920-25), Edwin S. Carman (fl.1920-30), and Alison De Nise (fl.1920-29). Their purpose was to reach the world for Christ and to awaken Baptist churches in the United States to the Great Commission (Matthew 28:19, 20). The working name of the mission was "Mid-Africa Mission," owing to the choice of the first field as French Equatorial Africa. The name "Baptist Mid-Missions" was introduced in 1952 to replace the cumbersome corporate title.

The first BMM missionaries appointed were **William and Genevieve Haas**, Rowena Becker (1883-1963), Arthur and Blanche Young (fl.1920), and a Swedish preacher whom Haas recruited at Moody Bible Institute, Gust Pearson (1895-1989). The fact that William Haas had earlier worked with the Africa Inland Mission and the Heart of Africa Mission set the stage for a beginning thrust into Africa. Later the number of fields of endeavor was expanded to include 37 countries and five types of domestic missions in the United States and **Canada**. The places of endeavor have included: French Equatorial Africa, **Venezuela**, **Chad**, **Brazil**, **India**, **Haiti**, **Jamaica**, **Liberia**, **Czechoslovakia**, **France**, **Germany**, **Italy**, the **Netherlands**, **China**, **Hong Kong**, **Indonesia**, **Japan**, **Peru**, **Dominican Republic**, **Honduras**, **West Indies**, **Congo**, **Australia**, **New Zealand**, United Kingdom, **Ivory Coast**, **Ghana**, **Bangladesh**, **Spain**, **Puerto Rico**, **Finland**, **Taiwan**, **Korea**, **Mexico**, **Ecuador**, and Canada (British Columbia, Quebec). Domestic ministries include migrants, Appalachia mountain villages, Native Americans, Alaska, and Jewish **evangelism.** Early in its history, Mid-Missions enjoyed the support of **fundamentalist** Baptist churches and groups in Canada, including **T. T. Shields** of Toronto, and the agency was separately organized in Canada in 1967. Over the years, BMM has often closely paralleled the work of the **Association of Baptists for World Evangelism**, a similar body representing both Baptistic identity and fundamentalistic theology. The international headquarters is located in Cleveland, Ohio, and the organization has published *Mid-African Mission* (1921-25), *Mid-Missions Bulletin* (1925-38), *Mid-Missions* (1938-43), *Mid-Missions News* (1943-54), and *Harvest* (1954-).

BAPTIST MISSIONARY ASSOCIATION OF AMERICA (BMA). Formerly called the North American Baptist Association until 1969, this group was formed in Little Rock, Arkansas, in May 1950. Partially a reaction to alleged violations of church sovereignty and authoritarian leadership in the **American Baptist Association**, the Association coalesced around militant Baptist **fundamentalism**, including the verbal plenary inspiration of **Scripture**, literal creation, the virgin birth and deity of Jesus Christ, his blood atonement, salvation by grace alone, and the personal, imminent return of Christ. "Missionary Baptists," as they are called, oppose open communion, alien **baptism**, pulpit affiliation with unacceptable ministers, conventionism, and unionism. Interstate missionaries serve the Association within the United States and foreign missionaries are found in **Brazil**, Central America, **Korea, Philippines, Australia**, and the Cape Verde Islands. In 1956 the North American Theological Seminary was founded, to become in 1970 the Baptist Missionary Association Theological Seminary, at Jacksonville, Texas. The Association publishes *The Gleaner* (1953-). As of 1995 there were 1,360 churches and 230,171 members in the Association.

BAPTIST MISSIONARY SOCIETY (BMS). The oldest foreign missionary sending agency in Baptist experience. The organization, chartered as the Particular Baptist Society for the Propagation of the Gospel Among the Heathen (abbreviated BMS), was founded in Kettering, England, on October 2, 1792, by **William Carey, Andrew Fuller** and ten other leaders, including **Samuel Pearce, John Ryland, William Staughton**, Abraham Greenwood (1749-1827), and Thomas Blundell (1752-1824). The founders desired an **evangelical** and **ecumenical** society, but realized the need for a particular constituency and chose to be specifically Baptist. The organization itself was a simple **voluntary** association which depended upon contributions from churches and individuals. Almost immediately the Society organized auxiliary societies to itself, located throughout England and later the British Empire.

The first field of the BMS was **India**, established by William Carey in 1793. Next were **Ceylon** (1812), the West Indies (1813), **Cameroon** (1841), **Canada** (1843), **China** (1860), **Congo** (1877), Angola (1899), Mizoram (1901), **Bangladesh** (1971), **Nepal** (1954), and **Brazil** (1953). The focus of the Society was broadened in 1843 when the Society was merged with the Baptist Colonial Missionary Society, a group which fostered work in the province of Upper Canada (the predecessor of modern Ontario). This led to the Society accepting limited responsibility for locations of British settlement.

The BMS had the advantage of outstanding leadership throughout most of its early history. The first secretary was the venerable Andrew Fuller, followed by James Hinton (d.1823) and John Ryland (1815-1825). John Dyer (1817-1840) was the secretary who commenced an official office for the Society in London in 1819 and presided over resolution of the schism which emerged among the Serampore missionaries, as they differed over terms of their support and lifestyle. **Joseph Angus** served 1840-1849 during a period of growth, succeeded by **Edward Bean Underhill**, 1849-1876. Underhill visited churches, restoring confidence, and reduced the Society's debt, largely due to his association with the benefactor and later treasurer of the BMS, **Samuel Morton Peto**. Overseas, Underhill also spearheaded an expansion of the fields; in 1865 he became embroiled in a political uprising in **Jamaica**, due to his social advocacy of the poor. From 1876 to 1906, Alfred Henry Baynes served as secretary, one of his outstanding accomplishments being the amalgamation of the General Baptist Missionary Society (1816) with the BMS in 1891.

In many locations the Society has cooperated with both Baptists and others in maintaining mission stations. Over the years the BMS has retained its independent organizational status, preferring to relate to the several British Baptist Unions and their congregations directly, rather than to become an auxiliary of a single union. In the 1990s the links have become closer and the Society has relocated its headquarters to Didcot, Oxfordshire, in proximity with the **Baptist Union of Great Britain**. See also **Baptist Union of Great Britain; Particular Baptists**.

BAPTIST MISSION UNION OF AMERICA. See **Finnish Baptist Union of America.**

BAPTIST UNION OF AMERICA. See **Finnish Baptist Union of America**.

BAPTIST UNION OF GREAT BRITAIN AND IRELAND (BU). The Baptist Union of Great Britain and Ireland ("and Ireland" was deleted in 1989) is the main body of Baptists in Britain, comprising congregations in England and others affiliated to it, which also maintain membership with the Baptist Union of **Wales** and the Baptist Union of **Scotland**. The Union traces its origins back to efforts by leaders like **John Rippon** and **Joseph Ivimey** in the early years of the 19th century to unite the Baptist cause throughout Great Britain. Churches in fellowship with the Baptist Union have been called "Union Baptists."

Through the *Baptist Annual Register*, begun in 1798, Rippon advocated a union which he thought should be international; Ivimey wrote an article for *The Baptist Magazine* in 1811 that stated: "union was essential to prosperity." The outcome of these catalysts was a meeting at Carter Lane Church in June 1812 at which 60 ministers agreed that union was desirable. The articles drawn up advocated cooperation for better communication among the churches and support of **missions.** One year later, again in Rippon's vestry, the Union was given shape by 45 ministers who signed 12 articles. The doctrinal basis, shorter than the ancient confessions, was **Particular Baptist** in substance and reflected the congregations represented by the ministers. During the early period of the Union's fragile history, the term "denomination" came into popular usage among those associated with the body. A combination of over-arching political events, the crisis among the missionaries at Serampore, and interest in other forms of domestic mission, however, engendered disinterest and doomed the Union after 1817.

In 1831 a new attempt was made to reshape the Union by involving more churches, largely in response to initiatives among the Congregationalists to form a union, and the vast changes wrought in English society by the introduction of the Reform Bill. Although small in scope, the 1831 reorganization is usually considered the birth of the modern union. Gradually important related organizations, including the missionary societies, the **Hanserd Knollys** Society (historical), and others began to meet and to function in closer cooperation, and national periodicals like *The Baptist Magazine* and *The Baptist Record* began to give space to the interests of the Union. Over the years, by mid-century, a long list of distinguished Particular Baptist leaders also came to be associated with offices in the Union, including **Francis A. Cox, John Howard Hinton, John Mockett Cramp, William Harris Murch, James Hoby,** and **Edward Steane.** The focus of the Union included issues of public concern in education, political recognition of dissenters, and theological differences.

The latter half of the 19th century witnessed vast changes in the life of the Union. In 1865 the missionary efforts relating to Ireland were brought under the aegis of one society and this led to the natural inclusion of Ulster congregations in the lists of what became the Baptist Union of Great Britain and Ireland. In 1866 a separate Welsh Baptist Union (see **Wales**) was formed with a similar body taking shape in Scotland in 1869. These bodies became affiliates of the Union in 1872. While the Union remained essentially a body politic of churches, theological colleges, associations, and recognized societies began to send representatives to the sessions as well. From 1863 a merger of General Baptists of the New Connexion and the Baptist Union was discussed, and this was achieved in 1891. In 1887 a major theological controversy, which caused great strife in the Union, surfaced in the ministry of **Charles Haddon Spurgeon**, who opposed both theologically **liberal** trends and the closer affiliation with General Baptists, constituting as Spurgeon called it a "downgrading of the Union's purposes" (see **Downgrade Controversy**). In 1887 Spurgeon withdrew from the Baptist Union.

In 1898 **John Howard Shakespeare** became secretary of the BU and moved the cause beyond the "Downgrade troubles." A Twentieth Century Fund added to the resources of the Union and through Shakespeare the Union became a charter member of the National Free Church Council. In 1891 the Union began publishing *The Baptist Times*, a weekly newspaper, which in 1910 was amalgamated with *The Baptist*. A new hymnbook appeared in 1900, a Young People's Union in 1904, a Baptist Insurance Company in 1905, and the Baptist Women's League and the Baptist Colonial Society in 1910 (actually the second usage of that term). In 1905 the Baptist Union became a charter member of the **Baptist World Alliance** (BWA) and hosted its first World Congress meeting at London. Symbolic of the maturity of the Union, an imposing edifice on Southampton Row in London opened in 1903, known as "Baptist Church House."

In the 20th century, the Union has facilitated participation by British Churches in all of the major events of the international family, including the **European Baptist Federation** (EBF), and the World Council of Churches, of which it became a founding member. In addition, important advances at home have also been the result of closer cooperation within the Union: Regent's Park College was moved to Oxford in 1938; a plan for a Northern Baptist College at Manchester, first proposed in 1903, was realized in 1964; Carey Press and Kingsgate Press were united in 1949; and after many years of debate, a strategic new location at Didcot in Oxfordshire was achieved in cooperation with the Baptist Missionary Society in 1989. Important leaders such as **Ernest Payne**, an historian, and David S. Russell (1916-), a renowned biblical scholar, have given leadership to the Union in the post-World War II era.

The Baptist Union consists of local churches, associations of churches (32 in number), colleges, and a variety of related organizations such as the Baptist Historical Society, Baptist Men's Movement, Baptist Ministers' Fellowship, the Federation of Lay Ministries, the National Council of Baptist Women, and the Alliance of Baptist Youth. It is divided into 12 areas with 12 area superintendents. There are seven affiliated theological colleges and the Baptist Missionary Society is the recognized overseas agency of the churches.

As of 1995, there were 2,130 churches and 156,939 members affiliated with the Baptist Union of Great Britain. See also **General Baptists; Particular Baptists; Scotland,** and **Wales.**

BAPTIST UNION OF LATIN AMERICA (UBLA). As part of the regional development within the **Baptist World Alliance** (BWA), the major Baptist conventions/unions of South and Central America formed in 1976 the Union Bautista Latina America (Baptist Union of Latin America). A structural reorganization took place in 1982. The purpose of the Union is to promote cooperation within the affiliated organizations for mission, education, and **evangelism** in the region, and to advance the purposes of the BWA. An executive secretary administers the programs of UBLA and a board of directors sets policy. The Union holds an assembly every three years.

BAPTIST WORLD ALLIANCE (BWA). The international body of Baptists to which most Baptist unions and conventions worldwide belong. Founded in 1905, the Alliance was the idea of **J. H. Shakespeare, William H. Whitsett,** and **J. H. Rushbrooke,** as well as being in some ways the successor to the **Baptist Congress.** The first international congress of the Alliance was held in London, England, where 3,250 delegates attended. The BWA has grown steadily over the years to a membership of 180 unions/conventions and members. A **voluntary** association of the unions, the Alliance provides a forum for fellowship, witness, and study, and addresses in particular the issue of **religious liberty.** Its divisions include **Evangelism** and Education, Study and Research, Promotion and Development, and Baptist World Aid. There are three auxiliaries: the Women's Division, the Men's Department, and the Youth Division. Internationally, the BWA constituency is divided into regions: **European Baptist Federation, All-Africa Baptist Fellowship,**

the **Asian Baptist Fellowship**, the **Latin American Baptist Fellowship**, and the **North American Baptist Fellowship**.

Annually, the General Council of the BWA meets to debate resolutions and hear reports from each division, and to reflect and represent the members in a particular region where the meetings are held. Every five years, or quinquennium, a World Congress is held where 5,000 to 10,000 Baptists assemble to hear reports, derive inspiration, and pass resolutions, including election of officers and adoption of a budget and a five-year theme. Upon action of the Congress, the Alliance may engage in dialogue (called "theological conversations") with other Christian groups; the BWA has concluded conversations with Roman Catholics, Lutherans, the World Council of Reformed Churches, the Mennonite World Conference, and begun discussions with the Orthodox Ecumenical Patriarchate. While the BWA is not a constituent member of the World Council of Churches (WCC), officers of the Alliance attend WCC committee meetings and administrative and educational events from time to time.

The Alliance has no authority over any church or union and consists primarily of denominational heads and elected denominational representatives. The BWA is funded by contributions of its member bodies, much of its budget being made up from North American bodies and individuals. The U. S. **Southern Baptist Convention** (SBC) provides the largest single amount.

The BWA has produced several periodicals, notably the *Baptist World* (1905-) and the *Proceedings of the Baptist World Congress* (1905-) and has administrative offices at McLean, Virginia, a suburb of Washington, D.C. Presidents of the Alliance have included **John Clifford**, **J. H. Rushbrooke**, and F. Townley Lord (1893-1962) (U.K.); Robert S. MacArthur (1841-1923), **Edgar Y. Mullins**, George W. Truett (1867-1944), C. Oscar Johnson (1886-1965), V. Carney Hargroves (1900-1986), Theodore F. Adams (1898-1980), and Duke K. McCall (1914-) (U.S.); **William Tolbert** (Liberia); G. Noel Vose (1921-) (Australia); Knud Wumpelmann (1922-) (Denmark); Joao F. Soren (1908-) and Nilson Fanini (1932-) (Brazil); John MacNeill (1855-1933) (Canada). General secretaries of the BWA (with years of service) have been: J. H. Rushbrooke, 1928-1939; Walter O. Lewis 1939-1948; Arnold T. Ohrn 1948-1960; Josef Nordenhaug, 1960-1969; Robert S. Denny, 1969-1980; Gerhard Claas, 1980-1988; Denton Lotz, 1988-.

As of 1995 the Baptist World Alliance includes 187 Baptist unions and conventions comprising a membership of over 40 million persons and over 150,000 churches.

BAPTIST WORLD MISSION (BWM). In the 1950s two theological traditions emerged within the **Conservative Baptist** movement in the United States. One known as the "soft policy" group maintained relations with neo-evangelicals, while the other, called the "hard core" was composed of more militant **fundamentalists**. Eventually in 1961 the "hard core," continuing as the Conservative Baptist Fellowship and led by Bryce Augsburger (1922-1988), Ernest Pickering (1928-), and **Richard Clearwaters** organized a new mission agency, the World Conservative Baptist Mission, after 1966 known as Baptist World Mission. Its emphases were fundamentalistic and separatist, and to ensure doctrinal purity a self-perpetuating board was provided for in 1967. In 1997 the Grace Independent Baptist Mission of Sellersville, Pennsylvania (founded c.1965), merged with Baptist World Mission, enlarging its outreach. BWM specializes in **evangelism**, church planting, and Christian education. Work is conducted in over 25 countries on every continent, and over 4,000 independent Baptist churches support the organization. The home base is in Decatur, Alabama, and a newsletter, *World Witness*, is published.

BAPTISTERION, BAPTISTRY. The names variously given to the container of the water of **baptism**. In Baptist practice, baptism most authentically occurs in "living waters" (meaning running water) in an outdoor setting. Among the early English Baptists, public baptisms were forbidden in rivers or ponds until after toleration. Prominent laymen sometimes constructed outdoor baptisterions on private property for the rite. Such a baptisterion survives at Rhual near Mold in North **Wales**.

However, as the technology of heating water improved and the baptismal ceremony became part of a regular service, and was required throughout the entire year, (not to mention human convenience), provisions were made for indoor baptisms. Architecturally, these were called baptisterions. Often, groups of congregations would pool their resources to construct a common baptisterion, as was the case at the Horsley-down Church. In 1716 the Barbican Church constructed a new baptisterion which was intended for the use of several congregations. The **Thomas Hollis** family paid for the construction and laid down specific rules about who should use it. A "license" was issued to appropriate ministers and a charge of two shillings per person was made (this included the use of changing rooms); a register of those baptized was also kept. These conditions offended the London ministers who responded by raising funds for the repair of the Horsley-down baptisterion, which had fallen into disrepair.

Early baptisterions were made to resemble stone-lined graves, approximately four to six feet deep. The baptisterion was filled prior to the baptismal service with fresh water. The officiant then called the candidates into the pool in waist deep water, and performed the baptism. Afterward, the candidate left the pool to change clothes and return to the congregation.

In many churches of the 19th century, the baptistry, as it came to be called in North America, was located in an inconspicuous place usually beneath the pulpit or under the floor. When not in use, it was not visible. Church **architecture** shifted in the United States in the 20th century to emphasize the public witness nature of the rite and the baptistry was moved to an elevated or prominent position, usually behind or to the side of the pulpit or choir area. Many churches painted a river scene on the wall behind the baptistry to evoke an impression of the Jordan River baptism of Jesus Christ.

With travel to the Middle East more common, numbers of pastors have encouraged baptismal candidates to be baptized in the Jordan River at a location which the Israeli government has declared appropriate. For those who cannot make such a trip, water has been transported from the actual Jordan River and poured from a vial into a local church baptistry, adding to the poignancy of the rite.

Technology affected the use of the baptistery in other ways. In the mid-19th century, deacon **William Colgate** of New York City offered his friend **Pharcellus Church**, pastor at First Baptist Church, Rochester, New York, a pair of rubber pantaloons to wear underneath his baptismal robes. While the initial pair shrank under the lower water temperature, the concept caught on and most Baptist ministers today wear either waist boots or waterproof clothing for an expeditious transition to and from the baptistery.

BARBADOS. Southern Baptist work in Barbados commenced in 1972, originally known as the Windward Islands Mission. The Barbados Baptist Convention was founded in 1974, with headquarters at St. Michaels. In 1978 Barbados Baptist Theological College was started, later named the Baptist Theological College for the Caribbean.

As of 1995 there were 421 members in four churches affiliated with the Barbados Baptist Convention.

BARBUDA. See **Antigua**.

BARNES, WILLIAM WRIGHT (1883-1960). Southern Baptist educator and church historian, born at Elm City, North Carolina. He was educated at Wake Forest College and Southern Baptist Theological Seminary where he earned the Th.D. degree in church history. He began his career as a teacher in Cuba under the Home Mission Board (1904-1905) and served as principal of El Colegio Cubano-Americano in Havana (1909-1912). In 1913 following **A. H. Newman**, he was elected to the position in church history at Southwestern Baptist Theological Seminary in Ft. Worth, Texas, which he held until 1953. Barnes was a widely published historian of the **Southern Baptist Convention** (SBC), sometimes to the irritation of Convention leaders. His *Southern Baptist Convention 1845-1953* (1954) was highly edited to obscure problematic interpretive comments he had made, and his *Southern Baptist Convention: A Study in Ecclesiology* (1923) became a classic treatise in American church historiography.

BARROW, DAVID (1753-1819). American Baptist minister, born in Brunswick County, Virginia. Barrow was ordained in 1774 and served a circuit of churches at Black Creek, Virginia. He itinerated in Virginia and North Carolina and served in the War for Independence. In 1778 he was molested and nearly drowned by a crowd of mockers. Following the war, he moved to Kentucky and served the church at Mount Sterling. There he became a zealous abolitionist and his congregation divided over the issue of **slavery**. In 1807 he helped to form an **association** of emancipators, and the following year, he published the earliest defense of abolition among the Baptists of the United States, *Involuntary, Unmerited, Perpetual, Absolute, Hereditary Slavery Examined, on the Principles of Nature, Reason, Justice, Policy and Scripture* (1808).

BEDDOME, BENJAMIN (1717-1795). English Baptist minister and theologian, born in Henly-in-Arden. He was educated at Bristol Baptist College and the Independent College at Mill End, London. Beddome served the congregation at Bourton-on-Water for over 50 years and exhibited the high caliber of Calvinistic Baptists of the 18th century. He was the first to produce a Baptist catechism in a series of questions and answers (1752) and he composed numerous hymns for worship, including the oft-used, "Father of Mercies, Bow thine Ear." He also published in 1820-1822 an eight-volume guide to worship. The College of Rhode Island awarded Beddome the honorary M.A. degree.

BEISSEL, JOHANN CONRAD (1690-1768). American German Seventh Day Baptist minister, born at Eberbach, Germany. He was apprenticed as a baker, but due to his extraordinary religious beliefs, he was banished from the Palatinate in 1720. He emigrated to the colony of Pennsylvania where he was influenced by Peter Becker (1687-1758), the founder of the

Church of the Brethren. In 1721 Beissel formed his own colony at Mill Creek, Pennsylvania, who referred to themselves as **Solitary Brethren**. In 1725 he was baptized by Becker and he created yet another colony at Ephrata near Lancaster, Pennsylvania. He composed over 1,000 hymns and a unique musical genre, "Paradaisical Wonder Music."

BELARUS. When the Baptist movement reached what became Belarus, the churches were part of the Russian Empire and thus included in the historical development of Russian Baptists. For instance, L. D. Priimachenko went to Tiflis (Tblisi) in Georgia to investigate the Baptist position and was baptized in 1884 at Vladikavkaz. He returned to Belarus to start the first Baptist church in the region. Growth in the Baptist community occurred after the turn of the century with churches at Kha'ch in 1907 and Gomel in 1908. The Grodzensky region was fertile soil for early Baptists. With more freedom under the early Communist regimes, Baptists in Belarus organized a Belorussian Union at Minsk in 1927, which was closed under Stalin after 1929. Congregations in Belarus then related to the Russian Union and later the All Union Council of Evangelical Christians-Baptists when it was organized from 1991 to 1993. At that time, a separate union for Belarus was again organized, the Sayuz Yevangel'skikh Khrystsiyan Baptystav Belarusy (Union of Evangelical Christians-Baptists of Belarus).

As of 1995 there were 154 churches and 9,399 affiliated with Sayuz Yevangel'skikh Khrystsiyan Baptystav Belarusy.

BELCHER, JOSEPH (1794-1859). English, Canadian, and later American Baptist minister, born in Birmingham, England. He was ordained to the **ministry** at Somersham, Huntingdonshire, where he served as pastor, 1819-1825. He then was minister at Folkstone (1825-1831), Paradise Chapel, Chelsea (1831-1834), and Greenwich (1834-1842). During his tenure as a Baptist minister in Britain, Belcher was a leader in denominational affairs. He was active in the **Baptist Home Mission Society** (BHMS) and the Baptist Board charged him in 1832-1833 to collect statistics and a membership roster for Baptist ministers in the newly formed **Baptist Union** (BU), which he served as first secretary, 1832-1840. In 1843 he emigrated to North America, serving Granville Street (1845) and Salem Chapel (1846), both in Halifax, Nova Scotia, Mount Tabor, Philadelphia (1847), and East Thomaston, Maine (1849-1851?). In the United States, Belcher was a prolific author, writing biographies of George Whitefield (1714-1770), Robert Raikes (1735-1811), **William Carey**, and **Robert Haldane**, as well as editing the works of **Andrew Fuller**. Belcher's ministry in Halifax, Nova Scotia, was cut short by a highly publicized schism in the church there, largely instigated by Belcher's personality and his overly British perspective on matters of **polity** and the question of open communion.

BELGIUM. An outgrowth of Baptist missions in France, Baptist work began in 1895 when French Baptists started the church at Ougrée and later at Mont-sur-Marchienne. Missionary work has been sponsored by U.S. Southern and American Baptists, as well as Canadian Baptists and the **Baptist Bible Fellowship** (BBF) since 1962. More recently, the **Conservative Baptist** Foreign Mission Society (CBFMS) opened a mission in Belgium at Brussels. In 1922 the Unie van baptisten in Belgie (Union of Baptists in Belgium) was formed, and as of 1995 the Unie included 19 churches and 850 members.

BELIEVER'S BAPTISM. See **Baptism**.

BELIEVER'S CHURCH TRADITION. Baptists in England, North America, and beyond have been classified as believer's churches. The first Baptistic confession of faith described the congregation as a "true church of true believers." By this is meant that individuals exercise faith in Jesus Christ as personal Saviour and accept the Lordship of Christ in their lives. Congregations are composed of believers rather than by definition of a parish or by assumption through a **sacramental** process like paedo-baptism followed by confirmation.

Believer's churches have been identifiable since New Testament times: Jesus said "where two or three are gathered together, there I am." Throughout the historical record of the Church, believer's churches have existed as in the examples of the Cathari and the Lollards. Beginning in the 15th century, related groups of reformed congregations banded together in the Radical reformation to constitute what historians now refer to as believer's churches as a stream or type of Protestant Christianity. A working definition according to Donald Durnbaugh (1927-), an historian of the movement, is "a covenanted and disciplined community of those walking in the way of Jesus Christ." This includes an earnest desire to be a Christian, regular meetings together, good works, **discipline**, mutual aid, **baptism**, attention to **Scripture** and submission to Jesus Christ. From the 16th century, those in the close circle of the believer's churches include the Mennonites, Brethren, Baptists, Amish, and Hutterites, to name the major subcategories. In more modern development, particularly in North America, many sects and smaller churches, such as the Pentecostals, may consider themselves believer's churches by this definition.

Beginning in 1967 leaders of several believer's churches began to meet periodically together to reflect theologically on their growing similarities. This was in part a response to the ecumenical movement, and in part a *sui generis* coming together. Conferences have dealt with the ordinances, the nature of the church, **missions**, **voluntarism**, dissent, and renewal. The Believer's Church Conferences now represent a wide variety of groups and scholars as well as leaders of the churches. Primary to the Baptist participation are the **Southern Baptists**, **American Baptists**, and Canadian convention Baptists.

BELIZE. Formerly called British Honduras, Baptist missionary effort was undertaken in 1822 by the **Baptist Missionary Society** (BMS). A church was constituted in 1825 and the work grew slowly. In 1977 **Southern Baptists** began missionary work in British Honduras, and in 1979 the **Baptist Bible Fellowship** (BBF) began its work.

As of 1995, there were 48 churches with 1,965 members affiliated with the Baptist Association of Belize.

BELLAMY, FRANCIS (1855-1931). American Baptist minister, born at Mount Morris, New York. He was educated at the University of Rochester and Rochester Theological Seminary; he was ordained at Little Falls, New York Baptist Church, which he served 1879-1884. Subsequently Bellamy was pastor at Dearborn (1884-1890) and Bethany (1890-1891) Baptist churches in Boston, Massachusetts. Increasingly liberal in his views, he felt uncomfortable in the Baptist movement and left the ministry for a career in journalism. First, he served as an editor for *The Youth's Companion*, later he was the editor of *The Illustrated American Magazine*. At the conclusion of his career he worked in advertising and for the Silver Burdette Publishing Company. With the support of his publisher, Daniel Ford, and his editor James B. Upham, Bellamy submitted a model pledge of allegiance to the American flag to *The Youth's Companion*. The pledge was published anonymously on September 8, 1892, and, owing to the wide distribution of American flags by Mr. Ford, it became a national institution. U.S. presidents Grover Cleveland (1837-1908) and Benjamin Harrison (1833-1901) both lent support to its being widely adopted.

BENEDICT, DAVID (1779-1874). American Baptist minister and historian, born at Norwalk, Connecticut. He graduated from Brown University and was ordained to serve the church at Pawtucket, Rhode Island. Benedict had a great interest in Baptist history and particularly the expansion of the denomination. In 1813 he published the first of his

Baptist histories, followed by a definitive edition in 1848. His work was considered a reliable source of congregational and associational data in the mid-19th century. His subsequent autobiography, *Fifty Years Among the Baptists*, is useful for its pre-Civil War reflections on the maturing denomination. His half-brother, Stephen (1801-1868), was a prosperous cotton manufacturer and Baptist deacon in his brother's church, who left a considerable legacy to the **American Baptist Home Mission Society** (ABHMS). Benedict College in South Carolina was named for Stephen.

BENIN. Earlier known as Dahomey, Baptist development dates back to 1851 when T. J. Bowen (1814-1875), a missionary to Nigeria, visited what is now Benin. In 1969 the Southern Baptist **Foreign Mission Board** appointed its first missionary who helped to begin a church at Abomey in 1974 and another at Porto Novo in 1976. Two associations have been formed, no convention as yet exists.

As of 1995, there were 72 churches and 2,746 members in the Baptist associations.

BENNETT, CEPHAS (1804-1885). American Baptist missionary, born at Homer, New York. Bennett was a printer, following that trade all his career. He developed an interest in religious publishing and produced a **bible** dictionary in 1827 while he printed the *New York Baptist Register*. In 1827 he indicated an interest in publishing the bible which **Adoniram Judson** was producing, and the **Baptist Board of Foreign Missions** (BBFM) appointed him to **Burma** for the project. In 1829 he became the first American missionary printer, settling first at Moulmein and later at Rangoon. He began the American Baptist Missionary Press and in 1862 he organized the Burma Bible and Tract Society. A long-time resident of Rangoon, Bennett published major historical works relating to Burmese life.

BERMUDA. The Baptist movement in Bermuda is traced to **Southern Baptist** missionary work, which began in 1956 among American military personnel. The **Foreign Mission Board** (FMB) has sponsored several initiatives over the years which have resulted in successful church planting. Also, the **National Baptist Convention U.S.A.** sponsored a congregation in Hamilton.

As of 1995, there were three churches and 336 members affiliated with the Bermuda Baptist Fellowship.

BIBLE. Baptists have held from their beginning that they are "people of the Book." This means practically that the bible serves as a guide for faith and practice and instructs local churches and individual believers on faith, conduct, and **polity**. The version of the bible which Baptists first used was the Geneva edition of 1560. Baptists also widely used Alford's *New Testament* and Young's *Literal Translation* (1862).

Only in response to the large number of copies available in the early 19th century through the Bible Society movement did Baptists in the United States adopt the *Authorized* or *King James Version* (1611) as their standard. Some even declined in this context, preferring to prepare an edition which recognized the proper translation of *baptizo* as "immerse"; this "Baptist Bible" which appeared in 1850, was short-lived. **Scripture** memorization, doctrinal formulation, and devotional aids all popularized the *King James Version* through the mid-20th century.

When the *Revised Standard Version* (RSV) was issued by the National Council of Churches of the United States in 1946, many Baptists declined to use or authorize the new version because of its translation of Isaiah 7:14: "Behold a young woman shall conceive..." This led to a proliferation of scripture translations from **conservative evangelical** sources which found widespread use in Baptist churches in North America. These have included the *Berkeley Edition* (1958), the *Amplified Bible* (1965), and the *New International Version* (1973). Many Baptists use a modernized edition of the KJV, known as the *New King James Version* (1982). Popular across the denomination in the United States are various editions of Scripture with notations, including the *Scofield Reference Bible* (1909, 1967), the *Thompson Chain Reference Bible* (1908, 1978), and the *Ryrie Study Bible* (1976). Also widely used are paraphrase editions like the *Charles Williams Translation* (1937), *The New Testament in Modern English* by J. B. Phillips (1961), and the *Good News Bible* (1976). In recent years, in Great Britain, Baptist churches have gravitated to the *New English Bible* (1970), the *New International Version* (1979), or the *Revised English Bible* (1989). More recently in North America many congregations have adopted the *New Revised Standard Version* (1989), and in study use the *Jerusalem Bible* (1966). The major concerns for new translations include nuances suggested by archaeology and linguistics and the use of inclusive English language. See also **Scripture, Authority of**.

BIBLE COLLEGES, BAPTIST. Perhaps the oldest example of a bible college among Baptists was the **Free(will) Baptist** Biblical School founded at Parsonfield, Maine, in 1840. This institution was so-called because it stressed the priority of **Scripture** studies in preparation for **ministry**. Its curriculum and approach to the **bible** was progressive for the era. Next in order was the Gordon Missionary Training School, opened in 1881 in Boston, Massachusetts.

In the 20th century the bible college movement has been associated with emerging Baptist groups and those groups which are antagonistic to higher education, as found in church-related or "Christian" liberal arts colleges, universities, and graduate theological seminaries. The differentiating characteristics are: (1) a more practical ministry and missionary curriculum; (2) a confessional statement which mandates the entire curriculum is based upon and derived from the bible; (3) practical **missionary** work is required of all students. Examples of the use of bible colleges among emerging Baptist groups are the schools of eastern Europe, such as at Odessa, **Ukraine**, and Bucharest, **Romania**. Institutions which have an inherent bias against "higher" education are found among the **General Association of Regular Baptists**, the **Baptist Missionary Association**, the **Baptist Bible Fellowship**, the **Liberty Baptist Fellowship**, and other independent Baptists in the United States. Bible colleges, not necessarily of a **fundamentalist** theological persuasion, are also found among **Black Baptists**, notably the American Baptist Theological Seminary (1924) and The National Baptist Missionary Training School (1936) in Nashville, Tennessee, related to the **Southern Baptist Convention** and the **National Baptist Convention, Inc**. In Great Britain, a number of Baptists have been trained at London Bible College, founded in 1943. See also **Theological Education**.

BIBLE DEFENSE LEAGUE. Part of the **Fundamentalist - Modernist** division among 20th century Baptists was the Bible Defense League in the **Seventh Day Baptist** tradition. Akin to the **Baptist Bible Union** among First Day Baptists, the Bible Defense League was formed in May 1925 at Milton, Wisconsin, by and for Seventh Day Baptists who desired "to throw off the incubus of rationalism" which threatened evangelical Christianity. Seventh Day Baptists involved in the Bible Defense League were less divisive than others in Baptist Fundamentalism and essentially carried forth an editorial campaign in a bimonthly magazine called the *Exponent*. For three years there were also meetings of the League between sessions of the General Conference (1925-1927), after which a Committee of Six on Denominational Harmony recommended that freedom of private judgment should be exercised and both sides of the debate should be presented in the columns of the *Sabbath Recorder*. From 1928 to 1931, a "modernist" page appeared and from 1929 to 1931, the "Fundamentalist" page was regularly issued. Seventh Day Baptists ultimately settled down to a moderate evangelical position, concluding for the most part that Modernism had reached its peak and did not reflect the majority of Seventh Day congregations.

BICKEL, LUKE WASHINGTON (1866-1917). American Baptist missionary, born at Cincinnati, Ohio. In his youth he was an apprenticed seaman and rose to the rank of captain in the merchant marine. After studies at Spurgeon's College and a missionary appointment with the British Baptist Publication Society, Bickel applied to the **American Baptist Missionary Union** for appointment. A gift from a Glasgow merchant for a gospel ship made possible Bickel's appointment in the Far East. In 1898 he began a mariner's mission in the Inland Sea of Japan aboard the *Fukuin Maru*. At many of the islands he created **Sunday Schools** and preaching stations; in 1916 he reported work on 60 islands in cooperation with other denominational groups.

BILL, INGRAHAM EBENEZER (1805-1891). Canadian Baptist minister, editor, and historian, born at Cornwallis, Nova Scotia. He was baptized by **Edward Manning** in 1824 and served the church at Nictaux 23 years. Bill also served churches in Fredericton and St. John, New Brunswick, and was one of the popular preachers and **revivalists** of his era. An ardent advocate of education, though lacking a formal education himself, Bill travelled to the United States and Great Britain in support of Acadia College, raising in the United States over $3,000 in 1844. In 1852 he became editor of the *Christian Visitor*, which he edited for 20 years. Bill was a far-sighted **pastor** and leader, advocating female education and progressive worship forms. He introduced the use of pipe organs to his church at Nictaux. In 1880 he published *Fifty Years With the Baptist Ministers and Churches of the Maritime Provinces of Canada*, a major primary source for the region.

BISHOP, NATHAN (1808-1880). Educator and denominational leader, born at Vernon, New York. Bishop graduated from Brown University and became school superintendent in Providence, Rhode Island, and Boston. Bishop moved to New York City in the 1880s and became involved in denominational work. He served from 1874-1876 as corresponding secretary of the **American Baptist Home Mission Society** (ABHMS) and at his retirement he paid its debt of $30,000. He was particularly interested in **Black Baptist** education and in his honor the ABHMS named its college in Texas after Bishop.

BITTING, CHARLES CARROLL (1830-1898). Baptist minister and denominational leader, born at Philadelphia, Pennsylvania. Following collegiate studies at Lewisburg and Madison Universities, Bitting served churches in Virginia. While **pastor** at Alexandria, Virginia, during the Civil War, he refused to take the Oath of Allegiance to the United States and was forced to ride as a hostage on the front of a railroad locomotive against Southern raiders for the day's trip from Alexandria to Orange County Courthouse. After the Civil War, he became secretary of the Southern Baptist **Sunday School Board** and in 1872 regional secretary for the **American Baptist Publication Society** (ABPS). Later Bitting again served congregations in Virginia and Maryland. He was one of a select group of post-Civil War leaders to serve in both the major Conventions, thus reversing the trend toward regionalism in Baptist life.

BLACK BAPTISTS. The Black Baptist tradition is culturally diverse and involves congregations in North America and the Caribbean Islands. Essentially the Black experience reflects an admixture of African-American and/or Caribbean cultures with Regular Baptist polity.

The initial Black Baptist expressions were found among the slave communities in the British colonies in North America. White preachers preached among the slaves and underground congregations emerged, notably on William Byrd III's (1728-1777) plantation in Virginia in 1742. Freedom of interpretation and spontaneity in worship attracted large numbers of Blacks to the Baptist tradition even before emancipation.

The first formally organized Black Baptist church began in 1778 at Silver Bluff, South Carolina, under the direction of **George Leile** and **Andrew Bryan**. Later in 1787 the Springfield Baptist Church was founded at Augusta, Georgia, and the First African Baptist in Savannah, Georgia (1788).

In the Canadian context, Black Baptist churches date from 1782 when **David George** started a congregation at Shelburne, Nova Scotia. From this eventually stemmed the African Baptist Association in 1854.

Black Baptist institutional life includes **associations**, national **conventions,** and educational institutions. While early congregations were related to Regular associations in northern cities, by the 1850s Black leaders sought control of their own relationships and structures and joined forces with abolitionists and sympathetic Republican Party members. This led to the **American Baptist Free Mission Society** (ABFrMS), which was established in 1843 in part to affirm Afro-American social equality. The **American Baptist Home Mission Society** (ABHMS) also assisted in the formation of many churches, cooperative bodies, and schools in the Black communities. Their work began directly in 1862 in the District of Columbia and later in South Carolina. The major effort of the ABHMS was in training leaders for work among the Freedmen, thus much money was raised to assist a group of academies, colleges, and universities across the South to train Black leaders. The yearning for Black organizations, however, led predictably to the formation of the **American Baptist Missionary Convention** (ABMC) in 1840 and the Western Colored Baptist Convention in 1853. This led eventually to the uniting of the Consolidated American Baptist Missionary Convention (CABMC) in 1866, and later to the **National Baptist Convention** (NBCUSA) in 1896, a heritage of Black-led organizations (see below) which won the support and cooperation of the White societies.

Early Associations. The first associations emerged in the Ohio Valley in the antebellum era: Providence (1834, Meigs County, Ohio), Union (1836, Cincinnati, Ohio), Wood River (1839, St. Clair County, Illinois). In Upper **Canada** (now Ontario), the Amherstburg Association was formed along the northern shore of Lake Erie in 1841. There were approximately nine Black Baptist associational bodies active in the United States before the Civil War and two in what is now Canada.

Black Baptist Education. Among the major Black Baptist educational institutions were Roger Williams University (Nashville, Tenn., 1864), Shaw University (Raleigh, N.C., 1865), Wayland Seminary (Washington, D.C., 1865), Storer College (Harper's Ferry, W.Va., 1866), Richmond Theological Seminary (Richmond, Va., 1867), Atlanta Baptist College (Atlanta, Ga., 1867), Mather School (Beaufort, S.C., 1869), Benedict College (Columbia, S.C., 1870), Florida Institute (Live Oak, Fla., 1873), Bishop College (Marshall, Tex., 1881), Jackson College (Jackson, Miss., 1877), Leland College (New Orleans, La., 1870), Alabama Colored Baptist University (Selma, Ala., 1878), Spelman College (Atlanta, Ga., 1881), Simmons University (Louisville, Ky., 1873), Hartshorn Memorial College (Richmond, Va., 1884), Walker Institute (Augusta, Ga., 1885), Arkansas Baptist College (Little Rock, Ark., 1887), Bible and Normal Institute (Memphis, Tenn., 1887), Coleman Academy (Gibsland, La., 1887), Spiller Academy (1891), Waters Normal Institute (Winton, N.C., 1887?), Houston Academy (Houston, Tex., 1893), Jeruel Academy (Athens, Ga., 1893), Hearne Academy (Hearne, Tex., 1896). Southern Baptists cooperated with the National Baptist Convention, Inc. in 1924 to establish the American Baptist Theological Seminary, a bible college and missionary training institute in Nashville, Tennessee. The National Theological Institute was formed in 1864 to sponsor schools in Washington, D.C., Virginia, South Carolina, and Georgia. In many cases, either the ABHMS or the **Freewill Baptists** early assisted the majority of the schools.

In addition, another group of colleges emerged on a more independent basis: Guadaloupe College (1884); Houston College (1885);

Virginia College and Theological Seminary (1888); Western College, Missouri (1890); Friendship Baptist College, South Carolina (1891); Meridian Baptist Seminary, Mississippi (1897); Central City College, Georgia (1899); Central Texas College (1903); Morris College, South Carolina (1905); Lee and Hayes University, Maryland (1914); Williams and Jones University, Maryland (1928); Central Baptist Seminary, Topeka, Kansas (1921); and Northern Baptist University, Rahway, New Jersey (1921). Several of these schools enjoyed the patronage of Black Baptist State conventions.

Formation of State Conventions. As associations grew in number and benevolent concerns proliferated, Black Baptists organized numerous state conventions, the General Association of Colored Baptists in Kentucky (1865), Florida Bethlehem Baptist State Convention (1874), Colored Baptist Convention of Maryland (1898), Baptist Missionary and Educational Convention of Tennessee (1872), to cite several examples. Most were linked directly from their beginnings with the National Baptist Convention or one of its predecessors.

Formation of Black Baptist National Conventions. Responding to the need for Black led national missionary organizations, the Consolidated American Baptist Missionary Convention was formed at Nashville, Tennessee, in August 1867. This organization sponsored **Sunday School** agents and missionaries throughout the southern states, until its demise in 1879. The next national organization was the Baptist Foreign Mission Convention of the United States, organized in Montgomery, Alabama, in 1880. In the west, the American National Baptist Convention was formed at St. Louis in 1886. In 1895 these two regional bodies merged their interests to form the National Baptist Convention. In order to have a Black-led foreign mission enterprise, the **Lott Carey Baptist Home and Foreign Mission Convention** was founded in 1897. In 1907 Black Primitive Baptists in the South formed a national body, the National Primitive Baptist Convention of the U.S.A., mostly as a racially defined outgrowth of the White Primitive Baptists. A disagreement over management of the publication house of the National Baptist Convention led **Richard H. Boyd** in 1915 to form the National Baptist Convention of America (Unincorporated) (NBCA). In 1961 under the influence of **Martin Luther King, Jr.** and Gardner C. Taylor (1918-), the **Progressive National Baptist Convention** (PNBC) was formed. A schism in the NBCA in 1988 led to the establishment of the **National Baptist Missionary Convention** (NBMC). See also **Primitive Baptists**.

BLACK ROCK CONVENTION. See **Primitive Baptists**.

BOARDMAN, GEORGE DANA, JR. (1828-1903). American Baptist minister and educator, born at Tavoy, **Burma**. The son of **George Dana Boardman, Sr.** and **Sarah Hall** (later **Judson**), he was the first surviving child of the missionary children born overseas to an American Baptist missionary. At the death of his father, he was sent to the United States to be raised and became the stepson of **Adoniram Judson** when his mother married Mr. Judson in 1834. George was educated at Brown University and Newton Theological Institution, after which he entered the pastoral ministry. He served Barnwell, South Carolina, Baptist Church (1855-1856), then Second Baptist, Rochester, New York (1856-64), and finally First Baptist Church, Philadelphia, Pennsylvania (1864-1894). Boardman was a widely regarded orator in Philadelphia and taught at Temple University and the University of Pennsylvania. Brown University awarded him an honorary doctorate in 1866, as did the University of Pennsylvania in 1889. His lectures on **bible** exposition were well attended in Philadelphia and published widely during his lifetime.

BOARDMAN, GEORGE DANA, SR. (1801-1831). American Baptist missionary, born at Livermore, Maine. He was in the first graduating class of Waterville College and remained briefly as a tutor on its faculty in 1822. In 1823 he sought an appointment of the **Baptist Board of Foreign Missions** (BBFM) and was accepted. He moved to Andover, Massachusetts, where he planned to enter seminary, but was diverted to serve as missionary to African people in that town. He was ordained at North Yarmouth, Maine, and entered the mission service in 1825. He and his wife, **Sarah Hall Boardman Judson**, embarked for **Burma**, but were detained at Calcutta where they lived with the English Baptist missionaries for two years. Eventually the Boardmans settled at Moulmein, Burma. After some years he served at Tavoy where he became the pioneer missionary to the Karens. He travelled extensively in the backcountry and gathered the first church at Tavoy. His health failed from respiratory illness and he died at Tavoy after an arduous journey.

BOGARD, BENJAMIN MARCUS (1868-1951). Southern Baptist and later Missionary Baptist minister, born at Elizabethtown, Kentucky. He was educated at Georgetown College and Bethel College in Kentucky and ordained at Woodland Church in 1888. He served a series of country churches in Kentucky (1888-92); congregations at Princeton (1892-1894) and Fenton (1894) Kentucky; Charleston, Missouri (1894-1899); and Searcy, Arkansas (1899-1903). Bogard, a leading **Landmarkist**, became a well-known debater among Southern Baptists, taking exception to what he called "conventionism." His major public debates occurred in Texas,

Indiana, Kentucky, and Arkansas, over Campbellism, evolution, and Christian union. In 1900-1905 he joined forces with other Landmarkists in Arkansas and challenged the basis of representation in the **Southern Baptist Convention** (SBC) and the basis of support for missionary work which Bogard and others thought included too much administration. Bogard's following left the Southern Baptist Convention and became organized in 1902 as the General Association in Arkansas and later the **Baptist Missionary Association** (BMA). He was a staunch defender of Baptist Successionism, the view that an unbroken line of Baptist churches existed from the year A.D. 31. His lasting institutional legacy was the Missionary Baptist Seminary in Little Rock, Arkansas.

BOHEMIAN BAPTISTS. See **Czechoslovak Baptist Convention of the United States and Canada**.

BOLIVIA. Baptist life in Bolivia is dated from the establishment at Oruro in 1898 of the first congregation by **Archibald Reekie**, a Canadian Baptist. In 1941 a biblical institute was founded at Cochabamba (later to become a theological seminary), and the Unión Bautista Boliviana was organized in 1936. Following the construction of a railroad from **Brazil** to **Peru**, the Brazilian Baptists began an aggressive missionary outreach in Bolivia in 1952 and formed the Convención Bautista Boliviana. In 1961 they organized a theological school at Santa Cruz, the Seminario Teológico Bautista del Oriente Bolivia. The Southern Baptist **Foreign Mission Board** (FMB) entered Bolivia in 1977 at the invitation of the Brazilian work and the Maranatha Baptists, International Baptist Missions entered the field in the 1960s, and the **Baptist Bible Fellowship** (BBF) began a mission in 1978.

As of 1995 there were 160 churches and 16,200 members affiliated with the Union, and 38 churches and 2,500 members affiliated with the Convención. The periodical, *El Centinela Boliviano* (The Bolivian Sentinel) (1945-), is associated with the Unión.

BOOTH, ABRAHAM (1734-1806). English Baptist pastor, born at Alfreton. He was converted during a revival in the Midlands and became superintendent of a congregation at Kirkby Woodhouse in 1760. Although this church was related to the **General Baptists**, Booth became a Calvinist and published significant theological treatises, including *Glad Tidings to Perishing Sinners* (1796). He was called to Little Prescot Street Church, Goodman's Fields, where he was ordained, and from this church he became a leading figure among London Baptists. He was a prime mover in founding the theological college at Stepney as well as the Itinerant

Society; he was also the first London minister to lend support to the **Baptist Missionary Society** (BMS). It was Booth who introduced **William Carey** to Dr. **John Thomas** in the service of the British East India Company, who in turn quickened Carey's interest in that region. He was remembered as an unostentatious man who gave large sums of money to benevolent causes, among which was the antislavery movement. Booth was one of the most widely read Baptists of the 18th century; among his many works were *The Reign of Grace; From Its Rise to Its Consummation* (1768), and *Paedobaptism Examined* (1784).

BOSNIA. Baptist experience began in Bosnia during the period of the Austro-Hungarian Empire. In 1862 Franz and Maria Tabory were baptized in Bucharest, Romania, and they moved shortly afterward to Sarajevo with Franz becoming a bible **colporteur**. The next year, August Liebig, a German missionary in Romania, also moved to Lukovac and conducted baptisms. A third stream of Baptist life in Bosnia began with the ministry of Adolf Hempt, a Serbian. Hempt was baptized in Budapest and conducted missionary work in Sarajevo, actually creating the first congregation about 1877. Following World War I, the Baptist Churches in Bosnia joined the Baptist Union in Yugoslavia. In 1992 with the dissolution of Yugoslavia and the ravages of war, Bosnian Baptists are rebuilding.

As of 1995, there were five churches (Tuzla, Zivinice, Sarajevo, Zenica, Novi Tranik) with about 100 members in Bosnia

BOTSWANA. The South African Baptist Missionary Society was first to enter the territory now called Botswana in 1966. This work was transferred to the Southern Baptist **Foreign Mission Board** (FMB) in 1968. The first congregation was formed at Francistown in 1970, and the churches organized a **convention** in 1978.

As of 1995, there were 17 churches and 720 members affiliated with the Baptist Convention of Botswana.

BOYCE, JAMES PETIGRU (1827-1888). Southern Baptist minister and educator, born at Charleston, South Carolina. He was educated at the College of Charleston, Brown University, and Princeton Theological Seminary. His mentors were **Francis Wayland** at Brown and A. A. Hodge (1823-1886) and Charles Hodge (1797-1878) at Princeton. From 1848-1849 he edited the *Southern Baptist* and then served First Baptist Church, Columbia, South Carolina (1849-1851). In 1855 Boyce became a professor of theology at Furman College and in 1859 a founder of Southern Baptist Theological Seminary. At Southern he was the first chair of the faculty and taught in New Testament, theology, homiletics, and church history. It was he who induced **Basil Manly, Jr**. and **John A. Broaddus** with others to join the original Southern Seminary faculty. When the Civil War forced the closure of the school, Boyce raised funds for its reopening and eventual removal to Louisville, Kentucky. He was president of the **Southern Baptist Convention** (SBC) from 1872-1879 and again in 1888. A double predestinarian Calvinist, Boyce also defended **Richard Fuller**'s views on **slavery**. He published in 1882 *Abstract of Systematic Theology*, reprinted for many years by the Southern Baptist **Sunday School Board**. A connoisseur of fine wines, he died in France while seeking a cure for gout.

BOYD, RICHARD HENRY (1843-1922). Black Baptist minister and publisher, born at Noxubee, Mississippi. Raised a slave in Mississippi and Texas, upon emancipation he was converted and soon ordained to the Baptist ministry. In 1872 he rallied Black congregations to form the first Black Baptist **association** in Texas and he rose to important positions in the General Baptist Convention of Texas. In 1896 he was elected the manager of the National Baptist Home Mission Board. An entrepreneur, Boyd negotiated a publishing arrangement with the Southern Baptist **Sunday School Board** to offset the influence of the **American Baptist Publication Society** (ABPS), and later formed the publishing board for the **National Baptist Convention** (NBCUSA) in 1897. He was financially very successful in this endeavor, but differed greatly with the leadership of the National Baptist Convention about matters of ownership and control. Between 1905 and 1915, Boyd engaged in an acrimonious debate with the Convention, and he finally withdrew and helped to form a new group of Black Baptists, the National Baptist Convention of America (NBCA). Boyd was the author or editor of numerous practical works for the churches, including the *National Baptist Pastor's Guide* (1900), the *National Baptist Hymnal* (1903), and *A Story of the National Baptist Publishing Board* (1915).

BRAZIL. As early as 1859 Southern Baptists in the United States planned to begin **missions** work in Brazil. Thomas J. Bowen (1814-1878) preached in Rio de Janeiro in 1859-1860. A church of American emigrants was formed in 1871 at Santa Barbara. The first missionaries were dispatched from the Southern Baptist **Foreign Mission Board** (FMB) in 1881. At Bahia the first Brazilian congregation was constituted in 1882, largely the work of William Bagby (1855-1939). In 1907 the Convención Bautista Brasilena was formed and the next year a college and seminary were opened at Rio de Janeiro. In 1953, as British missionaries left China, the

Baptist Missionary Society (BMS) began a new work in Ponta Grossa in cooperation with Southern Baptists. British influence upon the formation of the Parana Baptist Convention was significant thereafter.

In addition to the missionary efforts mentioned above, U.S. independent Baptist mission work was started in the Amazon Valley in 1922 when Eric Nelson (1862-1939), gained support of the Amazon Valley Faith Baptist Mission; in 1935 **Baptist Mid-Missions** (BMM) from the United States established an extensive mission in Brazil at Juazerio, and later at Manaus and Boa Vista; the **Association of Baptists for World Evangelism** (ABWE) started a mission in 1942; Conservative Baptists began a church planting mission in 1946 and sponsored seminaries in Brasilia, São Luis, and Teresina; the Baptist General Conference opened a mission in 1955 in cooperation with the Brazilian Baptist Convention, the **Baptist Bible Fellowship** (BBF) started its mission in 1952, and in 1963 the Japan Baptist Convention also appointed missionaries to Brazil. In 1913, the first Seventh Day Baptist congregation was started in Brazil.

Brazilian Baptists themselves developed an aggressive overseas missionary program after World War II, opening fields in **Portugal**, Macao, and **Angola**. Extension also occurred into **Bolivia**. The Convention publishes *O Jornal Batista* (Baptist Journal) (1901-). In 1942 the Baptist Publishing House was founded in Rio. The Convention encompasses an **evangelism** board, a Christian ethics commission, and a woman's missionary union. Theological schools exist at Recife (1902), Rio (1908), São Paulo (1901), and Belém (1955). Brazilian Baptist life was greatly advanced by the Tenth Baptist World Congress in Rio in 1970, which drew approximately 170,000 people.

As of 1995, there were 4,810 churches and 902,000 members affiliated with the Brazilian Baptist Convention, and 900 churches with 200,000 members affiliated with the National Baptist Convention of Brazil. Brazil has the most theological schools of any single Baptist national group. Thirty-six institutions or programs are dispersed throughout the country, several in key cities: Bauru, Teresina, São Paulo, Santo Andre, Pôrto Alegre, Rio de Janeiro, Itaperuna, Natal, São Goncalo, Ijui, Goiânia, Osasco, Brasília, Curitiba, Fortaleza, Juazeiro do Norte, Campinas, Campo Grande, Niterói, Feira de Santana, Vitória, Belo Horizonte, Dourados, Recife, Manaus, Salvador, Campos Goitacazes, Araguaina, Cuiabá, São Luis, and Belém.

BRINE, JOHN (1703-1765). English Baptist minister, born at Kettering. He was self-taught, and converted under **John Gill**. In 1726 he was called to serve Jordan's Well, Coventry, church, and in 1729 he was elected pastor at Curriers' Hall, St. Paul's Alley, Cripplegate, which he served until his death. Closely allied with **John Gill**, Brine was among the most theologically Calvinistic of the **Particular Baptists**. The author of over two dozen sermons and pamphlets published in seven volumes, he declined to address the condition of the unconverted and this caused his ministry to wither by mid-century, an obvious product of extreme Calvinism. Among his most famous works were *Certain Efficacy of the Death of Christ* (1743) and *A Vindication of Divine Justice* (1754).

BRISBANE, WILLIAM HENRY (1906-1878). Baptist physician and editor, born at Black Swamp, South Carolina. He was educated at Charleston Medical School, and became a plantation farmer and editor, in addition to his medical practice. **Francis Wayland**'s book, *Elements of Moral Science* (1835) influenced Brisbane against **slavery** and he freed his slaves and began a career as an abolitionist. Opposition to his views caused him to move to Ohio and later Wisconsin, where he wrote on **antislavery** topics. During the Civil War, he served as a chaplain in the Wisconsin Cavalry and later as tax commissioner in South Carolina during Reconstruction. He helped to organize the Port Royal Experiment, which assisted in the training of former slaves. Brisbane published a famous antislavery work, *Slaveholding Examined in the Light of the Holy Bible*, in 1847.

BRITISH HONDURAS. See **Belize**.

BRITISH VIRGIN ISLANDS. The **Baptist Missionary Association of America** (BMA) started a Baptist Mission in the islands in 1956. As of 1995, there were fewer than five churches and about 250 persons affiliated with the work.

BROADDUS, ANDREW (1770-1848). American Baptist minister, born in Caroline County, Virginia. He was self-educated in a frontier cabin, converted and baptized about 1789. He entered the Baptist pastoral ministry and served churches in central Virginia: Upper King and Queen, Salem, Bethel, and Fredericksburg. Repeatedly offered prestigious congregations in urban areas in the South and North, Broaddus declined and favored the small, rural church. He was a well-known preacher and scholar, writing for the *Religious Herald*, and various philosophic subjects, notably a response to the writings of Thomas Paine (1737-1809). Also an accomplished hymn writer, he published three volumes, among which were: *Sacred Ballads* (1790) and the *Dover Selection of Spiritual Songs* (1828). His son, Andrew Broaddus, Jr. (1818-1900), succeeded him as pastor at Salem Church in Caroline County, and a third generation in Andrew Broaddus III (1853-1926) followed in that pastoral ministry and leadership among Virginia Baptists.

BROADDUS, WILLIAM F[POSSIBLY FERGUSON] (1801-1876). American and later Southern Baptist minister, born at Woodville, Virginia. Privately educated, he was first a schoolteacher. He was ordained in 1824 at the "F.T." Church in Rappahannock County, Virginia, after which he served the Shiloh and Mt. Salem churches. In his early career, Broaddus was an opponent of **revivalistic** techniques, but this changed dramatically in 1831 at Upperville where he observed the benefits of protracted meetings and other new measures, and he became a promoter of these strategies. This won for him the criticism of hyper-Calvinists in Virginia, yet he persisted in holding meetings and organizing new congregations and **associations** along these lines. Because of his stand, he was denied a seat in the Ketocton Association in northern Virginia. In 1833-1836 he served the churches at Bethel and Long Branch, and then he moved to Kentucky for a decade. From 1840-1850 he served pastorates in Lexington, Shelbyville, and Versailles, Kentucky. Returning to Virginia in 1853, Broaddus served Fredericksburg Baptist until captured in the Civil War. He was arrested by Union troops in 1862 and taken to prison in Washington, D.C., where he was retained for a political prisoner exchange with the Confederate government. Following his release, Broaddus was minister at Charlottesville, Virginia (1863-1865), and again served the congregation at Fredericksburg until his death (1865-1876). He was one of the most effective promoters of education and mission among Virginia Baptists, a charter trustee of Richmond College (for which he raised $20,000) and of the Virginia Baptist Education Society. Broaddus was also known for his stance against strong drink, being an author of a plea to the Shiloh Association for total abstinence in 1840. Broaddus published several important tracts on **baptism**, 1835-1858.

BROADUS, JOHN ALBERT (1827-1895). Southern Baptist theological educator, born at Culpeper County, Virginia. Educated in a private school, he taught school 1844-1846 and then studied at the University of Virginia where he graduated with an M.A. in 1850. That year he became pastor of the Baptist church in Charlottesville, Virginia, and tutor in classical languages at the University of Virginia. In 1858 he became one of the founding faculty members of Southern Baptist Theological Seminary in Greenville, South Carolina. During the Civil War he was a chaplain in Robert E. Lee's (1807-1870) Army, after which he returned to the Seminary and facilitated its rebuilding and move to Louisville, Kentucky. While he taught New Testament and homiletics, his primary publications were in preaching: *On the Preparation and Delivery of Sermons* (1870), *Lectures on the History of Preaching* (1876). His *Harmony of the Gospels* (1893) was a standard text for many years. In 1889 Broadus delivered the Lyman Beecher Lectures in Preaching at Yale University, one of two Southern Baptists selected for that honor.

BRONSON, MILES (1812-1883). American Baptist missionary, born at Norway, New York. He was educated at Hamilton Literary and Theological Institution (later Colgate University) and upon graduation was appointed a missionary to Assam for the **Baptist Board of Foreign Missions** (BBFM). Arriving in northeastern **India** in 1837 he set up work among the hill tribes and pioneered work among the Garo people in 1863. In 1841 he began a school at Nowgong and he commenced his literary work creating the first Assamese-English dictionary, which he finished in 1867. Bronson theorized that the Assamese language was the key to reaching the remote tribes and this proved to be correct and productive of thousands of Christian converts in northeast India. During his only furlough he served as pastor of the Springfield, New York, Baptist Church. Bronson published nineteen works in Naga, Garo, and Assamese, including the *Naga Catechism* (1839) and *A Dictionary in Assamese and English* (1867).

BROTHERHOOD OF THE KINGDOM. Founded on July 9, 1892, in the New York City apartment of **Walter Rauschenbusch**, a young German Baptist minister. The group of six founding clergy, including Samuel Zane Batten (1859-1925), Spencer B. Meeser (1859-1939), **Nathaniel Schmidt, William Newton Clarke**, and Leighton Williams (1855-1935), was an outgrowth of the **Baptist Congress** and focussed on the reassertion of the doctrine of the Kingdom of God and its practical application in human society. The organization was kept to a minimum and the members engaged in **bible** study, theological revision, social reform, and advocacy of Christian unity. Over the next 30 years the Brotherhood became an international fellowship and helped to influence church organizations to accept the **social gospel** agenda. Notable among its converts were the leaders of the **Northern Baptist Convention** (NBC), formed in 1907, which in 1910 formed a social service department of the denomination.

BROWN, JOHN NEWTON (1803-1868). American Baptist minister and denominational publisher, born at New London, Connecticut. He was educated at Hamilton Literary and Theological Institution (later Colgate

University) and served pastorates in Exeter, New Hampshire (1829-1839), and Lexington, Virginia (1845-1849). For six years 1839-1845 he taught theology and pastoral relations at New Hampton Institute. In 1849 Brown was appointed educational secretary of the **American Baptist Publication Society** (ABPS), where he remained for a key decade, building the printed resources of the Society in response to the growth of frontier and overseas missions. Brown will ever be associated with the preparation of the New Hampshire Confession of Faith (1830-33), which he principally authored with two other ministers, for use among the Baptist churches in New Hampshire. The **Confession** became widely used, as well as his church **covenant**, because he included both in his *Baptist Church Manual* (1853) of church **discipline**, distributed to virtually every missionary Baptist congregation in the United States.

BROWN, NATHAN (1807-1886). American Baptist missionary, born in Ipswich, New Hampshire. He was educated at Williams College and studied at Newton Theological Institution before serving a church at Rutland, Vermont, teaching school, and editing the *Vermont Telegraph*, a weekly religious paper. In 1832 the **Baptist Board of Foreign Missions** appointed Brown and his wife to join the **Adoniram Judson**s in **Burma**. Judson convinced Brown to open a new field in Assam, and he settled at Sadiva. He translated several tracts and hymns into Assamese and organized an **association** of churches in Assam. While on furlough in the United States in 1855, he resigned from the Board and joined the **American Baptist Free Mission Society** (ABFrMS), editing their periodical, *The American Baptist,* and the *Journal and Messenger*. His strongly held abolitionist views were widely known. After the Civil War and the merger of the ABFrMS and the **American Baptist Missionary Union** (ABMU), Brown returned to Japan to translate the New Testament into Japanese, a project he finished in 1879. A highly regarded linguist, Brown helped to organize the American Philological Society. Brown published over 35 works, including *Catechisms in Thai and Assamese* (1837), the *First Assamese Hymnbook* (1845), and a *History of Assam, by a Native Pundit* (1844).

BROWN, NICHOLAS (1729-1741). Baptist entrepreneur and philanthropist, born at Providence, Rhode Island. He was a merchant in the spermacetti candle business, the first American businessman to create formally a monopoly, which he did among candlemakers in New England. During the French and Indian War he was a privateer and during the American Revolution he secretly obtained clothing for the Continental troops. In the constitutional debates in the 1780s he was a Federalist and helped to secure Rhode Island's support. In 1767 his contribution to the Baptist college secured its relocation to Providence and his firm built the first building, University Hall, on Brown family property. He was also a principal benefactor to the Charitable Baptist Society, the corporation of First Baptist Church in Providence.

His son, Nicholas (1769-1841), was educated in University Hall, and developed a lifelong affection for the College of Rhode Island, serving as a trustee and its treasurer. In 1804 he gave $5,000 for the endowment of a professorship in belles lettres, and the name of the university was changed to honor the family's generosity. In 1823 the younger Brown gave funds to erect Hope College named for his sister, and he built Manning Hall.

BRYAN, ANDREW (1737-1812). American Black Baptist minister, born in Goose Creek, South Carolina. Named for his master, Jonathan Bryan (fl.1780-1800) who was converted under **George Leile**, Bryan rose to leadership in the Savannah community of **Black Baptists**, following the pastorate of Leile. At length, Bryan was ordained by his uncle, **Andrew Marshall**, and in 1788 he organized the first African Baptist Church of Savannah at Yamacraw, near Savannah. He purchased his freedom and bought a lot for his church of 700 members. The growth of the congregation was such that twice it divided into two more congregations. Collectively, these African congregations were known as "**Ethiopian**" churches.

In a celebrated incident in the 1780s, Andrew and his brother, Sampson, held night meetings of his congregation and, suspected of inciting insurrection, they were publicly whipped for the incidents. In 1790 Bryan and his church were admitted to the Georgia Baptist Association, bringing important recognition to his congregation and ministry.

BULGARIA. Baptist congregations in Bulgaria are the result of **missionary** work, immigration, spontaneous **bible** study groups, and Bulgarians who travelled abroad. The first church was founded at Kazanlik in 1876 by Ivan Kargel (1849-1937), a German from St. Petersburg. The second congregation at Ruse (1888) led to the formation of a Romanian-Bulgarian Association (Evangelski Baptistki Alliance) in the 1890s. A congregation at the capital, Sofia, was started in 1899. Under the leadership of Peter Doycheff (1859-1913), the Soius na Evangelski Baptistki Zurkvi v Bulgaria (Bulgarian Baptist Union) was formed in 1908. Especially as a result of the **London Conference of 1920**, the **North American Baptist Conference** (NABC: German) in the

United States assumed sponsorship of missions in Bulgaria from 1924. For a time in the 1920s the Danish Baptists also supported a mission to Plovdiv. In 1995 the **Baptist Bible Fellowship** (BBF) opened a mission in Bulgaria.

As of 1995 there were 39 churches and 2,850 members affiliated with the Soius na Evangelski Baptistki Zurkvi v Bulgaria. The periodical is *The Evangelist* (1920-1938), afterwards *Khristiyanski priyatel* (Christian Friend) (1939-).

BUNYAN, JOHN (1628-1688). English Baptist minister and writer, born at Elstow, Bedfordshire. At first Bunyan was a tinker by trade. He was converted in the mid-1650s and baptized in 1655 by John Gifford, the Baptist minister in Elstow. Bunyan became pastor of the church in Elstow which was related to the **Particular Baptists** and the Independents. In 1660 he was arrested for preaching and imprisoned for 12 years. During this time he left prison frequently to preach outdoors and also composed the *Pilgrim's Progress*, an allegory considered to be one of the finest pieces of English literature in print. Upon his release in 1672, he became England's most celebrated preacher. He produced a tract in 1673 in which he declared that **baptism** should not be an obstacle to admission to the Lord's Table. In his posthumous autobiography, *Grace Abounding to the Chief of Sinners* (1679), Bunyan revealed that his conversion had been influenced by his reading of a passage from the Apocrypha, *Ecclesiasticus* 2:6, another extraordinary circumstance among the Particular Baptist community, which limited its understanding of the biblical canon to 66 books. Bunyan is recalled by a memorial window in Westminster Abbey in London, the only Baptist so honored.

BURKINA FASO. Formerly called Upper Volta, Baptist **missionary** work in this nation was an outgrowth of work in **Ghana**. In 1971 the **Southern Baptists** commissioned a missionary to Burkina Faso. Centers of Baptist work include Ouagadougou and Koudougou. The National Baptist Convention was formed in 1977. In 1994 the **Baptist Bible Fellowship** (BBF) also opened a mission in Burkina Faso.

As of 1995 there were 122 churches with 11,600 members affiliated with the National Baptist Convention of Burkina Faso. There is a school, the Rural Baptist Training Center, located at Kondougou.

BURMA. See **Myanmar.**

BURROUGHS, NANNIE HELEN (1883-1961), American Black Baptist denominational leader, born at Orange, Virginia. The child of skilled slaves, she received an education in Washington, D.C., and sought a teaching position in the Washington schools. Turned aside on the basis of color, she became a clerk and bookkeeper for the newly formed **National Baptist Convention** in 1895 and settled at Louisville, Kentucky. She was elected the first president of the Women's Auxiliary of the National Baptist Convention (NBCUSA) and became the corresponding secretary in 1900. She used her position to organize Black women, establishing a voluntary organization, the Association of Colored Women, and in 1909 the National Training School for Women and Girls, in Washington, D.C. She followed **Booker T. Washington**'s program of self-help for Blacks, calling her version "the bible, the bath, and the broom." Her work eventually extended across denominations and she was recognized as a pioneer in the National Association for the Advancement of Colored People (NAACP).

BURTON, ERNEST DEWITT (1856-1925). American Baptist minister and educator, born in Granville, Ohio. He was educated at Griswold College and Denison University, where he graduated. At first he taught in public schools in Xenia and Cincinnati, Ohio, later entering Rochester Theological Seminary, from which he graduated in 1882. In 1883 he was ordained to the Baptist ministry and became professor of New Testament Greek at Newton Theological Institution until 1892 when he was elected to the chair of the Department of New Testament and Early Christian Literature at the University of Chicago. In that position Burton worked in tandem with president **William Rainey Harper** in the area of Old Testament and Oriental Studies. In 1922 he became acting president of the university and a year later president. In his short two years in that role he increased the endowments to over $54 million, and greatly expanded the medical school. Burton was a widely renowned scholar, editing *The Biblical World* and *The American Journal of Theology*. He published a *Harmony of the Gospels* (1894) and was chair of the China Education Commission, which influenced theological education in the Orient.

BURUNDI. Baptist witness in what was formerly Ruanda-Urundi dates from 1928 when Danish Baptist missionaries Johann and Niels Peter Andersen went there and established a church in 1931. A Union of the Baptist Churches of Ruanda-Urundi was constituted in 1960, but divided in 1962 when the two countries were politically divided. In 1980 the (U.S.) Southern Baptist **Foreign Mission Board** (FMB) opened a mission in Burundi, strengthening ties with the wider Baptist world.

As of 1995, there were 87 churches and 32,000 members affiliated with the Union.

BUSHER, LEONARD (fl.1615-1620). Baptist writer, about whom little is known. He was probably of Dutch descent, but part of his life was spent as a citizen of London, perhaps in exile. His vocation, at least in London, was that of laborer. About 1614 he petitioned Parliament with a plea for freedom of conscience, entitled *Religion's Peace*. In this famous treatise he argued that coercion by fire and sword was dangerous to king and state, a means of increasing the kingdom of antichrist. His book appears to have been written in Amsterdam and carried to England to support the Baptist case for **religious liberty**. Significantly, Busher also advocated adult **baptism** by immersion, becoming one of the first Baptists to do so. In his older years, he appeared again at Delft.

BUTLER, JOHN JAY (1814-1891). American **Freewill Baptist** minister, theologian, and educator, born at Berwick, Maine. Butler was educated at Berwick Academy, Parsonfield Seminary, Bowdoin College, and Andover Theological Seminary. Holding several teaching appointments before seminary graduation, Butler was one of the first faculty members at the Free Baptist Biblical School in Whitestown, New York, in 1844. In 1854 he moved to the chair of systematic theology at New Hampton Institution in Vermont. In 1870 he relocated with that institution to Cobb Divinity School of Bates College in Maine. From 1873 to 1883 he taught sacred literature at Hillsdale College in Michigan. Butler published a one-volume systematic theology, *Natural and Revealed Theology* (1861) and a *Commentary on the New Testament* (1870-71). He was considered the principal theologian of the Freewill Baptist movement in the 19th century, a virtual authority on matters of doctrine. Butler is credited with keeping the mainstream of the theologically **Arminian** Free(will) Baptist movement from joining the **holiness** movement by maintaining a progressive stance on the doctrine of "entire sanctification."

BUZZELL, JOHN (1766-1863). American Freewill Baptist minister and editor, born at Barrington, New Hampshire. He became a school teacher and was influenced by the preaching of **Benjamin Randal**. He was baptized by Randal in 1791 and began preaching in the **Freewill Baptist** Connection. In 1798 he moved to Parsonfield, Maine, where he served for 65 years. He became Randal's successor as the leading minister in the Connection and started many congregations across northern New England. Buzzell edited *A Religious Magazine* (1811-13) and was a founding editor of *The Morning Star*, the official newspaper of the denomination. During his pastoral years in Parsonfield, he was also principal of Parsonfield Seminary, the first educational institution of the Freewill Baptists. His published *Life of Benjamin Randall* (1827) was the first history of the movement, and he also compiled *Psalms, Hymns and Spiritual Songs* (1823), the first hymnal of the Freewill Baptists.

C

CALL TO MINISTRY, BAPTIST CONCEPT OF. Baptists have joined other Christians, primarily in the Reformation traditions, in affirming the nature and necessity of a call to **ministry**. John Calvin (1509-1564) in particular noted the importance of a calling to ministry in his Ecclesiastical Ordinances of 1541. Likewise, English Congregationalists distinguished between an "immediate" call from God and a "mediate" call through the church. Baptists speak consistently of an internal or "secret" call from God to ministry. This is not to be for material reasons, but one based on a true and pure sense of service to God and edification of the Body of Christ. In the interview process with potential candidates for ministry, Baptists typically will expect to hear of the experience of the internal call and how it appears to derive from God alone. There is also the importance of the external call of a congregation. Church leaders will recognize the validity of the inner calling and respond with support for use of one's gifts to ratify a call. This may be accompanied by a license to ministry or license to preach. During the licentiate period, the effectiveness of one's gifts come to ratify one's verbal articulation of an internal call. Ultimately, the external call is an invitation from a congregation to practice ministry in a specified place. **Ordination** may follow among most Baptist groups. Typically, Baptists maintain that an internal call is for life, while an external call may be related to a particular set of circumstances. During the 18th and 19th centuries, Baptists joined others in being concerned about "hireling ministers" and an "unconverted ministry." This has led to high expectations of personal commitment and a genuine sense of call to ministry.

CALLENDAR, ELISHA (1680-1738). American Baptist minister, born at Boston, Massachusetts. Callendar graduated from Harvard College in 1710, the first native-born American Baptist minister to obtain a higher education. His education and **ordination** recognition indirectly were made possible by the influence of **Thomas Hollis**, an English Baptist philanthropist. Cotton Mather (1663-1728) attended Callendar's ordination, representing the regional Congregationalist Standing Order. Callendar served the First Baptist Church in Boston for 20 years (1718-1738) and helped to extend its influence as the center of New England Baptist life.

CALLENDAR, JOHN (1706-1748). American Baptist minister and historian, born at Boston, Massachusetts. Callendar was educated at Harvard College, receiving support from the **Hollis** foundation in England. In 1731 he succeeded **John Comer** as co-pastor in Newport, Rhode Island, where he served until his death. He collected early Baptist historical materials, which **Isaac Backus** used in his history. He also authored *An Historical Discourse on the Civil and Religious Affairs of the Colony of Rhode-Island and Providence Plantations in New England in America* (1739), a pioneering work in American religious history.

CAMBODIA. Baptist work in Cambodia is limited and recent, owing to earlier Roman Catholic and Buddhist traditions and military conflicts of the mid-20th century. Several U.S. Baptist groups have attempted missionary work indirectly and more directly of late. The **Association of Baptists for World Evangelism** (ABWE) opened its mission in 1996, as did the **Baptist Bible Fellowship** in 1997.

CAMEROON. Baptists were the first Protestant group to evangelize Cameroon. In 1845 the **Baptist Missionary Society** (BMS) began work there, led by **Alfred Saker**, and in 1886 they transferred the work to the Basel Mission, sponsored by the Reformed Church in Switzerland. Within three years, a "Berlin Committee" was organized of German Baptists and this gradually evolved into the support base for a permanent Cameroon mission. In 1890 August Steffens (1861-1893), an American German Baptist, opened a mission in Cameroon, which signalled a new era of **missionary** work as well as support from the American churches. Eventually the center of Baptist work became Soppo. A German-based organization, the Neuruppin Mission Society, handled all of the appointments. Gradually the American German churches assumed the leadership for Cameroon and in 1931-1935 the **North American Baptist Conference** adopted the country as a major mission priority, creating the Cameroon Baptist Mission. In 1951 the Cameroon Baptist Convention was founded, as well as a bible training center which later became the Cameroon Baptist Theological College. Significant medical missionary work followed, beginning at Mbingo in 1948. The European Baptist Mission Society, following the earlier German Baptist involvement, joined in support in 1954.

As of 1995, there were 745 churches with 73,160 members affiliated with the Cameroon Baptist Convention, 376 churches and 48,050 members affiliated with the Union of Baptist Churches, and 142 churches with 50,851 members affiliated with the Baptist Churches of Cameroon.

CAMPBELL, ALEXANDER (1788-1866). Presbyterian, and for a time American Baptist minister, born at Ballymena, Ireland. In 1807 Alexander joined his father Thomas (1763-1854), emigrating to western Pennsylvania, following studies at the University of Glasgow. Alexander had come under the influence of the **Haldanes**, and with his father he tried to create a fellowship which was **evangelistic** and non-creedal. At length, the Presbyterian Synod in western Pennsylvania rejected the admission of the Campbells' "Christian Association" and the group organized itself as a separate church at Brush Run, Pennsylvania. Alexander was ordained in 1812 and began a dialogue with local Baptists. His family was baptized by immersion and after a sustained doctrinal dispute in which Alexander rejected the **Philadelphia Baptist Association**, the church was admitted to the Redstone Baptist Association in 1813.

Over the next several years Campbell's views on **baptism,** the **Lord's Supper**, Christian organizations, and **ordination** (to mention a few of the areas in which he differed), separated him from the mainstream of Baptists and he withdrew in 1829 to create the "Reformer" movement, later to became the Disciples of Christ. From 1823 to 1830 he edited and published *The Christian Baptist*. Between 1825 and 1830 numerous Baptist congregations were swayed to the Campbellite position; eventually a western apologetic grew up among Baptist **associations**, producing new periodicals, numerous public debates, and at least two camps of Baptists, those supportive of missionary societies and the antimission Baptists. After his Baptist career concluded, Alexander Campbell enjoyed a long-term leadership of the Christian Church/Disciples of Christ tradition. Among Baptists, Campbell is best known for his publication, *Christian Baptism with Its Antecedents and Consequents* (1851) and published accounts of debates over baptism and church **polity** in which he participated, 1820-1850.

CANADA. The first Baptist congregations emerged from the New Light movement in Nova Scotia. About 1765 **Ebenezer Moulton**, a Baptist from Massachusetts, formed preaching stations along Nova Scotia's Annapolis Valley, including a permanent one at Horton (now Wolfville). The congregation languished before the American Revolutiom, and was reconstituted in 1778. In the same period another early congregation of the Six Principle type was started at Sackville, New Brunswick, but it ceased within a decade. By 1800 there were nine congregations represented at the first meeting of the Nova Scotia Baptist Association. An academy was started to train Christian leaders in 1828 at Horton, which later evolved into Acadia University.

Maritime Baptist life also grew with the settlements of New England planters (and after the Revolution, United Empire Loyalists) in New Brunswick. A separate **association** was formed in that province in 1821. Sensing the need for ministerial training there, New Brunswick Baptists started in 1836 the New Brunswick Seminary, which survived until 1872.

The **Freewill Baptists** of the New England region of the United States entered the Maritime Provinces via itinerant preachers in the early 1800s and started several churches. In 1836 the quarterly meetings in Canada organized the first Free Christian Baptist movement, which evolved to the Free Baptist General Conference (1866, 1898), distinct from the U.S. branch. With a close theological affinity to the Allinite tradition, the Free(will) Baptists spread through the provinces and even created a few congregations in Quebec and Upper Canada (later Ontario), before merging with the regional associations and **conventions** of regular Baptists after 1890. In the 1880s the **holiness** movement affected the Free Baptists in Canada and after a schism, the **Reformed Baptist Alliance** (RBA) of holiness congregations was formed.

In the central Canadian provinces, the earliest Regular Baptist congregations were found at Caldwell's Manor (1794), Hallowell (1796), Thurlow (1796), Bastard (1803), Clinton or Beamsville (1807), and Charlotteville (1810). North and east of Lake Ontario, it was Baptist ministers from upstate New York and Vermont who first planted churches. Likewise, the churches of the Niagara peninsula were largely the result of Baptist missionaries from New England and central New York state. Later, in the Ottawa Valley, **John Gilmour** and John Edwards (1780-1842) led a group of Scottish Baptists who had experienced the **Haldanite** revivals in Scotland, to form several churches. The earliest congregations in the Montreal region were from time to time sponsored by British Baptists, who through the Baptist Colonial Missionary Society, and later the **Baptist Missionary Society** (BMS), supported missionaries from 1838-1850. The first association in Upper Canada met in 1802 at Thurlow.

Gradually, four epicenters of Baptist life in central Canada grew up in the mid-19th century: Montreal, Woodstock, Brantford, and Toronto. The struggle to establish a theological school illustrated the competition between these communities. At Montreal in 1838 Canada Baptist College was begun; in Woodstock in 1860 the Canadian Literary Institute opened; in Toronto in 1881 the Toronto Baptist College began its institutional pilgrimage to what became McMaster University in 1888; at Brantford in 1959 the Baptist Training Institute held its first classes.

In the western provinces, it was missionary labor from Ontario and Quebec and to a lesser degree, the Maritime Baptists, which led to the formation of churches. **Alexander "Pioneer" McDonald** assisted in the constitution of the first church at Winnipeg in 1873. Immigrant families were a focus for American Baptist domestic missions as well as Canadian efforts; this work included Russians, Galicians, Ukrainians, Germans, and Swedes. Eventually, four separate conventions formed the Baptist Union of Western Canada in 1909. Educational institutions include Brandon University, Manitoba (1899), Baptist Leadership Training School, Calgary, Alberta (1948), and Carey Hall Theological College in Vancouver, British Columbia (1979).

Mention should also be made of the Francophone Baptist community in Quebec province, which also had its origin in the **Haldanite Movement**. **Louis Roussy**, an evangelist for the Commission of the Churches of Switzerland Associated for Evangelization (supported by the Haldanes), joined **Henriette Feller** in 1835, and the two of them pioneered the development of an institute which trained children at the secondary level. In 1966 the Union des Eglises Baptistes Françaises au Canada was formed from the former Grand Ligne Mission by the eight surviving congregations. Centered in Montreal with the Union is the Faculté de Théologie Evangélique, a **bible college** level training school opened in 1982.

Canadian convention Baptist organization has historically been focused on the regional level. Four major conventions/unions are constituted to provide interchurch relations, **missions**, and educational resources: the United Baptist Convention of the Maritime Provinces (1905) (later the Atlantic Provinces 1963), the Baptist Convention of Ontario and Quebec (BCOQ), the Union des Eglises Baptistes Françaises, and the Baptist Union of Western Canada (BUWC). Congregations also cooperated in the Baptist Federation of Canada from 1944 to 1994, at which time it was merged with the Canadian Baptist International Ministries to form Canadian Baptist Ministries, headquartered in Mississauga, Ontario. Built largely on the pattern of the U.S. **Baptist Joint Committee on Public Affairs**, the Federation created in 1983 a Canadian Baptist Public Affairs Committee which focused upon church-state issues and was staffed by volunteers in Ottawa. It was superceded in 1983 by a reorganized Committee on Public Affairs, a more internal group, based in Mississauga, Ontario. The oldest of the national organizations is the foreign mission enterprise, variously called the Foreign Mission Board of the Baptist Convention of Ontario and Quebec, the Canadian Baptist Foreign Mission Society, the Canadian Baptist Overseas Mission Board, Canadian Baptist International Ministries, and most recently, Canadian Baptist Ministries; it was founded in 1866 as an auxiliary to the **American Baptist Missionary Union** (ABMU).

Outside the main streams of the three "conventions" of Canadian Baptists are the **Fellowship of Evangelical Baptist Churches in Canada**, the **North American Baptist Conference** (NABC), the **Baptist General Conference** (BGC), and missionary work by U.S. **Southern Baptists**. The NABC churches are an outgrowth of the mission among German-speaking Baptists in the United States, as the BGC in Canada was the result of missions among Swedish churches in the U.S. The General Conference Baptists in 1955 assumed control of the Vancouver Bible College and operated the school until 1978. In 1953 Southern Baptists began support for Canadian work, beginning at Vancouver, British Columbia, from which other missions have spread across Canada. As of 1995, there were 28 congregations related to the Baptist Bible Fellowship, a **fundamentalist** Baptist group working in Canada since 1971. In the area of **theological education** Baptists in Canada of varying kinds operate eight schools from Vancouver to Nova Scotia.

In **polity** and style, Canadian Baptists are a blend of English, Scottish, and American traditions. Emphasis is upon the local congregation which calls its pastors, and is usually formally constituted. Organization beyond the local church is centered on regional **conventions**. Mission and benevolent work as well as education are conducted through cooperative agencies, the "convention" Baptists controlling the executive boards of denominational bodies, while others cooperate with interdenominational evangelical groups or parent organizations in the United States. "Convention" Baptists, Southern Baptists, and the NABC are affiliated with the **Baptist World Alliance** (BWA). Only the Baptist Convention of Ontario and Quebec is affiliated with the **Canadian Council of Churches**.

Mainstream Baptists published *Baptist Missionary Magazine* (1827); the *Christian Messenger* (1837-84); *The Messenger and Visitor* (1885-1905); *The Maritime (Atlantic) Baptist* (1905-); the *Canadian Baptist (1854 -1998)*, while Fellowship Baptists publish *The Evangelical Baptist* (1952-). The Canadian Baptist Historical Society, founded in 1865, has been reconstituted at McMaster Divinity College and carries forth programs of heritage education and conferences.

As of 1995, there were 1,120 churches with 131,500 members affiliated with the conventions/unions in Canadian Baptist Ministries. See also **Black Baptists; Conventions; Fellowship of Evangelical Baptist Churches in Canada**.

CAREY, LOTT (1780-1829). Black Baptist pastor and missionary, born near Charles City, Virginia. Carey was born on a plantation and went to work as a hired laborer in a tobacco warehouse in Richmond, Virginia. He purchased his freedom and attended classes at William Crane's School. He attended services at First Baptist Church, where he was pastor and began preaching among the Black population. He became interested in foreign **missions** and in 1815 he helped to found the Richmond African Missionary Society, which became an auxiliary to the **General Missionary Convention**. In 1821 Carey was appointed a missionary to western Africa by the **Baptist Board of Foreign Missions** (BBFM), in conjunction with the American Colonization Society and his Richmond Society. At first, Carey worked in **Sierra Leone** but was forced to go to Cape Montserado, later **Liberia**. There he set up a school and a medical service in the new colony. He also organized and served Providence Baptist Church at Monrovia. In 1828-1829 he served as vice governor, and then acting governor, of the colony of Liberia. He was killed in an accident while defending the capital against insurgents.

CAREY, WILLIAM (1761-1834). English Baptist pastor and missionary, born at Paulerspury. He was educated through the efforts of his schoolteacher father and read widely, especially in the subject areas of natural science and geography. He was apprenticed to a shoemaker and associated with people who held Dissenter views and strong Christian convictions. In 1782 he met **Andrew Fuller** and was baptized. He served a church at Moulton and continued to study politics and geography. At a meeting of the Northampton Baptist Association in 1786, he presented a plan for evangelizing the heathen, and was largely dismissed by **John Collett Ryland** and others. Later in 1792, Carey published a book, *A Solemn Enquiry*, which asserted the obligation of Christians to evangelize the heathen peoples of the world. This book became the most quoted tract in the history of modern missions.

   Carey and 12 others organized in 1792 the Particular Baptist Society for Propagating the Gospel Among the Heathen, in short the "**Baptist Missionary Society**" (BMS), of which he became the first appointee to **India**. Arriving in India in 1793, he set up a mission at Serampore and turned to large translation projects. He organized a press and built a church, the Lall Bazaar Chapel. His translation work produced results in six languages, and his numerous publications include a *Dictionary of the Bengalee Language* (1815-39) and a *Memoir Relative to the Progress of the Translations of Sacred Scriptures, in the Year 1815* (1816). Considered the most learned man of his era in India, he was appointed a professor of Sanskrit at Fort William College. Thanks to scores of biographies, Carey became a model as a premier international citizen and missionary builder.

CARIBBEAN BAPTIST FELLOWSHIP (CBF). As part of the regional organization of the **Baptist World Alliance** (BWA), the Caribbean Baptist Fellowship was organized at Lake Yale, Florida, in 1970. Thirteen member bodies comprised the original Fellowship from the islands of the Greater and Lesser Antilles. The CBF was a direct result of the combined efforts of the Crusade of the Americas, which began in 1965. The Fellowship describes itself as a **voluntary association** which advances education, **mission**, communication, relief, **evangelism**, Baptist **polity** and practice and justice, and **religious liberty**. The Fellowship is one of the six regional fellowships of the BWA. The Fellowship publishes *The Caribbean Baptist*.

CARPENTER, CHAPIN HOWARD (1835-1887). American Baptist missionary, born in Milford, New Hampshire. Educated at Harvard College and Newton Theological Institution, he was appointed by the **American Baptist Missionary Union** (ABMU) in 1863 to **Burma**. Commencing in 1864 he taught in the Karen Theological Seminary and superintended the Bassein Mission of 70 congregations. For two years, 1874-1875, he was president of the Rangoon Theological Seminary, after which he returned to Bassein. Working for 11 years among the Karens, he developed a policy of self-support and urged the Union to adopt this plan for all of their missionary work. The Board declined the plan and Carpenter resigned from the ABMU in 1886. Later he and his wife Harriet began an independent Baptist mission among the Ainos of **Japan**, on a self-support principle. Carpenter's publications include *The Anglo-Karen Handbook and Reader* (1875) and *Self-Support, Illustrated in the History of the Bassein Karen Mission from 1840 to 1880* (1883).

CARROLL, BENJAMIN HERVEY (1843-1914). Southern Baptist minister and educator, born in Carroll County, Mississippi. He was educated at Baylor College and invested much of his professional career there. Following military service in the Civil War as a Texas Ranger (he was among the last Confederates to surrender), he held pastoral ministries in Texas, from 1870-1899. He became professor of theology and **bible** at Baylor in 1872 and retired in 1905. Carroll built the Bible Department into a distinguished faculty, out of which emerged Southwestern Baptist Theological Seminary. He was the first president of the seminary from 1908-1914. He advocated the re-establishment of the Southern Baptist Sunday School Board (BSSB) and he defended the Home Mission Board against incursions of the **Gospel Mission** movement. Carroll wrote a 13-volume commentary on the bible, *An Interpretation of the English Bible* (1916-1917), intended for the use of preachers, and in his era he was one of the most popular preachers in the **Southern Baptist Convention** (SBC).

CARROLL, JAMES MILTON (1852-1931). Southern Baptist minister and educator, born at Montecello, Arkansas, the brother of **Benjamin Hervey Carroll**, who baptized him. He was educated at Baylor University, graduating with a B.A. in 1877. Following **ordination** in 1874 he served numerous small churches in central Texas: Dog Town, Anderson, Oakland, Macedonia, Washington, Good Hope, and finally Corpus Christi (1880-1882) and Lampeseas (1882-1887). He became active in promoting **Sunday Schools** and church planting, and was appointed a missionary for the Texas Baptist State Convention 1889-1892 and General Superintendent of Missions 1892-1894; he also served as an agent for the Texas Baptist Education Commission 1898-1899. Carroll edited the *Missionary Messenger* and *Texas Baptist Statistics* (1895). President of Howard Payne College in 1911, concluding his career as pastor at Riverside Park, San Antonio, in 1912. Among his outstanding achievements was a *History of Texas Baptists* (1923), and his famous lecture, "The Trail of Blood" (1931), which he delivered thousands of times in defense of historic Baptist sacrifice and an unbroken line of Baptists throughout history, later referred to as "**successionism**."

CARSON, ALEXANDER (1776-1846). Scotch-Irish Presbyterian, and later Baptist, minister, born at Stewartstown, County Tyrone, Northern Ireland. He was educated at the University of Glasgow. His first pastorate was the Presbyterian church in Tubbermore, Ireland (1798-1805). Under the influence of Haldanite itinerants, Carson was converted to Baptist principles about 1805. He preached in rented halls and open fields after leaving his Presbyterian pastorate. In 1814 he built a new meetinghouse at Tubbermore and was highly regarded in the region. Carson was a gifted intellectual, first demonstrating his linguistic abilities when he refuted a translation by Professor Lee, a specialist in Oriental Languages at Cambridge, and later with his treatises, *Baptism: Its Mode and Subjects* (1831) and *History of Divine Providence* (1833). He also provided the linguistic basis for **Robert Haldane**'s *Commentary on the Romans*. Following his preaching the annual sermon for the **Baptist Missionary Society** (BMS) in 1846, his ministry was cut short by a fall from a pier in Liverpool from which he died a few days later.

CARVER, WILLIAM OWEN (1868-1954). Southern Baptist minister and educator, born in Wilson County, Tennessee. He was educated at the University of Richmond and Southern Baptist Theological Seminary where he earned the Th.D. degree. He served churches at Concord (1889-1891) and Deatsville (1896-1907), Kentucky, and Hermitage, Tennessee (1891-1893). Carver began his teaching career at Boscobel College (1893-1896) and then at Southern Seminary from 1896 to 1953. He first taught New Testament, then comparative religions, finally moving to **missions**, where he formed the first missiology department in Southern Baptist life in 1899. Carver was one of the most widely traveled and highly respected Southern Baptists of his era. He toured the mission fields of the **Foreign Mission Board** (FMB) in 1900, 1907-1908, and 1922-1923. He was active in the Faith and Order Movement and the World Council of Churches. His great legacy was the formation of the Women's Missionary Training School at Louisville, later named the Carver School of Missions and Social Work. Of his 20 published books, he wrote *Missions in the Plan of the Ages* (1909) and *Christian Mission in Today's World* (1942).

CASE, ISAAC (1761-1852). New England Baptist missionary, born at Rehoboth, Massachusetts. With no formal education, Case was ordained in 1783 as an evangelist. He was influenced by **Isaac Backus** and Job Macomber (d. 1820), a Baptist church planter in Maine, and itinerated in Massachusetts and Vermont. He started a congregation at Thomaston, Maine, in 1784, the first of several churches which owe their origins to him: Bowdoinham, East Brunswick, and Readfield. In 1800 Case began his work as a **missionary**, first for the Bowdoinham (Maine) Association, then in 1802 for the Massachusetts Baptist Missionary Society (MBMS). He was the first appointed American missionary to **Canada** and helped to organize the Maritime Baptist associations. In 1804 he formed the Maine Baptist Missionary Society on the MBMS plan. Case's missionary endeavors did much to launch American Baptist influence into the Maritime Provinces of Canada.

CASE, SHIRLEY JACKSON (1872-1947). Canadian and American Baptist historian and educator, born at Hatfield Point, New Brunswick. Raised in a **Free(will) Baptist** family and educated at Acadia University, he taught at Horton Academy (1896) and Greek at New Hampton Institute (1897-1901). He then continued his studies at Yale (B.D., Ph.D.) where he majored in biblical studies and early Christianity. He served as pastor at two Congregational churches in Connecticut, Bethlehem (1902-1903) and Beaver Falls (1903-1906). He took a teaching post in history at Bates College in 1906 and in 1908 moved to the University of Chicago Divinity

School where he first taught New Testament and later was chair of the Church History Department. In 1925, due to Case's international influence, he was designated "professor of the history of Christianity," a trend-setting title. As dean of the Divinity School 1933-1938, he developed the "**Chicago School**" of interpretation, creating a prestigious graduate program in religious studies and recruiting faculty such as William Warren Sweet (1881-1959). In retirement he taught at Bexley Hall (1938-1939) and the Florida School of Religion in Lakeland (1940-1947). An advocate of the socio-historical method, he revitalized the American Society of Church History as its president, and edited the influential *Journal of Religion*. Among Case's book-length publications are *The Evolution of Early Christianity* (1914), *Jesus Through the Centuries* (1932), and *The Origins of Christian Supernaturalism* (1946).

CASTLE, JOHN HARVARD (1830-1890). American and Canadian Baptist minister and educator, born at Philadelphia, Pennsylvania. Castle was educated at the University of Lewisburg and Rochester Theological Seminary. He served pastorates at Newburgh, New York, and West Philadelphia, Pennsylvania; in 1872 he accepted the call of Bond Street Church in Toronto, Upper Canada. Castle developed a close friendship with Senator **William McMaster** and became the choice as the first principal of the Toronto Baptist College, over which the senator exerted great influence. Castle designed the curriculum and taught theology at the College, which at McMaster's death in 1887 became McMaster University.

CASWELL, ALEXIS (1799-1877). American Baptist minister and educator, born at Taunton, Massachusetts. Upon his graduation from Brown University, he became one of the original faculty members at Columbian College in Washington, D.C., where he taught ancient languages. Caswell also studied theology under **William Staughton** and Hebrew under **Irah Chase** while at Columbian. He left the College in 1827 to start the first Baptist church in Halifax, Nova Scotia, where he was ordained. In 1828, after only a year, he returned to Brown to the chair in mathematics and natural philosophy under President **Francis Wayland**. Caswell introduced new scientific techniques to Brown and was one of the most highly respected scientists of his era. In 1868, at an advanced age, Caswell became president of Brown University and enhanced its reputation greatly. In 1867-1868 he served as president of the **American Baptist Missionary Union** (ABMU), the highest-ranking elective position among Baptists in the northern United States.

CATHCART, WILLIAM (1826-1908). English and American Baptist minister, born at Londonderry, Northern Ireland. Cathcart was educated at the University of Glasgow and Rawdon Academy. He served the Baptist church at Barnsley in Sheffield (1850-1853) and then emigrated to the United States on account of anti-establishment principles. In 1853 he went to the church at Groton, Connecticut, and four years later to Second Baptist, Philadelphia, Pennsylvania (1857-1884), which he served for 27 years until his health failed. He served as president of the American Baptist Historical Society (1876-1884), greatly increasing its collections, and he wrote on the papal system and Baptists in the American Revolution. His monumental work was a two volume *Baptist Encyclopedia* (1881), which made him a household word in church libraries, while his lesser-known work, *The Papal System; From Its Origin to the Present Time* (1872) marked an important emphasis. Bucknell University conferred on him the doctor of divinity degree in 1873.

CENSURE. See **Discipline, Church**.

CENTRAL AFRICAN REPUBLIC. In 1921 **William Haas** of **Baptist Mid-Missions** in the United States established a mission in the area of French Equatorial Africa that would later become the Central African Republic; important stations were at Sibut and Bangui and later at Kaga Bandoro. Two years later, in the extreme southwestern part of the country, a Swiss Baptist Mission was established in 1923. A third effort was established in 1928 by the **World Baptist Fellowship** (WBF), an American **fundamentalist** group.

As of 1995, there were 147 churches and 41,000 members affiliated with the Fraternal Union of Baptist Churches of the Central African Republic.

CEYLON. See **Sri Lanka**.

CHAD. Although Baptist presence in Chad is not numerically great, Baptists were the initial Protestant witness in the country. **William Haas** of **Baptist Mid-Missions** (BMM) in the early 20th century opened a work at Balimba in 1925 and there was later work at Koumra, which included a hospital and **bible** institute in the 1930s. In 1963 an association of Baptist congregations in Chad was separated from the main work in **Central African Republic**, but the mission was closed in 1974, in response to government demands. Many Baptists were persecuted.

Beginning in 1993 U.S. **Southern Baptists** began a mission in Chad, with the work centered at N'djamena.

CHAMBERLEN, PETER (1601-1683). English Seventh Day Baptist physician and prominent layman, of Huguenot stock. Chamberlen graduated from Emmanuel College, Cambridge, studied at the universities of Heidelberg and Padua, and was admitted to the Royal College of Physicians of London in 1628. As royal physician to three monarchs of England, he had access denied to many others. A progressive doctor, he urged the organization of midwives into a sisterhood and he pioneered new techniques of medical practice. He belonged to the Baptist church at Lothbury and was given to **Fifth Monarchy** ideas. In 1659 at his urging, the congregation adopted sabbatarian views and migrated to Mill Yard as one of the earliest **Seventh Day Baptist** congregations. He favored greater cooperation among the sects and brought much prominence to his despised group by his medical reputation. Chamberlen was a powerful advocate of the Baptist persuasion, as illustrated in his *Master Bakewell's Sea of Absurdities Concerning Sprinkling Calmly Driven Back* (1650).

CHAMPION, LEONARD GEORGE (1907-1997). English Baptist minister, educator, and historian, born at Bristol. He was educated at Bristol Baptist College and studied New Testament under Martin Dibelius (1883-1947) at the University of Heidelberg where he received a Th.D. Following graduate studies, he served as pastor at Minehead (1934-1938) and Rugby (1938-1951) before returning to Bristol Baptist College as tutor and later as principal until his retirement in 1972. In his groundbreaking study of **Andrew Gifford**, *Farthing Rushlight* (1961), he challenged the prevailing historiography of **W.T. Whitley** and **A.C. Underwood** (who stressed the London Baptist community) with the importance of Bristol Baptists and the West Country. Champion also contributed key essays on evangelical Calvinism as well as the Baptist ministry. His publications include *The Church in the New Testament* (1951).

CHAPEL CAR EVANGELISM. A program initiated by the **American Baptist Publication Society** and the **American Baptist Home Mission Society** (ABHMS) which focused upon new church development and **evangelism** in the western and southern United States, 1891-1946. The idea of applying railroad technology to evangelism was first proposed by Wayland Hoyt (1838-1910), pastor of First Baptist Church, Minneapolis, Minnesota, in 1890. With Boston W. Smith (1851-1908) of the Publication Society, he formed a Chapel Car Syndicate on New York's Wall Street to finance the idea; the syndicate was composed of business leaders such as Charles L. Colby, John R. Trevor, James B. Colgate, Eugene J. Barney, and others. The first car, "Evangel," was dedicated in May 1891, to be followed by "Emmanuel" (1893), "Glad Tidings" (1894), "Good Will" (1895), "Messenger of Peace" (1898), "Herald of Hope (1900)," and "Grace" (1914). The chapel cars were modified Pullman train cars that included a miniature chapel with a pump organ provided by the Estey Company, and a fully furnished apartment for the missionary family. The cars were originally towed free of charge by major railroads onto sidings of new towns where worship services were held and **Sunday Schools** organized. Once the church was underway and plans were laid for a more permanent structure, the car and missionary were moved to another location. Among the states/territories where the cars were employed were West Virginia, the Pacific Northwest, Montana, the Dakotas, Minnesota, Nevada, Colorado, California, Arizona, Arkansas, and Idaho. The chapel car program was ended in 1946 when the railroads no longer moved the vehicles without charge and the cars themselves needed costly repairs. Several of the chapel cars were transformed into permanent structures or museum exhibits; one of the wooden cars is on display at Prairie Village, South Dakota, and one of the metal cars is at the American Baptist Assembly at Green Lake, Wisconsin. See also **Colporteurs**.

CHASE, IRAH (1793-1864). American Baptist minister and educator, born at Stratton, Vermont. Chase was educated at Middlebury College and Andover Theological Seminary. Ordained an evangelist, he itinerated in western Virginia and in 1818 joined **William Staughton** as a theological teacher in Philadelphia and later as a member of the first faculty at Columbian College in Washington, D.C., for seven years. In 1825, New England friends lured Chase from Washington to accept the first professorship at the new Newton Theological Institution in Massachusetts. In addition to teaching biblical theology for 20 years at Newton, Chase designed the curriculum on the Andover model for the first post-collegiate theological school of the Baptists in the United States. Chase published several devotional and doctrinal works, the most significant of which was *The Design of Baptism, Viewed in Its Relation to the Christian Life* (1851).

CHATER, JAMES (1802-1829). English Baptist missionary, born at Bourton-on-Water. A graduate of Bristol Baptist College, he was appointed by the **Baptist Missionary Society** (BMS) in 1806. He arrived in Serampore later that year, but was informed that the governor-general of **India** had ordered an end to itinerant preaching and decreed that Chater should leave the colony. Chater first explored the possibility of a mission to **Burma**, and travelled between Serampore and Rangoon until 1812, involved in translation work. When the BMS abandoned its Burma plans in 1812, he moved to Colombo, Ceylon where he opened the Society's Sinhalese work. His outstanding accomplishment there was the translation of the entire bible into the Sinhalese language. Chater died at sea en route to Britain. His published works introduced the Sinhalese mission to Baptists: *Dialogue Between a Buddhist and a Christian* (1825) and *A Grammar of the Cingalese Language* (1815).

CHICAGO SCHOOL. Refers to the development of a particular intellectual tradition at the University of Chicago in the first three decades of the 20th century. Beginning with the reorganized University of the 1890s under **William Rainey Harper**, theologians, biblical scholars, and historians began to apply the social sciences to the study of religious subjects. This led to an elaborate system of investigation of the contextual issues surrounding theological formulations. Basic to the Chicago School was the presupposition that ideas and institutions evolved and therefore that historical study was absolutely essential to proper interpretation of text and tradition. Advocates like **Shirley Jackson Case** held that there must be a concern for the total environment in which historical events occurred, and he and his colleagues utilized other methodologies such as literary analysis and archaeological evidence to support historical hypotheses. The evolutionary pattern underlying the Chicago School implied not only that history emerged from one epoch to another but also that ideas and institutions evolved from lower to more sophisticated forms, which many termed a "genetic approach."

The chief proponents of the Chicago School were William R. Harper in Old Testament, **Ernest Dewitt Burton** in New Testament, Shirley Jackson Case in church history, and **George Burman Foster** in theology and philosophy of religion. The impact of these thinkers was enormous, considering the number of people who studied at Chicago and served on faculties elsewhere, and the development of curriculum studies and publications which affected the Association of Theological Schools in the United States and **Canada** and educational developments outside North America. Among Baptists, most faculties in northern Baptist circles included at least one Chicago-trained member, if not large dependencies: Crozer, Rochester, Central, McMaster, Newton, and the liberal arts colleges like Bucknell, Bates, Colby, Rochester, and Colgate. Likewise, in the Southern Baptist tradition, both Southern Baptist Theological Seminary and Southwestern Baptist Theological Seminary had faculty members trained in the Chicago School.

CHILE. The Baptist movement entered Chile in the 1890s under the leadership of Daniel T. MacDonald (1852-1939). At Cajon in 1908 the Unión Evangélica Bautista de Chile was formed; with the entry of U. S. Southern Baptists in 1917, the term "**convention**" in 1936 replaced the term "Union." Under the auspices of the **Foreign Mission Board**, many churches were started in the 1930s and 1940s; an antimission schism occurred in 1940, which led to the creation of the Iglesia Bautista Nacional. At Temuco since 1936 there is a Baptist College, with a second institution later established there, and a theological seminary operates at Santiago. In 1953 the **Association of Baptists for World Evangelism** (ABWE) began church planting in Chile; in 1954 **Baptist Bible Fellowship** (BBF) missionaries arrived in Chile.

As of 1995, there were 247 churches and 28,406 members affiliated with the Convención Evangélica Bautista de Chile, and 36 churches with 1,690 members affiliated with the Iglesia Bautista Nacional.

CHINA. The first Baptist missionary to the Chinese people was **William Dean**, appointed by the **Baptist Board of Foreign Missions** (BBFM) in 1834. Dean worked in the Chinese community in Bangkok, **Siam**, and later transferred his work to **Hong Kong**. At the conclusion of the First Opium War in 1842, Baptist missionary work began in earnest in the coastal cities and South China. American Baptists concentrated in Hong Kong and Swatow, while **Southern Baptists** focused upon Canton. British Baptists first commenced a China mission at Ningbo through the General Baptist Missionary Society in 1845, but discontinued it in 1854. British interest shifted to the North in 1860, first at Shanghai, then at Yantai; this effort was renewed considerably after 1870 under the leadership of **Timothy Richard**.

An American Baptist, **William Ashmore**, opened a theological school at Swatow in 1871, and in 1899 a China Baptist Publication Society was started, as Swedish Baptists also opened their mission in Shantung. In East China, American Baptists began work in Shanghai and Nanjing; in 1906 the two groups, U.S. Northern and Southern Baptists, jointly opened a seminary at Shanghai. In Szechuan Province, work also began in West China in 1889, and in 1893 missions were conducted in Central China in cities like Hankow, Hanyang, and Wuchang. Indigenous Chinese Baptist associational life emerged in the late 19th and early 20th century as a product of the **missionary** conferences and as a response to anti-foreign uprisings: the Chekiang Baptist Association (1873) was reorganized in 1918 as the Chekiang-Shanghai Baptist Convention; the

Hakka and Ling Tong Conventions in 1925; and the China Baptist Council in 1922 as a national coordinating body.

Other Baptist groups organized mission efforts to China in the new century, including the U.S. **Baptist General Conference,** which assumed support for a mission to Manchuria, begun in 1909 and which later included Russian refugees in that province. The **Baptist Bible Fellowship** (BBF) began a mission in China in 1933 as its oldest field. In the aftermath of World War II, **Baptist Mid-Missions** (BMM) from the United States established a mission at Shanghai in 1947, which was closed three years later.

After the Chinese field was closed in general to foreign missionaries in 1949-1953, Chinese Baptists suffered greatly and in many cases participated in the Three Self Movement, emerging in 1986 in a post-denominational society. Some also joined the underground movement of churches. External missions involving Western support have recently been conducted through the Amity Foundation and indirectly through the China Christian Council. It is not possible to calculate the numbers of Christians in China who might consider themselves Baptists, especially since government policy dictates a "post-denominational era" of Christian presence in the country.

CHIPMAN, THOMAS HANDLEY (1756-1830). Canadian Baptist minister, born in Newport, Rhode Island. His family emigrated to Nova Scotia when he was a child. Chipman was converted under the preaching of evangelist **Henry Alline** and baptized at Horton, the oldest congregation. In his first churches, he took an open communion stance, later converting to closed communion, Baptistic principles. The pastor at Bridgetown, Nova Scotia, he was a founder of the first **association** in that province in 1800. In 1809 he went to Nictaux where he served for 20 years. With **Edward Manning** and **Harris Harding**, Chipman is considered one of the patriarchs of the Baptist movement in the Canadian Maritimes.

CHRIST, DOCTRINE OF. Among Baptists the doctrine of Christ is of fundamental importance. The earliest English **confessions of faith** expressed in detailed terms the nature and importance of Jesus Christ. The divine nature and special lineage of Jesus is affirmed as well as Mary's virginal conception. With the historic creeds of the church, Christ is affirmed to have lived as a human being, to have been crucified and buried, and to have risen from the dead as Saviour and Lord. As mediator of a new covenant, Jesus becomes perfectly and fully Prophet, Priest, and King of the Church of God, and these roles cannot be transferred to any other. Other names given to Christ are "Doctor," "Apostle of our profession," and "Angel of the Covenant." Christ is said to govern His church and His church expects his second coming to reign amongst the saints. Christ is the chief expression of the Godhead which empowers and defines the church. In contrast to the Roman Catholic doctrine that Christ gave special authorities to St. Peter, Baptists believe that Christ gave power to every congregation to receive and cast out, and to excommunicate members. Twenty-one of the articles of the First London Confession dealt with Christology, and the doctrine is the subject of one major article devoted to Christ's role as mediator in the Second London Confession. The Orthodox Creed gave six articles to Christ and is similar to the First London Confession.

The Lordship of Christ is also an important concept to Baptist Christians. Early English Baptists spoke of the doctrine in terms of the "Crown Rights of the Redeemer." In other words, since Jesus redeemed His people, they in turn owe Him their allegiance in every phase of their lives. Just as subjects of an earthly monarch owe that person loyalty, so also do God's people owe it to Christ to abide by His teachings. As **William Kiffin** said in 1639: "Christ's kingly power in His Church was committed not to a Hierarchy, neither to a National Presbytery, but to a Company of Saints in a Congregational Way." This idea was modified in the democratic context of the United States and elsewhere to become the Lordship of Christ or in the **social gospel**, the "righteous rule of God in all human affairs."

From time to time among Baptists, varying interpretations of the nature of Christ have created sharp differences of opinion. Among the **Strict Baptists** in England, for instance, a debate arose in the 1860s over whether Christ's human nature pre-existed the Incarnation. This "Sonship" question produced at least three divisions among the Strict Baptists. In contrast, Baptists in New England found **Asa Messer**'s Arian understanding of Christ unacceptable: he held that Jesus was pre-eminently the Son of God, but such of himself, not from God. Messer was forced to resign as president of Brown University in 1836.

No major modification in mainstream Baptist understanding of the doctrine of Christ occurred until the later 19th century. Under the influence of the social gospel and higher critical views of **Scripture**, the humanity of Jesus became more relevant than the question of divinity for some. Jesus was seen as an example of total submission to God and an ethical teacher who personified His ideals. Ultimately, the authority of Christ emerged when He sacrificed his life for the ideals He taught. **Liberal** Baptist theologians such as **William Newton Clarke, Douglas Clyde MacIntosh, Gerald Birney Smith,** and later process theologians held this view; related to this position was that of Michael Taylor, former principal of Northern Baptist College in Manchester, England, who in a speech to the 1971 Assembly of the Baptist Union emphasized that Jesus was fully and completely man. This had very serious repercussions in the British Baptist community and spawned a new interest in orthodox Christology. Most Baptists, however, have continued to hold orthodox views of the person and work of Jesus Christ.

CHRISTIAN, JOHN TYLER (1854-1925). Southern Baptist educator and historian, born at Lexington, Kentucky. He was educated at Bethel College and served pastorates at First Baptist, Chattanooga, Tennessee (1883-1886), East Baptist, Louisville, Kentucky (1893-1900), Second Baptist, Little Rock, Arkansas (1904-1911), and First Baptist, Hattiesburg, Mississippi (1913-1919). Christian was a prime mover in the establishment of a theological school at New Orleans, Louisiana, in 1917 and served as professor of church history at Baptist Bible Institute (1919-1925). He was a consummate collector of books and built a substantial collection at what became New Orleans Baptist Theological Seminary. His publications include *Close Communion* (1892), *Baptism in Sculpture and Art* (1907), and *History of the Baptists* (1923).

CHURCH, BAPTIST DOCTRINE OF. The Baptist understanding of the church is fundamental to Baptist theology and practice. It is based upon characteristics inherited from the Puritans and Separatists as well as some unique elements. Key passages of **Scripture** inform Baptist understanding: I Cor. 1:1-17; Ephesians 4:1-8: Col. 1:17-18; Hebrews 6:1-2; Rev. 2-3. **John Smyth**, pioneer of the English Baptist movement, characterized the church as a "true church of true believers." By this he meant to emphasize the basis of Christian experience and faith commitment of an authentic Christian fellowship. Other examples of the church, such as the Church of England, Smyth held to be "antichrist."

In the confessions of both the **General** and **Particular** Baptists, the church is primarily a local congregation, but there is recognition of the catholicity of Christ's body, namely, by the church universal.

Across the 17th and 18th centuries, a debate arose among English Baptists over the primary purpose of the church. Particular Baptists such as **John Gill** stressed the elect nature of the church and held that the primary purposes of the church were worship, nurture, and fellowship of the saints. Later in the 18th century, however, others such as **Andrew Fuller** argued that a primary purpose of the church and the Christian **ministry** was to preach the gospel, to offer salvation to non-believers. This position has been widely regarded as "**Evangelical** Calvinism" and opened the Baptist movement to placing a high value upon **missions** and **evangelism**.

Important to the Baptist concept of the church are **confessions of faith** and **covenants**. From the Puritan and Separatist traditions, Baptists followed the practice of writing confessional documents which described their theological beliefs. The purpose of confessions was to hold out the precise details of belief for new members and **discipline** of errant members, and to assert the identity of a congregation among other churches in the community. A covenant, on the other hand, served as a commitment between members and before God concerning membership responsibilities and ethics. The purpose of the covenant was to bind together voluntarily the members of a congregation to each other.

As early as the 17th century, Baptist theological writers have recognized the mixture of persons in the church body. Some are given to pure doctrine and others to error; no church is perfect. But Baptists have equally believed that each church is called of God to be faithful and contains under the Lordship of Christ all that is needful to be the church.

From the doctrine of the church flows the Baptist understanding of the **sacraments/ordinances** and mission. See also **Discipline, Church; Polity, Baptist**.

CHURCH, PHARCELLUS (1801-1886). American Baptist minister, born at Geneva, New York. Church graduated from the Hamilton Literary and Theological Institution and served the church at Poultney, Vermont, for three years, from 1825-1828. In 1836 he became pastor at First Baptist, Rochester, New York, where he spearheaded a relocation movement for the Baptist college in Hamilton, New York. When this failed, Church helped to organize the Baptist-related University of Rochester and Rochester Theological Seminary. For a brief time he was pastor at First Baptist, Montreal, Lower **Canada** (1852-1853). Church was a close friend of **William Colgate**, a New York manufacturer, who invited him to experiment with what was probably the first set of rubber pantaloons for baptismal services. Church wrote on a wide variety of topics, including *The Philosophy of Benevolence* (1836), *Permanency of the Pastoral Relation* (1845), and *Danger and Death of Missionaries* (1847).

CLARENDON CODE. A series of English parliamentary statutes passed between 1661 and 1665 to nullify religious dissent, named for Edward Hyde (1609-1674), the first Earl of Clarendon and lord chancellor of England, though his actual influence on this legislation was indirect at best. The first statute, The Corporation Act (1661), required members of municipal bodies to take the oaths of supremacy and allegiance, and that future applicants were to have taken the Sacrament in the Church of England in the 12 months prior to their appointment. This measure made it impossible for Baptists and other dissenters to have employment or commissions in government. A second law, the Act of Uniformity (1662), required from all Anglican clergy that they fully consent to all prescriptions in the *Book of Common Prayer*. This included all university professors, schoolmasters, and private tutors. Imprisonment and severe fines were levied for non-compliance. Baptists and other dissenters were thus effectively barred from university and educational posts. The Conventicle Act (1664) disciplined all persons over 16 years old who attended a **Nonconformist** service at which more than four people joined the family. Repeated offenders could be transported out of England for seven years. Under this statute many Baptists had to resort to clandestine meetings as their meetinghouses were seized. A fourth statute, the Five Mile Act (1665) targeted clergy and lecturers who might try to return to a town in which they had previously served in the **ministry**, unless they took an oath not to alter the government of the church or state. Those ministers who had left the Church of England to pursue Nonconformist ministries could thus not legally serve in the same communities.

The result of this total legislation was to exact much difficulty and privation upon numerous dissenters and in particular Baptists. In 1667 Clarendon was dismissed as lord chancellor and limited relief ensued for Nonconformists in the intriguing policies of King James II who attempted to restore Catholicism under the guise of being more tolerant toward Anglican Nonconformity. The enforcers of the Clarendon Code were a combination of Royal troops and Anglican clergy.

CLARKE, JOHN (1609-1676). English, and later American, Baptist minister and physician, born in Suffolk. He attended a university, most likely Cambridge, and became a physician in London in the 1630s. Clarke was devoted to the issue of **religious liberty** and this led others to accuse him of antinomianism. He joined a company of settlers and the group purchased land from the Indians and established in 1638 a colony on Aquidneck near Rhode Island, which they named Newport. There Clarke established himself as a leading citizen. He was a physician, pastor of the Baptist Church, which he helped to found (actually the second oldest in the United States), and a political leader. In 1652 he wrote *Ill Newes From New England,* which made the case against religious persecution and carried forth the principle of the two spheres of authority, and he returned to England for 12 years, among other duties to enable the colony of Rhode Island to obtain a charter. Clarke was the principal author of the Rhode Island charter, which guaranteed religious rights and liberties. In

1669, following five years in the Rhode Island Assembly, he was designated deputy colonial governor. Theologically, Clarke was a Calvinist and a gifted student of biblical languages. More than anyone else, Clarke deserved the title, "Father of American Baptists."

CLARKE, WILLIAM NEWTON (1841-1911). American and Canadian Baptist minister and theologian, born at North Brookfield, Massachusetts. He was educated at Hamilton College and the Theological Department of Madison University. In 1863 he entered the pastoral ministry at Keene, New Hampshire, followed by the First Baptist Church, Newton Centre, Massachusetts. In 1880 Clarke moved to Montreal to be pastor at Olivet Baptist Church, which he served for 11 prosperous years. In 1883, he became the first New Testament professor at Toronto Baptist College, remaining there through 1887. That year he returned to the American scene as pastor of First Baptist Church in Hamilton, New York. Upon the sudden death of Madison University President **Ebenezer Dodge**, Clarke stepped in and became the professor of theology at what became Colgate Theological Seminary. In several important works, including *An Outline of Christian Theology* (1909), Clarke pioneered the theological position of "**evangelical liberalism**." At his death he was one of the most highly respected and quoted theologians in North America. Clarke's autobiography, *Sixty Years With the Bible* (1909), is considered a classic in defining the transition to the New Theology.

CLEARWATERS, RICHARD VOLLEY (1900-1996). American Baptist, and later independent Baptist minister and educator, born at Wilmot, Kansas. He was educated at Moody Bible Institute, Kalamazoo College (B.A.), Northern Baptist Theological Seminary (Th.B.), and the University of Chicago (M.A.). He served student pastorates at Wilton Center, Illinois, and at Lawton and Kalamazoo, Michigan (1929-1935). In 1935 he became pastor at Calvary Baptist Church, Cedar Rapids, Iowa. In 1940 he accepted the call to serve Fourth Baptist Church, Minneapolis, Minnesota, which he served until 1982. Clearwaters worked with **William B. Riley** to lead the Minnesota Baptist Convention away from the control of the **Northern Baptist Convention** (NBC), which Riley thought was dominated by modernists. Clearwaters taught and served as an administrator in Riley's Northwestern Schools, 1942-1957.

With the passing of Riley, Clearwaters aligned himself with the **Conservative Baptist** Fellowship (CBF) in the NBC, and was one of the founders of the Conservative Baptist Association (CBA), which he served as president in 1951-1953. In 1956 he founded in his church Central Baptist Seminary, intended to be a major institution of the Conservative

Baptist movement; he was president of the school from 1956-1987. A schism occurred in the denomination, however, leaving Clearwaters alienated from the Conservative Baptist movement and the school became an independent seminary. In the early 1950s Clearwaters led in the reorganization of Pillsbury Academy, formerly affiliated with the Minnesota Baptist Convention, and he helped to found the Pillsbury Baptist Bible College at Owatonna, Minnesota. In 1942 he was awarded the honorary doctorate by Northern Baptist Theological Seminary.

CLIFFORD, JOHN (1836-1923). English Baptist minister and denominational leader, born at Sawley, England. Clifford was educated at Midland Baptist College and the University of London. A General Baptist, he served the Praed Street Baptist Church in Paddington and was a prime mover in uniting the old **General** and **Particular** Baptist factions in the **Baptist Union of Great Britain and Ireland** (BU). Clifford applied the principles of the **social gospel** in his ministry and as president of the Union, he advocated progressive thought, in keeping with the intellectual and moral trends of a progressive era. He was considered the chief adversary of **Charles H. Spurgeon** in the theological strife of the Union in the 1880s. Clifford was elected the first president of the **Baptist World Alliance** (BWA), 1905-1911. Clifford was a prodigious author, completing over 70 works, the most enduring of which were *The Attitude of Men of Science to Christianity* (1874), *Is Life Worth Living?* (1880), *The Free Churches of London: Their Faith and Future* (1895), *Socialism and the Teaching of Christ* (1898), and *Clericalism in State Education* (1912).

CLOSED COMMUNION. See **Lord's Supper**.

CLOUGH, JOHN EVERETT (1836-1910). American Baptist missionary, born at Frewsburg, New York. He was educated at Burlington College and Upper Iowa University, after which he was a schoolteacher. He became interested in foreign **mission** service after hearing **William Dean** tell of his China experiences, and was accepted by the **American Baptist Missionary Union** (ABMU) for **India**. The Cloughs arrived in Nellore in 1865, and a year later moved to Ongole to work with the Telugus. His work prospered greatly and the extra demands of his mission almost broke Clough's health. In 1876 a famine occurred which affected 60 million people; Clough devised a plan to employ hundreds of workers in the construction of the Buckingham Canal and in food distribution. Hundreds of converts were made from among the Telugus and in one day, July 3, 1878, Clough supervised the **baptism** of 2,222 persons in the

Gundlacumma River at Velumpilly. Twenty-four native ministers were ordained on April 16, 1880, to meet the needs of the Ongole field. In 1894 he married Emma Rauschenbusch (1859-1940), sister of Walter, and during a second major famine in India in 1896-1897, Clough again set up a work camp to organize relief and employment. During this period he experimented with some of **Walter Rauchenbusch**'s ideas concerning the **social gospel**. At the conclusion of his active career, Clough was highly regarded in missionary annals as well as enjoying heroic status in India. He was the principal literary exponent of the Great Revival in *From Darkness to Light: A Story of the Telugu Awakening* (1882), and his own story was told by his wife in *Social Christianity in the Orient: The Story of a Man, a Mission and a Movement* (1914).

COFFEEHOUSE MEETINGS. Beginning in the late 17th century, **Nonconformist** ministerial gatherings began to associate in coffeehouses, which for social purposes rivalled the public houses and provided an alternative to alcoholic consumption. Baptists in London began meeting this way and the result was the formation of permanent **associations** and funds. In 1714 **Benjamin Stinton** established a group at the Hanover Coffeehouse in London, composed of both **General** and **Particular Baptists**. This soon divided in 1724 and the Particular Baptists opened their own ministerium at the Gloucestershire Coffeehouse. The Hanover Coffeehouse club accomplished several worthwhile objectives, including assisting French refugees after the revocation of the Edict of Nantes (October 1685), improvement of the overall Baptist reputation by discouraging public disputes with radical groups like the Quakers, the repair of the Horsley-down Baptistry for use of the London congregations, and the formation of a united Baptist **ministry**, which eventually would join other Nonconformists in the **Three Dissenting Denominations**. The Baptist Board met at the Jamaica Coffeehouse, Coles Coffeehouse, and Blackwell Coffeehouse between 1767 and 1820. The General Baptist Fund and the Particular Baptist Fund were direct results of the respective coffeehouses, and the establishment of the Sunday School Society was at the King's Head, Swithin's Alley. At times, the Crown and the Church of England held the coffeehouse gatherings in contempt, such as the one kept by James Jones in Southwark in the 17th century, as seditious associations.

COLBY, GARDNER (1810-1879). American Baptist philanthropist, born at Bowdoinham, Maine. Colby opened a dry goods store in Boston in 1830, eventually becoming involved in the **China** trade and real estate speculation in Boston. During the Civil War, he amassed a fortune in producing woollen clothing for the Union Army and thereafter he became president of the Wisconsin Central Railroad, which he helped to build in the northern plains states. Colby used his money to support several educational institutions, including Newton Theological Institution and Waterville College, the latter of which changed its name in his honor after receiving a gift of $50,000. Colby was also a trustee of Brown University and was involved in the work of the **American Baptist Missionary Union** (ABMU).

COLGATE, WILLIAM (1783-1857). American industrialist and Baptist lay leader, born at Hollingbourne, England. In his early years he was apprenticed to John Slidell of New York in soapmaking; within three years he started his own company and perfected processes for scenting soaps and manufacturing various soap and petroleum products. His interest in the church was manifested in his generous support of scores of Baptist **voluntary** causes from home **missions** to education and **bible** translation. He was a member of most of the societies in the northern Baptist community, and he helped to sustain several projects, including a translation of **Scripture** by the American Bible Union in 1850. One of the leading philanthropists in the Baptist tradition, his work was carried on through his two sons, James (1818-1904) and Samuel (1822-1897). The legacy of the Colgate family in higher education was honored in 1888 when Madison University in Hamilton, New York, was renamed Colgate University.

COLLIER, THOMAS (fl.1650-1690). English Baptist minister, born in Wessex. Little is known about his early life. His opponents referred to him as a "base, mechanical fellow, a husbandman," which suggests he was a farmer and lay preacher. At one time Collier was expelled from Guernsey and later imprisoned at Portsmouth. He was ordained at Bridgwater in 1654. He evangelized widely and formed an **association** of churches in the West. In 46 years he published as many tracts, he engaged in significant debates at Axbridge and Wiveliscombe, and he championed the rights of Jews. In 1655 he was appointed a general **messenger** to the associated churches of Wessex and in 1656 and 1678 he issued **confessions of faith**. His emphases kept the churches of the West from fanatical directions, particularly the **Fifth Monarchy** ideas of **Henry Jessey**. In the 1660s he was involved in planting new churches, in 1672 taking out a licence for North Bradley. Collier issued a systematic theology of sorts, called *Body of Divinity*, which contained anti-Calvinistic thinking and which caused his enemies to refer to him as an Arian and Socinian. Five prominent London **Particular Baptists**, including **William**

Kiffin and Nehemiah Cox (fl.1670), visited Collier about 1676 to moderate his theological views, apparently without success. Shortly thereafter in 1677, they issued the Second London Confession of Faith to affirm the theology of the Westminster Confession. Collier convened a similar meeting of the association in the West and issued yet another confession in 1691. Despite his often brash behavior, Collier was the most significant figure among Baptists in the West before 1689, and he survived to see the effects of toleration. Among his several published works were *A Brief Discovery of the Corruption of the Ministry of the Church of England* (1647) and *A Looking-Glass for the Quakers* (1657).

COLOMBIA. Initial Baptist missions in Colombia began in 1941 when Southern Baptists J. L. Hart (1877-1966) and Henry Schweinsberg (1910-1996) investigated the possibilities of church development in Colombia. Schweinsberg began the first congregation in 1942 at Barranquilla. An initial coalition of churches formed in 1949 the Convención Colombo-Venezolana and later a separate Convención Bautista Colombiana in 1952. The Convención publishes *Heraldo Bautista* (Baptist Herald) (1942-) and supports a theological school at Cali since 1952. In 1929 the **Association of Baptists for World Evangelism** (ABWE) established churches resulting in the Iglesia Bautista Independiente. In 1971 the **Baptist Bible Fellowship** (BBF) entered Colombia, and the **American Baptist Association** (ABA) has a mission in the country.

As of 1995 there were 115 churches and 10,873 members affiliated with the Convención Bautista Columbiana. A theological school, Seminario Teológico Bautista Internacional, is located at Cali.

COLPORTEURS. Beginning in the 19th century and first associated with the **bible** society movement in Britain and the United States, **Scripture** distribution agents were sent forth to conduct **evangelical** missions in Europe, Africa, Asia, and Latin America. A significant number of them were Baptists and remained in the field to start churches, notably **J. G. Oncken** in Germany and James Thompson in Latin America. The **American Baptist Publication Society** (ABPS) employed numerous colporteurs from the 1830s to conduct horseback missions in conjunction with the **American Baptist Home Mission Society** (ABHMS) in the western and southern states. The first of the horsedrawn colportage wagons was placed in service in Jackson, Michigan, in 1897, with about 80 others put in service over the following two decades. The wagons contained storage room for bedding, clothes, food, and a tent and cookstove. In 1891 the first railroad **chapel cars** were placed in service by the mission agencies. In 1906 a chapel cruiser boat, the "Mamie Beal" was commissioned in Coos Bay, Oregon, with five others which plied the western coastal routes in California, Oregon, and Washington through 1921. Chapel car automobiles were used in the United States beginning in 1923. Outside the United States, other Baptists used the methods of the colporteurs, including **Luke Bickel** in **Japan** who commanded the boat, *Fukuin Maru*, and the **Evangelical Baptist Mission** in Mali, which in 1960 employed the "Niger Gospel Boat" on the Niger River. See also **Chapel Car Evangelism**.

COLUMBIA BASIN MISSION. An independent **fundamentalist** Baptist domestic mission founded in 1940. The work was started to evangelize small towns in the Pacific Northwestern United States, specifically the region created by the Columbia Basin Irrigation Project of the United States Government. Mission works were established in Washington state in 1940 and in 1941 in Idaho. With the formation of the **Fellowship of Baptists for Home Missions** in 1950, the Columbia Basin Mission merged its efforts with that larger work.

COMER, JOHN (1704-1734). American Baptist minister, born at Boston, Massachusetts. Originally apprenticed in the glover's trade, Comer sought an education and was assisted by Increase Mather at Harvard; he also attended Yale College as its first Baptist student. Comer was ordained by his uncle, **Elisha Callendar** and served the church in Newport, Rhode Island, 1726-1729. Comer advocated the "sixth principle" of the **laying on of hands**, which proved to be unpopular. He moved to Swansea to a congregation which accepted this view. His death at 30 deprived the early New England Baptists of an educated leader who showed promise among the urban churches. Comer's diary, published in 1893, is an important source for New England Baptist history in the first half of the 18th century.

COMMUNION, HOLY. See **Lord's Supper**.

COMPERE, LEE (1789-1871). English and later **Southern Baptist** minister and missionary, born in Harborough, England. Compere studied theology with **John Sutclif** and embarked upon a mission to **Jamaica** in 1815. Attempting to work at Old Harbor and Kingston, he succumbed to the tropical climate and went to the United States in 1817. With the assistance of **Richard Furman** he made further studies and moved about the South conducting **missions** with the Indians and starting churches. Remarkably, he was present at the formation of most of the early Baptist state **conventions** in the South, including South Carolina, Georgia,

Alabama, and Mississippi. While serving as superintendent of the **General Missionary Convention**'s Creek Mission in Alabama in the 1820s, he prepared a complete vocabulary and translated portions of **Scripture** into the Creek language.

CONE, SPENCER HOUGHTON (1785-1855). American Baptist minister, born at Princeton, New Jersey. Cone studied at Princeton College and took up a career in the theatre. He served as a journalist in the War of 1812 and wrote in support of the James Madison presidential administration. Eventually he entered the Baptist **ministry**, preaching at a small church in the Washington, D.C., Navy Yard. His success led to his appointment as chaplain to the U.S. House of Representatives, 1815-1816. He became pastor of the Baptist church in Alexandria, Virginia (1816-1823), moving in 1837 to the Oliver Street Church in New York City, which he served for 18 years (1823-1841) and finally First Baptist, New York (1841-1855). With Deacon **William Colgate,** Cone assisted the formation of many benevolent enterprises, housing the **American Baptist Home Mission Society**'s (ABHMS) office in his church, and was president of the Baptist Triennial Convention from 1838-1841. Cone's most important literary achievement was *The Terms of Communion at the Lord's Table* (1824).

CONFESSIONS OF FAITH. Historically, Baptists have understood themselves as "non-creedal." By this is meant that the historic creeds of the churches are non-binding on the conscience and thus may not be used for **discipline**, worship, or definitional purposes. Rather, Baptists affirm **liberty of conscience** and prefer to interpret the **bible** as guided by the Holy Spirit and the church. Confessions of faith, however, are a popular means of expressing doctrinal definition and the theological traditions of congregations, **associations,** and institutions. The idea of a confession of faith derives from a **voluntary** statement of specific beliefs. Based on Matthew 28:19-20, Baptists believe that Christians have a responsibility to witness to their faith and to agree on matters of common understanding.

The first confessional statements were issued by individuals, notably **John Smyth** the Se-Baptist. Smyth wrote a series of twenty doctrinal assertions in 1610 (and probably another in 1611) to define his beliefs for possible dialogue with the Dutch Mennonite community. This became a pattern among early English **General** and **Particular** Baptists, as they sought to differentiate themselves from heterodoxy on the one hand and also from each other.

The primary examples of English Baptist confessions of faith of the 17th century were the First and Second London Confessions. The First

London Confession was issued by seven congregations in the greater London area to define Baptist beliefs against critics who slandered Baptists as Münsterites. It contained 52 articles on topics such as Jesus Christ, the church, the **ordinances**, and the magistracy. In 1677 a second London Confession was written to demonstrate Baptist theological affinity with Presbyterians and Congregationalists as all sects faced persecution under the **Clarendon Code**. The Second London Confession was based upon the Westminster Confession of Faith and was decidedly more Calvinistic than the First London Confession of 1644. It contained 32 articles. Other important 17th century confessional statements included the Midland Confession (1655), the Somerset Confession (1656), and the Orthodox Creed (1679).

In the American colonies, the Second London Confession became the Philadelphia Baptist Confession, first issued by Benjamin Franklin (1706-1790) in 1742. A number of congregations put forward confessions of faith, notably the First Baptist Church of Boston (1665) and the Swansea Baptist Church, which had originated in Wales.

In order to provide a uniform format, if not a theological tradition, publishers issued many editions of the Philadelphia Confession along with standard covenants and rules of order.

In 1833 the New Hampshire Baptist Convention authorized the preparation of a new confession and this became a popular doctrinal statement for many local churches, notably in the southern states. The New Hampshire Confession affirmed concepts of biblical inerrancy and spoke only of the local congregation when defining the church.

As the debate over the authority of **Scripture** broke out in the early 20th century, various groups created confessional statements which asserted high views of Scripture and the autonomy of local congregations. **Strict Baptists** in Britain, **Fundamental** and **Conservative** Baptists in the United States, and **Fellowship** Baptists in **Canada**, to name the major groups, still adhere to confessional statements, usually based upon the 1689 London Confession or the 1832 New Hampshire Confession or some derived statement. American Baptists rejected any confession save the New Testament, and **Southern Baptists** (SBC) adopted "**Baptist Faith and Message**." Likewise, institutions also wrote doctrinal statements into their identities to serve as protocols for governance. Examples of the use of theological statements in the institutional setting were Spurgeon's College in Great Britain (1856), and Northern Baptist Theological Seminary (1913) and The Eastern Baptist Theological Seminary (1925) in the United States. Most fundamentalist schools and Baptist bible colleges followed this pattern as well. While the confession of faith has not usually been binding upon membership, it has been used to define faculty orthodoxy and assess missionary appointments.

CONGO, DEMOCRATIC REPUBLIC OF. Formerly known as Zaire, and prior to that the Belgian Congo, Baptist missionaries from the **Baptist Missionary Society** began work along the Congo River in 1878. At São Salvador, Lukolela, Bolobo, Yakusu, Leopoldville, and Kimpese in the east, British Baptists focused upon church planting and education and created a system of schools. In 1884 the Livingstone Inland Mission offered its Congo field to the **American Baptist Missionary Union** (ABMU) and the Union accepted the seven stations and nine missionaries. The primary outreach of the American Baptist mission was at Banza Manteke, Palabala, and later at Vanga and Sona Bata. A significant revival broke out at Banza Manteke in 1886 under the ministry of **Henry Richards**; a thousand converts were won in a few weeks in what came to be known as the "Pentecost on the Congo." In 1929 American Baptists opened a station at Kikongo which led to hundreds of converts. Baptist missionaries from Sweden conducted a successful mission in the Bandulu region, and later the **Conservative Baptist** Foreign Mission Society (CBFMS) in Goma and **Baptist Mid-Missions** (BMM) to the east and north of Kikwit, where they have established a **bible** school and medical work.

Baptist missions in the Congo grew organizationally by the turn of the century. In 1903 a General Conference of Missionaries of the Protestant Societies Working in Congo Land was organized and included Baptists, a Native Council was created in 1936, and later the American and British Baptist work joined in the collective efforts of the Protestant Council of the Congo. Education became a primary investment of Baptists in the Congo, including the Lower Congo Training School, which was merged in 1908 with the Congo Evangelical Training Institution at Kimpese. In 1933 the school became the Ecole de Pasteurs et d'Instituteurs (Pastors' and Teachers' School), offering a theological course, a bible college curriculum, and a teacher training course.

Following independence from Belgium in 1960, and subsequent Protestant ecumenical reorganization of the Eglise du Christ au Zaire, missionary and indigenous work has been divided according to "communities" with three Baptist communities originally emerging: Communauté Baptiste du Bas-Fleuve (CBBF), Communauté Baptiste du Moyen-Fleuve (CBMF), and Communauté Baptiste du Haut-Congo (CBHC). After further negotiations, the Communauté Baptiste du Fleuve Zaire (CBFZ) was formed which related to the British Baptist Missionary Society, the Communauté Baptiste du Zaire Ouest (CBZO) relating to the

American Baptist Foreign Mission Society (ABFMS), and the Communauté Baptiste au Bandundu related to the Swedish Baptists. Independent Baptist congregations, sponsored by **Baptist Mid-Missions** (BMM) and other agencies, have existed since 1921 at several locations in the country, including Sibut, Crampel, and Ouango. The Conservative Baptist Foreign Mission Society began a mission in 1946, centered in Kivu and Shaba provinces. The **Baptist Bible Fellowship** (BBF) began a mission in Congo in 1957.

As of 1995 there were 30 churches and 24,371 members affiliated with the Communauté Baptiste au Bandundu, 274 churches and 93,800 members affiliated with the Communauté Baptiste au Kivu, 600 churches and 252,000 members affiliated with the Communauté Baptiste du Zaire Ouest, 221 churches with 274,092 members affiliated with the Communauté Baptiste du Fleuve Zaire, and 15 churches with 15,488 churches affiliated with the Communauté des Eglises Baptistes Autonomes. There are seven Baptist-related institutions in the Congo located at Bendela, Bolobo, Kimpese, Kinshasa, and Kisangani.

CONGO, REPUBLIC OF. Baptists are not numerically strong in this nation, which was formerly the French Congo. In its early colonial history, Baptists from the U.S. **American Baptist Missionary Union** organized churches, which became part of the Evangelical Church of the Congo. The Örebo Mission of Baptists in Sweden established itself in the north of the Congo and significant growth was seen in the 20th century, including a **bible college** established in 1954. **Baptist Mid-Missions** (BMM) likewise assumed responsibility for a mission in Congo in 1953, which had previously belonged to the Unevangelized Fields Mission and the Congo Gospel Mission.

With a change of governments in 1978 mission work ceased and Baptists were outlawed. What churches survived became part of the Evangelical Church of the Congo, which numbers over 50 churches and 2,000 members.

CONGREGATION OF THE DEAD. See **Strict Baptists**.

CONNER, WALTER THOMAS (1877-1952). Southern Baptist theologian and educator, born in Cleveland County, Arkansas. He was educated at Hardin Simmons and Baylor Universities and Southwestern Baptist Theological Seminary. He also studied at Rochester Theological Seminary and the University of Chicago; he earned the Ph.D. from Southern Baptist Theological Seminary. He was professor of theology at Southwestern Seminary from 1910 to 1949 and gave shape to its theological position.

The author of 15 books, Conner was the link between founders **B. H. Carroll** and **L. R. Scarborough**, and the more modern Southern Baptist conservative evangelical stance. His position included an understanding on the inspiration of **Scripture** without espousing a theory such as inerrancy, and a balanced view of the divine and human elements in the **bible**. His publications were far ranging, covering doctrinal issues, the Holy Spirit and the cults, especially the Jehovah's Witnesses and Mary Baker Eddy (1821-1910). Conner was one of the most respected theologians of his era in the **Southern Baptist Convention** (SBC). He authored *Christian Doctrine* (1924) and *The Work of the Holy Spirit* (1949).

CONSERVATIVE BAPTIST ASSOCIATION OF AMERICA (CBA). A fellowship of autonomous congregations which originally withdrew from the **Northern Baptist Convention** (NBC) in the United States in 1947. For two decades previous to the schism, numerous pastors expressed opposition to the trend of Northern Baptists toward more **liberal** interpretations of **Scripture** and historic Baptistic theology. Of major concern in the 1930s and 1940s was the "inclusive policy" of the **American Baptist Foreign Mission Society** (ABFMS), which allowed for missionaries of widely differing theological positions to be commissioned for international service. This led to the first stage of the Conservative Baptist movement, a Fundamental Baptist Fellowship among NBC churches, and subsequently a foreign mission organization. For many years, Conservative Baptist congregations were forbidden to have fellowship with the American (Northern) Baptist Convention. The Fundamental Baptist Fellowship became in the 1940s the Conservative Baptist Fellowship and for many years maintained ties with the Conservative Baptist Foreign Mission Society (CBFMS) and what became the Conservative Baptist Association. In 1961 a schism occurred and the "hard core" Conservative Baptist Fellowship broke its ties with the Conservative Baptist movement (see **Baptist World Mission**).

Comprising what has been known as the "Conservative Baptist movement" are the Conservative Baptist Association, the Conservative Baptist Foreign Mission Society (1943), after 1994 CB International, and the Conservative Baptist Home Mission Society (1950), neither of which is controlled by the Association. There are 20 state and area associations, representing 29 states. Foreign mission work is conducted in 46 countries. Also related to the movement are three seminaries, Western Conservative Baptist Seminary in Portland, Oregon, Denver Seminary in Colorado, and with the **Baptist General Conference** (BGC), the Conservative Baptist Seminary of the East in Dresher, Pennsylvania. Undergraduate schools include Judson Baptist College in Portland, Oregon, Southwestern Baptist Bible College in Phoenix, Arizona, and International College in Honolulu, Hawaii. The Association publishes the *Conservative Baptist* (1971-) and, as of 1995, includes 1,084 churches and about 200,000 members.

CONSERVATIVE TRADITION. Conservative or conservative evangelical tradition can be identified in North American Baptist thought at about the turn of the 20th century. As schools and writers questioned time-honored values such as the authority of **Scripture**, others responded by "conserving" the great truths of the faith. After the publication of the Fundamentals in 1915-1919 and the formation of the World's Christian Fundamentals Association in 1919, many conservatives took the name **"fundamentalist"** because it identified them with a particular set of doctrinal formulae. In the 1920s fundamentalism evolved as a shrill and schismatic critique of **liberalism** and modernism. For many this was too strong a position and they sought a moderating stance which became "conservative," and later under the influence of Baptist theologians like Carl F. H. Henry (1913-), "conservative evangelical." Specifically this means a doctrinal stance which is orthodox, evangelical, and not dogmatic in nonessential areas such as the inerrancy of Scripture and the second advent of Christ. In the area of social ethics, conservatives tend to support right to life, traditional marriages, heterosexuality, Christlike speech, and abstention from the use of tobacco, alcoholic beverages, and the illegal use of drugs. Manifestations of a conservative stance among Baptists are found in the moderate **Southern Baptist** movement, the American Baptist evangelical tradition, the Conservative Baptist Association, and several **Black Baptist** groups in the United States. See also **Fundamentalism and Baptists**; **Liberal Tradition**.

CONTINENTAL BAPTISTS. Related to the **Reformed Baptist** movement, a group of Calvinistic Baptists located in the southern United States began to hold conferences in 1981 to revive Calvinistic theology and the thought of **C. H. Spurgeon** in particular. One of the leading pastors in the movement, Ronald McKinney, began a periodical which emulated Spurgeon's paper, *The Sword and Trowel* in 1978 and sponsored conferences on Baptist theology. McKinney's group for a time was close to the Reformed Baptist position, but preferred the First London Confession of Faith (1646) to the 1689 Confession. Further distinguishing them was an affirmation of preaching and a broader doctrine of the church. Referred to as the "Sword and Trowel Baptists," they adopted the name "Continental Baptists" in 1983 and followed an associational **polity**. Many of the approximately 40 congregations also share an affinity with the **General Association of Regular Baptist Churches** (GARBC).

CONVENTIONS. Use of the terminology "convention" among Baptists arose in the United States in the first decades of the 19th century. Probably derived from the political use of the term to designate a gathering of persons according to a certain perspective or with a common agenda, exemplified in the Constitutional Convention of 1787 and the Hartford Convention of 1814, Baptists used the term to organize themselves at the national and then state levels. In 1813 **Luther Rice** recalled that he had originated the idea of a national convention to which state conventions or auxiliaries would relate. The result was the **General Baptist Missionary Convention of the Baptist Denomination in the United States of America for Foreign Missions**, also known as the Baptist General Convention or the General Missionary Convention (GMC); it became a model for further organizations in the United States and where American missionary work has been conducted. The first state convention was the South Carolina Baptist Convention (1821), of which **Richard Furman** was a leading proponent.

In **Canada** the convention terminology was borrowed from U.S. experience and the first provincial use of the term was the Baptist Convention of Nova Scotia, New Brunswick, and Prince Edward Island in 1846. Subsequent provincial conventions were formed in the central provinces as follows: the Regular Baptist Missionary Convention (1854) and the Canada Baptist Missionary Convention East (1858); these two were united in 1888 as the Baptist Convention of Ontario and Quebec. In the western provinces the first convention formed was the Baptist Convention of Manitoba (1880), which was reorganized in 1884 as the Baptist Convention of Manitoba and the Northwest, followed by the British Columbia Baptist Convention in 1897. A Baptist Convention of Western Canada was formed in 1907 to unite the mission programs of the scattered churches; it became in 1909 the Baptist Union of Western Canada. Subsequent to the formation of the Union, separate conventions were organized as units of the Union in Alberta (1910), British Columbia (1910), Manitoba (1910), and Saskatchewan (1910). An attempt in 1908-1909 to create a national Baptist Union of Canada was aborted in Ontario and Quebec. See also **Polity, Baptist**.

CONWELL, RUSSELL HERMAN (1843-1925). American Baptist minister and educator, born at South Washington, Massachusetts. He graduated from Yale College and entered the U. S. Army during the Civil War. Afterward he became a lawyer in Minnesota, ultimately becoming an immigration agent for that state. In 1879, following the death of his wife, he turned to religion and was converted. Soon afterward he assumed the pastorate of a small church in Lexington, Massachusetts, and revived the church. In 1881 he moved to Grace Baptist Church in North Philadelphia, a struggling, debt-ridden congregation. Within 10 years, he was pastor of a church of over a thousand and easily one of Philadelphia's outstanding orators. The Baptist Temple became, under his pastorate, a leading example of an institutional church, providing education and community services to a wide variety of people. In 1884 he founded Temple University and later the Good Samaritan Hospital, the beginnings of the medical school. He is best remembered for his oft-preached sermon, *Acres of Diamonds* (1888), which was based on his startling Civil War encounter with personal valor in a young soldier named Johnny Ring. Conwell was a popular author on a variety of subjects, including *Why the Chinese Emigrate* (1871), *History of the Great Fire in Boston* (1873), *The Story of the Presidents from Grant to Arthur* (1878), *The Life of Charles Haddon Spurgeon* (1892), and *Why Lincoln Laughed* (1922).

COOK, HENRY (1886-1970). English Baptist minister, born near Tillicoultry, Scotland. His family emigrated to Canada, but he remained in Britain where he was educated at the Baptist College in Glasgow, becoming a prize student. He served pastorates at Govan, Leamington Road, Blackburn (1910-1921), Blenham, Leeds (1921-1925), and Ferme Park, London (1925-1939). He entered denominational service on various committees of the **Baptist Union (BU)**, served as president of the **Baptist Missionary Society** in 1940, and as General Superintendent of the London Area for the Baptist Union (1941-1955). He was elected president of the BU in 1955. From 1955-1959 he was associate general secretary of the **Baptist World Alliance** (BWA). His books, *The Why of Our Faith* (1924) and *What Baptists Stand For* (1947), were considered definitive of Baptist beliefs in the era. William Jewell College in Missouri awarded Cook an honorary doctorate in 1955.

COOK, THOMAS (1808-1892). English Baptist philanthropist and evangelist, born at Melbourne, Derbyshire. Early in life he was apprenticed to his uncle in the trade of wood turning. He was converted in the **General Baptist** Church at Leicester and was influenced by Joseph Winks, a publisher in that town. From 1828-1832 Cook served as a General Baptist associational bible reader and evangelist in Rutland County, travelling over 2,500 miles in one year. Later, as a wood-turner at Market Harborough, he was converted to the **temperance** movement by a Roman Catholic priest and he also became an advocate of antitobacco smoking. To assist a local temperance association, Cook organized an excursion trip by train from Leicester to Loughborough in 1841, the first of its kind. This was so successful that he took up organizing excursions in Britain and abroad and became wealthy as a result. His travel agency at Leicester published schedules and handbooks, and Cook himself organized the first round-the-world tour in 1872-1873. He travelled throughout the world, touring the **mission** stations of both **General** and **Particular** Baptists, making his reports in prominent periodicals. His work in the travel industry aided especially teetotalers, who often travelled together as a cultural experience. In 1840 Cook founded the *Children's Temperance Magazine*, four years later the *National Temperance Magazine* and the *Youth's Temperance Magazine*. Cook's own books included numerous tourist guides and a *Memoir of Samuel Deacon* (1889).

COOPERATIVE BAPTIST FELLOWSHIP (CBF). A coalition of mostly American **Southern Baptists** who felt the need to respond to the changes in the life of the Southern Baptist Convention, which was perceived to be moving in a theologically and administratively unacceptable direction. The Fellowship was formed in 1991, with a primary emphasis upon global **missions**. The CBF cooperates with other Baptist and Christian groups, notably the **American Baptist Churches**, emphasizing unreached peoples and a team approach to missions. Currently, there are 140 missionaries under appointment among 20 people groups, particularly in Europe, Asia, and North Africa. The Fellowship is administered by a Coordinating Council of 83 members, who are elected at a General Assembly. The executive offices of the Cooperative Baptist Fellowship are located in Atlanta, Georgia, with about 1,500 congregations supporting the program. The CBF cooperates in several programs with the American Baptist Churches USA.

COSTA RICA. A significant number of early Baptists in Costa Rica were Blacks, the result of efforts by the Baptist Missionary Society of Jamaica. In 1888 a church was established in Puerto Limón. In 1941 Landmarkist **Southern Baptists** opened a church in the country and Southern Baptist mission work commenced in 1947. Six congregations organized the Convención Bautista de Costa Rica in 1947, and in 1951 a Baptist seminary, Instituto Teologico Bautista, opened at San José. Other Baptist groups in Costa Rica include La Iglesia Bautista Nacional (1945), the Asociación Bautista Costarricense (1955), an ultrafundamentalist group, and the **Baptist Bible Fellowship** (BBF) since 1970. The **American Baptist Association** (ABA) also sponsors work in Costa Rica.

As of 1995 there were 26 churches with 1,560 members affiliated with the Convención Bautista de Costa Rica, and 17 churches with 1,040 members affiliated with the La Iglesia Bautista Nacional de Costa Rica.

CÔTE D'IVOIRE. See **Ivory Coast**.

COTTON GROVE RESOLUTIONS. Between 1846 and 1850 **James R. Graves** and John L. Waller (1809-1854) carried on a literary debate on Baptist identity in their respective Tennessee and Kentucky Baptist newspapers. Waller, editor of the *Baptist Banner* and later the *Western Recorder*, stressed the faith of persons baptized, while Graves emphasized the proper form, later to be known as a "**landmark**." Often ridiculing Waller, Graves challenged him to a public confrontation. A mass meeting of concerned Baptists (Waller was not present) met at Cotton Grove in Hardeman County, Tennessee, on June 24, 1851. They considered a presentation by Graves, who presented five propositions which stemmed from the question of whether recognition should be given to paedo-baptists. He questioned whether Baptists could recognize churches with a different government, different standards of membership, and different doctrines, practices, and **ordinances**. He held that ministers of such churches should not be recognized and that Baptists should not call such practitioners "brethren." Following a broad discussion, the meeting agreed to endorse the position or "resolutions" and Graves achieved much publicity from the event, holding that it was as definitive as Martin Luther's Ninety Five Theses. The Cotton Grove Resolutions are generally held to be the first definition of the Landmark Baptist movement. See also **Landmark Baptists**; **Local Church Protectionism**.

COUNCIL OF CHURCHES OF THE EVANGELICAL CHRISTIANS AND BAPTISTS (CCECB). See **Russia, Baptists in**.

COVENANTED BAPTISTS OF THE UNITED STATES AND CANADA. See **Primitive Baptists**.

COVENANTS. Since their earliest development, Baptists have understood the value of covenants as **voluntary** promissory statements. Borrowing heavily from Puritan and Separatist theology and practice, the first Baptists under **John Smyth**'s leadership covenanted together in 1607-1608 "as the Lord's free people... to walk in all his wayes made known, or to be made known to them, according to their best endeavors whatsoever it should cost them, the Lord assisting them," closely resembling the words of the covenant of the Ancient Church in 1591. Puritans had written covenants to remind themselves of God's provisions for the saints and their obligations toward God and the visible church. The use of covenants has a much broader history among Baptists in the United States than elsewhere. This was perhaps due to the widespread use of covenants in the New England Congregationalist community.

Unlike their predecessors in Nonconformity, Baptists usually stress the horizontal relational nature of covenants, that is the relationships and obligations between church members. Typically, a covenant is a statement of relationships and expectations of members which is signed at least originally by all of the membership. When a covenant has been written and signed, a church is said to be constituted; as such it reflects the consensus of the membership and is entirely voluntary. Among the more famous church covenants are the **William Screven** Covenant of 1682, Samuel Jones's (1735-1814) covenant printed in his 1798 *Treatise of Church Discipline*, and the covenant published in 1836 as an appendage to the New Hampshire Confession of Faith (1833), likely the work of **J. Newton Brown**. The Brown covenant is widely accepted in varying versions as "**the** church covenant."

On regular occasions, many congregations recite the covenant together, such as at celebrations of the **Lord's Supper** or in the reception of new members. In the latter 19th century some American churches had a Saturday set aside for a Covenant Service, prior to the Lord's Supper on Sunday. Covenants can also be used to define the boundaries of church membership in order to **discipline** an errant member who appears to be in violation of a provision of membership. Similarly, new converts may be instructed in the faith and life of a congregation by use of the covenant. Most covenants are not more than a few paragraphs in length. The provisions of a church covenant usually include a definition of membership, obligations concerning the sacraments/**ordinances**, care for each other, financial support for the church and attendance at its meetings. Some covenants also list ethical expectations of members such as abstinence from antisocial behavior, alcoholic beverages, and criticism of the church. Theologically, it is assumed that the grace of God allows (if not enables) the performance of covenanted obligations.

In recent years, covenants have lost relevance in North America, while elsewhere the confession of faith may have more meaning. An interesting use of the concept of the covenant is found among the **American Baptist Churches U.S.A.**, where beginning in 1973 each of the regional organizations agreed to a "covenant of relationships" with the national societies and the local churches. The covenant thus provides the uniting force in a voluntary polity of complex church corporations.

COX, FRANCIS AUGUSTUS (1793-1853). English Baptist minister, born at Leighton Buzzard. He studied at Bristol College under **John Ryland** and then graduated from the University of Edinburgh. He served the church at Clipstone and for 42 years at Hackney in London. Cox was a promoter of foreign missions, the Baptist Irish Society, and relations with Baptists in the United States. He and **James Hoby** visited the United States in 1836 and wrote extensively of their findings. Cox served as secretary to the Body of Ministers of the **Three Dissenting Denominations** and was a founder of the Liberation Society. A devoted voluntarist, he was a member of the Evangelical Voluntary Church Association, the British Anti-State Church Association, and led the anti-Maynooth drive and the Anti-Corn Law League. Fond of educational projects, he played a prominent role in the founding of University College and London University in 1827. At the jubilee of the **Baptist Missionary Society** (BMS) in 1842, Cox was its official historian and he was president of the **Baptist Union** (BU) in 1834, 1845, and 1852. Cox was widely published and his works include *Female Scripture Biography* (1817), *The Baptists in America* (1836), *History of the Baptist Missionary Society* (1844), and *On Christian Union* (1845).

CRAMP, JOHN MOCKETT (1796-1881). English, and later Canadian, Baptist minister and educator, born at St. Peter's, Isle of Thanet, England. He was educated at Canterbury and Stepney Theological College in preparation for his **ordination** to the Baptist ministry. In England he edited the *Baptist Magazine* (1825-1828), was a publisher, and was active in various denominational boards and societies. In 1844 he accepted under missionary appointment the presidency of Canada Baptist College in Montreal, operated by the Canada Baptist Missionary Society and the Baptist Colonial Missionary Society in England. The school collapsed in 1849 and Cramp moved to Acadia College in Nova Scotia in 1851 as the second president of that school. He revived the college's sagging finances, was active in the **temperance** movement, and served the Horton (Wolfville) Baptist Church. In 1853 he became the first principal of Acadia's theological institute, serving again as president from 1860-1869. Cramp was an active writer, completing *An Essay on the Obligation of Christians to Observe the Lord's Supper Every Lord's Day* (1827), a *History of the Baptists* (1871), *A Memoir of Madame Feller* (1876), several anti-Catholic works, and a series of newspaper articles chronicling the history of Maritime Baptists (1860-1863).

CRANDALL, JOSEPH (1761-1858). Canadian Baptist minister, born at Tiverton, Rhode Island. Crandall was converted under the evangelistic ministry of **Henry Alline** in the Chester, Nova Scotia, area. He was further awakened under the influence of **Harris Harding** and **Joseph Dimock** in 1795. Following a vivid vision of a call to preach and baptize, Crandall began his ministry in Liverpool, where he was a founding pastor until 1799, when he went to New Brunswick. He became the first regularly ordained Baptist pastor in New Brunswick, being set apart by **Edward Manning** and Joseph Dimock in Sackville. He served at Salisbury until his death. He was a founder of the Nova Scotia Association in 1800 and the separate New Brunswick Association in 1822. Crandall was elected to the New Brunswick Assembly in 1818, campaigning broadly for civil and **religious liberty**, and president of the New Brunswick Baptist Education Society in 1836. He died at 97 having preached his last sermon six weeks before.

CRAWFORD, ISABEL ALICE HARTLEY (1865-1961). American Baptist missionary, born at Cheltenham, Ontario. The daughter of a Canadian Baptist educator, Isabel was educated at the Baptist Missionary Training School in Chicago. She was appointed a missionary by the Woman's American Baptist Home Mission Society (WABHMS) in 1893 to the Kiowa Indians of Oklahoma. During her tenure at Elk Creek, she advocated Indian rights in the face of encroachment upon lands dedicated to the tribe. At Saddle Mountain in 1901 she superintended the construction of a church building. In 1905 while serving there she assisted in the celebration of the **Lord's Supper**, perhaps the first Baptist woman to do so. She was heavily criticized for this action by the **American Baptist Home Mission Society** (ABHMS) and the Indian Baptist Association; she was ultimately forced to resign her commission. In later years she lectured widely on Indian rights and in 1918 interceded in a dispute between the Presbyterians and Baptists on the Allegany Reservation in western New York. She was the first white woman missionary to be buried in the Indian Cemetery at Saddle Mountain, Oklahoma, a tribute to her affection for Indian peoples. The story of her early work is found in her *Kiowa: The History of a Blanket Mission* (1915).

CRAWFORD, TARLETON PERRY (1821-1902). Southern, and later Independent, Baptist missionary, born in Warren County, Kentucky. He graduated from Union University in Murfreesboro, Tennessee, and was appointed a missionary to **China** in 1851 by the Southern Baptist **Foreign Mission Board** (FMB). He and his wife served at Shanghai (1852-1863) in an educational mission, and later in North China at Tengchow (1863-1893). During the American Civil War, Crawford invested in Chinese real estate and became independently wealthy; this prompted a connection with his **Landmarkist** upbringing, and he began to argue that missionaries ought to be self-supporting. After an unsuccessful attempt to persuade the FMB to accept his position, which he called "gospel missionism," he left the service of the Board and became an Independent. Crawford's ideas were popularized in his *Evolution in My Mission Views* (1903).

CRAWLEY, EDMUND ALBERN (1799-1888). Canadian and American Baptist minister and educator, born at Ipswich, England. Crawley emigrated as a child to Cape Breton Island and graduated from King's College, Windsor, Nova Scotia. His first career was that of a Halifax lawyer, but in 1828 he entered the **ministry**, having been converted by area **evangelicals** and drawn into the Baptist movement. He took courses at Brown University and Andover Theological Seminary, under the influence of **Alexis Caswell**. Ordained in Providence, Rhode Island, he returned to be the pastor at Granville Street Baptist Church in Halifax, his home congregation. Crawley spearheaded the drive for a Baptist university in the Maritimes, which became Acadia University. A founder of the Nova Scotia Baptist Education Society on the New England plan, he was associated with Acadia at various times as professor of theology, president, and fundraiser from 1838 until his death. Between 1856 and 1865 Crawley went to the United States and was involved in a disastrous financial scheme involving a mining company; he also founded Mt. Auburn Female Seminary in Cincinnati, Ohio, and was president of Limestone Springs Female Academy in Spartanburg, South Carolina, from 1856 to 1860. During the Civil War he taught at a private school in Shelby, North Carolina. Returning to Acadia, he became the first principal of Acadia's theological school. Crawley was awarded a doctor of divinity degree by Brown University in 1844. His most notable publication was *A Treatise on Baptism* (1835).

CROATIA. Heinrich Meyer, the Baptist apostle to Hungary, indirectly originated the work in what is now Croatia. Meyer baptized Nicola Zrincak of Zagreb who in 1883 began a mission in Zagreb. Other early missions were commenced by Julius Peter, a German missionary who travelled throughout Yugoslavia, and Adolf Hempt, a convert of Germans who focused his efforts in Novi Sad. Under the leadership of Vinko Vacek, a Croatian Conference was organized in 1921, followed by a Serbo-Croatian Union, organized in 1922. This second body became the Savez Baptistickih Crkava (Baptist Union of Croatia) in 1924, which survived until World War II. During the period when Croatia was included in Yugoslavia, 1945-1991, Baptists in Croatia cooperated as part of the Baptist Union of Yugoslavia; with the independence of Croatia in 1991, the Savez Baptistickih Crkava u Republici Hrvatskoj was reconstituted. *Glas Evandjelia* (1923-1941; 1959-as *Glasnik*) was begun as the official newspaper of the Union, published first at Daruvar.

As of 1995, there were 34 churches and 2,000 members affiliated with the Savez Baptistickih Crkava u Republici Hrvatskpo. In 1997 the **Baptist Bible Fellowship** (BBF) also entered Croatia.

CROSBY, THOMAS (1683-1751). English Baptist educator and historian, born at London. Early in his life he went to sea and trained at the Royal Mathematical School. He was supported by the Church of England but adopted Baptist views and was baptized. He joined the strategic Horsley-down Church under **Elias Keach** and married the daughter of the next pastor, **Benjamin Stinton**. Stinton introduced Crosby to many **associations** and the larger **Nonconformist** community in London. When Stinton died in 1719, Crosby advocated **John Gill** and, under some adversity, managed to have the pastoral selection prevail. Crosby was accused of fraudulent accounting practices and was expelled from the church. He joined a congregation at Unicorn Yard and was expelled from there in 1742 on account of business practices and a bad temper. Over several decades he compiled the first published *History of the Baptists* (4 vols.,1738-40), based on the work of Benjamin Stinton, and partly as a reaction to inadequate treatments in existing religious histories.

CROWN RIGHTS OF THE REDEEMER. See **Christ, Doctrine of**.

CROZER, JOHN PRICE (1793-1866). American Baptist industrialist and philanthropist, born at Springfield, Pennsylvania. His career started as a laborer in a lumber mill where he developed clever mechanical adaptations to water power. He opened his own cotton milling center at Upland, Pennsylvania, and successfully marketed his goods in nearby Philadelphia. Crozer was baptized by **William Staughton** and was greatly influenced by his pastor's interest in **voluntary associations**. He was elected to prominent positions in the **American Baptist Home Mission Society** (ABHMS) and in the **American Baptist Publication Society** (ABPS), which his son-in-law, Benjamin Griffith (1821-1893), managed. He took a special interest in book distribution and **Sunday Schools**. During the Civil War, his profits soared, and he became one of the leading philanthropists in the Baptist community. He gave an endowed chair to the Baptist University at Lewisburg, Pennsylvania (later Bucknell University),and established an orphanage. After his death, his family used his estate to endow a theological school in Upland, Pennsylvania, named Crozer Theological Seminary.

CUBA. Baptist work relating to Cuba dates from 1886 when Southern Baptists first worked among Cubans in Florida. Foreign mission effort commenced at the conclusion of the Spanish-American War in 1898. Following consultation between the **American Baptist Missionary Union** (ABMU) and the **Southern Baptist Convention** (SBC), it was agreed that Southern Baptists would take missionary responsibility for the four western provinces, while the **American Baptist Home Mission Society** (ABHMS) took the same responsibility for the two eastern provinces and **Puerto Rico.** The first church was started at Santiago in 1899 by Hartwell R. Mosely (1863-1926), an appointee of the ABMU. By 1903 the Convención Bautista de Cuba Oriental (Convention of the Eastern Provinces) was formed and in 1920 a Cuban Baptist Home Mission Society was founded. In 1905 a Cuban-American College was started at Havana, out of which emerged El Cristo Colegios Internacionales. The first attempts in theological education came in 1947 when a seminary was started at Matanzas in cooperation with the Southern Baptist mission, plus Presbyterians and Methodists; however, this soon proved inadequate. Therefore in 1949 the Cuban Baptist Convention of the East established at Santiago its own theological school with the support of American Baptists. Owing to a significant number of Haitian refugees in eastern Cuba, missionary work was conducted and in 1940 in the Province of Camagüey, a Haitian Baptist Convention was organized, eventually with over 30 congregations. The first Southern Baptist congregation was started at Havana in 1905. American **Freewill Baptists** (FWB) began missionary work on the island in 1941, with whom the Convención Bautista Libre de Cuba has been affiliated. La Convención Bautista Occidental published *La Voz Bautista* (The Baptist Voice) (1908-1965) prior to the Revolution of Fidel Castro. In 1955 the **Baptist Bible Fellowship** (BBF) commenced a mission in Cuba in the **fundamentalist** tradition.

As of 1995, there were 100 churches with 6,200 members affiliated with the Convención Bautista de Cuba Oriental, 127 churches with 6,550 members affiliated with the Convención Bautista de Cuba Occidental, and 16 churches with 1,040 members associated with the Convención Bautista Libre de Cuba (Free Baptist Convention of Cuba). Presently, there are two schools in Cuba, Eastern Cuba Baptist Theological Seminary at Santiago de Cuba, and Seminario Teologico Bautista de Cuba Occidental at La Havana.

CUSHING, ELLEN HOWARD WINDSOR (1840-1915). American Baptist missionary and educator, born at Kingston, Massachusetts. Converted at a Charles G. Finney crusade in Boston in 1857, she was first a Congregationalist then a Baptist. At 21 she volunteered for service with the Port Royal Experiment, where she assisted freed slaves in entering post-war society. Later, married to Josiah N. Cushing (1840-1905), she and her husband went to **Burma**, where they collaborated on an English-Shan dictionary. In 1892, on furlough, she accepted a position with the Woman's American Baptist Foreign Mission Society of the East; realizing the need of a school to train single women missionaries, she started the Baptist Training Institute in Philadelphia (later Ellen Cushing College). Back in the mission field in 1905, when Josiah died, she completed his massive dictionary project. With her husband, she published *A Grammar of the Shan Language* (1871) and *A Shan and English Dictionary* (1881).

CZECHOSLOVAK BAPTIST CONVENTION OF THE UNITED STATES AND CANADA. An organization of Czech-speaking Baptist congregations in North America, this Convention was established by leaders in the German Baptist community in Chicago in 1909 to serve the needs of the immigrant Slovaks and Czechs in that area. Between 1909 and 1913 Polish work was also supported, but a decision was made to separate the conventions. Originally there were two Bohemian Baptist churches, as they were called in the United States. A publishing ministry began among the Slavic churches, as well as a missionary outreach to Czechoslovakia. During the Marxist era emphasis shifted to missionary work in **Haiti**, until 1993 when support was redirected to the unions of **Slovakia** and the **Czech Republic**. A General Board of 51 members directs the work of the Convention, which holds an annual assembly at Phillippi, West Virginia, the headquarters. The Convention publishes *Slavna nadeje* (Glorious Hope). As of 1995 there were six churches in the United States and **Canada** with about 400 members affiliated with the Convention.

CZECH REPUBLIC. Czech Baptists identify with early Hussite and Czech Brethren traditions, although modern Baptist witness is traced to the mid-19th century. **Colporteurs** of the British and Foreign Bible Society baptized believers in the 1860s in the region of Bohemia. **Henry Novotny** formed a church at Hledsebe near Prague in 1885 and a Baptist Union was founded in 1919. Mission assistance was provided by the British and American Baptists plus the Scottish Bohemian Mission. With the downfall of Marxist government in Czechoslovakia in 1992, the Czech Republic and the **Slovak Republic** emerged as separate nations, thus necessitating separate Baptist organizations in 1993. In 1994 the Baptist Theological Seminary in Rüschlikon, Switzerland, relocated to Prague, the Czech Republic, where it affiliated with the Protestant Faculty of Charles University; degree programs at the institution were closed temporarily in 1998. The Union publishes *Rozsievac* (The Sower) (1930-). The **Baptist Bible Fellowship** (BBF) opened a mission in 1992, and the following year the **Conservative Baptist** Foreign Mission Society (CBFMS) began a mission in Prague.

As of 1995 there were 25 churches and 2,412 members belonging to the Bratrska Jednota Baptistu (Baptist Union of the Czech Republic).

D

DAGG, JOHN LEADLEY (1794-1884). Southern Baptist minister and educator, born at Middleburg, Virginia. Early career positions included schoolteacher and physician's apprentice. He also served in the military in the War of 1812. Dagg became an itinerant preacher in 1817 and won an invitation to succeed **William Staughton** at Fifth Baptist Church, Philadelphia, in 1825. In 1834 he turned to education, first as president of a manual labor school in Pennsylvania, and ultimately as professor of theology and president of Mercer University in Macon, Georgia. Dagg was the first published theologian of the **Southern Baptist Convention** (SBC), producing its first systematic theology in 1859. He set the tone of later Southern Baptist theologians by laying down the rule of a biblical basis for all doctrine. Throughout his career he suffered from a crippled body and partial blindness. Among Dagg's significant works were *Essay in Defense of Strict Communion* (1845), *A Treatise on Church Order* (1858), *Elements of Moral Science* (1859), and *A Manual of Theology* (1871).

DAHOMEY. See **Benin**.

DANA, HARVEY EUGENE (1888-1945). Southern Baptist educator, born at Vicksburg, Mississippi. Dana was educated at Mississippi College and Southwestern Baptist Theological Seminary where he earned the Th.D. in New Testament. From 1920-1928 he served as professor of New Testament and Greek at Southwestern, then took further studies at the University of Chicago and Dubuque Theological Seminary. Dana went to Central Baptist Theological Seminary in Kansas City, Kansas, where he assumed the chair in New Testament and was president from 1938-1945. Central was jointly sponsored by the **Southern** (SBC) and **Northern**

Baptist Conventions (NBC) and Dana had an unusual opportunity to influence students north and south. His scholarly work included New Testament criticism, the application of form criticism to the fourth gospel, and an exhaustive study of the New Testament term "ecclesia." He collaborated with Julius R. Mantey (1890-1981) at Northern Baptist Theological Seminary in the authorship of a textbook in introductory Greek, which was a classic textbook for many generations. His published works include *A Manual for the Study of the Greek New Testament* (1923), *The New Testament World* (1928), and *A Manual of Ecclesiology* (1941).

DANISH AND NORWEGIAN CONFERENCE(S). As Norwegian emigrants moved into the American Midwest, the **American Baptist Home Mission Society** (ABHMS) took the opportunity to conduct **missions** amongst them. An immigrant, Hans Valder (1813-1899), was the first Norwegian appointee of the Society and he organized the first American Norwegian congregation at Indian Creek, Illinois, in 1848. The first Danish congregation was established at Raymond Township, Wisconsin, in 1856. Because the Danish and Norwegians shared a common European heritage and often settled in close proximity, the two congregational groups easily blended into an associative life. In the 1850s churches were started in Wisconsin, Minnesota, Michigan, and Iowa, most from former Lutheran relationships. Five congregations--four Danish and one Norwegian--comprised the first meeting of the "Danish-Norwegian Baptist Conference of the Northwestern States" in 1864 at Raymond, Wisconsin.

One of the chief obstacles to the expansion of the Conference was the lack of a trained ministry. At first, the Danish and Norwegian candidates joined the Swedish educational program at Morgan Park in Chicago. When the Swedes decided upon a separate seminary in St. Paul, the Scandinavian Department of the reorganized University of Chicago Divinity School, as it came to be called, came under the influence of the Danish-Norwegians. This program attracted a number of students from **Denmark** and **Norway** who later returned to Europe. In 1910 the Norwegian educational interest was moved from the University to an affiliation with the Northern Baptist Theological Seminary, where it continued for a number of years.

Attempts were made over the years from 1890 to 1910 to organize a general conference encompassing Danes and Norwegians, similar to the national conferences for the Germans and Swedes. A consensus was not reached between the two groups and in 1910 separate conferences were incorporated. The Norwegian Conference created a mission board, which sent workers to the Dakotas, the eastern states, the far West and **Canada**. The churches in Canada became the joint responsibility of the Baptist Union of the Western Provinces. Close relations in the United States with the **Northern Baptist Convention** were strengthened in 1939 with associate membership for the Conference in the Convention; eventually in 1957 the Norwegian Baptist Conference was merged with the **American Baptist Convention** (ABC).

Among the Danes, several state conferences were organized in the late 19th century, notably in Minnesota, Wisconsin, Illinois, and Iowa. In 1910 the Danish Baptist General Conference held its organizing session at Harlan, Iowa, with 48 congregations represented. By 1915 a pension fund and women's and youth work had been organized under the Conference. Canada was adopted as a mission field in 1928 with the first church established at Calgary in 1929. From 1912 to 1925 the Conference supported a seminary program at Des Moines University in Iowa, after which the program affiliated with the Northern Baptist Theological Seminary in Chicago. Like the Norwegian Conference, the Danish Baptist General Conference also accepted associate membership in the Northern Convention and merged with the ABC in 1958.

In addition to producing a hymnal, the Danish and Norwegian churches cooperated in publishing *Oliebladet* (Olive Leaf) (1877-1887) and *Vaeteren* (Awakener) (1887-1910). From the separation of the two conferences, the Norwegians produced *Missionaeren* (The Missionary) (1910-1956), while the Danes published *Vaeteren* until 1958.

DAVIES, BENJAMIN (1814-1876). Welsh and Canadian Baptist minister and educator, born at Werne, Carmarthenshire. He was educated for the ministry in **Wales**, at Bristol Baptist College, and the University of Glasgow; he received a Ph.D. degree in Oriental studies at the University of Leipzig. Davies emigrated to **Canada** in 1838 on the recommendation of **John Gilmour** to head up the new faculty of Canada Baptist College in Montreal. As such, he became the first theological educator in Canada to have an earned doctorate. The College failed from an overly scholastic program and lack of local support; Davies returned to England to become principal at Stepney College, 1843-1846. His tenure was short due to lack of administrative ability, and in 1847 he went back to Canada for 10 years as professor and chairman of classical literature at McGill University in Montreal. In 1857 Davies returned to England as tutor in Old Testament and classical languages under **Joseph Angus** at Stepney and later Regent's Park, distinguishing himself as a teacher and scholar. He was one of the principal revisers of the English **bible** and brought the fruits of German higher criticism to English **Nonconformity**. Davies was the translator of

Gesenius's *Hebrew Grammar* and *Lexicon* and he compiled and translated *The Paragraph Bible*.

DAVIS, NOAH (1802-1830). American Baptist minister and publisher, born at Salisbury, Maryland. Early in life he worked as a clerk in the Philadelphia firm of Fassitt & Langstroth. In 1819 he was baptized at Sansom Street Baptist Church by **William Staughton**. Licensed to the **ministry** by his home church in Salisbury, he returned to Philadelphia to study in Staughton's theological school and moved with the school to Washington, D.C., when it became Columbian College. Frustrated in his attempts to become a foreign missionary because of frail health, he moved to a pastoral ministry at Drummondtown, Virginia (on the eastern shore), and then to a church in Norfolk, Virginia. While in Norfolk, he preached to the soldiers at Old Point Comfort and started a Seaman's Friend Society. In 1824 he wrote to a friend in Washington (likely **Luther Rice**) urging the establishment of a denominational tract society on the model of the American Tract Society. Thus the Baptist General Tract Society (BGTS) was organized in 1824 with Davis as its manager. He moved the Society to Philadelphia in 1826 and it prospered under his leadership. Never of strong stamina, he died after a brief illness. His epitaph indicated that he was born, baptized, ordained, married, and died all in the month of July.

DEACON. The office of deacon in Baptist **polity** and practice is derived from the biblical tradition in acts of lay **ministry**. Based upon the Greek term "diakonos," meaning "servant", it was originally a person who waited upon tables, and this evolved to apply to those lay persons in each congregation who took care of the needs of the congregation, both financial and pertaining to the **sacraments/ordinances**. Early Baptists recognized the need for a regular lay ministry and elected deacons from among the church membership, according to the qualifications in I Timothy 3:8-13. Generally, deacons serve for a stated term, some congregations limiting their re-election, while others do not.

In the United States, deacons can be the governing board in a congregation. They may supervise the ministry, provide care for the membership themselves and adjudicate matters of church **discipline**. Among Southern Baptists, deacons may be ordained by the **laying on of hands** and may be elected for life. In general deacons would be considered the lay spiritual leadership of a congregation.

DEAN, WILLIAM (1807-1895). American Baptist missionary, born at Eaton, New York. He was educated at Hamilton Literary and Theological

Institution (later Colgate University), and was appointed by the **Baptist Board of Foreign Missions** (BBFM) to **Siam** to work among the Chinese. When **Hong Kong** was transferred to British sovereignty in 1842, Dean moved there and organized the first Protestant church among the Chinese. Later he returned to Bangkok where as a missionary of the **American Baptist Missionary Union** (ABMU), he became a close confidante of the Siamese king, Chulalongkorn (1868-1910). Among Dean's literary achievements were translations of **Scripture** into Chinese, a catechism, and a hymnal. Dean has the distinction of being the first American missionary to work among the Chinese and he helped train most of the first generation of Baptist missionaries to the Chinese people. His published works include *Chinese Scriptures* (1849) and *The China Mission; Embracing a History of the Various Missions of all Denominations Among the Chinese* (1859).

DENMARK. The Baptist movement in Denmark, though small, claims the oldest congregation in Scandinavia. It was founded in 1839 at Copenhagen, the result of mission efforts by **J. G. Oncken** and his close associate, **Julius Köbner.** The church at Copenhagen suffered much persecution and its early pastors, the Monster brothers, were several times imprisoned. Köbner returned to the Copenhagen church as pastor in 1865 and a period of growth and extension ensued. From 1849 to 1952 the Baptists were a non-recognized **dissenter** group, receiving assistance from time to time from the **American Baptist Missionary Union** (ABMU). For a time, Danish Baptists were part of the German Baptist Union and many of their pastors were trained at the Danish-Norwegian Seminary in Chicago, Illinois.

As of 1995, the Danske Baptistsamfund, formed in 1865, had 44 churches and 5,761 members. A Folkehojskole was opened at Gistrup in 1899 and expanded to seminary status in 1918. Later the theological seminary was moved to Tollose near Copenhagen. A periodical, *Baptisternes Ugeblad* (Baptist Weekly), is published (1853-). In addition to the indigenous work, the **Baptist Bible Fellowship** (BBF) has a mission in Denmark, begun in 1980.

DENNE, HENRY (fl. 1640-1660). Anglican and later English Baptist minister and controversialist, born at Well, Ickham. He was educated at Cambridge and in 1630 ordained at St. David's. He became curate at Pirton and remained there for a decade. About 1642 he became convinced of the wrongfulness of infant **baptism** and he converted to Baptist principles. He was baptized in 1643 and became a member of the church in Bell Alley, where he also preached. In 1644 authorities apprehended him for preaching and he was jailed at Cambridge and London. One of his fellow prisoners in London was Daniel Featley (1582-1645), author of *The Dippers Dipt*, whom Denne challenged to a debate in 1645. Denne's printed version became the classic treatise, *The Foundation of Children's Baptism Discovered and Rased* (1645). He preached in the outdoors and baptized candidates in rivers, drawing persecution upon himself. In 1646 he joined Cromwell's Army where he served with distinction. In 1658 he held a two-day disputation at St. Clement Dane's Church, which brought him much attention. Denne published six works, including treatises on the Quakers and Levellers. Among his other significant works were *The Doctrine and Conversation of John Baptist* (1642) and *Antichrist Unmasked in Two Treatises* (1646).

DIGGERS. One of the several dissenter sects which emerged in England in the mid-17th century around greater freedom to interpret **Scripture** and find new ethical applications. Diggerism was a radical outgrowth of the **Leveller** movement, which blended egalitarian politics with theology. Gerard Winstanley (fl.1648-1652) was likely the original Digger; he preached a reorganization of land cultivation in England, so as to benefit the poor and attach all classes more directly to agrarian means. He used Scripture to justify communal cultivation of town commons, paraphrasing Scripture, "True religion and undefiled is to let every one quietly have earth to manure." Calling themselves "True Levellers,", the Diggers were so-called because in some places, notably St. George's Hill in 1649, they dug up and planted public lands. A number of colonies were started across southern England from 1647-1650.

Digger thinking always placed a high value on education and particularly on women's education. As Winstanley's own theology became more radical and the seizure of public lands drew negative reaction from the Commonwealth, Diggerism faded into other religious pursuits. The Digger movement for a time included Levellers, **Ranters**, and Baptists, notably **Henry Denne**. Like other groups, the Diggers reflected the fluidity of 17th century English dissenter identity. See also **Levellers**; **Nonconformity**; **Ranters**; **Seekers**.

DIMOCK, JOSEPH (1768-1846). Canadian Baptist minister, born in Newport, Nova Scotia. Self-educated, he was swept into the **New Light** revival of **Henry Alline** and immersed in 1787. He preached as a New Light for a time and became gradually more orthodox in his views, being ordained at Chester, Nova Scotia, in 1793. Dimock was a leading player in the transition of many New Light congregations into the Baptist tradition. In 1800 he was elected moderator of the Nova Scotia Baptist

Association at its first meeting. He also advocated education and **missionary** organizations and was considered one of the "Maritime Baptist fathers."

DISCIPLINE, CHURCH. Discipline of members and congregations has taken a variety of forms in the Baptist tradition. As early as the 1660s Baptist congregations in Great Britain and North America responded to breaches of the **covenant** or **confession of faith**, or aberrant behavior, with degrees of punitive or corrective action. First was admonition, which involved a meeting with deacons and the pastor who presented the allegations and sought conformity with membership expectations. If this did not produce desired results, censure was next. Censure involved public announcement of the infraction and, through embarrassment and peer pressure, again the desired result was expected. Failing these two measures, excommunication was the last disciplinary action and this amounted to being removed from the membership by vote of the members, as well as being deprived of all benefits of the church. Such excommunicated persons could be restored by vote of the members.

In the United States during the 19th century, many Baptist congregations instituted Prudential Committees, which handled matters of church discipline and freed the deacons from what was essentially a negative task. Formal acts of church discipline have become rare among many Baptist groups, as the pastor and deacons prefer counselling to discipline and, in general, congregations have become more lenient or timid about such matters.

Church discipline could also take place among congregations within an **association**. If a church breached the rules of the association, perhaps by allowing an unorthodox practice or doctrinal position, the congregation could be admonished and, if uncorrected, disfellowshipped. This has remained a practice in many associations in the United States, where for instance a congregation which expressed support for **women** in ministry by calling a woman to be its senior pastor, was disfellowshipped by its association in 1987, and others have been disfellowshipped in Ohio and California for openness to the practice of homosexuality.

DISFELLOWSHIPPING. See **Discipline, Church**.

DISPENSATIONALISM. A theological tradition which divides world history, biblical history, and teleology into a series of periods or dispensations of God's relationships with humanity. Often associated with chiliasm, or the belief in a literal one-thousand- year reign of Christ at the future end of human history, evidence of a kind of dispensationalism is found in the early church fathers, notably Ignatius (c.35-c.107), Justin Martyr (c.100-c.165), and Tertullian (c.160-c.220). Later, the Waldensians and Paulicians evinced this tendency in doctrine. In the 17th century, some members of the Baptist community adopted dispensationalist views as part of the **Fifth Monarchy Movement**.

Dispensationalists hold that God relates differently to humans in different periods of human history. In the Age of Law, for instance, God called upon the faithful to observe the Mosaic Law and this was accounted to them for righteousness. In contrast, during the "Age of the Church," God required people to accept Christ as Saviour and become members of the church universal. Following the Great Tribulation, the Millennial Kingdom or "Kingdom Age" when all will acknowledge the Lordship of Jesus Christ. The last dispensation is the New Heavens and Earth, wherein the saints of God will dwell eternally. A feature of many dispensational calculations is "pretribulationism," whereby the church will be "raptured" from the world prior to the beginning of seven years of worldwide calamity, culminating in the Battle of Armageddon. Such raptured saints, plus the "dead in Christ" will return with Christ at his Second Coming to reign with him on earth. Other dispensationalists opt for a "mid-tribulation," "partial rapture," or "post-tribulation" rapture theory concerning the translation and gathering of the saints. Dispensationalists base their theological system upon literalistic interpretations of prophetic utterances such as Ezekiel 38-39, Daniel 9-12, Matthew 24-25, and the entire book of Revelation, to identify the major biblical passages.

Modern dispensationalism owes its origins to the teachings of John Nelson Darby (1800-1882), an English **bible** teacher and founder of the Plymouth Brethren movement. Darby held a pessimistic view of human history and taught that through a series of prophetic events, Jesus would secretly rapture the true church and return triumphantly to establish his literal kingdom. He organized his understanding of God's relations with mankind into seven dispensations covering all of **Scripture**. Darby's influence was felt in the United States and **Canada** through his personal visits, via Dwight L. Moody, and through the bible conference movement. Baptist teachers such as **Henry G. Weston, William Bell Riley, Elmore G. Harris** of Toronto, and Arno C. Gaebelein (1861-1945) of New York were early leaders of the dispensationalist revival of the 20th century. The *Scofield Reference Bible*, edited by Cyrus I. Scofield (1843-1921) and first published in 1909, was popular among Baptists as the first annotated version of the Scriptures popularly produced for laypersons. In the period 1915-1930 dispensationalist theology became permanently wedded to **fundamentalism** when **conservative evangelical** ministers accused **liberal** teachers of denying supernaturalism, including the literal second coming of Christ. Dallas (Texas) Theological Seminary, under the leadership of Lewis Sperry Chafer (1871-1952) and John F. Walvoord (1910-) prepared numerous Baptist ministers and teachers in the dispensationalist position, although non-denominational itself. Among the categories of Baptists in which dispensationalism is popular are the **General Association of Regular Baptist Churches** (GARBC), **Landmark** Baptists, the **Baptist Bible Fellowship** (BBF), and most independant fundamentalist Baptists.

DISSENTERS. See **Nonconformity**.

DIXON, AMZI CLARENCE (1854-1925). American Baptist minister, born at Shelby, North Carolina. He was educated at Wake Forest College and briefly at Southern Baptist Theological Seminary, and he served pastorates at Immanuel Baptist, Baltimore, Maryland (1882-1890); Hanson Place, Brooklyn, New York (1890-1900); Ruggles Street, Roxbury, Massachusetts, and the independent Chicago Avenue Church, Chicago, Illinois. Just after the turn of the century, Dixon became a devotee of Dwight L. Moody (1837-1899) and followed his revivalistic methods. Dixon opposed theological modernism, evolutionary teaching, and the **social gospel**. In 1909 he began editing a series of tracts called *The Fundamentals*, thus creating a major watershed in American religion. His own contribution to the series defended the infallibility of **Scripture**. When other Baptist pastors, notably **T. T. Shields** and **William B. Riley** created the **Baptist Bible Union** (BBU) in the 1920s, Dixon joined their efforts until he noticed that the movement was too stridently critical of mainstream church relationships. One of the authors of the BBU **confession of faith** in 1923, Dixon resigned from the board in 1925. He was characterized as a moderate **fundamentalist**, the author of numerous **evangelical** works, including *Evangelism: Old and New* (1905).

DOANE, WILLIAM HOWARD (1832-1915). Baptist industrialist and composer, born at Preston, Connecticut. A graduate of Woodstock Academy, he became a bookkeeper in his family's firm. He developed several tools and machines for woodworking and amassed a fortune in his own firm, the J. A. Fay Co. In 1862, following a severe illness, he became interested in music and spent the remainder of his life writing and publishing Christian music. He collaborated with **Robert Lowry** and Fanny J. Crosby (1820-1915). Lowry edited the *Baptist Hymnal* in 1888, the most widely used hymnal in the denomination. His compositions included "Take the Name of Jesus With You," "To God Be the Glory," and "Jesus, Keep Me Near the Cross."

DODGE, EBENEZER (1819-1890). American Baptist minister and theological educator, born at Salem, Massachusetts. He was educated at Brown University under the tutelage of **Francis Wayland** and later at Newton Theological Institution. In addition he studied theology in Berlin under the noted teachers F. A. G. Tholuck (1799-1877) and August J. Dorner (1846-1920). He taught at the Western Baptist Theological Institute in Covington, Kentucky, in the 1840s, and then served as pastor at New Hampton and New London, New Hampshire. In 1853 he was elected professor of biblical criticism and interpretation at Hamilton Theological Seminary and to a chair in evidences of revealed religion at Madison University. In 1861 this role evolved into a professorial chair in doctrinal theology, which he renamed Christian Theology. In 1868 Dodge was elected president of Madison University, having turned down professorships at Rochester and Newton seminaries. He led the university into one of its prominent periods, following the Removal Controversy, which sought to relocate the school to Rochester, New York, and resulted in a damaging split among faculty and the churches. In addition to his administrative duties, Dodge also acquired the status of senior theological faculty member in the institution. **William Newton Clarke** and **Nathaniel Schmidt** greatly admired Dodge as their mentor. Among his published works were *The Evidence of Christianity* (1869) and *Lectures in Christian Theology*, made available to his students at Madison.

DOMESTIC MISSIONS. See **American Baptist Home Mission Society**; **Baptist Home Mission Society**.

DOMINICAN REPUBLIC. The first Baptists in the Dominican Republic were **Baptist Mid-Missions** (BMM) from the United States who established a mission in the Republic in 1947. Next were the **Southern Baptists** (SBC) who arrived in 1962 to begin work at Santo Domingo and later Santiago; more recently the **Baptist Bible Fellowship** (BBF) started a mission in 1996. The Convención Bautista Dominicana was organized in 1968. An important chapter in Baptist history was written in 1971 when Paul and Nancy Potter, Southern Baptist missionaries, were killed at Santiago (see **Martyrology, Baptist**).

As of 1995, there were 22 churches and 1,299 members affiliated with the Convención Bautista Dominicana.

DOUGLAS, THOMAS CLEMENT (1904-1986). Canadian Baptist minister and politician, born at Falkirk, **Scotland**. First trained as a printer, he studied for the ministry at Brandon College and served the Baptist church at Weyburn, Saskatchewan, in 1931-1933. A product of the **social gospel** movement, Douglas during the Great Depression developed an interest in programs to relieve poverty and unemployment. In 1935 he was elected from the Weyburn District to the Federal House of Commons on the Canadian Commonwealth Federation (CCF) ticket. In 1944 he switched to the provincial CCF ticket for Saskatchewan and won a landslide victory. For the next 17 years, Douglas was premier of that province and head of the first socialist government in North America. In 1961 he resigned to become head of the national New Democratic Party. When he was premier in Saskatchewan, he fostered legislation in support of collective bargaining, minimum wages, social welfare, free medical care, and rural electrification. His ideas on socialized medical care became the basis for Canadian national policy in the 1960s.

DOWNGRADE CONTROVERSY. A theological and ecclesiastical disgreement among English Baptists in the last two decades of the 19th century. By the 1880s **Charles H. Spurgeon** and a following of Baptist ministers were increasingly concerned over trends in the Baptist and **Nonconformist** communities toward a departure from traditional Calvinistic doctrines such as eternal punishment, the substitutionary atonement of Christ, and, at the root, the authority of **Scripture**. From Spurgeon's perspective as one of London's leading pastors and Christian voluntarists, the antidote was to develop and affirm a doctrinal statement such as that of the Evangelical Alliance. In the spring of 1888 Robert Shindler (1823-1903), a Baptist minister at Addlestone and friend of Spurgeon, published two unsigned articles in Spurgeon's paper, *The Sword and Trowel*, which under the title "Downgrade," attacked the **General Baptists** for their **Arminian** doctrines, which Schindler thought would lead to Arianism and Socinianism. Presumably the articles had Spurgeon's approval. Spurgeon himself became openly critical of other Baptists whom he suspected of unhealthy tendencies: John G. Greenhough (1843-1911?), James Thew (1846-1922), W. E. Blomfield (1862-1934), Richard Glover (1837-1919), and **Samuel G. Green**. Spurgeon considered **John Clifford** leader of the General Baptists in the Union, his main adversary, and sometimes described him as the "arch-heretic."

In October 1887 Spurgeon withdrew from membership in the **Baptist Union** (BU) and this sent a shockwave through an unsuspecting Baptist community. While some of Spurgeon's associates withdrew with him, most, even those members of his Pastor's College, remained to seek a way of reconciliation. **Joseph Angus** drafted a "Declaration" in which the history of the Union and its basic theological tenets were clearly stated, and he presented it to Spurgeon's representatives. Spurgeon declined to accept it and in January 1887 a delegation consisting of James Culross (1824-1899), John Clifford, and Samuel H. Booth (1824-1902) met with him to try to convince him to reverse his opinions. Spurgeon refused and accused the Union of being a "confederacy in evil," not naming anyone in particular. The rift opened wider, fueled by further phrases of condemnation from Spurgeon, and patience among the leadership of the Union declined. In January 1888 Spurgeon's resignation was accepted, in February Angus' Declaratory Statement was adopted, and John Clifford's leadership in the BU was solidified. The BU went on to receive the full integration of the General Baptists, a six-point doctrinal statement was adopted, and perhaps the largest and most prestigious of its churches, the Metropolitan Tabernacle, was permanently dissociated from both the Union and the London Baptist Association.

Within the greater British Baptist family, the issues profoundly affected relations with Irish Baptists, where Hugh D. Brown (1858-1917), a close follower of Spurgeon, led the churches away from affiliation with the BU. The Downgrade Controversy had far reaching effects upon the Baptist community on both sides of the Atlantic, legitimating the practice of schism over doctrinal differences, and laying a sure foundation for the type of doctrinal purity witnessed in the **fundamentalist** crusade in the next century.

DUNKERS. See German Baptist Brethren.

DUNSTER, HENRY (1612-1659). English and later American paedo-baptist minister and educator, born at Bury, England. He graduated from Magdalen College, Cambridge University, and entered the Anglican ministry. Disliking King Charles I and Presbyterians alike, he moved to New England in 1639. Almost immediately due to his rare educational attainments among dissenters, he was selected to be president of the fledgling Harvard College and he thrived in that role for almost a decade. About 1652, however, he changed his mind about **baptism** and he refused the **sacrament** for his third child. He was admonished and put on trial 1653-1655, ultimately resigning from his presidency and losing his residence. He assumed a baptistic position on the matter of believer's **baptism** and moved to Plymouth Colony in Massachusetts where he joined an Independent Church.

DUTTON, ANN WILLIAMS COLES (1692-1765). English Baptist writer, born at Northampton. Not formally educated, she became a member of John Hunt's Baptist congregation at Castle Hill in Cambridgeshire. She moved to London about 1720, marrying twice and being widowed. She married a third time to Benjamin Dutton, a clothier, and they moved to Great Gransden where he became a **Nonconformist** minister. Ann was a prolific writer of about 50 pamphlets and tracts, covering topics as diverse as the Christian life, the Holy Spirit, and biblical themes. Her theological perspective was Calvinistic and she was marked as a woman of great poetical gifts. Among her many works were *A Narration of the Wonders of Grace* (1734), *Brief Hints Concerning Baptism* (1746), and *A Letter on Perseverence Against Mr. Wesley* (1747?).

E

EARTHEN VESSEL **BAPTISTS.** See **Strict Baptists.**

EATON, ISAAC (1724-1772). American Baptist minister and educator, born at Montgomery, Pennsylvania. Self-educated in theology, he also studied medicine. Eaton became pastor of the Hopewell, New Jersey, Baptist Church in 1746, which he served until his death. In 1756 the **Philadelphia Baptist Association** voted to support the establishment of a Latin grammar school under Eaton's care at Hopewell, which he operated concurrently with his pastoral work. The prime purpose of this school was to train ministers for the Association, and since it was a preparatory institution, it was expected that graduates would enter collegiate studies at Princeton or Philadelphia. Among Eaton's students were **Samuel Jones**, **Hezekiah Smith**, and Isaac Skillman (1740-1799), in addition to several graduates who became lawyers and physicians. Eaton is credited with establishing the first educational institution among Baptists in America. A sample of Eaton's thinking about ministerial formation is found in *The Qualifications, Characters and Duties of a Good Minister of Jesus Christ* (1755), a sermon he preached at the ordination of **John Gano.** See also **Education.**

ECUADOR. Two missionaries of the Southern Baptist **Foreign Mission Board** (FMB), Bill M. Haverfield (1917-1991) and E. Gordon Crocker (1922-), began work at Quito in 1950 and several associations formed in the mid-1960s. In 1972 the Convención Bautista del Ecuador was constituted. A theological seminary at Guayaquil opened in 1961, later relocated to Quito. In 1975 the **Baptist Bible Fellowship** (BBF) opened a mission in Ecuador.

As of 1995, there were 157 churches with 12,530 members affiliated with the Convención Bautista de Ecuador.

ECUMENISM, BAPTIST INVOLVEMENT. From their beginnings Baptists have been involved in dialogue and sometimes cooperation with other Christian groups. In the first three decades of the **General Baptist** movement in England, Baptists were closely allied with the Dutch Mennonite community. This led to the first congregation under **John Smyth** seeking refuge with the congregation at Singelkerk in Amsterdam. Ultimately some withdrew under **Thomas Helwys** and returned to England where correspondence was carried forth until about 1630. The Mennonites declined serious relations with the General Baptists due to the schismatic nature of the latter movement. In the 1670s the **Particular Baptists** in England drew close to the Presbyterians and tried to demonstrate their doctrinal affinities (except for **baptism**) with the Westminster Confession of Faith. Toward the end of the 17th century several English General Baptists were friendly with the **Unitarian** movement and numerous congregations adopted that theological position.

The advance of **William Carey** in 1792 in calling for cooperation in world missionary outreach, signalled a major interest among British Baptists toward cooperation with other Christians at the end of the 18th century. Similarly, Baptists were at the forefront in England and **Wales** in forming **voluntary** societies, often in conjunction with other Christians. Among the outstanding examples were the **Sunday School** Society (1785) and the British and Foreign Bible Society (1804).

In the United States, Baptists often evolved along fairly sectarian lines. Doctrinal differences over the mode of baptism caused wide differentiation between Baptists and other Protestant groups and open criticism of Roman Catholics by prominent authors like **William Cathcart** separated them from Catholics. But, with other evangelical Protestants, many Baptists also supported the American Bible Society (1816) and the Sunday School Union (1817), exhibiting an early cooperative spirit. Toward the middle of the 19th century, many Northern Baptists participated in the Evangelical Alliance and came to understand themselves as mainstream evangelicals. **Freewill Baptists** cooperated with Free Communion Baptists and frequently joined causes with Regular or Calvinistic Baptists. There were serious differences expressed in several published debates between Baptists and Campellites (Disciples of Christ/Christian Church).

Serious engagement of organized ecumenism began in the American Baptist community with the merger of the **Northern Baptist Convention** (NBC) and the Free Baptist General Conference (FWB) in 1911. In 1913 the NBC joined the Federal Council of Churches of Christ as a charter member. This alienated many and encouraged others, causing Northern Baptists, for instance, to decline discussions in 1918 with the Presbyterians toward organic union. In the wake of this sentiment, however, numbers of Northern Baptists joined in local and regional ecumenical relations, such as holiday observances, councils of churches, relief projects, and the Home Mission Council. In 1948 the NBC joined the World Council of Churches, the first North American Baptist body to do so. Among the several ecumenical organizations which American Baptists have participated in are: the International Council of Religious Education, the Foreign Missions Conference of North America, the Missionary Education Movement, the Home Missions Council, the National Protestant Council on Higher Education, the United Stewardship Council, the United Council of Church Women, and Americans United for the Separation of Church and State. Subsequent to the American Baptists joining the World Council of Churches, the **Seventh Day Baptist** General Conference (SDB) also joined. Membership in the National Council of Churches and other educational organizations has allowed some Baptists to be aware of church school curriculum writing, social action projects, and theological education among other major Protestant groups. Perhaps the most extensive amount of ecumenical relationships are enjoyed in the Association of Theological Schools in the United States and **Canada**, where Baptists of almost all persuasions who have accredited seminaries interact and attend policy-making meetings on at least a biennial basis. This has led to countless projects in cooperative education across confessional lines.

Southern Baptists have rather staunchly resisted most formal ecumenical involvement. Influenced by the **Landmarkist** movement, they have not joined, for theological reasons, most regional or national cooperative bodies. The high-water mark of irenic feeling was reached in 1914 when Southern Baptists expressed a desire to participate in the Faith and Order movement, but soon the tide turned to supporting only Convention-related efforts. In the case of the **North American Baptist Fellowship** (NABF), the **Baptist World Alliance** (BWA), and the **Baptist Joint Committee on Public Affairs** (BJCPA), the SBC has joined, but it makes certain to provide the largest contribution and thus has a major role in charting the course of the bodies. During the 1960s and 1970s Southern Baptists supported observer status in World Council of Churches discussions of faith and order and meetings of the National Council of

Churches, but this drew sharp criticism and was curtailed in the 1980s. In the far-reaching missionary context of the Southern Baptist Convention, non-cooperation with ecumenical missions and local councils is required by Southern Baptists for aid to those churches and this greatly impedes Southern Baptist involvement worldwide. Against this prevailing disinclination toward ecumenism, many Southern Baptists take pride in the establishment of the Ecumenical Institute at Wake Forest University in 1968, which has sponsored dialogues with several Protestant groups and Roman Catholics.

The **Black Baptist** movement in the United States has a long record of involvement in ecumenical concerns and organizations. Together with White Baptist groups, Black Baptists have been related to other groups in significant ways, for instance the **National Baptist Convention, USA** (NBCUSA), related to the American Baptist movement, and the National Baptist Convention of America (NBCA) related to the Southern Baptist Convention. Beyond Baptist organizations, both major Black conventions supported cooperation with the Society for the Advancement of Colored People (NAACP) and the National Equal Rights League as early as 1916. In 1918 a campaign for membership in the NAACP was launched among National Baptists. With the advent of the Progressive National Baptist Convention in 1961, fully committed to ecumenism, Black Baptists cooperated with the Congress on Racial Equality (CORE), the Southern Christian Leadership Conference (SCLC), and the National Council of Churches of Christ in the USA. A number of prominent Baptist Black Americans were leaders in the ecumenical task, including **Adam Clayton Powell, Jr.**, **Martin Luther King, Jr.**, **Howard Thurman, Benjamin E. Mays**, and **Jesse Jai MacNeill**.

In Great Britain, Baptists pioneered international ecumenism and it was the founding of the Evangelical Alliance in 1846 which brought Baptists into a recognition of cooperative Christianity. **Baptist W. Noel, Charles H. Spurgeon**, and others favored cooperation with other evangelical voluntarists in both the Alliance and the Exeter Hall meetings. Later, the establishment of the Free Church Council drew Union Baptists into a new form of ecumenism with Presbyterians, Congregationalists, and Methodists. Over the years, the close ecumenical relations have been maintained by British Baptists with the Congregationalists.

John Clifford, a leader among the Baptists, joined Hugh Price Hughes (1847-1902) in 1892 in convening in Manchester the first congress of Nonconformists. This Free Church council became an annual gathering which organized free churches in the face of Anglican influence in Parliament and the Conservative Party. **J. H. Shakespeare**, the secretary of the **Baptist Union** (BU), called for the establishment in 1919 of the Federal Council of Evangelical Free Churches, in which Baptists were heavily involved. In 1939 the Federal Council and the Free Church Council merged (with the support of the Baptist Union) into the Free Church Federal Council. When the British Council of Churches was formed in 1942, Baptists were among its members, as Baptists were represented in each phase of the International Missionary Council, Life and Work, and Faith and Order movements leading up to full membership with the establishment of the World Council of Churches in 1948. In recent years, **Ernest A. Payne** led the BU into playing important roles in the World Council of Churches.

Elsewhere in the international family of Baptists there is considerable support for involvement in ecumenical affairs. In western Europe it is common for Baptist unions to participate in national ecumenical bodies; in eastern Europe it became important to unite a Christian witness under Marxist regimes. Thus, in the Baltic States, **Hungary,** and **Poland**, to name a few places, cooperation in the face of anti-Christian governments was necessary and proved productive from the 1940s through the downfall of Marxist regimes. In **Canada**, Baptists in one convention are members of the Canadian Council of Churches, and in two other conventions are part of the Evangelical Fellowship of Canada. Officially, in various parts of the world, Baptists have related to Methodists, Presbyterians, and other Reformed bodies; Lutherans and Catholics have in the last few decades also opened discussions with Baptists. In **India**, major cooperation and even integration has occurred as large numbers of congregations in West Bengal, Orissa, and Bihar voted to enter the Church of North India after it was constituted in 1970.

The **Baptist World Alliance** (BWA) has been a major catalyst toward introducing a reluctant Baptist family to Christian cooperation. From its inception, the Alliance has maintained cordial relations with other world communions and with the advent of the World Council of Churches, the BWA has supported observer status at most major meetings and activities of the World Council of Churches. Significantly, the BWA has engaged in theological dialogues with Roman Catholics, the Lutheran World Federation, the World Alliance of Reformed Churches, and the World Mennonite Conference. Negotiations have also been held with the Ecumenical Patriarchate of the Eastern Orthodox Churches. See also **Baptist World Alliance**.

EDUCATION, BAPTIST VIEWS ON. Baptist views on, and involvement in, education have varied across time and cultures. In their early development as **General Baptists**, **Particular Baptists**, and **Seventh Day Baptists**, leadership in these traditions came from a fairly high level of educational attainment, including academies, universities, and professional training. Among some early Baptists, there was a distinct disinclination toward formal **theological education** as competitive with spiritual preparation and fitness for **ministry**. Nevertheless, Baptists attended dissenter academies and after Toleration in 1689 opened their own schools, frequently associated with a church. In the 18th century American Baptists pioneered educational efforts with **Isaac Eaton**'s Grammar School (1756) in Hopewell, New Jersey, and the College of Rhode Island in Providence (1764). More and more Baptist ministers by the 19th century studied at least partially in a college or seminary (see **Higher Education**), except those in the **Primitive** and **Old School** Baptist groups. As the missionary expansion took place both at home and abroad, the opening of academies, schools, colleges, and seminaries became essential steps in establishing Baptist institutional life. Many of these, unfortunately, lacked sufficient funding and interest from Baptists and either closed or devolved into public or private institutions. Rare historically has been the Baptist collegiate institution whose student population is primarily Baptist. It is of interest that even modern **fundamentalist** Baptist groups, who often strenuously oppose "higher education," have created a significant number of educational institutions, holding to the importance of reinforcing their beliefs in a context of Christian education.

EDWARDS, MORGAN (1722-1795). British and later American Baptist minister and historian, born at Trevithin, **Wales.** Edwards was educated at Trosnant Academy under John Mathews, and later Bristol Baptist College under Bernard Foskett; initially, he was ordained to serve a church in Cork, Ireland, where he remained for nine years. In 1761 he took the advice of Dr. **John Gill** and accepted the pastoral call of the First Baptist Church of Philadelphia, Pennsylvania. He served that church until 1771 when a dispute about his drinking habits caused his severance. Edwards also itinerated in the colonies as one of the first commissioned evangelists of the Philadelphia Baptist Association. After 1771 Edwards travelled and lectured from his base at Pencader, Delaware. He compiled the first history of Baptists in the United States, entitled *Materials Toward a History of the Baptists* (7 vols, 1770-1772), based on a model suggested by the work of Welsh Baptist historian, Joshua Thomas (1719-1797). In the 1760s Edwards was a prime mover in the **Philadelphia Baptist Association** for the establishment of the College of Rhode Island and he suggested a union of Baptists in the United States. During the American Revolution he was a Loyalist, which caused him great difficulty in the Baptist community.

EGYPT. Baptist witness in Egypt commenced in 1931 with the establishment of a congregation by **Southern Baptists**. The **Baptist Bible Fellowship** (BBF) opened a mission in Egypt in 1963. The organization of Baptists, formed in 1955, is known as the General Baptist Evangelical Convention of Egypt, as it is registered with the government.

As of 1995, there were 12 churches with 550 members affiliated with the General Baptist Evangelical Convention of Egypt, 10 churches with 320 members affiliated with the Baptist International Mission in Egypt, a U.S.-based **fundamentalist** group.

ELDER. Term used among Baptists for a variety of purposes to designate both lay and clergy persons. Beginning in the 17th century, following the usage of the New Testament the pastors of local Baptist congregations were called elders. This term in the United States, especially, in New England, became the title of pastors rather than "reverend" which was associated with the episcopal or presbyterial churches. Later, most likely under the influence of Brethren or Presbyterian usage, senior lay leaders in the congregation were called "elder," usually understood to be superior to **deacons** in their election to their office.

Among some Baptist groups, like the **Freewill Baptists** in the Northeast, there was a distinction between the "teaching elder" who administered the **ordinances/sacraments** and preached the Word, and the "ruling elder" who led the congregation when the teaching elder itinerated. The ruling elder cared for the welfare and **discipline** of the congregation in addition to supervising the officers, such as **deacons.** In the mid-twentieth century, **Reformed Baptists** in the United States, some American and **Southern Baptists**, and some congregations in **Canada**, have adopted a multiple eldership, by which is meant a group of spiritual leaders who as a body provide for the various ministries of the congregation. In this case, there is not necessarily a single pastor; rather the pastoral office is divided among those of various personal gifts: teaching, pastoral care, administration, etc. Generally speaking, the deaconship is the more common terminology among Baptists to designate lay spiritual oversight within a local congregation. See also **Polity, Baptist**.

ELLA THING MEMORIAL MISSION. In 1895 amidst the expansion of missionary endeavor from North America, an independent Baptist mission was launched at Clarendon Street Baptist Church in Boston, Massachusetts. With pastor **A.J. Gordon**'s encouragement, S. B. Thing, a deacon in the Clarendon Street Church, set up a memorial fund in 1895 to honor his only daughter, Ella. The first candidates were drawn from the Gordon Missionary Training School and went to **Korea**. The concentration of the Mission was in the Korean hinterland, specifically at Kongju and Kanggyung. In 1905 the Mission withdrew from Korea to **Japan**, perhaps because of Korean aversions to bathing and the impact of this thinking upon baptismal practices. The work in Korea was assumed by **Malcolm Fenwick** and the Church of Christ in Korea. See also **Korea; Fenwick, Malcolm.**

EL SALVADOR. William Keech (fl. 1890-1915), a missionary of the **American Baptist Home Mission Society** (ABHMS), entered San Salvador in 1911, placing emphasis upon development of schools. The centers of American Baptist work were San Salvador and Santa Ana. The first organization of churches, the Baptist Convention of El Salvador, was organized in 1934. A second organization, the Associación Bautista de El Salvador, was formed among the churches in 1967. The **National Baptist Convention in the U.S.A.** (NBCUSA) began a work there in 1937. Through connections with U.S. **Southern Baptists** in Guatemala, an agreement for cooperation was struck and the Associación took on support from the Southern Baptist **Foreign Mission Board** (FMB). In 1976 the **Baptist Bible Fellowship** (BBF) opened a mission in El Salvador in the **fundamentalist** tradition.

As of 1995, there were 61 churches with 5,402 members affiliated with the Associación Bautista de El Salvador. A publication, *Boletin de Fraternidad Bautista (Bulletin of the Baptist Fraternity)*, is published by the Associación. The Baptist-related theological seminary for El Salvador is located in Santa Ana.

ENGLAND. See **Baptist Union of Great Britain and Ireland; General Baptists; Leg of Mutton Baptists; Particular Baptists; Seventh Day Baptists.**

EPHRATA COMMUNITY. See **Solitary Brethren; Beissel, Conrad.**

ESTONIA. In the 19th century there were several attempts made to establish evangelical churches in Estonia, which were always met with intense persecution from Lutherans and Orthodox. German Baptists were influential in teaching believer's **baptism**, beginning in the late 1870s and a baptism was held at Hapsal in 1884. This action, which was held in frozen waters, impressed the public and many converts were added. In 1922 a revival occurred with about a thousand converts, and the same year a seminary was opened at Kegel, the result of the **London Conference of 1920**; it was later removed to Tartu.

As of 1995, there were 86 churches and 6,474 members in the Eesti Evangeeliumi Kristlaste ja Baptistide Koguduste Liit.

ETHIOPIA. Baptist missionary work in Ethiopia commenced in 1950 with missionary appointments by the **Baptist General Conference of America** (BGC). Their first congregation was organized at Ambo, with later works at Bekoji and Gendeberet. In 1965 when **Southern Baptists (SBC)** entered the country, they set up a station in the Menz-Gishe District. Through 1977 Southern Baptist missionaries worked closely with the Orthodox churches, since Baptists were forbidden to work independently in Ethiopia. A Baptist organization, the Ethiopian Evangelical New Covenant Baptist Church, has, since 1978, assisted several groups in coordinating a Christian witness. The **Baptist Bible Fellowship** (BBF) has had a mission in Ethiopia since 1960.

As of 1995 there were 51 churches and 8,009 members affiliated with the Baptist Evangelical Association in Ethiopia.

ETHIOPIAN BAPTIST CHURCHES. Name applied to Black Baptist churches in the American South. In the 1780s the congregations of the Savannah, Georgia, region started by **George Leile**, **Andrew Bryan**, and **Andrew Marshall** were referred to by White Baptists as "Ethiopian," doubtless as a generic term for Africa, indirectly inspired by scriptural usage. It was also used to signify Black churches for **Black Baptists**.

EUROPEAN BAPTIST CONVENTION (EBC). Following World War II mission work sponsored by the **Southern Baptist Convention** (SBC) in the United States created churches of English-speaking people across Europe. Congregations were largely associated with U.S. military installations in the NATO command network and had a common Southern Baptist perspective. In 1958 an Association of Baptists in Continental Europe was formed and in 1964 an association of almost 50 churches became the European Baptist Convention (EBC). As of 1995 there are 30 churches and 2,379 members in the Convention. The Convention produces a periodical called *Highlights* (1963-).

EUROPEAN BAPTIST FEDERATION (EBF). The root of a continental organization of Baptists in Europe can be traced to the **London Conference of 1920** where comity agreements and relief projects following World War I were agreed upon under the aegis of the **Baptist World Alliance** (BWA). Turmoil again ensued with the instability in Europe in the 1930s followed by World War II. As the various unions of Baptists in Europe matured after the war, a federation of national Baptist unions was formed in 1949 under the sponsorship of the Baptist World Alliance. Since that time various programs and divisions have been formed. The EBF holds congresses every five years and promotes mission and education projects. Its divisions include Theology and Education, Mission and **Evangelism**, Communications, and External Relations. The Federation has oversight also of the International Baptist Theological Seminary in Prague, the **Czech Republic**. Among other organizations associated with it are the International Baptist Lay Academy in Budapest, **Hungary**, the European Baptist Mission, the European Baptist Press Service, the European Baptist Women's Union, and several institutes relating to Baptist and Anabaptist studies, training and education, and mission and evangelism. Its offices are located at Bad-Hamburg, Germany, and it is one of the six regional fellowships of the BWA.

As of 1995 there were 49 **conventions**/unions in 44 countries belonging to the Federation.

EVANGELICAL BAPTIST MISSIONS (EBM). In September 1928 a missionary from Africa, a pastor, Edward Drew, and six members of the Madison Avenue Baptist Church in Paterson, New Jersey, met to form a new mission sending agency, the Africa Christian Missions. The first missionary was Joseph McCaba (1899-1973) who had served as an independent missionary in **Nigeria** from 1925 to 1927; McCaba returned to the Niger Colony of French West Africa, later the Republic of **Niger**, and served until 1948 when he became the field director of the Mission. The Mission was adopted by the **General Association of Regular Baptists** in 1938 and changed its name twice: Christian Missions, Inc. (1946), and Evangelical Baptist Missions (1957). Since its founding, the EBM has supported work in Africa, **Canada**, **Martinique**, and **Algeria**, primarily in francophone areas. Its doctrinal stance is premillennial and **fundamentalistic**.

EVANGELICALISM, AND BAPTISTS. The term "evangelical" has an evolved meaning in the history of Christianity. In the early church, "evangelical" pertained to the "good news" or gospel of Jesus Christ, derived from the Greek term "euangellos." During the Reformation of the 16th century, the German form of the word, "evangelische" denoted the Protestant churches, such as the Lutheran and Reformed. The watermarks of such churches were the authority of **Scripture**, the Lordship of Christ, and a practising Christian discipleship referred to as the **priesthood of all believers**. In the 18th century, **revivals** associated with John Wesley (1703-1791) and Jonathan Edwards (1703-1758) among others, also known in North America as the **Great Awakening**, produced a following known as "evangelicals" who were considered proponents of renewal or revival in the churches. There was an increasing emphasis upon religious experience and overt manifestations of religious enthusiasm.

In the 19th century, as revivalism became more widespread and under leaders like Charles G. Finney (1792-1875), more doctrinaire and formulaic, the term "evangelical" became less an adjective and more a noun to define a growing number of people who wanted to be classed as supportive of certain emphases. These included the authority of the **bible**, the need for conversion, a new life in Christ, and a passion for **evangelism** and **missionary** outreach. As mainstream denominational life grew more complex and defined, those with evangelical sentiments seized upon the **voluntary association** form of organization and produced scores of new Christian endeavors using an essentially entrepreneurial form of Christianity which became synonymous with evangelicalism. In 1846, organized evangelicalism took a great leap forward in the formation of the Evangelical Alliance, which gave widespread respect to the term amidst the traditional and established churches.

In the 20th century, the term "evangelical" was adopted by those wanting to defend or recover the fundamentals of the faith, until several **liberal** theologians, notably **William N. Clarke**, spoke of their position as "evangelical liberals", because they did not want to loose the warmth of religious experience in their own theological systems. This led to the more definitive use of the word "fundamentalist," and the temporary abandonment of the term "evangelical." Those who wanted a more generic term were caught in the theological middle and were accused of compromising their faith principles by being too open. In the 1950s a movement, somewhat derisively called "neo-evangelicalism," grew up among open fundamentalists who wanted dialogue with more liberal and orthodox mainstream thinkers. Also to be accounted for were the younger scholars and leaders of an evangelical disposition who came to pastorates and teaching positions in the denominational circles. Carl F. H. Henry (1913-) was a primary Baptist leader of this movement.

Gradually, evangelicalism emerged again among smaller groups and individuals as a viable term in the 1960s. The revitalized National Association of Evangelicals in the United States, the Evangelical Fellowship of **Canada,** the World Evangelical Fellowship, and the Lausanne Covenant tradition gave new life to organized evangelicalism, which now included charismatics and those who argued for a social conscience in tandem with evangelism. Baptist evangelist **Billy Graham** has been a leading proponent of bridging the traditional denominations and the more highly doctrinally defined evangelical community.

Baptists have always inculcated the historic emphases of evangelicalism, such as authority of Scripture, necessity of conversion, the Lordship of Christ, a missionary imperative and discipleship. In this sense, adjectivally, Baptists are "evangelical". In addition, Baptists have for the most part been supportive of **revival** traditions, themselves becoming in the United States one of the chief beneficiaries of the revivals. Baptists in Great Britain likewise joined in significant individual numbers the Evangelical Alliance, marking Baptists among the evangelical coalitions. In the 20th century, Baptists can be found among all of the shades of the evangelical tradition: **fundamentalism**, neo-evangelicalism, the World Evangelical Fellowship, and the National Association of Evangelicals (NAE) and others. However, many Baptists in the mainstream convention and union organizations have declined to be entirely classed as evangelicals, in part because they hold that Baptists predated the formal organization of evangelicals, Baptists having pioneered the same emphases. Also, some Baptists believe that evangelicalism's demand for doctrinal statements and confessions is contrary to the historic Baptist emphasis of non-creedalism. Many Baptists feel that in cooperating with other non-Baptist groups, their doctrine of the church and **ordinances** is diluted, and thus Baptist identity is compromised.

Outside the United States, many Baptist groups have been collectively referred to as "evangelical churches" where there is a particular establishment church in existence, in contrast particularly to Roman Catholic and Orthodox Christians. This is the case in eastern Europe where under Marxist governments, and later under Orthodox establishment, Baptists, Mennonites, Adventists, and Methodists are called evangelicals. In Latin America non-Protestants are referred to as evangelicals and this includes the Baptists of varying sorts. Even in **Canada**, Baptists are historically known as part of the evangelical denominations, along with Methodists, Presbyterians, and the Free Church of Scotland.

Baptists then typically defend their right to the use of the adjective "evangelical," and it may even be imposed upon them, while separating themselves necessarily from the organizational side of the evangelical movement. There are numerous outstanding Baptists who adopt the dual terminology of also being individual evangelicals in order to maintain fellowship with other believers across confessional lines.

EVANGELISM, BAPTIST VIEWS ON. From their earliest development, Baptists have understood evangelism as both a command of Jesus Christ and a process of sharing the Gospel or Good News. In the written gospel narratives (Matt. 28:19,20; Mark 16:7-9; Luke 24:48; John 20:21) and the Acts of the Apostles (1:8), Jesus clearly commissioned his disciples to move throughout the world to share the Good News that "God so loved the world that He gave His only Son that whosoever believes in Him might have eternal life" (John 3:16). Baptists have taken this commission specially (though not exclusively) to themselves and evangelism has thus become an important characteristic of Baptist faith and life. Theologically, Baptists assume that salvation is entirely of God, not of works (Eph. 2:8ff), but that God graciously ordains that other humans should be part of the announcement of the Good News as well as exemplifying its effects in their lives. Most Baptists hold that evangelism should be followed by a commitment to become a member of a local congregation, which implies believer's **baptism** by immersion and other acts of personal discipleship and faithfulness (Acts 8:26-39; 16:30-34).

In their early development some Baptists in Britain and North America debated whether evangelism was to be conducted for all persons or for an "Elect" of God (see **Primitive Baptists; Strict Baptists**). Some held that evangelism was an awakening by the Holy Spirit of the Elect, while others believed it was the church's responsibility to preach the gospel so that people led of God's Spirit could respond at will. These differences have survived in the Strict, Primitive, or Calvinistic Baptist groups on the one hand, and the more open or "**Arminian**" groups on the other.

Evangelism has been a high priority in local church activity. Most Baptists believe it is the responsibility of every believer to share the gospel. Some groups, such as the **Southern Baptists** and others in the **fundamentalist** groups, pray for evangelism, witness to others, and hold special services or opportunities where evangelists can call forth public decisions in response to a sermon. **Billy Graham**, following earlier evangelists like Billy Sunday (1862-1935), has come to symbolize "crusade" evangelism. Still other Baptists in North America and Europe can be seen preaching in public places, or conducting house-to-house visits, two other long-used Baptist strategies of evangelism. In the 1960s and 1970s Baptists in the **American Baptist Convention** (ABC) affiliation stressed "corporate evangelism," in which they emphasized a Christian witness to social and economic structures in addition to a call for personal acceptance of Christ, generated from the **social gospel** thinking of **Walter Rauschenbusch** and others. Symbolically, evangelism occupies a prominent place among many Baptist groups. Many Baptist newspapers and journals are titled "messenger" or "herald" or "sower."Proclamation is also a common term which emphasizes sharing the Gospel through preaching and teaching.

EVANS, BENJAMIN (1803-1872). English Baptist minister, educator, and historian, born at Bilston. Early in life he was employed as an artist, later studying theology with **William Steadman** at Horton. He was pastor at Scarborough (1825-1862), the largest and most influential congregation in the northeast of Yorkshire. Evans was active in many of the **voluntary** associations of his day, including the Society for Liberating Religion from State Patronage and Control, the Archaeological Society, and the Bethel Mission to Seamen. He is said to have travelled thousands of miles in an open gig in support of denominational causes. At 64 years old Evans founded the Theological College at Bury and assumed the chair in ecclesiastical history there. He established and edited the *Baptist Record*, largely for the benefit of **Strict Baptists**. His historical work was considerable: he wrote a two-volume history, *The Early English Baptists* (1862-1864), in which he undertook pioneering research in the British Museum and the archives in Amsterdam, and he completed the histories of Rawdon College and Horton Academy (1854). He corresponded officially with Baptists in the United States and contributed to the library of the American Baptist Historical Society. The University of Rochester in New York awarded Evans an honorary D. D. in 1857.

EVANS, CHRISTMAS (1766-1838). Welsh Baptist minister and evangelist, born at Llandyssul. He was first a farmer; from a study of the **bible** he began to preach informally. Baptized as an adult by Timothy Thomas in 1788, he was ordained two years later by the Welsh Baptists as an itinerating **missionary**. Early in life he suffered several mishaps, including being waylaid and beaten, the result of which was the permanent loss of one eye and facial disfiguration. This made him somewhat of a curiosity, and coupled with his great preaching abilities, he drew vast crowds. While he spent much of his focused **ministry** in Anglesey, he held open air campaigns across **Wales** and in parts of England. Not only did his preaching renew the Baptist movement in the first decades of the 19th century but also his work helped to revive the Welsh language. He was well known for his narrative sermon on the Gadarene Demoniac, whom he portrayed. Evans was Calvinistic, much appreciative of **John Gill**. He supported mission societies and a compensated ministry. Christmas Evans's published sermons were reprinted regularly in Welsh and English well into the 19th century. See **Wales, Baptists in**.

EXECUTIVE MINISTER. Terminology which is applied among American Baptist Churches and certain Canadian Baptists to describe the senior executive officer of a state **convention**, city society, or regional convention. The title succeeds that of "agent," "corresponding secretary," "executive secretary," or "general secretary," found in early 19th century Baptist polity at the provincial, state, or city level of administration in North America.

Before the American development of Baptist polity and terminology, "general superintendent" and "**messenger**" were used in the English tradition, and the compensated corresponding secretary (at least for expenses!) of a missionary society was typical, as in the **Baptist Missionary Society** (BMS) from 1792 and the **Baptist Union** (BU) from 1832. In the United States this pattern was seen in Massachusetts from 1802.

The executive staff of the early American societies were also voluntary. The first state convention paid employee appears to have been John Peck (1780-1849), general, agent of the Baptist Missionary Convention of the State of New York, beginning in 1825. As the statewide Baptist communities organized and became involved in missionary activity, a definite need for supervision arose and each one in turn appointed such persons to administrative and traveling tasks. When the **American Baptist Home Mission Society** (ABHMS) was organized in 1832, it developed patterns of cooperation with the various state **associations** and conventions, and this often led to funding of the general secretary role as a missionary superintendent. The ABHMS followed this pattern in the development of western U.S. state conventions, appointing its senior missionary as an administrator, for instance in Minnesota, the Dakotas, California, and Washington State.

In 1919 the **New World Movement** called for the state secretaries to become collecting agents for the **Northern Baptist Convention** (NBC) and its auxiliaries, and this led to a national role for the secretaries and the formation of the Organization of State Convention Secretaries in the 1920s. The use of the term "corresponding" or "executive secretary" continued to be popular through the 1950s.

Reorganization of state and national bodies took place in the 1960s with fundamental changes occurring in 1972-1973. The first instance of the new title "executive minister" in the United States occurred in 1977 among regional secretaries of the **American Baptist Churches**. This title, provided for in the Report of the Study Commission on Relationships (SCOR) of December 9, 1976, became the title of all state and city secretaries, originally 37 in number. It conveyed both a regional and national accountability. Among Canadian Baptists the term "executive minister" appears to have been adopted in the later 1970s first in the Baptist Union of Western Canada, in response to the Janssen Report, issued by an ABHMS consultant to the Baptist Convention of Ontario and Quebec, Lawrence H. Janssen (1921-1995).

The executive minister is usually accountable to a board or council of a convention and has oversight of the staff and program of the organization. The office has influence only in the life of member congregations and limited ceremonial importance at assemblies where the elected voluntary officers preside over sessions. In certain circumstances, the executive minister may be the supervisor of the area or of regional ministers. Sociologically, the executive minister assumes many of the functions associated with the episcopacy in other denominations, including registrar of the ministerial roster, conflict resolution, and pastoral ministry to local church **pastors**. See also **American Baptist Home Mission Society; Area Minister; Polity, Baptist.**

F

FAMILISTS. Name applied to a 17th century English religious sect related to the early Baptist movement. The "Family" or "House of Love" was established about 1540 in Emden, Westphalia, by Hendrik Nicklaes (1502-1580?). Although the Elizabethan Act of Uniformity attempted to eliminate groups like the Familists, they continued underground in conventicles. The Family was organized as a perfectionist brotherhood with hopes for the establishment of a thousand-year reign of Christ and the saints, which would be ushered in by an outpouring of the Holy Spirit. Familist organization drew upon **Anabaptist** patterns, with three classes of priests, and no apostolic succession. Members were subject to the **discipline** of the brotherhood. Ethically, the Family was pacifistic and refused to take oaths. Seventeenth-century writers, notably the Presbyterian Thomas Edwards (1599-1647), considered the Familists as the root of radical ideas and behavior, influencing Quakers, Baptists, and **Fifth Monarchists.** A significant number of Familists evolved into Quakers, some surviving into the 1680s in Ely, England. See also **Diggers; Levellers; Ranters; Seekers.**

FAUNCE, WILLIAM HERBERT PERRY (1859-1930). American Baptist minister and educator, born at Worcester, Massachusetts. He was educated at Brown University and Newton Theological Institution, later spending a year in advanced studies at the University of Jena in **Germany.** He served the pastorate of State Street Baptist Church in Springfield, Massachusetts, and from 1889-1899, Fifth Avenue Baptist in New York City. An able orator and thinker, he served as lecturer at the University of Chicago and as campus preacher at Harvard University.

Faunce was elected president of Brown University in 1899 and expanded the program of the university in buildings and curriculum. Among his accomplishments, Faunce had the charter changed to allow for a non-Baptist president, in defense of religious freedom of the institution. This caused a great uproar in the **Northern Baptist Convention** and led ultimately to the separation of Brown as a church-related institution. A second tumultuous incident occurred in Faunce's career when McMaster University in **Canada** conferred upon him an honorary degree and drew the wrath of conservative evangelicals in the Baptist Convention of Ontario and Quebec.

Faunce was a leading **liberal** thinker of his era, interested in the historical-critical study of **Scripture** and the ethical issues inherent in the Christian faith. He defended United States entry into World War I and later championed the League of Nations. His Lyman Beecher Lectures at Yale in 1908 were published as *The Educational Ideal in Ministry*. In retirement he toured the mission fields of the Baptists, taking particular interest in **China**, and he was president of the World Peace Foundation. Faunce's published works include *The Social Aspects of Foreign Missions* (1914), *Religion and War* (1918), and *What Are the Fundamentals?* (1923).

FELLER, HENRIETTE ODIN (1800-1868). Canadian Baptist educator, born at Montmagny, **France**. About 1833 Henriette Feller met Henri Olivier (fl.1800-1840), who introduced her to the Swiss Evangelical Movement and she joined his church at Lausanne. At length, Olivier and his wife moved to Lower **Canada** (now Quebec) in 1834 to conduct missionary work. They induced Henriette and another young person, **Louis Roussy**, to come to Canada and Henriette arrived in 1835. In 1836 she moved to a rural location at Grand Ligne where she and Roussy started a school and did evangelistic work as the Mission de la Grande Ligne en Canada. Frequently they suffered persecution and fled to upstate New York, for instance in 1837. Support for Feller's work was broadened and a permanent mission house was erected in 1840. Over the next 20 years, Baptist congregations increased in the region, leading to the eventual formation of the Union des Eglises Baptistes Françaises (French-Speaking Union of Canadian Baptists).

FELLOWSHIP OF BAPTISTS FOR HOME MISSIONS (FBHM). An independent American domestic missionary agency which conducts **evangelism** and church planting in the United States. Formed in July 1941 of missionaries and laymen at the First Baptist Church, Elyria, Ohio, the Fellowship grew out of **fundamentalist** discontent with the **Northern**

Baptist Convention and was adopted by the **General Association of Regular Baptist Churches** (GARBC) as its home mission agency. Its stated objectives were evangelization of the unsaved and establishment of New Testament churches. Several organizational mergers have taken place: the Montana Baptist Fellowship (1941) joined in 1948, and in 1950 the Western Baptist Missions (including the **Columbia Basin Mission**) and the West Virginia Fundamental Baptist Mission united with the Fellowship. A national council and an advisory council guide the work of the mission, whose headquarters are located in Elyria, Ohio. The Mission published the *Home Fellowship News*.

FELLOWSHIP OF BRITISH BAPTISTS. Formed in 1994, the Fellowship owes its origin to the suggestion in 1991 of **Baptist Union of Great Britain** (BU) General Secretary Bernard Green (1925-) that those with common interests should consult and plan together. The Fellowship is composed of representatives of the Baptist Unions of **Scotland**, **Wales**, Great Britain, and the **Baptist Missionary Society** (BMS); it meets at least annually for fellowship, consultation, and mission planning. The Fellowship represents all of the mainstream Baptists in Britain and Northern Ireland in a less formal mode than in the historic national/regional structures.

FELLOWSHIP OF EVANGELICAL BAPTIST CHURCHES IN CANADA (FEBC). In the mid-1920s against the background of the **Fundamentalist**-Modernist controversy in the United States, a schism broke out in the Baptist Convention of Ontario and Quebec. Led by **Thomas Todhunter Shields** an investigation was launched in 1923-1925 into modernist tendencies at McMaster University, specifically concerning the appointment of **L. H. Marshall** as professor of pastoral theology. The 1926 Convention adopted a resolution of censure against Shields and the following year the Convention voted to **disfellowship** 13 churches. Immediately a new group was formed behind the leadership of Shields, the Union of Regular Baptist Churches of Ontario and Quebec. A further split occurred in 1931-1933 which spawned a loosely knit group in 1933, the Fellowship of Independent Baptist Churches of Canada. The doctrinal basis of this fellowship affirmed **voluntary association** and premillennialism. Related to this movement were the Fundamentalist Baptist Young People's Association (1927) and the Muskoka Baptist Conference (1931).

In the late 1920s several Baptist churches in Alberta and British Columbia also coalesced around fundamentalistic principles and formed the British Columbia Regular Baptists (1927) and the Regular Baptist

Missionary Fellowship in Alberta (1930). For a time, these western movements sought a relationship with the U.S. **Southern Baptists (SBC)** who had started mission churches in the region. Ultimately, the Southern Baptist connection broke down and Southern Baptists organized their own separate work in Canada. Between 1950 and 1953 merger discussions took place between the major groups of fundamentalist Baptists, and the result was the establishment of the Fellowship of Evangelical Baptist Churches in Canada in Toronto in October 1953. Over the years, Fellowship Baptists have supported mission work through **Baptist Mid-Missions** and the **Association of Baptists for World Evangelism** (ABWE), two U.S.-based organizations, as well as their own work, the **Japan** Regular Baptist Mission at Takaoka (1952), and missions at Ellichpur, **India** (1963), and in **Indonesia** (1967).

In 1938 the Fellowship formally began a francophone mission in northern Quebec which encompassed 76 churches and 4,700 members as of 1995. There is also a theological school, Seminaire Baptiste Evangélique du Québec, in Montreal.

For educational purposes, in the central region, the Fellowship related to the London (Ontario) Baptist Bible College and Central Baptist Seminary in Toronto, which were merged in 1993 to become Heritage Baptist College and Seminary in Hespeler, Ontario. In the Western provinces, a separate educational heritage evolved: in 1934 the Regular Baptist Churches of the Prairies founded the Western Baptist Bible College, which closed in 1940. In 1945 the Regular Baptists of British Columbia and the Prairies opened the Northwest Baptist Bible College at Port Coquitlam, British Columbia, which in due course became the Northwest Baptist Theological College, now a member of the Associated Canadian Theological Schools (ACTS) in Langley, British Columbia. Numerous ministerial students in the Fellowship family have been trained at the Ontario Theological Seminary (later Tyndale Theological Seminary) in Toronto and also at various conservative evangelical schools in the United States. The group publishes the *Evangelical Baptist* (1953-) and claims 512 congregations and 65,246 members across Canada (1995).

FELLOWSHIP OF EVANGELICAL BAPTIST CHURCHES IN EUROPE. An organization of conservative **evangelical** Baptists who in 1967 banded together for fellowship and mission to greater Europe and beyond. Included in the coalition are the **Strict Baptists** of England, Evangelical Baptists of **France**, and the Irish Baptists. The Fellowship is characterized by a doctrinal statement and opposition to ecumenical organizations such as the **Baptist World Alliance**.

FENWICK, MALCOLM (1863-1935). Canadian evangelical and later Korean Baptist missionary and minister, born at Markham, Ontario. He worked on a model farm in Ontario and then went to Manitoba. He was called to foreign mission service while attending the Niagara Bible Conference. He married Fanny Hinds, who had taught for the Methodists in **Korea** and studied under **A. J. Gordon.** About 1893 Fenwick met Gordon and was influenced by his teaching. In 1894 with Joseph Douglas of Toronto, Fenwick started the Corean Itinerant mission which supported him later in Korea. His ministry in Korea was based in Sorai and Wonsan, where he conducted a school. In 1901 Fenwick merged his work with the **Ella Thing Memorial Mission** to form the Church of Christ in Korea. Fenwick served from 1909-1914 as the "kammok," or superintendent-**pastor** of this body and earned a reputation as an authority figure in the church. Over the years of his missionary work, Fenwick gradually evolved into a Baptistic thinker, with definite leanings toward the conservative **evangelical** tradition. See also **Korea.**

FIFTH MONARCHY MOVEMENT. A 17th century movement among Baptists and others in England which exhibited biblical literalism applied to the political context. Among the **General** and **Particular** Baptists and other Nonconformists in the 1640s were those who understood the **Scriptures** literally and took a special interest in the apocalyptic passages in the biblical books of Daniel and Revelation. A few hundred people during the last years of the reign of King Charles I, led by Col. Thomas Harrison (1606-1660), concluded that Christ was due to return to earth as a king and establish the fifth monarchy of Daniel 7:1-8. The new kingdom was thought to be composed of saints, without priest or **sacrament**, law or oath, king or government. They expressed an interest in putting Charles I to death in order to hasten the coming of Christ's kingdom.

Fifth Monarchists also in due course opposed Oliver Cromwell's (1599-1658) taking the title of king and proclaimed him an apostate and the little horn of Daniel's prophecy, when in December 1653 he accepted power over the Commonwealth. That event brought calculations of the biblical 1260 days and plans for an insurrection to overthrow the "beast." Fearing an insurrection, Cromwell had many Fifth Monarchists, including Harrison, thrown into prison. In 1660 Harrison was hanged, drawn, and quartered; this incited Thomas Venner (d.1661), a cooper, to rise up against the government, resulting in a violent defeat of the Fifth Monarchists at Cripplegate. Such political events, plus errors of calculation, proved the falsity of the fifth monarchy idea, and most of the chiliastic sentiment died.

Many of those who held a literalistic biblical hermeneutic, however, found in the recovery of the sabbath a new cause, and they shifted to the **Seventh Day** movement, which included some Baptists and others. The major Baptist activists and writers in the Fifth Monarchy Movement were **Henry Jessey, Hanserd Knollys,** John Pendarves (1622-1656), Henry Danvers, **Peter Chamberlen,** and **Vavasor Powell.** In order to clear the name of Baptists from charges of extremism, both General and Particular Baptists published a document, *The Humble Apology of some commonly called Anabaptist* (1660), the first joint effort of all Baptists. The contributions of Fifth Monarchist Baptists include the application of new hymns to old tunes. See also **Diggers;** **Dispensationalism; Levellers; Ranters; Seekers.**

FINLAND. Baptist development in Finland evolved as an outgrowth of Swedish Baptist missionary endeavor and from crosscurrents of relationships. As early as 1854 Carl J. M. Mollersvard (1832-1901) preached on Foglö Island and a chapel was erected at Jakobstad in 1871. In 1870 Esaias Lundberg, baptized by a Swedish sailor, founded the first Finnish-speaking congregation; later John Hymander (1803-1877) went to Stockholm to be baptized and returned to form a congregation at Parikkala. A District Union of the Swedish-speaking churches was established in 1883 and renamed in 1893 "Conference of the Baptist Denomination in Finland." Some strife occurred between the Swedish-speaking churches and what became the Suomen Baptistiyhdyskunta (Finnish Union), formed in 1903; the Swedish-speaking congregations separated from the Finnish-speaking churches in 1922, essentially creating a second organization, Svenska Baptisternas i Finland. A newspaper, *Kodin ystava* (Friend of Homes), began publication in 1896 and a **bible** institute opened in 1949. The Swedish churches publish *Missions Standaret* (1914-) and the Finnish churches publish *Tootuuden kaiku* (Echo of the Truth). Theological education is conducted at a bible school in Tampere. In addition to the indigenous work, **Baptist Mid-Missions** from the United States established a mission in 1980.

As of 1995, there were 11 churches and 655 members in the Suomen Baptistiyhdyskunta and 21 churches and 1,461 members in the Svenska Baptisternas i Finland.

FINNISH BAPTIST UNION OF AMERICA. At the beginning of the 20th century, significant numbers of Finnish emigrants went to the United States and intermingled particularly with the Swedish communities in the Great Lakes region. At length missions were conducted and two congregations emerged in 1900: Worcester, Massachusetts, and Felch,

Michigan. The preaching of pioneer evangelist Matts Esselstrom (1868-1949) and Albert M. Wickstrom (1872-1951), a physician and **bible** teacher, were important catalysts in church development.

A conference, the Finnish Baptist Mission Union of America (also known as the Baptist Union of America and, after 1947, the Baptist Mission Union of America), was formed in 1901 at Austin, near Chicago, Illinois. It served primarily to send out evangelists to Finns and Swedes in the United States and **Canada**, focusing mainly on Michigan, Minnesota, Wisconsin, and Illinois. The Union published for a time *Finnoka Missions Posten* (Mission Post) (1906-). In the 1940s, the Union included about 19 churches and 1,000 members. After 1948 the congregations were invited to affiliate with the **Baptist General Conference** (Swedish) and most were absorbed into its work. For a period in the 1940s the Union was also affiliated with the **Northern Baptist Convention**.

FIVE PRINCIPLE CALVINISTIC BAPTISTS. In the U.S. colonial New England context, a coalition of churches emerged between 1639 and 1740 in Massachusetts, Rhode Island, and Connecticut known as Five Principle Calvinistic Baptists. The name signified their affirmation of historic Calvinistic doctrines as stated in the Westminster **Confession of Faith** (1646): total depravity, unmerited favor, limited atonement, irresistible grace, and the perseverance of the saints. The Five Principle Calvinistic Baptists were divided into two camps, those who worshipped on the first day and those who worshipped on the **seventh day**. The sabbatarians had two congregations before 1740, Westerly and Newport, Rhode Island. The first day churches included those at Boston, Swansea, Tiverton, Rehoboth, Sutton, Bellingham, Leicester, South Brimfield, and West Springfield in Massachusetts, and at Wallingford in Connecticut. Generally, the Five Principle Calvinistic Baptists in New England closely imitated the **Particular Baptists** in England and **Wales** in the 17th century. See also **General Six Principle Baptists**.

FLEISCHMANN, KONRAD ANTON (1812-1867). American German Baptist minister, born in Nuremberg, Germany. In his youth he travelled in **Switzerland** and **Germany**, ultimately being converted under the Swiss Separatists. He studied for the ministry under Karl von Rodt, experienced persecution from the Reformed Church in Switzerland and emigrated to America in 1839. He came under **American Baptist** influence and was commissioned by the **American Baptist Home Mission Society** as a missionary to the Germans in eastern Pennsylvania. In the winter of 1841 he was part of a great revival in central Pennsylvania. The next year he moved to Philadelphia where he baptized five candidates and gathered the first German Baptist Church in the United States. In 1851 he organized the first German Baptist Conference and in 1853 he began publication of *Der Senbote des Evangeliums* (The Gospel Messenger). Fleischmann is considered the founding father of the German Baptist movement in the United States. See also **North American Baptist Conference**.

FOOTWASHING. A recognized **ordinance** among several Baptist groups, including some **Primitive Baptists**, **Black Baptists**, **Glasites**, and the **Scotch Baptists** of the 19th century. The washing of feet in the ancient Near East was done for practical purposes of cleanliness and comfort where people travelled by foot and wore open sandles. Usually a servant in the family or household washed the feet of newly arrived travellers (Gen. 18:4; Judges 19:21; II Sam. 11:8; Canticles 5:3).

Three passages in the New Testament indicate that the washing of feet was relevant to the early Christian community. In John 13: 14-15 Jesus washed the feet of His disciples and asserted that they ought to wash the feet of each other. This passage has meant for some in the Brethren tradition (and some Baptists) that it should become a gospel ordinance practiced by believers in the church. In the early 19th century, a debate arose among New England Baptists to that end. Among the objections raised were whether footwashing was meant to be universal, that it had never being recorded as part of New Testament liturgy, the excessive time that it would take, that it would be difficult for men and women to wash each other's feet, and that the task seemingly implied by I Timothy 5:9-10 in which a woman appears to have the task of washing people's feet as part of her household service would be deemed too exclusive. These objections prevented footwashing from becoming a widely accepted gospel ordinance among Baptists.

In the instances where footwashing is practiced, the ceremony, called the pedalavium, is simple. At a service which begins with self-examination, the text is commonly John 13. The congregation is divided according to sex, with men serving men and women serving women. Among **German Baptist Brethren**, the oldest sibling first washes the feet of the first sibling on the right and that person in turn washes the feet of the one on his/her right, until the entire company has participated. The leader uses a small basin of tepid water to dip a towel, then with dried hands, may shake the hand of the one served and perhaps use the kiss of peace or offer a prayer. The first male and female initially gird themselves with the drying towel, in the form of a servant.

Most Baptists have taken footwashing as a symbolic gesture to teach humility and servanthood, actually practicing it rarely, such as only during Lent or Passion Week.

FOREIGN MISSION BOARD, SOUTHERN BAPTIST CONVENTION (FMB). The Southern Baptist Foreign Mission Board in the United States is the largest missionary organization belonging to the Baptist family. In 1845 with the organization of the **Southern Baptist Convention**, one of the first tasks was to promote foreign missions and a "Board of Foreign Missions" was set up in Richmond, Virginia. The original governing body included officers of the Convention, plus several elected by the Convention, and a board of managers local to the Richmond area. **James B. Taylor** was chosen corresponding secretary and served until 1871. The first mission fields were **China** and Africa and, after the American Civil War, **Italy**. Negotiations were held with the **Baptist Board of Foreign Missions** (BBFM), with which Baptist churches in the South had previously cooperated; one missionary under appointment to that Board, **J. Lewis Shuck**, transferred to the Southern Board. During the American Civil War, operations of the Foreign Mission Board virtually closed down for four years. Afterward, under the leadership of **Henry A. Tupper**, expansion into China, **Nigeria**, Italy, **Mexico**, and **Japan** took place. Tupper also resurrected the appointment of female missionaries with Lulu Whilden and the **Moon** sisters in 1873 and shepherded the establishment of the auxiliary Woman's Missionary Union in 1888. Important steps were taken in 1851 with the first female appointment, Harriet Baker (fl.1850), and its first commissioning service that year, and in 1875 with the appointment of Black missionaries W. J. David (1850-1919) and W.W. Colley (1847-1879) to Yoruba Land.

During the early years of its evolution, the Foreign Mission Board experimented with several scenarios of appointment and work, as in **Sierra Leone** where in 1855 it assumed the support of personnel from other sources. In its expanding witness after the turn of the century, however, the Foreign Mission Board confronted the issue of cooperation in world mission with other Baptist and Christian organizations. In 1916 the Board approved a policy of complete autonomy at home and abroad, rejecting arbitrary territorial boundaries, and any form of cooperation which was not accountable to the Convention and under its control. This has often meant that Southern Baptist missionaries work in fields already occupied by other Baptists. Much of the initiative of the Board, however, has been in previously unevangelized fields. Since 1845 Southern Baptists have worked in 155 countries; presently they operate in 117 nations/people groups with over 4,000 missionaries. The Foreign Mission

Board has received 50 per cent of the annual Cooperative Program receipts since 1925, and the remaining funds for overseas work have come from the annual Lottie Moon Christmas Offering.

In 1997 with the reorganization of the Southern Baptist Convention, the Foreign Mission Board became the International Mission Board of the Southern Baptist Convention. The Board's official publication has been *The Commission* (1849-1850; 1938-).

FORTRESS MONROE CONFERENCE. Following the era of Civil War and Reconstruction in the United States (1861-1877), the Baptist communities of the North and South competed in missionary efforts, particularly among the Black population. Representatives of the **Southern Baptist Convention** (SBC) requested a meeting with the **American Baptist Home Mission Society** (ABHMS), which had long operated schools, colleges, church planting programs, and **chapel car evangelism** in the southern states. Ostensibly the SBC wanted the ABHMS to cease its work in the region. On September 12-14, 1894, the representatives met at Fortress Monroe, Virginia, the site of a federal prison during the Civil War where President of the Confederacy Jefferson Davis had been incarcerated. A series of agreements were reached which provided for assumption of greater influence in the schools for **Black Baptists**, cooperation in mission work among Blacks, and that a principle of comity be agreed upon whereby the two Baptist groups would not compete in the same region and focus their energies upon fields not already occupied by either. The Fortress Monroe Conference established a principle of mutual recognition of the two major U.S. Baptist groups until the SBC voted in the mid-1940s to establish churches in the northern states because of migration of southerners to the North.

FOSDICK, HARRY EMERSON (1878-1969). American Baptist minister, born at Buffalo, New York. He was educated at Colgate University and Union Theological Seminary and later took a master's degree at Columbia University. His early mentor was **William Newton Clarke** at Colgate. He served three pastorates, First Baptist, Montclair, New Jersey (1904-1915), First Presbyterian Church, New York (1918-1925), and Park Avenue Baptist Church, New York City. Under Fosdick's leadership, Park Avenue evolved into Riverside Church in the Morningside Heights area of New York's Upper West Side. During World War I he served with the American Expeditionary Forces in Europe and developed a pacifist position. As a pulpiteer, Fosdick had few equals and he quickly became one of the most highly quoted clergymen of his era. In his Park Avenue congregation were **John D. Rockefeller** and James **Colgate**; Rockefeller built a new edifice on Fosdick's irenic theology, Riverside Church, dedicated in 1931.

At the outbreak of the **Fundamentalist** crusade, Fosdick preached a sermon "Shall the Fundamentalists Win?" which became a battle cry for both the liberal camp and fundamentalists. His pastoral approach to the **bible** and popular dependence upon the documentary hypothesis of the origins of the Pentateuch (*The Modern Use of the Bible*, 1924) brought popularity as well as scorn, and his stance on civil rights and against war likewise galvanized people. Fosdick also devoted his communications gifts to Union Seminary, teaching practical theology there from 1908-1946. He was the weekly preacher on the "National Vespers Hour," an influential ecumenical radio broadcast. Fosdick was awarded an honorary doctorate from the University of Glasgow. Memorable Fosdick publications include *What Shall We Do With Jesus?* (1922), *Science and Religion* (1924), and *The Unknown Soldier* (1934).

FOSTER, GEORGE BURMAN (1857-1918). American Baptist minister and theologian, born at Alderson, West Virginia. He graduated from West Virginia University and studied theology in German universities at Berlin and Göttingen. In the 1880s he served congregations at Morgantown, West Virginia, and Saratoga Springs, New York, preferring a career in academic life. In 1892 he took a teaching position in philosophy at McMaster University in Toronto, Ontario, later moving to the University of Chicago in 1896 at the invitation of **William Rainey Harper**. A controversial systematic theologian, he developed his theology on the basis of human experience and moved in the then fashionable streams of pragmatism in American intellectual thought. A member of the famous "**Chicago School**," he was described as one of the most intellectual theologians ever to develop in the Baptist tradition and he influenced many **liberal** thinkers, including **Douglas Clyde Macintosh**. Foster's major works include *The Finality of the Christian Religion* (1906) and *The Function of Religion in Man's Struggle for Existence* (1909).

FOX, WILLIAM (1736-1826). Baptist businessman and humanitarian, born at Clapton, England. He was apprenticed a draper and mercer and operated his own successful business at an early age. He was a member of **Benjamin Beddome**'s congregation at Bourton-on-Water, but later moved to London. He became a **deacon** at Prescott Street Church in London under the **ministry** of **Abraham Booth** and engaged in numerous humanitarian efforts, including feeding and clothing the hungry. In May 1785 at the King's Head Tavern in the Poultry, London, he introduced a plan for universal education and this reached the attention of a number of important thinkers, including Robert Raikes (1735-1811). In collaboration with Raikes, Fox began in 1785 the Society for the Establishment and Support of **Sunday Schools** throughout the Kingdom of Great Britain, which aimed to teach children to read the **bible** and fulfilled Fox's dream of universal education. He was treasurer of the **Baptist Home Mission Society** (BHMS) and a friend of political leaders, Granville Sharp (1735-1813) and William Wilberforce (1759-1833).

FRANCE. Early France was the scene of several significant baptisteries, and during the Middle Ages, the Albigensians and Waldensians found refuge in the eastern mountains. Modern Baptist life in France reaches back to 1810 in French Flanders when, through a home **bible** study at Nomain, persons were first baptized and a church was organized after 1815 by Henri Pyt (1797?-?), a disciple of **Robert Haldane**. Some of Pyt's followers became active **colporteurs** for various societies in France. Later, with assistance from the **American Baptist Missionary Union** (ABMU), another mission began with **Casimir Rostan** and Isaac Willmarth (1804-1891). The first church was constituted in 1835 at Douai, while Rostan and Willmarth concentrated their efforts at Paris. A "school of the prophets" to train Christian workers was formed at Douai about 1839 and later moved to Paris. The Fédération des Eglises Evangéliques Baptistes de France (French Baptist Federation) was formed in 1919, uniting the Fédération des Eglises Baptistes du Nord de la France with the Association des Eglises Baptistes Franco-Suisses. In 1920 Arthur Blocher led a secession over theological issues and in 1921 R. Dubarry and M. G. Guyot with six churches formed the Association Evangelique d'Eglises Baptistes de Langue Française, with congregations in France, **Belgium**, and **Switzerland**, plus missions in Madagascar and **Martinique**.

There were also British Baptist missions in Brittany (BMS) and the Welsh Baptists sponsored missions among the Bretons, centered in Morlaix. The **Conservative Baptist** Foreign Mission Society (CBFMS) since 1962 has conducted a mission in conjunction with the Baptist Evangelical Alliance of East and North Paris. **Baptist Mid-Missions** (BMM) from the United States have a French center, located at Bordeaux with a bible institute, and the **Baptist Bible Fellowship** (BBF) began a mission in 1970. In 1984 the **Association of Baptists for World Evangelism** (ABWE) opened a mission in France.

As of 1995, there were 111 churches and 6,404 members in the Fédération des Eglises Evangéliques Baptistes de France. The French Baptist periodical is *Croire et Servir* (Believe and Serve) (1924-). There is a Baptist-related theological school in Paris.

FREE BAPTISTS. See **Free(will) Baptists**.

FREE CHRISTIAN BAPTIST CONFERENCE. See **Free(will) Baptists**.

FREE COMMUNION BAPTISTS. See **Free(will) Baptists**.

FREE GRACE GENERAL BAPTISTS. See **General Baptists**.

FREEDOM OF CONSCIENCE. Terminology common among Baptist writers on **religious liberty**. On the basis of Acts 5:29 and Galatians 5:1 humans possess in the image of God a conscience or moral decision-making capability which is free to choose good or evil. Conscience is coerced by other individuals, the church, or the state. Baptists oppose any form of coercion of the conscience. This generally includes freedom to decide whether to worship or not, to join with a congregation, to change ecclesiastical affiliations, to nurture children and new adherents to the faith, to choose religious instruction, to express and propagate one's faith, to travel in the interests of religion, to associate for religious purposes, to contribute to religious causes, to make judgments on issues for religious reasons, and to have free access to religious information. The key element in freedom of conscience is the **voluntary** nature of one's choice. See also **Religious Liberty; Voluntarism**.

FREE(WILL) BAPTISTS (FWB). A North American phenomenon which began in the **ministry** of several preachers in the colony of New Hampshire in the 1770s. Theologically, Freewill Baptists are akin to, but not connected with, the **General Baptist** movement. **Benjamin Randal** was foremost among the early itinerants in advancing the Freewill Baptist "Connexion." Like other 18th century awakeners, he travelled to preaching stations in Vermont, New Hampshire, and Maine in the United States across a period of three decades, emphasizing free grace, free will, and free communion. Many of Randal's preaching stations eventually became permanent monthly meetings. Elder **John Buzzell**, successor to Randal, is credited with shaping the denominational structure.

As the "connexion" multiplied, the monthly meetings combined to form "quarterly meetings," roughly equivalent to regular Baptist associations. By the 1820s several quarterly meetings had united to form a "Yearly Meeting," the equivalent of a state convention. Finally, in 1827 the first Freewill Baptist General Conference met at Tunbridge, Vermont, uniting the entire movement nationally with a single purpose, reporting procedure, and statistical directory. Later, other **voluntary** associations followed: the Freewill Baptist Book Concern (1831), the Freewill Baptist

Foreign Mission Society (1832), the Freewill Baptist Home Mission Society (1834), and the Freewill Baptist Education Society (1840). The unusual terminology, "meetings," employed by the Freewill Baptists to identify their **polity**, was derived from Randal the founder, who appears to have syncretized elements of Quaker, Methodist, and Congregationalist polities into his own experience.

In 1841 the Freewill Baptists merged with the Free Communion Baptists, a group of churches mostly located in New York State. Free Communion Baptists affirmed open communion, experiential religion, trinitarianism, and high ethical standards. The group was supportive of voluntary organizations for benevolent purposes and liberally gave to Freewill Baptist enterprises. The resulting denomination was referred to as the "Free Baptists." The Freewill Baptist congregations in the Canadian Maritime provinces in 1836 organized themselves as the Free Christian Baptist Conference and cooperated fully with the U. S. Free Baptist General Conference. *The Morning Star* (1826-1911), a Freewill Baptist newspaper, was merged into *The Watchman.*

The Free(will) Baptists maintained correspondence with several theologically Arminian groups, including the New Connection of General Baptists in England. This led to the visit of a delegation of New Connection Baptists, **Jabez Burns** and **Joseph Goadby**, to the United States in 1848 and a reciprocal visit by Noyes to Britain the same year. On an earlier visit by British General Baptist missionary, **Amos Sutton**, the Freewill Baptists formed their own foreign mission society and adopted him as their first missionary.

The Free Baptists in the northern states were the sole major theologically **Arminian** group in the 19th century in the United States and **Canada** not to adopt perfectionistic theology. As much as any influence, this was due to the writing and teaching of **John J. Butler** at Cobb Divinity School in Maine. A group of churches in the Canadian Maritime Provinces, however, left the main movement in 1888 and formed the **Reformed Baptist Alliance**, emphasizing holiness themes.

Merger conversations with the Regular (Calvinistic) Baptists of the North began in 1904. Alfred Williams Anthony, brought the union discussions to fruition in 1911. A publicity campaign took place between 1904 and 1911 to convince local congregations to accept the union. Yearly Conferences were integrated into the respective regular state conventions and several of the institutions were adopted by the **American Baptist** Board of Education. Many of the isolated congregations, notably the mother congregation at New Durham, New Hampshire, identified with a rural **evangelicalism** and declined the merger; some later joined one of the conservative Baptist denominations. Of the roughly 1,100 congregations at the time of the merger, about one half joined the Convention. For several years the Free Baptists also considered merger with the Christian Church and the Congregationalists, declining both.

At the time of Union, the following educational institutions existed: Bates College (Maine, 1855), Hillsdale College (Michigan, 1855), Rio Grande College (Ohio, 1876), Keuka College (New York, 1888), and Storer College, (West Virginia, 1867). Earlier institutions which had closed before Union, include Parsonfield Academy (Maine, 1832), Stratford Academy (New Hampshire, 1834), Smithville Seminary (Rhode Island, 1839), the Biblical School (Dracut, Massachusetts, 1842), Geauga Seminary (Ohio, 1844), Whitestown Seminary (New York, 1844), New Hampton Institute (New Hampshire, 1853), Cheshire Academy (Ohio, 1858), Pike Seminary (New York, 1859), Wilton Collegiate Institute (Iowa, 1860), Green Mountain Seminary (Vermont, 1862), Lyndon Literary and Biblical Institute (Vermont, 1869), and Cobb Divinity School at Bates College (Maine, 1870). Later, in a related group, the Holiness Bible Institute in Woodstock, New Brunswick (1936), evolved into the Bethany Bible College in Sussex, New Brunswick, related to the **Reformed Baptist Alliance**, a holiness offshoot of the Freewill Baptist movement in Canada.

Southern or Original Freewill Baptists. This terminology is applied to a U.S. southern group of Arminian Baptists who emerged in North Carolina in the first decade of the 19th century. There is no evidence for a connection with the General Baptists of the coastal region who were defunct by the late 18th century, but some modern Freewill Baptist historians find their origins in the collection of diverse Arminian Baptists in the wake of that former movement in the 1790s. Perhaps as early as 1812, but more likely about 1829, an annual conference commenced meeting in eastern North Carolina, centered at New Bern and led by two elders, James Roach and Jesse Heath. These pastors corresponded with *The Morning Star* and styled themselves "Original Baptists" and later "Original Freewill Baptists," also adopting an English General Baptist confession of faith of 1660.

The Bethel Conference, as it came to be called, continued to be the epicenter of the movement in North and South Carolina, beset by theological struggles in the 1840s caused in large measure by the influence of the Disciples of Christ, with which many of the churches affiliated in 1845. Those remaining 38 congregations constituted the North Carolina General Conference of Original Freewill Baptists the same year. By 1904 14 conferences or **associations** from six states constituted the General Conference. In 1916, under the influence of the **holiness movement** and growing opposition to the union of Freewill Baptists in the northern states with Calvinistic Baptists, a renewed body was born, the Co-operative General Association of Freewill Baptists. In 1921 the southern churches coalesced with the midwestern churches to form the General Conference of Original Freewill Baptists in the United States. Over the years, the denomination has constituted mission departments, ladie's aid societies, orphanages, and **Sunday School** work. A denominational paper, the *Freewill Baptist Advocate* (1873-) was published beginning at Elm City, North Carolina.

From 1898 to 1925 the Freewill Baptists operated the Freewill Baptist Theological Seminary at Ayden, North Carolina; designed as a training school for ministers, it evolved as a church-related high school program. Its successor, Eureka College, operated from 1926-1929, and was closed due to financial insolvency. Thereafter churches in the Freewill Baptist movement operated **bible** colleges such as Zion Bible School at Blakely, Georgia (1930), the Bible School at Smithfield, North Carolina (1933), and the Carolina Bible Institute at Pine Level, North Carolina (1975). The Freewill Baptist Bible College, Nashville, Tennessee opened in 1938, just as the denomination became a "national" entity, the National Association of Freewill Baptists (1935). This educational tradition, under the influence of graduates of Bob Jones University, provided a **fundamentalist** alternative to Mount Olive College, Mount Olive, North Carolina, the mainstream school founded in 1945.

As of 1995 Freewill Baptists operate a denominational press, foreign and home mission agencies, an assembly ground at Cragmont, North Carolina, and a national headquarters at Antioch, Tennessee. There were at that date 2,491 churches and 213,716 members in connection with the National Association of Freewill Baptists.

Pentecostal Freewill Baptist Church. The holiness movement influenced the Freewill Baptist movement in the southern states and eventually created a new form of the denomination. In 1912 a holiness minister, G. B. Cashwell, introduced the emphases of the Azusa Street Revival into the churches of the Cape Fear (North Carolina) Conference of the Freewill Baptist movement and soon thereafter "Freewill Baptist Holiness," which referred to the second blessing or "entire sanctification," became a dominant motif in this regional conference. Three other conferences were organized along these lines, and in 1959 the body incorporated as the Pentecostal Freewill Baptist Church. The headquarters of the organization of churches is at Dunn, North Carolina, as is the official school, Heritage Bible College. The publication is *The Messenger* (1912?-).

Connections with other Freewill and General Baptists. Attempts have been made by some modern historians of the movement in the

American South to connect it to either the General Baptists organized by **Paul Palmer** in North Carolina or the English General Baptists. These connections involve only similarity of ideas rather than actual historical connections. More appropriately, the southern Freewill Baptists have considered relationships with groups like the Disciples of Christ, the **General Association of General Baptists** (GAGB), and the Churches of God, General Conference (Winebrennarians).

FRENCH-SPEAKING BAPTIST CONFERENCE OF NEW ENGLAND. In the late 19th century, significant numbers of francophone emigrants moved from Quebec to New England for seasonal employment and jobs in factories. In conjunction with the Grande Ligne Mission in Canada, efforts were made at **evangelization** and church planting. In 1895 a Conference was organized to coordinate missionary outreach in the region. In the 1940s the Conference was affiliated with the **Northern** (American) **Baptist Convention** and the Conference shared the publication *L'Aurore* with the Grande Ligne Mission.

FULLER, ANDREW (1754-1815). English Baptist minister and denominational leader, born at Wicken. Raised on a farm and lacking much formal education, he read widely, much interested in the writings of **John Bunyan**. He was converted at 16 and five years later he became the **pastor** at the Baptist Church in Soham. In 1782 he moved to the church at Kettering, which he served until his death. Fuller was the principal advocate of a renewal movement among **Particular Baptists**, called "**evangelical** Calvinism." He held that God has a grand redemptive design in which the church has an important role to hold up the free grace of God. It was Fuller's theological stance, as articulated in his famous treatise, *The Gospel Worthy of All Acceptation* (1781) that catalyzed the formation of the **Baptist Missionary Society** (BMS) in 1792. Fuller was a close confidant to and exerted considerable influence on **William Carey**, with whom he labored in establishing the denomination in overseas missions. He served as the secretary of the BMS from 1792 to 1815. The movement of renewal which followed his teaching, called "Fullerism," broke the rigid determinism of "Gillism," which had prevailed among Particular Baptists since the ministry of **John Gill**. Fuller's other notable published works include *Life of the Rev. Samuel Pearce* (1799), *Thoughts on Open Communion* (1800), and *Strictures on Sandemanianism* (1812).

FULLER, RICHARD (1804-1876). Southern Baptist minister, born at Beaufort, South Carolina. He was educated at Harvard College and first entered a career in law. In 1832 he was converted under the **revival** ministry of Daniel Baker and became convinced of a call to **ministry**. Fuller left his career and became **pastor** of the Beaufort Baptist Church in 1832, where his ministry extended to the slaves of the plantation community. In 1846 he moved to the pastorate of Seventh Baptist, Baltimore, and later formed a new congregation, Eutaw Place Baptist, Baltimore. He engaged in a series of published debates with President **Francis Wayland** of Brown University in which Fuller advocated a proslavery position. He was a principal advocate of the formation of the **Southern Baptist Convention** and preached its first annual sermon. He supported the rebuilding of Southern Baptist Seminary after the Civil War, and he did much to attempt to heal the rift between **Northern** and Southern Baptists. Fuller was considered one of the great oratorical preachers of the 19th century and had numerous sermons published. Among Fuller's published works were *The Psalmist; A New Collection of Hymns for the Use of the Baptist Churches* (1843), *Domestic Slavery Considered As a Scriptural Institution* (1845), and *Baptism and Terms of Communion* (1850).

FUNDAMENTAL BAPTIST CONGRESS OF NORTH AMERICA. See **Fundamentalism, Baptists.**

FUNDAMENTAL BAPTIST FELLOWSHIP. See **Baptist World Mission; Conservative Baptist Association of America.**

FUNDAMENTALISM, BAPTIST. The fundamentalist agitation among Baptists in the United States began in 1906 over the teaching of perceived **liberal** ideas in denominational schools, especially the theological seminaries. Concerns emerged in Chicago over teachers and approaches at the University of Chicago (see **Chicago School**), in Philadelphia at Crozer Seminary, in Toronto at McMaster University, and in Boston at Newton Theological Institution. The Baptist community followed the lead of the World's Christian Fundamental Association, an interdenominational body, and pockets of concern began to meet regularly, notably in the Northeast and Great Lakes regions. In New York City, **Cortland Myers**, pastor at Calvary Baptist Church, first raised the issues as a national concern, followed by articles in the widely read newspaper *The Watchman Examiner*; articles by S. M. Lindsay and **W. B. Riley** were widely quoted. Subsequently in 1919, 25 Baptist pastors from metropolitan New York called for a meeting for prayer and consultation. The next year 3,000 "delegates" assembled in Buffalo, New York to, organize. A "Group of Seven" was appointed to continue as an executive committee on "Conferences on Baptist Fundamentals," the name given to the ongoing body.

At least two groups were evident among the Baptist fundamentalists, the militant leaders including W. B. Riley of Minnesota, **John Roach Straton** of New York City, **Thomas T. Shields** of Toronto, and **J. Frank Norris** of Fort Worth, Texas, and the moderates who included **Curtis L. Laws** of Philadelphia, Frank M. Goodchild (1860-1928), **A. C. Dixon**, and **Jasper C. Massee**. The militants, whose spokesman was often W. B. Riley, made sharp demands, while the moderates, led by Massee, preferred to work for change through Convention structures. Various views were exhibited including, for example, on the doctrine of the Second Coming of Christ.

Moderate fundamentalists came to define what would evolve into Baptist evangelical thought. J. C. Massee at first held to five fundamentals: the inspiration of **Scripture**, the deity of Christ, the spiritual nature of the church, a divine call to the **ministry**, and an emphasis upon **evangelism**. He was also a premillennial Calvinist, but not of the familiar Princetonian variety associated with Benjamin B. Warfield (1851-1921) and J. Gresham Machen (1881-1937), two defining Presbyterian theologians of the era. Frank M. Goodchild, similarly, was not opposed to critical study of the **bible**, a high educational standard, **religious liberty**, and social service. The moderate faction eventually gravitated to three epicenters: Philadelphia, Chicago, and Boston. In Chicago, Northern Baptist Theological Seminary became the graduate school of fundamentalists, in Philadelphia, The Eastern Baptist Theological Seminary developed an evangelical doctrinal stance, and in Boston, Gordon Missionary Training School became an alternative to Newton Theological Institution. Each of these schools devised a doctrinal statement which reflected identifiable constituencies affirming the infallibility of Scripture and the classic evangelical positions on the virgin birth of Christ, the atonement, the depravity of man, and the return of Christ, without a necessarily premillennial interpretation.

Militant fundamentalism, on the other hand, focused on the inerrancy of Scripture, literal damnation of unsaved people after death, the absolute substitutionary atonement of Christ, his return according to a pretribulational, premillennial scheme, restrictive lifestyle (anti-alcohol and anti-smoking), and an insular public and foreign policy which emphasized the forward march of western capitalism. The more militant factions focused their efforts on the formation of doctrinally restrictive training schools, devoid of ideas like evolution, social science theory, **ecumenical** relationships, and the value of comparative religions. T. T. Shields and W. B. Riley took over the operation of Des Moines

University in Iowa for a time. When that failed, Shields opened Toronto
Baptist Seminary in Ontario and Riley began the Northwestern Schools in
St. Paul, Minnesota. J. Frank Norris started a **bible college** in his church
at Fort Worth, eventually called the Bible Baptist Seminary.

Organized fundamentalism in the first generation took several
forms among Baptists in North America. Among the first were the
General Association of Regular Baptist Churches in the United States
(1932) and the **Fellowship of Independent Baptist Churches of Canada**
(1933), the latter of which became the **Fellowship of Evangelical Baptist
Churches in Canada**. Under the leadership of J. Frank Norris, a third
stream evolved, first called the Premillennial Baptist Missionary
Fellowship, later the **World Baptist Fellowship** (WBF, 1931), then the
Bible Baptist Fellowship, out of which grew the **Baptist Bible
Fellowship** (BBF, 1950). Also included in this category was be the
Liberty Baptist Fellowship, formed in 1977 by Jerry Falwell (1933-)
of Lynchburg, Virginia. Various smaller movements of Baptist
Fundamentalists can also be found among independent groups, notably the
Independent Fundamentalist Churches of America and those in harmony
with Bob Jones University in Greenville, South Carolina. Because of their
doctrinal stances, other small bodies could be considered fundamentalistic,
including the **Landmarkist** groups in the southern states, the **General
Association of General Baptists**, and the Original Freewill Baptists.
Baptist Mid-Missions (BMM) and the **Association of Baptists for World
Evangelism** (ABWE) coordinate the overseas efforts of many of the
fundamentalist Baptist churches in the United States.   Among Seventh
Day Baptists, fundamentalism was manifested in the **Bible Defense
League**.

A second generation of Baptist fundamentalists can be identified
during the era of World War II. Disaffection with the appointment policy
of the **Northern Baptist Convention** (NBC) in its overseas work, plus
continued concern for educational philosophies of the older theological
schools, led to the formation of the Fundamental Baptist Fellowship, and
later, a schism. In 1943 a Conservative Baptist Foreign Fellowship was
formed to reflect the need for change in the Northern Convention. This
led ultimately to the **Conservative Baptist Association** with its loose
federation of schools and programs. This generation had little impact upon
the **Southern Baptist Convention** (SBC), which was beginning to move
aggressively north and west in its home mission programs.

Noteworthy in the second generation of fundamentalists was the
evolution of both the moderate and militant positions from that of the first
generation. Replacing Massee, Laws, and Goodchild in the northern states
were Carl F. H. Henry (1913-), Culbert H. Rutenber (1909-), James D.

Mosteller (1915-), and even later theological writers like Clark Pinnock (1937-), **Dale Moody**, and Millard Erickson (1932-). These "neo-evangelical" writers favored cooperation and dialogue and thus often made a greater contribution to a broader alliance of evangelicals than to the ongoing denominational battles of the 1950s and 1960s. Characteristic of these theologians was the desire to work within the existing conventions, Henry, Rutenber, Mosteller in the **American Baptist Convention** (ABC), Erickson in the **Baptist General Conference** (BGC), and Clark Pinnock in the **Southern Baptist Convention** (SBC) and later the Baptist Convention of Ontario and Quebec (BCOQ; Canada). But the militant fundamentalists also gained strength through men like **John R. Rice, Robert T. Ketcham, Richard Clearwaters**, and Lee Roberson (1909-) in both the North and South. Rice and Roberson helped form the **Southwide Baptist Fellowship** (SBF), Ketcham was a founder of the **General Association of Regular Baptist Churches** (GARBC), and Richard Clearwaters found fellowship first among the Conservative Baptists, but later became an independent Baptist.

A third generation of fundamentalists among Baptists evolved within the two major conventions in the United States in the 1970s. Among Southern Baptists, widespread disaffection arose over unacceptable (to some) interpretations expressed in official bible commentaries in 1962 and 1970. Pastors of leading Southern Baptist congregations such as W. Amos Criswell (1909-) of First Baptist, Dallas, Adrian Rodgers (1931-) of Bellevue Baptist Church, Memphis, Tennessee, and Charles Stanley (1932-) of First Baptist, Atlanta, Georgia, used their growing constituencies to launch a platform of change from the theological moderation of the Convention. Criticism of the six theological seminary faculties across the Southern Baptist Convention widened and a hardened doctrinal position was evident at annual meetings of the national Convention. Under the careful planning of H. Paul Pressler III (1930-), a judge from Houston, Texas, who vowed to restore the biblical basis of the S.B.C., officers were elected to transform the Convention structures to be in perceived harmony with its roots and their agenda. Eventually by 1995 each of the seminaries had been reorganized with new faculty leaders and trustees, and the Convention's boards were reorganized and staffed by sympathetic leadership. Spokesmen external to the Convention, such as Jerry Falwell of Lynchburg, Virginia, and Pat Robertson (1930-) of Virginia Beach, Virginia (himself a former Southern Baptist), were influential in creating a rarified national media atmosphere for change.

In the **American Baptist Churches**, a gradual decline in membership statistics and a seemingly perpetual need to reorganize led to concern for a more well-defined evangelical direction. Although a series of quiet ecumenical evangelicals were elected to prominent positions from the 1970s, the social activism and broad inclusivity positions of the national agencies led to the establishment of **American Baptist Evangelicals** (ABE), an aggressive group calling for a return to a biblically defined position and rejecting alternative lifestyles and politically correct policies.

Baptist fundamentalism has coalesced at regional, national, and international levels as well as within existing conventions or unions. For instance in Europe, the Fellowship of Evangelical Baptists in Europe has met periodically since an initial conference in 1967 at Northwood in the United Kingdom. Similarly, the Fundamental Baptist Congress of North America has met in conferences, 1963-1978. An International Baptist Fellowship, which sponsored the first congress of fundamental Baptists, has held meetings in 1962, 1965, 1973, 1976, 1979, and 1992 in various locations.

Because Baptists revere Scripture and tend toward a transparent or literal understanding of the **bible**, the temperament of fundamentalism continues to be evident in the various branches of the denomination. See also **Conservative Tradition**; **Evangelicalism, and Baptists**; **Liberal Tradition**.

FURMAN, RICHARD (1755-1825). American Baptist minister, born at Esopus, New York. The family moved in the 1750s to the colony of South Carolina where Richard received an informal education. At 19 he became the Baptist pastor at High Hills, South Carolina Church, and he became a regionally known orator. During the American Revolution he was a prominent patriot and was sought by British general Lord Cornwallis. For a time, Furman fled the state for Virginia where he came in contact with tidewater politicians like Patrick Henry (1736-1799). Following a continued pastorate with High Hills, in 1787 Furman became **pastor** of First Baptist, Charleston, the oldest and most prestigious congregation in the state. He followed the lead of Baptist organizers in the North and helped to form missionary societies and educational ventures. In 1814 he was a principal mover in the founding of the **General Missionary Convention** of Baptists in the United States and served as its first president. He responded quickly to the call of the **Judson** Mission in **Burma** and was **Luther Rice**'s closest confidant in the South. In 1821 he shaped the South Carolina Baptist State Convention, which he saw as an auxilliary to the national convention. Furman promoted higher education for the southern churches as a part of the work of the Triennial Convention in 1817 and was a founder of Columbian College in

Washington, D.C. Furman University in Greenville, South Carolina (1850), was named in his honor. Furman's famous sermon on the death of George Washington was entitled *Humble Submission to Divine Sovereignty the Duty of a Bereaved Nation* (1799) and represents one of the best examples of a public eulogy offered by a Baptist in the United States.

FYFE, ROBERT ALEXANDER (1816-1878). Canadian and American Baptist minister and educator, born in St. Philippe, Quebec. He spent a year at Hamilton Literary and Theological Institution (later Colgate University) and graduated from Newton Theological Institution. He served churches at March Street, Toronto (1844-1848), and Perth, Ontario (1848-1849), and was on the faculty of Canada Baptist College in Montreal, 1843-1844. During the 1840s debate over the distribution of the Clergy Reserves, Fyfe led a courageous crusade against church establishment in Upper Canada and became the chief advocate of religious voluntarism in the province. He also favored a national body of Baptists and he worked hard for the short-lived Canada Baptist Union in 1844 and following. In 1849 Fyfe took the pastorate in Warren, Rhode Island, which he served until 1853 when he moved to the Baptist church in Milwaukee, Wisconsin, 1853-1854. He returned once again to a Toronto pastorate at Bond Street (formerly March Street) until, in 1857, he helped to organize the Canadian Literary Institute at Woodstock. The founding principal of the Institute, Fyfe gave many of the lectures, particularly specializing in theology. He engineered a curriculum of Christian education, which became a model for Toronto Baptist College and McMaster University. Among his protégés were John McLaurin (1839-1912) and **Alexander McDonald,** two pioneer Canadian missionaries. Fyfe was able to persuade his good friend, Senator **William McMaster** of Toronto, to support the idea of a Christian university, but Fyfe died before the dream was realized.

G

GADSBY, WILLIAM (1773-1844). English Baptist minister, born at Attleborough, Warwickshire. He had no formal education and as a youth was apprenticed to the craft of ribbon-weaving. He was converted and turned to preaching part-time. He served **Particular** Baptist congregations at Hinckley and Desford from 1798-1800, settling at Hinckley until 1805. From 1805 to 1844 he was minister at Back Lane Chapel, Manchester. Gadsby was a masterful preacher and built a considerable following among the working classes for his views, forming 40 congregations in the Lancashire, Yorkshire, Cheshire, and Derbyshire regions. Frequently he travelled to London to preach at Red Cross Street, Gower Street, and Zoar chapels to raise money for his ministries in the North of England. He is said to have travelled over 60,000 miles and preached nearly 120,000 sermons in his career. Gadsby was a firm opponent of Fullerism, advocating instead a high Calvinism; he also opposed the formation of the **Baptist Union of Great Britain and Ireland** (BU), with which he had no fellowship. He and his followers, called "Gadsbyites," are considered the origin of what would become a major branch of the **Strict Baptist** position. Gadsby's thought is well articulated in his published works, including *Doctrinal Antinominianism Refuted* (1850?) and *An Everlasting Task for Arminians* (1828).

GALUSHA, ELON (1791-1856). American Baptist minister and social reformer, born at Shaftsbury, Vermont. In 1816 he became a member of the Whitesboro, New York, Baptist Church, which he appears to have served as pastor until 1830. From 1830-1833 he was pastor of Second (Broad Street) Baptist in Utica, New York. While a pastor he served as a missionary to Michigan Territory and founded the first Baptist Church at Pontiac. He was elected president of the Baptist Missionary Convention of New York in 1823, and in 1824 he founded the *Baptist Register*, a prestigious denominational paper. Active in the establishment of a firm financial basis for Hamilton Literary and Theological Institution (later Colgate University), he moved to Rochester, New York, in 1834 and formed the Second Baptist Church, which institution was later instrumental in forming Rochester Theological Seminary. While in western New York he was an **antimasonic** enthusiast in the late 1820s, and he helped form a local **antislavery** society in Rochester. In 1842 he moved to Lockport and the next year announced his adoption of Millerite views. Galusha alienated himself temporarily from the Baptist mainstream and was forced in 1844 to withdraw to the Baptist Church at Perry, New York, where he worked hard for the **Adventist** cause. Even when **William Miller**'s predictions of the end of the world did not materialize, Galusha held the movement in western New York together and did much to ensure the evolution of the Adventist denomination. Highly regarded by Joshua Himes (1805-1895) and William Miller, Galusha was restored to the Baptist movement in 1856; however, he did not withdraw his Millerite views.

GAMBIA. In 1978 the **Association of Baptists for World Evangelism** (ABWE) opened a mission in the country. Later **Southern Baptist**

missionaries arrived in Gambia in 1982. As of 1995 there were three churches and 130 members in the Baptist community in Gambia.

GAMBRELL, JAMES BRUTON (1841-1921). Southern Baptist educator and editor, born in Anderson County, South Carolina. He fought in the American Civil War, earning a reputation as a sharpshooter and a scout for General Robert E. Lee (1807-1870). At the conclusion of the war, he became pastor of the Oxford, Mississippi, Baptist Church (1865-1877) and was educated at the nearby University of Mississippi. In 1877 Gambrell became editor of *The Baptist Record* for 16 years. For a term 1893-1896 he was president of Mercer University in Macon, Georgia. In 1896 he moved to Texas and became a home missionary for the state convention until 1910 when he became editor of the *Baptist Standard*, where he served for four years. In 1912 Gambrell was a founder of Southwestern Baptist Theological Seminary, continuing to serve the Consolidated Board of Missions of Texas, and he was president of the **Southern Baptist Convention** (SBC) for four terms from 1917 to 1921. Gambrell's published work includes *Baptist, Why and Why Not* (1900) and *Lectures on Ecclesiology* (1919).

GANO, JOHN (1727-1804). American Baptist pastor and military chaplain, born at Hopewell, New Jersey. Originally a farmer and self-educated in a Presbyterian home, Gano early converted to Baptist principles, uniting with the Hopewell, New Jersey, congregation. Following a tour of the southern colonies in which he met George Whitefield (1714-1770), he was ordained in 1754 and became pastor of the Scotch Plains, New Jersey, church. In 1756 he moved to the South, but returned in 1760 to become the founding **pastor** of the First Baptist Church in New York City, where he remained for 26 years. In 1777 he joined Governor George Clinton's (1739-1812) New York Brigade in the Revolution and served with distinction, often under fire. There was a popular belief that he baptized George Washington (1732-1799), but no evidence exists for this event; General Washington did commend his military exploits. After the war Gano travelled to the West and started a church at Duck Creek (now Cincinnati, Ohio), and served a congregation at Town Fork, Kentucky. The brother-in-law of **James Manning**, Gano was a promoter of Rhode Island College and the missionary expansion of the Baptists. Although disabled by a stroke, he was carried to camp meetings in Kentucky, where he preached with power.

GATES, FREDERICK TAYLOR (1853-1929). American Baptist educator and businessman, born at Maine, New York. He was educated at the

University of Rochester and Rochester Theological Seminary; he served the Central Baptist Church in Minneapolis, Minnesota, 1880-1888. As part of his service to the Minnesota Baptist Convention, **George A. Pillsbury** asked Gates to head up a campaign to raise $50,000 to endow Pillsbury Academy at Owatonna, Minnesota. Gates's success with this project led to his being named executive secretary of the newly formed American Baptist Education Society (ABES) in 1889. That year **John D. Rockefeller** asked Gates to raise one million dollars toward the newly constituted University of Chicago, which Rockefeller planned to match. In time this friendship grew and Gates came to manage Rockefeller's iron ore projects in Minnesota, coordinating resources, finance, and transportation interests. By 1893, Gates devoted himself entirely to Mr. Rockefeller's philanthropic work, distributing millions of charitable dollars to Rockefeller's interests. He was president or chair of 13 different companies and the **Northern Baptist Convention**'s (NBC) General Education Board, 1907-1917. During the years he worked with John D. Rockefeller, Gates managed over $600 million in charities and helped set up the Rockefeller Foundation, with estimated assets of over $125,000,000.

GAUNT, ELIZABETH. See **Martyrology, Baptist**.

GENERAL ASSOCIATION OF GENERAL BAPTISTS (GAGB). See **General Baptists**.

GENERAL ASSOCIATION OF REGULAR BAPTIST CHURCHES (GARBC). An outgrowth along theological lines of the **Northern (American) Baptist Convention** (NBC) in the United States. In 1932 22 congregations withdrew from the NBC to form the GARBC. Their concerns included modernist teachings, inequality of representation in the Convention, control of missionary work, and the principle of conventionism. The member churches are considered part of Baptist **fundamentalism**, along with, for instance, the **Conservative Baptist Association**, the **Baptist Bible Fellowship** (BBF), and the **Baptist Missionary Association** (BMA). The term "**association**" is preferred, in contrast to "convention." "Regular" Baptist refers to their understanding that they are the true heirs of consistent Baptist teachings, rather than the two great conventions. Association churches are Calvinistic and subscribe to the New Hampshire Baptist **Confession of Faith** (1833), with a premillennial interpretation.

The Association is governed by a Council of Eighteen; it maintains the Regular Baptist Press and is related to the **Association of Baptists for**

World Evangelism (ABWE), **Evangelical Baptist Missions** (EBM), Baptist Church Planters, **Baptist Mid-Missions** (BMM), Baptist Missionary Builders, and other domestic missionary organizations. Four **bible colleges** are approved: Baptist Bible College of Pennsylvania, Clark's Summit, Pennsylvania, Faith Baptist Bible College, Ankeny, Iowa, Spurgeon Baptist Bible College, Mulberry, Florida, and three undergraduate schools: Cedarville College, Cedarville, Ohio; Cornerstone Baptist College, Grand Rapids, Michigan; and Western Baptist College, Salem, Oregon. There are four approved theological seminaries: Baptist Bible Seminary, Clark's Summit, Pennsylvania; Faith Baptist Bible Theological Seminary, Ankeny, Iowa; Grand Rapids Baptist Seminary, Grand Rapids, Michigan; and Northwest Baptist Seminary, Tacoma, Washington. The periodical is *The Baptist Bulletin*, (1935-). As of 1995, there were 1,458 churches and 136,380 members in the GARBC.

GENERAL BAPTIST MISSIONARY CONVENTION OF THE BAPTIST DENOMINATION IN THE UNITED STATES OF AMERICA FOR FOREIGN MISSIONS (GMC). Name given to the first national organization of Baptists in the United States. The **Convention** was formed at Philadelphia on May 18, 1814, and chartered in the state of Pennsylvania. The idea of a national body originated with **Luther Rice** while travelling from Richmond, Virginia, in a stage coach. Doubtless the term **"convention"** was borrowed from political discourse of the era (e.g. "constitutional convention") and involved delegates from the state and local **associations** and individual contributing members, the latter category reflective of the single purpose **voluntary** society particularly popular in New England. Elements of the plan of the American Board of Commissioners for Foreign Missions (Congregationalist) were also seen in 1814, as the central purpose was originally to support overseas missionaries.

In 1817 the Convention's work was enlarged to include domestic missions and education for ministers, and in 1820 the actual purpose statement was expanded to include "other important objects relating to the Redeemer's kingdom." Another fundamental change occurred in 1826 when the Convention was reduced essentially to a single purpose missionary society, reflecting the financial woes suffered from the overextension into education and western U.S. missionary activity. A final modification was made in 1846 when the Board structure was changed to reflect the departure of newly organized **Southern Baptist Convention** (SBC) elements and the General Missionary Convention (GMC) became the **American Baptist Missionary Union** (ABMU).

The Convention was popularly known as the "General Missionary Convention," the "Baptist General Convention," and the "Triennial Convention," the latter because its principal manifestation involved a meeting of all the delegates every three years from 1814-1844, in an assembly. During the three interim years in each triennium, the Convention's work was carried out by the **Baptist Board of Foreign Missions** (BBFM) or the Acting Board. See also **American Baptist Churches; American Baptist Foreign Mission Society**.

GENERAL BAPTISTS. The term "general" has usually been applied to groups of Baptists who hold to an unlimited view of Christ's atonement, that is, they believe that Christ died for all persons. In some contexts the terminology "General Baptist" is used synonymously with the **Arminian** theological tradition, but this is not always accurate.

English General Baptists. The first General Baptists emerged in England following the teachings of the earliest Baptists, including **Thomas Helwys** and others. Helwys clearly advocated a general view of the atonement of Christ. About 1626 churches of this persuasion were in correspondence with Waterlander Mennonites in Holland. The first **confession of faith** which was undeniably General Baptist was published in 1660 and reputedly had the sanction of over 20,000 persons. Two other confessions were issued in 1679 and by the General Baptists of Somersetshire in 1691. English General Baptists had a threefold order of **ministry: messengers, elders**, and **deacons**. The office of messenger was based upon 2 Cor. 8:23 and was widely successful in holding together the disparate congregations. **Thomas Grantham** wrote of the role of the messenger and was the earliest systematic **theologian** of the General Baptist sort. The local churches were organized into **associations** and then into a national General Assembly, which first met in 1660. The Assembly became a court of appeals for the entire connection and may have led to its demise for that reason. Another popular distinction of the General Baptists in England was the "sixth principle" based on Heb 6:1,2, in which it is held that the **laying on of hands** should be done to all newly baptized believers. English General Baptists also practiced **footwashing**, anointing the sick with oil (James 5:14,15), and some refused to eat blood, on the basis of Acts 15:20. A much debated issue in the Assembly after the Revolution was psalm-singing, the decline of which retarded their distinctive music.

As the 17th century waned, so also did the English General Baptists. Their churches were not well distributed in the towns, many congregations met in homes, their doctrine was rigid, ministerial education was frowned upon and, significantly, many followed a leading and long-lived messenger, Matthew Caffyn (1628-1715), into Hoffmanite Christology and Socinian views. Throughout the eighteenth century several congregations retained their General Baptist nomenclature while evolving into **Unitarian** meetings or cooperating with **Particular** or **Seventh Day** Baptists. The remaining Old General Baptist congregations and associations for the most part joined fellowship with the reorganized **Baptist Union** (BU) in 1831.

New Connexion of General Baptists. This movement originated in the ministry of **Dan Taylor**, a Midlands preacher. On June 6, 1770, the Assembly of Free Grace General Baptists, soon to be called the "New Connexion," was founded to distinguish the **evangelical** zeal of Taylor and Gilbert Boyce from the rigidity and doctrinal laxity of the older General Baptists. Taylor wrote a doctrinal statement which was unabashedly Arminian and with a high Christology. By 1820, the Connexion had over 7,000 members in slightly less than 100 churches. Taylor and his following exhibited a mild form of **holiness** ethics particularly attractive among the working classes. Beginning in the 1850s, movement toward cooperation and later amalgamation with the Baptist Union began; under the leadership of **John Clifford**, the consummation of merger took place in 1891. The General Baptists operated a theological academy/college from 1797 to 1914 (cf. **Theological Education**). Periodicals include the *General Baptist Magazine* (1798-1800), succeeded by the *General Baptist Repository*, published at London from 1802-1821.

Colonial General Baptists in North America. Early in American Baptist history, General Baptists appeared in both New England and the South. As early as the 1680s General Baptists were situated in South Carolina, and in North Carolina **Paul Palmer** apparently led in the formation of several General Baptist churches, according to **Morgan Edwards**. In New England, many of the first congregations were known as General Six Principle Baptists (see next).

General Six Principle Baptists. Among the early Baptists in New England, this group took their doctrinal basis from Hebrews 6:1,2 and included the **laying on of hands** in their practices. Although mildly Calvinistic at first, most churches became Arminian. At one time in the late 17th century, the **Six Principle** Baptists claimed many of the prominent congregations, including First Baptist Church in Providence. Rhode Island was the center of their influence (12 in Massachusetts and Rhode Island and three in Connecticut) and they probably can claim the oldest associational meeting among Baptists in America, held in 1670. In most respects, the General Six Principle Baptists resembled their English General Baptist counterparts. In the 20th century only a handful of congregations remain.

Freewill Baptists. The **Freewill Baptists** (FWB) of New England and the Canadian Maritimes are also included in most discussions of the General Baptists, owing to their position on the atonement of Christ. The **Free Communion** Baptists, merged with the Freewill group in 1841, also held a general atonement position (see the article on **Free(will) Baptists**).

General Association of General Baptists. In 1823 a movement in the Old Northwest began with the preaching of **Benoni Stinson** who articulated Arminian views. In 1870 an association was formed, the General Association of General Baptists (GAGBC). With congregations in 15 states, the Association supports Oakland College and theological school in Indiana and publishes the *General Baptist Messenger* (1885-). As of 1995, there were 823 churches and 73,129 members in the GAGB. The historians of this movement argue for a connection with the original General Baptists of England; however, this is not historically established.

GEORGE, DAVID (1743-1810). American and Canadian Black Baptist minister, born in Essex County, Virginia, the son of slaves. Suffering cruel treatment, he ran away as a young man to the colony of Georgia where he lived and worked with the Creek Indians. Later he was converted under the preaching of **George Leile** and Wait Palmer (c1740-1780). About 1775 he became the first regular **pastor** of the Silver Bluff Baptist Church, Georgia, the oldest **Black Baptist** congregation in North America. In 1782 he was granted freedom and he joined the exodus of British Loyalists from Charleston, South Carolina, to Halifax and later Shelburne, Nova Scotia. There he gathered a congregation and preached broadly in Nova Scotia and what later became New Brunswick. In 1792 in response to limited political and social opportunities, George joined 1,200 other Black settlers and emigrated to **Sierra Leone**, West Africa. Following a visit to England by George, the **Baptist Missionary Society** (BMS) agreed to support missions in **Sierra Leone** and George carried on extensive correspondence with **Samuel Pearce** and John Newton (1725-1807). George himself served a church at Freetown, supplementing his income by keeping an alehouse. George's principal publication was his autobiographical "Account of the Life of Mr. David George, from Sierra Leone in West Africa...", printed in **John Rippon's** *Annual Register* in 1793.

GEORGIA. The oldest Baptist church in the Asian Republic of Georgia dates from 1919 at Tbilisi. An Armenian congregation was founded in the region in 1926. Over the years of socialist government, the Baptists in Georgia were included in the All Union Council of Evangelical-Christians Baptists; in 1991 this changed and the churches in Georgia later formed

Siouz Evangelskikh Christian-Baptistov Gruzii. Additionally, the **Baptist Bible Fellowship** (U.S.) opened a **fundamentalist** mission   to the Republic of Georgia in 1995.

As of 1995, there were 41 churches and 4,500 members affiliated with the Soiuz Evangelskikh Christian-Baptistov Gruzii.

GERMAN BAPTIST BRETHREN. Name applied to the congregations of German **Anabaptists** who emigrated to the colony of Pennsylvania in the 1720s, also known as Dunkers, Taufers, or Tunkers, the latter being a term of derision. The movement dated back to 1521 and the Zwickau Prophets who first preached and practiced adult **baptism** in Saxony. In 1708 a congregation was gathered at Alexander Mack's (1679-1735) home in Schwarzenau where there was a baptism and commitment made to move to Pennsylvania. The small group settled in the Wissahickon Valley near Philadelphia. In 1723 on Christmas Day a church was constituted near Roxborough, Pennsylvania, after which the group spread to Chester County and Conestoga country. The congregations practiced an eclectic group of experiences, unrelated to other Baptists, including the **Love Feast**, Kiss of Peace, and **footwashing**. The term "Brethren" was derived from Matthew 23:8, "...you have only one master and you are all brethren."

As the movement grew, divisions occurred and two primary bodies emerged, the Brethren and the Ephrata community, or Beisseliander. Surrounded by English-speaking Baptists, the German Baptist Brethren came to look more like Anabaptists than Baptists. In more recent times, a fraternal ralationship between **American Baptists** and the Church of the Brethren emerged, which recognizes a common theological heritage and shared delegates to national **conventions**. See also **Footwashing**; **Love Feast**; **Solitary Brethren**; **Zionitic Brotherhood**.

GERMAN BAPTIST CONFERENCE. See **North American Baptist Conference**.

GERMAN SEVENTH DAY BAPTIST BRETHREN. See **Solitary Brethren**.

GERMANY. Baptist life in Germany is almost inseparable from the ministry of **Johann G. Oncken**. His work for various religious societies and eventually the **American Baptist Publication Society** (ABPS) and the **American Baptist Missionary Union** (ABMU) was critical in the development of both churches and institutions. In 1834 Oncken opened the first congregation at Hamburg; although authorities tried numerous times to close its worship and work, this became the center for Baptist witness. **Julius W. Köbner** and **Gottfried W. Lehmann** joined Oncken as a triumvirate of missionaries and German Baptist leadership. In 1849 a Bund der vereinigten Gemeinden getaufter Christen in Deutschland und Dänemark (Union of United Baptist Churches in Germany and Denmark) was founded with Oncken as chairman; this union included churches in **Switzerland**, the **Netherlands**, and eastern Europe as well. Lehmann led in the formation of the Predigerseminar (Preacher's Seminary) in 1880 at Hamburg, which served most of the churches in Europe. The publishing house, Oncken Verlag, was founded in 1878. The union also worked in both domestic and foreign missions.

Under pressure from the government, the Union of Free Church Christians (Bruedergemeinden plus Elimgemeinden) merged with the "Open" Brethren (Bruedergemeinden) to form in 1937 the Union of Free Christians (Bund freikirchlicher Christen-BfC); in 1941 this church body merged with the German Baptist Union (Bund Deutscher Baptisten), to form the Union of Evangelical Free Churches (Bund Evangelisch-Freikirklicher Gemeinden-K.d.oe.R.). Following World War II, Germany was divided and the Baptists of the German Democratic Republic (East Germany) had to create their own theological school, Theologisches Seminar, at Buckow im 1959, and in 1970 their own Union, the Bund Evangelisch-Freikirchlicher Gemeinden in der DDR. **Baptist Mid-Missions** (BMM) from the United States established a German mission at Munich in 1951, the **Baptist Bible Fellowship** (BBF) began a mission in 1970, the **Association of Baptists for World Evangelism** (ABWE) in 1989, and the **American Baptist Association** (ABA) also has a mission in the country.

In 1991 the two German Baptist unions were reunited, reflecting the political reunification of Germany. As of 1995 there were 623 churches with 87,926 members. The Bund publishes *Wort und Werk* (Word and Work) (1880-). There is a theological school at Elstal, which is heir to the one founded by J. G. Oncken.

GHANA. In 1914 **William Haas** of the **Baptist Mid- Missions** commenced a work at Bambili in what became Ghana. From 1957 this effort included church planting in Gold Coast, Ashanti, and British Togoland. The main Baptist work in this West African nation was the initiative of the Nigerian Baptists, beginning in 1947 with congregations at Tamale and Sekondi. **Southern Baptist** (SBC) missionaries began work in Ghana in 1949. The Ghana Baptist Convention was formed in 1954 and separated from the Nigerian Convention in 1964. The **Baptist Bible Fellowship** (BBF) began a mission in Ghana in 1987, as did the **Association of Baptists for World Evangelism** (ABWE) in 1993.

As of 1995, there were 548 churches with 52,000 members affiliated with the Ghana Baptist Convention. A Baptist Training Center is located at Tamale and a seminary at Kumasi.

GIFFORD, ANDREW (1700-1784). English Baptist minister, born in Bristol. One of the most eminent pastors of his era, Gifford was educated at Tewksbury Academy and Gresham College. He was called to the church at Wild Street in London in 1729. A long forgotten moral lapse from his youth, involving allegations of homosexuality, became known and the congregation split. Gifford withdrew and formed the Eagle Street Church and served there until his death. Although ostracized by his fellow Baptist ministers in London, he was befriended by influential members of Parliament and was a well-known collector of coins. Through Marischal College, Edinburgh University conferred on him the Doctor of Divinity, and he worked for a time at the British Museum as a librarian. Gifford bequeathed his books, which included a copy of the *Tyndale New Testament* (sold in 1994 to the British Library) to the Bristol Baptist College, where they became the special collection known as the "Andrew Gifford Remains."

GILL, JOHN (1697-1771). English Baptist minister and theologian, born in Kettering. Gifted in the Classics, Gill was educated at a local academy. He was called to be pastor of the Horsley Down, Southwark Church in London in 1720; he died in that role 51 years later. Gill was an avid student of biblical literature and the Hebrew language, and in 1748 the University of Aberdeen awarded him the doctor of divinity degree for this scholarship. Gill became known for his extreme Calvinism, "unable to offer Christ to sinners because it did not respect the sovereignty of God." His **ministry** concentrated on the edification of an elect church. He published a major commentary on the books of the **bible** (1728-1767) and a comprehensive systematic **theology** called *A Complete Body of Doctrinal and Practical Divinity* (1769). His influence upon churches in Great Britain and North America was termed "Gillism" and stood in contrast with "Fullerism" as the position of **Andrew Fuller** came to be called. Beyond his local congregation, Gill was a member of the Baptist Board and the **Three Dissenting Denominations**, one of the most influental Baptist leaders of his era. John Gill continues to be the preferred theologian of theologically Calvinistic Baptists, including especially many **Strict Baptists** (SB) in Britain and **Primitive** or **Old School** Baptists in North America.

GILMOUR, JOHN (1792-1869). Canadian Baptist missionary, born at Ayr, Scotland. An apprenticed seaman, he was captured in 1809 and imprisoned in France for five years. In 1814 he was baptized, studied for the ministry, and began itinerant preaching. Gilmour was influenced by William Fraser (1800-1883) and John Edwards (1780-1842) to emigrate to **Canada** and he settled at Montreal in 1830. He formed the St. Helen Street Church (later First Baptist) and served there for five years. At length he travelled in the Ottawa Valley and founded churches across Upper Canada (now Ontario), his base being at Peterborough. His itinerant parish ran from Montreal to Dundas and he wielded a considerable influence of the **Scottish Haldanite** tradition. He helped to form the Ottawa Association, the Canada Baptist Missionary Society, and the *Canada Baptist Missionary Magazine*. In 1838 he was the prime mover in the establishment of Canada Baptist College at Montreal, the first Baptist institution of higher learning in central Canada. He travelled to Britain in 1836 to appeal for funds to begin a college and support missionaries, a trip which resulted in the **Baptist Missionary Society**'s (BMS) appointment of educational and church planting missionaries in Canada and the formation of the Baptist Canadian Missionary Society.

GLASITES. Term used to designate the followers of John Glas (1695-1773), a minister of the Church of Scotland who in 1728 founded a sect which aimed to restore the primitive church. Glasite congregations developed in the vicinity of Dundee, with a principal one at Perth. The practices of Glasites included **love feasts, footwashing,** the holy kiss, and abstinence from eating blooded meats; unanimity in congregational decision-making was practiced and a strict **separation of church and state** adhered to. Because of their advocacy of the kiss of peace, Glasites were also derisively called "Kissites." Numerous **dissenters** from the Church of Scotland vacillated between Glasite convictions and Baptist practices; the principal flow of Glasite ideas came through Robert Sandeman, **Archibald McLean,** and **Alexander Campbell**. Glas himself became known as a "father of voluntarism." See also **Sandamanians; Voluntarism**.

GLOVER, TERROT REAVELY (1869-1943). English educator and Baptist leader, born in Bristol. The son of a Baptist minister, Richard Glover (1837-1919), he graduated from Cambridge University and for most of his career was a fellow and lecturer in Classics at St. John's College, Cambridge, where in later years he was University Lecturer in Ancient History. In 1896 he emigrated to Canada where he was professor of Latin at Queens University until 1901, when he returned to Cambridge where he held the prestigious office of Public Orator at the University. He was a popular lecturer (speaking on many occasions in Latin) well known for his scholarship. His book, *Conflict of Religion in the Early Roman Empire* (1909), was regarded as a piece of first-rate scholarship on both sides of the Atlantic, and his later work, *The Jesus of History* (1917), was widely circulated. His scholarship was confirmed in 1918-1921 when Oxford University appointed him Wilde Lecturer in Natural and Comparative Religion. Glover served as president of the **Baptist Union of Great Britain and Ireland** (BU) in 1924. Among Baptists, he was identified with the **liberal** tradition and often took severe criticism for his views. Followers of **C. H. Spurgeon** attacked him in British circles and **T. T. Shields** branded him the "English Pippin of Three Rotten Apples" along with **L. H. Marshall** and **Shailer Mathews** in **Canada** in 1928. He was awarded the LL.D. degree by Queens University and McMaster University in Ontario and by the University of St. Andrews in Scotland.

GOADBY, JOSEPH (1801-1859). English Baptist minister, born at Ashby-de-la-Zouch in Leicestershire. Educated by his father, who was a **General Baptist** preacher, Joseph was apprenticed as a watchmaker. He studied at the General Baptist Academy at Wisbech and served the churches at Manchester (1825-1826) and Dover Street, Leicester (1826-1848). In 1847 Goadby and Jabez Burns (1805-1876) were deputed by the General Baptist Assembly to visit the **Freewill Baptist** (FWB) Triennial Convention in the United States, which resulted in close relations between the two **Arminian** groups. Goadby was recognized as one of the outstanding General Baptists of his era, serving as secretary to the General Baptist College, publisher of the *General Baptist Magazine*, and the chief advocate of the Orissa Mission. He concluded his ministerial career as pastor at Wood-Gate, Loughborough, 1848-1859.

GOBLE, JONATHAN (1827-1896). American Baptist missionary, born at Wayne, Steuben County, New York. Raised on a farm, he was convicted of arson and sentenced to jail in 1844. In a second altercation in 1846 he threatened the life of a Syracuse grocer and was sentenced to prison at Auburn, New York, for two years. While in prison he became a Christian and was baptized three years later. He resolved to become a **missionary** and joined the U.S. Marine Corps to embark on the expedition of Commodore Matthew C. Perry (1794-1858) to **Japan** in 1851. Among the influences on Goble was Bernard John Bettelheim (1811-1850), a medical missionary to Okinawa who served as a translator for the Perry expedition. In 1854, following his return to the United States, Goble studied at Madison University. Preferring to act rather than study, he was commissioned in 1859 by the **American Baptist Free Mission Society** (ABFrMS) to serve as the first Baptist missionary to Japan. He arrived in Japan in 1860 and set up at Kanagawa. In 1868 he moved to Yokohama where he conducted an evangelical and translation ministry. At the end of 1864 he had completed the first Japanese translation of the Gospels. With the merger of the ABFrMS and the regular Baptist movement, Goble was appointed by the **American Baptist Missionary Union** (ABMU) as a missionary in 1872. The next year he was involved in a violent act in Yokohama and he withdrew from the ABMU. He became engaged in a war of words with senior Baptist missionary **Nathan Brown** and this destroyed his reputation at home.

Among Goble's claims to fame was his patent in 1870 for the jinrikisha, a popular and convenient personal conveyance for cities; it originated as a cart for his disabled wife. In the later 1870s Goble served as a **bible colporteur** for the American Bible Society in distant areas of Kyushu. His health worn out, he returned a widower to the United States in 1884 and settled in Germantown, Pennsylvania. At length his conduct was again unbecoming and he was expelled from the Baptist-sponsored George Nugent Home for the Aged. He died after a diagnosis of dementia at St. Louis, Missouri. To his death he continued to be a vocal critic of the ABMU. Goble clandestinely kept a diary during his voyage with Commodore Perry and this has survived to become a document of singular importance to historians.

GOEN, CLARENCE CHARLES (1924-1990). Southern and later American Baptist minister and historian, born at San Marcos, Texas. He was educated at the University of Texas, Hardin Simmons University, and Southwestern Baptist Theological Seminary, completing a Th.D. in church history. For a time he was pastor of congregations in Texas and Oklahoma and ordained a Southern Baptist in 1948. Encouraged by **Robert A. Baker**, the senior historian at Southwestern, Goen completed his Ph.D. at Yale under Sidney Ahlstrom (1919-1984) and Roland Bainton (1894-1984). In his absence, a promised post at Southwestern closed and he took a teaching position at the newly formed Methodist-related Wesley Theological Seminary in Washington, D. C., and remained there from 1960 to his retirement. His principal contribution was *Revivalism and Separatism in New England, 1740-1800,* which focused on the development of the **Separate** Baptists of New England. He also examined the factors leading to separation of northern and southern Baptists before the Civil War. Goen served as president of the American Society of Church History (1982) and the American Baptist Historical Society

(ABHS) (1974-1976) as well as holding positions among American Baptist churches in the Washington, D.C. area.

GOING, JONATHAN (1786-1844). American Baptist minister and educator, born at Reading, Vermont. He was educated at Brown University and remained after graduation to study theology with Asa Messer (1769-1836). He served two pastorates: Cavendish, Vermont (1811-1815), and Worcester, Massachusetts (1815-1831). At Worcester, he was a statewide leader in educational issues, promoting a public school system, and within the New England region, the creation of Newton Theological Institution in 1825. In 1831 Going made a recuperative trip to the Old Northwest where he encountered **John Mason Peck** in Illinois. Peck convinced him of the urgent missionary needs of the West, and Going became a devoted advocate of a separate domestic mission agency for the Baptists. At an adjourned meeting of the Seventh Triennial Convention in New York City in 1832, he helped to organize the **American Baptist Home Mission Society** (ABHMS) and he became its first corresponding secretary. In 1838 he resigned to become president of Granville Literary and Theological Institution (later Denison University) in Ohio. As president at Granville, he established the faculty and institutional reputation and was highly regarded for his pastoral care of students.

GOLD COAST. See Ghana.

GOOD SHEPHERD MINISTRIES. An **independent** Baptist missionary organization founded in 1974 to conduct church planting, literacy work, and relief aid. With its home base in Rockledge, Florida, the organization focuses upon work in **Haiti.** Its periodical is *Good Shepherd Newsletter.*

GOODSPEED, THOMAS WAKEFIELD (1842-1927). American Baptist minister and educator, born near Glens Falls, New York. He studied at the old University of Chicago, finishing his degree at the University of Rochester with theological studies at the Rochester Theological Seminary. He served the Baptist church at Quincy, Illinois (1866-1871), then as associate pastor to his brother Edgar at Second Baptist Church, Chicago (1871-1875). That year he was named agent for the Baptist Union Theological Seminary and raised funds for the struggling institution while also serving as pastor at Morgan Park Baptist Church. Goodspeed's reputation as a fundraiser was considerable (he raised over $500,000 in 13 years) and he came to know closely **John D. Rockefeller** and **Frederick Gates**, the corresponding secretary of the American Baptist

Education Society. Goodspeed helped Rockefeller to formulate a plan for a modern university in Chicago and he brought both Rockefeller and Gates into the project. As well, he enlisted the leadership of **William Rainey Harper** as president of the institution in 1890. Beginning in 1890 Goodspeed was for 23 years the secretary of the Board of Trustees of the University of Chicago, writing its first history as well as biographies of **Ernest D. Burton** (1926) and William R. Harper (1928).

GORDON, ADONIRAM JUDSON (1836-1895). American Baptist minister, born at New Hampton, New Hampshire. He was educated at Brown University and Newton Theological Institution, choosing a lifelong pastoral **ministry**. For 26 years he served Clarendon Street Baptist Church in Boston (1869-1895), making it a center of **evangelism** and **missions**. Gordon relied heavily upon evangelistic strategies of the era, including those of Dwight L. Moody (1837-1899). His theological bent became increasingly **dispensationalist**, thus making him a popular speaker at **bible** conferences. Within denominational circles, his church became a major contributor to the work of the **American Baptist Missionary Union** (ABMU), earning for him the presidency of the organization. He eschewed rationalism and modern theological trends, and singlehandedly revived the denomination's missionary program, adding for instance the African **Congo** field to the American Baptists. Gordon's educational legacy became the Boston Missionary Training School that he founded in his church in 1881 (later Gordon College and Gordon Divinity School). Gordon published a number of popular works, including *The Holy Spirit in Missions* (1893), *How Christ Came to Church* (1895), and *Is Christianity True?* (1897).

GOSPEL FURTHERING FELLOWSHIP. An **independent** Baptist missionary organization founded in 1935 by George Rhodes, a missionary in Africa. The agency is based in Lebanon, Pennsylvania, and focuses on **evangelism**, church planting, and theological education in **Canada**, **Spain**, and Africa. The Mission publishes *News and Views of GFF*.

GOSPEL HERALD **BAPTISTS.** See **Strict Baptists**.

GOSPEL MISSION OF SOUTH AMERICA. An **independent** Baptist missionary organization founded in 1923 to foster **evangelism**, church planting, theological education, and broadcasting. Its home base is in Ft. Lauderdale, Florida.

GOSPEL MISSIONARY UNION. An **independent** Baptist missionary agency founded in 1892. It focuses its effort on church planting, broadcasting, **theological education**, and missionary orientation. With a home base in Kansas City, Missouri, the Union operates in 19 countries. It publishes *The Gospel Message*.

GOSPEL MISSIONISM. A movement among Baptists in North Amercica which stresses the role that local churches should play over the interests of societies in conducting missionary activity. A form of **local church protectionism**, and related to **Landmarkism**, Gospel Missionism was advanced primarily by **T. P. Crawford**, and to a lesser extent by **James R. Graves**. Gospel Missionists believed that the sole purpose of missions is **evangelism** and that local churches could choose their missionaries and support them directly. Further, missionaries should eventually be self-supporting. The Gospel Mission movement reached the apex of its influence in 1892 when several missionaries resigned from the service of the Southern Baptist **Foreign Mission Board** (FMB) and followed T. P. Crawford.

GOSPEL STANDARD **BAPTISTS.** See **Strict Baptists**.

GOTCH, FREDERICK WILLIAM (1808-1890). English Baptist minister and educator, born at Kettering, England. He was educated at Bristol Baptist College and graduated from Trinity College, the University of Dublin.   For a time he served the Baptist church at Boxmoor, Hertfordshire, and his first teaching position was in philosophical studies at Stepney College. He took a permanent teaching position at Bristol Baptist College (1845-1883), serving as president from 1868-1883. In 1868 he was chair of the **Baptist Union of Great Britain** (BU). Among other theological concerns, Gotch rejected theories of inspiration for a system of interpretation he called non-creedal Christocentrism. His scholarship was well respected. He contributed to the *Encyclopaedia Britannica* and was author of the "Genesis to Deuteronomy" section of the *Revised English Bible* in 1881. Gotch was awarded an honorary doctorate by the University of Dublin in 1859.

GRACE BAPTISTS. See **Strict Baptists**.

GRAHAM, WILLIAM FRANKLIN (1918-). Southern Baptist minister and evangelist, born at Charlotte, North Carolina. He was educated at Bob Jones University and Florida Bible Institute, graduating from Wheaton College. Raised a Presbyterian, he met **Mordecai F. Ham**

(1877-1961), an evangelist, who greatly influenced his conversion and call to full-time **evangelism**. During World War II "Billy," as he became popularly known, preached on the radio and toured American military installations, conducting crusades. In 1947 **William Bell Riley** persuaded Graham to become president of Riley's **fundamentalist** school, the Northwest Bible Training Institute in Minneapolis, Minnesota, for five years.

In 1949 Graham held his first major crusade in the Rose Bowl stadium in Pasadena, California, and a year later he organized the Billy Graham Evangelistic Association with a team of evangelists, musicians, and the well-known soloist, George Beverly Shea (1909-). Graham's relation to the Baptist community includes membership in a local Baptist church and addresses at national denominational meetings and the **Baptist World Alliance**. During his crusades outside North America, he has enjoyed support from many groups and he has advocated for Baptist communities, notably **Poland** and the former U.S.S.R. Graham has been a kind of unofficial chaplain to presidents and other public figures, delivering the prayer at several U.S. presidential inaugurations and prayer breakfasts.

GRENADA. Baptists came late to the islands, evangelizing from South American conventions. **Southern Baptist** missions in Grenada date from 1975, involving a transfer of missionaries from Guyana. Church development has been slow and the community has remained a missionary enterprise.

As of 1995 there were four churches and 316 members in the Baptist community of Grenada.

GRANTHAM, THOMAS (1634-1692). English Baptist minister and theologian, born at Halton-Holegate, Lincolnshire. Originally a tailor, then a farmer, Grantham was baptized in 1653 and three years later became a **General Baptist** pastor at Halton-Holegate, where he assisted in forming several congregations. In 1666 he was ordained a "**messenger**" and for the next several years started churches at Norwich, Yarmouth, and Lynn. Several terms in jail allowed him the time to study and write, and he composed the first General Baptist **theology** in 1678, *Christianismus Primitivus*. He was ecumenically-minded and was buried in St. Stephen's Church, Norwich, owing to his friendship with the Anglican vicar. Grantham's theological works, more than any other General Baptist writer, were formative in establishing the theological position of the General Baptists. He was the first systematic theologian of any breadth in the Baptist movement.

GRAVES, JAMES ROBINSON (1820-1893). Southern Baptist minister and editor, born at Chester, Vermont. Self-taught, Graves took positions as a schoolteacher in Ohio and Kentucky. Moving to Nashville, Tennessee, in 1845 he studied for the **ministry** and was ordained. The next year he became editor of *The Tennessee Baptist* and exerted a wide influence across the South and beyond. He wrote on issues of Baptist **polity** and **theology**, emphasizing "landmarks" of the faith. He debated leaders of other denominations, notably the Methodists and Disciples of Christ. In a dispute with the Southern Baptist Publication Society, he formed the Southwestern Publishing House, which produced many controversial works. A great preacher and enthusiast, he raised an endowment for Union University in Jackson, Tennessee, and established Mary Sharpe College in Winchester, Tennessee. He is generally accorded the leadership of the **Landmarker** Baptist movement, in which strict views of the authority of a local church and the requirement of **baptism** by immersion are propounded. See also **Cotton Grove Resolutions; Landmarkism; Local Church Protectionism**.

GREAT AWAKENING. The term "Great Awakening" applies to the revival movement in the American colonies in the mid-18th century and less directly to some influences of the Wesleyan Revival in Great Britain during the same era. Renewal occurred beginning in the 1720s in New Jersey among the Dutch Reformed congregations. Later, Presbyterians experienced revival in New Jersey and Pennsylvania. In the 1740s and 1750s the Awakening was carried forth by several exponents, including Jonathan Edwards (1703-1758), George Whitefield (1714-1770), and James Davenport (1710-1757). Of the three, Whitefield probably had the greatest direct impact upon the Baptists.

A significant number of "separate" congregations grew up around the emphases of the **revival**, perhaps as many as 300 in 10 colonies. Originally the churches were primarily part of varying shades of the Congregationalist movement, but by the 1740s and 1750s many adopted Baptistic principles and as congregations made the transition to "Separate Baptists." Leaders of that movement include **Isaac Backus** and **Ebenezer Moulton**.

Benjamin Randal, a sailmaker of Portsmouth, New Hampshire, heard Whitefield preach, was eventually converted, and formed an itinerant **ministry** called the **Freewill Baptist Connexion**, which spread the revival fires through northern New England. Two other products of the Awakening were **John Gano** and **Oliver Hart**, who were both influenced by Whitefield.

In the Canadian provinces the Awakening reached the Maritimes via **Ebenezer Moulton** and **Henry Alline**. In the 1760s Moulton itinerated in the Annapolis Valley and formed at least two churches of the New Light persuasion. Alline itinerated throughout Nova Scotia and New England, focusing his efforts especially in the Annapolis Valley where several of his preaching stops survived as congregations. Alline established a peculiar revivalist, experiential understanding of the faith which characterized the Baptist communities in Nova Scotia long after his death.

In 1754 a pastor in Toland, Connecticut, **Shubael Stearns** joined the revival movement, and with **Daniel Marshall**, moved south to Virginia where, at Mill Creek, their evangelism produced extraordinary results. At length, Stearns and Marshall removed to Sandy Creek, North Carolina, where the Separate Baptist movement in the South took shape. Overall, the Baptists seem to have experienced the greatest surge of numerical growth in all regions, among all the denominations in the 18th century.

GREAT BRITAIN. See **England**; **Scotland**; **Wales**.

GREECE. In 1836 American Baptists, through the **Baptist Board of Foreign Missions** (BBFM), commenced evangelistic work in Greece, but withdrew due to opposition and shortage of funds. Two more later attempts were made by the **American Baptist Missionary Union** (ABMU), in 1851 and 1871, that Board withdrawing in 1886. In more recent history, Baptists entered Greece, the first modern church being planted by Marcus Bousios at Athens in 1969. The Baptist movement is assisted by the Southern Baptist **Foreign Mission Board** (FMB) and is officially designated the Evangelical Baptist Church of Greece. In 1993 the **Baptist Bible Fellowship** (BBF) began a mission to Greece.

As of 1995 there were three churches and approximately 220 Baptists in Greece.

GREEN, SAMUEL GOSNELL (1822-1905). English Baptist minister and educator, born at Falmouth, England. He was educated at Stepney College and graduated from the University of London. He served two churches, High Wycombe (1845-1847) and Taunton (1847-1851), before taking a position at the Yorkshire Baptist College (Rawdon) as tutor in Classics, 1851-1863. In 1863 Green became principal at the College, serving until 1876. In 1876 he became the secretary of the Religious Tract Society through 1891. Among the most widely circulated popular writers on various biblical subjects, Green was the author of 18 books, including *A*

Handbook to Grammar of the Greek New Testament (1870). His leadership at Rawdon College was considered progressive by some and latitudinarian by others; he was a catalyst in the establishment in 1866 by closed communion Baptists of the Bury Baptist College, later Manchester Baptist College.

GRENFELL, GEORGE (1849-1906). English Baptist missionary, born at Sancreed, England. Active as a young person in the Birmingham Young Men's Missionary Society, he was educated at Bristol Baptist College. There he met **Alfred Saker**, who influenced his decision for missionary work in Africa. Convinced that mission stations should be established in the interior, he began his work for the **Baptist Missionary Society** (BMS) in 1875 in present-day **Cameroon**. Eventually his river explorations took him to the Upper **Congo** in the steps of Henry M. Stanley (1841-1904), and where he helped to found the mission at Saõ Salvador. In order to advance the work, Grenfell supervised the construction of a steamboat, financed by Arthington which was disassembled and reassembled up river in 1884. He established stations at Lukolela, Yakusu, and Bolobo where he built his home. For his work in exploring the interior of the Congo, Belgian King Leopold II presented Grenfell the "Chevalier of the Order of Leopold." His published work includes *The Upper Congo as a Waterway* (1902), a significant geographical account.

GUADALOUPE. Baptist presence in the French West Indies, including Guadaloupe, has been small. **Southern Baptists** began missionary work on the islands in the 1970s, stressing medical ministries and **Sunday School** outreach.

As of 1995, there were seven churches and 694 members in the Baptist community of Guadaloupe.

GUAM. Baptist presence on Guam began in 1922 with a **General Baptist** mission. Then followed U.S. military occupation, with a Baptist fellowship in 1959-1961, which related to the **Southern Baptists** (SBC). Southern Baptists also have mission work among the numerous Vietnamese refugees living in Guam. **Conservative Baptists** (CBFMS) have had a mission since the early 1960s, and the **Baptist Bible Fellowship** (BBF) also opened a mission on Guam in 1975.

As of 1995, there were five churches with about 400 members affiliated, since 1993, with the Hawaii Baptist Convention (SBC), and four churches with approximately 300 members related to the General Baptist Mission.

GUATEMALA. Paul C. Bell, Sr. (1928-) and William J. Webb (1912-1973), U. S. **Southern Baptists** (SBC) from **Costa Rica** and **Panama**, visited Guatemala in 1946, which resulted in the **baptism** of 300 people and the formation of five new Baptist congregations that year. Later in the year, La Convención Bautista de Guatemala was formed. In 1947 a library, **colporteur** program, and Instituto de Pastores were begun. Southern Baptist support of missions in Guatemala commenced in 1947 when the president of the Baptist Seminary in Mexico transferred to Guatemala City and became the primary missionary there. In 1975 **Baptist Bible Fellowship** (BBF) began its mission in Guatemala.

As of 1995 there were 163 churches with 17,500 members affiliated with the Convención Bautista de Guatemala. The Convención publishes *Nueva Era Bautista* (New Era Baptist). The Pablo Bell Baptist Bible Institute is located at Solala and a theological seminary is in Guatemala City.

GUYANA. The first **Southern Baptist** (SBC) missionaries arrived at Georgetown, Guyana, in 1962. Brazilian Baptists were next to begin a mission in Guyana, with the assistance of the Baptist Missionary Society (BMS) in 1991. In 1993 the **Baptist Bible Fellowship** (BBF) opened a mission to Guyana. The Baptist Cooperative Convention was organized in 1973, relating to Southern Baptist work.

As of 1995 there were 16 churches and 1,607 members associated with the Cooperative Convention of Guyana. A Baptist-related theological institute is located in Georgetown.

H

HAAS, WILLIAM CLARENCE (1873-1924). American Baptist minister, and later **Independent** Baptist missionary, born at Mendon, Michigan. He was educated to be a schoolteacher and taught from 1889-1894. He became a pastor at Union City, Michigan (1894-1902); Manchester Baptist Church, Caldwell, Ohio (1902-1906); and Memorial Baptist Church, Columbus, Ohio (1906-1908). That year he resigned to become a missionary to Africa. Frustrated in his attempts to gain appointment through the **American Baptist Missionary Union** (ABMU), he accepted a call from the Africa Inland Mission in 1911 and served for a time at Mombasa, East Africa. His interest lay in French Equatorial Africa, however, which he entered in 1914 first at Bambili and later at Rafai. Following returns to the United States in 1916 and 1920, Haas was a principal organizer of **Baptist Mid-Missions** (BMM), soon to become the most extensive **fundamentalist** Baptist mission work in the United States. Just prior to his death he had firmly established the Mission's work in Sibut and earned a reputation as a respected pioneer of African missionary work.

HAITI. Baptist mission labors in Haiti date from 1823 when the Massachusetts Baptist Missionary Society (MBMS) commissioned **Thomas Paul** of Boston to do work there on a short-term basis. Paul opened a church at Cap Haitien but returned to New England in 1824. During the 1840s William Jones of Philadelphia went to Haiti under the auspices of the **American Baptist Free Mission Society** (ABFrMS) to train Christian workers for Africa. A century after Thomas Paul, American Baptists commenced work in Haiti in 1923 through the **American Baptist Home Mission Society** (ABHMS). The first church became the re-opened facility at Cap Haitien. A second stream of Baptist missions was started in 1848 by the **Baptist Missionary Society** (BMS) at Jacmel on the southern coast. In 1885 the English mission was transferred to the Jamaican Baptist Missionary Society and later this mission was supported by the **Lott Carey Baptist Foreign Mission Convention** (LCBFMS). The Carey mission concentrated its efforts particularly on the island of La Gonave. **Baptist Mid-Missions** (BMM) from the United States established a station at Marigot in 1934, and in 1982 the **Baptist Bible Fellowship** (BBF) opened a mission.

As of 1995, there were 91 churches with 49,100 members affiliated with the Convention Baptiste d'Haiti (organized 1923), and 345 churches with 17,423 members affiliated with the Conservative Baptist Mission. The Baptist theological seminary of Haiti is located at Cap Haitien.

HALDANE, JAMES ALEXANDER (1768-1851). Scottish Baptist minister and mariner, born at Dundee, Scotland. Following studies at the University of Edinburgh, he served in the Merchant Marine and returned to Scotland about 1795. He began to preach at various rural locations and came under the influence of John Campbell, an iron worker and itinerant Congregationalist preacher. In 1797 James made his first preaching tour of the North of Scotland, based on the methods of Campbell. The next year with the assistance of his brother, **Robert**, he started a **voluntary** organization, the Society for Propagating the Gospel at Home, and he recruited numerous young protégés. In 1799 he began a **ministry** at what was called the Tabernacle or Circus Church in Edinburgh, which in 1801 was moved to Leith Walk to occupy a building which his brother helped to finance. In 1808, under the influence of writings of Archibald MacLean, a **Scotch Baptist**, and Lachlan Macintosh, James was baptized.

He was **pastor** at the Tabernacle for half a century and with his brother, Robert, exerted much influence on the development of **evangelical** and Baptist ministries through a theological school and the sending forth of missionary-**pastors**. James's published works include *The Voluntary Question Political Not Religious* (1839) and *Man's Responsibility (1842)*.

HALDANE, ROBERT (1764-1842). Scottish Baptist theologian and philanthropist, born at London. He began studies at the University of Edinburgh, but quit to join the Royal Navy. Completing his term at sea, he settled at the family estate at Airthney, near Stirling, and with his brother, James Alexander, he devoted himself to various forms of Christian endeavor. Robert's initial plan was to sell Airthney and set up at Benares in India a Christian colony of 30 persons to conduct **evangelism** and publish literature; the East India Company, however, declined his proposal. In 1808 he was baptized and moved about the circles of **Scotch Baptists** with increasing influence. He had an interest in the Serampore Mission, but this was channelled into mission work in **Scotland**. He supported tract societies, **Sunday Schools**, and the resettlement of former **slaves** in **Sierra Leone**, West Africa. He went to Geneva and **France** in 1816-1819 to study and write; a number of students gathered about him and a **revival** occurred among Protestant churches in the French-speaking communities. Among his students at Montauban, France, were Louis Gaussen (1790-1863) and J. H. Merle d'Aubigne (1794-1872). Haldane published a major study of the nature of the inspiration of **Scripture** and aided in establishing the Continental Society. His generosity extended to aid for many houses of worship in Scotland, including the Tabernacle in Edinburgh that his brother served. Robert's most significant theological work was *The Evidence and Authority of Divine Revelation* (1816).

HALDANITE TRADITION. Terminology applied to the emphases and personalities involved in the outreach of James and **Robert Haldane** of **Scotland**. Many writers characterize the work of **revivalism** wrought through the brothers as nothing short of a Wesleyan Revival. Against the infidelism generated by the French Revolution and troubles within the Church of Scotland, the Haldanes brought renewal through **voluntary associations** of outreach, publications, educational efforts, and **evangelical** preaching. Their philanthropy led to the establishment of institutions which transformed churches at home and abroad. The formation of the Free Church of Scotland in 1843 was influenced greatly by the Haldanes. Their seminary produced student **pastor**-missionaries who fanned out over Scotland, England, and **Wales**, as well as the

Canadian provinces and indirectly in the United States. In **Canada**, for instance, John Edwards (1780-1842), William Fraser (1801-1883), and **John Gilmour**, three primary church planters,were of the Haldanite tradition. Although the work of the Haldanes came to an end in 1851 when James Haldane died, the tradition could be found wherever their disciples took up **ministry**.

HALL, ROBERT (1764-1831). English Baptist minister and theological controversialist, born at Arnesby, England. The son of **Robert Hall, Sr.**, Hall was educated at Bristol Baptist College and King's College, University of Aberdeen. He took an assistant pastoral position under Caleb Evans (1737-1791) at Broadmead, but owing to rivalry with Evans, he moved to Cambridge to succeed **Robert Robinson**. At Cambridge he developed a reputation as the city's finest preacher; he later served at Leicester and at Bristol a second time. He wrote widely on subjects such as freedom of the press, infidelity, and terms of communion. He was opposed to hyper-Calvinism and energetically supported open communion. A critic of **John Gill**, Hall referred to Gill's theology as "a sea of mud."

HALL, ROBERT, SR. (1728-1791). English Baptist minister and theologian, born in Northumbria. Hall was credited with having changed the course of the theological tradition of Old Calvinism when in 1770 he preached a sermon encouraging **evangelism**. His book, *Help to Zion's Travellers* (1781), was a major catalyst in the thinking of **William Carey**. Hall settled at Arnsby in Leicestershire in a poor parish and to support his family he kept a small farm, all the while writing materials which defended the new directions of **evangelical** Calvinism among Baptists. His sermons were widely published after his death.

HAM, MORDECAI (1877-1961). Southern Baptist minister and evangelist, born in Allen County, Kentucky. He began his **ministry** in Bowling Green, Kentucky, and served First Baptist Church, Oklahoma City (1927-1929). As an evangelist he itinerated widely; among his converts were **William F. "Billy" Graham** and Grady Wilson (1919-1987). Ham was a popular radio preacher who spoke of conversions numbering over one million during his ministry.

"HARD CORE" BAPTISTS. See **Baptist World Mission**.

HARDING, HARRIS (1761-1854). Canadian Baptist minister, born at Horton, Nova Scotia. Harding was converted under the ministry of John

Payzant (1749-1834), a **New Light** Congregationalist preacher, and he united with the mixed communion congregation at Cornwallis. He went to Yarmouth as an evangelist in 1790 and settled there in 1797, serving the church for 60 years. Although he became a Baptist in 1799, his church did not join the Association until 1806, preferring a mixed communion stance. Harding suffered from personal defeats in his professional development, notably from a romantic affair in 1796 which led to a forced marriage, and accusations in 1798 of "new **dispensationalism**," which referred to his denial of structures and rules. In both instances he presented a contrite response and rebuilt his **ministry** with solid **evangelism.** In 1806 and again in 1812-1813 he was involved in major awakenings in his community, the former resulting in 150 new converts. Exemplifying the **Second Great Awakening** in the Maritimes, he was considered one of the "fathers" of the Baptist movement in that region.

HARDING, THEODORE SETH (1773-1855). Canadian Baptist minister, born at Barrington, Nova Scotia. He was converted under the influence of Harris Harding, **Joseph Dimock**, and the Methodist, Freeborn Garrettson. He was further converted to Baptist principles in 1795 and was called to the Horton (later Wolfville, Nova Scotia) Church in 1796. He served that congregation for 60 years. Harding was an active promoter of establishing Horton Academy, and the Nova Scotia Baptist Education Society. He travelled extensively among the Baptist communities in the United States and gave spiritual insight to the founding of Acadia College. He was considered one of the "fathers" of the Maritime Baptist community. Between 1814 and 1820, opposed to closed communion, Harding served as a home missionary in New Brunswick. He returned an advocate of closed communion. Two great **revivals** occurred during his ministry, 1841 and 1848-1849; both the church and the College were involved in the protracted meetings. Between 1832 and 1841 he baptized over 350 persons at Horton.

HARPER, WILLIAM RAINEY (1856-1906). American Baptist educator, born at New Concord, Ohio. He graduated from Muskingum College, Baptist Union Theological Seminary, Chicago, and Yale University (Ph.D.). Harper had a gift for the study of languages and completed his doctorate at 19. For a time he lectured at Denison University Academy and at his theological alma mater. Yale created a chair for him in linguistics and he taught there with great success in 1886-1890. Harper became **Thomas Goodspeed**'s and **John D. Rockefeller**'s choice to build a great university at Chicago and Harper designed the institution's curriculum. Among his achievements were a school that in five years counted over 2,000 students, a university press and extension school, and a scholarly publication, *Biblical World*. With **Ernest DeWitt Burton** and **Shailer Mathews**, Harper was a leader in the first generation of what became known as the **Chicago School** of religious scholarship.

HARRIS, ELMORE (1854-1911). Canadian Baptist minister, born at Beamsville, Ontario. He was heir to the family of Massey-Harris Industries, a major producer of farm machinery. Educated at the University of Toronto, he turned immediately to pastoral **ministry**. He served at Centre Street, St. Thomas (1876-1882), Yorkville, which became Bloor Street, Toronto (1882-1889), and Walmer Road in Toronto (1889-1895). Under his leadership, congregations expanded greatly and required new facilities. His pastoral ministry at Bloor Street included many of the faculty at Toronto Baptist College (later McMaster University); in 1908-1909 he led an investigation of perceived modernist teachings by Professor Isaac G. Matthews (1871-1959) at McMaster. For several years, Harris himself lectured at McMaster in **bible**. Following his retirement from active pastoral leadership, Harris remained as a senior spiritual counsellor in the Walmer Road congregation, which he had founded and the property of which was donated by his family. He moved into the field of religious education in 1894 when he founded the Toronto Bible Training Institute (later Toronto Bible College). Serving as the first president of the school, he used the opportunity to showcase the institution to a wide variety of conservative **evangelical** leaders of the era, including Arno C. Gaebelein (1861-1945), C. I. Scofield (1843-1921), and W. H. Griffiths Thomas (1861-1924). These associations brought Harris a reputation as a leading bible teacher and inclusion as a member of the editorial board of the first edition of the *Scofield Reference Bible* (1909). He died of smallpox while on a missions exploratory trip in Delhi, **India**.

HART, OLIVER (1723-1795). American Baptist minister, born at Hopewell, New Jersey. Early influenced by **Great Awakening** preachers George Whitefield (1714-1770) and Gilbert Tennent (1703-1764), Hart adopted an **evangelistic** style and embarked on an itinerant ministry in the southern colonies. During the Revolution he was an ardent patriot, serving as a member of the South Carolina Committee of Safety. He fled Charleston with a British bounty on his head, settling in Hopewell, New Jersey, as **pastor** from 1780-1795. Hart was firmly convinced of the associational principle and built up cooperation among churches wherever he served. In Charleston, shortly after his arrival in 1751, the first **association** in the South was formed. In Philadelphia he greatly strengthened the oldest association in the United States. One of the most esteemed clergy of the 18th century, two memorial sermons were preached for Hart, one by **Richard Furman** in South Carolina, the other by **William Rogers** in Philadelphia. Hart wrote a few works which were published, including *Dancing Exploded* (1778) and *A Gospel Church Portrayed* (1791).

HARTSHORNE-FROYD REPORT. Following a reorganization of the **American Baptist Publication Society** in 1944, the **Northern Baptist Convention** (NBC) undertook a study of theological training in its churches. Hugh Hartshorne (1885-1967) and Milton C. Froyd (1908-1985) canvassed colleges, universities, theological seminaries, and ministers to make their report to the Board of Education and Publication in 1945. They found that 31.9 percent of the ministers serving in the Convention had no formal college training of any kind, and 19.1 percent had no theological training. Of the 68.1 percent who had at least one year of college, 19.8 percent received it in Baptist colleges, while 36.1 percent received it in other than denominational schools, and 12.3 percent received their education in theological schools founded after 1900. Fifty-three percent of all Northern Baptist ministers had no training in Baptist schools, an alarming result of the survey. The report, published in 1945 as *Theological Education in the Northern Baptist Convention*, prompted the denomination to take steps to enhance leadership development, one of which was the calling of a Conference on Professional and Lay Leadership at Green Lake, Wisconsin, in August 1950. Scholarship funds were also increased for use in denominational schools. The Hartshorne-Froyd Report proved groundbreaking among Baptists in that it defined in sociological and organizational terms the profile of **ministry** and marked the participation of a Baptist group in social scientific research.

HARVEY, HEZEKIAH (1821-1893). American Baptist minister and theological educator, born at Hulven, Suffolk, England. As a child he emigrated to the United States and was converted under the **ministry** of **Jacob Knapp**. He was educated at Madison University and Hamilton Theological Seminary, and owing to his prowess with languages, remained in Hamilton as a tutor for two years. He served as pastor at Homer, New York (1849-1857), and Hamilton, New York (1857-1858). Due to poor health he left the pastorate for a teaching career at the seminary, lecturing in church history and pastoral **theology**. In 1861 his teaching fields expanded to biblical criticism. For one year he returned to the pastorate, in Dayton, Ohio, but soon health failure forced him back to Hamilton, New York. In 1869 he resumed his teaching career at Hamilton and remained in biblical studies and pastoral theology for the rest of his career. He was one of the first seminary professors among Baptists to conduct a study tour of the Holy Land (1874), about which he was widely published. Harvey's works on Baptist **polity** were definitive for many generations. They include *The Church: Its Polity and Ordinances* (1879) and *The Pastor* (1879).

HASSELTINE, ANN (1789-1826). American Baptist missionary, born at Bradford, Massachusetts. She was educated at Bradford Academy and read widely in religious classics. In February 1812 she married **Adoniram Judson** of Malden and in 1813 the couple became America's first foreign missionaries to **India**. Although sent out under the sponsorship of the Congregationalist American Board of Commissioners for Foreign Missions, Ann and her husband adopted Baptist sentiments upon landing in India. Ann was baptized by **William Carey** at Serampore. Difficulties with the colonial government forced the Judsons to relocate to **Burma**, where Adoniram became the pioneer Baptist missionary. She became involved in children's work and maintained an extensive correspondence. Owing to health problems, she returned to the United States in 1821 and worked to modify the policies of the newly formed **Baptist Board of Foreign Missions** (BBFM). Returning to Burma in 1822, Ann encountered trying circumstances. Her husband was imprisoned in the Burmese civil war and she continuously pled for his release. She died of a liver ailment and became an instant heroine of missions. Her inspiring story was told by **Emily Judson**, Adoniram's third wife.

HAZZARD, DOROTHY (fl. 1640). English **Separatist** and, later, Baptist leader. She was the spouse of Anthony Kelly and then Matthew Hazzard (both of Bristol), the latter an Anglican priest who held Parliamentary sympathies in the English Civil War. About 1640 she refused to conform and began a meeting of Nonconformists at a private home in Bristol. Described as a "Mother in Israel," she was among the first Separatists in Bristol. She fell under the influence of a Baptist preacher named Cann and followed his gospel order in organizing what became the Broadmead Church in the City of Bristol.

HELWYS, THOMAS (c.1570-1616). English Baptist pioneer, born at Bilbrough, England. Details of Helwys's early life are sketchy. He appears to have attended Gray's Inn where he prepared for the practice of law. His home at Broxtowe Hall, Nottinghamshire, was the venue for a conventicle formed by **John Smyth** about 1605. Helwys likely funded the removal of this group of **Separatists** to Amsterdam in 1608. The next year the group adopted Baptist practices and became the first Baptist congregation. In Holland Smyth and Helwys differed on doctrinal and social issues, Helwys determining to return to England. Back in England in 1612, Helwys published the first exposition of complete **religious liberty** in the English language, *The Mistery of Iniquity*, and addressed his case to King James I. He also helped to form that year the first Baptist congregation in England at Spitalfields, outside London. Because of Helwys's understanding of the unlimited nature of Christ's atonement, the church was considered the progenitor of the **General Baptist** tradition. Helwys likely died in Newgate Prison before 1616. Among his other published works were *A Short and Plaine Proofe By the Word and Workes of God that God's Decree is Not the Cause of Any Man's Sinne or Condemnation and that All Men are Redeemed By Christ* (1610?).

HIAWATHA LAND INDEPENDENT BAPTIST MISSIONS. An **independent fundamentalist** Baptist domestic mission founded in May, 1942, at Escanaba, Michigan. The prime mover was Arthur A. Glen (? -1952), a **colporteur** for the **American Baptist Home Mission Society** (ABHMS), 1926-1933, who became disenchanted with the **liberalism** of the **Northern Baptist Convention** and resigned. A **pastor** in upstate Michigan for four years, Glen gathered several sympathetic pastors and formed the Hiawatha Land Independent Baptist Mission, whose objectives were **evangelism,** church planting, and assistance for ministers in the northern central states. In 1943 the Mission was recognized by the **General Association of Regular Baptist Churches** (GARBC).

HIGHER EDUCATION. The interest of Baptists in Christian higher education goes back to the origins of the denomination in England in the 17th century. Among the earliest **General** and **Particular Baptists** in England were several university-trained ministers of the Anglican or Puritan persuasion. Such names as **John Smyth, Thomas Helwys, Hanserd Knollys, Roger Williams,** and **Henry Denne** give ample evidence of the learning of the leadership.

In the years of the Puritan Commonwealth and the Restoration, Baptists and other **Nonconformists** were denied the opportunity to study in the universities at Oxford and Cambridge, as well as the schools and academies where the Established Church offspring received their primary educations. This led to clandestine academies and later recognized secondary institutions where Independents, Presbyterians, and Baptists were educated. In 1679 Edward Terrill (fl.1680) of Bristol took the significant step of setting up a trust whereby ministers could be trained in the apprenticeship style by the pastors of his church, Broadmead Baptist in Bristol. This evolved in the 18th century into Bristol Baptist College.

Several other theological schools were founded by the English Baptists in the 18th and 19th centuries, meeting the needs of the professional clergy (see **Theological Education**). Others who aspired to be physicians, lawyers, or teachers found their way into the system and excelled at both Oxford and Cambridge, plus the "red brick" universities founded in the 19th century. The founding of the University of London upon non-sectarian principles, but with heavy Dissenter influences (and related colleges and lectures), was an exception to the English trend to send students through the ancient universities to receive a higher education.

In the United States, however, different circumstances ensued. Christian colleges emerged from the mid-17th century as bastions of the religious confessions which gave them life. Indeed it has been shown by historians of higher education that the foundation of the American collegiate system was the church-related college. Baptists were privileged to make their mark in the pre-Revolutionary era with the establishment of the College of Rhode Island at Providence in 1764. This was the first of scores of institutions.

Throughout the 19th century, the Baptist system of state conventions, established before 1850, gave rise to state Baptist institutions, like Colby College (Maine, 1817), Colgate University (New York, 1819), Columbian College (Washington, D.C., 1821), Mississippi College (Mississippi, 1826), Furman University (South Carolina, 1827), Georgetown College (Kentucky, 1829), Denison University (Ohio, 1831), Richmond College (Virginia, 1832), Shurtleff College (Illinois, 1832), Kalamazoo College (Michigan, 1833), Mercer University (Georgia, 1833), Franklin College (Indiana, 1834), Union University (Tennessee, 1834), Wake Forest University (North Carolina, 1834), Howard College (Alabama, 1842), Baylor University (Texas, 1846), Bucknell University (Pennsylvania, 1846), Linfield College (Oregon, 1849), William Jewell College (Missouri, 1849), and Stephens College (Missouri, 1856).

Later collegiate level institutions which enjoyed wide patronage in their respective states were Des Moines University (Iowa, 1865), Ottawa University (Kansas, 1865), Alderson, Broaddus (West Virginia, 1871), Pillsbury College (Minnesota, 1877), Sioux Falls University (South Dakota, 1883), Colorado Women's College (Colorado, 1888), Grand Island College (Nebraska, 1892), Oklahoma Baptist University (Oklahoma, 1914), and Ouachita University (Oklahoma, 1886). Several of these institutions did not survive financial crises caused in large part by insufficient interest and support from their Baptist constituencies. Others left the church relationship in favor of nonsectarian higher education: Brown University, University of Rochester, Bucknell University, Colby College, Colgate University, and the University of Chicago.

In **Canada** the American style of school was seen in the development of Acadia University (1838), Canadian Literary Institute (1860) (later McMaster University), Prairie College (1879), Brandon College (1899), Okanagan College (1906), Atlantic Baptist University (1949), and Carey Theological College (1960). Similar to the secularization process in the United States, Canadian Baptists lost control over their three most prestigious universities in the 20th century: McMaster, Acadia, and Brandon. Baptist influence continues at McMaster and Acadia in the form of Divinity Colleges related to private, non-sectarian universities.

In other parts of the world where Baptist missions have been established, schools, universities, and special colleges have resulted from concerted efforts to offer egalitarian education. Notable are the Serampore College founded by **William Carey** in **India** and the Reekie School (1898) in Oruro, **Bolivia**. See also **Education**.

HINDUSTAN BIBLE INSTITUTE. An **independent** mission agency of Baptistic doctrine, founded in 1952 by Paul Gupta, a converted Hindu in Madras, **India**. The U.S.-based organization raises funds for educational and **evangelistic** efforts in India and sponsors short-term teams to India. The office is in Union Mills, North Carolina.

HINTON, JOHN HOWARD (1791-1873). English Baptist minister, **theologian**, and denominational leader, born at Oxford. He was educated in surgery at Oxford University, but under the influence of **Andrew Fuller** and **John Sutcliff**, he transferred to Bristol Baptist College where he completed two years. In 1811 he graduated from the University of Edinburgh. From 1816-1820 he served Haverfordwest, and later Hosier St. Chapel, Reading (1820-1837), and Devonshire Square in London (1837-1863). In 1837 he was elected secretary of the **Baptist Union of Great Britain** (BU) and in the ensuing quarter of a century his leadership saved the feeble union. Hinton strongly favored **voluntarism** and the authority of local congregations and lamented the priority of overseas over domestic missions. A moderate Calvinist, he repeatedly stressed human responsibility in conversion and was severely criticized by the *Gospel Standard* and **Strict Baptist** movements. At the end of his **ministry** he rejected the moralising tendencies of **Nonconformist** theologians, favoring a more **evangelistic** approach and opposing the growing cooperation with the Congregationalist Union. A **pastor** again in Reading from 1863-1868, Hinton compiled seven volumes of his theological writings, as well as a history of the United States.

HISPANIC BAPTISTS. Since the establishment of American and Southern Baptist missions in the Caribbean and Mexico in the 19th century, Spanish-speaking Baptists have constituted a growing minority in the denominational family. There is a Baptist Convention in **Spain** (1928) and conventions in every Spanish-speaking republic in Latin America. Significant Hispanic communities in North America are located in Florida, New York, Pennsylvania, Texas, and southern California. In 1928 a Spanish American Baptist Convention was founded in California. It sponsored the Spanish American Baptist Seminary in Los Angeles and a periodical, *El Paladin* (The Champion). The Convention, which included about 10 congregations in 1940, was associated with the **Northern Baptist Convention**.

In **Puerto Rico**, the Baptist community is related primarily to the **American Baptist Churches** and within the United States there is the American Baptist National Hispanic Caucus, formed in 1970 at Green Lake, Wisconsin. The Hispanic community related to the American Baptist family is derived primarily from **Puerto Rico**, **Cuba**, **Mexico**, and **Nicaragua**. Likewise, **Southern Baptist** Hispanic churches tend to be derived from **Mexico**, and Central and South America. One of the most recent developments in North America is the emergence of an Hispanic Baptist community in **Canada**, where there is a seminary, founded in 1997 at Montreal, Quebec. The Hispanic community in Canada has been formed largely from emigrants from the Central American republics and is concentrated in Quebec, Ontario, and British Columbia. The Spanish Baptist Publishing House in El Paso, Texas, founded in 1906, is a major producer of Hispanic language educational materials.

HISTORICAL COLLECTIONS. Early in their history, Baptists began to collect historical materials for use in writing an official history. Probably the first to do so was **Benjamin Stinton**, brother-in-law of **Thomas Crosby**. Evidently **Joseph Ivimey** also used a wide variety of primary sources.

Morgan Edwards took an interest in uniting the many clusters of Baptists from New York to the southern colonies and prepared notes for further publication in a full-blown history. Several sets of his manuscripts were discovered after his death, only some of which were published. Edwards's notes became the important beginnings of Baptist materials in North Carolina, Virginia, South Carolina, and Pennsylvania. Similarly, **Isaac Backus**, in compiling his history of Baptists in New England, brought together a substantial amount of letters and firsthand accounts of the various streams of Baptists from his section of the country.

In the first decade of the 19th century, **David Benedict** and **Luther Rice** collected a wide variety of materials for differing purposes. Benedict collected not only minutes of associations but he also requested regional leaders to write essays on the development of Baptist church life in their midst. Luther Rice, peripatetic missionary promoter among the Baptists in the United States, amassed a large amount of **associational** literature, which later found its way into the American Baptist Historical Society (ABHS).

The American Baptist Historical Society was the first systematic attempt in the United States to preserve materials relating to the Baptist enterprise. **Howard Malcolm,** a missionary promoter and writer, **John Mason Peck**, and William R. Williams (1804-1885) were among the originators of the society, which was created in Philadelphia in 1861. In 1896 a tragic fire destroyed much of the Historical Society's collections. A parallel collection was started by **Samuel Colgate** of Orange, New Jersey, in 1888 and presented to Colgate University. This collection featured published reports and a rare book library of early English Baptist publications. In 1955 the Historical Society merged its reconstituted holdings housed at Crozer Theological Seminary in Chester, Pennsylvania, with the Colgate Collection to form the largest body of Baptist historical literature and records in the world. The merged libraries were given a new home at Colgate Rochester Divinity School in Rochester, New York. In 1983 the Historical Society opened an American Baptist Archives Center at Valley Forge, Pennsylvania, to administer the American Baptist denominational records at the headquarters site, in addition to the Colgate Library in Rochester. Also in 1983 a small museum with changing exhibits was started at the American Baptist Assembly at Green Lake, Wisconsin.

In most of the state regions in both the Southern and American Baptist families there are important regional collections; among the oldest and largest are Virginia, North Carolina, Georgia, Texas, Illinois, Oregon, South Dakota, and Berkeley, California. Additionally the **Baptist General Conference**, the **North American Baptist Conference**, and **Seventh Day Baptists** have archives related to their organizations. In 1949 the **Southern Baptist Convention** (SBC) created an Historical Commission, which in 1985 took over the Dargan-Carver Library of the **Sunday School Board**. This library and archives was for a time the repository for the national Southern Baptist agencies. However, due to reorganization of the commission structure of the Southern Baptist Convention in 1995, the Southern Baptist Historical Society and many program facets of the Historical Commission broke away from the Nashville center in 1996 to be recreated at Oklahoma Baptist University.

Canadian Baptist efforts in historical preservation are also extensive. **John Mockett Cramp** collected many details for his serialized essays in Maritime Baptist history in the *Christian Messenger*. **Edward Manning**, pastor in Nova Scotia, left a large body of letters and associational items. In 1845 the Maritime Baptists organized a collection later to become the Baptist Archives at Acadia University. In the central provinces, historical preservation efforts began with the formation of the Canadian Baptist Historical Society in 1865, associated with **Robert A. Fyfe** at Canadian Literary Institute and later McMaster University in Toronto and Hamilton, Ontario. This collection also includes materials for the French Union, the national organizations, and the Baptist Union of Western Canada.

In Great Britain, the most significant collection of materials is the Angus Library, associated with Regent's Park College at Oxford. The provenance of this collection was Joseph Angus's personal library. Its strengths are original publications of 17th and 18th century Baptist literature, and records of **associations** and societies, notably the **Baptist Missionary Society** (BMS). The **Strict Baptists** maintain their historical collection at Dunstable in Bedfordshire. Less extensive collections are to be found at Bristol Baptist College, Dr. Williams' Library in London, and the John Rylands Library at the University of Manchester. A small but significant collection of Welsh Baptist materials is kept at the Union offices of the Welsh Baptist Union in Swansea, and a Scottish collection is kept at Union offices in Glasgow.

In Europe, many unions have made efforts to preserve their historical materials. In Hamburg (since 1996 at Elstal) at the Baptist seminary are many items relating to **German** Baptists, notably papers associated with August and **Walter Rauschenbusch**. At Betelseminariat in Stockholm, the **Swedish Baptists** have an extensive collection, emphasizing education and missions as well as a museum exhibit. Likewise the theological seminaries in Tolose, **Denmark**, Stabekk, **Norway**, and Budapest, **Hungary**, maintain historical materials. The Southern Baptist-originated seminary at Rüschlikon, **Switzerland** (recently removed to Prague, **Czech Republic**) has a Baptist/**Anabaptist** collection of mostly secondary materials.

Elsewhere in the Baptist family, many colleges maintain historical collections. Among these are the Baptist Historical Society of New South Wales, **Australia** (1974), Serampore College in **India**, **Hong Kong** Baptist College, and Central **Philippines** University.

Baptist historical serial publications include *The Chronicle* (1938-1957), *Foundations* (1958-1982), *American Baptist Quarterly* (1982-) by American Baptists; *Baptist History and Heritage* (1965-) by Southern

Baptists; and *Transactions of the Baptist Historical Society* (1908-1921) and its successor, the *Baptist Quarterly* (1922-) by British Baptists.

HOBART, ALVAH SABIN (1847-1930). American Baptist minister and theological educator, born in Whitby, Ontario, **Canada**. Upon the death of his mother, he was raised in Vermont by his grandfather, the distinguished American Baptist minister, Alvah Sabin (1793-1885). He was educated at Madison (later Colgate) University and Hamilton Theological Seminary. Ordained at Morris, New York, he served that church from 1874-1879 and then Mt. Auburn, Cincinnati, Ohio (1879-1885), First Baptist Toledo, Ohio (1885-1889), and Warburton Avenue, Yonkers, New York (1889-1900). Crozer Theological Seminary appointed him professor of English New Testament in 1900, a post he held for 20 years. In the classroom he became a master of biblical hermeneutics. From 1920-1923 he returned to the pulpit of Warburton Avenue and then retired. As a denominational statesman, he was in much demand, for instance as a member of the investigation committee at Colgate in the **Nathaniel Schmidt** incident, and also as one of the committee on the union of **Free Baptists** (FWB) and **Northern Baptists** (NBC), a merger which Hobart was the first to suggest. Among theological educators he was an advocate of English **bible** instruction. At Crozer, he dropped the Greek and Hebrew language requirements and modernized the entire curriculum. Hobart also pioneered the extension course of education at Crozer which assisted scores of pastors in remote locations. His published works include *Key to the New Testament* (1910) and *Religion for Men* (1912).

HOBBS, HERSCHEL HAROLD (1907-1995). Southern Baptist minister and denominational leader, born at Talladega Springs, Arkansas. He was educated at Howard College (later Samford University) and Southern Baptist Theological Seminary, where he was awarded the Ph.D. in New Testament. A pastor for most of his career, he served Vinesville (1929) and Berney Points, near Birmingham, Alabama (1929-1932); Crestwood, Kentucky (1937-1938); Calvary Baptist, Birmingham (1938-1939); Clayton Street, Montgomery, Alabama (1939-1941); Emmanuel Baptist, Alexandria, Louisiana (1941-1945), Dauphin Way, Mobile, Alabama (1945-1949); and First Baptist, Oklahoma City (1949-1972). Hobbs was one of the most widely respected leaders of the **Southern Baptist Convention** (SBC) of his era, serving as president, 1962-1963, chair of the Peace Commission in 1985, and preaching the annual sermon in 1957. Hobbs wrote hundreds of lessons for the Baptist Sunday School Board and preached over 700 sermons on the *Southern Baptist Hour*, a popular radio broadcast. In 1962-1963 he chaired the prestigious committee to revise the **Baptist Faith and Message** and this earned him a place as a prominent moderate theological voice among Southern Baptists.

HOBY, JAMES (1788-1871). English Baptist minister, born in London. He was educated at Bristol Baptist College and served as assistant pastor at Maze Pond Baptist Chapel (1812-1823) and then as **pastor** at Birmingham, Weymouth, and Twickenham. In 1836 on behalf of the **Baptist Union** (BU) he joined **Francis A. Cox** and made an extensive tour of the Baptists in the United States and **Canada**. The report was published and became a major resource in Britain for understanding the development and splintering of Baptist life in North America.

HOLINESS MOVEMENT AND BAPTISTS. The holiness movement was a collection of themes derived from the Methodist and revival traditions in the United States and Great Britain. From the time of John Wesley (1703-1791), some Methodists emphasized Christian perfection and wrote much about the doctrine of entire sanctification. With the **Second Great Awakenings**, particularly the stream fostered by Charles G. Finney (1792-1875), a Presbyterian **evangelist** in upstate New York, the notion of the perfectibility of individual Christian experience received new attention. In the revivals of 1858, led particularly by Walter C. (1804-1883) and Phoebe (1807-1874) Palmer and A. B. Earle (?-1892), a holiness **theology** took definite shape. Advocates of the holiness position held that sanctification was instantaneous, not progressive, and this led to a recogition of a second work of grace after salvation. Theologically and ethically, the doctrine teaches that the roots of sin are removed by sanctification, but that the possibility of a lapse remains. Typically, persons could experience this work of grace in revival meetings or the regional camp meetings being held throughout the United States and Britain in the 1860s and 1870s.

Baptists in the northeastern United States in limited numbers responded to holiness preaching and a few professed to have had an experience of entire sanctification. Likewise, during revival services in New Brunswick and Nova Scotia, **Canada**, in 1882-83 prominent **Free Christian Baptists** (FWB) had experiences. The result was a prolonged debate among the **Freewill Baptists** whose **Arminian** theology provided a context for emphasizing Christian experience. In 1888 a schism took place in which the mainstream Free(will) Baptists rejected holiness theology on the grounds that it was unbiblical and that it was contrary to the teachings of their systematic theologian, **John J. Butler**. Those who favored an instantaneous experience in turn formed the **Reformed Baptist**

Alliance, which in 1968 merged with Wesleyan Methodists in the United States. A similar set of circumstances occurred among Freewill Baptists in the southern United States when G. B. Cashwell in North Carolina had an experience of grace and led in the formation of the Cape Fear Conference of Freewill Baptists, later the Pentecostal Freewill Baptist Church. See also **Freewill Baptists**; **Reformed Baptist Alliance**.

HOLLIS, THOMAS (1659-1731). English Baptist philanthropist, born at Rotherham. Hollis was an active supporter of the Pinner's Hall open membership church in London. Hollis paid for the elaborate **baptisterion** at the church in Barbican for Baptists in London to use. He helped to found the Particular Baptist Fund in 1717. In response to the plight of Baptists in New England, he established at Harvard College the Hollis professorships, in exchange for recognition of Baptist ministers by the Congregationalist Standing Order. His gift gave preference to Baptists, and thus established Baptists on a sound footing among New England sects. See also **Architecture, Baptist**.

HOLMES, ELKANAH (1744-1832). American and Canadian Baptist missionary, born at Canterbury, New Hampshire. He served in the British military during the French and Indian War and later in the American Revolution as a chaplain. A frontiersman at heart, he left his pastorate at Staten Island, New York, to volunteer for **missionary** service among the Iroquois of western New York. He first worked for the New York Missionary Society from 1796-1807, but his insistence on believer's **baptism** led to a rift, and the New York Baptist Missionary Society was formed, for which he also worked. He evangelized the British settlements on the Niagara Peninsula, starting several congregations, and lived in Upper **Canada** (now Ontario) during the War of 1812. In 1797 he published an important manual of **polity** which was widely used on both sides of the border.

HOLMES, OBADIAH (1607-1682). American Baptist minister, born at Manchester, England. Holmes emigrated to Massachusetts as part of the Puritan migration under Archbishop William Laud (1573-1645). He settled first at Salem, then at Rehoboth, Massachusetts. In 1650 he adopted Baptist views and moved to Newport, Rhode Island, to enjoy greater religious freedom. In 1651 Holmes, **John Clarke**, and John Crandall travelled to Lynn, Massachusetts, to witness to a friend, and were imprisoned and fined. His whipping became the subject of works on persecution by John Clarke and **Roger Williams**. He served as pastor of the Newport Baptist congregation from 1651-1663, in the absence of John

Clarke. He maintained correspondence with London **Particular Baptists** and withstood a schism in the congregation, which eventually became Second Baptist Church. Holmes's steadfast opposition to Seventh Day views ·led to the establishment in Newport of a separate **Seventh Day Baptist** (SDB) church in 1668.

HOLY COMMUNION. See Lord's Supper.

HOLY SPIRIT, BAPTIST UNDERSTANDING OF. A universal Baptist "doctrine" of the Holy Spirit cannot be easily identified or summarized in a single, convenient statement. There is a long tradition of Baptist recognition of the work of the Spirit, with increasing attention to the gifts of the Spirit and the Spirit-filled life in the later 20th century.

 None of the early Baptist confessions of faith have a separate section devoted to the Holy Spirit, as is the case, for instance, with the doctrines of Christ and the church. Instead, discussion of the Holy Spirit occurs in the context of the Trinity, the gathering of the church, witness to the person of Christ, and teacher of truth. As Quakers, **Seekers**, and **Ranters** spoke openly of "being in the Spirit" or "led by the Spirit" in the 17th century, Baptists clearly wanted to differentiate themselves from these more radical enthusiastic sects. Most early Baptists therefore adopted a generally Reformed view of the Holy Spirit as paraclete and guide, preferring instead to emphasize the pre-eminence of **Christ**.

 Beginning in the 18th century, and probably under the influence of the Wesleyans in Britain and the revivalist movement in the United States, Baptists began to awaken to manifestations of the Spirit in individual and collective spiritualities. **New Lights** emphasized the work of the Spirit in regeneration and sanctification, while Old Lights stressed education, nurture, and confessionalism. Camp meetings, revivals, outdoor **evangelism** and missionary endeavor of many kinds, all necessitated a strong belief in an immanent and personal manifestation of God, namely, the Holy Spirit. The influence of the **Holiness** tradition upon particularly the **Freewill Baptists** led to correctives by theologians such as **John J. Butler**, who urged a traditional progressive understanding of sanctification, rather than instantaneous manifestations purportedly wrought by the Spirit.

 With the growing attention in the 20th century to the Pentecostal traditions and the Charismatic renewal movements, Baptist were forced to respond to the stimuli of media evangelists, small group development, and massive literature output about the Spirit upon church members. Not atypically, many Baptists in the United Kingdom were involved in the Spring Harvest movement, and in North America the Vineyard

movement, both of which emphasized the extraordinary work of the Holy
Spirit. In a few cases, ongoing **associations** of "Spirit-filled Baptists"
exist in denominational families, such as the American Baptist
Charismatic Fellowship, more recently called the Holy Spirit Renewal
Fellowship.

In terms of doctrinal statements, Baptists generally have stressed
the personhood of the Holy Spirit and referred to the Spirit in the third
person. Additionally, the Spirit is understood to have been active in
Creation, the inspiration of **Scripture**, the exaltation of Christ, the calling
of believers, cultivation of Christian character through presence in every
believer, and the empowerment of believers for worship, evangelism, and
service.

HONDURAS. Baptist life in Honduras was an outgrowth of missions in
Guatemala and **El Salvador**. In 1946 the first congregation was
organized at Choluteca and U. S. **Southern Baptist** William J. Webb
(1912-1973) conducted preaching tours and established the work. In 1958
the Asociación de Iglesias Bautistas de Honduras was founded with five
churches; a theological institute was opened a short time later at
Tegucigalpa. The **Conservative Baptists** (CBFMS) from the United
States in 1951 began a substantial work with a radio station, in 1955
Baptist Mid-Missions (BMM) opened a mission at Utila on the Day
Islands, in 1974 the **Baptist Bible Fellowship** (BBF) opened a mission,
and the **American Baptist Association** also has mission work in
Honduras.

As of 1995 there were 113 churches and 8,267 members with the
Convención Nacional Bautista de Honduras.

HONG KONG. The presence of Baptists in the city and province of Hong
Kong may be dated from 1842 when **William Dean** and **J. Lewis Shuck,**
missionaries of the American **Baptist Board of Foreign Missions**
(BBFM), embarked upon a church planting mission with the support of
the **British Baptist Missionary Society** (BMS). Eventually American
Baptists were to leave Hong Kong to indigenous leaders in favor of other
ports in South **China**. Shuck became a missionary of the **Southern**
Baptist Convention (SBC) and for a time carried on the work under their
auspices. In the 20th century as the fields in mainland China closed, Hong
Kong once again became a major focus of American and Southern Baptist
missionary work in its own right, often connected with missions in
Macao. Hong Kong Baptist College was established in 1956. In addition
to regular Baptist work, **Baptist Mid-Missions** (BMM) from the United
States established a mission in Hong Kong in 1951, as an outgrowth of its

closed China work, as did the **Association of Baptists for World Evangelism** (ABWE) the same year, the **Conservative Baptist** Foreign Mission Society (CBFMS) began a mission in 1963 in Kowloon and the New Territories, and the **Baptist Bible Fellowship** (BBF) established a mission in 1969.

As of 1995, there were 77 churches with 51,924 members affiliated with the Baptist Convention of Hong Kong. The Hong Kong Conservative Baptist Association includes about 10 churches with 500 members. There are two Baptist-related schools in Kowloon and one in Sha Tin.

HOOTEN, ELIZABETH (c.1600-1672). English Baptist preacher, born in Nottinghamshire. From scant evidence, recent historians hold that Elizabeth Hooten probably was one of the earliest Baptist "she-preachers." In Thomas Edwards's (1599-1647) book, *Gangrena*, a **woman** preacher who was believed to conduct **baptisms** ministered in the vicinity of Skegby, near Mansfield. She may well have been one of the **"shattered Baptists"** whom George Fox (1624-1691) encountered in 1648. Hooten was said to be Fox's first convert; later she went on a mission for the Society of Friends and died in **Jamaica**.

HOVEY, ALVAH (1820-1903). American Baptist minister and theological educator, born at Greene, New York. A graduate of Dartmouth College and Newton Theological Institution, Hovey began his career as a schoolteacher. He returned to Newton in 1849 to teach Hebrew and church history. Later he became professor of **theology** and Christian ethics. From 1868 to 1898 he was president of the seminary, one of the longest and most distinguished tenures of a Baptist seminary administrator. His published writings include a biography of **Isaac Backus** and a systematic theology. During the Civil War era, he forcefully opposed **slavery** and he chaired the trustee committee at Brown University which admitted women students. Hovey was also one of the organizers of the **Baptist Congress** (BC).

HOWARD, JOHN (1726-1790). English Baptist philanthropist and reformer, born at Hackney. Early in life he was apprenticed as a grocer, but declined to continue in that trade. In 1756 he took a sea voyage, was captured and imprisoned in France. During his incarceration he cared for sailors and took note of the deplorable conditions in the prison system. Returning to England he was made a Fellow of the Royal Society in 1756 and he settled at Cardington, Bedfordshire. On his property he constructed a model village and conducted education for **Nonconformist** children. From 1773 to his death he travelled widely in England and Europe, at his own expense conducting a tour and assessment of prisons, hospitals, lazarettos, and military encampments. In 1773 he was elected high sheriff of Bedfordshire and from this position he brought about reform of prison conditions in the counties. In 1777 he published a widely acclaimed study, the *State of the Prisons in England and Wales*, which initiated much reform of the system. A teetotaler and vegetarian, Howard was also an active Baptist layman, involved in **Samuel Stennett**'s church at Little Wild Street, London. He held Stennett in high esteem and wrote affectionately of his worship services. Howard died at Khersom in southern **Russia**, while inspecting military outposts.

HOWELL, ROBERT BOYTE CRAWFORD (1801-1868). Southern Baptist minister and denominational leader, born in Wayne County, North Carolina. A graduate of Columbian College, his **ministry** began in Norfolk, Virginia, after which he moved to the pastorate of First Baptist, Nashville, Tennessee, from 1834-1850. Next he served Second Baptist, Richmond, Virginia, from 1850-1857. In each of these pastorates he served with distinction, building large congregations. Howell served as president of the **Southern Baptist Convention** (SBC) from 1851-1853 and again in 1855 and 1857, resigning under pressure from **James R. Graves** and the **Landmarkist Movement**. One of the most prolific writers of the Baptist family in the United States, he wrote major works entitled *The Deaconship* (1846) and *The Terms of Communion* (1854). He debated with Campbellites and within his own denomination, with James R. Graves. Howell favored a strong denomination which was missionary-minded in contrast to other more exclusivist views of the church.

HUBMAIER, BALTHASAR (c. 1480-1528). German religious reformer, born at Friedberg. He was educated at the University of Freiberg where he earned an M.A. under the tutelage of Johann Eck (1486-1543), and in 1512, he was awarded the Th.D. degree at the University of Ingolstadt, again largely under Eck. Hubmaier earned a wide reputation as a pulpit orator from his service as a chaplain at the Church of the Virgin. In 1516, he moved to Regensburg as a preacher, where he became embroiled in an anti-Jewish movement. At length, he went to Waldshut in Württenberg as a zealous Catholic. Influenced by Swiss reformers and Erasmus (1469-1536), in 1522 he began to rethink his theological position. In 1524, much affected by **Huldrych Zwingli** in Zurich, Hubmaier announced to his congregation at Waldshut 18 theses, which included the principle of *sola fide* and an end to the Mass. He was married the same year. In 1525, Hubmaier moved beyond Zwingli to a position in support of believer's **baptism** and he was baptized by William Roublin of Wytiken.

Hubmaier's tract, *The Christian Baptiam of Believers* (1525), summarized his new beliefs. In 1526, he moved to Nikolsburg in Moravia where he mingled with chiliastic **Anabaptists**. By edict of Ferdinand of Austria, he and his wife were imprisoned at Greisenstein near Vienna. Under pressure, Hubmaier made several concessions to Catholicism and his having conspired against the state. His continuing anabaptist views, however, led to his martyrdom on March 10, 1528, at Vienna, while his wife was drowned in the Danube. Recovered historically in the 19th century, Hubmaier became an heroic figure among advocates of believer's baptism and his defense of the position is considered the earliest and best theological presentation of the sacrament/ordinance.

HUMAN RIGHTS, AND BAPTISTS. Many Baptists have difficulties with the terminology of "human rights" because of their Calvinistic heritage of the doctrine of the sovereignty of God. However, this has not diminished Baptist interest in and support for human rights concerns: physical, political, and spiritual.

The primary human rights issue for Baptists has been **religious liberty**, almost to the exclusion of other needs. From the time of **Thomas Helwys**, religious liberty has included the rights to **freedom of conscience**, education of children, propagation of the faith, and freedom to organize churches and religious **associations**. (see **Religious Liberty**).

In the early 19th century human rights for many was equated with the abolition of **slavery**. Progressive Baptists in the American South, such as **David Barrow** and **William H. Brisbane**, advocated emancipation of **slaves** as an act of Christian responsibility. In the 1830s **Freewill Baptists** (FWB) and Regular Baptists in the northern states advocated abolition of slavery on the grounds of moral law and human rights. In the British context, **William Knibb** reminded readers of his observations of life in **Jamaica** in decrying the evils of slavery, and he advocated the emancipation of slaves to numerous members of Parliament in the 1832 session. Slavery was the overriding violation of human rights and it consumed Baptist moral energies well into the 1850s.

Later, Baptist **associations** in the northern United States organized various **voluntary** societies to alleviate poor housing conditions, exploitation of women and children, and the plight of Black and immigrant communities. The Long Island Baptist Fresh Air Society (actually a camping ministry) and the Friendship House movement in northern Baptist cities illustrated these responses.

The Baptist community spoke out dramatically in the 1930s as totalitarian governments seized control in several European countries. Of particular concern were Nazi **Germany** and Stalinist **Russia**. In 1939, the three major U.S. Baptist groups, **Northern**, **Southern**, and **National**, jointly issued the **American Baptist Bill of Rights**, which upheld basic human rights to personal spirituality, unconstrained religious expression, a free church in a free state, and complete religious freedom for all peoples, regardless of faith commitment. It was said that the governments of the United States and Great Britain were influenced by the position of their Baptist constituencies.

When the United Nations was formed in 1945, Baptists were granted Non-Governmental Organization (NGO) status through the **Baptist World Alliance** (BWA), and this has ficilitated a constant flow of human rights data as well as a forum for Baptists to express their concerns to representatives of various world governments.

From the 1960s through the 1980s, many Baptists focused their energies on the civil rights struggle in the United States as well as on the apartheid conditions in South Africa. Support was forthcoming from the **American Baptist Convention** and several historically **Black Baptist** groups for the work of **Martin Luther King, Jr.** Likewise, it was a stated position of the General Board of the **American Baptist Churches** in the 1980s to support the **Sullivan Principles** which increased pressure on U.S. corporations to withdraw investments from South Africa.

Currently Baptist concerns for human rights focus on the abuse of governments with respect to the treatment of children, refugees, prisoners (political and military), genocide, minority groups, and military action as a tool to resolve conflict. Hunger, famine, natural disasters, sustainable development, violence against believers, churches, and ministers, vandalism borne of racial or ethnic strife, and uncontrolled disease epidemics are also of particular interest to several Baptist groups. Some would even argue that religious harassment within some Baptist groups over political control or doctrinal differences is a violation of human rights in a free society.

Advocacy for human rights is seen in the Human Rights Study Commission of the BWA (which has been under pressure since the 1980s to create a higher level of divisional status), the American Baptist Churches, the Southern Baptist Convention (SBC), the **Baptist Union of Great Britain** (BU), the regional fellowships of the BWA, and the **Baptist Peace Fellowship of North America** (BPFNA). In 1998 the BWA developed a format to receive complaints and reports of the violation of human rights, which are reported to the general secretary for appropriate action. Increasingly, the language of human rights as intoned in the United Nations is being used in BWA circles, such as the widespread advocacy of "life, liberty, and security" as stated in the Universal Declaration of Human Rights. Locations of particular concern to Baptists in the last 25 years have included, **Zaire** (Congo), **Myanmar** (Burma), **China**, the Soviet Union, **Uganda, Rwanda, Liberia, South Africa, Ireland, Nicaragua, Mexico, Bolivia, Colombia, Peru, Argentina**, Australian Aborigines, **Kenya, Angola, Mozambique**, Afghanistan, **Iran**, Palestine, and Tibet.

HUNGARIAN BAPTIST UNION OF AMERICA. Part of the **American Baptist Home Mission Society**'s (ABHMS) witness to Slavic immigrants to the United States in the late 19th and early 20th centuries was the formation of Hungarian Baptist congregations. Many of these churches were clustered in northeastern Pennsylvania and the Great Lakes region. In 1908 at Homestead, Pennsylvania, the Hungarian Baptist Union was formed, which at once began publication of a newspaper, *The Gospel Messenger* (1908-). In 1913 a Hungarian Baptist Seminary was started at Scranton, Pennsylvania, later to be merged with the International Baptist Seminary in East Orange, New Jersey. Over the years, the Union came to include about 30 churches in Pennsylvania, Ohio, and New Jersey. In 1940-1941 the Union became an "Associated Organization" with the **Northern Baptist Convention** (NBC).

HUNGARY. In the interests of the free church tradition, Hungarian Baptists maintain an ideological historical connection with Swiss **Anabaptists** from the 16th century. Officially, Baptist work in Hungary is traced to the ministry of **Heinrich Meyer** who arrived in Budapest in 1873 as an agent of the British and Foreign Bible Society. Also working for **J. G. Oncken**, Meyer baptized several candidates and a church was formed by 1874. Eventually two distinct groups emerged, a German-speaking and a Hungarian-speaking association. In 1892 a mission board was organized and the Hungarian Baptist Union was formed in 1900 with a **confession of faith** adopted in 1902. In 1920 the separate factions were united in the Magyarorszagi Baptista Egyhaz. A theological school was founded at Budapest in 1921 as a result of the **London Conference of 1920**. In 1990 the International Baptist Lay Academy (IBLA) was established under the auspices of the **European Baptist Federation**. The **Association of Baptists for World Evangelism** (ABWE) started a mission in 1988 and in 1990 the **Baptist Bible Fellowship** (BBF) opened a mission in Hungary, as did the **Conservative Baptist** Foreign Mission Society (CBFMS) the same year.

    As of 1995, there were 241 churches with 10,960 members in the Magyarorszagi Baptista Egyhaz. A newspaper, *Bekehirnok* (Messenger of Peace) (1894-), is published by the Union.

I

ICELAND. Baptist mission in Iceland has followed the presence of U.S. military personnel. **Southern Baptists** began a mission in Iceland in 1963, but four years later closed down the effort. The **Baptist Bible Fellowship** (BBF) opened a mission in Iceland in 1982. One congregation located at Njardvik is independent of any outside group and has over 100 members.

INDEPENDENT BAPTISTS. The term "independent" has been applied to Baptist congregations and some associative bodies who are distinguished for their opposition to mainstream Baptist organizations. The term is usually employed in the American context, though it is found among Baptists in **Trinidad** from 1890.

In the 18th century United States, for instance, **Isaac Backus** stood outside the regular association for several years and was ""independent," as was **Elias Smith** of Haverhill, Massachusetts, when he became critical of the leaders of the Warren Association. Deep antagonisms emerged in the 19th century among the antimission Baptists and later the "gospel mission movement." Many in the **Landmarker** movement were independent of "conventionism." As the **fundamentalist** movement emerged in the first decades of the 20th century, leaders like **J. Frank Norris, John R. Rice, T. T. Shields,** and others first tried to reform the conventions to which they related, then they organized various **associations** "independent" of any existing Baptist body. A new wave of "independent" Baptists came forth after World War II, mostly in the United States, but expanding in the missionary context, which are not related strongly to any extra-congregational body. These congregations cherish their **autonomy** and exhibit strong individual pastoral leadership. The terminology "independent" must be understood in a context of selective associationalism, however, as most congregations which employ the label "independent" cooperate with some organization, for instance the **Baptist Bible Fellowship** (BBF), the **World Baptist Fellowship** (WBF), the **Southwide Baptist Fellowship** (SBF), or the **Liberty Baptist Fellowship** (LBF). Independent Baptist missionary agencies have allowed the independent church movement to carry forth the same outreach programs that "convention-related Baptists" enjoy. Among the prominent independent Baptist mission agencies are the **Association of Baptists for World Evangelism** (ABWE), **Maranatha Baptists, Baptist Mid-Missions** (BMM), and **Evangelical Baptist Mission** (EBM). There are also several colleges, **bible schools**, and seminaries which meet the needs of independent Baptists, for instance, Bob Jones University (South

Carolina), Tennessee Temple Schools (Tennessee), Baptist Bible College (Missouri), Dallas Theological Seminary (Texas), Liberty University (Virginia), Moody Bible Institute (Illinois), Baptist Bible College and Seminary (Pennsylvania), Toronto Baptist Seminary (Ontario), and the Northwestern Schools in Minnesota. See also **World Baptist Fellowship**.

INDEPENDENT GOSPEL MISSIONS. An American independent Baptistic missionary organization founded in 1968 by David Bovard and Henry Campbell. It focuses its effort on **evangelism** and church planting with about 150 missionaries in Africa, **India**, South America, the Caribbean, **Philippines**, and **Korea**. Its home base is in Sharon, Pennsylvania.

INDIA. The first Baptist missions in India were commenced in the early 1790s through the work of **John Thomas**. He informed **William Carey** of the opportunity he had observed in two previous visits, and the two became the first Baptist missionaries to Bengal in 1792; they were sent by the newly organized Particular Baptist Society for Propagating the Gospel Among the Heathen (later the **Baptist Missionary Society**). The first Baptist congregation in India was organized by Carey and his cohorts in November 1795 at Serampore, with the first **baptism** of a Hindu convert in 1800. With the translation and evangelization work supervised by Carey, the growth of Baptists in India through an extension of mission stations was slow and dependent upon the missionary society for many years. The first association on the British model was formed in Bengal in 1842, and a loose association in Barisal District from about 1880. American Baptist missionaries passed through India to other fields and eventually claimed their own Indian territory in Assam in the northeast in 1836. **Amos Sutton**, originally a British Baptist missionary, came under the sponsorship of the American **Freewill Baptists** and began church planting in Orissa. Canadian Baptists began the Telugu work at Vizagapatam in 1836.

The development of indigenous Baptist organizations in India was much influenced by the ecumenical movement and the strength of certain regions. In Assam a Baptist association on the American model was organized in 1851, followed by the All Assam Baptist Christian Convention, organized in 1914. In 1928 the convention of Manipur State was first held. In 1950 the work in Assam was united as The Council of Baptist Churches in Assam, and took its place in the Assam Christian Council. Over 400 schools and five hospitals were part of this legacy. In Bengal Orissa, a field originally opened to the Free(will) Baptists, but transferred to American Baptists in 1911, the Yearly Meeting was nationalized in 1918 and a Home Mission Board was formed in 1935. The following year, with the support of American Baptists, the Bengal-Orissa Mission joined the All India Baptist Union, a body of mission coordination for the country. In the South India Baptist Mission, also an outgrowth of American Baptist efforts, the American Baptist Telugu Mission became the Telugu Baptist Convention in 1918.

Cooperation has characterized Baptist work in India. In the state of Assam, the Assam Baptist Christian Convention merged with the Assam Baptist Missionary Conference in 1950 to inaugurate the Council of Baptist Churches of Northeast India. Further cooperation in Indian Baptist organization ensued in 1939 with the formation of the Baptist Union of India, which included six former missions from American Baptists, **Canada, Australia, New Zealand,** and Britain, plus seven language groups fron India itself. In 1998 over 700 Baptist churches from several conventions and unions joined together to form the All India Baptist Federation.

The oldest educational institution among Baptists in India is Serampore College, begun in 1818. American Baptists started a theological seminary in 1872 under the tutelage of **A. V. Timpany** at Ramapatnam; the school was originally known as Brownson Theological Seminary and in 1920, with the merger of the Canadian Baptist school, Union Theological Seminary. A significant educational center was developed at Jorhat, beginning in 1906 and inclusive of four kinds of education; in 1950 this became the location of Eastern Theological College. Perhaps no other national context has witnessed so widespread growth of Baptist schools, hospitals, clinics, social service centers, and other institutions as in India. The vast majority of these institutions were indigenized after 1948 when India won its independence from Great Britain and thereafter placed restrictions upon foreign mission influences. Presently, there are 20 theological schools related to various Baptist bodies in India, several in key centers: Andhra Pradesh, Assam, Manipur, Mizoram, Nagaland, Serampore, and Tripura.

Aside from the historic Baptist work in India, U. S. **Southern Baptists** (SBC) entered the country by appointing Dr. Jasper McPhail (1930-), a thoracic surgeon, to the Vellore Christian Medical College. McPhail urged the establishment of a hospital at Bangalore in 1962 with a medical mission, under the direction of Ralph Bethea (1919-). The (U.S.) **Baptist General Conference** (BGC) assumed in 1944 responsibility for mission work begun in 1912-1917 in Assam on the north bank of the Brahmaputra River at Manipur. Also, **Baptist Mid-Missions** (BMM) from the United States established in 1935 a mission in Assam, as did the **Conservative Baptist** Foreign Mission **Society** (CBFMS) in

1945 at Calcutta, Madras, and in Maharashtra and Madhya Pradesh states (where they work with Serampore College and Calcutta Bible College), and the **Baptist Bible Fellowship** (BBF) established a mission in 1952. The **American Baptist Association** (ABA) also has a mission in India. In 1925, a Seventh Day Baptist Church was recognized in Calcutta, with another established among the Telugus in 1950.

As of 1995, there were 16 Baptist bodies in India as follows: Assam Baptist Convention (266 churches, 24,360 members); Baptist Church of Mizoram (379 churches, 70,000 members); Baptist Christian Association, affiliated with Conservative Baptists (250 churches, 2,369 members); Baptist Union of North India (131 churches); Bengal Baptist Fellowship (45 churches, 1247 members); Bengal-Orissa-Bihar Baptist Convention (70 churches, 9,500 members); Council of Baptist Churches in North India (470 churches, 60,000 members); Garo Baptist Convention (1,541 churches, 166,375 members); India Association of General Baptists (40 churches, 10,300 members); Karbi Anglong Baptist Convention (197 churches, 16,835 members); Karnataka Baptist Convention (105 churches, 13,000 members), Convention of Baptist Churches of Maharastra (54 churches, 8,125 members); Manipur Baptist Convention (1,294 churches, 134,594 members); Nagaland Baptist Church Council (1,244 churches, 298,678 members); North Bank Baptist Christian Association (666 churches, 49,157 members); Samavesam of Telugu Baptist Churches (893 churches, 475,639 members); and Tripura Baptist Christian Union of India (363 churches, 30,000 members). The total of Baptists in India as of 1995 was about 8,008 churches with 1,232,585 members.

INDONESIA. Baptist work in Indonesia commenced in 1952 when a **Baptist Mid-Missions** (BMM) missionary, Ernest Loong left **China** to minister to Chinese in Indonesia. He started the initial Baptist congregation in Djakarta. Also in 1952 **Southern Baptist** (SBC) missionaries entered Indonesia and organized their first church in 1953 at Bandung. In 1954 the Baptist Theological Seminary of Indonesia was opened at Semarang. By 1961 work began on Sumatra at Palambang; a station opened on Madura and one on Bali in 1970. The growth of Baptist missions led to the organization in 1973 of the Union of Indonesian Baptist Churches. Conservative Baptists (CBFMS) have had an extensive mission in Indonesia since 1961 at locations like Java, Jakarta, and Sumatra; they established the Gospel Baptist Association of Indonesia. The **Baptist Bible Fellowship** (BBF) opened a mission in Indonesia in 1972.

As of 1995, there were 82 churches with 6,935 members affiliated with the Convention of Indonesian Baptist Churches, 260 churches and 60,000 members affiliated with the Fellowship of Baptist Churches in Irian Jaya, 120 churches and 4,294 members affiliated with the Gospel Baptist Association of Indonesia, and 165 churches and 37,532 members affiliated with the Union of Indonesian Baptist Churches. There are four recognized Baptist theological schools in Indonesia: Pontianak, Manado, Semarang, and Tobelo.

INERRANCY OF THE BIBLE. See **Scripture, Authority of.**

INGALLS, MARILLA BAKER (1828-1902). American Baptist missionary, born at Greenville, New York. Educated in local schools, she met in 1850 Lovell Ingalls (1808-1856), a furloughed American Baptist missionary to Burma who had served under **Adoniram Judson.** She returned to Burma with her husband in 1851 to continue his mission at Arracan. When Lovell died in 1856, Marilla travelled to the United States and arranged an appointment from the **American Baptist Missionary Union** (ABMU) for independent work in Burma. She returned to Lower Burma and settled at Thonze, a village located on the verge of the jungle. She endured persecution and health difficulties at Thonze, but remained as the railroad construction reached the village; her ministry consisted of tract distribution, libraries, and reading rooms. The nearby Buddhist monastery was a special object of her witness and it was said that she led over 100 Buddhist priests to faith in Christ. On her return trip in 1866 through England, she secured a copy of the **bible** signed by Queen Victoria, which she presented to the Queen of Burma at Mandalay in 1872, obtaining recognition of the Bible Women's Movement of Burma.

INITSIATIVNIKI. See **Russia.**

INSTITUTIONAL CHURCHES. Terminology applied to urban congregations in the later 19th century United States which adapted their roles and outreach to an all-encompassing program. Beginning as inner city congregations which grew to substantial size and accompanying edifices, the churches were confronted with several social classes, variegated educational needs, and many opportunities for **evangelism** and outreach. An institutional church came to be defined as an organized body of Christian believers who found themselves in an uncongenial social environment and supplemented the ordinary methods of **ministry** with a system of "organized kindness" which reached all in its shadow. New programs included language training, vocational classes, soup kitchens, recreation, shelter, and summer camping outside the urban areas for school age children. Such congregations sought to combine in the church the work of welfare agencies, social clubs and settlement houses, on the premise that the church alone contains the potential cure for all social ills. The institutional churches were in many ways the embodiments of the ideals of the **social gospel movement**. **Edward Judson**, pastor of the Memorial Church on Washington Square in New York City, wrote the defining pastoral theology for institutional churches, and others like **Russell Conwell** in Philadelphia and **A. J. Gordon** of Boston also followed the pattern. In the latter two cases major educational institutions were rooted in the local congregations.

INTERNATIONAL BAPTIST FELLOWSHIP. See **Fundamentalism, Baptists.**

INTERNATIONAL BOARD OF JEWISH MISSIONS. An **independent** Baptistic missionary organization founded in 1949. It focuses its effort on **evangelism**, church planting, and broadcasting ministries among Jewish communities in Asia, **Brazil**, **France**, and **Spain**. Its home base is in Chattanooga, Tennessee.

INTERNATIONAL CRUSADES, INC. An **independent** Baptistic missionary organization founded in 1971. Support is given to **evangelistic** crusades, particularly in the **Philippines**. Its home base is in Dallas, Texas.

INTERNATIONAL MINISTRIES TO ISRAEL. An **independent** Baptistic missionary agency founded in 1944. Its focus is on Jewish missions in **Israel** and **Mexico**. It publishes *The Covenant Newsletter*.

INTERNATIONAL PARTNERSHIP MINISTRIES. An **independent** Baptistic missionary organization founded by Chester Joines, pastor of Calvary Bible Church in Hanover, Pennsylvania, as American Technical Outreach Ministries in 1982. The agency focuses on theological education and leadership development in Africa, Asia, South America, and the Caribbean. Its publication is *Partnership News* and the home base is Hanover, Pennsylvania.

INTERNATIONAL URBAN ASSOCIATES. A Baptistic missionary organization founded in 1989 by Northern Baptist Theological Seminary urban missiologist Raymond Bakke (1938-). It focuses on leadership development, research and training, and management consulting for the mission context. With a home base in Chicago, Illinois, it publishes the *International Urban Associates Newsletter*.

IRAN. U. S. **Southern Baptist** missionaries began work among Muslim students at the University of Teheran in 1968. A congregation was established in Teheran in 1972, with others created in Shiraz, Ahwaz, and Isfahan. The **Baptist Bible Fellowship** (BBF) opened a work in 1966. In 1978, with the Islamic Revolution, Baptist missionaries were withdrawn.

IRELAND. Baptist work in Ireland began in earnest during the Cromwell Protectorate: 11 churches were established between 1652 and 1654 and the English governor-general was a member of the movement. The congregation at Dublin later became the center for Irish Baptist life; it became the Baptist Society for Propagating the Faith in Ireland and related to the Baptist Irish Society, which was founded in England in 1813 by **Joseph Ivimey** and others. Another root of Baptist faith was in the work of **Alexander Carson** who brought the Scottish **Haldanite** movement to Ireland and formed a congregation at Tobermore where he spent 30 years. English Baptists organized the Irish Baptist Home Mission and in 1888 this was transferred to the Irish Baptist Association in a move toward "home rule." In response, in 1895 the Association upgraded itself to become the Baptist Union of Ireland, partly in response to the **Downgrade Controversy**. Within this new Union, two **associations** were formed in 1897, the Northern and Southern. In the 1920s a separate relationship was recognized for the churches in northern Ireland which belong to the **Baptist Union of Great Britain and Ireland** (BU).

In cooperation with the Baptist Union of Ireland are several voluntary organizations: Irish Baptist Home Mission (1888), Annuity Fund (1902), Total Abstinence Society (1904), Prayer Union (1908), Sunday School Union (1913), Orphan Society (1917), Irish Baptist Foreign Mission (1924), Women's Auxiliary (1928), Baptist Youth Fellowship (1943), and Irish Baptist Historical Society (1968). Irish Baptists carry forth missionary work in **France, Belgium, Peru**, and **Spain** and support a theological college at Belfast, which was founded by Hugh D. Brown as the Irish Baptist Training Institute in 1892 at Dublin. Generally separatistic, Irish Baptists declined to join the **Baptist World Alliance** (BWA) and maintain fellowship with **evangelical** and **Strict Baptists** in Europe and Britain through the **Fellowship of Evangelical Baptist Churches in Europe**. The *Irish Baptist* (1876-) is published by the Union. In 1977 **Baptist Bible Fellowship** opened a mission in Ireland, and in 1993 the **Conservative Baptist** Foreign Mission Society (CBFMS) opened a mission in conjunction with the Baptist Union of Ireland.

As of 1995, there were 109 churches with 8,421 members affiliated with the Baptist Union of Ireland.

IRELAND, JAMES (1748-1806). American Baptist minister and evangelist, born in Edinburgh, Scotland. As a child with his family he emigrated to Virginia and by 1766 was a schoolteacher in the Shenandoah Valley. In 1769 he was baptized at Sandy Creek, North Carolina, and allied himself with the **Separate Baptists** who in due course, ordained him. He was a popular preacher in the region and was imprisoned in 1769-1770 at Culpepper, Virginia, for his public preaching. Accounts of his imprisonment indicate that local interests tried several means to kill Ireland, including suffocation with gunpowder smoke. He was ultimately released under the provisions of the Toleration Act, his incarceration becoming one of the most celebrated cases of Baptist persecution in the American colonies. He served as pastor at Buck Marsh (Berryville) and Water Lick Churches in Virginia. In the year 1802 Ireland received 52 members in one day into his church.

ISRAEL. Baptist missionary work in Israel began in 1921 when a Syrian, Shukri Mosa, established a church at Nazareth. Following the **London Conference of 1920**, Israel has evolved as part of the Southern Baptist **Foreign Mission Board**'s (FMB) Europe and Middle East Section. Before World War II there were four congregations: Nazareth, Jerusalem, Tel Aviv, and Haifa. With additional missionary support, schools have been opened and the Association of Baptist Churches in Israel (officially the Baptist Convention in Israel) was organized in 1964(?). The **American Baptist Association** (ABA) also has a mission in Israel. From 1954-1956 Conservative Baptists also had a mission in Jerusalem and Haifa.

As of 1995, there were 15 churches with 1,139 members affiliated with the Association of Baptist Churches in Israel.

ITALIAN BAPTIST ASSOCIATION OF AMERICA. Missionary work among the Italian community in the United States began at Mt. Pleasant Baptist Church in Newark, New Jersey, in 1887. The first congregation was constituted in 1894 in Buffalo, New York. In the 1890s an Italian Department was formed at Colgate Theological Seminary to train ministers for these churches, and in 1898 the Italian Baptist Association of America was formed and the number of congregations by 1940 grew to over 40. Largely an eastern states association, the churches publish *L'Aurora (Dawn)* and most of the congregations are affiliated also with the **American Baptist Churches U.S.A.**

ITALY. Baptist life in Italy began in 1863 with the work of English missionaries, James Calne in Bologna and Edward Clark in La Spezia. Following the dissolution of Roman Catholic establishment in 1871, the **Baptist Missionary Society** (BMS) and the Southern Baptist **Foreign Mission Board** (FMB) began support for missionaries and the Southern Baptists commissioned George Boardman Taylor who began his work in 1873. Churches were started in Rome (1871), Turin, and other urban centers. In 1923, as an outgrowth of the **London Conference of 1920**, Baptist work was united, with the Baptist Federation founded in 1939. An Italian Baptist Union, separate from the mission work, was formed in 1956 and this assisted in the gaining of **religious liberty** in the country. Baptists cooperate with Methodists and the Waldensians in educational work; there is an educational program, Centro Filadelfia, at Rivoli and the periodicals are called *Il Testimonio* (The Testimony) (1883-), *Il Seminatore* (The Sower) (1876-), and *Bilychnis* (1912-). Literature distribution to various constituencies is a major thrust of Baptist mission in the country. Other groups include the **Conservative Baptist** Foreign Mission Society (CBFMS) since 1947, **Baptist Mid-Missions** (BMM) from the United States established works at Naples (1951) and Salerno (1956), the **Baptist Bible Fellowship** (BBF) has had a mission in Italy since 1978, and the **Association of Baptists for World Evangelism** (ABWE) opened its work in 1989.

As of 1995 there were 88 churches and 4,695 members in the Unione Cristiana Evangelica Battista D'Italia.

IVIMEY, JOSEPH (1773-1834). English Baptist minister and historian, born in Hampshire. Originally a tailor, Ivimey was a pastor at Wallingford and then Eagle Street, London. As a pastor he added 800 new members to the church and 20 candidates to the **ministry**. Ivimey was a strict communionist and Calvinist. A consummate **voluntarist**, he advocated abolition of **slavery**, education for the poor, and public almshouses. He was a devotee of the **Baptist Missionary Society** (BMS), the Baptist Irish Society, and the **Home Missionary Society** (BHMS). In 1811 he proposed a **Baptist Union,** which was finally realized in 1831. Ivimey opposed the open communionism of **Robert Hall** and he staunchly supported "Fullerism" or **evangelical** Calvinism. He wrote a five-volume *History of the Baptists*, published in 1811.

IVORY COAST. The first Baptists in Ivory Coast came from **Nigeria** to work with Yoruba people. Beginning in 1947 **Conservative Baptists** began their mission, as did **Freewill Baptists** and later **Southern Baptists**; these three groups worked together in various types of **mission**.

Freewill Baptists concentrated their efforts in bible translation for the tribespeople. After 1966 Southern Baptists worked with the indigenous French, rather than the Yorubas. Abidjan became the center of Southern Baptist francophone missions in Africa. By 1979 the French-speaking churches near Abidjan organized an association and by 1984 this became the Association Baptiste Evangélique de Côte d'Ivoire and eventually the Eglises Evangéliques Baptistes Méridionales en Côte d'Ivoire. In addition to the older work, the **Baptist Bible Fellowship** (BBF) opened a mission in Ivory Coast in 1988.

As of 1995, there were 57 churches and 1,539 members affiliated with the Eglises Evangéliques Baptistes Méridionales de Côte d'Ivoire.

J

JACOB, HENRY (1563-1624). English Separatist and Independent minister, born at Cheriton, Kent. He was educated at St. Mary Hall, Oxford, but did not enter the Church of England's ministry, holding that church to be in need of reformation. In 1590 he joined the Brownist sect and fled to Holland where he conferred with other Marian exiles. Over the next 15 years he moved between England and Holland in the communities of Separatists. In 1616 he formed at Southwark a congregation on the plan of John Robinson (1576-1625); this became the first Independent or congregational church in England. Later, as it evolved in the 1630s, the church became the first **Particular Baptist** congregation. Jacob wrote on the subject of **religious liberty** and eventually moved to the colony of Virginia where he formed a settlement named after him, "Jacobopolis." He died in London.

JACKSON, JOSEPH HARRISON (1900-1990). American Black Baptist minister and denominational leader, born at Jamestown, Mississippi. He was educated at Jackson College, Colgate Rochester Divinity School, and Creighton University and served pastorates in rural Mississippi and Omaha, Nebraska, and Philadelphia, Pennsylvania. In 1934 he became the corresponding secretary of the **National Baptist Convention** Foreign Mission Board, the leading position in the largest Black Baptist denomination. In 1941 he assumed the pastorate of Olivet Baptist in Chicago (which he served for over 40 years), which positioned him to become the president of the denomination in 1953. He served in that capacity through 1982, longest in the denomination's history. During his presidency, the Convention expanded into several relief projects and Jackson courted government relationships. He opposed the militancy of the civil rights crusade and stood against the attempts of Gardner C. Taylor (1918-) and **Martin Luther King, Jr.** to take control of the National Baptist Convention in the U.S.A. (NBCUSA). His leadership style led to the schism in 1961 which created the **Progressive National Baptist Convention** (PNBC). Among Jackson's publications are *Many But One: The Ecumenics of Charity* (1964) and *A Story of Christian Activism: The History of the National Baptist Convention, USA, Inc.* (1980).

JAMAICA. **George Leile**, a slave from Virginia, arrived in Kingston in 1782 and began preaching on the local race course. He gathered a congregation and in 1791 built the first Baptist church in Kingston. In 1814 John Rowe was appointed by the **Baptist Missionary Society** (BMS) to Jamaica; he settled at Falmouth and opened a school for the children of slaves. Other British missionaries followed, including **Lee Compere**, J. M. Phillippo (1798-1879), and Thomas Burchell (1799-1846). Among the most outstanding missionaries were **William Knibb** who led the drive for emancipation of the slaves. With a church in every parish on the island by 1841, Baptists made extensive contributions to Jamaica's history.

The Jamaica Baptist Union was organized in 1849, which in recent development includes departments for youth work, a women's federation, and **evangelism**. In 1842 the Jamaica Baptist Missionary Society was founded to support missions in Africa and Central America. Efforts in **Cuba**, **Costa Rica**, **Haiti**, Cayman Islands, and West Africa have resulted. In 1843 Calabar Theological College was opened, later in 1964 to be federated with 10 other denominations in the United Theological College of the West Indies at Kingston, a major theological school for the region. From 1865-1871 the Union published the *Jamaica Baptist Reporter* (1966-) succeeded by various periodicals. In addition to the regular Baptist work, **Baptist Mid-Missions** (BMM) from the United States established a Jamaican mission in 1929 with the assistance of Canadians; the Fairview Baptist Bible College, founded in 1963 at Savanna-la-Mar, resulted from this effort. The **Baptist Bible Fellowship** (BBF) established a mission in Jamaica in 1972.

As of 1995 there were 301 churches and 42,500 members affiliated with the Jamaica Baptist Union.

JAPAN. Baptist witness in Japan dates from **Jonathan Goble**, a sailor on Commodore Matthew Perry's ship in Tokyo Bay in 1853. Goble returned to Japan in 1860 under the auspices of the **American Baptist Free Mission Society** (ABFrMS) and worked for 10 years. Later, the **American Baptist Missionary Union** (ABMU) commissioned **Nathan**

Brown to Japan in 1873, also assuming the mission of Goble. Brown formed the first church in Yokohama about 1873, and in 1884 a theological school was founded also at Yokohama. The first Baptist church in Tokyo was founded in 1876. A number of the outer islands of Japan were reached by Capt. **Luke Bickel** for the ABMU; he operated a **colporteur** boat to over 400 outposts from 1898 to the opening of World War I. In 1890 the Yearly Japan Baptist Conference of Missionaries was formed and the Japanese Baptists organized the Japan Baptist Union at the same time. For a brief time, the Australian Baptist Missionary Society supported a mission at Hiroshima (1874-1877), begun by Wilton Hack (1843-1923). American **Southern Baptists** began work in Japan in 1889; it was seriously interrupted by World War II, after which the work was reorganized in 1947 as the Japan Baptist Convention.

The post-war mission of the **North American Baptist Conference** opened in Japan in 1951. Among the other American missions, the **Baptist Bible Fellowship** (BBF) opened a mission in 1948 and **Baptist Mid-Missions** (BMM) established a work at Tokyo in 1950, one of its earliest fields; the **Association of Baptists for World Evangelism** (ABWE) started a Japan mission in 1953; the **Conservative Baptist** Foreign Mission Society (CBFMS) started a mission in Japan in 1947 and has over 70 churches together with the Sendai Baptist Seminary affiliated with the Conservative Baptist Association of Churches, begun by missionaries. The **American Baptist Association** (ABA) also has a mission in the country, and since 1952 the **Fellowship of Evangelical Baptists of Canada** have a mission at Takaoka.

As of 1995 there were 237 churches with 31,854 members affiliated with the Japan Baptist Convention, 57 churches with 4,814 members affiliated with the Japan Baptist Union, 37 churches with 3,092 members affiliated with the Okinawa Baptist Convention, and eight churches with 471 members affiliated with the Japan Baptist Conference. The Conservative Baptist Association of Churches includes about 65 churches with 2,019 members. There are six recognized Baptist-related colleges or theological schools in Japan: Fukuoka (2), Sendai, Yokohama, Kyogo-ken, and Kitakyushu.

JASPER, JOHN (1812-1901). American Black Baptist minister, born in Fluvanna County, Virginia. Raised a slave, he worked on various plantations in Virginia. He became a Christian in 1839 and was baptized in the Richmond African Baptist Church. He began preaching and attracted throngs of listeners, owing to his rhetoric. During the American Civil War, Jasper was employed to preach among the sick and wounded in the Confederate hospitals. He received his freedom in 1864 and organized several Black congregations, including Brown's Island, Third Baptist, Petersburg, Virginia, and Weldon, North Carolina. In accord with the Zetetic school of philosophy, Jasper advocated a curious theory of the rotation of the sun which in his sermons brought him both ridicule and applause because of its affinity with Joshua 10:14. His sermon "The Sun Do Move" was one of the classic sermons of the **Black Baptist** tradition. He served as pastor of the Sixth Mount Zion Baptist Church in Richmond, which included over 1,000 members in 1885.

JESSEY, HENRY (1601-1663). English Anglican and Baptist minister, born at West Rounton, England. He graduated a top scholar from St. John's College, Cambridge, his favorite subjects being Hebrew and rabbinical literature. He became a personal chaplain to Brampton Gurdon (fl. 1650), a wealthy Puritan, and took up the study of medicine. In 1627 he was episcopally **ordained**, but was without a charge until he took Aughton in Yorkshire in 1633. Jessey was soon discharged for removing a crucifix and neglecting the use of parts of the liturgy; subsequently he became chaplain to Matthew Boynton of Barnston (d. 1651). With Boynton he went to London in 1635 and later to Uxbridge. In midsummer 1637 he became pastor of the Separatist Independent congregation founded by **Henry Jacob** and **John Lathrop** in Southwark. This congregation had suffered a schism in 1633 over **baptism**, and a second occurred when Jessey became pastor. Jessey examined the question, took on believer's baptism (by **Hanserd Knollys**) and held immersion to be imperative.

Jessey's congregation suffered persecution and actually split in 1640 to avoid discovery. During the time he served the Baptist congregation he also preached at St. George's, Southwark, until he was ejected in 1660. He was one of the first missionaries to **Wales** in 1639, planting a congregation at Llanvaches. In 1646 he was reported to have participated in a healing service for a blind woman at Aldgate. During the Commonwealth he served as a Trier and Expurgator for Cromwell (1654), and his minute knowledge of the **bible** led to his appointment in 1652 to a committee to approve any new English translation of the **Scriptures**. In addition to serving as a teaching minister at Swan Alley, Coleman Street, Jessey also travelled extensively among the Baptist churches in the West and the eastern counties. He advocated citizenship for Jews and contributed generously to the charitable maintenance of 30 families. Suspected of **Fifth Monarchy** views, he was arrested in 1660 and later imprisoned until 1663. Following a trip to Holland to defend the rights of some of his parishioners, he died at London.

JETER, JEREMIAH BELL (1802-1880). Southern Baptist minister and denominational leader, born in Bedford County, Virginia. He was self-educated and early in his career he served as an itinerant minister in the valley of Virginia and a small church at Morattico. In 1836 he became **pastor** at First Baptist, Richmond, moving to Second Baptist, St. Louis, Missouri in 1849-1852. His final pastorate was at Grace Street Baptist, again in Richmond. Jeter used his Richmond base to broaden his denominational influence considerably. For 15 years he edited the *Religious Herald*, one of the outstanding state Baptist papers of the South. He was the first president of the Southern Baptist **Foreign Mission Board** (FMB) and set the denominational tone for overseas work. He was convinced of the need to improve relations between Blacks and Whites in his congregation, and against the advice of the city fathers, he provided a building for separate services which became the First African Baptist Church in Richmond. He used **revivalistic** techniques in his church and city and was himself a popular preacher in northern Baptist pulpits. Conciliatory toward his fellow Baptists of the North following the Civil War, he was an ardent opponent of **Alexander Campbell**'s teachings.

JOHNSON, WILLIAM BULLEIN (1782-1862). Southern Baptist minister and denominational leader, born at John's Island, South Carolina. He first studied law, then under the influence of Baptist luminaries like **Richard Furman** and **Oliver Hart**, he entered the **ministry** and served churches at Euhaw and Columbia, South Carolina, and then Savannah, Georgia. Also an educator and champion of women's education, Johnson supported the establishment of the **General Missionary Convention** (GMC) in 1813 and Columbian College in 1821. President of the GMC from 1841-1844, he offered the **Baltimore Compromise** and later feared the predisposition of the national body to **antislavery** supporters. In 1845 he was a prime mover in the organization of the **Southern Baptist Convention** (SBC) and served as the first president of that body. It was his influence which caused the SBC to adopt many of the characteristics of the GMC.

JOHNSONIANS. Name applied to followers of John Johnson (1706-1791) of Liverpool, an English **Particular Baptist** minister who advocated high Calvinism. Johnson, originally a **General Baptist**, developed a unique theological system which destabilized many churches in the Lancashire and Yorkshire **associations** well into the 19th century. Because faith is a grace, Johnson taught, lack of it is no sin. He held to a modalist understanding of the Trinity, a millennarian interpretation of prophecy, and he was vehemently **local church protectionist** and opposed to cooperation even with other Baptists. Johnsonian churches practiced the

laying on of hands and one **ordinance**, water **baptism**. In the 18th century, **John Brine** and Samuel Fisher (1742-1803) opposed Johnson's teachings and later John Fawcett and **Andrew Fuller** were among his critics. Churches sympathetic to Johnson's teachings numbered 13 and were found in Liverpool, Halifax, Towchester, Chesterfield, London, Newark, Todmorden, Norwich, and Wisbech. The last of the Johnsonian congregations had disappeared by 1850.

JONES, SAMUEL (1735-1814). American Baptist minister born at Cefn y Gelli, Glamorganshire, **Wales**. His father was a wealthy emigrant to America in 1737 and Samuel was accorded an education in the College of Philadelphia, graduating with an M.A. in 1762. He was ordained by First Baptist Church of Philadelphia in 1763 and became **pastor** at the Baptist churches of Southampton and Pennypack, a united parish. In 1770 Jones resigned the church at Southampton and served the congregation at Pennypack (Lower Dublin) for 51 years. He became one of the leaders of the **Philadelphia Baptist Association (PBA)**, and by extension the denomination at large. The Association appointed him to compile a system of **discipline** (1798) and a *Book of Hymns*, published in 1790. He also drew up a map of the churches, probably the first of its kind in the United States, and served numerous years as either the moderator or composer of the circular letter of the Association. Jones' booklet on the **laying on of hands** was a longtime authority in the American Baptist community. He was frequently called upon to constitute new churches in Pennsylvania and New Jersey and in 1763 helped to write the draft of a charter for the College of Rhode Island. The College of Rhode Island conferred the M.A. on him in 1769 and the College of Philadelphia the D.D. in 1788.

JORDAN. Baptist presence in Jordan can probably be traced to military personnel presence and Holy Land tourists early in the 20th century. In 1952 **Southern Baptists** took responsibility for a hospital at Ajloun, which also became an educational center. The Jordan Baptist Convention was organized in 1955. The **Baptist Bible Fellowship** (BBF) opened its Palestine Mission in 1955, and the following year the **Conservative Baptist** Foreign Mission Society (CBFMS) began its work in Amman and Aqaba and helped to form the Free Evangelical Church.

As of 1995 there were 12 churches and 900 members affiliated with the Jordan Baptist Convention. The Free Evangelical Church includes about nine churches with 600 members.

JORDAN, LEWIS GARNETT (1854-1939). American Black Baptist minister and denominational leader, born at Meridian, Mississippi.

Educated at Roger Williams University in Nashville, Tennessee, he initially served churches in Yazoo City, Mississippi (1876-1883) and successively at Second Baptist, San Antonio, New Hope, Waco, and St. Emmanuel in Hearne, Texas (1883-90?). He served the pastorate of Union Baptist Church in Philadelphia, Pennsylvania (1890?-1896), after which he became a canvasser for the National Prohibition Party, which ultimately nominated Jordan for congressman-at-large in Pennsylvania. In 1896 he was elected corresponding secretary of the Foreign Mission Board of the **National Baptist Convention, U.S.A.**, (NBCUSA) where he gave substance to the structure and program of overseas missions in the 25 years of his service to the Board. Among his accomplishments were the establishment of the headquarters in Louisville, Kentucky, central to the **Black Baptist** community, the beginning of the Providence Industrial Mission in Nyasaland in 1900, and the Suehn Mission in **Liberia** in 1912, and recognition of the pioneering work of **George Liele**. As part of his administrative successes, Jordan urged the creation of the Women's Auxiliary in 1900, and in 1896 he began the *Afro-American Mission Herald*, the first national Black Baptist foreign mission periodical in the United States. In 1915-1916 when **Richard H. Boyd** led a schism of the National Baptist Convention, Jordan was a vocal opponent, and his leadership helped to avoid a larger defection of cooperating congregations. Jordan's historical work, *Up the Ladder in Foreign Missions* (1901) is considered a pioneering work in Black Baptist studies. Jordan was a well-travelled denominational statesman, making four trips to Africa, two trips to Latin America, and four trips to the West Indies.

JUDSON, ADONIRAM (1788-1850). American Congregationalist, and later Baptist missionary, born at Malden, Massachusetts. He was educated at Brown University and Andover Theological Seminary, graduating in the Seminary's first class. In 1812 he became a catalyst in the formation of the American Board of Commissioners for Foreign Missions and was the leading candidate of that body for commissioned service in **India** in 1812. He and his wife, **Ann Hasseltine**, became America's first foreign missionaries to the East; upon arrival in Serampore after much study on the subject of **baptism**, he turned to Baptist principles and was baptized by **William Carey**. Judson was not allowed to remain in India and went to **Burma**, where he opened a new field for the newly formed **Baptist Board of Foreign Missions** (BBFM). He concentrated on language study and produced a Burmese dictionary and a translation of the **Scriptures** into Burmese. His work was interrupted by imprisonment and great deprivation during the civil war in 1824. He remained in Burma, except for a furlough in 1845-1846, and married three times—to Ann Hasseltine,

Sarah Hall Boardman, and Emily Chubbock, each of whom made literary and mission contributions in their own right. See also Hasseltine, Ann.

JUDSON, EDWARD (1844-1914). American Baptist minister, born at Moulmein, Burma, the son of Adoniram and Emily Judson. He was educated at Brown University, earning the A.B. and M.A. degrees. For several years, 1867-1874, Judson taught languages at Madison (later Colgate) University, after which he was a pastor at Orange, New Jersey (1875-1881), and Judson Memorial Church in New York City. The Judson Memorial Church was designed to be a model institutional church in the Progressive Era, organizing projects and ministries to assist persons in special need. Judson also intended the downtown church to be a memorial to his father, and he prevailed upon his friendship with the Rockefeller and Colgate families to contribute to its construction and programs. Frequently, Judson travelled with John D. Rockefeller and Frederick Gates. In addition to his pastoral responsibilities, he taught pastoral theology at Colgate, 1897-1900, and 1905-1914, and homiletics at the University of Chicago, 1904-1905. One of his last projects was the completion of the Judson Centennial celebrations in 1914.

JUDSON, EMILY CHUBBOCK (1817-1854). American Baptist writer and missionary, born at Eaton, New York. As a child she lived a life of drudgery, collecting firewood and working in a woolen mill. Self-educated, she taught school in various central New York towns from 1832-1840, after which she took classes and taught English at Utica Female Seminary. She published several articles in national magazines and became a widely known fiction writer under the pseudonym, "Fanny Forester." In 1845 she met Adoniram Judson and, though he disapproved of her writings, they were married. She took on the project of producing the memoirs of Sarah B. Judson. The couple returned to Burma in 1846 and Emily assisted in her husband's translation work. Ill for the years 1848-1850, she left Burma after Adoniram died and devoted herself to an official edition of his memoirs. Among her published works were *Tripping in Author Land* (1846) and *The Memoirs of Sarah B. Judson* (1848).

JUDSON, SARAH HALL BOARDMAN (1803-1845). American Baptist missionary, born at Alstead, New Hampshire. She was educated in Danvers, Massachusetts, and married George Dana Boardman (1801-1831), a student at Waterville College in Maine. In 1825 the Boardmans were appointed as missionaries to Burma by the American Baptist Board

of Foreign Missions (BBFM) and they arrived at Moulmein that same year. Following early work at Tavoy among the Karens, George Boardman died in 1831 and Sarah was encouraged by **Adoniram Judson** to continue the work. She travelled widely in the jungles of Burma, evangelizing, translating, conducting **women's missions**, and organizing schools. By 1832 she was superintending five day schools with about 170 students. Her work was part of the Bengali school system and she received a regular stipend from the government. She married Adoniram Judson in 1834 and assisted him in several translation projects. A gifted writer and poet, Sarah died in 1845 of complications from the birth of her tenth child.

K

KAZAKHSTAN. As part of the socio-political results of the collapse of the Union of Soviet Socialist Republics in 1991, Baptist history in Kazakhstan has been separated as a distinct movement of its own. In 1917 eight families, primarily from Ukraine, moved to Alma Ata and established the first congregation of Baptists. Over the years, as scattered churches were formed, most related to the All Union Council of Evangelical-Baptists. In 1992 the Soyuz Tserkvey Evangel'skikh Khristian Baptistov Kazakhstana (Union of Evangelicals-Christians Baptists of Kazakhstan) was formed. The Conservative Baptist Foreign Mission Society (CBFMS) began missionary work in Central Asia in 1994.

As of 1995, there are 190 churches with about 24,000 members affiliated with the Soyuz Tserkvey Evangel' Khristian-Baptistov Kazakhstana, three churches with 500 members affiliated with the Korean Baptists in Kazakhstan, and about 25 churches with 2,750 members in the unregistered Baptist churches in Kazakhstan.

KEACH, BENJAMIN (1640-1704). English Baptist minister and writer, born in Buckinghamshire. Keach was a tailor by trade who became a **General Baptist** pastor at Winslow. For his catechetical work, *Child's Instructor* (1664), he was jailed and his book was burned. He rewrote the book from memory and it was sold widely. In 1668 he went to serve the Southwark church in London and was the first **Nonconformist** ordained since the Restoration. In moving to London, Keach also moved to the **Particular Baptist** persuasion, probably under the influence of **Hanserd Knollys** and **William Kiffin**. He established the Horsley-down Church and introduced hymn singing, perhaps the first in all of England to do so. He operated a bookshop to supplement his income and to sell his over 40 works, defended the **laying on of hands** at **baptism** among the Particular Baptists and managed to write a full-scale allegory before **John Bunyan** published *Pilgrim's Progress*. Keach was one of the most celebrated and quoted Baptist ministers of his era on both sides of the Atlantic. Among his many published works were *The Breach Repaired in God's Worship* (1691), *Spiritual Melody* (1700), and *Gospel Mysteries Unveiled* (1701).

KEACH, ELIAS (1667-1701). English, and later American, Baptist minister, born at Winslow, England. The son of the celebrated **Benjamin Keach**, he emigrated to Philadelphia at 19 and supported himself by masquerading as a minister. In a moment of self-disclosure he recognized the error of his ways and sought the counsel of a local Baptist minister, Thomas Dongan (fl.1680), of Cold Spring, Pennsylvania. Keach was subsequently baptized and ordained and served the congregation at Lower Dublin faithfully from 1688-1692. He returned to London and organized a congregation at Pinner's Hall where he preached to hundreds. Among his published works was *The Glory and Ornament of a True Gospel-Constituted Church* (1697).

KEITHIAN BAPTISTS. In the late 17th century a division among Quakers occurred in Pennsylvania which led to a small, short-lived company of Quaker-Baptists. Following the leadership of George Keith (1638-1716) that coalesced around differences over the doctrine of Christ and human ability in salvation, several meetings split from the main Quaker movement in 1691 and formed their own organization centered in Burlington, New Jersey. Some of the meetings, notably at Philadelphia, Southampton, and Lower Dublin, Pennsylvania, pursued New Testament practices like the **Love Feast**, Kiss of Charity, anointing of the sick, and believer's **baptism**. Probably the practice of baptism was introduced in 1797 by Abel Noble (fl.1690-1700), a **Seventh Day Baptist**. But in 1700 a division arose among the new group over keeping of the Sabbath, and the Keithian Baptists gradually dissolved into other Christian fellowships. The last of the congregations was reorganized at Brandywine, Pennsylvania, as a Regular Baptist Church in 1715. The Keithian Baptists were characterized by plain speech and dress, pacifism, and a **confession of faith** composed in 1697 and based upon the Apostles' Creed.

KENYA. Baptist history in Kenya is quite recent. In 1956 a Southern Baptist missionary, Davis Saunders (1925-) arrived in Nairobi and the following year James Hampton (1929-) settled in Mombasa. With mission stations established among the tribespeople, the work grew rapidly. In 1971 the National Baptist Convention of Kenya was organized, and the same year the **Baptist Bible Fellowship** (BBF) opened its mission. **Conservative Baptists** (CBFMS) began their Mission in 1972 and created the Conservative Baptist Fellowship of Kenya. In 1983 the **Association of Baptists for World Evangelism** (ABWE) started a Kenya mission.

As of 1995 there were 2,036 churches and 210,000 members affiliated with the Baptist Convention of Kenya. There are about four churches with about 150 members affiliated with the Conservative Baptist Fellowship of Kenya.

KETCHAM, ROBERT THOMAS (1889-1978). American and later Independent, Baptist minister and denominational leader, born in Nelson, Pennsylvania. Educated by correspondence, he entered the pastoral **ministry** in 1912 and served at Brookville (1915-1919) and Butler (1919-1923), Pennsylvania, Niles (1923-1926) and Elyria (1926-1932), Ohio, Gary, Indiana (1932-1939), and Waterloo, Iowa (1939-1948). Almost from the outset of his ministry, Ketcham was identified with the Baptist **fundamentalist** movement. In 1919 he opposed the **New World Movement**, he joined the fundamentalists in Buffalo in 1920, and addressed the **Baptist Bible Union** (BBU) in 1923. Ketcham was among the first to announce separation from the **Northern Baptist Convention** (NBC) in 1928, and he organized the Ohio Association of Independent Baptist Churches in Columbus that year. When the **General Association of Regular Baptist Churches** (GARBC) met to organize a national movement in 1932-1934, Ketcham was a principal founder and was elected president in which he served, 1934-1938.

As editor of the paper, *Baptist Bulletin*, and GARBC National Representative from 1948-1966, Ketcham exercised a wide influence on Baptist churches in the northern United States. Frequently, he interfered in the affairs of a congregation to influence withdrawal from the Convention, as in the case of Smethport, Pennsylvania. Ketcham was considered *persona non grata* with the NBC, and he also had a bitter disagreement with other fundamentalist Baptists, notably **J. Frank Norris** in the 1930s. Elected president of the interdenominational, fundamentalist American Council of Christian Churches, he was awarded an honorary doctorate by Bob Jones University in 1961. Among his published works were *Communism in Baptist Ranks* (1935) and *Let Rome Speak for Herself* (1956).

KIFFIN, WILLIAM (1616-1701). English Baptist minister and theologian, born in London. Kiffin lost both his parents to the plague and was an apprentice to a glover. He attended Independent churches beginning about 1638 and by 1642 became a Baptist under the influence of **John**

Spilsbury. About 1643 he helped to form what became the Devonshire Square Church in London, which he served as **pastor**/leader for 60 years. After an illness, Kiffin traded in Holland and became a highly successful woollen merchant, as well as becoming an esteemed member of the Leathersellers Guild of London. During the Protectorate, he served Cromwell and was a member of Parliament for Middlesex in 1656. During the Restoration, Kiffin loaned King Charles II £10,000 and frequently secured the release of Baptist friends, imprisoned under the terms of the Conventicle Act. Two of Kiffin's grandsons were executed in the cause of **religious liberty**. King James II named him to be an alderman for the City of London, a task Kiffin found onerous. Kiffin lived to see the results of the "Glorious" Revolution of 1688 and helped to compose both the First and Second London Baptist Confessions of Faith. He was critical of **John Bunyan**'s stance on open communion and was an exponent of the **Particular Baptist** persuasion. Kiffin was the first Baptist known to have written an autobiographical sketch and his portrait, which hangs in Regent's Park College, Oxford University, is one of the oldest known depictions of an early English Baptist. Kiffin's life was detailed in *Remarkable Passages in the Life of William Kiffin, Written By Himself* (1823).

KINCAID, EUGENIO (1797-1883). American Baptist missionary, born at Wethersfield, Connecticut. He was educated at Hamilton Literary and Theological Institution (later Colgate University) and served pastorates in Galway, New York, and Milton, Pennsylvania, from 1822-1827. In 1828 he served as a domestic missionary for the Pennsylvania state **association**; in 1829 the **Baptist Board of Foreign Missions** (BBFM) appointed him a missionary to **Burma**. Following great difficulty with the government, Kincaid established himself among the Karens at Arracan. In 1837, he pioneered a mission to the Kachin peoples in the northern hills. In his later years in Burma he became widely respected in the diplomatic community and in 1857 actually served as an official emissary of the United States to the Court of Ava. During his furlough in the United States in 1842-1849 he travelled on deputation for the BBFM and became a legendary hero in Alfred S. Patton's book *The Hero Missionary* (1858) for his stories of daring work in Burma.

KING, MARTIN LUTHER, JR. (1929-1968). American Baptist minister and civil rights activist, born in Atlanta, Georgia. He was educated at Morehouse College, Crozer Theological Seminary, and Boston University, the latter where he earned the Ph.D. degree, mentored by E. J. Brightman (1884-1953). King served in the pastoral ministry at Dexter

Avenue Baptist Church, Montgomery, Alabama (1954-1959), and finally as co-**pastor** with his father, Martin Luther King, Sr. (1899-1984), at Ebenezer Baptist Church in Atlanta, Georgia (1959-1968). Later influenced by Mahatma Gandhi (1869-1948) and **Walter Rauschenbush**, King developed a theology of non-violent opposition to injustice which he exhibited in several key demonstrations for civil rights of Blacks. With **Ralph Abernathy**, he was an organizer of the Southern Christian Leadership Conference (SCLC) in 1957 and was active in the National Association for the Advancement of Colored People (NAACP). He led major civil rights marches in Birmingham, Alabama (1962), Washington, D.C. (1963), and Selma, Alabama (1965). In 1964 King was awarded the Nobel Prize for Peace. As a Baptist leader, he helped to organize the **Progressive National Baptist Convention** (PNBC) in 1961, to affirm the values of the civil rights crusade and ecumenism. He was the first Black minister to address the **American Baptist Convention** (ABC) meeting in Philadelphia in 1957. While speaking publicly in Memphis, Tennessee, in 1968, King was assassinated. Among his published work was *Strength To Love* (1963) and *Why We Can't Wait* (1964).

KINGHORN, JOSEPH (1766-1832). English Baptist minister, born at Gateshead-on-Tyne, Newcastle-upon-Tyne. He was educated at Bristol Baptist College and shortly thereafter was pastor at Fairford, Gloucestershire in 1788. In 1789 he embarked on a lifelong ministry at St. Mary's **Particular Baptist** Church in Norwich. Kinghorn, a bachelor, became a beloved member of the community, a self-professed **conservative**. When **Robert Hall**, for instance, advocated open communion, Kinghorn responded by defending a strict Baptist position and became widely known for his views on the matter. Kinghorn was an exceptional scholar and was offered a tutorship at Stepney Academy when it opened in 1810, which he declined in order to continue his pastorate. He travelled on behalf of the **Baptist Missionary Society** (BMS), challenging in particular the **Scottish** churches to greater support for missions. Among Kinghorn's numerous published works were *Scriptural Arguments for the Divinity of Christ* (1813) and *Baptism, A Term of Communion at the Lord's Supper* (1816).

KIRKCONNELL, WATSON (1895-1977). Canadian Baptist educator and denominational leader, born at Port Hope, Ontario. He was educated at Queen's University where he obtained the bachelor's and master's degrees; later at Oxford University he earned the B.Litt in Economics. He taught English at Wesley College, Winnipeg, and later at McMaster University, where in addition to his wide interest in humanities and linguistics, he launched a vigorous anti-communist writing and speaking campaign during World War II. In 1944 he was one of the prime movers of the establishment of the Canadian Baptist Federation. From 1948 to 1964 he was president of Acadia University, the Baptist institution of the Canadian Maritime Provinces. Kirkonnell was well known for his linguistic skills, translating numerous works from Polish, Hungarian, and Slavic into English. Among his many published works were *Liberal Education in the Canadian Democracy* (1948) and *Seven Pillars of Freedom* (1952).

KISSITES. See **Glasites**.

KNAPP, JACOB (1799-1874). American Baptist minister and evangelist, born in Otsego County, New York. He was educated at Hamilton Literary and Theological Institution, served as a schoolteacher, and was **pastor** for a time at Springfield and Watertown, New York. In 1833, Knapp entered a full-time **ministry** of itinerant **evangelism**. He adopted the New Measures of Charles G. Finney (1792-1875) and became the Baptist exponent of the **Second Great Awakenings**. He held major protracted **revival** meetings in Rochester, New York, New York City, Washington, D.C., and Boston, Massachusetts. His style was often excessive and he created deep divisions in the Baptist community. In upstate New York he was a leader in the Removal Controversy, an unpopular campaign to move Baptist-related Madison University to Rochester. In Boston, he was accused of fraudulent practices and accepting gifts for his services. In 1837 he claimed that he had baptized 60 people in 28 minutes at Crooked Lake, New York. Knapp published a popular collection of revival hymns in 1845 and an autobiography in 1868.

KNIBB, WILLIAM (1803-1845). English Baptist missionary, born in Kettering, England. As an appointment of the **Baptist Missionary Society (BMS)**, he went to Jamaica and served several churches and taught school at Kingston. He was pastor at Port Royal, then at Savanna-la-Mar. In 1830 he was called to the church at Falmouth, on the north shore of the island. Gradually Knibb became openly critical of the slave code, becoming a popular hero with the Black population, but a pariah in the planter class. In 1832 he returned to Britain to travel widely on behalf of abolition; his was a major contribution to the bill of 1834 which abolished **slavery** in the British Empire. Again due in large part to his influence, slavery was abolished in Jamaica in 1838. Following his return to the island, he advocated education for the freed slaves and later died of yellow fever. Knibb's published work, *Colonial Slavery, A Defense of the*

Baptist Missionaries from the Charge of Indicting the Late Rebellion in Jamaica (1832), was a catalyst in marshalling the forces of British **antislavery sentiment**. See also **Jamaica**.

KNOLLYS, HANSERD (1598-1691). English, and for a time American, Baptist minister and writer, born at Cawkwell, Lincolnshire, England. Knollys graduated from Cambridge University and was ordained in the Church of England in 1629. In 1636 he resigned his membership in the church and was imprisoned for **Nonconformist** preaching. He escaped prison and fled to New England; he was turned away by the Congregationalists in Boston and he served a church in Dover, New Hampshire 1639-1641. Afterward, he was a pastor for a short time on Long Island (1641), likely with Baptist sentiments. This congregation survived and relocated to Piscataway, New Jersey, naming the village for the town where Knollys had first gathered the congregation. He returned to England in 1643 and was co-pastor with **William Kiffin** and others in the early **Particular Baptist** community, often preaching to hundreds. A strong Calvinist, he was jailed several times for preaching, and he wrote 11 works on historical, doctrinal, and linguistic topics. Among his works were *Christ Exalted* (1646) and *An Exposition of the Whole Book of the Revelation* (1689). Knollys was honored by the early naming of the British Baptist historical enterprise, the Hanserd Knollys Society.

KÖBNER, JULIUS (1806-1884). Danish Baptist minister, born at Odense, **Denmark**. The son of a Jewish rabbi, he was trained as an engraver, settling in Schleswig-Holstein. In Hamburg he encountered **J. G. Oncken** and was baptized in 1836. In 1839 Köbner visited Denmark and with Oncken organized the first Baptist church at Copenhagen. Years later he served as **pastor** of the church, 1865-1879. A **revival** occurred during his **ministry** and the membership rose to 400. Köbner helped to organize the Baptist churches on the German plan, and served as a resident theological professor for the other pastors. He composed the first Danish Baptist hymnbook, writing many of the poems himself. With Oncken and **G. W. Lehmann**, Köbner formed the "Kleeblat" (cloverleaf) or great triumvirate of European Baptist pioneers. Among Köbner's published works were *Die Glaubenstimme* (1849) and *Das Lied von Gott* (1873).

KOREA. Baptist history in Korea is dated from 1889 when **Malcolm Fenwick** (1863-1935), a Canadian **independent**, and later Baptist, arrived to begin **evangelism**. Under the auspices of the Corean Itinerant Mission, which he helped to create, in 1896 he began a church at Sorai and later organized several congregations in the Tuman District. Another important stream of Baptist work commenced in 1895 when the first missionaries of the **Ella Thing Mission** arrived in Seoul. It was an outgrowth of Clarendon Street Baptist Church in Boston, Massachusetts and it concentrated its effort in Kongju and Kanggyung. In 1901 the Corean Itinerant Mission merged with the Ella Thing Mission under the leadership of Fenwick and the result was the formation in 1905 of Daihan Kitokkyohuay (Church of Christ in Korea).

The Baptist cause was fairly minimal until after the Korean War (1949-1953) when, following U.S. military presence, the **Southern Baptist** work in South Korea began in earnest. Daihan Kitokkyo Chimneyhuay, the Korea Baptist Convention, was formed in 1949. The first missionaries were the John Abernathys (1896-). A schism occurred in 1959 over relations between the Convention (which was under intense theological pressure from the International Council of Christian Churches) and the Southern Baptist Mission; the separate entities were reunited in 1968 as the Hankook Chimneyhuay Yunmaing (League of Korean Baptist Churches). In the 1980s large churches have emerged in the vicinity of Seoul, the scene of the Baptist World Congress in 1990.

In addition to the regular Baptist work, **Baptist Mid-Missions** (BMM) from the United States established in 1974 a work related to the Korea Baptist Convention, and in 1958 the **Baptist Bible Fellowship** (BBF) opened its mission. Also, the **American Baptist Association** (ABA) has a mission in Seoul which includes a school.

As of 1995 there were 1,548 churches and 323,750 members affiliated with the Daihan Kitokkyo Chimneyhuay (formerly the Hankook). There are two recognized Baptist theological schools in Korea: Kyungkido and Tae Jun City.

KOREA GOSPEL MISSION. An **independent** Baptistic missionary agency founded in 1952. The Mission focuses on education and **evangelism** in South Korea. Its home base is in Seoul, South Korea, with recognition in the United States.

KYRGYZSTAN. Baptist beginnings in Kyrgyzstan are traced to 1882 when Mennonites from Ukraine entered the region. Mennonites and Baptists developed in tandem with each other, the Mennonites creating German-speaking congregations. In 1907, R.G. Bershadsky and his wife, while travelling near Frunze, established a Baptist church at Pischpek (later Bischkek). Others were planted, and the churches associated with the All Union Council of Evangelical Christians - Baptists until 1991. With the reorganization of the U.S.S.R., and the recognition of Kyrgyzstan as a separate state, 16 churches met in a congress in 1992 and formed the Union of Evangelical Christians - Baptists in Kyrgyzstan.

As of 1995, there were 34 churches and 24 groups with approximately 3,200 members affiliated with the Union.

L

LAGERGRAN, CARL GUSTAF (1846-1941). Swedish and later American Baptist minister and educator, born at Ostersund, Jamtland, Sweden. He was educated at a local gymnasium and at the University of Uppsala where he studied languages and philosophy. **Anders Wiberg** recommended him to serve the congregation at Uppsala, after which he was pastor at Sundsvall from 1883-1889. While in the pastorate he helped organize a domestic missionary effort for **Sweden** and **Finland**, and he conducted a **bible school**. In 1889 he was called to be dean of the Swedish Baptist Theological Seminary, then a part of the Baptist Theological Union in Morgan Park, Chicago, Illinois. He also served as professor of theology in that institution through 1922, writing a major systematic **theology** (1924), as well as his autobiography (1927). In 1912-1914 he supported the combination of Bethel Academy and the Swedish Baptist Seminary in Chicago, and the removal of both schools to St. Paul, Minnesota. For his distinguished service over many years, he was named a Knight of the Royal Order of the North Star by Swedish King Gustav V.

LAMBE, THOMAS (fl. 1635-1673), English General Baptist minister, whose birthplace is unknown. He first appears in records at Colchester where he was imprisoned in 1639-1640 for preaching and baptizing. He is significant to Baptist history as a bridge figure between those who sprinkled and those who immersed, and as one of the first to conduct itinerant preaching among the **General Baptists**. Likely a soapboiler by trade, he is not to be confused with the Thomas Lambe, pastor and merchant of London of about the same era. He was a **Leveller** to the end of that party's progress and preached widely, presaging the General Baptist office of **messenger**. He served the church at Bell Alley, London, and was remembered by the Presbyterian Thomas Edwards (1599-1647) for his openness and revivalistic style. Sometime in the early 1640s Lambe moved the congregation to Spitalfields and a split occurred over the **laying on of hands** at **baptism**, which he opposed. In his classic book, *The Fountains of Free Grace Opened* (1645), he helped give General Baptists a theological reputation by openly advocating an **Arminian** position. He drew other preachers to his itinerating style, among whom were **Henry Denne**, Samuel Oates (1610-1683), and

Jeremiah Ives (fl.1653-1674). Lambe was imprisoned in 1663 for attending a conventicle service and, according to **Thomas Crosby**, he died in 1673.

LANDMARKISM. A form of **local church protectionism** which emerged among Baptists in the United States in the 19th century. While Landmarkism is usually associated with Baptist life in the southern region, its origins are in New England.

Based upon Scriptural references such as Proverbs 22: 28, "Remove not the ancient landmarks which thy fathers have set" and Deuteronomy 19:14 "Thou shalt not remove thy neighbor's landmark, which they of old time have set in thine inheritance, which thou shalt inherit in the land that the Lord thy God giveth thee to possess it," the originators of the movement sought to observe strictly their definitions of Baptist identity, which was synonymous with unadulterated, historic Christian identity.

Within the frame of reference of New England Baptist congregational life in the early decades of the 19th century, rural Baptist churches and **associations** became alarmed with the buildup of extra-congregational organization. These new organizations included societies of various kinds and involved a push toward a national convention, thus creating a sense of Baptist denominationalism. The newer forms were advocated by leaders in the Middle States and South, and were particularly well supported by urban churches in the eastern cities. When the funding for many of the nationalists' agenda (including domestic and foreign missions, education, and publication) proved inadequate in the 1820s, New England Baptists moved to control the development of the new organizations and in their place instituted a style of limited purpose societies which historians have later referred to as the "society model" of Baptist life. Well-educated thinkers such as **Francis Wayland** of Brown University advocated the society model, while others like **J. Newton Brown** and I. M. Person (fl.1830) in New Hampshire provided a theological basis for local church protectionism. The movement also found adherents among the isolated churches of the Old Northwest and what became the **Primitive** or **Old School Baptists**.

James M. Graves held that the "Landmark" movement began in his own spiritual pilgrimage starting from confusion over different modes of **baptism** and the spiritual fitness of certain ministers and leading to a clear articulation of Baptist principles according to seven landmarks. He began to write about his positions in *The Tennessee Baptist* in 1846, and in 1851 called a major debate at Cotton Grove, Tennessee (see **Cotton Grove Resolutions**), where he claimed to have convinced a significant number of churches to accept his positions. In 1854 **James M. Pendleton** actually coined the term "Landmark" in a pamphlet which Graves published under the title, *An Old Landmark Reset*. Graves argued that **William Kiffin**, the English **Particular Baptist, John Clarke** of Rhode Island, and **Jesse Mercer** of Georgia were all Landmarkists because of the way each sharply defined Baptist identity, before anyone actually used the term. For Graves and Pendleton, the issue was to carry out in their practice those principles which all true Baptists, in all ages, have professed to believe.

Modernity set in more rapidly in the East and North than in the South, and the churches in those two sections turned to missionary expansion at home and abroad, as well as to more sophisticated institutions of **higher education**. In the rural South, Landmarkism became a powerful force which some historians believe has been determinative in the making of **Southern Baptist** identity, especially with respect to **ecumenical** relations and denominationalism. Landmarkism may be identified as a critical factor in regions of the Southern Baptist Convention as diverse as the Southwest and Upper Mississippi Valley. It was a contributing factor in the **Gospel Mission Movement** of the 1880s, and one of the negative factors which retarded the growth of a unified publishing program and educational system of Southern Baptists in the period 1860-1910.

Several schisms in Southern Baptist life have followed Landmark emphases. The anti-conventionism of leaders like **Ben M. Bogard** and **J. Frank Norris**, plus the organizational rifts at the state level which led to the **Baptist Missionary Association** (BMA) and the **American Baptist Association** (ABA), reveal strong Landmarkist tendencies. Landmarkism has become a tradition which includes a number of organizationally distinct bodies. Some Baptist bodies are both Landmarkist and **fundamentalist**. The more missionary-minded Landmarkists have carried the ideals far beyond North America to Asia, Africa, and Latin America in particular.

As fully elaborated, Landmark theology includes beliefs such as the purity of Baptist churches as the truest churches in the world and that the church is essentially visible and local, the church is composed only of regenerate persons, repentence must precede baptism ("blood before water"), only a true church can perform the **ordinances** of the **Lord's Supper** and baptism, the Lord's Supper is not intended for fellowship with unbelievers, and a non-believer must not be admitted to a Baptist pulpit nor to the Lord's Supper. In more recent embellishments of Landmarkism, some advocates have equated the use of the term "kingdom" in **Scripture** with "church," and the historical position of

"**Successionism**" is assumed by many writers. Among the important literature of the Landmark movement are works written by James M. Pendleton, *An Old Landmark Reset* (1854); James R. Graves, *Old Landmarkism: What Is It?* (1880); A. C. Dayton, *Theodosia Ernest:or the Heroine of Faith* (1856); Ben M. Bogard, *The Baptist Way-Book* (1927); and D. B. Ray, *Baptist Succession* (1949).

LATHROP, JOHN (d.1653). English Independent minister. Almost nothing is known of his background except that he likely attended Cambridge University and accepted the curacy of Egerton. He resigned his position in 1622 and assumed the pastorate of **Henry Jacob**'s **Independent** Church in Southwark. In 1632 the Bishop of London had the church raided during a meeting in the home of Humphrey Barnet, a brewers clerk; 41 of the members and Lathrop were imprisoned at the Clink for 12 years. During Lathrop's incarceration, a schism took place, one group remaining true to Independency, the other following **John Spilsbury** and the practice of believer's **baptism**. Lathrop was given permission in 1634 to go into foreign exile, but reorganized his congregation, which included **William Kiffin**. Lathrop fled to New England accompanied by 32 church members, and they settled at Scituate, and later Barnstable, Massachusetts. The Southwark portion of his congregation was apparently led for a time by **Samuel Eaton**, who was succeeded by **Henry Jessey**.

LATOURETTE, KENNETH SCOTT (1884-1968). American Baptist historian and educator, born at Oregon City, Oregon. He was educated at McMinnville (later Linfield) College and Yale University, receiving his Ph.D. at Yale in 1909. He travelled for two years as a staff member and later missionary of the Student Volunteer Movement in China, teaching in the Yale in China program in Hunan Province in 1910. Being forced to return home due to illness, he taught at Reed College in Oregon (1914-1916) and Denison University in Ohio (1916-1921), before taking the D. Willis James Professorship in missions at Yale Divinity School in 1921. Soon he began teaching courses in the university on the Far East and his title was expanded in 1927 to include Oriental History. Latourette awakened scholarly and popular interest in the Far East, influencing many university departments around the world. In 1949 he was named Sterling Professor at Yale. His contribution to the discipline of Church History was enormous, as witnessed in his major publications, *A History of the Expansion of Christianity* (7 volumes, 1937-1945) and his encyclopedic one-volume *History of Christianity* (1953). His peers elected him president of the American Society of church history (1945) and of the

American Historical Association (1948), and the Far Eastern Association (1954). In 1952 he was elected president of the American Baptist Convention, in part recognizing his many years of service on the board of the **American Baptist Foreign Mission Society** (ABFMS).

LATVIA. The first baptism of believers in Latvia was observed in 1861 near Libau in the secrecy of night to avoid being detected by police. Under much persecution, Baptist representatives presented a petition to Russian Czar Alexander II who granted full **religious liberty** in 1879 to the Baptist community. Largely under the direction of the Memel Church in Lithuania, considered the mother congregation of the Letts, congregations were started at Windau, Sakkenhausen, and Riga. Beginning in 1875 Lettish Baptist Conferences were held. Under the leadership of Janis A. Frey (1863-1950), pastor at Dunamunde, the Latvian cause grew to include **Sunday Schools** and a publishing house. A Bund of Baltic Baptists was created in 1885, renamed in 1891 the Association of Latvian Baptists and again in 1908 the Union of Latvian Baptists. Missionary work among Lettish people was carried out in **Russia**, Siberia, **Brazil**, and later in **India** and **China**. With the coming of war all Baptist meetings were banned and the leadership was exiled to Siberia in 1916. Frey returned to Riga in 1922 to start a theological school there as a result of the **London Conference of 1920**. In 1940 the Soviet government forbade the activities of the Union, but the Germans restored it in 1942. In 1945 the Baptist churches in Latvia were incorporated in the Soviet All-Union Council of Evangelical Christians-Baptists; this status ensued until 1991, when with Latvian independence, the Union was reestablished as Latvijas Baptistu Draudzu Savieniba. The theological school at Riga was closed in 1940 but reopened in 1991.

As of 1995 there were 75 congregations and 6,056 members affiliated with Latvijas Baptistu Draudzu Savieniba.

LAWS, CURTIS LEE (1868-1946). American Baptist minister and editor, born at Aldie, Virginia. He was educated at the University of Richmond and Crozer Theological Seminary. Laws served pastorates in Baltimore, Maryland (1893-1908), and Brooklyn, New York (1908-1913). While in the charge of Greene Avenue Baptist in Brooklyn, Laws facilitated the merger of *The Watchman* (Boston) and *The Examiner* (New York). In 1911 he became editor for 27 years of the combined *Watchman-Examiner* weekly newspaper, the most widely circulated Baptist periodical in the United States. As a respected **evangelical** editorial opinion, Laws sought to recover historic Baptistic and biblical principles to the denomination, especially in the **Northern Baptist Convention** (NBC). He was an organizer in 1920 of the **fundamentalist** movement at the Buffalo meeting of the NBC, always a moderate and pro-Convention voice. Eschewing terms like "**conservative**," "premillennial," and "**Landmarker**," he coined the term "fundamentalist" in an editorial in the *Watchman Examiner* in 1920. Believing fundamentalists were part of an "historic and holy succession," he held to the Philadelphia and New Hamphire Baptist **confessions of faith** as definitions of the theological traditions. He was associated in 1925 with the founding of The Eastern Baptist Theological Seminary in Philadelphia, whose chapel bears his name. Among Laws's book publications was *Baptist Fundamentals* (1920).

LAYING ON OF HANDS. Also known as "imposition," and considered by some to be an **ordinance**, the laying on of hands occurs at three occasions in Baptist practice: for some following believer's **baptism**, the **ordination** of **deacons**, and the ordination of **pastors**.

Following believers baptism. In Acts 8:14-18 the order of reception into the Christian faith involved preaching, prayer, baptism, and the laying on of hands to impart the Holy Ghost. Early Baptists in England, particularly the **General Baptists**, coupled this teaching with the supposed confession of Hebrews 6:1-2, to require the laying on of hands on all believers following baptism. In the North American colonies from the late 17th century through the late 18th century, both General **Six Principle** and Calvinistic Baptists ordained the laying on of hands for this purpose. The Philadelphia Confession of Faith (1742), a modification of the Second London Confession of Faith (1677), included an article on the laying on of hands, but asserted that the purpose was not to receive extraordinary gifts of the Spirit, but to receive the promise and graces of the Spirit, such as comfort, strength, and confirmation of the presence of the Spirit in one's life. The practice was abandoned by the end of the century among most Regular Baptist congregations in the United States.

The ordination of pastors. In the tradition of Old Testament identification of leaders, as in I Samuel 16:12-13, the New Testament churches practiced "setting apart" candidates for **ministry**; "fasting, prayer, and the laying on of hands" were observed (Acts 13:2, 3). I Timothy 4:14 suggests that the New Testament church believed that a gift was conveyed and that the presbytery (eldership or ordained ministry) had the responsibility for the act. Baptists with other Christians make this act an important component of an ordination service. After appropriate remarks have been made, the candidate kneels in front of the congregation or **associational** gathering and ordained clergy are asked to come forward to place their hands on the head of the candidate, offer remarks quietly to the candidate, and/or say a personal prayer. An alternative form is to have several clergy place a hand on the candidate's head at the same time and one person offers a prayer of ordination. By placing the hands on the head of the candidate, Baptists believe that the spiritual power of ministry is symbolically passed to the candidate, the participating ministers affirm personally their support of the candidate, and the candidate signals his/her submission to the authority of the church. When the laying on of hands is concluded, the candidate rises and is recognized as a minister in full standing.

The ordination of deacons. Among some Baptists, **deacons** may also participate in a laying on of hands ceremony. Deacons may be asked to represent the congregation as part of the ordination of a **pastor**. Deacons themselves may be ordained and the laying on of hands is carried forth much as above, except that deacons join pastors in placing their hands on the head of the candidates. In the case of deacons, several may be ordained at once. Early Welsh Baptists and later **Southern Baptists** in the United States (among others) practice the laying on of hands with deacons.

LEBANON. Baptist presence in Lebanon doubtless stems from British and American military personnel and tourists in the middle years of the 20th century, while occupying various sites in the region. The first Baptist **mission** was established by **Southern Baptists** in 1948; the first congregation was located at Beirut and subsequent church planting occurred throughout the Christian sectors. In 1955 the Lebanese Baptist Convention was organized, later the Arab Baptist Seminary was opened in 1960, and a major Arabic language press was begun, which became the center for Baptist witness among Arab peoples. In 1958 the **Baptist Bible Fellowship** (BBF) opened a mission in Lebanon, broadening the Baptist presence in the country.

As of 1995 there were 25 churches and 1,500 members affiliated with the Lebanese Baptist Convention. There is a recognized Baptist theological school at Beirut.

LEE, ROBERT GREENE (1886-1978). Southern Baptist minister, born at Fort Mill, South Carolina. He was educated at Furman University and Chicago Law School. He highly esteemed the president of Furman, **Edwin Poteat,** and modelled his life on Poteat's oratorical abilities. Greene turned aside careers in law and teaching at Furman to be a pastor. He served churches at Saluda (1918), Edgefield (1918-1921), and Chester (1921-1922) South Carolina; First Baptist, New Orleans, Louisiana (1922-1925), Citadel Square, South Carolina (1925-1927), and Bellevue Baptist Church in Memphis, Tennessee (1927-1960). Lee became one of the most outstanding preachers of his day, the quintessential Southern Baptist style of the 20th century. He was well known for his **evangelistic** sermon "Pay Day...Some Day," first preached at Edgefield, South Carolina, and 900 times thereafter. Lee developed a widespread reputation for large numbers of decisions for Christ and **baptisms** at his church in Memphis. He was elected a rare three times to the presidency of the **Southern Baptist Convention**, in 1949, 1950, and 1951.

LEG OF MUTTON BAPTISTS. Marius D'Assigny (1643-1717) in his survey of Baptists of 1709 found that at Lambert Street, Whitechapel, there was a congregation that practiced eating meat, particularly leg of mutton, at the **Lord's Supper**. Presumably this was a recognition of the connection with the Passover Meal and earned the group the name "Leg of Mutton Baptists."

LEHMANN, GOTTFRIED WILHELM (1799-1882). German Baptist minister and denominational leader, born in Hamburg, **Germany**. As a youth he was in contact with Mennonites in Friesland and followed his father's occupation as an engraver. Lehmann came to know **J. G. Oncken** and followed his example in converting to Baptist principles. In 1837, immediately after his **baptism**, Lehmann became **pastor** at a new church in Berlin where he remained for many years. With Oncken and **Julius Köbner**, Lehman constituted the "Kleeblat" (cloverleaf), a trio of German Baptist leaders.

LEILE, GEORGE (c.1750-c.1800). American and later Jamaican Black Baptist minister, born a **slave** in Virginia. About the beginning of the American Revolution he was converted under the **ministry** of Matthew Moore of South Carolina, who also baptized him and received him into his church. Ultimately, his master gave him his freedom in order to become a minister. Among the Savannah River plantations, Leile preached, was ordained, and gathered a congregation which became the first African Baptist Church in the United States. Fleeing his former owners who attempted to reclaim him as a slave in the 1780s, he fled to **Jamaica** in 1782 and became the first missionary there. To support himself he worked at the Customs House in Kingston, and preached at the race course. In 1791 he reported to the English Baptist **John Rippon** that he had baptized 500 people, who became the nucleus of the Windward Road Church in Kingston. This led English Baptists to begin their support for missions in Jamaica. Leile wrote an early church covenant for Jamaica and quietly advocated **religious liberty** and **human rights**, as well as mentoring other ministers, notably Moses Baker who served in St. James Parish.

LELAND, JOHN (1754-1841). American Baptist minister, born at Grafton, Massachusetts. Leland was not formally educated, and was quickened in his religious profession under the **ministry** of **Elhanan Winchester**. In 1773 he conducted a preaching tour of Virginia and returned there for 15 years of ministry. He was finally ordained in 1786, and two years later reported 300 baptisms on a preaching tour of the South and Middle States. In 1791 he returned to Cheshire, Massachusetts. Leland resisted a settled pastorate and wrote widely on various subjects, notably **religious liberty**. He opposed governmentally established religious holidays and chaplains to governments paid by tax dollars. In 1804, in a celebrated incident, he delivered a large gift of Cheshire cheese to U.S. President Thomas Jefferson (1743-1826), for whom Leland had great affection. It is widely held that Leland had a significant impact at least indirectly upon James Madison (1750-1836) in his political understanding of the **separation of church and state**. Among Leland's most famous published works were *The Rights of Conscience Inalienable* (1791) and *The Government of Christ a Christocracy* (1804).

LEVELLERS. A mid-17th century English **dissenter** movement which coincided and interacted with the rise of the Baptists. Inspired by religious, political, and economic motives which opposed monopolies, religious compulsion, property taxes, debt imprisonment, and capital punishment, the Levellers reached a peak of influence about 1645. The movement was diffuse, united by three leaders: John Lilburne (1614-1657), Richard Overton (fl. 1642-1663), and William Walwyn (fl. 1649). Leveller propaganda shared a common heritage with **Separatists** and Baptists and it was not uncommon for Baptists to have Leveller sympathies. Overton, a printer, had been a follower of **John Smyth** in 1615, but by the 1640s he developed a radical position denying the immortality of the human soul, and while a distant **General Baptist** associated with the church at Bell Alley, London, he was a leading Leveller. Other Baptists known to be part of the movement were **Thomas Lambe** (c.1635-1673), Samuel Highland (fl.1645-1649), William Allen (1614-1677), and Edmund Chillenden (fl.1645-1656). Levellers in fact helped to give a clear focus to Baptists and other dissenters as soldiers, artisans, skilled workers, and "mechanicks."

   As the theological and political position of Leveller writers became increasingly radical, many Baptists broke ranks. In addition, Levellers were an increasing irritant to Oliver Cromwell (1599-1658), and the

Leveller plan for a coming democratic kingdom conflicted with the eschatological aspirations of millennialists and a theocratic kingdom. Some Baptists, such as **William Kiffin**, openly opposed the Levellers before various tribunals. Ultimately, the defeat of the King's forces at Burford and the death of Charles I in 1649 brought the Leveller cause to a bitter conclusion, with its Baptist adherents having drifted back to their more conservative positions. As with other dissenter traditions, Baptist engagement with radical ideas illustrated the fluidity of 17th century dissenter identity. See also **Diggers**; **Fifth Monarchy Movement**; **Ranters**; **Seekers**.

LIBERAL TRADITION. Among Baptists the term "liberal" has both negative and positive connotations, depending upon the context. In the positive sense, liberal usually refers to thinkers and positions which affirm progressive social thought and religious ideals, **human rights**, and social reform. From the later 19th century, particularly in North America, liberalism was a flowering of at least two elements inherent in the Baptist character. As several theological analysts have shown, the liberal spirit owed much to the pietism and experiential bases of religion on the one hand, and the heritage of religious liberty on the other. Among Baptists, religious fervor, such as that felt in the **revival** tradition, replaced orthodox creedalism and confessionalism. This, coupled with an impulse of free thought, can be seen in many of the avant garde Liberal theologians from about 1880 to 1930, a substantial number of whom were Baptists. Liberal thought among Baptists, however, also has a much older history.

In the 17th century, at least from an Establishment point of view, Baptists (especially **General Baptists**) were considered a liberal sect. Ideas like **religious liberty**, **separation of church and state**, believer's **baptism**, and belief in free will, plus some Baptists' identification with **Seekers**, **Levellers**, and **Ranters**, reinforced the liberal reputation of the movement. Baptist liberal thinking was also applied to an openness on key theological issues, such as admission to the Lord's Supper, and the nature of the atonement. But other concerns were also evident, including singing in the church, the role of women, involvement in contemporary political and social movements, and relations with other churches and theological traditions.

Eighteenth-century liberal Baptist thinkers were associated with opposition to **revivalism** and enthusiastic expression, like Harvard alumnus Jeremiah Condy (1709-1768) of First Baptist, Boston. Others were advocates of education, ordination, soul freedom, and separation of church and state, like **John Leland**. Some liberal thinkers, such as

Elhanan Winchester, held **unitarian** or **universalist** views. In the early 19th century those who supported missionary activity, the formation of **associations** and **conventions**, higher education, and social reforms were often labelled liberals. **Freewill** and **Free Communion** Baptists were among those groups considered liberal among Regular Calvinistic Baptists in the United States, largely because of their openness to inclusion of persons regardless of social status. In Britain, in the early 19th century, **Robert Aspland**, formerly a **Particular Baptist** minister who studied at Bristol and Aberdeen, and then joined the General Baptist movement, became successively a Unitarian and then a Presbyterian, editing the *Universal Theological Magazine*, a publication associated with contemporary liberal thought. Later, advocates of the **Baptist Union of Great Britain and Ireland** and those who favored a lessening of the distinctions of Calvinism were among those considered "liberal," among whom were **Robert Hall**, **Andrew Fuller**, and **Joseph Ivimey**. More recently, Michael H. Taylor (1937-), principal at Northern Baptist College in Manchester from 1970-1985, espoused a liberal position on the doctrine of **Christ** in his 1971 address before the Baptist Union Assembly, which caused quite a stir among the Union churches.

Liberal Baptist thinkers since the mid-19th century have utilized a critical historical or scientific approach to the interpretation of **Scripture**, rather than a simple proof text method and assumptions about the divine origins of the **bible**. Among such writers and scholars in the British context were **Samuel G. Green**, S. A. Tipple (1828-1910), and **James Martin**, and in the United States, **Asa Messer**, **William Newton Clarke**, **Nathaniel Schmidt**, and **Crawford H. Toy**. Messer was forced to resign from the presidency at Brown over doctrinal matters early in the century. Schmidt and Toy were actually the defendants in educational heresy proceedings and dismissed from their respective institutions for their liberal positions. Toward the end of the 19th century in the United States, influenced by progressive thought, university education in the sciences, and a growing awareness of social problems, some Baptist thinkers became more interested in Christian social reform than in personal **evangelism** and church planting; among these were **Walter Rauschenbusch**, Leighton Williams (1855-1935), and **William H. P. Faunce**. The **"Chicago School"** came to be synonymous with liberal thought, emphasizing critical scientific investigation of the Scriptures, a comparative religions approach to the uniqueness of Christianity, interfaith dialogue, and the application of the social sciences to theological disciplines. Exponents of this tradition included **William Rainey Harper**, **Shirley Jackson Case**, **Ernest Dewitt Burton**, **George Burman Foster**, and **Douglas Clyde Macintosh**.

In the Canadian Baptist context, liberalism has been termed "modernism" and has been associated with McMaster University and to a lesser degree Brandon University in Manitoba and Acadia University in Nova Scotia. Each of these schools was influenced by the methods at the University of Chicago in the early decades of the 20th century. In the mid-1920s the theological faculty at McMaster was reorganized and some of the churches in the Toronto region felt the trend pointed toward an unacceptable view of Scripture and teaching of scientific theories of the earth's origins. The arts faculty became predominant over the theological studies. For those who remained in the Baptist Convention of Ontario and Quebec, liberalism became synonymous with the university's right to explore knowledge; for those who left the affiliation of the Convention, liberalism became a negative decription of mainstream Baptist life.

As a pejorative label, Baptist **evangelicals** and **fundamentalists** have frequently categorized their theological and ethical adversaries as "liberals." Among the typical liberal tendencies noted by these groups are, not holding to an orthodox view of the authority of Scripture, denying in many cases the deity of Christ and the personhood of the Holy Spirit, the transcendence of God, miraculous events, the physical return of Christ, and a literal understanding of direct theistic creation. Traditional **Conservative Evangelicals** often associate certain ethical liberties and attitudes with liberalism, including the enjoyment of alcoholic beverages in the North American context, smoking tobacco products, use of drugs for other than medicinal purposes, dancing, rock music, premarital sex, permission of divorce, use of profanity, and human sexual orientations other than heterosexual. Also considered liberal in the realm of social and political thought are aggressive civil rights advocacy, support for abortion rights, pro-feminist thought, liberation theology, toleration of Marxist ideology and governments, membership in **ecumenical** organizations, and openness to socialist and pluralistic religious policy in government legislation. See also **Conservative Tradition; Evangelicalism, and Baptists; Fundamentalism.**

LIBERIA. Baptist mission in Liberia dates from the arrival of **Lott Carey** in 1821. He established a church at Monrovia in 1822 under the auspices of the **Baptist Board of Foreign Missions.** Many early missionaries died of fevers in Liberia; Ezekiel Skinner was a notable medical missionary who served for four decades, arriving in 1834. A Liberia Baptist Association was formed at Monrovia in 1835. In 1856 the **American Baptist Missionary Union** (ABMU) transferred its Liberian Mission to the **Southern Baptists** (SBC) who were assisted by **Black Baptists** in the United States. Southern Baptists terminated their work in 1875 until 1960, leaving the mission to a U.S. Black body, the Consolidated American Baptist Foreign Mission Convention (CABMC) in 1880 and Jamaican Baptists. In 1880 various churches and **associations** combined to form the Liberia Baptist Missionary Convention at Marshall, later to be called the Liberian Baptist Missionary and Educational Convention. This body has worked closely with U.S. Black Baptists. An outgrowth of this work was the establishment of Ricks Institute in 1887.

In addition to the regular Baptist work, **Baptist Mid-Missions** (BMM) from the United States established a mission in 1938 among the Kpelle people at Sua Koko. In 1954 this mission established the Baptist Bible Institute in Monrovia and two years later a Baptist press. Likewise, the **General Association of Regular Baptists** (GARBC) established their mission in 1968. In 1976 a theological seminary was opened under Southern Baptist auspices.

As of 1995 there were 229 churches and 60,000 members affiliated with the Liberia Baptist Missionary & Educational Convention, Inc. The Liberia Baptist Theological Seminary is located at Paynesford City.

LIBERTY BAPTIST FELLOWSHIP (LBF). Formed in 1977 to support and enlarge the emphases of Jerry Falwell (1933-), a fundamentalist **pastor/evangelist**, and the Thomas Road Baptist Church in Lynchburg, Virginia. From its beginning it has been chaired by Falwell and influenced by graduates of Liberty University, a **fundamentalist** Baptist institution in Lynchburg. The purposes of the Fellowship include providing fellowship for pastors of like faith, mutual accountability, support for planting new churches in the United States, assistance for pastors of new congregations, and a certifying body for licensing and recognition of chaplains. The fellowship elects officers from a church constituency of about a hundred pastors and a periodical, the *Liberty Baptist Fellowship Newsletter*, has been issued since 1977. Several of the pastors in the Fellowship are also identified with the **Baptist Bible Fellowship** (BBF) or the **Southwide Baptist Fellowship** (SBF). Also associated with the Fellowship is Liberty Baptist Mission, founded in 1978 at Thomas Road Baptist Church. The Mission has work in seven countries and focuses on **evangelism** and **theological education**.

LIBYA. In the 1960s with the production of oil, American presence in Libya was expanded and Baptist missionaries entered the country on a limited basis. In 1962 U.S. **Southern Baptist** (SBC) missionaries created a church, consisting of Americans, at Tripoli. In 1970, the American presence left the country and mission work ceased.

LITHUANIA. In 1841 The German Baptists formed a Baptist congregation at Memel, which had great impact upon the Lettish peoples. Similarly, in 1879 a second German Baptist congregation was commenced at Kaunas, eventually to be independent in 1889. Following World War I, other Baptist works were started among Russian-speaking emigrants and a theological school was started as a result of the **London Conference of 1920.** In 1933 a Lithuanian Baptist Union was formed at Klaipeda, and reformed in 1989 in the same city. In 1991 the **Baptist Bible Fellowship** (BBF) opened its mission in Lithuania and in 1997 the **Conservative Baptist** Foreign Mission Society (CBFMS) began a work in Lithuania.

  As of 1995 there were seven churches and 422 members associated with the Lietuvos Evangeliku Baznyciu Sajunga (Lithuanian Evangelical Baptist Union).

"LIVING FAMILY." See **Strict Baptists**.

LOCAL CHURCH PROTECTIONISM. A term applied to the tendency among Baptists in the United States to safeguard the rights and privileges of the local congregation. In the 1820s the antimissionary spirit resisted all interference and competition from societies, **conventions**, and **associations**. In 1833 the Baptist Convention of New Hampshire published a **confession of faith** in which the church was defined in purely local terms. Later in the 1840s and 1850s the **Landmarkist** Movement in the Upper South spawned a whole new round of local church protectionism which influenced greatly the entire future of the **Southern Baptist Convention**. Doctrinally, the idea of local church protectionism is defended on the basis of New Testament evidence of the strength and power of the local church. In many Baptist circles, it has been called a Baptist distinctive usually referred to as the **"autonomy of the local church."**

LONDON CONFERENCE OF 1920. A watershed event in modern Baptist history whereby agreements were reached on the post-war relief and development of Baptists in Europe. During World War I, much of the Baptist community established in the 19th century was scattered, if not destroyed. Representatives of the U.S. Southern Baptist **Foreign Mission Board** (FMB), the **American Baptist Foreign Mission Society** (ABFMS) **(Northern Baptist Convention)**, and the British **Baptist Missionary Society** (BMS) toured Europe in 1920 to ascertain appropriate rebuilding steps in the Baptist community.

  At a meeting in London, England, on July 19-23, delegates from the mission agencies and representatives of most of the European bodies met to plan for the future. A three-year relief program under the aegis of the **Baptist World Alliance** (BWA) was undertaken and certain mission territorial "mandates" were agreed upon, some jointly supported: **Spain**, **Italy, Yugoslavia,** Hungary, **Ukraine, Romania,** southern **Russia** to be administered by the U.S. **Southern Baptist Convention; France, Belgium, Switzerland,** Czechoslovakia, **Poland, Norway, Denmark,** northern Russia, and the Baltic States by the U.S. **Northern Baptist Convention** (NBC); France, Italy, Czechoslovakia, **Finland,** all three Baltic States, and the **Netherlands** by the **Baptist Missionary Society** (BMS); **Bulgaria, Poland,** and **Austria** by the German Union and the German Conference in North America; and **Portugal** by **Brazil**.

These relationships were to be completely voluntary, and native work was to be preferred over missionary appointments. **Religious liberty** was to be a top priority and sound relations with civil authorities were a goal. The Conference authorized the establishment of a "commissioner" to coordinate relief efforts and make presentations to respective European governments. The venerable **James H. Rushbrooke** of Great Britain was chosen as commissioner, and his report was published in 1923 as *The Baptist Movement in the Continent of Europe*, a classic source on European Baptists. New **theological schools** were started in Spain, Portugal, **Latvia, Lithuania, Estonia,** Czechoslovakia, Hungary and Romania. Much of the complexity of relations between European Baptists and their North American counterparts may be traced to the London Conference of 1920.

LORD'S SUPPER. The ordinance of the Lord's Supper, also called the breaking of bread, the **sacrament** of Holy Communion or the Eucharist, is considered of primary importance to Baptists. Baptist understanding of the Lord's Supper is derived from Matthew 26: 26-29, Mark 14: 22-25, Luke 22: 17-20, and I Corinthians 11: 23-34.

Early English Baptists followed the patterns their ministers had learned in the Anglican and Puritan traditions. The Supper was considered by many to be sacramental, though this terminology was often eschewed because of its connection with Roman and Anglican superstitions. More appropriate was the Calvinistic understanding of a sacrament, namely, a sign of the grace of God which nurtures and confirms true believers. The term "**ordinance**" was used to designate a teaching of Christ for the whole church and this was more palatable to the nascent Baptist community. It is referred to as an ordinance in most of the early confessions, excepting the Orthodox Creed (1679) where the term sacrament is also used.

The Lord's Supper was usually prepared for church members who had been baptized as believers and this practice was called "closed or close communion." In "open communion" congregations, such as that of **John Bunyan** at Bedford, the invitation was given to all professing believers, regardless of baptized status as an infant or adult. The term "mixed communion" was used in Britain and later in the American colonies to denote the practice of admitting baptized believers and paedo-baptized Christians to the Table.

In normative Baptist practice, a table is set in the midst of the congregation around which gather the **deacons** and **pastor**, who will serve the elements. Two elements are used: bread and wine, later to be replaced by grape juice. Usually the bread is cut into one-inch cubes and the grape beverage is served in either a single chalice or individual communion cups. The deacons take the bread first, and then the wine (grape juice), to the congregation in their places. A deacon offers a prayer of thanksgiving over each element, and after the minister serves the deacons and a deacon serves the minister, all partake of the bread, then the cup in the same manner. After all have been served, a hymn is sung and the congregation is dismissed. Great care is taken to re-enact the Last Supper of Jesus and his disciples, as recorded in the Gospels and I Corinthians 11. The Pauline passage is more common than the gospels as a reference in the service for many Baptists, particularly because it lays stress upon the spiritual preparation of the believers.

Baptists have disagreed and written widely on various aspects of the Lord's Supper. In the beginning, the controversy centered on who should be admitted. In Britain, **Robert Hall** understood the Lord's Supper as a sign of the church's unity and thus practiced open communion. **Joseph Kinghorn**, on the other hand, held that communion belongs to the church and only those admitted to the church through the waters of **baptism** should be invited to the Lord's table. In the United States, these positions were advocated by **Benjamin Randal** and the **Landmarkist** movement, respectively, the latter led by **James R. Graves** and others.

Some Baptists also debated over the terminology of "sacrament" and "ordinance." Then followed the question of wine or grape juice. In Britain between 1820 and 1880 a transition from wine to unfermented grape juice took place. Francis Beardsall (1799-1842) in 1835, Jabez Burns (1806-1876) in 1841, and the **Strict Baptists** (SB) by 1850 all led in the transition, which reflected the teetotal movement and new theological/biblical rationales. In one congregation at Bolton in the 1870s a "two-cup" solution emerged for a time, with both wine and grape juice served as alternatives in the same service. Similarly in the United States with the processing of grape juice and the introduction of germ theories of disease transmission, grape juice served in small glasses became the preferred administration of the cup in most Baptist churches by the 1880s.

Alvah Hovey defended the use of wine on scriptural grounds and Abraham Coles (1813-1891) propounded the use of unfermented grape juice.

In the 19th century, there was some interest in taking the ordinance to sick or invalid persons, but in England this was overrruled by those who believed it was too close to the high church practice of a priest taking the reserved sacrament as an act of mercy. Moreover, it was held that ordained persons wherever possible should preside at the Table in order to maintain proper church order. This hearkened back to **John Gill** and later **Andrew Fuller** among the **Particular Baptists. Scotch Baptists**, who recognized a plurality of elders, were an exception to this practice in Britain and North America. In the United States elders as pastors presiding at the Supper were the common practice; a question arose over women and unordained presiding when **Isabel Crawford** celebrated the Lord's Supper in 1905 at Saddle Mountain, Oklahoma, and had to resign from her **missionary** work for violating mission Board policy.

Typically, among Baptists, the Lord's Supper is celebrated on the first Sunday of each month and on special occasions throughout the year, such as Holy Week and Advent. Among some groups, the Pedalavium (**footwashing**) Service and **Love Feast** may accompany the Supper. In the mid-19th century there was an attempt by several English Baptists, notably **John M. Cramp, James Haldane**, and **C. H. Spurgeon** to adopt a weekly celebration, but again this was viewed as too close to the Establishment sacramentarian practice. Some English Baptists and many American Baptists have recovered the sacramental dimension in recent years, while most Baptists prefer the terminology of "ordinance ." See also **Baptism; Footwashing; Love Feast.**

LOTT CAREY BAPTIST FOREIGN MISSION CONVENTION (LCBFMC). One of the major national expressions of **Black Baptist** organizations in the United States, named for **Lott Carey**, a pioneer Baptist missionary to Africa. As the new **National Baptist Convention in the United States** took shape under the leadership of **Elias C. Morris**, several pastors objected to the Convention's attitude of Black separatism toward White Baptists. This led to a schismatic movement in 1896-1897. A coalition met at Shiloh Baptist Church in Washington, D.C., in December 1897, led by several prominent clergy, including Joseph E. Jones (1850-1922), A. W. Pegues (1859-1929), Calvin S. Brown (1859-1936?), and William T. Johnson (1866-1942), to form the Lott Carey Baptist Foreign Mission Society. Most of the pastors were from eastern states, were employed by the **American Baptist Home Mission Society**, and were educated at either Shaw University in Raleigh, North Carolina, or the Richmond Theological Institute in Virginia, both schools supported by the ABHMS. A distinct contribution to the development of Black Baptist foreign missions, the Society changed its name to a Convention in 1903. It is the only distinct Baptist foreign missionary convention in the United States, and as such, it administers 133 missionary efforts in **Guyana, India, Kenya, Liberia,** and **Nigeria.** Sixteen states and the District of Columbia have affiliate organizations. The purpose of the Convention includes **evangelism,** education, and healing ministries. In the national convention, there are four divisions: Parent Body, Women's Auxiliary, Layman's League, and the Auxiliaries. A number of churches which are affiliated with the Lott Carey Convention are dually aligned with one of the **National Baptist Conventions** or the **American Baptist Churches U.S.A.** The Convention publishes the *Lott Carey Herald* (1908-).

LOVE FEAST. The Love Feast, also called by some the Agape Meal, is an historic **ordinance** among **German Baptist Brethren** and some other Baptist groups. Celebrated in conjunction with the **Lord's Supper,** the Feast is a re-enactment of the Last Supper which Jesus celebrated at the Feast of the Passover. Following the Pedalavium, or **footwashing** service, participants face each other across large tables and prepare for a full meal. In some instances, a meal consisted of many staples like lamb stew, while in other situations, the meal has symbolic elements like coffee or chocolate and wheat biscuits. For strangers or newcomers, bread and apple butter are common in the German Baptist tradition. The meal is eaten in absolute silence and prayerfully. When this portion of the meal is concluded, members turn to the distribution of the unleavened bread and the wine which constitute the traditional Lord's Supper or Holy Communion. The purpose of the Love Feast is both to fulfill the scriptural drama of Matthew 26: 17-25, and to allow a time for communal fellowship and reconciliation with other members of the congregation. See also **Lord's Supper; Footwashing.**

LOWRY, ROBERT (1826-1899). American Baptist minister and hymnist, born at Philadelphia, Pennsylvania. Lowry graduated from the University at Lewisburg (later Bucknell) in 1854 with valedictory honors. He was called the same year to First Baptist Church, West Chester, Pennsylvania. In 1858 he moved to Bloomingdale Baptist in New York City, and thence to Hanson Place Baptist in Brooklyn, where under his leadership 400 new members were added. In 1869 Lowry took the position of Crozer Professor of Rhetoric at the University of Lewisburg, concurrent with a call to the First Baptist Church of Lewisburg. He retired from teaching in

1875 and became chancellor of the University until 1882. With the reorganization of the University, Lowry moved to a church in Plainfield, New Jersey, which he served for nine years, until he lost his hearing. He was the author of scores of popular hymns and gospel songs, including "Shall We Gather at the River," "Nothing But the Blood," and "Low in the Grave."

LUND, ERIC (1852-1933). Swedish, and later American, Baptist missionary, born at Selja, Mora, **Sweden**. He was educated at Betelseminariat in Stockholm and Harley College, London. While studying at the H. G. Guiness Mission Institute, he became interested in missionary work and went to **Spain** where he preached and distributed **bibles**. For his **evangelistic** work he was imprisoned. In 1882 Lund became a missionary of the **American Baptist Missionary Union** (ABMU), having established relationships with Filipino Baptist students. When the ABMU decided to enter the Philippine field after the Spanish-American War, Lund was one of the first missionaries appointed. In 1900 he founded the American Baptist mission among the Visayas at Jaro. At length he took charge of the **bible school** at Jaro and taught preaching and Baptist doctrine from 1900-1912. His **theology** was dogmatic and anti-Catholic, as revealed in over 200 tracts, a bible dictionary in Visayan (1931), and translations of the New Testament into Panayan, Cebuan, and Samaryan. He edited the journal *Revista Homiletica* (Homiletic Review) for many years and was awarded an honorary doctorate by Des Moines University in 1913.

M

MABIE, HENRY CLAY (1847-1918). American Baptist minister and educator, born in Belvidere, Illinois. Influenced by **Charles Hill Roe**, he was educated at the University of Chicago where he received the B.A. and B.D. He was ordained at Rockford, Illinois, in 1869 and served as pastor (1869-1873), and later at Oak Park, Illinois (1873-1876). In 1876 he moved to First Baptist, Brookline, Massachusetts (1876-1879), and First Baptist, Indianapolis, Indiana (1879-1884); Belvidere, Illinois (1884-1885); First Baptist, St. Paul, Minnesota (1885-1888), and Central Baptist Church, Minneapolis (1885-1890). In 1890 Mabie was named corresponding secretary of the **American Baptist Missionary Union** (ABMU), which he served until 1908. After leaving the mission board, he served as Davis Professor of Systematic Theology at Rochester Theological Seminary (1908-1909), and subsequently at the Seminary as lecturer on the theory and practice of **missions**. In his retirement he lectured across the United States on various university and seminary campuses, including a number of distinguished lectureships, one of which was published as *Unshaken Kingdom* (1917). His "Personal Manifesto," delivered in 1917, included a full blown declaration of **religious liberty** and the purposes of **voluntary** organizations as *ecclesiolae in ecclesia*. His best remembered work was *The Meaning and Message of the Cross* (1906).

MACAO. Baptist work in Macao dates from 1836 when **J. Lewis Shuck** went there for the **Baptist Board of Foreign Missions** (BBFM). In 1910 a pre-existing independent **mission** in Macao was assumed by the **Southern Baptists** and their work began in earnest. With the flood of refugees from mainland **China** after 1949, missionary staffing was increased and included many of the missionaries formerly in China. In 1952 the **Hong Kong**-Macao Baptist Mission was organized, which evolved into the Hong Kong Baptist Association. As of 1995 there were five churches with 577 members in the Baptist community in Macao.

   The **Conservative Baptist** Foreign Mission Society also established a mission in Macao in 1986. Still largely considered a mission field for Baptists, there are three congregations with about 75 church members associated with the Macao Baptist Mission.

MACEDONIA. Baptist work in Macedonia can be dated from 1928 when the Methodist congregation at Radovis turned to the Baptists because the Methodists were not legally recognized. That same year Vinko Vacek visited Skopje, the capital of Macedonia, baptized several persons, and established **missions** throughout the region. Later, beginning in 1936, Macedonian congregations were an outgrowth of missionary work of the Belgrade church and part of the Baptist Union of Yugoslavia. The ravages of civil war in the wake of the 1991 dissolution of Yugoslavia left the Baptist movement greatly reduced. In 1991 the Sojuz na Hristijanite-Baptisti vo Republika Makedonija (Union of the Baptist Christians in the Republic of Macedonia) was formed.

   As of 1995 there were three congregations with less than 250 members which are related to Sojuz na Hristijanite-Baptisti vo Republika Makedonija.

MACEDONIA WORLD BAPTIST MISSIONS.   Founded in 1967, Macedonia World Missions has work in 16 countries with about 65 missionaries overseas. With headquarters in Lawrenceville, Georgia, the mission publishes *Focus on the Field*.

MACEDONIAN MISSIONARY SERVICE. Founded in 1973 by Harold Williams (1936-) and Leon Jasper (1936-), the Macedonian Missionary Service has work in 30 countries and about 40 short-term missionaries. Major support is derived from churches affiliated with the **American Baptist Association** (ABA). The organization is headquartered in Lakeland, Florida, and publishes *The Macedonian Call*.

MACINTOSH, DOUGLAS CLYDE (1877-1948). Canadian, and later American, Baptist minister and theologian, born at Breadalbane, Ontario. Macintosh served **mission** congregations in the Baptist Convention of Ontario and Quebec, after which he was educated at McMaster University and the University of Chicago where he earned the Ph.D. degree. Macintosh taught for two years at Brandon College in Manitoba where he organized the Department of Theology and then he took a position in **theology** at Yale Divinity School in the United States. Ordained at the Hyde Park Baptist Church in Chicago, he became the Timothy Dwight Professor at Yale. Macintosh evolved into one of the leading **liberal** thinkers of his era, espousing first a pragmatism and later an empirical approach to theology. In the 1930s he was involved in a celebrated case with the U.S. government over his application for U.S. citizenship, which was denied because he refused to take an oath to bear arms in defense of the United States. His position was that he was loyal ultimately to God in such matters. Among his 18 published books were *The Reasonableness of Christianity* (1925) and *The Problem of Religious Knowledge* (1940).

MACKENZIE, ALEXANDER (1822-1892). Scottish, and later Canadian, Baptist political leader, born in Perthshire, **Scotland**. Trained as a stonemason, in 1842 he emigrated to **Canada** settling at Sarnia in Upper Canada as a builder. He became editor in 1852 of the Liberal *Lambden Shield* and in 1861 he was elected to the provincial parliament. With the establishment of the Dominion of Canada in 1867, Mackenzie was elected to the House of Commons and became prime minister in the first Liberal government, 1867-1878. Among his outstanding achievements as prime minister were the building of the Canadian Pacific Railroad, which he personally advocated, and the establishment of the Supreme Court of Canada. Mackenzie joined a Baptist congregation in Irvine, Scotland, which was influenced by the **Haldane** brothers. Later in Canada, he was an active member of the Bunyan Baptist Church near Sarnia, Ontario, where he led in worship services. When he moved to Toronto, he became a member of historic Jarvis Street Baptist Church. Mackenzie followed

the pattern of leaders like **R. A. Fyfe** in advocating a **voluntary** religious
system.

MACLAREN, ALEXANDER (1826-1910). English Baptist minister, born
in Glasgow, **Scotland**. He was educated at Stepney College and first
served the church at Portland Chapel, Southampton. In 1858 he went to
Union Chapel, Manchester, where he remained until 1903. At Union
Chapel he became the premier expository preacher of his day and
attracted throngs of hearers. He disdained pastoral work, keeping records,
organization, and elaborate music. He was twice elected to the presidency
of the **Baptist Union** (BU) and presided over the first congress of the
Baptist World Alliance (BWA) at London in 1905. MacLaren published
32 volumes of sermons, as well as works on mysticism, religious equality,
and Free Church history. His literary popularity extended to North
America where his expository materials were used across Protestantism.

MACLAY, ARCHIBALD (1778-1860). American Baptist minister, born
in Killearn, **Scotland**. Maclay came under the influence of **Robert
Haldane** who assisted him in preparing for the **ministry**. His first work
was as a supply preacher in Fifeshire. As a Congregationalist, he took an
appointment as a missionary to **Jamaica**, but owing to government
opposition, he went to New York instead. He started Congregational
Church on Rose Street in that city, but after studying the **Scriptures** was
led to Baptist sentiments. He and friends then began the Tabernacle
Baptist Church (later Mulberry Street Church) and this prospered for
many years under Maclay's leadership (1809-1837). He was heavily
involved in **voluntary** associations, notably the **bible** society movement.
He left his pastorate in 1837 to become a general agent for the American
and Foreign Bible Society. Dissatisfied with translation policies in the
Society, Maclay assisted in establishing in 1850 the American Bible
Union, a breakaway movement to protect Baptist emphases in translation.
His literary efforts produced works about bible translation, hymnology,
and published sermons.

MACNEILL, JESSE JAI (1913-1965). American Black Baptist minister
and educator, born in North Little Rock, Arkansas. He was educated at
Shurtleff College, Union Theological Seminary, and Columbia University.
His first **ministry** was pastoral, serving Tabernacle Baptist Church,
Alton, Illinois (1932-1939), after which he became editor of young
people's literature with the **Sunday School** Publishing Board of the
National Baptist Convention, USA (1943-1944). In 1944 he became
dean of the School of Religion at Bishop College and also completed his

seminary degree at Virginia Union School of Theology. He became involved in the World Council of Churches (WCC) in 1947, as a member of which he attended the Ecumenical Institute at Bossey. He gave international lectures at the **Baptist World Alliance** Youth Meeting in Stockholm, Sweden, in 1949 and was a consultant to W. A. Visser't Hooft (1900-1985) for the Second Assembly of the WCC in 1954. MacNeill served as pastor at Tabernacle Baptist Church in Detroit, Michigan (1947-1961), and pioneered ecumenical activity in that metropolitan area. Through travel seminars, personal advocacy, and membership in urban and statewide councils of churches, MacNeill became one of the foremost **Black Baptist ecumenists** of the 20th century.

MADAGASCAR. As early as 1813 American Baptist pioneer missionaries **Adoniram Judson** and **Luther Rice** planned a Baptist **mission** in Madagascar. Independent Baptists from the United States began a mission in the country in 1932, which embodied a split from an earlier mission established by the London Missionary Society. The **Conservative Baptist** Foreign Mission Society likewise entered Madagascar in 1966, with work at Antananarivo, Fianarantsoa, and Mahajanga. Finally the Southern Baptist **Foreign Mission Board** began its mission in 1987.

As of 1995 there were about 40 churches with 1,400 members associated with the Malagasy Baptist Association, which is associated with the Conservative Baptists.

MALAWI. In 1892 Australian Baptists formed a mission near Blantyre, which was the first Baptist effort in the former British colony of Nyasaland. Shortly afterward, the **Seventh Day Baptist**s entered the country in 1899 and developed about 50 congregations; also from the United States came the **National Baptist Convention in the U.S.A.** in 1900, eventually helping to form the African Baptist Assembly in 1945. **Southern Baptist**s entered Malawi in 1959, and an outgrowth of Southern Baptist work was the formation of the Baptist Convention of Malawi in 1970.

As of 1995 there were 784 churches and 56,694 members affiliated with the African Baptist Assembly, Malawi, Inc., 507 churches with 87,178 members affiliated with the Baptist Convention of Malawi, and 300 churches with 19,000 members affiliated with the Evangelical Baptist Church of Malawi.

MALAYSIA. The first Baptists in Malaya, later Malaysia, came from Swatow, **China,** in 1905. Church development began in 1937 at Alor Star and Perek. In 1952 the U.S. **Southern Baptist**s organized a Malayan

Mission with stations at Kuala Lumpur and Singapore. As the China mission field closed, both North American personnel and Chinese leadership emigrated to Malaya and strengthened the work there. The church in Kuala Lumpur, organized in 1952, became a point of church planting for all of Malaya. In the 1960s and 1970s Baptist missions were extended into Borneo, Sarawak, and Brunei. In 1953 the Malaya Baptist Theological Seminary opened at Penang.

As of 1995 there were 80 churches and 7,000 members affiliated with the Malaysia Baptist Convention. The Convention publishes the *Malayan Baptist* (1920-).

MALI. Beginning in 1951 the Evangelical Baptist Missions of the United States began a work in what is now Mali in the city of Gao and another at Timbucto in 1952. In 1964 **Conservative Baptist**s from the United States opened a mission and **Southern Baptist**s entered the country in 1983.

As of 1995 there were approximately 10 congregations and 250 members in the Baptist community of Mali.

MALTA. Malta has a small community of Baptists of recent origin. The **Baptist Bible Fellowship (BBF)** opened a mission in 1983. As of 1995 there were two congregations not affiliated with an internal **association**.

MANLY FAMILY. A prominent family in U.S. Southern Baptist life in the 19th and early 20th centuries. The first of the family was **Basil Manly, Sr.** (1798-1868), born in Pittsborough, North Carolina. He was educated at the College of Charleston with honors and ordained to serve the Edgefield, South Carolina, Church, 1822-1826. He became pastor of prestigious First Baptist Charleston, which he served until 1837. Manley became the president of the University of Alabama for 18 years and enlarged its interests greatly. During this period, Manly was active in Alabama state Baptist work and prepared the resolution in 1844 which posed a hypothetical case to the **General Missionary Convention** (GMC) to determine if they would appoint a **slave**holder as a missionary. This was considered inflammatory and the responses led to a hardened position of southern regionalism, which Manly advocated. His term as president of the university ended, Manly returned to Charleston to serve the Wentworth Street Church in 1855, and after a short time he served as an evangelist in Alabama. He was active with his son, Basil, in establishing the Southern Baptist Theological Seminary at Greenville, South Carolina, in 1859 and in promoting what became Furman University. **Basil Manly, Jr.** (1825-1892), the son of Basil, Sr. was also a **Southern Baptist**

minister and educator, born at Edgefield, South Carolina. He was educated at the University of Alabama, Newton Theological Institution, and graduated from Princeton Theological Seminary in 1847. He served in the pastoral ministry of small churches in Sumter County, Alabama (1848-1850), and later First Baptist Church, Richmond, Virginia (1850-1854). He founded the Richmond Female Institute in 1854 and was its president from 1854-1859. In 1859 **James Boyce** asked Manly to join the inaugural faculty of Southern Baptist Theological Seminary in Greenville, South Carolina, as professor of Old Testament. Manley drew up the Seminary's doctrinal basis, the "Abstract of Principles." During the American Civil War, he served various churches and in 1871-1877 was president of Georgetown College in Kentucky. During this same era he helped to establish the Southern **Baptist Sunday School Board** (BSSB) and was its first president. In 1877 he returned to Southern Seminary, now in Louisville, Kentucky, and during his final term until 1892 he helped to build the outstanding reputation of its faculty. His book, *The Biblical Doctrine of Inspiration* (1888), helped to countermand the difficulties raised by his colleague, **Crawford H. Toy**. Manly was a gifted and prolific writer of about 20 hymns, the most famous of which is "Soldiers of Christ in Truth Arrayed." His literary efforts produced catechetical aids for young people, historical treatises, published sermons, and collections of hymns. Finally, the family included **Charles Manly** (1837-1924), second son of Basil Manly, Sr. He was educated at the University of Alabama, and Princeton Theological Seminary. Charles was ordained to serve the Tuscaloosa, Alabama Baptist Church from 1859-1871, after which he was pastor at Murfreesboro, Tennessee (1871-1873), and Staunton, Virginia (1873-1880). While in Alabama, he taught and was president at Alabama Female College, and in Tennessee, he was president of Union University. He was pastor of the Greenville, South Carolina, Church from 1880-1881, after which for 18 years he was president at Furman University (1881-1897). Having set the school on firm foundations, Manly returned to pastoral **ministry**, serving churches in Lexington, Missouri, and Lexington, Virginia from 1897-1914.

MANNING, EDWARD (1766-1851). Canadian Baptist minister, born in Ireland. He was converted under the **evangelistic ministry** of Congregationalist John Payzant (1749-1834) and ordained to serve the Congregational church at Cornwallis, Nova Scotia. He embraced Baptist sentiments and was baptized by **Thomas H. Chipman** in 1798. Soon thereafter, he brought his church into the Baptist association and he served the congregation for over 50 years. Considered one of the "fathers" of the Maritime Baptists, Manning was one of the founders of Horton Academy and Acadia University, and an historian of the Maritimes, supplying **David Benedict** with materials for his *History of the Baptists* (1848).

MANNING, JAMES (1738-1791). American Baptist minister and educator, born at Elizabethtown, New Jersey. Manning was educated at the Baptist academy at Hopewell, New Jersey, under **Isaac Eaton** and the College of New Jersey, earning the highest honors in his class. After a year of travel in the colonies, Manning accepted the invitation of the **Philadelphia Baptist Association** (PBA) to start a grammar school in Warren, Rhode Island. This he did in 1764, as well as commencing a new Baptist congregation. Upon the securing of a charter in that year, Manning became the first president of the College of Rhode Island. In 1767 he assisted in the formation of the Warren (Rhode Island) Baptist Association. The decision was made to move the college to Providence in 1770 and Manning set about building the campus. In addition, he accepted the call of First Baptist Church in Providence and superintended the construction of their meetinghouse in 1774 (see **Church Architecture, Baptist**), one of the most impressive church edifices of the era. In 1786 Manning was chosen to represent Rhode Island in the Confederation Congress; he later shifted to support the new constitution in 1787 and used his considerable influence to carry the support of the state. His long-time friendship with the **Nicholas Brown** family made possible the firm establishment of the College and the family later honored Manning by building the chapel in his memory.

MARANATHA BAPTIST MISSION. Founded in 1961 by James W. Crumpton, Maranatha Baptist Mission is an **independent** Baptist overseas agency which relates to the Independent Fundamental Baptist Churches. As of 1995, the organization has missions in 24 countries, including **Australia**, Europe, Africa, South America, and the Far East, with 1,180 missionaries. Headquarters is located in Natchez, Mississippi, and the mission publishes *Maranatha Publications*.

MARING, NORMAN HILL (1914-1998). American Baptist minister and church historian born at Crozer Theological Seminary in Upland, Pennsylvania. He was educated at Furman University and the Collegiate Division of The Eastern Baptist Seminary, after which he earned the M.A. and Ph.D. degrees at the University of Maryland under Richard Hofstadter and Wesley Gewehr. Following his theological degree from Eastern, he served churches in Berwyn and Cumberland, Maryland. In 1948 he became professor of church history at Eastern and served the school for 35 years. From 1972 to 1978 he was academic dean of the seminary. Maring was a valued resource for three generations of American Baptists, particularly in the areas of denominational polity and identity. He offered a "conservative, but progressive" theological position and was mentor to several senior American Baptist leaders. His outstanding publication, *A Baptist Manual of Polity and Practice* (1963, 1991), has been used broadly in the Baptist family and his *Baptists in New Jersey: A Study in Transition* (1964) was hailed for its approach to regional church history. In retirement, Maring served on the American Baptist Denominational Identity Commission (1984-1986) and taught at Southern Baptist and Southeastern Baptist seminaries.

MARKS, DAVID (1805-1845). American Freewill Baptist minister and evangelist, born in Shandaken, New York. In 1818 he walked over 300 miles and return to enroll at Brown University, only to be disappointed with an inadequate offer of financial assistance. Marks was baptized in 1819 and embarked upon an itinerant **ministry** among **Freewill Baptist** churches in western New York and Canada at only 15 years old. Known as the "boy preacher," he finally settled in a pastorate at Portsmouth, New Hampshire (1834-1836), but moved to plant a congregation in Rochester, New York (1836-1837), and afterward at Varysburg, New York (1838-1842). Marks was the principal founder of the "Freewill Baptist Book Concern" for his denomination. In 1842 he moved to Oberlin, Ohio, to further his studies, establishing high schools at Strafford, New Hampshire, and Chester, Ohio. Ultimately the strain of his efforts took its toll and he died at 40 years old. A remarkable feat for his age, he wrote on religious experience, catechetical subjects, and hymnology.

MARNEY, CARLYLE (1916-1978). Southern Baptist minister, born at Harriman, Tennessee. He was educated at Carson Newman College and Southern Baptist Theological Seminary. In 1946 he received the Th.D. degree from Southern Seminary in church history, his dissertation entitled, "The Rise of Ecclesiological Externalism to 337 A.D." He served churches at Ft. Knox (1941-1944), and Immanuel, Paducah, (1946-1948) Kentucky; Austin, Texas (1948-1958); and Myers Park Baptist Church in Charlotte, North Carolina (1958-1967). During his Texas pastorate Marney served as adjunct professor in Christian Ethics at Austin Theological Seminary and published an acclaimed book, *Faith in Conflict* (1957). In 1967, with assistance from foundations and the denomination, he opened at Lake Junaluska, North Carolina, The Interpreter's House, a **ministry** of renewal, instruction, and self-integration. Openly critical of denominational structures and alienated from the administration of the **Southern Baptist Convention**, Marney moved in an **ecumenical** direction and was increasingly critical of racism and **fundamentalism**. He became a nationally recognized lecturer and commentator on religious experience. His academic activities included serving as adjunct Professor of Preaching at Duke University Divinity School from 1972-1978 and in 1978 as Visiting Professor of Humanities at Virginia Military Institute. In 1976 he was awarded an honorary doctorate at the University of Glasgow, largely for his work in clergy professional rehabilitation. Marney was the author of over 20 books, including *The Recovery of the Person* (1963).

MARSHALL, ANDREW (c.1755-1856). American Black Baptist minister, born in South Carolina, the son of an English soldier and a slave woman. He was raised on a plantation and owned by several masters. He purchased his freedom in 1785 and became a Christian about the same time. When President George Washington (1732-1799) toured the southern states in the 1790s, Marshall accompanied him as a servant and wrote of his experiences. Considered one of the outstanding preachers of his era, Marshall succeeded **Andrew Bryan** in 1806 as pastor of Second Baptist Church (later named the First African Baptist Church) in Savannah, Georgia, which he led to over 3,000 members. During the course of his **ministry** he is said to have baptized 3,800 persons and seen over 4,000 converted. About 1820 Marshall was whipped publicly for advocating the plight of his slave brothers, and this increased his notoriety in Georgia. His theology was Calvinistic, based upon an appreciation of **John Gill**, the English Baptist writer. In order to raise money for a new building for his church, he toured the northern states in 1856, preaching in many prominent Baptist pulpits. His funeral was one mile long with over 58 carriages in train, including persons of both races.

MARSHALL, DANIEL (1706-1784). American Baptist minister and evangelist, born in Windsor, Connecticut. He was converted in 1745 under the preaching of George Whitefield (1714-1770) and became a self-proclaimed **missionary** to the Mohawk Indians of upstate New York. In 1746 he moved to Conecocheague, Pennsylvania, and then to Winchester, Virginia. In Winchester in 1754 he joined a frontier Baptist congregation related to the **Philadelphia Baptist Association**. About 1756 in response to French frontier hostilities, he moved to Hughwarry, North Carolina, and then to neighboring Abbot's Creek where he was ordained **pastor**. Closely associated with **Shubael Stearns**, his brother-in-law, Marshall became an itinerant **Separate Baptist** pastor in the next few years, serving Beaver Creek, South Carolina, and then Horse Creek, Georgia, near Augusta. At length, he was ordered not to preach in the colonies of South Carolina and Georgia. But, against government decrees, he settled in 1771 at Kiokee, Georgia, and conducted a successful ministry, organizing the first Baptist congregation in the colony. Daniel's wife, Martha Stearns Marshall (fl.1750), was said to be a church planter and evangelist herself, of no little reputation. In 1784 Marshall presided over the inaugural meeting of the Georgia Baptist Association.

MARSHALL, LAURENCE HENRY (1882-1953). English, and later Canadian, Baptist minister and educator, born at Louth, England. Initially educated at Rawdon College, he graduated in arts and divinity from the University of London, gaining both the Dr. Williams and **Baptist Union** scholarships. He spent two years studying in **Germany**, first under C. G. A. von Harnack (1851-1930) and G.A. Deissman (1866-1937) at Berlin, then under Adolf Julicher (1857-1938) and Wilhelm Heitmuller (1869-1926) in Marburg. After post-graduate work, he was **pastor** at Prince's Gate, Liverpool (1911-1919), and Queen's Road, Coventry (1920-1925). In 1925 Marshall was elected to the vacant chair in theology at McMaster University in Toronto, a move which caused much controversy in Ontario. **T. T. Shields** led an attack upon Marshall's reputation in the Baptist Convention of Ontario and Quebec, which prompted Marshall to deliver an able defense of **religious liberty**. Although the McMaster administration won the floor fight at the Convention, Marshall returned to England in 1930 to become pastor at Victoria Road, Leicester. In 1936 he returned to Rawdon as Tutor in New Testament and Pastoral Theology and became principal in 1948 on the death of **A. C. Underwood**. Marshall's book, *The Challenge of New Testament Ethics* (1946), was long considered a classic in the field. In **Canada** his appointment at McMaster became a symbol of the **liberal** tradition adopted at the university.

MARSHMAN, HANNAH (1767-1847). English Baptist missionary, born at Bristol, England. Educated in local schools and orphaned at 12, she lived in London and was baptized at Westbury Leigh Church. In 1791 she married **Joshua Marshman** and they settled at Bristol where Joshua studied at Bristol Baptist Academy. The couple offered themselves for missionary service and embarked for **India** in 1799, settling at Serampore with **William Carey**. Aside from her family responsibilities, Hannah helped to organize the school plan her husband initiated. She returned to England in 1820 for two years, during which time she promoted the Indian schools and the Serampore Mission. Upon her return to India she took over the administration of Serampore's female schools after **William Ward** died and she assumed the care of several families in the Christian community. Hannah Marshman is credited among Christians and educators in India with introducing and advocating **women's** education. She is recalled throughout the century as a role model for aspiring missionary candidates.

MARSHMAN, JOSHUA (1768-1837). English Baptist missionary, born at Westbury Leigh, England. He was educated in primary school and read very widely. At Bristol in 1794 he took charge of a school and was baptized at Broadmead Baptist Church. He studied at Bristol Baptist College with an emphasis in Hebrew and Syriac. In 1799 he and his wife offered themselves to the **Baptist Missionary Society** (BMS) for service in **India**. He worked with **William Carey** in translation and the operation of boarding schools with his wife, Hannah. With Carey and **William Ward**, Marshman was considered part of the "Serampore Trio." Following an extensive study of Chinese, Marshman produced a Chinese grammar in 1814 and the first Chinese bible in 1821. His literary efforts were wide-ranging on topics relating to Christian witness in India, education, translation missions, and a memoir of the first Serampore missionaries (1827). Brown University in Rhode Island conferred the Doctor of Divinity degree on him in 1811.

MARTIN, JAMES (1821-1877). English Baptist minister and scholar, born at Hackney, England. He was educated at Madras House School and later at Stepney College under **Benjamin Davies** and **F. W. Gotch**. After his graduation from the University of London, he studied under Dr. Ward's Trust in Germany at the University of Bonn in 1847. He served pastorates at Lymington (1848-1855), Charlotte Chapel, Edinburgh (1856-1858), Derby Road, Nottingham (1858-1869), then Collins Street, Melbourne, Australia (1869-1877). Martin was a catalyst for the publication of German theological scholarship into English, translating 20 works for the Edinburgh publisher, T & T Clark, notably his contemporaries, Karl F. Keil (1807-1888), Franz Delitsch's (1813-1890) Old Testament commentaries, and E. W. Hengstenburg's (1802-1869) *Christology of the Old Testament* (1856).

MARTINIQUE. Martinique, formerly part of the French West Indies, has a small Baptist population. The first Baptists were likely associated with **Evangelical Baptist Missions** (EBM), beginning in 1945. This group numbers about four churches and 300 members. In 1977 **Southern Baptists** began missionary work on the island as part of their work in **Guadaloupe**; in 1978 this work was separated from Guadaloupe to form a new mission **association**.

As of 1995, there were 30 churches with about 1,200 members and 4,000 adherents.

MARTYROLOGY, BAPTIST. From the earliest period of Baptist development there have been instances of persecution and loss of life for one's religious principles, or in the conduct of **ministry** and missionary service. One of the founders of the **General Baptist** persuasion in England, **Thomas Helwys,** likely died in prison for his religious convictions. Others in the 17th century who gave their lives include Benjamin and William Hewling, grandsons of **William Kiffin**. Benjamin (c.1663-1685) and William (c.1665-1685) took up arms against the Duke of York (later King James II) because of his perceived Catholic tendencies, and were imprisoned at Newgate, and executed at Lyme and Taunton, respectively, in September 1685. The last woman to be executed in England for her religious views was a Baptist, Elizabeth Gaunt (fl. 1660-1685). She was found guilty of harboring a man named Burton who was suspected of complicity in the Rye House Plot, and she was tried and burnt at the stake at Tyburn near London on October 23, 1685.

While there is ample evidence of persecution, loss of property and position and corporal punishment in the early American scene, there is no known case of martyrdom among Baptists in the American colonies in the 17th or 18th centuries. A famous example of punishment of Baptists involved **Obadiah Holmes** who joined Joseph Crandall and **John Clarke** in 1651 on a visit to Lynn, Massachusetts, to provide spiritual care for a blind friend, William Witter (fl.1650). When the authorities found out the plan, they imprisoned Holmes, and after a trial in which he refused to pay his fine of 30 pounds, he was flogged 30 times. Likewise in the next century, **James Ireland** in Virginia was imprisoned for preaching in Culpeper; while he was in prison, attempts were made upon his life to halt his witness.

It is in the missionary context that several Baptist ministers and laypersons lost their lives in the 19th century. **Lott Carey** was killed in an explosion in **Liberia**, apparently the victim of an insurrection in 1829. Many writers hold that **Ann Hasseltine Judson** and **Sarah Hall Boardman**, to mention just two missionary wives, essentially died for the cause of missions in **Burma**.

A famous story among the Baptist communities of eastern Europe concerns a boy named "Frank" who in the 1870s attended the **Sunday School** started by Henry and Amalie **Novotny** in Prague. Warned not to return to the Baptist church, the boy was beaten and abused by a local Catholic priest who opposed Protestantism. Frank's love for the **Scriptures** and Sunday School were widely known, and as he died from his injuries he became a folk hero among Sunday School students across Czechoslovakia.

During much of their history, Baptists in **Russia** have suffered greatly from government persecution. Pastors such as Andreas Erstratenko (1863-?), who was banished to Siberia in 1891 and remained to begin a church there, and Ivan Savelieff (1858-?), who was banished from Transcaucasia to Siberia from 1894-1904, illustrate the harsh treatment inflicted on Baptists by the government of Imperial Russia. Although many names are not available, it is certain that numerous Baptists lost their lives in prisons during the Stalinist purges and later. For instance, N. Odintsov (1871-1939) suffered a violent death for **evangelical** labors, as did Peter Vins, a missionary in Siberia who died in a prison in 1929, a victim of the "Anti-God" law of that year.

Likewise, **China** was the scene of Baptist martyrdoms. During the period of the Boxer Rebellion (1900), in Shansi Province 112 of the Chinese Christian community were killed for their connection with the English Baptist Mission. Choa Hsi Mao, with his wife and sister and mother, were beheaded in July 1900.

Two outstanding examples of martyrdom occurred in the **Phillipines** and **Bolivia** in the 1940s. On the Island of Panay in the Philippines, **American Baptists** maintained hospitals, which were placed in jeopardy by the advance of the Japanese army in April 1942. In accord with the "scorched earth" policy of the Allied forces, the hospital buildings were destroyed and the missionary personnel fled to a prearranged mountain retreat called "Hopevale." For several months up to 22 people survived, until the Japanese located them and executed 11 missionaries and relatives on December 19, 1943. Those who gave their lives were: a nurse, Jennie Clare Adams (1896-1943); a teacher, James Howard Covell (1896-1943); his wife, Charma Moore Covell (1895-1943); an educational administrator, Dorothy Antoinette Dowell (1889-1943); a teacher, Signe Amelia Erickson (1898-1943); a medical doctor, Frederick Willer Meyer (1892-1943); his wife, Ruth Schacht Meyer (1892-1943); a college administrator, Francis Howard Rose (1884-1943); his wife, Gertrude Coombs Rose (1885-1943); an evangelist, Erle Frederick Rounds (1901-1943); his wife, Louise Cummings Rounds (1904-1943); and their son, Erle Douglas Rounds (1934-1943).

A celebrated Baptist martyrdom occurred in **Bolivia** in 1949. While on a preaching tour of the interior altiplano, the Rev. Norman Dabbs (1912-1949), a Canadian Baptist missionary, and seven other Bolivian Baptist leaders were stoned and killed, while six others were left for dead on August 8, 1949, at Merk'Amaya. The murder of Dabbs became an instant international incident and the Christian community responded with horror. Many new leaders in Bolivia were recruited for ministry as a result of the martyrdom.

Baptist leaders in **Korea** lost their lives in the military advance of the Communists following World War II. At a rate comparatively higher than other Korean Christian groups, Baptists were martyred in significant numbers: in 1950 61 Baptists were killed by the Communists. A specially remembered incident involved the president of the Korean Baptist Convention, Jong-Duk Yi (1884-1950), who was shot to death in the marsh of the Kum on September 28, 1950.

More recently, **Southern Baptist** missionaries to the **Dominican Republic**, Paul E. (1932-1971) and Nancy (1935-1971) Potter, were killed at their home in Santiago on July 7, 1971. The Potters had been serving in the Dominican Republic since 1966, opening the mission station in Santiago. The deaths were apparent homicides and may have been related to robbery. While not directly associated with Christian witness, the Potters died in the course of their **ministry**.

Over the three and a half centuries of their development, Baptists have suffered persecution, estrangement of goods, property, and family, and some have died for their faith. In this regard they fit the pattern of religious dissenters through the course of Christian history.

MASON, FRANCIS (1799-1874). American Baptist missionary, born at York, England. In his youth he was an apprenticed shoemaker, self taught in literature and mathematics. He emigrated to the United States in 1818 and studied theology at Newton Theological Institution. He was appointed a missionary to **Burma** in 1829 by the **Baptist Board of Foreign Missions** (BBFM). Mason settled at Tavoy, replacing **George Dana Boardman**, serving 20 years as a translator, administrator, and seminary teacher. He is especially remembered for the growth of the **mission** at Toungoo: more than 6,000 converts were baptized and over 100 churches begun in a decade under his leadership. In the late 1850s his wife Ellen (1817-1894) assumed leadership in the mission, and caused a stir by claiming a special revelation from God. From 1865-1871 the **American Baptist Missionary Union** (ABMU) withheld its support until Ellen's teachings were withdrawn, ultimately restoring his funding. Mason was a linguistic scholar with few peers, publishing over 30 **Scripture** translations in Pali, Burmese, and Sanskrit. He also published a scientific study on natural life in Burma, historical mission treatises, and mathematical subjects for which he was elected a member of the Royal Asiatic Society. His biography is told in *The Story of a Workingman's Life* (1870).

MASSEE, JASPER CORTENUS (1871-1965). American Baptist minister, born at Marshallville, Georgia. He graduated from Mercer University and attended Southern Baptist Theological Seminary for one year. He served congregations in Kissimmee, Florida (1893-1896), Orlando, Florida (1897-1898), Lancaster, Kentucky (1899-1901), Mansfield, Ohio (1901-1903), Raleigh, North Carolina (1903-1908), Chattanooga, Tennessee, (1908-1913), Dayton, Ohio (1913-1919), Brooklyn, New York (1919-1922), and Boston, Massachusetts (1922-1929). Following pastoral ministry he pursued a career as an evangelist and was professor of homiletics at The Eastern Baptist Theological Seminary from 1938-1941. Massee perfected an **evangelistic** style which included thematic nights in protracted meetings, pulpit responses to contemporary social phenomena, pledge cards for ethical commitments, and **bible** exposition. During his pastoral **ministry** at Tremont Temple in Boston, 2,500 persons joined the church in seven years.

With **Curtis L. Laws** and **William B. Riley**, Massee joined the **fundamentalist** crusade in 1920 and became the presiding officer of the newly formed Fundamentals of the Faith Conference at Buffalo, 1920. As president of the Fundamentalist Federation (1920-1925), he led an investigation of Baptist schools to ferret out modernism. Massee, considered a moderate fundamentalist, became increasingly concerned over the bitter spirit of more radical colleagues in the movement, notably **John R. Straton** and **J. Frank Norris**. Opposing a split in the **Northern Baptist Convention**, Massee left the fundamentalist movement in 1925, blaming the **Baptist Bible Union** (BBU) for divisiveness in the denomination. He held to five "fundamentals of the faith," and while openly centrist in the denominational struggles, he exhibited anti-intellectual characteristics and opposed the **social gospel**. Massee was a widely circulated author, publishing over 30 books on topics ranging from doctrine to ethical issues and sermons.

MASTER'S MISSION, THE. An independent, doctrinally-baptistic missionary organization, founded in 1979 by Paul Tisdale and Robert Van Campen. Tisdale was a former Africa Inland Missionary in **Kenya**. The Mission currently supports about 40 projects or missionaries in Kenya and elsewhere in Africa, and **Mexico**. Its publication is *Mission News* and the headquarters are located in Robbinsville, North Carolina.

MATHEWS, SHAILER (1863-1941). American Baptist educator and denominational leader, born at Portland, Maine. He was educated at Colby College and Newton Theological Institution. He began his teaching career at Colby, where he first taught history and later New Testament

Interpretation from 1889-1897. **Ernest D. Burton** induced him to accept a position at the new University of Chicago where his efforts flourished. Mathews introduced the scientific study of religion and guided the school to a distinctive approach utilizing the social sciences and called the **"Chicago School."** He argued for contextual studies and evolutionary patterns of history to understand Christian dogma. His book, *The Faith of Modernism* (1924), was a cogent and positive response to the attacks of **fundamentalists.** Mathews was not ordained, but was one of the shapers of the **Northern Baptist Convention** (NBC) and particularly its social action emphases. He was also one of the most popular teachers in the religious lecture circuit of his era. Mathews's published works number over 50 items, notably *The Life of Christ* (1901) and *Creative Christianity* (1935).

MAURITIUS. Originally known as the Isle of France, Baptist work began here with the arrival of **Adoniram Judson** and **Luther Rice** in 1814. For a short time the American missionaries remained on Mauritius until Judson left for **Burma** and Rice returned to the United States. Not until 1978 did Baptists return, via the Southern Baptist **Foreign Mission Board** (FMB), among Chinese believers. As of 1995, there was a small association of two churches, numbering 150 members.

MAYS, BENJAMIN ELIJAH (1894-1984). American Black Baptist minister and educator, born at Epworth, South Carolina. He was educated at South Carolina State College, Bates College, and the University of Chicago, where he received the Ph.D. degree. He taught mathematics at Morehouse College (1921-1924), while also serving as pastor at Shiloh Baptist Church in Atlanta, Georgia. From there he moved to teach English at Orangeburg State College in South Carolina (1925-1926). He then served as executive secretary of the Urban League in Tampa, Florida (1926-1928), national student secretary of the Y.M.C.A. (1928-1930), and he conducted research on the Black church in America for the Institute of Social and Religious Research (1930-1932). In 1934 Mays entered educational administration, his lifelong ministry. He served as dean of the School of Religion of Howard University (1934-1940) and president of Morehouse College (1940-1967). One of the eminent leaders in Black higher education, Mays was a consultant to government and private organizations, including the Ford Foundation, the Peace Corps, and the United Nations. He served as president of the United Negro College Fund from 1958-1961, and he received over 50 honorary degrees, probably the most among the Baptist family worldwide in any era. Mays was an authority on the Black church in America and the symbolic leader of the movement to establish a high standard for Black education. He was the author of several published works, including *Seeking to Be Christian In Race Relations* (1957) and *Born to Rebel* (1971).

MCCOY, ISAAC (1784-1846). American Baptist missionary, born in Fayette County, Pennsylvania. Lacking an adequate education, he was ordained to the Baptist ministry in 1810 at Maria Creek, Indiana, where he was pastor from 1810-1817. He was appointed by the **Baptist Board of Foreign Missions** (BBFM) to work with the Miami Indians in Illinois and Indiana. In 1822 he moved to Michigan and settled among the Potawatomi Indians and became a government teacher. In 1825, as the government moved the tribes west of the Mississippi, McCoy devised an enlightened plan for an Indian Territory and he worked for the government during the removal. He operated a mission among the Delawares and Shawnees in Kansas in the 1830s. In 1842 McCoy created the American Indian Mission Association (AIMA) to unite all Indian missions. Ultimately, he moved his allegiance from the BBFM to the newly formed Domestic Board of the **Southern Baptist Convention** in 1846. Because of his dealings with the U.S. government, McCoy was often the target of criticism of the antimissionary Baptists led by **Daniel Parker**.

MCDONALD, ALEXANDER (1837-1911). Canadian and American Baptist missionary, born at Osgoode, Ontario. He was educated at Canadian Literary Institute (later McMaster University) under the tutelage of **Robert A. Fyfe** and a close friend of Robert McLaurin (1839-1912), the first Canadian Baptist overseas missionary. In 1873 McDonald arrived in Ft. Garry (later Winnipeg), Manitoba Territory. Within two years he established the first Baptist congregation there, which came to be the first in the Canadian West. He started a second church at Stonewall in 1879 and assisted in the constitution of the Red River Association in 1880. In 1882 McDonald transferred to Grafton, North Dakota, where he served that congregation as a home missionary **pastor**. In 1893 he became the first pastor of the First Baptist Church in Edmonton, Alberta, where he served for two years before commencing a new congregation at Strathcona, near Edmonton. For his many church plantings he was popularly known as "Pioneer McDonald" and is the parent of the Baptist movement in western **Canada**.

MCGLOTHLIN, WILLIAM JOSEPH (1867-1933). Southern Baptist educator and historian, born at Gallatin, Tennessee. He was educated at Bethel College, Southern Baptist Theological Seminary, and the

University of Berlin, where he received his Ph.D. He was professor of church history at Southern Baptist Seminary (1894-1919), after which he was president at Furman University (1919-1933). He greatly enlarged Furman and brought it accreditation. The first David T. Porter Professor of Church History at Southern Baptist Seminary (1904-1919), McGlothlin published *Baptist Confessions of Faith* (1910), *Infant Baptism in History* (1915), and *The Course of Christian History* (1917). He was instrumental in critically examining the original documentation exhibiting relationships between Baptists and Swiss **Anabaptists**.

MCKINNEY, BAYLUS BENJAMIN (1886-1952). Southern Baptist minister and hymnist, born in Heflin, Louisiana. He was educated at Louisiana College and Southwestern Baptist Theological Seminary, and later at the Bush Conservatory of Music in Chicago. In 1919 he joined the faculty of music at Southwestern Seminary and taught there until 1931. McKinney developed a popular following as a music minister in **evangelistic** meetings and special events in the **Southern Baptist Convention**. In 1931 he became the director of music at Travis Avenue Baptist Church in Ft. Worth, Texas, the city's most prestigious congregation. The **Sunday School Board** (BSSB) of the Southern Baptist Convention called McKinney in 1935 to be its first music editor, and his greatest accomplishment in that role was the compilation of the *Broadman Hymnal* in 1940. He was the author or composer of 483 pieces of work, including gospel songs, hymns, and choruses. Among his better known hymns are "Send A Great Revival!," "Glorious Is Thy Name," and "Wherever He Leads I'll Go."

MCLEAN, ARCHIBALD (1733-1812). Scotch Baptist minister, born at East Kilbride, Lanarkshire. As a young man he heard George Whitefield (1703-1770) preach and was much impressed. He was apprenticed a printer in 1746 and followed that trade as a printer and bookseller in Glasgow from 1759-1766. After a year in London, McLean left the Presbyterian Church and became a follower of the **Glasites**. He continued in the printing business as a superintendent for the Donaldson Company, printers in Edinburgh from 1767-1785. In 1763 he was involved in a dispute with the Glasgow Glasites over a point of church **discipline**, and left their fellowship with Robert Carmichael (?-1774) to build a New Testament Church. The two leaders sought the advice of **John Gill** who baptized Carmichael, who in turn baptized McLean in 1765.

In 1768 McLean and Carmichael became co-elders of a congregation in Edinburgh calling themselves and their new movement "Scotch Baptists." Following the principles of Robert Sandeman (1718-

1771) plus a stricter ethic and believer's **baptism**, McLean interacted with leaders of the Baptist community, notably **Andrew Fuller**, with whom he frequently debated. After the death of Carmichael in 1774, McLean became the sole pastor of the church at Edinburgh. His influence was felt in northern England, in Yorkshire and Lancashire, basically characterized by a multiplicity of church elders and primitivist practices; McLean was popular in North Wales among the **Particular Baptist** churches. His following were often referred to as "McLeanists" or "McLeanites." His works were published in six volumes and he was awarded an honorary M.A. degree in 1793 by Brown University in Rhode Island.

MCLOUGHLIN, WILLIAM GERALD (1922-1992). Historian of Baptist life and thought, born at Maplewood, New Jersey. He was educated at Princeton and Harvard Universities (A.M., Ph.D.), where he specialized in American civilization. He taught his entire career at Brown University, emphasizing in his scholarship from time to time Baptist experience and **religious liberty**; in 1981 he was named Annie McClelland and Willard Prescott Smith Professor of History and Religion at Brown. McLoughlin trained numerous Baptist students and was the author of 16 books. Among his most important works were *New England Dissent* (2 vols., 1971), an updated, comprehensive history of Baptists in New England, the *Diary of Isaac Backus* (3 vols, 1979), and *Modern Revivalism* (1958). His biography of **Billy Graham** (1958) was based upon careful observation of Graham at crusades, etc., and was expected to be the authoritative work on the life of the 20th century **evangelist**. However McLoughlin made some assessments of the revivalist's techniques that the Graham organization felt were unfair and damaging, and the Graham organization protested McLoughlin's material. He continued to turn out major scholarly works about **evangelical** life and characters, **revivalism**, and Indian **missions**, while espousing numerous activist causes.

MCMASTER, WILLIAM (1811-1887). Canadian Baptist denominational leader, born in Tyrone County, Ireland. He was not formally educated and after emigrating to York, Upper Canada (now Ontario), took a minor position with a dry goods company and later took over the business, moving it to Toronto. To further his trading interests, McMaster founded his own financial house, the Bank of Commerce, becoming its first president in 1867. He served on the Legislative Council of the province of Upper **Canada** and was appointed to the first Senate of the Dominion of Canada in 1867. He was an active Baptist layman, a member of the Jarvis Street Church in Toronto and various societies and boards of the denomination in Ontario and Quebec. He took an interest in **Robert A.**

Fyfe's plan for a Christian university at Woodstock, Ontario, but later shifted his support to a Toronto-based institution called the Toronto Baptist College, which he largely founded in 1881, also writing its doctrinal basis. McMaster helped to secure a charter for the College, which was renamed McMaster University at his death in 1887. His estate, which amounted to just under one million dollars, was the most substantial gift of its kind in all of Canada to be given at that time to a religious institution.

MERCER, JESSE (1769-1841). Southern Baptist minister, denominational leader, and historian, born in Halifax County, North Carolina. Lacking formal education, he plunged into pastoral **ministry** at several towns in Georgia and was remembered as an effective revivalist. Mercer opposed the New Measures of Charles G. Finney (1792-1875) and others, preferring long periods of prayer and exhortation. He served three congregations simultaneously while conducting a far-reaching career in education. He began an academy at Salem, Georgia, in 1796 and wrote an authoritative history, based upon his own observations, *History of the Georgia Baptist Association* (1838). He believed strongly in the **associational** principle and **missions**, writing major treatises on these topics, as well as Baptist **polity**. Mercer was president of the state Baptist convention for almost 20 years, and Mercer University in Macon, Georgia, was named in his honor. Brown University conferred an honorary doctorate on Mercer in 1835.

MESSENGER, BAPTIST UNDERSTANDING OF. The title of messenger first began to appear in Baptist usage among the English **General Baptists** in the 1650s. It designated travelling ministers who visited the churches, celebrating the **Lord's Supper**, resolving questions of church **polity**, and sometimes doing **evangelical** work. **Particular Baptists** also employed the office of messenger in the 17th century. Messengers came to symbolize the larger connection and eventually served as superintendents of areas of England. The office of messenger was fully defined in the work of **Thomas Grantham** and seems to have had an effect upon American colonial General Baptist development in the Carolina Colony. As the General Baptists declined in the 18th century, so the office of messenger dropped out of usage. It was ultimately recovered in the **Baptist Union** development of area minister.

A second usage of the term "messenger" was developed among **Southern Baptists** and others in the United States. Under the influence of **Landmarkism**, Southern Baptists eschewed the northern churches' use of representatives to associational meetings, holding that no one could "represent" a Baptist congregation. Those persons who attended **convention** and **association** meetings on behalf of local churches thus came to be called "messengers" because they carried messages between their congregations and other bodies.

MESSER, ASA (1769-1836). American Baptist minister and educator, born in Methuen, Massachusetts. He turned from farming to tutorial studies under **Hezekiah Smith**, who prepared him for Rhode Island College, where he graduated in 1790. Messer, a brilliant student, was appointed tutor at the College in 1791 and rose to professor of languages and natural philosophy by 1799. He was ordained to the Baptist **ministry** at First Baptist, Providence in 1801, although he never served a congregation. From 1802-1836 he was president of Rhode Island College, during which time he was an able administrator and developer of what emerged as Brown University. He secured the Brown family munificence, started a medical school, and extended the faculty. Messer cherished **liberty** of speech and conscience, and this led him into difficulty with Baptist authorities. Described as an Arian, he held an unorthodox position on the doctrine of **Christ**. At length, he was forced to resign as president and turned to local politics and farming in Rhode Island. The University of Vermont gave him an LL.D. in 1812 and Harvard Divinity School awarded him the doctor of divinity degree in 1820.

MEXICO. Protestant and Baptist works in Mexico are synonymous in the earliest period of development. In 1827 James Thompson (fl.1825-1845), a **colporteur** for the British and Foreign Bible Society, conducted **evangelical** work; he was followed by James Hickey (1800-1866), a colporteur and Baptist minister from Texas who started the first Baptist church at Monterrey. Later Thomas Westrup (1837-1909) commenced missionary efforts for the **American Baptist Home Mission Society** in 1870. Due to legal restrictions in Mexico, leaders were trained at the Spanish-American Baptist Seminary in Los Angeles, California, until 1947 when a theological school was opened at First Baptist Church in Mexico City. In 1880 the Southern Baptist **Foreign Mission Board** set up their first work at Saltillo, with the center of American Baptist missions in Mexico City. In 1894 a unifying step was taken with the organization of the Baptist Association of Central and Southern Mexico. Later, in 1903 the Convención Nacional Bautista was founded and it cooperated with both major U.S. Baptist mission bodies, American and Southern Baptists. In 1946 the **fundamentalist Baptist Bible Fellowship** (BBF) opened one of its earliest fields in Mexico and for a time it drew congregations away from affiliation with the Convención. A Seventh Day Baptist work was established in Mexico in 1965.

As of 1995 there were 791 churches with 65,398 members affiliated with the Convención Nacional Bautista de Mexico. The Convención publishes *La Luz* (The Light). There are two Baptist-related seminaries in Mexico, one in Mexico City and the other at Edo de Mexico.

MEYER, FREDERICK BROTHERTON (1847-1929). English Baptist minister, born in London, England. Following an early career in business, he studied at Regent's Park College and the University of London, receiving his B.A. He served a student pastorate at Richmond, then as assistant at Pembroke, Liverpool (1870-1872), and pastor at Priory Street, York (1872-1874), Victoria Road, Leicester (1874-1888), Regent's Park Chapel, London (1888-1892), Christ Church, Lambeth (1892-1907), a second pastoral **ministry** at Regent's Park Church (1909-1915), and a second term at Christ Church, Lambeth (1915-1922). Meyer was a greatly influential pastor, serving as president of the **Baptist Union** in 1906 and taking world **mission** tours in 1889, 1901, and 1907. He made 12 preaching tours to North America, the last one in 1922. Beginning in 1878, his preaching filled Melbourne Hall. Dwight L. Moody (1837-1899) was a close friend of Meyer, stemming from the 1873 tour Moody made to Britain, in which he preached in Meyer's church. Later in 1891, Meyer was Moody's guest at the Northfield, Massachusetts Bible Conferences Moody hosted. Meyer's published works totalled over five million copies of over 500 titles in his name, distributed worldwide. His important works include *The Exalted Life* (1896), *My Daily Prayer* (1913), and *A Winter in South Africa* (1908). McMaster University in **Canada** conferred the doctor of divinity degree on Meyer in 1911.

MEYER, HEINRICH (1842-1919). German Baptist minister and missionary, born at Grossbussek, **Germany**. He became a **colporteur** and conducted missionary tours into eastern Europe, choosing **Hungary** as his home in 1873. His work was supported by the British and Foreign Bible Society and he ministered in the tradition of a Baptist throughout Hungary and **Serbia**. Twelve Baptist congregations in Hungary alone are said to be the result of Meyer's **ministry**. He created a connection among the churches he served, the so-called "Free Baptist Convention," which crossed numerous national boundaries. Meyer is considered the father of the Hungarian Baptist movement.

MIDDLE ASIA. Following the political reorganization of the U.S.S.R. in 1991-1992, Baptists in the Soviet republics which had cooperated with the All Union Council of Evangelical Christians-Baptists, sought to reorganize on a state-by-state basis. Where there were insufficient Baptists to support a single union or convention in the Asiatic republics, several joined in 1992 to form Soyuz Evangel'skikh Khristian Baptistov Srednoy Azyi (the Union of Churches of Evangelical Christians-Baptists of Middle Asia). This body includes churches in Tadzhikistan, Turkmenistan, and Uzbekistan. The Union cooperates with the Evro-Asiatskaya Federatsia Evangel'skikh Khristian Baptistov (Euro-Asiatic Federation of Evangelical Christians-Baptists) and the **European Baptist Federation**.

MILLER, WILLIAM (1782-1849). American Baptist preacher and later **Adventist** leader, born in Pittsfield, Massachusetts. Self-taught, he became a farmer in Poultney, Vermont in 1803, and later Low Hampton, New York, serving in local political offices and the U.S. army in the War of 1812. Taunted by his friends for his deistical religious beliefs, he began a serious study of the **bible** about 1816 and focused on the return of Christ's prophecies. Miller calculated that Jesus Christ would return in 1843 and announced this in a public lecture in 1831. In 1833 the Low Hampton Baptist Church granted him a license to preach and he circulated widely and spoke to large audiences on prophetic themes. His published lectures, *Evidence from the Scriptures and History of the Second Coming of Christ about the Year 1843* (1836), made him a sensation. Joshua Himes (1805-1895), a publicist, adopted Miller's views and campaigned in print for the "Advent" emphases. The two purchased a tent and toured the northeastern United States holding 120 camp meetings in 1842-1844. When Miller's predictions did not materialize in 1843, many of his followers suffered great disappointment. In 1845 he helped to organize the **Adventist** Church and became its titular head. Baptists eventually rejected Miller's views and charged **associations** and congregations to avoid contacts with the Adventists. See also **Adventism.**

MINISTRY, BAPTIST UNDERSTANDING OF. Baptists have understood ministry in terms of service, from the original language of the New Testament, "doulos." All members of the church or Body of Christ are servants, ministers, and are expected to be witnesses and provide care for one another. Clergy, or ordained ministers, are gifted for certain kinds of service and set apart accordingly. Ordained ministry concerns preaching, pastoral care, and the administration of the **sacraments/ordinances,** though the latter service is shared with **deacons.** Ministry is a gift from God, as well as an opportunity within the church empowered by the Holy Spirit. Baptists have typically understood the offices of ministry in the New Testament in a functional way, as opposed to a hierarchy as assumed by other denominations. Thus, the "episcopos" (bishop) is an overseer ministry of the pastor, and the "presbuteros" (**elder**) is likewise associated with the pastor of a local congregation. In this way, Baptists evolved with one of the most egalitarian ideas of ministry among Protestant sects.

Titles for Baptist ministers have varied through the centuries. In American colonial experience, the term "elder" was used up to the War of Independence. Perhaps as a concession to the egalitarian mood of the times or the maturation of the denomination in urban regions, many ministers adopted the use of the title "reverend," which had previously been reserved for the learned clergy of the established churches. Once the College of Rhode Island was functioning (1764), its graduates placed their degrees (A.B.,M.A.) after their names, and to this list was added a long list of those awarded honorary doctorates in divinity. **Samuel Stillman, Isaac Backus, Hezekiah Smith, Thomas Baldwin,** and **James Manning** all enjoyed the use of educational and ecclesiastical credentials in their titles. See also **Deacon; Elder.**

MINISTRY OF MISSION SERVICES. Founded in 1968, Ministry of Mission Services is interdenominational, but with a Baptistic tradition. Located in Apple Valley, California, it sponsors work in **Mexico** and publishes.

MISSIONARY BAPTISTS. Nomenclature applied to several groups of Baptists across the American South.

(1) A western branch is centered in Arkansas. At the 1901 meeting of the Arkansas State Baptist Convention in Hope, Arkansas, questions arose over the issues associated with **Landmarkism** and in particular the work of **W. H. Whitsett** and the organizationally centralizing tendencies of **Southern Baptist Convention** leaders. Behind the leadership of **Ben M. Bogard,** a collection of churches affirming the rights of local congregations and **associations** over conventions, met at Fort Smith to consider organizing a new association in which churches would control **missions** and benevolence. The result was the formation of the State Association of Missionary Baptist Churches of Arkansas, the first of the Missionary Baptist movement which later spread throughout the southwest as a reaction to the Southern Baptist Convention. In the beginning 150 churches comprised the Arkansas General Association, with later asssociations organized in Alabama, Missouri, Texas, Oklahoma, and Mississippi. In 1910 a Publishing Company was formed, in 1919 the

Missionary Baptist College was founded at Sheridan, which lasted until bankruptcy in 1933. An orphanage was operated at Texarkana from 1903. The Missionary Baptists are clearly Landmarkists, although they prefer not to use the terminology "Landmarkist" because of its sectarian tone. Rather, they stress the New Testament congregational principle, coupled with mostly local missionary outreach and **evangelism**.

(2) In the East, another group calling themselves Missionary Baptists and located in the Carolinas, Tennessee, and Kentucky have a more austere perspective: they oppose the sale of alcohol, the practice of abortion, and the teaching of sex education in public schools. These Appalachian Missionary Baptist churches are small, and rural, with characteristics of behavior similar to **Primitive Baptists**. They uniformly use the *King James Version* of the bible and are opposed to the use of indoor **baptistries**, robed choirs, theological education for ministers, and **women** in ministry. There is little to no relationship between the two groups using the name "Missionary Baptist," except that both are disinclined, if not adversarial, to the Southern Baptist Convention. See also **Baptist Missionary Association**.

MISSIONARY EVANGELISTIC FELLOWSHIP. Founded in 1940 by a missionary to **China** and **Japan**, John Rhodes, Missionary Evangelistic Fellowship is related to the **Independent** Baptist movement and sponsors work in six countries. It focuses on support for training national workers. Its headquarters are located in Buffalo Center, Iowa.

MISSIONARY FLIGHTS INTERNATIONAL. Founded in 1964, Missionary Flights International provides support for Baptist missionaries in aviation ministries. With headquarters located in West Palm Beach, Florida, it publishes *Flight Briefing*.

MISSIONS, BAPTIST. The missionary impulse among Baptists of most kinds stems from a literal and personalized interpretation of the Great Commission, Matthew 28: 19, 20. Most Baptists believe this was a challenge and command of Christ to go, teach, and baptize in His name. When coupled with Mark 16:15 and Acts 1:8, it becomes a fourfold task: in places familiar (Jerusalem), nearby and receptive (Judea), nearby and indifferent or antagonistic (Samaria), and virtually everywhere (to the "uttermost parts of the earth"). In the 17th century, Baptist missions concentrated on personal **evangelism** and local churches expended efforts on expansion of their ministries in the urban areas of Great Britain. Later in the century, missions were conducted in North America, such as in the Carolinas and New England, mostly on an individual basis.

High Calvinistic theology propounded by great London preachers like **John Gill** and **John Brine** did little to promote an interest in missions from the late 17th century to the first decades of the next. The 18th century, beginning with Baptists in the West of England, witnessed a resurgence of interest in missionary activity, with Baptists in the forefront of all English-speaking Protestants. Beginning in mid-century, prayer meetings were held in Britain, leaders like **Andrew Fuller**, **John Sutclif**, and **William Carey** laid a theological basis for the Great Commission, and **voluntary** groups sprang up for various benevolent enterprises. Chief among them was the **Baptist Missionary Society**, formed at Kettering, England, to evangelize the heathen, a relatively new concept for churches. Soon the missionary impulse hit the churches of the American colonies; in Philadelphia and New England **associations** sent forth commissioned evangelists or missionaries to take tours of regions in the summer months. This led to missionary endeavor in what became **Canada** and the continental interior. Indian missions were popular in the West and South. In the 1780s work among the slave and free **Black** communities in Georgia led to missionary work in **Jamaica** and other Caribbean islands.

The largest organizational outreach of missions occurred in the 19th century and followed denominational boundaries. In Britain, both **Particular** and **General Baptists** formed societies and concentrated upon different fields at home and in **Ireland**; high Calvinists formed the **Strict Baptist** Mission in 1861. From the United States, Baptist missionaries were commissioned from the **Baptist Board of Foreign Missions** (BBFM) (1814-1845) (later the **American Baptist Missionary Union**, 1846-1905; afterward the **American Baptist Foreign Mission Society,** 1905-), the **Freewill Baptist** Foreign Mission Society (1832), the **Foreign Mission Board** of the Southern Baptist Convention (1845-), the **Seventh Day Baptist** Mission Society (1842), and the **American Baptist Free Mission Society (ABFrMS)** (1843). In the European Baptist context, German Baptists in the later 19th century sent missionaries and trained indigenous leaders for much of eastern and southern Europe, and the Swedish Baptists cooperated with other Baptists in the **Congo**, **China**, and eastern Europe.

The 20th century has seen yet more organizations develop within the Baptist tradition and along theological lines, such as the **Strict Baptist** Mission (U.K.), Örebo Mission (**Sweden**), and in the United States: **Baptist Mid-Missions** (1920), Africa Christian Missions, later **Evangelical Baptist Missions** (1929), the **Association of Baptists for World Evangelism** (1928), **World Baptist Fellowship** (1928), the **Conservative Baptist** Foreign Mission Society (1943), and **Baptist International Missions** (1965).

Also, the growth of the older mainstream sending agencies has been phenomenal. The American Baptist Foreign Mission Society, in conjunction with the Woman's American Baptist Foreign Missionary Society as of 1995, has under appointment 131 missionaries in 23 countries. Likewise, as of 1995, the largest outreach of all is administered by the Southern Baptist International Mission Board, which employs 4,078 missionaries in over 110 countries.

Elsewhere in the international Baptist family, there are examples of the maturation of mission fields which in turn have assumed missionary responsibilities themselves. Included among these are the Canadian Baptist Foreign Mission Board (1873), the Brazilian Baptist Foreign Mission Board (1907), the Baptist Union of **South Africa** (1892), and the Jamaican Baptists. The **Baptist World Alliance**, formed in 1905, itself encourages missions through its programs of **evangelism** and education.

MIXED COMMUNION. See **Lord's Supper**.

MOLDOVA. The first Baptist congregations formed in Moldova were at Kishinev in 1908. Simyon V. Rakhmanov was among the early Baptist ministers in the region. Over the years of the 20th century, Moldovan churches became part of the All-Union Council of Evangelical Christians-Baptists in the Soviet Union. In 1992, however, as the Moldovan Republic declared its independence, the Baptist community organized its own body, the Uniunea Bisericilor Crestine Evanghelice-Baptiste Din Moldova (Union of Evangelical Christians-Baptists of Moldova), representing most Baptists in the Republic. The **Baptist Bible Fellowship** (BBF) appointed missionaries to Moldova in 1992.

As of 1995 there were 265 churches with 16,319 members affiliated with the Uniunea Bisericilor Crestine Evanghelice-Baptiste Din Moldova (Union of Evangelical Christians-Baptists of Moldova). Offices of the Union are located in Chisinau.

MONGOLIA. Baptist work in Mongolia is relatively recent, owing to government restrictions. **Southern Baptist** witness in Mongolia dates from 1992 when a small congregation was gathered in Ulaanbataar. In 1994 this congregation became the first formally recognized Baptist church in Mongolia. In 1995 the **Conservative Baptist Foreign Mission Society** (CBFMS) established a work in Mongolia. As of 1995 there are an estimated 100 Baptist adherents in Mongolia.

MONTANA BAPTIST FELLOWSHIP. An **independent fundamentalist** Baptist domestic mission in the United States founded in 1941. The object of the organization formed in Indianapolis, Indiana, in September that year was to plant new congregations in Montana. Eventually in May 1948 the Montana Baptist Fellowship was merged with the **Fellowship of Baptists for Home Missions**.

MONTGOMERY, HELEN BARRETT (1861-1934). American Baptist lay leader and mission promoter. Born at Kingsville, Ohio, she was educated at Wellesley College and became a schoolteacher. Helen married William A. Montgomery of Rochester, New York, who operated a successful component manufacturing business in the early automobile industry. His wealth gave Helen many social and civic opportunities, which she placed at the disposal of her church and denomination, the **Northern Baptist Convention**. She was a key figure in the unification of the western and eastern branches of the Woman's American Baptist Foreign Mission Societies (WABFMS) in 1914, and she wrote and travelled widely on behalf of women in missions. She advocated establishing the World Day of Prayer and she translated the Greek New Testament into a popular edition for the **American Baptist Publication Society** in 1924. Helen was elected president of the Northern Baptist Convention in 1920--the first woman president of any mainstream denomination in the U.S.--and in this role she presided over the stormy debates with **fundamentalists**. She collaborated in several **mission** trips and publications with **Lucy Waterbury Peabody**. Among Helen's several published works are *Western Women in Eastern Lands* (1910), *From Jerusalem to Jerusalem* (1929), and *The Preaching Value of Missions* (1931).

MONTSERRAT. As of 1995, a small Baptist community in one congregation of 75 members existed in Montserrat.

MOODY, DALE (1915-1992). Southern Baptist minister and theologian, born at Stamford, Texas. He was educated at Baylor University, Southern Baptist Theological Seminary and Oxford University, where he received the D.Phil. degree. In 1948 Moody assumed the chair at Southern Baptist Seminary in Christian Theology and taught there until 1983. He was a popular teacher and broadly involved in Baptist and **ecumenical** organizations. He was the only Baptist and second Protestant to teach at the Pontifical Gregorian University in Rome, Italy (1969-1970), and he was a visiting professor at the Ecumenical Institute for Advanced Studies in Jerusalem in 1973 and 1976. Moody, whose theological pilgrimage ran from **dispensationalism** to Southern Baptist biblicism, admitted being influenced by **A. T. Robertson** and **W. O. Carver** as well as Paul Tillich (1886-1965) and Emil Brunner (1889-1966).

As the theological reorientation of the **Southern Baptist Convention** took shape in the 1970s, Moody became an antagonist of the inerrancy movement and "unthinking **conservatism.**" In 1982-83 as a retired distinguished professor at Southern Seminary, he openly took exception with the Seminary's doctrinal statement, "The Abstract of Principles" on the matter of the "perseverance of the saints," holding to the possibility of apostasy. This drew the ire of Convention **conservatives** (particularly in Arkansas), who demanded Moody's dismissal. His post-retirement status became much celebrated and the seminary trustees voted not to renew his annual contact after 1983. Moody continued to teach at other schools, notably American Baptist-related Eastern Baptist Theological Seminary in Philadelphia, Pennsylvania. He was a widely published author, his outstanding books including *The Hope of Glory* (1964) and *The Word of Truth* (1981).

MOODY, DEBORAH (fl. 1630-1640). American colonial Baptist thinker who was likely born in England. In 1640 she settled in Salem, Massachusetts, and was admitted to the Congregational Church. In 1642 she concluded that infant **baptism** was not scriptural and persuaded others in the congregation of her position. The clergy sought to dissuade her but to no avail; subsequently she was brought before the court of sessions in Salem and admonished. Under intense pressure, she left to settle among the Dutch on Long Island in 1643 where her wealth and education gave her much influence in the colony of New Netherland. Eventually, she became a Quaker.

MOON, CHARLOTTE (1840-1912). Southern Baptist missionary, born at Viewmont, Virginia. She was educated at Virginia Female Institute and in the women's department related to the University of Virginia, one of the best-educated women of her era. Following a brief career in schoolteaching, "Lottie" was appointed by the **Foreign Mission Board** (FMB) of the **Southern Baptist Convention** to **China**, where she joined her sister, Edmonia (1851-1908) in 1873. Ultimately Edmonia returned to the United States and Lottie embarked on a long career in Shantung Province, China. She started schools, conducted **evangelism**, and cared for the plight of **women.** Her influence on Baptists in the United States was great: in the 1880s it was her idea to organize support which eventually became the Woman's Missionary Union. She also advocated greater opportunities for women missionaries under the FMB. An annual offering among Southern Baptists is named in her honor.

MOORE, JOANNA PATTERSON (1832-1916). American Baptist missionary, born in Clarion County, Pennsylvania. She was educated at Rockford Seminary (Illinois) and became a schoolteacher. During the American Civil War she experienced a call to **missions** which first focused on overseas work. She visited the Freed **Black** communities in the Mississippi River communities and decided to devote herself to domestic missions. She won a designation from the **American Baptist Home Mission Society** (ABHMS) without remuneration to work on Island 10 in the Mississippi. There she taught reading, personal hygiene, and skills to freed women. At Helena, Arkansas, after the War, she earned a wide reputation for teaching soldiers to read. With the formation in 1871 of the Woman's American Baptist Home Mission Society (WABHMS), Moore was its first appointee. With a base in Louisiana, amidst stiff opposition from White Christians, Moore worked among women in domestic education groups she called "fireside schools." This program was made formal in 1892 and promoted daily Bible reading and the development of personal spirituality in the Black community. Among the sick and poor she established the Bible Bands and she edited *Hope* magazine. At length she established a base in Nashville, Tennessee, from which she trained workers for the entire Reconstruction South. At her death, she was buried in a Black cemetery, honoring her work in that community. Her published works include *Fireside School Manual* (1895) and *In Christ's Stead* (1902).

MOREHOUSE, HENRY LYMAN (1834-1917). American Baptist minister and denominational leader, born at Bagnall, New York. He was one of the first graduates of Baptist-related University of Rochester and Rochester Theological Seminary, and first embarked on a political career in the Republican Party. His decision to enter the **ministry** took him on a tour of the Civil War southern states and he noted the needs particularly of the free Black population. A gifted administrator, Morehouse moved from pastorates in Saginaw, Michigan, and East Rochester, New York, to become in 1879 corresponding secretary of the **American Baptist Home Mission Society** (ABHMS) and greatly expanded its work among Blacks, French Canadians, and American Indians. In 1891 he stepped down to become field secretary of that Society, and observing antagonism with **Southern Baptists** over territorialism, Morehouse organized the **Fortress Monroe Conference** in 1894. In 1898 he recommended the unification of the northern Baptist societies and he became the chief architect of the **Northern Baptist Convention** (NBC), organized in 1905. For 38 years the head of the Home Mission Society, Morehouse was a highly respected leader of what became **American Baptist Churches in**

the U.S.A. (ABCUSA). Morehouse College, an undergraduate school in Atlanta, Georgia, founded for Black men, was named in his honor. Morehouse was the author of several definitive books, including *Baptist Home Missions in North America* (1883) and *Relationships Between the General Denominational Societies and State Conventions* (1913).

MOROCCO. Baptist witness in Morocco is late in origin and limited by government restrictions. In 1966 **Southern Baptist** missionaries began a work in Melilla with a Spanish congregation. Later the work was transferred to Rabat. Outreach is also maintained in Tangiers and Fes, particularly among the U.S. military personnel. As of 1995 the Baptist presence consisted mainly of personnel serving in international churches which include multinational employees and emigrant workers from the Middle and Far East.

MORRIS, ELIAS CAMP (1855-1922). American Black Baptist missionary and denominational leader, born in Murray County, Georgia. He was born in slavery and after the Civil War he took up shoemaking and secured an education. Settling in Arkansas, he worked closely with the **American Baptist Home Mission Society** (ABHMS) in founding Arkansas Baptist College, a school for Freedmen. He was elected president of the Negro state convention and helped to form the **National Baptist Convention U.S.A.** (NBCUSA). In 1915 he was president of the Convention when **Richard H. Boyd** sought control of the National Baptist Publishing Board. Morris stood firm, although he lost the publishing board to Boyd. Morris frequently represented **Black Baptists** across the United States and at the **Baptist World Alliance** and was widely respected among the Baptist family.

MOULTON, EBENEZER (1709-1783). American, and later Canadian, Baptist minister and controversialist. Born in Windham, Connecticut, Moulton was a leading pastor and itinerant in the **New Light** awakenings in New England and Nova Scotia in the 18th century.

Ordained in 1741 at Brimfield by regular Calvinistic Baptists from eastern Massachusetts, Moulton soon shifted to the New Light position and itinerated broadly. In 1748 he led a split in the Brimfield church, forming a new **Separate Baptist** congregation. With other Baptist pastors in Massachusetts concerned over oppressive taxation to support the Standing Order, Moulton was a primary leader in successive petition campaigns to the Massachusetts General Court on behalf of a united Baptist community. In the 1750s he is credited with helping to give New England Baptists a sense of identity and unity. For a time, in conjunction with his pastoral duties, he worked in mercantile pursuits, until he was bankrupted in 1763 and fled to Nova Scotia.

In Nova Scotia Moulton became the pioneer planter of the Baptist faith. He itinerated broadly along the eastern coast of the Bay of Fundy and in the Annapolis Valley, baptizing converts upon request. His New Light principles and closed communion **polity** soon made enemies in the isolated settlements. At Horton (later Wolfville), he formed in 1765 what became the oldest surviving Baptist church in **Canada**, but was forced to withdraw from the village by Congregationalists of the open communion kind. In 1773 Moulton returned to Brimfield, Massachusetts, his former debts having been forgiven.

MOZAMBIQUE. The Swedish Baptists were the first to establish churches in Mozambique, beginning in 1892. Later in 1949, Portuguese Baptists began a mission. A Baptist Convention was formed in 1960. Swedish Baptists in 1918 started a mission later to be developed as Missão Baptista Escandinava. This group has evolved as the Igreja União Baptista, the union of Swedish efforts and the **South Africa** General Mission.

As of 1995 there were 23 churches and 13,000 members affiliated with the Convenção Bautista de Mozambique, and 1,000 churches with about 200,000 members affiliated with the Igreja União Baptista. There is a Baptist-related theological school at Maputo.

MULLINS, EDGAR YOUNG (1860-1928). Southern Baptist theologian and educator, born in Franklin County, Mississippi. Early in life, he worked in several trades, becoming a telegrapher. Educated at Texas Agricultural and Mechanical College, and Southern Baptist Seminary, he became a **pastor** at Harrodsburg, Kentucky (1885-1888), Lee Street, Baltimore, Maryland (1888-1895), and First Baptist, Newton Centre, Massachusetts (1896-1899), one of the few Baptist pastors to serve in both the North and the South. In 1899 he began a 30-year teaching career at Southern Baptist Theological Seminary in the field of systematic theology. In that role he became the principal theologian of **Southern Baptists**, publishing widely; his books on Baptist doctrines became standard texts. Mullins became president of the Seminary in 1899 and led in the expansion and modernization of the school. As president of the Southern Baptist Convention (SBC) from 1921-1924, Mullins raised the consciousness of Southern Baptists to social concerns and as president of the **Baptist World Alliance** in 1928 he travelled extensively on behalf of religious liberty. Among the over 40 titles which Mullins published were *The Axioms of Religion* (1908) and *The Christian Religion in its Doctrinal Expression* (1917).

MURCH, WILLIAM HARRIS (1784-1859). English Baptist minister and educator, born at Honiton, England. Baptized by **John Rippon** at Carter's Lane, he began preaching at 14 years old. His education consisted of training at Wymondley College. In 1806 he became assistant pastor at Sheppard's Barton, Frome, in 1806 and three years later the sole pastor until 1827. That year he accepted the tutorship in theology at the Baptist Theological College at Stepney, where he remained until his health failed in 1844. From 1845 to 1851 he served the church at Rickmansworth, Hertfordshire, and in 1856 he started a new congregation at Kensington, Bath. At the denominational level, Murch was secretary of the **Baptist Union** from 1834-1846 and of the Baptist Board from 1837-1843. One of the most respected clergy of his era, he received an honorary degree from Brown University in Rhode Island in 1837. Murch was the editor of *A New Selection of Hymns* (1838), in wide use by the Baptist Union churches.

MUSIC, IN BAPTIST WORSHIP. See **Worship, in Baptist tradition**.

MYANMAR. Baptists established an early mission in what was formerly called Burma. In 1814 **Adoniram and Ann Judson** established the American Baptist mission in Burma in the city of Ava. After them, the mission expanded from the urban areas to the hill tribes and eventually to **Siam** and **China**. American Baptists invested heavily in Burma, especially with remote tribes: Elisha Abbott and Henry Van Meter began formal work among the Karens in Bassein in 1852; Josiah **Cushing** prepared a Shan translation of Scripture, beginning his work in 1867; **Francis Mason** commenced a mission among the Kachins in 1873. Institutional development by Baptists was extensive throughout the 19th century. At Insein the Karen Theological Seminary was established in 1845, and a widespread system of Baptist girl's and boy's schools added much to the denomination's rapid growth. In 1871 the **American Baptist Missionary Union** established Rangoon Baptist College, which eventually became Burma Baptist College. At the end of the 19th century there were 15 associations of Baptist churches, united by the Burma Baptist Missionary Convention, founded in 1865. At the high point of Baptist missionary activity in Burma (about 1880), there were the following missions: Rangoon (1813), Moulmein (1827), Tavoy (1828), Karen (1831), Bassein (1840), Henthada (1853), Swaygyeen (1853), Toungoo (1853), Prome (1854), Thongzai (1855), Zeegong (1876), and Bhamo (1877). An important asset to the Burmese Baptists was the establishment in 1830 by **Cephas Bennett** of the American Baptist Mission Press at Moulmein.

In 1966 all Baptist missionaries were withdrawn at request of the Burmese government. As of 1995 there were 3,640 churches with 555,063 members affiliated with the Myanmar Baptist Convention. The Myanmar **Seventh Day Baptist** Conference, established in 1964, encompasses 15 churches and 750 members. Over the years, the following periodicals have been associated with Baptist life in Burma (Myanmar): *Myitta Taman*, *Burma News*, and the *Burman Messenger*. There are presently 10 Baptist-related theological schools in Myanmar: Bassein, Chi State, Insein (3), Kutakai, Moulmein, Myitkyina, Rangoon, and Taunggyi.

MYERS, CORTLAND (1864-1941). American Baptist minister, born at Kingston, New York. He was educated at the University of Rochester and Rochester Theological Seminary. His pastorates included First Baptist, Syracuse, New York (1890-1893); First Baptist, Brooklyn, New York (1893-1909); and Tremont Temple, Boston, Massachusetts (1909-1921). Myers was a widely regarded pulpit orator, reflecting conservative **evangelical** views of his era. Among his published works are *Midnight in a Great City* (1896), *The Dangers of Crooked Thinking* (1924), and *How Do We Know?* (1927). His sermons at Tremont Temple were published in popular pamphlet form and circulated throughout the northeastern United States.

MYLES, JOHN (1621-1684). English, and later American, Baptist minister, born at Newton-Welsh, Hertfordshire. Myles matriculated at Brasenose College, Oxford, after which he began preaching in **Wales** about 1645, likely as an Independent. In 1649 he was in London as part of a Baptist Church at the Glasshouse, under Edward Draper. That same year he returned to Wales and formed the first Baptist church at Ilston on the Gower Peninsula. He became a Trier under the Cromwell government and did much to advance the Baptist cause in the 1650s. Myles and his Ilston congregation emigrated to Massachusetts in 1663 where they settled at Rehoboth. At times Myles was an irritant to the authorities and at other times he served as the sole town minister. At Swansea, a town he named for the Welsh seaport, he practiced **mixed communion** and conducted a school. He maintained cordial relations with his Congregationalist brethren and was one of the most respected Baptists of the 17th century. In 1656 Myles published *An Antidote Against the Infection of the Times; or a Faithful Watchword from Mt. Sion to Prevent the Ruin of Souls*.

N

NAMIBIA. In 1961 the South African Baptist Missionary Society began missionary work in Namibia, while three years later **Southern Baptists** entered the country. Major church centers were established at Tsumeb, Oshakati, and in Kavango. The Baptist Convention of Namibia was formed in 1984, supported by the Baptist Union of **South Africa** and composed largely of Caucasian members.

As of 1995 there were 49 churches and 3,500 members affiliated with the Baptist Convention of Namibia.

NATIONAL ASSOCIATION OF FREEWILL BAPTISTS. See **Freewill Baptists**.

NATIONAL BAPTIST CONVENTION IN THE U.S.A. (NBCUSA). The oldest and largest of the **Black Baptist** national denominations in the United States. The origins of the Convention lie in the merger of the National Baptist Educational Convention, the **Baptist Foreign Mission Convention of the United States**, and the **American National Baptist Convention** to form the **National Baptist Convention in the United States of America** in May 1895. In 1900 the Baptist Convention of the Western States and Territories joined.

Boards of the Convention originally included Home Missions (1886), Education (1893), **Sunday School** Publishing (1896), Baptist **Temperance** (1899), and the Women's Convention (1900). In recent years these have been reduced to three: Sunday School Publishing, Home Missions, and Foreign Missions. Auxiliary organizations include: National Baptist Layman's Movement, Women's Convention, and Congress of Christian Education. There are 171 state/regional affiliated organizations. Missionary work is conducted in **Sierra Leone, Malawi, Swaziland, South Africa, Nicaragua, Jamaica**, the **Bahamas**, and **Barbados**. The Convention supports the following schools: Shaw University, Shaw Divinity School, Central Baptist Theological Seminary, National Baptist College, Selma University, American Baptist Theological Seminary, and Morehouse School of Religion. Missionary work is conducted in two regions of the world, Africa and the Caribbean. The Convention publishes *The Mission Herald* (1897-).

As of 1995 there were 33,000 churches and 8.5 million members affiliated with the National Baptist Convention in the U.S.A.

NATIONAL BAPTIST CONVENTION OF AMERICA (NBCA).
Commonly referred to as the unincorporated convention of **Black Baptists** in the United States, and also formerly known as the "Boyd Baptist Convention" because of its connection with **Richard H. Boyd.** The Convention traces its origins to 1889-1890 with the founding of the Baptist Foreign Missionary Convention of the United States in Montgomery, Alabama.

The Convention was incorporated in Louisiana in 1987 and one of the initial actions was to assert that the National Baptist Publishing Board was not the property of any **convention.** Further organizational evolution occurred in 1988 when a controversy over the control of the National Baptist Sunday Church School, the Baptist Training Union Congress, and the National Baptist Publishing Board again became an issue. Five hundred leaders met in Dallas, Texas to form a new convention related to the Boyd family, the **National Missionary Baptist Convention of America** (NMBCA), while 700 leaders met in San Antonio to advocate central control of the **National Baptist Convention of America** (NBCA).

The NBCA has eight boards and 11 auxiliary bodies. The boards are autonomous: Foreign Missions, Home Missions, Benevolence, and Education to mention the major ones. Auxiliaries include Women, Brotherhood, Youth, Pastor's Conference, Ministers' Wives, and Matrons. There are 120 state/regional organizations related to the NBCA. The Convention supports missionary work in **Ghana,** West Africa, **Cameroon, Jamaica,** Virgin Islands, and **Panama.** Schools which have the approbation of the Convention are Union Baptist Seminary, Florida Memorial College, and Morris College. The denominational periodical is the *National Baptist Voice* (1915-).

As of 1995 there were 2,500 churches with an estimated membership of 3.5 million in the National Baptist Convention of America.

NATIONAL BAPTIST MISSIONARY CONVENTION OF AMERICA (NBMCA). A major Black organization of U.S. Baptists, founded in 1988 after a dispute within the **National Baptist Convention of America** over control of the National Baptist Publishing Board. The purpose of the Convention is to serve its constituent congregations as an agency of Christian education, church extension, and missionary efforts, both domestic and overseas. As well, the Convention seeks to safeguard **religious liberty** and engage in social and **ecumenical** development. The Convention is seen as a "restoration" of the original purposes of the **National Baptist Convention in the United States** (NBCUSA) of the 19th century. Among the agencies of the NBMCA are the home mission, foreign mission, education, and **evangelism** boards. An executive committee makes policy for the denomination. The headquarters of the NBMCA is at Greater Temple of God Missionary Baptist Church in Los Angeles, California. The Convention supports the publication, *National Baptist Union Review* (1896-).

As of 1995 there were about 1,500 churches and four million members associated with the National Missionary Baptist Convention of America.

NEPAL. In 1962 missionaries of the **Baptist Missionary Society** (BMS), in cooperation with the Council of Baptist Churches of Northeast **India**, began work in Nepal. The Baptist mission became part of the United Mission to Nepal, which focuses on development efforts rather than establishing a national church body. A separate mission thrust of Naga Baptists in India, some of whom were relocated Nepalese, led to the establishment of the Nepal Baptist Church Council in 1992, with seven churches. As of 1995 there were 40 churches or 200 fellowships with about 5,000 members affiliated with the Council.

NETHERLANDS. Baptist thought and practices in what is now the Netherlands is traceable to the early **Anabaptists** of the 16th century. However, modern Baptist development evolves from the 1840s. **Julius Köbner**, a Danish colleague of **J. G. Oncken** met Johannes E. Feisser, a Dutchman who had been pondering **baptism** as a believer. In 1845 Köbner baptized Feisser and several others at Gasselternijveen. Two other congregations soon followed at Amsterdam from a **bible** study group, and at Zutphen, from Mennonite foundations. Amidst a **revival** among mission works in the 1880s, a union was founded in 1881 with seven charter members. During the 1880s there was serious doctrinal controversy in which churches left the Union. At length the organization recovered its unity and the work was expanded to include young people's work and a **theological seminary** in 1958 known as "De Vinkenhof" at Utrecht. From its beginning, the Union has published *De Christen* (The Christian) (1883-). There are also other Baptists involved in the Netherlands, notably the **Baptist Bible Fellowship** (1979), **Baptist Mid-Missions** (BMM), the **Conservative Baptist** Foreign Mission Society, and Canadian Baptist Ministries, which works in conjunction with the Union.

As of 1995 there were 88 churches and 12,259 members affiliated with the Unie van Baptisten Gemeenten in Nederland.

NEWCOMEN, THOMAS (1663-1729). English Baptist minister and inventor, born at Dartmouth. He was apprenticed as an ironmonger and later he opened a business of this kind at Exeter. He read widely and experimented with engines, inventing in 1705 a steam engine which operated with an atmospheric chamber, and an arrangement of a rocking beam and pump. Newcomen's engine was soon constructed at numerous prominent collieries across England. For about 20 years at the turn of the century he was pastor of the Baptist congregation in Dartmouth.

NEW GUINEA. See **Papua New Guinea, Baptists in.**

NEW LIGHT BAPTISTS. During the 18th century in the American colonial context, the **Great Awakening** produced a profound effect upon religious development. Some churches were favorable to the **revival**, and scores were actually brought into being by revival preaching and turned to spiritual matters. These pro-Awakening churches were derisively dubbed "New Lights" because of their insistence upon a conscious conversion experience. The enthusiasm of Quakers and others for an "inner light" probably inspired the negative label. Originally, most of the New Light congregations in New England were Congregationalists, many of whom in the 1740s turned to Baptistic principles, particularly believer's **baptism** over infant baptism which the New Lights felt had no basis in **Scripture.** Frequently, Congregationalist church record books read "gone to the Baptists" to denote a member who had converted to Baptist principles. Among the many leaders of the New Light Baptists were **Isaac Backus, John Leland, Hezekiah Smith, Ebenezer Moulton, Shubael Stearns** and Wait Palmer (1711-1795). The New Light movement in Virginia, influenced by New Englanders, produced leaders such as **James Ireland,** Samuel Harris (1724-1799); and **John Waller.**

Those who were opposed to the Awakening were similarly called "Old Lights," particularly in New England. Among the Old Light Baptists were Jeremiah Condy (fl. 1750-1765), **John Callendar,** and **Edward Upham.** By the end of the 1700s the distinctions between Old Lights and New Lights were greatly diminished, most New England Baptists having formed **associations** of pro-revivalistic sentiments. In the South, the New Lights were known as **Separate Baptists** and many in this group largely merged with the Regular Baptists by 1801. See also **Separate Baptists.**

NEWMAN, ALBERT HENRY (1852-1933). American, Canadian, and Southern Baptist educator and historian, born in Edgefield, South Carolina. He was educated at Mercer University and Rochester Theological Seminary, as well as being trained in Middle Eastern languages under **Crawford H. Toy** at Southern Baptist Theological Seminary. In 1880 Newman was elected Pettengill Professor of Church History at Rochester Seminary, replacing R. J. W. Buckland (1829-1877) who died. Four years later, however, he accepted one of the inaugural professorships in Toronto Baptist College (later McMaster University), where he served with great distinction until 1901. At that time he went to Baylor University where he helped to create Southwestern Baptist Theological Seminary and taught there from 1907-1913. Thereafter Newman taught church history at Baylor, Mercer, Chicago, and again at McMaster. Newman was the premier Baptist and Free Church historian of his era in North America. He pioneered the study of anti-paedobaptism and wrote 16 textbooks on church history and the history of the Baptists, including *A History of the Baptist Churches in the United States* (1894), *A History of Antipaedobaptism* (1897), and *A Manual of Church History* (1903).

NEW WORLD MOVEMENT. Following World War I, Baptists in the **Northern Baptist Convention** (NBC) in the United States were influenced by the ecumenical movement and spurred forward by the needs of the post-war period. One manifestation was the New World Movement, the first major fundraising drive of the new Convention. Between 1919 and 1924 the Northern Baptist Convention sought to raise a single budget of $100 million from among its churches. Reminiscent of the Liberty Loan drives, each congregation was solicited once, thus ending the separate solicitations of the **independent** American Baptist societies. By 1924 about 50 percent of the $100 million was subscribed by 86 per cent of the churches. Although the financial results were disappointing, the unifying effect upon the Northern Baptist Convention and its overseas affiliates was remarkable in that schools and missions were combined into a single stewardship effort. One negative result of the New World Movement was the crystallization of **fundamentalist** identity, which opposed many of the directions of centralization in the Northern Baptist Convention. For them, the New World Movement symbolized modernism and unwanted **ecumenism**.

NEW ZEALAND. The first Baptist congregation was started in 1851 at Nelson by Decimus Dolamore, an English Baptist. The Baptist Union of New Zealand, encompassing both islands, was organized in 1882 and the New Zealand Baptist Missionary Society founded in 1885. A school, the Baptist College of New Zealand, commenced in 1924. Countering Baptist **ecumenism**, the **Baptist Bible Fellowship** (BBF) began a mission in 1971, and **Baptist Mid-Missions** established a church in New Zealand in 1974. In cooperation with the Australian Baptist Missionary Society, New Zealand Baptists sponsored missionary work in **India** and East **Bengal**, later **Bangladesh**, in the early 20th century. The Baptist Union publishes the *New Zealand Baptist* (1885-).

As of 1995 there were 253 churches and 23,259 members affiliated with the Baptist Union of New Zealand, and six churches with 135 members in the Australasian Conference of **Seventh Day Baptists**. Carey Baptist College is located in Auckland.

NICARAGUA. As early as 1852 a Baptist congregation was started on Corn Island, the result of work through Baptists in **Belize**. Later, in 1889 Baptists from **Jamaica** sponsored a missionary work. Both the **Northern** and **Southern Baptist Conventions** in the United States looked at Nicaragua as a potential mission field early in the 20th century. As a result of agreements reached at the missionary conference at Edinburgh in 1910, the **American Baptist Home Mission Society** (ABHMS) began evangelization in 1917 in Nicaragua. The first church, largely begun by Eleanor Blackmore (1873-1943), was located in Managua, which became the center of Baptist life. Institutional development evolved, including Colegio Bautista in 1917, a seminary was relocated from **El Salvador** to Masaya in 1941, and the Cranska Memorial Hospital in 1930. The Convención Nacional Bautista was formed in 1936. In 1951 the Seminary was relocated to Managua, where it has had a major impact on Baptist life in Central America. Beyond mainstream Baptist organization, the **Baptist Bible Fellowship** (BBF) opened a mission in Nicaragua in 1969.

As of 1995 there were 87 churches with 10,000 members affiliated with the Iglesia Bautista Internacionale. There is a Baptist-related theological School at Managua.

NIGER. Baptist work in this West African nation began in 1929 when Joseph McCabe started a mission for what became the **Evangelical Baptist Missions** (EBM) from the United States; this mission resulted in the creation of the Union des Eglises Evangéliques Baptistes in 1927. Later in 1973, the **Southern Baptists** entered Niger with an extension of their work among the Yoruba people.

As of 1995 there were about ten congregations with approximately 500 members in the Baptist mission communities in Niger.

NIGERIA. One of the important early fields of Southern Baptist foreign missions was Yorubaland, later Nigeria. Work began in 1850 with the preaching mission of Thomas J. Bowen (1814-1875). By 1853 he had organized a church and mission outpost at Ijaye. In the 20th century the **Lott Carey Baptist Foreign Mission Convention** (LCBFMC) and the **National Baptist Convention in the U.S.A.** (NBCUSA) began missionary works, now cooperating in the Pilgrim Baptist Mission of Nigeria. In 1987 the **Baptist Bible Fellowship** (BBF) began a mission in Nigeria.

As of 1995 there were 5,200 churches and 1,026,000 members in the Nigerian Baptist Convention. A smaller group, the Mambilla Baptist Convention, has 171 churches and 18,588 members. The Nigerian Convention publishes the *Nigerian Baptist* (1923-). There are six theological schools in Nigeria: Eku, Gongola State, Kaduna, Ogbomosho Western State, Owerri, and Oyo.

NILSON, FREDRIK OLAUS (1809-1881). Swedish and American Baptist minister, born near Gothenburg, Sweden. Baptized by a Danish minister, Forster, he was ordained at Hamburg by **J. G. Oncken**. Nilson organized the first congregation near Gothenburg in 1848. Seized for departing from the doctrine of the State Church, he was banished from **Sweden** in 1851 and became the **pastor** of the Baptist church in Copenhagen, 1851-1853. At length his following in Sweden persuaded him to emigrate to the United States where he was pastor at Rock Island, Illinois, from 1853-1860 of the first Swedish Baptist congregation in the United States. In 1860 his banishment from Sweden was lifted by King Charles XV and Nilson triumphantly went to Gothenburg as a Baptist pastor. In 1868 he again returned to the United States, settling at Houston, Minnesota, as a pastor. He later withdrew from the Baptist ministry, joining the Swedish Free Religious Society, a local **Unitarian** group.

NOEL, BAPTIST WRIOTHESLEY (1798-1873). English Baptist minister, born at Leightmount, Scotland. He was the son of a baronet and educated at Trinity College, Cambridge University. At first he was an Anglican priest and took the parish at St. John's Chapel, Bedford Row. His **evangelical** preaching was widely regarded and he was appointed a chaplain to Queen Victoria. With other prominent leaders, Noel was a founder of the Evangelical Alliance in 1846. At length his sermons caused much disturbance and he converted to Baptist principles in 1849, being publicly baptized that year. From 1850 to 1868 he was minister at John Street, Holborn, and he then embarked upon an evangelistic **ministry**, travelling in the interest of the Evangelical Alliance and the Exeter Hall meetings. An ardent **voluntarist**, Noel criticised **Charles H. Spurgeon** for causing division among evangelicals over baptismal regeneration and he refused to support united political action against state religion. Over 70 titles are attributed to Noel, including *Essay on Christian Baptism* (1849), *A Revival of Religion* (1851), and *The Rebellion in America* (1863). In 1859 Brown University (U.S.) conferred an honorary doctorate on Noel.

NONCONFORMITY. A term used in the Elizabethan English historical context to describe Christians who were in communion with the Church of England, but who refused to conform to specified practices in the *Book of Common Prayer*, 1559 edition. In 1662 when Parliament required Anglican clergy to give complete consent to the 1559 edition, many were left outside the Church and the term "nonconformist" took a more exclusive definition. Eventually, nonconformity evolved as a political term with respect to the state, and its adherents organized to represent a new religio-political force in English politics. The word "dissent" is close in meaning to nonconformity, originally referring to those Protestants who worshipped outside the Established Church.

By the mid-17th century, dissenters and nonconformists were roughly the same and included not only Presbyterians and Independents but also the Baptists, and in some instances a host of sects that included like **Diggers, Familists, Levellers,** Quakers, **Ranters,** and **Seekers.** Baptists, Congregationalists or Independents, Presbyterians, and sometimes Quakers constituted what was called "Old Dissent," while Methodists (divided between Calvinists and **Arminians**), from the 18th century were part of the newer dissent. Baptists originally were a sect, but by the Act of Toleration, sought recognition as a legitimate element of Nonconformity. Generally, Nonconformists held common principles such as high priority placed on religious experience, individual expression of the faith, **voluntarism, separation of church and state,** and **religious liberty.**

NORRIS, HANNAH MARIA (1842-1919). Canadian Baptist missionary and denominational leader, born at Canso, Nova Scotia. Educated at the Normal School in Truro, she taught school in her area, often visiting Micmac Indian camps. About 1869, while teaching at the Female Seminary at Acadia University, she was called to **mission** service in **Burma**. Lacking sufficient funds from the Canadian Mission Board, she began a crusade to organize **women** for missionary support and started the first of several societies in 1870 at Canso. In all, she organized 33 societies in three months, essentially creating the woman's missionary movement of the Canadian Maritimes. She married William F. Armstrong (1849-1918) and served for 48 years in Burma among the Telugus. Her specialty became "redemptive theologies" in Sgau Karen and Telugu folklore; she also developed strategies for **bible** study in schools, orphanages, and local churches. Hannah equipped a bible school for the **American Baptist Missionary Union** (ABMU) at Rangoon and travelled widely in its financial interest.

NORRIS, JOHN FRANKLYN (1877-1952). Southern Baptist, and later independent Baptist, minister, born at Dadeville, Alabama. Norris graduated from Baylor University and Southern Baptist Theological Seminary, but became vehemently critical of higher education. He served three pastorates in Texas: Mt. Calm (1899-1903), McKinney Avenue, Dallas (1905-1908), and First Baptist, Ft. Worth (1909-1951), the latter reportedly paying him the highest ministerial salary in the U.S. South. From 1908-1909 he was editor of the *Baptist Standard*, the official paper of Texas Baptists. In the early 1920s Norris joined with the **fundamentalist** movement and from his pastorate at Ft. Worth, he launched a lifelong crusade against the **Southern Baptist Convention** (SBC) and religious modernism, withdrawing from membership in the Convention in 1931. He also served Temple Baptist Church, Detroit, Michigan, simultaneously with the Ft. Worth congregation from 1935-1951.

Norris was a flamboyant fundamentalist preacher, often involved in controversial behavior such as a celebrated indictment in 1935 for murder, from which he was acquitted. He denounced the New Deal, the Congress of Industrial Organizations, Columbia University, and the Federal Council of Churches of Christ. His open criticism of Southern Baptist leadership caused his ouster from the Pastor's Conference in 1914, from the local association in 1922, and from the state convention in 1924. Norris, in turn, started a new Baptist movement, the Premillennial Fundamental Missionary Fellowship, later known as the **World Baptist Fellowship** (WBF), and a school, the Bible Baptist Seminary in Arlington, Texas. His authoritarian leadership in later years led to a split within his group from pastors like **G. Beauchamp Vick**, who began yet another movement, the **Baptist Bible Fellowship** (BBF) in 1950. Norris published several titles, including *The Gospel of Dynamite* (1933) and *New Dealism Exposed: Communism in Baptist Circles* (1935).

NORTH AMERICAN BAPTIST ASSOCIATION. See **Baptist Missionary Association of America**.

NORTH AMERICAN BAPTIST CONFERENCE. Formerly known as the German Baptist Conference, this body was formed in November 1851 at the First German Baptist Church of Philadelphia, Pennsylvania. Four churches and several laymen and missionaries created the conference to encourage the development of German-speaking Baptist Churches in North America. The total membership of the churches at the time of formation was over 600.

From the outset, the German Conference was integrally related to the work of the **American Baptist Home Mission Society** (ABHMS) and the **American Baptist Publication Society** (ABPS). The churches were listed among the English-speaking congregations for statistical purposes, ministerial candidates were trained in a special department of the Rochester Theological Seminary, and many of the churches received financial grants from the ABHMS.

The growth of the Conference depended upon German immigration patterns, and areas in New York, Illinois, Missouri, and the Dakotas and in Upper **Canada** and the Canadian Prairies were of special missionary concern. Early leaders of the Conference included **Konrad Anton Fleischmann** (1812-1867), August Rauschenbusch (1816-1899), and Alexander von Puttkammer (1801-1893).

Gradually, the scope of the Conference's work expanded with the establishment of a missionary society, a publication society, regional conferences; and **associations**. In 1902 a conference separate to Canada was organized as was a national women's union. By the 1970s the number of churches exceeded 350 with a foreign mission program in four countries: **Cameroon**, **Nigeria**, **Japan**, and **Brazil**. Many of the North American churches became bilingual, then mostly English-speaking in the 20th century.

Between 1920 and 1940 the relationship between the German Conference and the **Northern Baptist Convention** (NBC) was reevaluated by both parties. The ABHMS had long desired the foreign language groups to be assimilated into the mainstream, while the Conference affirmed the continuation of the German culture and language. When, in 1938, the NBC extended an invitation for associate membership in that body, the Conference declined. Among the reasons listed were the possible isolation of German-speaking churches, the loss of the organizational achievements of the Conference, and less, specifically, a perception of growing theological **liberalism** in the NBC. In 1946 the General Conference was incorporated as the North American Baptist Conference; in 1954 a similar incorporation took place in Canada for the several churches there.

The headquarters of the North American Baptist Conference are located at Oakbrook Terrace, Illinois. From 1853 to 1983 the Conference has published a German language paper, *Der Sendbote* (The Messenger), and since 1926 an English magazine, *The Baptist Herald*. In the United States the Conference supports one theological school, North American Baptist Seminary, and several homes and orphanages; in Canada there is a single campus for Edmonton Baptist Seminary and the Edmonton Baptist College.

NORTH AMERICAN BAPTIST FELLOWSHIP (NABF). One of the six regional fellowships of Baptist conventions/unions related to the **Baptist World Alliance** (BWA). The Fellowship was formed in 1964 and now includes ten member bodies: **American Baptist Churches in the U.S.A.**, **General Association of General Baptists**, **Southern Baptist Convention**, the **National Baptist Convention in the U.S.A.**, **National Baptist Convention of America**, **Baptist General Conference**, **North American Baptist Conference**, **Progressive National Baptist Convention**, **Seventh Day Baptist** General Conference, and Canadian Baptist Ministries. The Fellowship meets periodically to facilitate cooperative effort among the members.

NORTHERN BAPTIST CONVENTION (NBC). See **American Baptist Churches in the U.S.A.**

NORWAY. Two sailor-missionaries, a Dane, Frederik Rymker (1819-1884) and a Norwegian, Gotfred Hübert (1835-1922), and a Swedish blacksmith, Ola B. Hanssen (1842-1925), began the Baptist work in Norway. The first churches appeared at Porsgrunn and Larvik in 1860. An associational meeting was first held in 1872 at Skien, and the first all Norwegian Baptist Union meeting was in Bergen in 1877. The Union was officially organized in 1879 at Trondheim. The Norwegian Baptists in 1910 opened the first Free Church theological school at Christiana; later with the assistance of **American Baptists** a seminary, Baptistenes Teologiske Seminar, was opened at Stabekk, near Oslo. Baptists in Norway enjoyed a close relationship beginning in the 19th century with the Norwegian Baptist Conference in the United States, as well as leadership from the Scandinavian Department of the Divinity School at the University of Chicago. Norwegian Baptists produce the periodical, *Unions-Banneret* (Banner) (1880-1892; *Banneret* 1892-). In 1971 the **Baptist Bible Fellowship** (BBF) began a mission in Norway and in 1978 the **Association of Baptists for World Evangelism** (ABWE) started its work in Norway.

As of 1995 Det Norske Baptistsamfunn (Norse Baptist Union) included 64 churches and 5,302 members.

NORWEGIAN BAPTIST CONFERENCE. See **Danish-Norwegian Baptist Conference**.

NOVOTNY, HENRY (1846-1912). Czech Baptist minister and denominational leader, born near Nachod, Bohemia. Recruited by American Congregationalist missionaries, he was educated at the

Theological Institute on St. Chriscona in Basle, **Switzerland**; and at the Free Church College, University of Edinburgh. Following his studies he returned to Prague to begin pastoral work for the Congregationalists. Under the influence of a Russian Baptist from **Poland**, August Meereis (b.1847), he was persuaded to adopt Baptist sentiments. In 1885 at Hled'sebe near Prague, Novotny formed the first Czech Baptist congregation, the first services of which were held in his home under great persecution. Later he was also influential in the creation of the first Baptist congregation in Slovakia at Vavrisovo. He was the publisher of the first Czech Baptist periodical, *Pravda*, and the prime mover in the establishment of the Baptist Union of Czechoslovakia. Novotny wrote the first history of Czech Baptists, *The Baptist Romance in the Heart of Europe* (1939).

NYASALAND. See **Malawi**.

O

OLD GENERAL ASSOCIATION OF BAPTISTS. A regional body of **landmarkist** Baptists formed in November 1905 at Texarkana, Texas. Churches were represented by "**messengers**" from seven states and two foreign countries. The purpose of the Association was to unite congregations for **missionary** work and to coordinate a national fellowship. The name adopted was General Association of Baptists in the United States of America, shortened in 1924 to the "Missionary Baptist General Association." The effectiveness of the Association was short-lived, however, because the Baptist Missionary Association of Texas, for example, was older and larger. Thus in 1924 the Old General Association of Baptists merged with the Texas Association to become the **American Baptist Association**.

OLD LIGHT BAPTISTS. See **New Light Baptists**.

OLD REGULAR BAPTISTS. Name applied to a group of Baptists in the United States who date their founding in 1825 with the formation of the New Salem (Kentucky) Association. As Regular Baptists they are Calvinistic in the **Philadelphia Baptist Association** (PBA) tradition, and were once part of the United Baptist movement which brought together the Regular and **Separate** Baptists. Several of the churches, however, were unsatisfied with that union, on the one hand not accepting the **revivalism** of the Separates and also the modernizing tendencies of the

Regulars. "Old Regularism" emerged as a means to preserve older patterns in worship and lifestyle. The name was first applied in 1892.

The movement is characterized by basic Baptist principles, plus lined singing in worship, non-instrumental music, support for **Sunday Schools**, reluctance to cooperate with other Baptists, unaltered codes of conduct, the **ordinance** of **footwashing**, frequent handshaking, and much spontaneity. Theologically, the Old Regulars reject absolute predestination and position themselves deliberately between the hyper-Calvinistic **Primitive Baptists** and the **Arminian** groups like **Freewill Baptists**. The churches of Old Regular Baptists are simple white frame meetinghouses, mostly rural in location. Ministers include not only elders of one congregation, but also travelling **elders** who move about the constituency for special meetings and celebrations of the **Lord's Supper**. **Baptisms** tend to occur later in life than among other Baptists.

There are 13 associations of Old Regular Baptists, ranging from Michigan to Florida and the Mississippi Valley; the center of the movement is in Kentucky and Tennessee. Other than **associations**, there are few evidences of Old Regular institutional life; an exception was the Old Regular Baptist Orphanage in Letcher County, Kentucky, which existed from the late 1940s to 1959. Recent statistics (1990) indicate about 288 congregations with 15,000 members associated with the Old Regular movement.

OLD SCHOOL BAPTISTS. See **Primitive Baptists**.

ONCKEN, JOHANN GERHARD (1800-1884). German Baptist missionary and pastor, born at Varel. Self-taught, Oncken was first a schoolteacher and then he became a missionary for the Edinburgh Bible Society, and later the British Continental Society. He met an American Baptist theological educator, **Barnas Sears**, when the latter was touring Europe; Sears baptized Oncken on April 22, 1834. This propelled Oncken on a course as a Baptist missionary and church planter throughout Europe. He established a church at Hamburg in 1834 and served as its pastor for much of his career. His work was recognized by American Baptists and he became the senior missionary of the **Baptist Board of Foreign Missions** (BBFM) in Europe. He evangelized the Austro-Hungarian Empire, the Balkan states, **Russia**, and Scandinavia. In many cases he assisted in the establishment with governments of favorable conditions to preach and start congregations. Sometimes this meant imprisonment. No one was more important to the spread of Baptist principles and **religious liberty** in Europe. In 1849 Oncken was the prime mover in the establishment of a union among the German Churches and a publishing house, which was later named after him. His sermons were published under the title *Licht und Recht* (1901).

OPEN COMMUNION. See **Lord's Supper**.

ORDINANCES. In Baptist usage, the primary generic term for the religious rites of the church is "ordinance." In contrast with the term "**sacrament**" which some early as well as contemporary Baptists use, an ordinance is taught by Christ and clearly evidenced in the New Testament. The purpose of ordinances is symbolic and educational in that by participating in the ordinance, believers are drawn closer to Christ, their fellowship and witness is strengthened, and they act in obedience to a direct command of Christ. There are for most Baptists two ordinances, **baptism** and the **Lord's Supper**, but some would also argue that the **laying on of hands**, singing, **footwashing**, and preaching are also ordinances, that is, these are taught by Christ. See also **Baptism**; **Footwashing; Lord's Supper**.

ORDINATION. A term used among Baptists to designate those who are set apart for special **ministry**, called by some the "professional church leadership" of the denomination. In keeping with the practices of the New Testament churches (Eph. 4:12-13; Acts 6:4; 2 Cor. 4:1), ministry belongs to all, while some are set apart for the ministry of preaching, teaching, **evangelism**, pastoral care, administration, and missionary service (Eph. 4:11; Acts 13:2,3). The process of ordination involves the local church, the **association**, sometimes a regional or national body, and a candidate. Once the candidate announces to his/her local church that he/she has felt a call of God to ministry, the local church usually issues a license to preach in order that gifts for ministry may be observed. After a reasonable time of training, education, and evaluation, the formal steps toward ordination take place. This involves a committee of an association, which examines the candidate's sense of call, doctrinal beliefs, practical experience, and gifts. If the candidate passes the examination, a service of ordination, culminating in the **laying on of hands** will take place. Usually Baptist candidates are ordained with a clear place of ministry in view.

Ordination is considered a lifelong status as long as the candidate maintains his/her commitments, though some Baptists withdraw recognition of ordination from those who are not actively engaged in ministry. An ordained minister may be in full-time or part-time ministry. A certificate of ordination issued to the candidate has been common since the 18th century, and in the 20th century candidates are listed on a roster kept in the association or **convention** official records. The status of ordination usually carries the privileges of officiating at marriages, funerals, **baptisms**, and other occasions, and may in some cases allow the minister to enjoy tax/rate benefits in housing and income reporting, due to historically lower remuneration in ministry than other fields. Ordination of deacons is also recognized among Baptists, notably **Southern Baptists**, and allows for recognition of lay ministry. See also **Ministry, Baptist Understanding of.**

ORIGINAL AND ANCIENT BAPTISTS. Terminology applied by British writers to the New Testament churches, which they assumed practiced believer's **baptism** and held other Baptist principles, and later Baptistic adherents. Some **Strict Baptists** (SB) refer to the earliest Baptists of the Calvinistic tradition before the creation of the **Baptist Union of Great Britain** (BU) in 1831, as "Ancient Baptists," in contrast with the "Union Baptists" who in Strict Baptist teachings had erred from the faith. See also **Strict Baptists.**

ORIGINAL FREEWILL BAPTISTS. See **Freewill Baptists.**

ORTHODOX BAPTISTS. Name given to a movement of **fundamentalist** Baptists who emerged in Ardmore, Oklahoma, in 1931. W. Lee Rector (?-1945), a former professor at Oklahoma Baptist University and pastor at First Missionary Baptist Church in Ardmore, resigned to form the First Orthodox Baptist Church, also in Ardmore. His guiding principles included reaction to perceived modernism in the **Southern Baptist Convention** (SBC), a clear premillennial stance, and the basic Baptist **polity** and thought of **James M. Pendleton**. Eventually, Rector founded a school, the Orthodox Bible Institute, in 1944 and published a periodical, *The Illuminator* (1931- ; later the *Orthodox Baptist*). See also **Dispensationalism.**

P

PAKISTAN. Principally an Islamic republic, Pakistan has been a difficult field for Baptist missions. In 1954 the **Conservative Baptists** (CBA) embarked upon a mission, joined by Canadian Fellowship Baptists and in 1984 by **Southern Baptists** to which the official Baptist Convention is related. The Baptist community of approximately 1,000 members is centered in Karachi. The **Baptist Bible Fellowship** (BBF) also opened a mission in Pakistan in 1959, and the Conservative Baptist Foreign Mission

(CBFMS) relates to the Indus Christian fellowship in the Sindh province, begun in 1954. The Conservative Baptists work in partnership with the Fellowship Baptists of **Canada**.

As of 1995 there were about seven churches with 1,500 members affiliated with the Indus Christian Fellowship, and 17 churches with 470 members affiliated with the Baptist Convention.

PALMER, PAUL (fl. 1720-1740). American Baptist minister, whose origins are unsubstantiated; some historians believe he was born in the colony of Maryland, while others hold that he may have been born in England and emigrated to the colonies as a **General Baptist messenger**. The American thesis holds that Palmer was baptized at Welsh Tract Church in Delaware and ordained in Connecticut. In either case, in 1720 he started what became the first Baptist congregation in Maryland at Chestnut Ridge. Within seven years he settled in North Carolina colony and started the first Baptist congregation there in 1727. Over the next decade he started about eight other churches. **Morgan Edwards** visited Palmer in 1738 and proclaimed him the father of the General Baptists of the South. Palmer, who may have been formally elected a General Baptist "messenger" before he left England, corresponded with General Baptists in England to receive financial assistance, which the English General Baptist Assembly approved in 1702.

PALMQUIST, GUSTAF (1812-1867). American Swedish Baptist minister, born at Solberga, Småland, Sweden. Originally a schoolteacher, he was converted in 1844 to **evangelical** principles. He met **F. O. Nilsson** in Stockholm and was persuaded to emigrate to the United States to be **pastor** to persecuted **Swedish** emigrants. He was baptized and ordained at Galesburg, Illinois, and settled at Rock Island in 1852. Commissioned by the American Baptist congregation at Galesburg, he organized the first Swedish Baptist Church in the United States at Rock Island. In 1854-1855 he was a commissioned missionary of the **American Baptist Home Mission Society** (ABHMS) in New York City, but withdrew to Rock Island in 1855. He returned to **Sweden** in 1857 and spent the remainder of his life in ill health, contracted during a bitter winter experience in Illinois.

PANAMA. Baptist life in Panama has great variety, beginning with the **Jamaican** Baptist Mission Society in conjunction with the **Baptist Missionary Society** (BMS) in 1866. With the establishment of the Canal Zone in 1903, English language missions were established through the **Southern Baptist Convention** (SBC). The work in Panama became a base for **mission** expansion into other Central American countries. In 1959 the Convención Bautista de Panama was established and a theological school opened at Arraijan. The **Conservative Baptist** Foreign Mission Society (CBFMS) began in 1962 and the U.S. **Freewill Baptists** have a mission which began the same year. In 1976 the **Baptist Bible Fellowship** (BBF) also opened a mission in Panama.

As of 1995 there were 89 churches with 6,624 members affiliated with the Convención Bautista de Panama. Presently, there are two theological schools in Panama: Arraijan and Panama City.

PAPUA NEW GUINEA. Baptist witness in this nation began in 1949, the result of Australian missionaries with assistance from **New Zealand** Baptists. Early church planting was conducted at Baiyer River, Kompiam, Lumusa, and Tekin. By 1956 public baptismal services were held at Baiyer River and Lumusa. In 1969 a Baptist Bible College was opened and in 1973 the first portion of the **bible** translated into Kyaka Enga was completed. The **Baptist Bible Fellowship** (BBF) opened a mission in Papua New Guinea in 1961, and in 1967 the **Association of Baptists for World Evangelism** (ABWE) started its mission in the country.

As of 1995 there were 360 churches and 35,500 members affiliated with the Baptist Union of Papua New Guinea. There are two Baptist-related theological schools in Papua New Guinea: Sepik and Western Highland Province.

PARAGUAY. The first Baptist mission work in Paraguay was begun by Argentine missionaries in 1919. The first congregation was started at Asuncion in 1920 and churches were included in the Misión Bautista del Rio de la Plata after 1945. The Convención Evangelica Bautista del Paraguay was organized in 1956. The **Association of Baptists for World Evangelism** (ABWE) began its mission in Paraguay in 1976 and the **Baptist Bible Fellowship** (BBF) opened a mission in Paraguay in 1980.

As of 1995 there were 100 churches and 6,630 members associated with the Convención Evangelica Bautista. The Convención publishes *Centinela* (Sentinel) (1964-). There is a theological institute located in Asuncion.

PARKER, DANIEL (1781-1844). Baptist minister and publisher, born at Culpeper County, Virginia. He was little educated and took to living at various locations on the Old Northwest frontier. Beginning about 1815, he became an ardent critic of Baptist **missions**, favoring instead individual congregational **ministry**. He opposed **Sunday Schools**, education, and missionary societies. He moved among congregations, preaching his doctrine of the "Two Seeds," and organized a successful campaign against the efforts of men like **Luther Rice** and **Isaac McCoy**. He was the **pastor** of Pilgrim Predestinarian Church in Lamotte, Illinois, 1817-1836, and published a newspaper, the *Church Advocate* in 1829-1831. For one term he was elected to the Illinois State Senate from 1826-1827. Parker was well known for his publications, *A Public Address to the Baptist Society of the Baptist Board of Foreign Missions* (1820) and *Views on the Two Seeds: Taken From Genesis, 3rd Chapter and Part of the Fifteenth Verse* (1826).

PARTICULAR BAPTISTS. With the **General Baptists**, the Particular Baptists were a major type among early English Baptists. Particular Baptists were so-called because they held that Christ's atonement applied to the elect of God only, or a particular group of persons.

The first Particular Baptist congregation may be traced to a London Congregational **Separatist** group established in 1616. **Henry Jacob**, an Oxford graduate, founded the church and later emigrated to Virginia where he died. **John Lathrop**, a Kentish preacher, assumed pastoral duties until he emigrated to the New World about 1634. Three years later **Henry Jessey**, a Yorkshire man and Cambridge graduate, became pastor and served for the next few years. The question of **baptism** was debated among the congregation as early as 1630, with some members under **Samuel Eaton** accepting believers' baptism about 1633. In 1638 a group of Baptist sympathizers behind the leadership of **John Spilsbury** separated itself from the Jessey congregation as the first Particular Baptist congregation. Between 1638 and 1641 further enlightenment about baptism occurred as Richard Blunt (fl.1640), a **deacon** in the Spilsbury congregation, travelled to the **Netherlands** and recieved baptism by immersion from the Rhynsberger Collegiants, a practice which he brought back to England.

In 1644 seven London area Particular Baptist churches issued a **Confession of Faith,** which sought to distinguish the Particular Baptist movement from the maligned **Anabaptists** of Münsterite infamy. Among the signers were **William Kiffin**, John Spilsbury, Thomas Patience (d.1666), and Samuel Richardson (fl.1643-1658).

Particular Baptists grew dramatically under Cromwell's Protectorate, with numbers of the sect in the New Model Army who planted churches and **associational** life as the army moved about the countryside. In 1689 the first general "**convention**" (as Whitley, q.v., called it) of Particular Baptists was held for all of those who agreed to the Confession of 1677. At the turn of the 18th century, the Particular Baptists, strengthened in the urban areas, were the leading Baptist group in England.

During the 18th century Particular Baptist life matured at both the local church level and beyond. Numerous congregations developed substantial resources, for example the Horsley-down, Southwark church served by **John Gill** for 51 years. Baptist ministers met in meetings for regular advice (as in the Hanover **Coffeehouse**) and to address political concerns, as part of the **Three Dissenting Denominations**. Education funds and measures to care for widows were instituted in the first decades of the 18th century. In 1770 Particular Baptists of the West Country rallied behind Bristol Academy in the formation of the Bristol Baptist Education Society. In this new **voluntary** tradition, Particular Baptists in 1792 formed the first overseas missionary body in the denomination to reach heathen peoples. Particular Baptists in the North began itinerating missions which eventually became part of the home missionary movement. In 1813 Particular Baptist leaders like **Joseph Ivimey** worked to unite all Baptists in what became the **Baptist Union of Great Britain and Ireland** (BU) (1833). Some Particular Baptist congregations chose to retain the name to demonstrate their continuing Calvinistic ethos, following an historical lineage to **Strict** and later Grace Baptists. At length in 1891, with the diminution of Calvinism due to the Wesleyan Revival and other factors, most Particular Baptists dropped the label and were fused with the remaining General Baptists in the Union. English Particular Baptists published in London a periodical, *The New Baptist Miscellany and Particular Baptist Magazine* (1827-1832).

PASHKOVISM. A religious movement in Imperial **Russia** which emerged in the 1870s and culminated in part as a component of the mainstream Baptist tradition. Granville A. W. Waldegrave, Lord Radstock (1833-1913), a Plymouth Brethren missionary from England, began a mission at St. Petersburg in 1874. One of his most ardent converts was Vasilii A. Pashkov (d.1901), who gave himself vigorously to propagating the Christian faith in the Empire. Pashkov and his followers sought to renew the Russian Orthodox Church as a kind of pietistic movement and appealed to Russians on this basis. The "Pashkovites," as they were called, were open communionists and rejected the strict **discipline** of the Baptists.

In 1882 they organized the Society for Encouragement of Religious and Moral Reading, a group which ultimately won the approval of the Holy Synod. This Society led in the production of a Russian bible. Numerous people, including many early Baptist leaders, were led to faith by the literature the Pashkovites produced, and Pashkov himself aided the Baptists very generously, at one point purchasing a plot of land for a Baptist colony. Close cooperation ensued between Pashkovites and

Baptists until 1903, when the Pashkovites were formally accepted into the Russian Baptist Union and the name was changed to the Soyuz Yevangel' skikh Khristian-baptistov (Union of Evangelical Christians-Baptists), the term "evangelical" being preferred by the Pashkovites. See **Russia.**

PASTOR, BAPTIST UNDERSTANDING OF. Among almost all Baptist groups since the beginning of the 17th century, the pastor has been the spiritual leader of a local congregation. Baptists typically hold that the terms in the New Testament—presbyter (**elder**), bishop (episcopos), and pastor—all designate the same office.

Qualities required of a pastor include moral uprightness, an ability to lead one's family, graciousness, sobriety, temperance, self-control, spiritual discipline, trustworthiness, and honesty (I Tim. 3: 1-8; Titus 1:5-9). The duties of a pastor are derived from the apostolic churches and include preaching the gospel, administration of the **sacraments/ordinances,** leadership at weddings and funerals, and supervision of the governance and oversight of the congregation. Pastors of local churches also constitute together the presbytery of the associated churches (ee **Associations**).

Since the days of both the English **General** and **Particular Baptists,** the pastoral ministry has been understood as the primary ordained form of **ministry.** All others, such as missionaries, chaplains, educators, administrators, **evangelists,** and special workers, must be understood and assessed first for their fitness as pastors. Pastors are elected by the congregation, usually on nomination of a pulpit or selection committee, or in some cases by a committee of deacons. There is usually no term of office for pastors, the early experience being one of **ordination** for life in a given congregation and re-ordination where a pastor moves to another congregation. A long pastorate might be several decades, as with **John Gill** who served in London for half a century, or typically for 10 to 15 years. In North American experience in the 20th century, seven to 10 years is more typical, with British experience being a bit longer in one place.

Among the more **fundamentalist** Baptist congregations, "pastor" can be a title and noun of address. This may signal an unusually authoritarian role and perception of a Baptist pastor, rationalized upon the leadership of Christ as a singular great teacher and example. In contrast, British and North American Calvinistic Baptists may practice a multiplicity of elders (see **Polity**), and thus elect several "pastors" with differing and changing functions in the life of a congregation. Various bodies of Baptists frequently list the pastors of churches affiliated with an organization (i.e. ,**associations,** fellowships, and **conventions**), along with their credentials, and this establishes a formal ministerial roster of the approved and credentialled pastoral ministry.

PAUL, THOMAS (1773-1831). American Black Baptist minister and missionary, born at Exeter, New Hampshire. He was baptized in 1789 and ordained to the **ministry** at Nottingham, West, New Hampshire. He served the African Baptist Church in Boston from 1805-1831, also organizing the Abyssinian Baptist Church in New York City in 1809. In 1823 he secured a missionary appointment from the Massachusetts Baptist Missionary Society (MBMS) to serve in **Haiti**; this service lasted for six months during which he became a pioneer preacher on the island. His lack of knowledge of the French language inhibited his mission, however, and he returned to Boston. Reports of his missionary labors were printed in the *Massachusetts Baptist Missionary Magazine*.

PAYNE, ERNEST ALEXANDER (1902-1980). English Baptist minister, educator, and denominational leader, born at Clapton, England. He was educated at King's College, University of London, Regent's Park College and Mansfield College, Oxford University. Following his Oxford studies, he served from 1928-1932 as **pastor** at Bugbrooke. From 1932 to 1940 he served in several roles with the **Baptist Missionary Society** (BMS) and the **Baptist Union** (BU), resigning to accept a position as tutor at Regent's Park College, Oxford. In his 10 years with the College, he specialized in ecclesiastical history and mentored a number of future Baptist leaders. He wrote during this period a history of the Free Churches and advocated the **anabaptist origins** of the Baptist movement. In 1951 he became the secretary of the BU, and as such, one of the most influential voices in English **Nonconformity**. Under Payne's leadership, British Baptists participated fully in the World Council of Churches, Payne serving as one of its presidents and as a member of the Faith and Order Commission. Within the Union until 1967, and well into retirement, he was an advocate of **religious liberty** and international human rights causes. Among Ernest Payne's many literary contributions were *The Prayer Call of 1784* (1941), *The Free Church Tradition in the Life of England* (1944), *The Baptist Union : A Short History* (1959), and *Christian Baptism* (1959).

PEABODY, LUCY WHITEHEAD MCGILL (1861-1949). Baptist denominational leader, born in Belmont, Kansas. She attended classes at the University of Rochester and married a Rochester Seminary student, Norman Waterbury. Lucy taught for a time at Rochester School for the Deaf; later she and her husband were appointed missionaries to **India** by the **American Baptist Missionary Union** (ABMU). After five years work with the Telugus at Madras, Norman died and Lucy returned to the United States. In 1887 she accepted the position of corresponding secretary of the Woman's American Baptist Foreign Mission Society of the East and married a wealthy Salem merchant, Henry Peabody. Peabody died in 1908 leaving Lucy with a considerable estate, which she devoted to various mission causes. She made the acquaintance of **Helen Barrett Montgomery** and the two women campaigned widely on behalf of women's missionary work, particularly in 1910 during the International Jubilee of Women's Missions. During the theological debates among Northern Baptists in the 1920s, Lucy lent her support to the **conservative evangelical** camp. She helped to establish the **Association of Baptists for Evangelism** (ABWE) in the Orient in 1927. Resigning from all of her **Northern Baptist Convention** (NBC) responsibilities, she became an outspoken promoter of conservative causes, including The Eastern Baptist Theological Seminary in Philadelphia. Ultimately rebuffed as a woman in leadership, she reduced her outreach to writing on missionary subjects and managing her benevolent projects. Among her more enduring works were *Henry Wayland Peabody-Merchant* (1909) and *Just Like You: Stories of Children of Every Land* (1937).

PEACEMAKING, BAPTIST. While not one of the "historic peace churches," numerous Baptists have advocated various forms of peacemaking, based on the scriptural injunction, "Seek peace and pursue it" (Psalm 34:14). **Voluntary** associations and later denominational agencies have also taken pro-peace (or non-violence) stances among parts of the Baptist family. Many early English Baptists fought in the New Model Army and viewed military service as a part of their civic responsibility. However, linked with **religious liberty**, Baptists like **Leonard Busher** published works which reinterpreted the theme of peace, *Religion's Peace; or a Plea for Liberty of Conscience* (1614).

Likewise in the American colonies, Baptists took a non-resistance position, like the **Rogerenes.** In the early American Republic, Baptist ministers like Henry Holcombe (1762-1824) of Charleston, South Carolina, and Philadelphia, Pennsylvania, and **Francis Wayland** of Boston, and Providence, Rhode Island, Massachusetts were peace advocates and joined voluntary societies dedicated to peace concerns; Howard Malcolm (1799-1879) and **George Dana Boardman, Jr**. also joined the movement.

In Great Britain, with the formation of the Society for the Promotion of Permanent and Universal Peace in 1816, several Baptist ministers, including George Pilkington (1785-1858), James Hargreaves

(1768-1845), and William Stokes (d.1881) were prominent in its membership. Even greater interest among Baptists for the cause of peace emerged in the 20th century, with the formation in Britain in 1929 of the Baptist Peace Fellowship (BPF), gathered by a Baptist pastor, W. H. Haden (1875-1952) of West Bridgford. This followed clear advocacy by British leaders like **F. B. Meyer, James Rushbrooke**, and **John Clifford**. In the United States those who wished to offer support to concientious objectors in the era of World War II formed the Baptist Pacifist Fellowship in 1939, including **Harry Emerson Fosdick, Edwin M. Poteat Jr.**(see **Poteat Family**), and Edwin Dahlberg (1892-1986). This presaged in 1984 American and **Southern Baptists** in the U.S. forming the **Baptist Peace Fellowship of North America** (BPFNA). A major conference of 200 Baptists from 30 countries was held in Sjovik, Sweden, in 1988, at which a manifesto was issued. One of the important catalysts toward recognition among Baptists of the importance of pursuing peace was the endowment in 1964 of an award in the American Baptist Convention (ABC) by Victor and Eileen Gavel in honor of Edwin T. Dahlberg. Among the prominent Baptist leaders in the modern peace movement were **Martin Luther King, Jr.**, Muriel Lester (1883-1968), and **Howard Thurman**. The BPFNA publishes *Baptist Peacemaker* (1981-).

PEARCE, SAMUEL (1766-1799). English Baptist minister, born at Plymouth, England. Early in his life he had an **evangelical** experience and he was educated for the ministry at Bristol Baptist College. His sole pastorate was at Cannon Street Baptist Church in Birmingham from 1789-1799. Pearce knew **William Carey** before his missionary career and became one of Carey's most devoted supporters. He offered himself for **missions**, but owing to his organizational powers and reputation in the north of England he was encouraged to work for missions at home. This he did by organizing an auxiliary society and carrying forth a system of prayer for missions among the churches. He travelled widely, speaking in England and **Ireland** on behalf of the **Baptist Missionary Society** (BMS). In 1794 he wrote to **William Rogers** of First Baptist Church, Philadelphia, urging him to appeal to American Baptists to create an **American Baptist Foreign Mission Society**. Pearce died of consumption; it has been speculated this was the result of a wearing schedule, which entailed travel among the poorer classes and straightened living circumstances. Pearce produced one major treatise in his short career, *The Scripture Doctrine of Baptism, with Some Historical Remarks on the Subject* (1794).

PECK, JOHN MASON (1789-1858). American Baptist missionary and denominational leader, born at Litchfield, Connecticut. Peck was largely self-taught, although he received some lectures in William Staughton's Theological School in Philadelphia. Following a pastoral ministry in Amenia, New York, in 1813-1815, Peck accepted an appointment of the Massachusetts Baptist Missionary Society (MBMS) as a domestic missionary in the West. In 1817, along with **James E. Welch**, Peck became one of the first missionaries of the **Baptist Board of Foreign Missions** (BBFM) from 1817-1820. He positioned himself at St. Louis and turned his attention to the Indian tribes in the vicinity. After only three years, the Board withdrew its support, but Peck stayed in the field. He moved to Rock Spring, Illinois, where he began a school based on a combination of a high school and a literary and theological model coupled with a manual labor institute program. To support himself, he wrote extensively on the western territories and he edited newspapers, notably *The Pioneer and Western Baptist* (1830-1843). With the support of **Jonathan Going**, Peck helped to organize the **American Baptist Home Mission Society** (ABHMS) in 1832. In 1843 he became the corresponding secretary of the **American Baptist Publication Society** (ABPS) and reduced its debt and greatly extended its outreach. In 1853 he helped to found the American Baptist Historical Society (ABHS) in recognition of the need to address Baptist identity. As an editor, Peck was an **antislavery** thinker, but refused abolitionism as too extreme. Peck's journal, *Forty Years of Pioneer Life: Memoir of John Mason Peck* (1864) is considered an important resource for the study of the Mississippi Valley region.

PEDALAVIUM. See **Footwashing**.

PENDLETON, JAMES MADISON (1811-1891). Southern, and later American, Baptist minister, born in Spotsylvania County, Virginia. He was tutored by **Andrew Broaddus** and became a merchant. He moved to Kentucky, and further studied at an academy in Hopkinsville, Kentucky under James Rumsey. After a brief career in schoolteaching he served churches at Hopkinsville (1833-36), First Baptist, Bowling Green (1836-1849), and Russellville (1849-1857). About 1852 Pendleton met **James R. Graves** who promptly won Pendleton over to a closed **communion** position. Graves invited Pendleton to write for his paper, *The Tennessee Baptist*, and Pendleton's work was well received. Two important classics emerged from his pen, *Three Reasons Why I Am A Baptist* (1856) and *An Old Landmark Re-Set* (1857). Pendleton immediately became a leader in the emerging Landmarker movement, although he never advocated Baptist successionism and held to the doctrine of the universal church.

In 1857 Pendleton was named to an endowed chair in theology at Union University in Murfreesboro, set up by Graves. There he served also as president of the institution (1859-60) until it was forced to close at the threat of war. He also served as an editor of the *Southern Baptist Review* and of *The Tennessee Baptist*. He was an ardent opponent of Campbellism, Roman Catholicism, and infant baptism. His position against **slavery** (he was a gradualist) angered Graves and he was fired as associate editor of *The Tennessee Baptist* in 1861. In 1862 Pendleton became pastor at First Baptist Hamilton, Ohio, where he served until moving to the Upland Baptist Church in Pennsylvania in 1865. At Upland he had a close relationship with **Henry G. Weston** and the **Crozer** family and taught at Crozer Theological Seminary. At Upland he published a *Church Manual* (1867) and *Christian Doctrines* (1878), as well as other doctrinal and exegetical works.

PENTECOSTAL FREEWILL BAPTIST CHURCH. See **Freewill Baptists**.

PERRY, RUFUS (1834-1895). American Black Baptist minister and denominational leader, born a slave in Tennessee. Perry educated himself secretly, using the good resources of his Baptist preacher-father until his father ran away to Canada. Rufus was sold to a Mississippi slaveholder in 1852, but fled to Windsor, Ontario, where he taught school. Eventually he took theological classes at Kalamazoo College and was ordained in 1861 to serve the Second Baptist Church, Ann Arbor, Michigan. Later he was also pastor at St. Catherines, Ontario, and at Buffalo and Brooklyn, New York. In Brooklyn, he organized Messiah Baptist Church. After the Civil War, Perry devoted himself to educational efforts and administration. He superintended schools for freedmen and edited newspapers, including the *American Baptist* and the *National Monitor*. He became a corresponding secretary for the **Consolidated American Baptist Missionary Convention**, as well as the American Educational Association and the **American Baptist Free Mission Society** (ABFrMS). Perry was an outspoken devotee of Black leadership in black affairs. Following an electrifying address entitled "Light" at State University in Louisville, Kentucky, in 1887, that school awarded him the Ph.D. degree, possibly the first to a **Black Baptist** clergyman in the United States. Perry's booklet, *The Cushite or the Children of Ham* (1887) is considered a classic of African-American literature.

PERU. The initial Baptist work in Peru was an outgrowth of Argentine Baptist work. Under the influence of the Southern Baptist **Foreign**

Mission Board (FMB), Argentine missionaries began churches north from Lake Titicaca in 1933. Independent Baptists working for the Amazon Valley Baptist Faith Missions established a church in 1935 at Iquitos. In 1950 the Convención Evangelica Bautista de Peru was started; in the 1950s congregations opened in most of the major cities. Other Baptist developments included independent Baptists associated with Misión Evangelica Bautista Irlandesa (1927; the Irish Baptist Foreign Mission), Associación Bautistas Maranathas (1964), and the **Associación Bautistas para Evangelistas Mundial** (ABWE) initiated a work in 1929 related to another effort of **Baptist Mid-Missions** (BMM) in the United States, which began its mission in 1947 at Lima and Cuzco. The **Baptist Bible Fellowship** (BBF) opened a mission in Peru in 1958. Recently, the Baptists of eastern Peru have been involved in cooperative ministries with the Bolivian Baptist Union.

   As of 1995 there were 152 churches and 7,346 members affiliated with the Convención Evangelica Bautista del Peru. The Convención publishes *Destellos Bautistas* (Baptist Stars). There is a Baptist-related theological school located at Trujillo.

PETO, SAMUEL MORTON (1809-1889). English Baptist philanthropist, born at Woking, Surrey. He was apprenticed in various building trades and became a draftsman. He developed the firm of Griswell and Peto, a construction company. His firm constructed the Nelson Monument, the Houses of Parliament, and the Lyceum Theatre. The original firm dissolved in 1840, with Peto directing his energies into railroad construction on several continents, as well as in Britain. In 1846 he began railway construction on the Norwich section of the Northeastern Railway where he met William Brock, the minister of St. Mary's, Norwich. Two years later Peto built with his own money Bloomsbury Chapel in London, to which he persuaded Brock to come as **pastor**. Peto served in Parliament for Finsbury, Norwich (1859-1865), and later for Bristol (1865-1868). He led in the passage of the Church Rates Bill and the Peto Act, which prescribed the procedures for appointing trustees for dissenting places of worship. At length Peto went bankrupt, but recovered by entering the field of railroad building. Later in life he was again able to support numerous Baptist causes. Peto also served as treasurer of the **Baptist Missionary Society** (BMS) from 1855-1866. He published *The Resources and Prospects of America Ascertained During a Visit to The States in the Autumn of 1865* (1866).

PHILADELPHIA BAPTIST ASSOCIATION (PBA). The oldest Baptist association in the United States in continuous existence, the Philadelphia

Baptist Association was founded in 1707. Originally comprising five small congregations, Lower Dublin (Pennepack), Piscataqua (Piscataway), Middletown, Cohansey, and Welsh Tract, the association spanned the Delaware River in Pennsylvania and New Jersey. Based upon English and Welsh Baptist models, this prototype of all American Baptist **associations** and extra-parish bodies, the PBA pioneered many features of Baptist life. The Association handled queries about matters of order and church **discipline**, examination for **ordination**, supply of pastors, constitution of new churches, and special projects. In 1746 Benjamin Griffiths provided a classic definition of an association in the annual minutes, the next decade the first educational institution of Baptists in America was sponsored in Hopewell, New Jersey (see **Education**), and in 1764 the Association sponsored the establishment of a college in Rhode Island (see **Higher Education**).

During the 1770s the Association grew strong enough to commission travelling evangelists to the other colonies and the pattern of leadership was passed to the north (Warren Baptist Association) and south (Charleston Baptist Association). The Philadelphia Association was the nucleus of sentiment several times for a national organization of Baptists, notably in the 1760s and 1790s and again in 1812. Its churches, which numbered 81 (21,000 members) by 1940 included several of the most prestigious congregations in the United States. The PBA debated most of the significant social concerns of the day and affirmed typical Protestant positions, such as **religious liberty**, **antislavery**, **temperance**, and the need to maintain a watchful eye on the developing Roman Catholic community in the region. Following the Civil War, the PBA became essentially dominated by its urban congregations, although many historic churches in the surrounding Pennsylvania countryside remained faithful. This led in due course to the founding of the Philadelphia Baptist City Mission Society in 1880, which placed the association at the forefront of American Baptist urban mission development.

With the formation of a statewide **convention** in Pennsylvania, the PBA churches often dually aligned themselves with both bodies and this resulted in cooperation in many projects. In the reorganization of the American Baptist Convention in 1972 (see **American Baptist Churches, U.S.A.**), the PBA became one of 37 recognized regional, state, or city organizations in covenant with the national denomination. In its membership are churches of various ethnic and racial groups, including **Black Baptists**, Hispanic, German, and Chinese. As of 1995, the Association includes 116 churches with over 46,000 members. See also **Association, Baptist; Polity, Baptist**.

PHILIPPINES. The **American Baptist Missionary Union** (ABMU) was the first Baptist organization to send missionaries to the Philippines, beginning in 1900 after the Spanish-American War. Under a comity arrangement for **evangelization** of the islands by the Evangelical Union of the Philippines, Baptists were given Panay and Negros Islands, with primary emphasis upon the indigenous Visayan peoples. The centers of the effort were Jaro and Iloilo. From this mission came the Baptist Conference of the Philippines in 1904. Educational institutions, including Jaro Industrial School (1905), Filamer College (1906), and Central Philippine University (1923), were started by missionary support. In 1925 a Philippine Baptist Home Mission Society was organized. As a result of American Baptist divisions over missionary methods, the Association of Baptists for World Evangelism began work in the islands in 1929, founding the Doane Evangelistic Institute at Iloilo, Panay, in 1930, and the Luzon Baptist District Association with Manila at its center in 1935. This same effort produced the Baptist Bible Seminary in Manila in 1948.

In 1943 11 American Baptist missionaries were executed on the Island of Panay by the Japanese army (see **Martyrology, Baptist**). U.S. **Southern Baptist** interest in the Philippines commenced as large numbers of American troops were incarcerated on the islands during World War II and with the closing of the **China** field in 1949-1953. In 1948 Southern Baptist missionaries began work which would become the Convention of Philippine Baptist Churches and the Mindanao Baptist Convention of Southern Baptist Churches. The Philippine Baptist Theological Seminary was opened in 1952 at Baguio. Another U.S. group, the **Baptist General Conference**, began a mission in 1946 with a Baptist Theological College at Cebu. The **Baptist Bible Fellowship** (BBF) opened a mission in the Philippines in 1948, as did the **Conservative Baptist Foreign Mission Society** (CBFMS) the same year, with a theological school founded at Quezon City in 1968. In 1974, a Seventh Day Baptist mission was established in the Philippines.

As of 1995 there were five Baptist groups organized in the Philippines: the Baptist Conference of the Philippines, with 206 churches and 15,040 members; the Convention of Philippines Baptist Churches, with 672 churches and 95,155 members; the General Baptist Church of the Philippines, with 313 churches and 13,450 members; and the Mindanao Baptist Convention of Southern Baptist Churches, with 889 churches and 52,166 members. The Conservative Baptist Association of the Philippines includes about 150 churches with 21,000 members. There are 10 schools in the Philippines: Bacolad City, Baguio City, Cebu City (2), Davan City (3), Dagupan City, Iloilo City, and Negros.

PHILPOT, JOSEPH CHARLES (1802-1869). English Baptist minister and editor, born at Ripple. He was educated at Oxford University and elected a fellow of Worcester College in 1827. As an Anglican rector he served the parish at Stadhampton; he was a popular **evangelical** preacher and built a substantial congregation. Philpot was converted to the Baptist position and baptized in 1832 by John Warburton, a former weaver. He served **Strict** and **Particular** congregations the rest of his life, at Allington, Oakham, and Stamford. For over 20 years he edited the *Gospel Standard*, assuming the mantle of **William Gadsby**. Philpot's sermons were translated into Dutch and German as exemplars of the theme of sovereign grace. One of Philpot's favorite themes was to stand against **Arminianism** and he frequently denounced John Wesley (1703-1791) and the Methodists. Among Philpot's published works were *The Eternal Sonship of Christ* (1861) and *Strict Communion Vindicated* (1873).

PILLSBURY, GEORGE ALFRED (1816-1898). American Baptist denominational leader and philanthropist, born at Sutton, New Hampshire. After a secondary education he worked in the grocery business and sheet-iron manufacture. By 1848 he entered a partnership in dry goods and became a local politician. In Concord, New Hampshire, Pillsbury served as purchasing agent for a railroad and was elected mayor of the city and served one term in the New Hampshire State legislature (1871-1872). In 1878 he moved to Minneapolis, Minnesota, and entered a partnership in flour milling with his son and brother. This became the Pillsbury-Washburn Flour Mills Co., the largest in the world of its era. Again involved in politics, he was elected mayor of Minneapolis in 1884 and was an influential Republican. In Concord, he was a highly regarded lay member of First Baptist Church and in Minneapolis he superintended the construction at First Baptist Church of the largest ecclesiastical edifice west of Chicago, as well as the creation of the largest pipe organ in the West. He also virtually built the campus of an academy at Owatonna, later named Pillsbury Academy. He also served as president of the St. Paul/Minneapolis Baptist Union, the Minnesota Baptist Convention (1880-1887), and the **American Baptist Missionary Union** (1888).

POLAND. Polish Baptist development stems from the German Pietist movement and the mission work of **J. G. Oncken**. In 1858 Gottfried A. Alf (1831-1898) formed the first congregation at Adamow near Warsaw. In contrast with the German-influenced churches, Slavic and other language congregations also emerged. Under great persecution, partly because of their German origins, Polish Baptists finally united in 1942 and secured recognition from the government in 1946. The partition of lands to the East and West made it difficult to unite the Polish churches until the Marxist era. In 1907 a seminary was formed at Lodz (recently transferred to Radosc near Warsaw), and a newspaper, *Slowo Prawdy, (Word of Truth)* was started in 1925. Among the other groups represented in Poland, the **Conservative Baptist** Foreign Mission Society (CBFMS) began work in 1988, assisting in the establishment of a Baptist-related seminary at Wroclaw. In 1933, a division among Seventh Day Adventists led to the establishment of a Seventh Day Baptist work.

As of 1995 there were 61 churches and 3,810 members in the Koscio Chrzescijan Baptystow.

POLISH BAPTIST CONFERENCE IN THE U.S.A. With increasing numbers of immigrants from Poland and improved economic opportunities in the United States and **Canada**, significant numbers of Poles emigrated to the eastern industrialized regions of the United States. American and German Baptists began Polish mission work in Buffalo, New York, in 1890; Jozef Antozewski (1853-1934) founded the Fillmore Avenue Baptist Church in 1894. In the Chicago area, Polish mission was conducted by several German Baptist churches. By 1912 the scattered congregations formed the Polish Baptist Association at Pound, Wisconsin; this later became the Polish Baptist Conference in the U.S.A. By 1939 there were 38 churches; in Canada an additional seven were founded. The Conference supported missions to Polish people and raised support for aid to Poland. The Conference has published the following periodicals: *Naszc Zycic (Our Life)* (1910-1917); *Zrodlo Prawdy (Source of Truth)* (1917-1930); *Zwiastun Prawdy (Herald of Truth)* (1930-1939). The Conference has been related to the American Baptist Churches and the Baptist Convention of Ontario and Quebec.

POLITY, BAPTIST. Term applied to the organizational principles and behavior of a religious group. In Baptist experience of all kinds, the centerpiece of polity is the local congregation. All authority under Christ is vested in the local church and no external authority is superior. Its officers, mandate, relationships, and ministries are determined by its membership. A **confession of faith,** derived from the membership, may indicate the local church's theological identity, and a **covenant** agreed upon by the membership may define obligations and conditions of membership and **ministry.** A constitution and/or bylaws will likely profile the structures, procedures, and purposes of each local church. In some cases, mostly in North America and Great Britain, local churches will also be incorporated in order to achieve protection and opportunities under local laws. Among many Baptist groups, Baptist polity ends with the local church.

From the early 17th century English Baptists associated among congregations. This led inevitably to the formation of permanent **associations** which serve as advisory bodies to the local churches and help to facilitate certain functions which local churches prefer to do collectively. These functions include **ordination** of ministers, resolution of conflict, doctrinal interpretation and advice, and various forms of mission activity. Associations grew rapidly in the 18th century in England, **Scotland**, and **Wales** and the vehicle was transferred to North America as well. At the end of the 18th century, the identity of the Baptist denomination was seen primarily in the collection of associations. Associations are usually defined by rules of order and procedure and are entirely **voluntary** bodies.

Emerging from the British community was the voluntary association, which provided a variegated form of organization for Baptists. These societies were composed of individuals who focused upon a particular task and drew up their own rules and membership qualifications. Sometimes these societies existed within churches, while others developed alongside congregations, or involved a mixture of Christians from many denominations. The society model of polity influenced Baptists broadly in shaping future permanent organizations at the denominational level; the society had a great appeal to Baptists because it fostered individualism and freedom of choice. The Bristol Education Society and the **Baptist Missionary Society** (BMS) were pioneers of this model in British Baptist experience.

In 1813 and 1814, respectively, British and American Baptists created a new level of polity by organizing the Union or **Convention**. In Britain, this became eventually the national assemblage of Baptists from churches and **associations,** which coordinated mission programs, stewardship, and ethical/political concerns. In the United States the convention became a gathering of representatives of churches and associations interested in cooperating in mission–first overseas, then domestic–and education. With the formation of the **Southern Baptist Convention** (SBC) in 1845, the convention became a unifying symbol of Baptist identity in the United States and a model of cooperation and advice for smaller Baptist bodies. Inevitably, some Baptists objected to the organizational unity and preferred to stress the inviolable local church; these have variously been referred to as "Landmarkers," "antimissionary," or "**Primitive**" Baptists.

Beginning with associational rules and **Thomas Grantham**'s *Christianismus Primitivus* (1678), manuals of polity and practice have been produced to instruct churches and extraparish bodies on rules of decorum and structure. Among the more widely accepted authors have been **Elkanah Holmes** (1797), Samuel Jones (1798), Edward Hiscox (1859), **James M. Pendleton** (1867), **Hezekiah Harvey** (1879), **Ben M. Bogard** (1927), William R. McNutt (1935), **Henry Cook** (1947), and Norman H. Maring and Winthrop S. Hudson (1963, 1991). Many Baptist unions require candidates for **ordination** to complete courses in Baptist polity and practice. See also **Elder; Local Church Protectionism; Pastor**.

PORTUGAL. The first Portuguese Baptist was likely Ignatius Fernandez (1757-1830), a candlemaker in Dinajpur, **India**. He was brought under the influence of **Baptist Missionary Society** (BMS) personnel in India in 1796. As for Portugal itself, an English Baptist layman and protégé of **Charles Haddon Spurgeon**, Joseph Jones (1769-1868), began **evangelistic** work and formed the first Baptist congregation in 1888 at Oporto. In 1910 Brazilian Baptists heard of the work and sent Zachary C. Taylor (1851-1919), a **Southern Baptist** missionary, to Portugal. New congregations at Wisen (1913), Tondela (1914), and Lisbon (1922) resulted. A Portuguese Baptist Convention was started in 1920. Another Baptist beginning was the result of **Conservative Baptist** missionaries from the United States, who used the services of a former Brazilian Baptist missionary, João de Oliviera (1883-1958), who was associated with no less than 10 mission organizations, beginning in 1945. In 1949 they started several congregations and a seminary at Leiria was established in 1948; the seminary has changed hands several times and continues operation at present with Southern Baptist support. A cooperative body, União Baptista de Portugal, was formed in 1946, securing assent of 11 churches. Portuguese Baptists publish *O Semeador Baptista* (*The Baptist Sower*) (1925-). Separate from the other Baptist works, the Conservative Baptist Foreign Mission Society (CBFMS) began a work in central Portugal in 1945, the **Baptist Bible Fellowship** (BBF) opened a mission in 1987, as well as the **Association of Baptists for World Evangelism** (ABWE) in 1978.

As of 1995 there were 57 churches and 4,111 members affiliated with Convencão Baptista Portuguêsa. The Conservative Baptist Mission includes about three churches with 150 members. There is a Baptist-related seminary at Queluz.

PORTUGUESE BAPTIST CONGRESS IN THE UNITED STATES.
Portuguese mission work in the United States dates from the 1890s when Francisco C. B. Silva (1863-1926) accepted an appointment from the

American Baptist Home Mission Society (ABHMS) in Oakland, California. Later Silva attended Newton Theological Institution and worked among the Portuguese in Massachusetts, especially the Bethel Baptist Mission in Boston and vicinity. In 1894 a chapel was constructed in New Bedford, Massachusetts, becoming the first Portuguese Baptist Church in North America. The Congress was formed in 1919 to provide fellowship among the churches, which in 1940 numbered about 14. The Congress became a cooperating organization of the Northern Convention, later American Baptist Churches.

POTEAT FAMILY. A prominent Southern Baptist family of several generations. Among the leaders were William Louis Poteat (1856-1938), son of James and Julia Poteat, the president of Wake Forest College (1905-1927). William was educated at Wake Forest, then did graduate studies at the University of Berlin and the Marine Biology Laboratory at Woods Hole, Massachusetts. He taught at Wake Forest, 1878-1905, and blended science and religion in his teachings. He was active in the North Carolina Baptist Convention, the Anti-Saloon League, the North Carolina Academy of Sciences, and the North Carolina Conference of Social Services.

William's younger brother was Edwin McNeill Poteat, Sr. (1861-1937), president of Furman University (1903-1918). Edwin was educated at Wake Forest and Southern Baptist Theological Seminary, with further studies at Berlin, Yale, and Johns Hopkins Universities. He served pastorates at Chapel Hill, North Carolina (1884-1886) and Memorial Baptist Church, Philadelphia (1898-1903). Poteat was active in the Layman's Missionary Movement, and the Interchurch World Movement 1918-19, and worked for the **Northern Baptist Convention** (NBC) General Board of Promotion. Following his presidency at Furman he was professor of philosophy and ethics at the University of Shanghai in **China** and at Mercer University (1931-1934). Edwin McNeill Poteat, Jr. (1892-1955), son of Edwin McNeill Poteat, Sr., was a **Southern Baptist** minister and educator, born at New Haven, Connecticut. A graduate of Furman University and Southern Baptist Seminary, he joined the Student Volunteer Movement and became a missionary to China. For four years he taught philosophy at the University of Shanghai and then returned to the United States to be **pastor** at Pullen Memorial Baptist Church in Raleigh, North Carolina, and Euclid Avenue Baptist in Cleveland, Ohio (1937-1944). For one term (1944-1948) he was president of Colgate Rochester Divinity School in Rochester, New York. He was also a member of the Committee on Worship of the National Council of Churches (1941-1955) and president of Protestants and Other Americans

United for the **Separation of Church and State** (POAU). As a pastor he advocated scientific advances and wrote on a great many subjects, including history, poetry, and liturgy--18 books in all, including *Jesus and the Liberal Mind* (1934) and *Mandate to Humanity* (1953). In the Southern Baptist Convention he became known as an advocate of the **social gospel**, and even charged that Baptists had participated in social evils. He called upon his fellow Baptists to confess their sins and pursue racial and economic justice and **religious liberty**. In 1940 he delivered the Beecher Lectures in Preaching at Yale University. The Poteat family represented the liberal tradition in Southern Baptist life, raising questions of modernity and **ecumenism** within their own denomination and the larger Christian church.

POWELL, ADAM CLAYTON, JR. (1908-1972). American Black Baptist minister and political leader, born in New Haven, Connecticut. The son of a prominent **Black Baptist** clergyman, **Adam Clayton Powell, Sr.**, Powell was educated at Colgate University (B.A.) and Columbia University (M.A.). He became minister at Abyssinian Baptist Church in New York City in 1937 following his father, where he served until 1960. He entered city politics in the 1930s, being elected to the City Council of New York in 1941, and founding and editing a civil rights newspaper, *The People's Voice*, in 1942. Powell was elected to the U.S. Congress in 1945, and subsequently 10 more times through 1967. A flamboyant orator, he was irreverent, audacious, and prophetic in his advocacy of non-discrimination. Powell's personal life overwhelmed his career, however. In 1966 following an eight-year legal battle in which he was found guilty of slander, he took up residence on the island of Bimini. The following year, amidst charges of the misuse of public funds, the U.S. House of Representatives voted to censure him, and ultimately to remove him from his congressional seat. In 1969 he was stripped of his seniority, but later the Supreme Court reversed his removal order. To complicate matters further, at the time of his death, two women vied for the right to determine Powell's funeral arrangements. Powell received honorary degrees from Shaw University in Raleigh, North Carolina, and Virginia Union University in Richmond, Virginia. His outstanding literary achievement was *Keep the Faith, Baby!* (1967).

POWELL, ADAM CLAYTON, SR. (1865-1953). American Black Baptist minister, born at Martin's Mill, Virginia, the son of a German planter and a Negro-Indian woman slave. He was poorly educated and fled accusations in a gunshot incident in 1884. He worked in coal mines in Ohio and was dramatically converted in 1885, turning to the **ministry**.

For a time he worked in a hotel in Washington, D.C., and studied at Wayland Seminary. In 1892-1893 he was pastor at churches in St. Paul, Minnesota, and Philadelphia, Pennsylvania. In 1893 he was called to Emmanuel Baptist Church in New Haven, Connecticut, where he became a nationally famous Black preacher. Abyssinian Baptist Church in New York City, deeply in debt, called him as pastor in 1908 and he remained there until his retirement in 1937. In his years at Abyssinian, he cleared the debt, helped the congregation to move uptown to a new location, and became a major spokesman for Black racial pride. A long-time Republican, Powell switched to the Democrats in 1932 to support Franklin D. Roosevelt, and Powell led in the creation of programs to combat poverty in the Great Depression. A **liberal** social thinker who shifted from the position of **Booker T. Washington** to that of W. E. B. Dubois (1868-1963), Powell was a founder of the Urban League and the National Association for the Advancement of Colored People (NAACP). The community base which his ministry created became the political base of his son, **Adam Clayton Powell, Jr.**.

POWELL, VAVASOR (1617-1671). Welsh Baptist minister and evangelist, born in Radnorshire, **Wales**. He was a graduate of Jesus College, Oxford University, and entered the Anglican ministry. He was influenced by Puritan thought and converted to the Independant cause; he was baptized in 1655. Powell was considered the greatest **evangelist** of his era, preaching across Wales and at London to great crowds and starting new churches. At Dartmoor he started a congregation, but later returned to Wales. From 1650 Powell enjoyed opportunities under the Act for the Better Propagation and Preaching of the Gospel in Wales, which allied him with government interests. A significant number of Welsh congregations followed his teachings: Calvinistic, mixed communion, open membership, and **revivalistic**. His extreme republican views, such as advocating the right of lower classes to rule, and **Fifth Monarchist** sympathies drew the ire of Oliver Cromwell (1599-1658) and he had Powell imprisoned. Powell was incarcerated eight years in 13 prisons; he died at Fleet Jail in London in the eleventh year of his confinement. Powell managed to publish nine works, including one of the first biblical concordances (1671) produced by a Baptist. His biography, also published in 1671, was influential over many generations among Welsh Baptists. Powell was the author of several polemics, including *A Short View of the Praelaticall Church of England* (1641) and *Common Prayer-Book No Divine Service* (1660).

PRAYER MEETING. A customary devotional and worship experience among Baptists since the 17th century. While the precise origins of prayer meetings is not known, it is likely that they were an outgrowth of small groups which met as illegal conventicles when more public meetings were unlawful. This was typical of Puritans and **Separatists** from the 1580s. Early congregational records, notably at Broadmead Baptist Church in Bristol, England, in 1640, indicate that church members gathered in homes for prayer between Sunday worship services. Some churches connected such meetings with the **Lord's Supper** and met at least monthly. In the later 18th century, the New Connection of **General Baptists** produced tickets for participants in weekly prayer meetings, which in turn admitted members to the **Lord's Supper**; this was derived from the Methodists. It is also evident in British Baptist practice that prayer meetings were an occasion for lay leadership, many times in the absence of ministers, as at Birchcliff in Yorkshire. The General Assembly of **General Baptists** in 1724 urged the organization of "cottage meetings" to increase spiritual gifts.

The occurrence of prayer meetings among Baptists in America originated in the 17th century. Association circular letters enjoined prayer among the congregations as early as the 1720s. It appears that the idea of a mid-week prayer service was popularized in the mid to late 19th century in the **revivalist** tradition as a means of spiritual discipline between Lord's Days. With **Sunday Schools**, prayer meetings caught on as a regular part of church life for the faithful. In the 20th century, prayer meetings were common until the 1970s when family activities and schedules complicated the weekly routine. A typical prayer service consists of **Scripture** reading, a brief homily or reflection (hence the name of the service is often "prayer meeting and **bible** study"), followed by sharing of prayer needs and concerns and a "season of prayer" in which several persons pray extemporaneously. The entire experience lasts about one hour in North American practice and occurs typically on Wednesday evenings. When the service occurs in a home rather than in the church building, it is referred to as a "cottage" prayer meeting.

PRE-EXISTERIAN BAPTISTS. See **Strict Baptists.**

PRIESTHOOD OF ALL BELIEVERS. A generally accepted characteristic of most Baptists, the priesthood of all believers is an inheritance of the Reformation. Martin Luther (1483-1546) especially emphasized this doctrine. For Baptists of the 17th century, the notion of an hierarchical priesthood such as in the Church of England or Roman Catholicism was unacceptable and tended toward clericalism. Rather, each believer has direct access to God through Jesus Christ, the High Priest (Hebrews 7:17-28; 1 John 2:1). Based upon **scripture** references, such as Exodus 19:5-6, Revelation 1:6, 1 Peter 2:9, and Ephesians 4:12, Baptists teach that priestly **ministry** is conducted by one believer for others. Included in the priestly ministry of believers are intercessory prayer and service in the name of Christ for one another. Some Baptist writers also stress that the priesthood of all believers allows any believer to administer the **sacraments** (**baptism**, the **Lord's Supper**) to each other. In contemporary literature, the priesthood of all believers has often been expressed as the "ministry of the whole people of God" or the "mutual ministry of believers."

PRIMITIVE BAPTISTS. Also called the "Old School," anti-missionary, or "Hard Shell" Baptists, the Primitive Baptist movement originated in 1832 among rural Baptist congregations in Maryland and Delaware. On September 28 of that year, a group of 22 ministers convened as the "Black Rock Convention" to oppose tract societies, **Sunday Schools**, missionary societies, the Bible Society, colleges and theological schools, and protracted meetings. They issued a series of resolutions and an account of their proceedings, and called upon others to subscribe to a new periodical, the *Signs of the Times*. Their reasoning was that societies and new measures were human inventions of a modern age and were not found in the New Testament; as such, these were contrary to the spirit and power of Christ. They refused to cooperate with others in the regular Baptist **associations** on the basis of "Can two walk together, except they be agreed?" (Amos 3:3). They styled themselves "Old School Baptists" because it distinguished them as belonging to the School of Christ; in actuality, the terms "New School" and "Old School" had some currency among Presbyterians and Congregationalists on the matter of using "means" (human instrumentality) to advance the gospel (New School people used means).

A second emergence of this tradition occurred in the Chemung (New York) Baptist Association in 1835. Leaders there called for disassociation from other Baptist associations which supported missionary societies and educational institutions. The same rationale was used, namely, that there was no New Testament basis for such organizations. The desire of these churches was to adhere to the order of the "primitive" church. Within a decade, there were 1,600 congregations and over 60,000 members in the movement.

Primitive Baptists have provided various kinds of observers with opportunities to examine a microcosmic community of Baptists. The **German** social scientist Max Weber (1864-1920) visited the Primitive

Baptist community at Mt. Airy, North Carolina, in 1904. He drew several useful conclusions about the application of Calvinism in religious communities and typified the Primitive Baptists as a sect. Other more recent studies by various sociologists and anthropologists of Appalachian religious culture continue to mark the importance of the group.

As of 1995 there were approximately 1,600 churches and 20,000 members associated with various segments of the Primitive Baptist movement, including the "Absoluters," the "Old Liners," and the "Progressives." Primitive Baptists of different persuasions publish several periodicals, including *Signs of the Times* (1833-), *The Primitive Baptist* (1885-), *Baptist Witness* (1952-), and *Banner Herald* (1918-) (formerly the *Pilgrim's Banner* 1893-1918, merged with the *Primitive Herald* 1916-1918).

Following the Civil War, Black Primitive Baptists in the southern United States separated from the Caucasian churches and formed a movement of Black Primitive Baptists. As of 1995 there were about five churches per association (43 associations total), and about 3,000 members.

PROGRESSIVE NATIONAL BAPTIST CONVENTION (PNBC). The most ecumenical of the major American Black Baptist denominations. The roots of the organization are found in a 1961 dispute at the annual meeting of the National Baptist Convention in Kansas City over the election of the president of the **National Baptist Convention in the U.S.A.** (NBCUSA). **Joseph H. Jackson** sought his fourth two-year term as president against a movement among delegates to elect Gardner C. Taylor (1918-) of New York City. Jackson won, in part by manipulating the election. A related issue was the question of support for **Martin Luther King, Jr.** and the Civil Rights Movement, which the Taylorites wanted but the followers of Jackson opposed. When it appeared futile to bring about change in the "tenure" of the incumbent, 33 delegates from 14 states convened on November 14-15, 1961, at Cincinnati, Ohio, and founded the Progressive National Baptist Convention. Lavaughn Venchael Booth (1919-), pastor of Zion Baptist Church in Cincinnati, was considered the leading voice in the new movement. Timothy Moses Chambers (1899-) was elected president of the Progressive National Baptist Convention, while Taylor and King played a major role in shaping the principles of the organization.

Like the other national **Black Baptist** organizations, the PNBC includes boards for Home Missions, Foreign Missions, Christian Education, and Pensions. The Convention participates in most **ecumenical** bodies, including The National Association for the Advancement of Colored People (NAACP), the Southern Christian Leadership Conference

(SCLC), and the Urban League. From its inception, the PNBC has maintained a cooperative agreement with the **American Baptist Churches in the U.S.A**. Its support for educational institutions is extended to Chicago Baptist Theological Seminary, Central Baptist Theological Seminary, Morehouse School of Religion, Virginia Union School of Theology, Shaw University, and Howard University School of Divinity. Missionary work is sponsored in **Haiti**, **Liberia**, **Nigeria**, and other parts of West Africa.

The Convention periodical is *Baptist Progress* (1912-), an older Black Baptist news magazine. As of 1995 there were 1,800 congregations and an estimated 1.8 million members related to the Convention, many of which are dually aligned with other Baptist bodies.

PROKOFIEVITES. See **Russia.**

PUERTO RICO. From 1898 Baptist work in Puerto Rico has primarily been related to the American Baptists. Just after the United States occupied Puerto Rico in 1899, Hugh McCormick (1860-1929), a missionary of the **American Baptist Home Mission Society** (ABHMS), arrived at Rio Piedras to begin church planting. The location at Rio Piedras insured that it would become a center for education, including the University and the Evangelical Seminary (founded originally in Coamo in 1907), in which Baptists participate with five other denominations. Other educational ventures include the Grace Conaway Institute (1914) and the Barranquitas Academy (1926). A convention of churches, Iglesias Bautistas de Puerto Rico, was formed in 1902 and is a recognized regional organization of the **American Baptist Churches in the U.S.A.** Following U.S. military presence on the island, **Southern Baptists** (SBC) began mission work in Puerto Rico in 1964, having started a congregation in the early 1950s. In 1965 an association of Southern Baptists was formed.

As of 1995, there were 89 churches with 21,414 members affiliated with the Iglesias Bautistas de Puerto Rico.

PULSFORD, THOMAS (1793-1871). English Baptist minister and revivalist, born in West Ansty, Devonshire. Baptized at Tiverton, he served the church at Limpley Stoke and from 1819-1839 he served as **pastor** at Torrington. In 1839 he was appointed evangelizing agent for the **Baptist Home Mission Society** (BHMS). Pulsford focussed his efforts in northern England and produced a widespread **revival** experience among the churches in 1847. He used "means" much akin to those of American Presbyterian revivalist, Charles G. Finney (1792-1875): protracted meetings twice per day and three times on Sundays, tracts, prayer meetings, inquiry meetings, and the anxious bench. In the years 1842-1843 it was estimated that Pulsford helped to convert as many as 500 persons at towns like Newark and elsewhere in the North. Following an assessment of his work, it was agreed that he should not hold protracted meetings after 1844 and he took a settled pastorate in the southwest. Pulsford was the author of *Helps for Revival Churches* (1846).

PURITAN SEPARATIST HYPOTHESIS. An historical theory which seeks to explain the origins of the Baptist movement with reference to the English Puritan tradition. Since the later 19th century, British and American Baptist historians have debated whether Baptists were an outgrowth of the **Anabaptists** or a sect which emerged as part of the overall Puritan Reformation of 1560-1650. Following the clues laid forth in the studies of English **Separatism** and Congregationalism, where a congregational form of church government arose along with a strong commitment to biblical authority, proponents of this view hold that the earliest Baptists came to be connected with Francis Johnson (1562-1617), a Cambridge theologian, and his protégés, John Robinson (1572-1625) and **John Smyth**. A distinct connection of doctrinal and ecclesiastical similarity, if not personal relationships, has been demonstrated to exist from Johnson to Smyth and the first **General Baptists**, and also from **Henry Jacob** and what became the **Particular Baptist** movement. Those who propound this thesis see no necessary connection between English Separatists and European Anabaptists and hold that the burden of proof lies upon those who would affirm such a connection. Rather, it was a particular view of church government and the widespread influence of the **Scriptures** in the vernacular which produced the first Baptists as an entirely distinct group. Among the historians who have advanced the Puritan-Separatist hypothesis are **Henry C. Vedder**, **William T. Whitley**, Barrington R. White of Oxford, Winthrop S. Hudson at Colgate Rochester in New York, **Norman H. Maring** at Eastern Baptist Seminary in Philadelphia, Pennsylvania, Ken R. Manley at Whitley College in Melbourne, Australia, and H. Leon McBeth at Southwestern Baptist Seminary in Ft. Worth, Texas. See also **Anabaptist Kinship Theory**.

R

RAND, SILAS TERTIUS (1810-1889). Canadian Baptist minister and missionary, born at Cornwallis, Nova Scotia. He was self-taught, excelling in languages, including Latin, Greek, Spanish, French, German, and Italian. A bricklayer by trade, he became interested in Indian languages and mastered Mohawk, Micmac, and Malecite. He embarked upon a pastoral **ministry** among several Baptist churches at Parrsboro, Horton, Liverpool, and Windsor, Nova Scotia from 1834-47. His fascination with Indian cultures led him to declare himself a missionary to the Micmacs and the formation of the Micmac Missionary Society, an overtly anti-Catholic organization, resulted. His personal disinclination to rely on denominational resources and his adoption of Plymouth Brethren theology, followed by his public denunciation of the Baptist denomination, led to his being excommunicated from the Hantsport Baptist Church in 1872. He came to rely on Brethren leader, George Müller's (1805-1898) plan of "begging" for funds and these were never sufficient. He wrote a Micmac dictionary (1888), prepared a Micmac translation of the **Scriptures** (1875), and a collection of Indian legends (1894), the latter a credit to his lifelong cultural interests. In 40 years of evangelization of the heavily Roman Catholic tribe, he made only one convert.

RAND, THEODORE HARDING (1835-1900). Canadian Baptist educator, born at Canard, Nova Scotia. He was educated at Acadia College and took up a career in education. A public school teacher, Rand advocated in Nova Scotia the establishment of nonsectarian, state-supported schools. As a superintendent of schools, he introduced the theories of Horace Mann (1796-1859) and Egerton Ryerson (1803-1882), and he began the *Journal of Education* in 1866 to trumpet his ideas. An indefatigable worker, he put in place a licensing system for teachers, uniform standards across the province, and a grading system for student progress. Deposed in 1870 from the Nova Scotia position for political reasons, he moved to New Brunswick where he provided the same innovations in a similar role.

Also active in Baptist church life, Rand was twice elected president of the Maritime Baptist Convention and he recommended that Maritime and Ontario Baptists cooperate in theological education. He held the chair in education at Acadia, the first of its kind in Canada, until he accepted a professorship in apologetics, ethics, and didactics at Toronto Baptist College in 1885. Senator **William McMaster** and principal **John Castle** relied heavily on Rand's reputation to secure a charter for their new Christian university. At length, he became chancellor of McMaster University (successor to Toronto Baptist College) in 1892 and designed its curriculum, particularly advocating the arts. Rand had a wide-ranging literary interest and produced *A Treasury of Canadian Verse with Brief Biographical Notes* (1900).

RANDAL, BENJAMIN (1749-1808). Freewill Baptist evangelist and church planter, born at New Castle, New Hampshire. Randal had various occupations in his early career, including sailmaker and seaman. In 1770 he was converted under the preaching of George Whitefield (1715-1770) and over the next 10 years he moved to a full-time **evangelistic** ministry of his own. Randal came to Baptist principles from a plain reading of **Scripture** and was also influenced by the work of Nova Scotia evangelist, **Henry Alline**. In 1777 he began preaching regularly at New Durham, New Hampshire, from which he gathered a congregation which was formally established by covenant in 1780. He itinerated across the northern stretches of New England, establishing in 1783 a quarterly meeting system and in 1792 the first yearly meeting.

Randal described his theological position as "free grace, free will, and free communion," all three principles derived in response to the prevailing Calvinism in the New England Congregationalist order. He was influenced in his position by Edward Lock of Gilmanton, New Hampshire, and Tozier Lord of Barrington, New Hampshire, both earlier Baptist opponents of Calvinism. When confronted in 1779 by Regular or Calvinistic Baptists, Randal dismissed their position and had little fellowship with that group, claiming to be "owned by God." He was a tireless preacher and exhausted himself itinerating through the **Freewill Baptist** Connexion (FWB), which he largely founded.

RANTERS. In the first half of the 17th century in English religious development, a number of radical sects grew up in defense of free interpretation of **Scripture** and in opposition to any form of religious establishment. Among these were the Ranters, pejoratively so called because of their blasphemous public behavior and seemingly careless statements of doctrine. Essentially a movement of migratory, dispossessed craftsmen, Ranters lacked any spokesman or organization, some preferring simply to be known as "My one flesh." Positioned somewhere on a continuum between **Seekers** and Quakers, Ranters often equated themselves with God, frequented ale-houses where they sang blasphemous songs, publicly flaunted their misdeeds, and used tobacco to heighten their spiritual awareness. Some Baptists became Ranters or vice versa, while others were accused of having a ranting spirit or "being a loose person like a Ranter." See also **Diggers**; **Levellers**; **Seekers**.

RAUSCHENBUSCH, WALTER (1861-1918). American German Baptist theologian and educator, born at Rochester, New York. The son of a German Baptist pioneer church planter and educator, Walter was educated at the Evangelische Gymnasium at Gutersloh, Westphalia, the University of Rochester, and Rochester Theological Seminary. His seminary mentors were Howard Osgood (1831-1911) and **Augustus H. Strong**. After graduation, he went to the pastorate of Second German Baptist Church on New York City's West Side. There in "Hell's Kitchen" he developed advanced social theories and interacted with prominent reformers and theologians, including Henry George (1862-1916) and Richard Ely (1854-1943). In 1892 he, Samuel Zane Batten, and Leighton Williams (1855-1935) formed an international movement called the **Brotherhood of the Kingdom**, devoted to progressive Christian social thought, which came to be known as "social Christianity" or the "**social gospel**."

In 1897 Rauschenbusch took a faculty position at Rochester Seminary in the German Department where he taught undergraduate courses and New Testament. In 1902 he became the Pettengill Professor of Church History in the English Department of Rochester Theological Seminary. Through the years of his professorship he wrote extensively on social Christianity and Baptist identity. Among his outstanding works were *Christianity and the Social Crisis* (1907), *The Theology of the Social Gospel* (1917) and *For God and the People: Prayers for the Social Awakening* (1910). The outbreak of World War I crushed Rauschenbusch's plan for a better, peaceful kingdom under the righteous rule of God, and his health failed. Long hampered by profound deafness, he was greatly beloved by his students and colleagues, notably his lifelong friend, Augustus Hopkins Strong. See **Social Gospel**.

REEKIE, ARCHIBALD BROWNLEE (1862-1942). Canadian Baptist minister and missionary, born at Armow, Ontario. He was a farmer for several years and then returned to complete his education at Woodstock College and McMaster University. While still a student, Reekie studied the possibilities of a mission to **Bolivia** and convinced the Baptist Convention of Ontario and Quebec Foreign Mission Board to commence a work there. In 1897 he became the pioneer Protestant **missionary** to Bolivia, settling first at Oruro and later at Cochabamba and La Paz. Reekie used an educational approach to mission and began a school which bears his name in Oruro. He was influential in the development of a **liberal** policy toward Protestantism in Bolivia and served in the country until 1921. For a short time in 1917-1918 he served in **Cuba** for the **American Baptist Home Mission Society** (ABHMS). After missionary service Reekie was pastor at several small congregations in southern Ontario.

REFORMED BAPTIST ALLIANCE (RBA). Influenced by the **holiness movement**, particularly as advanced by Phoebe Palmer (1807-1874), several Baptist congregations in the Canadian Maritime Provinces withdrew from the Free Christian Baptist Conference (see **Freewill Baptists**) and formed an alliance of holiness-oriented churches. When the majority of Free Christian Baptist elders in New Brunswick and Nova Scotia refused to accept the doctrine of "instantaneous entire sanctification" and called for discipline of ministers who held this position, 75 "delegates" from New Brunswick, Nova Scotia, and Maine met at Main Street Free Baptist Church in Woodstock, New Brunswick, on November 1-3, 1888, to organize the "Reformed Baptist Denomination of the Dominion of Canada," popularly called the Alliance. The terminology "reformed" was used in the sense of "reformulated," rather than referring to any association with the Calvinistic churches of the Reformation. Among the original leaders of the Alliance were James E. Drysdale (1834-1914), William Kinghorn (1823-1893), W. B. Wiggins (1849-1924), Elisha Cosman (1835-1925), and Benjamin N. Goodspeed (1835-1922).

The RBA was incorporated in 1894. In 1889 a periodical began, *The King's Highway*, which was published through 1967. Over the years, Reformed Baptists held to **"bible** holiness," congregational **polity**, open communion, **Arminian** theology, and believer's **baptism** by immersion. By the 1950s many were unhappy with the terminology "reformed" because it connected in some minds with a Calvinistic theology; the principal doctrinal point became holiness perfectionism. Institutional developments included a college called the Holiness Bible Institute in Woodstock, New Brunswick (1936) (later renamed Bethany Bible College), Yarmouth, Nova Scotia, and then Sussex, New Brunswick (1959); a Sunday School Association, home mission board, and foreign missions in Natal and the Transvaal in **South Africa**. In 1968 the RBA merged with the Pilgrim Holiness Church and Wesleyan Methodists to form the Wesleyan Church.

REFORMED BAPTIST MISSION SERVICES. Founded in 1985 as part of the Reformed Baptist movement in the United States and **Canada**, Reformed Baptist Mission Services supports missionaries in six countries, including **Colombia**, **France**, **Israel**, **Jamaica**, **Kenya**, and the United Kingdom. With heaquarters in Carlisle, Pennsylvania, it publishes *Missionary Update*.

REFORMED BAPTISTS. One of the recent smaller bodies of Baptists in the United States, the Reformed Baptists emerged in 1949 and coalesced in the 1970s. Energized by the Banner of Truth Trust, an English Calvinistic organization which promotes the re-publication of Calvinist writers like A. W. Pink (1886-1952) and **C. H. Spurgeon**, churches in Pennsylvania and New Jersey formed in 1967 the Reformed Baptist Association. They consider themselves the true successors to the Calvinistic traditions of the Second London Confession of Faith (1689), the **Particular Baptists** of Great Britain, and in particular the English theologian, **John Gill**. Stressing "sovereign grace," the Reformed Baptists avoid relations with mainstream Baptists, and, in particular, certain **Arminian** groups. Most of the churches emphasize sovereign grace and particular election, and several practice multiple eldership rather than singular pastorates. The Reformed Baptist movement has been influenced by hyper-Calvinistic non-Baptist groups, notably Orthodox Presbyterians and members of Faith Theological Seminary in Elkins Park, Pennsylvania. The Association has distant relations with the **Continental Baptist Association**.

As of 1995, there were over 100 congregations scattered across the United States, united by the **Reformed Baptist Mission Services** and the periodical, *Baptist Reformation Review* (1972-), a publication which it shares with the Continental Baptists.

REGULAR BAPTISTS. See **General Association of Regular Baptist Churches**.

RELIGIOUS LIBERTY. A fundamental earmark of Baptist identity from the beginnings of the movement, religious liberty has occupied a prominent place in Baptist thought. Prior to the advent of Baptists per se, **Anabaptist** writers in England asserted their rights to freedom of conscience. For instance, Hendrik Terwoort (fl.1550-70), a Flemish Anabaptist, was burned at Smithfield in June 1575 for his religious convictions, according to Van Braght's *Martyr's Mirror*. Likewise, Anabaptists were accused in 1589 of holding the erroneous opinion that the civil power should not hinder their preaching. The concern for religious liberty was thus firmly planted in English culture at the seedtime of the Baptist movement.

A concern for religious liberty grew out of circumstances in which English **Nonconformists** found themselves at the turn of the 17th century. Early in the reign of King James I, **Separatists** realized that the Crown and the Established Church were formidable obstacles to the free expression of biblical Christianity and the propagation of their faith. Moreover, their desire to avoid the **sacraments** drew the wrath of the Anglican Church and stern measures were taken to bring about conformity. As the first Separatist-Baptistic congregation emerged under the leadership of **John Smyth**, many Separatists fled to Holland to avoid imprisonment and the loss of their property; Smyth and his small congregation did likewise and settled in Amsterdam. Able to discuss their views in greater liberty, they were still confined to the frame of reference of the Mennonites, with whom they boarded and worshipped. Smyth would write in his Confession of Faith that "Christ alone is the King and Lawgiver of the Church and the conscience." At length in 1609, one faction of this group under the leadership of **Thomas Helwys** decided to return to England and face the consequences. This led to Helwys's publication of the first tract in the English language to advocate complete religious liberty, *A Mistery of Iniquity*. Helwys argued in cogent terms that the king had no right to abuse his subjects, who were in spiritual matters required to abide by a higher law. Further, Helwys stated, persecution did not accomplish its objective, and finally he made the classic assertion that "God alone is Lord of the conscience." For his accomplishment, Helwys was imprisoned and likely died there.

A second generation of those advocating religious liberty, which began in the 1620s, is evident in the writings of **Leonard Busher**, a leader among the **General Baptists**. Busher took a slightly different tack, demonstrating first that **Scripture** never grants permission to use physical coercion in spiritual matters. He affirmed that "Christ hath given no such weapons to the Church." Rather, erring persons were to be disciplined and non-Christians were to be evangelized. Moslems, Busher reminded his readers, were more tolerant than some Christians.

By mid-century, English Baptists were clearly the leading spokesmen for religious liberty. The General and **Particular Baptists** held this truth in common. In the First London Confession of Faith (1644), there was found the bold statement among the emerging Particular Baptists concerning religious liberty: "concerning the worship of God; there is but one lawgiver...which is Jesus Christ...So it is the magistrate's duty to tender the liberty of men's consciences..." This position was to include all persons, regardless of religious affiliation: Protestants, Catholics, Turks, infidels, etc.

The third major theoretical base for the Baptist position on religious liberty was laid by the English and later Anglo-American thinker, **Roger Williams**, a short-term leader more appropriately identified with the **Separatists** and later the **Seekers**. In his book, *The Bloudy Tenant of Persecution* (1644), Williams recounted the instances of persecution of true believers in England and New England, and demonstrated the futility of using force to achieve religious ends. He argued that there was a wall of separation between the church and the Crown which must not be violated by the state. Williams was oft-quoted, particularly by Baptists in the American colonies.

The issues surrounding religious liberty were rejoined in the American colonies and Baptists were again in the vanguard. The Standing Order establishment of New England was intolerant of the kind of dissent which the Baptists posed. They were especially antagonized by the Baptist refusal to practice the sacrament of infant **baptism**. Names like **William Screven**, Roger Williams, **Henry Dunster**, and **Obadiah Holmes** all evince the Baptist penchant in 17th century New England for religious freedom. The theoretical case followed the pattern of the English Baptists and the course of events in the colonies closely paralleled those in England. When the Toleration Act in 1689 was passed, Baptists in New England used this achievement to call for toleration in their own situation.

During the 18th century, Baptists fanned out through the Middle Colonies and the South, and they stood firm in their claim for religious liberty. In Pennsylvania and the Jerseys, they enjoyed complete freedom based on Quaker constitutional provisions. In Virginia and the Carolinas, intense persecution set in from the Church of England, which desired to silence the preaching of Baptists. It was left to leaders like **Isaac Backus**, **James Ireland**, and **John Leland** to make the particular case for separation of church and state, a corollary to religious liberty (see **Separation of Church and State** entry). With the winning of independence and the creation of the U.S. Constitution and Bill of Rights, religious liberty was formally achieved in the United States. Many historians credit John Leland in particular for the contribution of this doctrine to the Constitution.

The 19th century saw yet another shift in the meaning and force of religious liberty among Baptists. As the great efforts were undertaken in world mission, Baptists moved their focus to advocating religious liberty as part of the missiological apologetic. **Burma** became the first battleground where Baptists called upon the government to recognize religious freedom. In **Liberia**, Baptists faced hostile insurgents and contended for a free state. In Europe, under the leadership of **Johann Gerhard Oncken**, Baptists called upon Lutheran authorities to grant the right of assembly and propagation of the faith. And in Latin America Baptists became part of the "**evangelical** movement" favoring the ideals of a free church in a free state. Much of this ideology was transplanted from the American political experience. By the end of the century, Baptists were taking credit for having given to the world a precious gift of religious liberty.

In the United States a curious set of circumstances led liberal Baptists to rediscover the heritage of religious liberty. In the 1940s when the Franklin Roosevelt Administration advocated recognition of the Vatican for purposes of foreign affairs, Baptists in the United States protested loudly and issued the **American Baptist Bill of Rights**. Later as **fundamentalism** sought to deprive more liberal theologians (see **Liberalism**) of their right of free expression, Baptists again sounded the chord of religious liberty, particularly **soul liberty**.

In the last decades of the 20th century, Baptists in the United States are divided on the relevance of religious liberty. Conservative and fundamentalist Baptists prefer to emphasize strict adherence to biblical authority and mandate **confessions of faith**; this retards the growth of pluralism and heterodoxy. Others emphasize complete freedom of conscience and maintain that nothing whatsoever should dictate to the human conscience, save the guidance of the Holy Spirit.

In the late 20th century there continue to be concerns for religious freedom, some with implications for the Baptist family. In **Belgium** Baptists are still classified as a cult, in **Romania** and **Bulgaria** Baptist pastors have been imprisoned and churches closed. In Saudi Arabia small congregations of Baptists are denied the right to have churches and are harassed when they meet in homes.

When Baptists create a biblical warrant for religious liberty the most frequently referenced passages are Galatians 5:1 and II Corinthians 3:17. See also **Human Rights, Baptists and**.

REVIVALS, REVIVALISM. Revivals have been an important component of Baptist experience since the 17th century in Great Britain and North America, primarily in the latter. The term technically applies to a renewal of Christian experience, based upon biblical passages such as 2 Kings 23:21-25, Psalm 51:10, Matthew 12:20-24, and Revelation 2:5. In North American and British usage, "revival" applies first to a period of intense religious interest, for instance in a single congregation, and also to a spiritual awakening in a region or country over a prolonged period of time.

Early in their history, English Baptists exhibited a revivalistic impulse, for instance in the 1640s when **Thomas Lambe** of London held open church meetings and called people to repentance. Lambe also conducted itinerant preaching tours in Gloucestershire and trained others in this style of conversionist **evangelism**. **General Baptist messengers** in the latter 17th century also helped to renew congregations on a visiting basis. In the 18th century, Baptists followed general evangelical patterns in periodically looking for renewal in their congregations, a greater sense of personal godliness, and congregational vitality. In many cases, this renewal was associated with evangelism and church planting because the revivals were the result of itinerant preachers in often remote areas. In

Wales leaders like **Vavasor Powell** travelled widely in this regard as did **Dan Taylor** in England, and much renewal was the result.

In the American colonies **Isaac Backus** and **Elias Smith** exemplified the revival tradition in the North, **Morgan Edwards** in the Middle Colonies, and **Shubael Stearns**, **John Leland**, and **Daniel Marshall** did so in the South. **David George** popularized the revival among **Black Baptists** in South Carolina and later in Nova Scotia. In the Canadian Maritime Provinces, **Henry Alline** preached the New Light emphases as did **Joseph Dimock**. Their primary method was preaching convictional sermons in public places (usually not in meetinghouses) accompanied by prayer, and allowing for overt responses from their audiences. Home visitations of possible candidates typically preceded actual preaching events.

In the 19th century, the fruits of **Second Great Awakenings** leaders like Charles G. Finney (1792-1875) among the Presbyterians with their "New Measures" had an impact upon American and British Baptists. In the United States, men like **Jacob Knapp** moved from city to city employing means that included protracted meetings, altar calls, mass **baptisms**, and invitations to participate in social reforms such as the **temperance** crusade. In **Canada Harris Harding** exemplified the fervor of the Second Awakenings. At length in the 1880s under the influence of the Keswick movement and the Niagara Bible Conferences, Baptists became sympathetic to crusades and conferences for personal renewal; these were led by pastors like **A. J. Gordon** and disciples of Dwight L. Moody (1837-1899). This "New Measures" style of revival meeting was translated to Britain in the **ministry** of **Charles Roe**, who in 1849 invited Finney to Britain to establish the "revival system." **Thomas Pulsford** held protracted meetings on the American model and employed many of Finney's strategies in his itinerant missions with the **Baptist Home Mission Society** in the 1840s. Sometimes Pulsford conducted two services a day, every day for several weeks.

In the 20th century Baptists regularly responded to the revivalist impulse in mass meetings and within the congregation. The mass appeal of Billy Sunday (1862-1935) and **Billy Graham** swept up many Baptists in large protracted crusade meetings. Graham, himself a Baptist, often addressed significant Baptist gatherings like the **Southern Baptist Convention** (SBC) and the **Baptist World Alliance** (BWA), thus reinforcing the symbols of the revival. International figures like Billy Kim of **Korea** and Nilson Fanini (1932-) of **Brazil** have itinerated broadly in the BWA circles as revivalists/evangelists. Within the local congregation, many Baptists frequently schedule one or two week revival services, usually inviting a guest preacher to follow a theme of personal renewal and invite people to make a public response. This phenomenon is popular in the Southern Baptist tradition, among **Black Baptists**, and many of the **conservative evangelical** Baptist groups in the United States. A small number of Pentecostal **Freewill Baptists** in the United States encourage a second overt work of grace, "entire sanctification," at revival services.

Typically the elements of a Baptist revival service are uplifting congregational singing, personal testimony reports of God's work in individual lives, a season of prayer, a convictional sermon emphasizing personal experience, and an invitation to public profession of faith, rededication of one's life to Christ, or the opportunity to surrender one's life to Christian service. A key element at the conclusion of the service is the singing of a hymn of commitment or invitation, several of which have been written for the purpose: "Pass Me Not, O Gentle Saviour," "Almost Persuaded, Now to Believe," "Just As I Am, Without One Plea," and "I Surrender All." The revivalist who holds meetings which result in numerous decisions quickly gains a reputation for this ministry and may embark upon a full-time ministry of evangelism or revivalism, thus making the role a permanent category of the Baptist ministry. See also **New Light Baptists**.

RHYS, MORGAN JOHN, SR. (1760-1804). Welsh Baptist minister, born at Llanbradach. He was educated in a school kept by David Williams, an Independent minister of Watford; later he attended Bristol Baptist Academy and was ordained a Baptist minister at Penygarn, Pontypool, in 1787. As a young pastor, Rhys adopted radical reform positions opposing **slavery** and welcoming the French Revolution as a democratic movement. Rhys in fact in 1791 took a trip to **France** to visit the site of the Bastille. Very much a supporter of America as a "Promised Land," Rhys advocated setting up a democratic republic and this drew criticism to the cause of **Nonconformists**. In 1794 Rhys and a company of Welsh Baptists emigrated to Pennsylvania where he made the acquaintance of **William Rogers** and Benjamin Rush (1746-1813) of Philadelphia. Eventually Rhys purchased a substantial tract of land which he named "Cambria" and settled a colony. His last settlement was in Somerset County, Pennsylvania, where he died. In Wales Rhys was a promoter of **missions** and **Sunday Schools**, as well as a plan for day and night classes. Rhys exprssed his **antislavery** views in an early pamphlet among the American Baptist community, *Letters on Liberty and Slavery* (1798).

RICE, JOHN RICHARD (1895-1980). Southern and later Independent Baptist evangelist, born in Cooke County, Texas. He was educated at Decatur Baptist College, Baylor University, Southwestern Baptist

Seminary and the University of Chicago. For two years (1920-1921) he taught English and was a football coach at Wayland Baptist College in Plainview, Texas. In 1923 he was **pastor** of the Shamrock, Texas Baptist Church, but under the influence of **J. Frank Norris**, he withdrew from the **Southern Baptist Convention** and embarked on a career as full-time evangelist. From 1932-1940 he was pastor of the Fundamentalist Baptist Tabernacle in Dallas, Texas, a congregation he started. Having begun a newspaper, *The Sword of the Lord*, in 1934, he devoted himself full-time to editorial responsibilities in 1940 and built the paper into a widely read platform for militant **fundamentalist opinion**. In 1955 he moved to the Chicago area where he started Calvary Baptist Church in Wheaton, Illinois; four years later he began the "Voice of Revival," a radio **ministry**. Rice moved to Murfreesboro, Tennessee, in 1963 and established the Sword of the Lord Foundation. He also became active in the **Southwide Baptist Fellowship** and related to Bob Jones University. His citywide crusades across four decades drew large crowds to his open air and stadium preaching from—Buffalo, New York, to Moncton, New Brunswick. He was the author of over 200 books, the most famous of which was his sermon, "What Must I Do to Be Saved?" (1949), which is said to have sold 32 million copies. His other titles include *Bobbed Hair, Bossey Wives, and Women Preachers*: *Significant Questions for Honest Women Settled by the Word of God* (1941) and *Amusements for Christians* (1955).

RICE, LUTHER (1783-1836). American Baptist missionary and denominational leader, born at Northborough, Massachusetts. He graduated from Williams College and Andover Theological Seminary a Congregationalist. Fresh from seminary, he joined the entourage of **Adoniram Judson** and others who persuaded the American Board of Commissioners for Foreign Missions to give him an appointment as a single missionary to the East. Rice was commissioned at Salem Tabernacle on February 19, 1812, and sailed for **India**. En route, he shifted to Baptist principles and was baptized by **William Ward** at Serampore. Rice took Judson's advice to return to the United States and build up the **missionary** enterprise among Baptists. This he did with singular devotion for the next two decades. He persuaded the Baptist leaders to expand the idea of **associations** to create a national **convention**, and he worked with **Richard Furman** and **William Staughton** to create a national collegiate and theological institution and denominational center at Washington D.C., the new nation's capital. Rice overextended himself in support of Columbian College and was caught in a difficult debt situation. An investigation was called for in 1826, which essentially exonerated Rice, but reduced his sphere of influence. He lost leadership to the New England interests and after 1827 was solely the agent for the College, itinerating mostly in the southern states where he died. In 1814 Brown University conferred the honorary master of arts degree upon Rice.

RICHARD, TIMOTHY (1845-1919). English Baptist missionary to **China**, born in Ffaldybrenin, Carmarthenshire, **Wales**. He studied at Haverfordwest College (where he won the Hebrew prize) and was appointed in 1869 by the **Baptist Missionary Society** to **China**. He served first at Shanghai, then Chefoo, and Chi'ing Chou-fu. Much influenced by J. Hudson Taylor (1832-1905), Richard desired to move into the interior of China, beyond western influence; in 1874 he gathered the first church in Shantung Province. During the great famine of 1876-1877, he became a household name for his relief efforts, which he summarized in a fourfold plan: famine relief, teaching Christian civilization, introducing new industries, and teaching spiritual truths. Richard founded Whitewright Institute in Sinan on these principles. At the Exeter Hall meetings in 1885 he stressed the social aspects of missionary work, which changed profoundly the direction of the **evangelical** community. From 1900-1910 Richard was the first chancellor of the Western University in Tai-yuan-fu, which he modelled on London University. During furloughs back in Britain and Europe, he participated in Welsh revival meetings, advocated an International Federation of Nations, disarmament, and a Peace Conference at Lucerne; he was also present at the Edinburgh Conference of 1910. In 1905 he was elected general secretary (in Shanghai) of the China Literature Society, which he served until 1914. Richard was one of the most highly honored Baptists of the new century, receiving degrees from Brown University (1895) and the University of Wales (1907), plus the Order of the Double Dragon from the Chinese government (1907). Richard collected his biographical experiences in *Forty-Five Years in China, Reminiscences* (1916).

RICHARDS, HENRY (1851-1928). English and American Baptist missionary, born in Somersetshire, England. With an Anglican upbringing, he worked for his father during his youth. He affiliated with the Congregationalists and then the Baptists, among whom he preached for a time. Alfred Tilly (1821-1905), a Baptist minister and founder of the Livingstone Inland Mission, recruited Richards for that mission, which prompted Richards to take studies in medicine at Harley College. In 1879, Richards arrived in the Congo River region in Africa; in 1884, the Livingstone Inland Mission was transferred to the **American Baptist**

Missionary Union (ABMU) and Richards continued in the new relationship. About 1886, following an intense study of the New Testament, Richards was involved in a remarkable conversion experience among the Bantu peoples: more than 1,000 people accepted the Christian message at Banza Manteke in August 1886, becoming known as the "Pentecost on the Congo." With the financial and prayer support of **Adoniram J. Gordon** in Boston, Richards superintended the establishment of evangelical work in the Upper Congo area and the construction of the mission station. His study of Congolese languages led to an important classification scheme.

RILEY, WILLIAM BELL (1861-1947). American Baptist minister and **fundamentalist** leader, born in Greene County, Indiana. He was educated at Hanover College and Southern Baptist Theological Seminary and served pastorates in Kentucky, Indiana, and Chicago, 1883-1897. In 1897 he became pastor at First Baptist Church, Minneapolis, Minnesota, where he served until 1947. In this role he won many converts to the church, drew national attention for his scorn of **liberal** theology and the **Northern Baptist Convention (NBC)**. He openly opposed Darwinism and tried to convince the Northern Baptist Convention to adopt the New Hampshire Confession of Faith. His services were characterized by **evangelism**, popular music, and a "hymn of invitation." In his **ministry** in Minnesota, he estimated that 7,000 people had joined his church. As a fundamentalist organizer, he started the World's Christian Fundamentals Association, the Northwestern Schools, and a charitable foundation which was to rival the generosity of **John D. Rockefeller**. His chosen successor was a young evangelist from North Carolina, **Billy Graham**. Among Riley's numerous published works were *The Perennial Revival, A Plea for Evangelism* (1904), *The Menace of Modernism* (1917), and *The Conflict of Christianity with Its Counterfeits* (1940).

RIPPON, JOHN (1750-1836). English Baptist minister, hymnist, and editor, born at Tiverton, England. He was educated at the British Academy and entered the Baptist ministry in the early 1770s. Rippon succeeded the eminent **John Gill** as minister at Carter Lane Church in London and became a premier minister of the denomination. He edited the *Baptist Annual Register* (1790-1802), which did much to unite Baptists on both sides of the Atlantic. He is remembered for his popular *Selection of Hymns from the Best Authors* (1787) which made him a comfortable income, as well as for his history of Bunhill Fields, the **Nonconformist** burial ground in London. Rippon was appreciated in the American Colonies for his support of the Independence movement; Brown

University conferred on him the degree of A.M. in 1784 and the D.D. in 1792.

ROBERT, HENRY MARTYN (1837-1923). American soldier and engineer, born at Robertville, South Carolina. Educated at the U.S. Military Academy at West Point, Robert was promoted through the ranks to brigadier general and chief of engineers. Before and following the Civil War, he taught at West Point and chaired the department of practical military engineering. During the war he designed the defenses of Washington and Philadelphia and afterward the causeway and seawall for Galveston, Texas. As a member of Second Baptist Church, Germantown, Pennsylvania, he took an interest in parliamentary procedure and wrote a summary, which became a household manual for due process in organizations. *Robert's Rules of Order* (1876) were widely adopted as the standard manual in Baptist and other churches in the United States. Heavily suggestive of Baptist **polity**, *Robert's Rules* give priority to the rights of the membership of the organization.

ROBERTSON, ARCHIBALD THOMAS (1863-1934). Southern Baptist minister and educator, born at Chatham, Virginia. He was educated at Wake Forest College and Southern Baptist Theological Seminary and held the position of professor of New Testament at Southern Baptist Seminary for 44 years. He concentrated his studies on Greek grammar and produced 45 books, including a *Harmony of the Gospels* (1922), *A Grammar of the Greek New Testament in Light of Historical Research* (1914), and *Word Pictures in the New Testament* (1930-1933). Robertson's stature as a Greek scholar was matched by few; his advocacy of an international Baptist conference led in large part to the establishment of the **Baptist World Alliance** (BWA) in 1905.

ROBINSON, EZEKIEL GILMAN (1815-1894). American Baptist minister and educator, born at Attleborough, Massachusetts. He was educated at Brown University and Newton Theological Institution, after which he was **pastor** of the Baptist church in Norfolk, Virginia, 1842-1845. During his Norfolk ministry, he took a leave to serve as chaplain at the University of Virginia. In 1845-1846 he was pastor at Cambridge, Massachusetts, adjacent to Harvard College. In 1846 he accepted the professorship in biblical interpretation at Western Baptist Theological Seminary in Covington, Kentucky, leaving in 1850 to serve the Ninth Street Baptist Church in Cincinnati, Ohio. Robinson became an illustrious name among Baptists and was elected professor of **theology** at Rochester Theological Seminary in 1853 where he served for two decades. Among his students was **Augustus Hopkins Strong**. In 1872, having served Rochester as president from 1868, he became president of Brown University, which he served until 1889. Having retired from Brown, he taught apologetics and ethics at the University of Chicago from 1892-1894. His published works include *The Relationship of Christianity to Ethics* (1883) and *Christian Evidences* (1895). In 1882 Robinson was the first Baptist to deliver the prestigious Lyman Beecher Lectures at Yale University.

ROBINSON, HENRY WHEELER (1872-1945). English Baptist minister born at Northampton. As a youth he worked for a leather merchant and attended extension lectures at Cambridge University. He studied at Regent's Park College in London and graduated from Edinburgh University with an M.A. in Classics and Philosophy. Later he studied theology under the esteemed Andrew M. Fairbairn (1838-1912) at Mansfield College, Oxford University, and at the Universities of Strassburg and Marburg. Robinson served two churches, Pitlochry (1900-1903) and St. Michaels, Coventry (1903-1906), before joining the faculty at Rawdon College in 1906, where he lectured in church history, doctrine, philosophy and New Testament for 14 years. His scholarship and service to the denomination increased considerably while he was at Rawdon, serving on several boards and committees. In 1920 he became principal of Regent's Park College and devoted his efforts to relocating the school to Oxford University, a process completed 1928-1940. Robinson thus opened the possibility of a Baptist foundation in an ancient university. A well-written scholar, he published the *Century Bible Commentary on Deuteronomy and Joshua* (1907), *The Faith and Life of the Baptists* (1927), *The Christian Experience of the Holy Spirit* (1928), and *Redemption and Revelation* (1942). A prize-winning student at Oxford, Robinson was also awarded the Burkitt Medal for Biblical Studies by the British Academy in 1944. He was president of the Society for Old Testament Study in 1929 and president of the Baptist Historical Society 1921-1945.

ROBINSON, ROBERT (1735-1790). English Baptist minister, born at Swaffham, England. He received an excellent education in grammar school but upon the death of his father, was apprenticed to a trade in London. He heard George Whitefield (1714-1770) preach and was eventually converted and joined Whitefield's circle as a protégé. He adopted Baptist sentiments in the late 1750s and began preaching among the churches. Robinson was called to the Baptist Church at Cambridge and remained their **pastor** from 1761-1783. His preaching drew large crowds and required a new meetinghouse to accommodate 600 persons. Toward the end of his career, he adopted unitarian views, and this caused a decline in his influence among Baptists. He is best remembered for his *History of Baptism* (1790) and *Ecclesiastical Researches* (1792), as well as for hymns which he composed, including "Come Thou Fount of Every Blessing."

ROCKEFELLER, JOHN DAVISON (1839-1937). American industrialist and Baptist philanthropist, born at Richford, New York. Educated in public schools, he started his career as a clerk and cashier in Cleveland, Ohio. In 1862 he entered the oil business, which through wise mergers eventuated in 1873 in the creation of the Standard Oil Company; by the 1890s the Company controlled three-quarters of the oil production and related industries in the United States. In 1896 he retired from active work in oil, and devoted his life to philanthropy, establishing in 1913 the Rockefeller Foundation, which was largely the work of **Frederick Gates**.

Rockefeller's religious leanings began with participation in the Erie Street Baptist Church, Cleveland, Ohio, where he was baptized in the 1850s. Later he helped to construct the 1869 edifice for Euclid Ave Baptist Church in Cleveland, known popularly as "Rockefeller's Church." He served as **Sunday School** superintendent for 60 years and the family attended the church **prayer meetings** and socials; among Mrs. Rockefeller's students in was Charles Evans Hughes (1862-1948). Rockefeller gave generously to Spelman College and Atlanta University, Rochester Theological Seminary, Brown University, and the Riverside Church in New York City, which he helped to create for the ministry of **Harry Emerson Fosdick**. Large gifts to the **Northern Baptist** and **Southern Baptist** pension and annuity boards led to retirement funds for Baptist ministers. In the 1890s with **William R. Harper**, he established the University of Chicago as a premier modern research university for the United States. Because of Rockefeller's frequent generosity to Northern Baptists, conservative elements in the Convention were often critical of his perceived control of Convention policies, but this did not daunt his work.

ROE, CHARLES HILL (1800-1873). English and later American Baptist minister and evangelist, born in King's County, **Ireland**. Early in his life he was converted through the Irish Baptist Mission and he determined to be a Baptist minister; he studied with **William Steadman** at Bradford and married Steadman's daughter. After studies, he served the church at Middleton-in-Teesdale from 1824-1835. In 1834 he became secretary of the **Baptist Home Mission Society** (BHMS) and there he exercised his considerable skills as a fund-raiser and **revivalist** among the churches of the Union. He became **pastor** of Heneage Street Baptist Church in Birmingham from 1841-1851 and thereafter emigrated to the United States to observe the **revival** methods of Charles G. Finney (1792-1875), whom he greatly admired. In 1849, during a visit to England, Finney held revival meetings in Roe's church. Roe decided to emigrate to America and in 1851 he settled at Belvidere, Illinois, following brief periods at Milwaukee, Wisconsin, and New York City. In 1861 Roe became chaplain of a U. S. army regiment and later superintendent of educational work among the Freedmen. An ardent abolitionist, he protested the British support of the southern cause during the American Civil War. In 1858 he became a founder of the first University of Chicago, taught there for two years and served as secretary-treasurer of the University. Roe's autobiography, *A Minister's Life* (1900), provides much data on the transition from Victorian British Baptist life to the Progressive Era in the United States.

ROGER WILLIAMS FELLOWSHIP (RWF). A **voluntary association** of Baptists in the United States dedicated to "fellowship, freedom, and faith" in honor of **Roger Williams**. Founded in 1935 at the annual meeting of the **Northern Baptist Convention** (NBC) in Colorado Springs, Colorado, the fellowship was made up of pastors of the younger generation who felt the need for open, free, and creative discussion of theological ideas and denominational issues. There was a sense of urgency in the midst of renewed **fundamentalist** reaction to perceived modernist tendencies in the Northern (American) Baptist Convention. From the beginning there have been no theological requirements for membership and persons of varying theological perspectives have been members. Beginning in 1952 a three-day conference was held at the University of Chicago with the faculty and trustees of the Baptist Theological Union; in the 1980s this institutional context was transferred to Colgate Rochester Divinity School in Rochester, New York. The RWF has published *Baptist Freedom* since 1944. Generally speaking, the Fellowship articulates a theologically **liberal**, socially active perspective within the **American Baptist Churches, U.S.A.**, although in recent years some wings of the **Southern Baptist** tradition have expressed interest. Prominent members over the years include Gordon Poteat (1891-1986), Dores R. Sharpe (1886-1981), Wilbur E. Saunders (1894-1979), H. Otheman Smith (1901-1971), and Gordon Torgerson (1916-).

ROGERENES. A colonial New England sect which arose in support of the teachings of **John Rogers**. In Great Neck, New York, a congregation was organized in 1674 around the principles of honoring the Sabbath on Saturdays, believer's **baptism**, non-resistance, and a healing **ministry** for the sick. The Rogerene church was opposed to formal prayers and conducted itself like a Quaker meeting. Rogers, however, denied that his church was Quaker in orientation, doubtless to avoid the stigmas attached to that group. The Rogerenes practiced some outlandish behavior among the other Baptists, such as appearing unclothed in public to affirm their freedom in Christ. No evidence of their existence beyond Rogers's ministry survives. Their presence on the colonial religious scene, however, did lend credence to the adversarial case that claimed some Baptists were extreme sectarians.

ROGERS, JOHN (1648-1721). Baptist minister born at New London, Connecticut. Little is known of his early years, except that his father was a well-to-do baker. In 1674 while visiting Newport, Rhode Island, John encountered the **Seventh Day Baptists** and was converted to their principles. Shunned by his family for this new direction, he relocated to Long Island where at Great Neck he organized a church. His principles included sabbatarianism, believer's **baptism**, and open membership for Negroes. Eschewed by other Christians, the group came to be called **"Rogerenes"** and gained a reputation for literalistic interpretation of the bible. Rogers was imprisoned in 1694 for blaspheming Governor Gurdon Saltonstall (1666-1724) of Connecticut. Concerned for those in need, he died of smallpox while in Boston caring for those stricken with the disease. Rogers's publications include *A Description of the True Shepherds of Christ's Flock and also of the Antiochristian Ministers* (1695?) and *Epistle to the Church of Christ Call'd Quakers, and to the Seventh Day Baptists* (1705).

ROGERS, WILLIAM (1751-1824). American Baptist minister and military chaplain, born at Newport, Rhode Island. He was the first student in the College of Rhode Island under **James Manning**. In 1770 he was baptized at Newport and two years later became **pastor** at First Baptist Church, Philadelphia. Among his adherents was the celebrated physician, Dr. Benjamin Rush (1746-1813). In 1775 he was named chaplain to the Pennsylvania regiments in the Revolution and he served in that capacity until 1780. George Washington (1732-1799) knew Rogers well and esteemed his work. In addition to his pastoral work he taught oratory and belles lettres at the University of Pennsylvania. For two years, 1816 and 1817, Rogers served as a delegate to the Pennsylvania State General Assembly. He was elected a vice president of the **General Missionary Convention** and was one of the architects of the American Baptist national organization. In 1814 Rogers joined with others of the **Baptist Board of Foreign Missions** (BBFM) in opposing appointments of single women missionaries, and in protest he dissociated himself from the Board for a time. Rogers's journal (1879), written while he served with the expedition of General John Sullivan (1740-1795) in 1779 provides a unique insight into the defeat of the Six Nations Indian confederacy.

ROMANIA. In addition to an appreciation for early **Anabaptist** influences in their history, there are four roots of the Baptist movement in what is now Romania. In 1845 Karl Scharschmiedt (1820-?), a disciple of **J. G. Oncken**, baptized converts near Bucharest. Russian Baptist immigrants from **Ukraine** began a congregation at Cataloi in 1862. Constantin Adorian, a graduate of the seminary in Hamburg, started several churches in the vicinity of Bucharest and Dobrogea. Over 100 Hungarian-speaking churches were started in Transylvania between 1871 and 1910 (where Baptists are referred to as "Repenters"), and in the region of Bessarabia in 1912 a congregation was started at Cetatea Alba (Akkerman), which led to the establishment of a Bessarabia Baptist Convention.

Baptists received official government recognition in 1905 and formed a union in 1919; by 1940 the All Romanian Union of Baptist Churches was established. A theological school was started in 1921, with assistance from U.S. **Southern Baptists**, who accepted responsibility for mission in Romania as of the **London Conference of 1920**. In recent years Romanian Baptists have also been influential in establishing ethnic congregations in **Serbia**, later Yugoslavia, beginning in 1931. In 1988 the **Association of Baptists for World Evangelism** (ABWE) began a mission in Romania, the **Baptist Bible Fellowship** (BBF) started its work in the country in 1990, and in 1991 the **Conservative Baptist** Foreign Mission Society (CBFMS) opened a mission at Oradea.

As of 1995 there were 1,323 churches and 75,000 members in the Uniunea Bisericilor Crestine Baptists din Romania and 100 churches and 9,081 members in the Conventia Bisericilor Crestine Baptiste Maghiare Din Romania. The Romanian Baptist Union publishes a periodical, *The Christian Guide*.

ROSTAN, CASIMIR (1774-1833). French scientist, diplomat, and Baptist missionary pastor, born at Marseilles, **France**. He was educated at the College of Tournon and joined his father's mercantile business. He continued to study oriental languages, natural sciences, and archaeology, an this led to an extensive tour to the eastern Mediterranean in 1792-1798. He became devoted to the cause of Greek nationalism and was instrumental in proclaiming political liberty among the Greek islands at

Ithaca in 1798. Frustrated in his attempts to secure a position in the government service, he returned in 1799 to Marseilles where he became professor of botany and natural history at the Botanical Gardens; he also edited a religious and philosophical journal and became city archivist, owing to his erudition.

Rostan was converted to **evangelical** Christianity and attached himself to the Society of Christian Morals where he again developed an interest in **Greece**. In 1825 he served in Havana, **Cuba**, as French Consul, after which he went to the United States in 1827. He became a minister, supported the revivalist tradition, and was involved with missionary societies while in the United States. In 1832 Rostan returned to Paris, began an **evangelical** church which was supported by the Society of Christian Morals and the **American Baptist Board of Foreign Missions** (BBFM) as one of its first forays into European missions.

ROUMANIAN BAPTIST ASSOCIATION OF AMERICA. The first Roumanian Baptist congregation in the United States was formed in 1910 in Cincinnati, Ohio, largely of recent immigrants from Europe. Within three years, eight small churches in Illinois, Indiana, and Ohio formed at Cincinnati the Roumanian Baptist Association to further cooperation and mission work among themselves. The Association was a simple **voluntary** union which published *Crestinus* (The Christian) from 1913. At its peak of organization, the Association included about 20 congregations and 1,200 members. In 1940 the Association joined temporarily with the **Northern Baptist Convention** (NBC).

ROUSSY, LOUIS (1812-1880). French **evangelical** missionary and later Canadian Baptist minister, born at Vevey, **Switzerland**. His parentage was Huguenot and as a young man he was apprenticed as a mason. He engaged in work as a **colporteur** in **France** and in the 1830s he served as a missionary for the Lausanne Institute. In 1835 **Henriette Feller**, a co-laborer in the Institute, invited Roussy to accompany her to a mission among the French of Quebec. First at Montreal and later at Grande Ligne, Roussy and Feller planted the first Protestant congregation in French-speaking Canada, out of which grew the Grande Ligne Mission and School. He superintended the construction of the school and mission buildings in 1840 and baptized new converts to the mission. Essentially **pastor** or preacher at the Grande Ligne congregation, 1837 to 1879-1880, Roussy was baptized in 1847 and enabled the Grande Ligne Church to affiliate with the Baptists in 1849. He continued to evangelize in Quebec and plant new congregations until his death.

RUSHBROOKE, JAMES HENRY (1870-1947). British Baptist minister and denominational leader, born at Bethnal Green, England. Baptized by **John Clifford**, he was educated at Midland Baptist College and London University, after which on a Pegg Scholarship he studied at the University of Berlin where he greatly admired Adolf von Harnack (1851-1930). In 1902 he commenced a pastorate at St. Mary's Gate Baptist Church in Derby, which he served until 1907. Thereafter he was pastor at Archway Road, London (1907-1910), and Hampstead Garden Suburb Free Church (1910-1920), a new congregation which brought together Baptist and Congregational elements. In 1919 Rushbrooke was selected to conduct a nine-week tour of post-war Europe for the **Baptist World Alliance** (BWA); this was owing to his familiarity with Europe and his ability to speak German fluently. In 1920-1925 the **London Conference** appointed him Commissioner for Europe, which involved supervision of relief, development, and mission for the united Baptist community. Rushbrooke became vice president of the BWA in 1926 and from 1926 to 1939 he served as general secretary of the organization. During the war years from 1939 to 1945 as president of the Alliance, Rushbrooke made several trips on behalf of the Baptist community, personally uniting the denominational family. Rushbrooke's publications give evidence of his critical role in the making of an international Baptist identity: *Baptist Work in Europe* (1920), *Baptists as Champions of Religious Freedom* (1938), and *Baptist Reconstruction in Europe* (1945).

RUSSIA. European Baptist pioneer, **J. G. Oncken** first visited Russia in 1864. He interceded on behalf of persecuted **evangelicals** in the south of Russia and planned a missionary venture into Russia. The first recorded **baptism** in what is now Russia occurred in the Kura River in August 1867 amongst the Molokans, an evangelical, non-sacramental sect in the country. Nikita Voronin (1840-1905) was the leader of this group, which called itself "baptist" because of their open professions of faith by baptism. Vasili G. Pavlov (1854-1924) was another leader of a pietistic group in Tiflis; he was baptized by Voronin and became a patriarch of the Baptist movement in Russia. Several aggressive Baptist congregations thus arose in the Caucasus region in Taurida, Samara, Astrakan, Tiflis, and Mihilev. Other congregations were located in Kiev, Rostov, and Moscow. On May 1, 1884, a Russian Baptist Union was formed at Novo Vasil'evka, largely the initiative of Germans living in Russia, but with solid Russian leadership.

Another important pioneer was Ivan S. Prokhanov (1869-1935), who was associated with the first Baptists in St. Petersburg and came to lead that part of the movement known as the Evangelical Christians. In

1888 Prokanov went to St. Petersburg as a student and developed a **dissenter** renewal among some Orthodox Christians. Early in his career Prokhanov developed a strategy of uniting Russian evangelicals (Baptists and others) as an alternative Christian movement to the Orthodox Church. In 1890 he started a periodical called *Besseda* (Dialogue) and left for theological studies at Bristol Baptist College in England and the Universities of Berlin and Paris, during which time he mailed his paper into Russia and published a hymnal, *Gusli*. He returned to Russia as an engineer and professor, also involved in preaching. Prokanov spearheaded a plan for a Baptist College (which the fall of the Czarist regime precluded) and he helped to organize in 1909 the first All-Russian Evangelical Christian Conference.

Elsewhere in the Russian Empire, other religious forces helped shape the Baptist tradition. In Ukraine it was the **Stundist** movement which gave birth to many of the first Baptist congregations in the 1880s.

By 1914 the two groups, All-Russian Baptists and the Evangelical-Christians, numbered over 100,000 members, even under intense persecution by the government. During the period between the wars, Baptists, like other evangelical groups, attempted to organize their own communal settlements, only to be halted by the government. One such scheme involved Prokhanov's 1926-1927 plan for a "City of the Sun" to be called "Evangelsk" in Siberia. Other advances during this era included a Baptist Congress at Moscow in 1926, at which 365 candidates were publicly baptized in the Moscow River, and in 1927 a Russian **bible** was printed in Leningrad and a theological seminary was opened in Moscow with Ivanov-Klishnikoff as rector. In 1929 the seminary was closed and its leaders sent to Siberia.

Despite persecution under Joseph Stalin (1879-1953) in the 1930s and 1940s during which time many churches were closed and the numbers of Baptists significantly decreased, Baptist growth resumed in the post-Stalinist era in Russia and the U.S.S.R., totalling perhaps as many as 3,000 churches and a half million members. In 1944 a major union occurred of the Baptists and Evangelical Christians; in 1945 the Union of Christians of Evangelical Faith, a Pentecostal **association**, joined to create the All Union Council of Evangelical Christians Baptists (AUCECB). In the late 1940s, however, many of the former Pentecostal churches dropped out of the Union. A fourth component in the history of the AUCECB, the Mennonite Brethren, was also added in 1963.

With the disintegration of the Soviet Union in 1991, a Baptist seminary was started in Odessa and a second theological program at Moscow began in 1993. A magazine, *Bratski Vestnik* (Brotherly Herald), has been published since 1945. Other Baptist efforts in Russia include the

U.S. **Baptist General Conference,** which had a mission in Siberia from 1922 to 1946.

In a context of isolation caused by persecution and ostracism, a number of Baptist pastors and congregations in the 1940s refused to join the formation of the AUCECB. Two primary groups, the "Prokofievites" and the Initsiativniki or "Action-group," coalesced to form a separatist movement known as the Council of Churches of the Evangelical Christians and Baptists (CCECB) in 1965. This body of "pure" Baptists and like-minded evangelicals opposed centralization of authority in the AUCECB, government registration of churches, and what they perceived to be a lessening of evangelistic interests. Leaders associated with various wings of this movement, sometimes described as the "non-registered or underground" Baptists, include Alexei F. Prokofviev (1915-), Gennadi K. Kryuchkov (1926-), and Georgi Vins (1924-). Worldwide attention was drawn to the group because of Vins's persecution by the Soviet authorities in the 1960s and 1970s, and the intervention of Baptist U.S. president Jimmy Carter in the late 1970s. In 1969 and later, several of these congregations were reconciled to the AUCECB. In recent years, the Initsiativniki have been associated with Donetsk Christian University in Donetsk, **Ukraine**, in which the president and some of the faculty are associated with this movement.

With the reordering of Baptist life after the organizational demise of the All Union Council of Evangelicals-Baptists in the U.S.S.R. in 1992, mainstream Russian Baptists reconstituted themselves as the Soyuz Yevangel'skikh Khristian-baptistov Rossiyskoy Federatsyi (Union of Evangelical Christians-Baptists of the Russian Federation). This body conducts denominational business and mission from headquarters in Moscow and relates to the European Baptist Federation, the Euro-Asiatic Federation of Evangelical Christians-Baptists, and the **Baptist World Alliance**. In 1992 the **Conservative Baptist** Foreign Mission Society opened a cooperative mission with Peter Deyneka Russian Ministries and the Evangelical Alliance Mission, and the **Baptist Bible Fellowship** (BBF) opened a mission in Russia in 1993.

As of 1995 there were 1,200 churches with 92,000 members affiliated with the Soyuz Yevangel'skikh Khristian-baptistov Rossijskoy Federatsi. Presently, there are four theological schools in Russia: Irkutsk, Moscow (2), and Volgograd.

RUSSIAN-UKRAINIAN EVANGELICAL BAPTIST UNION, U.S.A. (RUEBU). Founded in 1919 in Philadelphia, Pennsylvania, the Russian-Ukrainian Baptist Union united many of the immigrant churches in the United States and lends support to churches and projects in **Russia**,

Belarus, and **Ukraine.** Originally there were 20 congregations in the United States and **Canada,** located mostly in the Northeast and Great Lakes regions. Headquartered in Ashford, Connecticut, since 1952 and also in Union, New Jersey, with close ties to the **American Baptist Churches** and the **Baptist World Alliance** (BWA), the Union includes 24 churches and 1,200 members. The Union publishes *Sower of Truth* (1919-) and *Evangelical Baptist Herald* (1952-), formerly *The Pilot* (1934-52), together the oldest Russian language religious magazine in print.

RWANDA. Danish Baptists pioneered mission work in what became Rwanda in 1938. In 1977 **Southern Baptist** missionaries entered Rwanda and began work at Kigali. The **Conservative Baptist Foreign Mission Society** (CBFMS) established its mission also at Kigali in 1965 and later established the Association des Eglises Baptistes du Rwanda.

As of 1995 there were 64 churches and 53,000 members affiliated with the Union des Eglises Baptistes du Rwanda, and 114 churches with 53,202 members affiliated with the Association des Eglises Baptistes du Rwanda. Presently there are nine Baptist-related theological schools or colleges in Rwanda: Bugesera, Butare (3), Gisenyi, Kigali (3), Nyabisindu, Nyantanga, and Ruhengeri.

RYLAND, JOHN (1753-1825). English Baptist minister and educator, born at Warwick, England. Ryland was self-taught in the Classics, and as a prodigy, he taught in his father's school at age 15. Beginning in 1771 he assisted his father in the Northampton Church, ultimately becoming sole **pastor** in 1786. In 1793 he was called to be pastor of the Broadmead Church in Bristol and the president of the Academy there. From 1815 to 1825 he was secretary of the **Baptist Missionary Society** (BMS), which he helped to found. A Calvinist devoted to the position of American Congregationalist theologian/pastor Jonathan Edwards (1703-1758), Ryland inveighed against perceived Pelagianism and Antinomianism. He was credited with being a principal force in the revival of the churches in the West Country and the upgrading of Bristol Academy to a college status at the turn of the 19th century. He was a well-known Oriental scholar and was fond of natural history. Ryland's published works, which include *Advice to Students of Divinity* (1770), *The Difficulties of the Christian Ministry and the Means of Surmounting Them* (1802), and *The Practical Influence of Evangelical Religion* (1819), give evidence of his concern for ministerial training and spiritual nurture. Brown University in Rhode Island conferred on Ryland the doctor of divinity degree in 1792.

RYLAND, JOHN COLLETT (1723-1792). English Baptist minister, born at Bourton-on-Water, England. Ryland was a consistent Calvinist who exemplified the **Particular Baptist** tradition. He studied at Bristol Baptist Academy under **Bernard Foskett** and served congregations at Warwick, Northampton, and Enfield. He also managed schools in these villages. Ryland is best remembered as a gruff Calvinist delegate at the annual meeting of the Northamptonshire Baptist Association in 1792 who accused **William Carey** of enthusiasm and silenced his proposal about missionary endeavors. **Robert Hall** was terrified of Ryland when, as a child, Hall was admitted to Ryland's academy at Northampton. Ryland was considered ahead of his time in supporting the American War for Independence, a position for which Brown University rewarded him the honorary doctor of divinity degree in 1769. Ryland was one of the most widely published Baptists of his era, producing over 50 works, including *List of Baptist Churches in Great Britain* (1753), *A Contemplation on the Insufficiency of Reason* (1775), *The Preceptor, or General Repository of Useful Information* (1775), *An English and Greek Grammar* (1777), and *A Body of Divinity in Miniature* (1791).

S

SACRAMENTS. See **Baptism; Lord's Supper**.

SAKER, ALFRED (1814-1880). English Baptist missionary, born in Borough Green, Wrotham, England. In his youth he worked at the Devonport Dockyard and was active in the local Baptist church. Inspired by stories of Africa and the mission of **William Knibb**, Alfred and his wife Helen Jessup, offered themselves for service with the **Baptist Missionary Society** (BMS). They sailed in 1843, stopping briefly in **Jamaica** where they met Knibb, and landed finally on the island of Fernando Po, West Africa, in 1844. In 1845 he began work among the Dualla tribe on the mainland in **Cameroon**; he learned the language and ultimately translated the **Scriptures** into Dualla (1872). Despite the odds against Europeans surviving in the African tropical climate, Saker believed the British should colonize Cameroon as an entry to the interior of Africa and he set about to create a religious colony at Victoria. He preached, built churches and schools, and advocated the mission to a reluctant BMS board in London over the next three decades. From the coast he created settlements well into the interior and established a firm footing for British Baptist African missions. He became a virtual administrator of the territory, arbitrating tribal disputes, and influencing a number of later Africa missionaries, including **George Grenfell**. Saker's publications include a *Grammatical Elements of the Dualla Language* (1855), *Dualla Hymnbook* (1859), and translations of the **bible** into Dualla (1872-1882).

SAMPEY, JOHN RICHARD (1863-1946). Southern Baptist minister and educator, born at Fort Deposit, Alabama. He was educated at Howard College and Southern Baptist Theological Seminary. Upon graduation from seminary, Sampey was selected by **John A. Broadus** to assist him in teaching New Testament and homiletics. Later he studied Hebrew under **William Rainey Harper** at the University of Chicago and he adopted Harper's "inductive method." Eventually he held the chair in Old Testament and taught as many as 7,000 students in English and Hebrew. He authored textbooks in Old Testament and was editor of the Uniform **Sunday School** Lesson Series for 40 years, which influenced thousands of lay students in scores of Protestant denominations. In 1928 he followed **E. Y. Mullins** as president of Southern Baptist Theological Seminary and in the course of his 13 years in that office liquidated its debt. In 1935 Sampey served as president of the **Southern Baptist Convention** (SBC) and later in the decade he represented Southern Baptists at the Conference on Faith and Order and the Conference on Life and Work of what would become the World Council of Churches. Sampey was widely published and a chair in Old Testament at Southern Baptist Theological Seminary was named in his honor. He was the author of several significant works, including *Syllabus for Old Testament Study* (1903), *The Heart of the Old Testament* (1908), and *The International Lesson System* (1911).

SANDEMANIANS. Term used to designate followers of Robert Sandeman (1718-1771), the son-in-law of **John Glas**, a Scottish **dissenter**. A native of Perth, **Scotland**, Sandeman brought to London the ideas of recovering primitive Christianity and this created distress in the greater Baptist community in the 1760s. In 1764 he moved to Boston and planted several Sandemanian meetings, notably in Boston, Portsmouth, New Hampshire and Danbury, Connecticut, where Sandeman died and was buried. Two congregations in New England were known to have absorbed the Sandemanian position: Stratfield, Connecticut, and Chelmsford, Massachusetts.

Among the Sandemanian principles were literalistic interpretation of **Scripture**, multiple ruling elders of a congregation, unpaid clergy, celebrating the **Lord's Supper** each Lord's Day, **footwashing**, and a contempt for an educated ministry and proselytizing. Some were said to reject the practice of family prayer. Sandeman often spoke of faith as an intellectual assent and rejected the necessity of spiritual conversion. Some of Sandeman's followers held that the atonement of Christ as an external act of God's grace, was sufficient to human salvation. **Isaac Backus** wrote a polemic against Sandeman's teachings in 1767, and **Andrew Fuller** published in 1810 a major treatise in opposition to Sandemanianism. Sandemanianism lost out among American Baptists who preferred to emphasize heartfelt religious experience over legalistic formulations of Calvinism.

SAUNDERS, EDWARD MANNING (1829-1916). Canadian Baptist minister and historian, born at Tremont, Nova Scotia. A graduate of Acadia College, he served pastorates at Berwick and Halifax, Nova Scotia (1867-1881). In 1881 he resigned from Granville Street Baptist Church, Halifax, to edit and publish the *Christian Visitor*, the principal Baptist paper in the Maritime Provinces. He published a *History of the Baptist Churches of the Maritime Provinces*, long considered a standard. Saunders based much of his work on the earlier unpublished manuscript of **John M. Cramp**.

SAUNDERS, JOHN (1806-1859). English missionary and Australian Baptist minister, born in London, England. A member of **Edward Steane**'s Baptist church at Cold Harbor Lane, Camberwell, he studied for a career in the law, but felt called to missionary service. He studied at the University of Edinburgh, devoting some of his time to itinerant preaching. During the early 1830s he planted churches at Mason Court and Ball's Pond, and served an existing congregation at Shacklewell, all three near London. In 1834 he applied to the **Baptist Missionary Society** (BMS) and was referred to a group in **Australia** who were seeking a minister. Saunders and his wife, Elizabeth, arrived at Sydney, New South Wales, and in 1835 began preaching services at South Head Lighthouse and later at Court House Room. In 1836 this meeting became the Bathurst Street Baptist Chapel, the first congregation of the Baptists in Australia. From this strategic point, Saunders conducted **evangelistic** tours and helped to form several of the other churches in what became the New South Wales Baptist Association. Saunders is remembered as the first Baptist missionary to Australia.

SAVANNAH RESOLUTIONS. A series of resolutions presented on May 13, 1861, to the annual meeting of the **Southern Baptist Convention** (SBC) in Savannah, Georgia. In the midst of the secessionist movement to form the Confederate States of America, a Special Committee on the State of the Country was established to make appropriate recommendations to the Baptist churches of the southern states. **Richard Fuller** of Baltimore, Maryland, a state which had not yet seceded, made the report, which included nine resolutions disclaiming blame for dissolution of the Union, approving of the formation of the Confederacy, and accusing the U.S. government of "lawless terror in the North." Other resolutions included an injunction to prayer and an observance of a day of humiliation, fasting, and prayer in the month of June. The resolutions were signed by 10 leading pastors, including Richard Fuller, **James B. Taylor, R. B. C. Howell**, and Basil **Manly**, Sr. and transmitted to the Confederate Congress at Montgomery, Alabama. The Savannah Resolutions became a statement of rebellion in the North and Fuller was especially vilified for his part in the process. As president of the Convention he was targeted by northern sympathizers and the 1861 SBC convention delegates therefore offered their collective prayers for his safety.

SCARBOROUGH, LEE RUTLAND (1870-1945). Southern Baptist evangelist, pastor, and educator, born at Colfax, Louisiana. He was reared in hardship in frontier Texas in a cowboy society where his father was a Baptist minister. His education included bachelor's degrees from Baylor and Yale Universities, plus additional work at Southern Baptist Theological Seminary. Upon completion of his studies, he served as pastor at First Baptist, Cameron (1896-1901) and First Baptist, Abilene, Texas (1901-1908). Scarborough was in great demand as an evangelist and came to prominence in the Texas Baptist Convention and the **Southern Baptist Convention** (SBC). In 1919 he was director of the Convention-wide $75 Million Campaign, following which he held strategic positions in the Baptist General Convention of Texas and president of the SBC, 1939-1940. He was named to the first chair of **evangelism** at Southwestern Baptist Theological Seminary in 1908 and president at Southwestern (1914-45) during its period of greatest growth. In 1936 he made an evangelistic tour of South America for the **Foreign Mission Board** (FMB) and drew international attention to his gifts. Scarborough was the author of over 30 books, among which were *Christ's Militant Kingdom* (1924), *How Jesus Won Men* (1926), and *A Modern School of the Prophets* (1939). He was awarded the honorary doctorate by Baylor and Union Universities.

SCHMIDT, NATHANIEL (1862-1939). American Swedish Baptist educator, born at Hudiksvall, Sweden. He was educated at the University of Stockholm and Colgate University where he received an M.A. degree. His mentor at Colgate was **Ebenezer Dodge** a **liberal** and irenic theologian. After a brief return to **Sweden** he was pastor of the Swedish Baptist congregation in New York City, 1887-1888. Colgate invited Schmidt back to teach languages in 1888 and in 1891 at 29 years old he was given a professorship in Semitic Languages and Literature in view of his attainments in scholarship. He began and edited the seminary's scholarly journal in 1892. During the 1890s Schmidt brought concern to the faculty and trustees for his application of scientific principles to biblical interpretation. Ultimately accused of holding **unitarian** views and weakening the confidence of young seminarians in the authority of **Scripture**, Schmidt was dismissed from the faculty at Colgate in 1896. He was immediately offered an endowed chair in Semitics at Cornell University by **Jacob Schurman**. He became one of America's most distinguished scholars at Cornell through his retirement in 1932. His major works included *The Prophet of Nazareth* (1905), in which he asserted that Jesus did not claim to be the Messiah, and *The Coming Religion* (1930), in which he advocated new religious ideals, free, ethical, and scientific as well as devoid of creeds and dogma. He also authored 1,500 encyclopedia articles. Schmidt was president of the Society of Biblical Literature in 1914 and the Jewish Institute awarded him the degree D.H.L. in 1931.

SCHURMAN, JACOB GOULD (1854-1942). Canadian and later American Baptist educator, born at Freetown, Prince Edward Island. Raised in a Baptist home, he was educated at Prince of Wales College, Acadia College, and the University of London where he completed his B.A. with first class honours. For a time he studied religion and moral philosophy at Manchester New College under James Martineau (1805-1900), and then he studied concurrently at the University of Edinburgh where he earned a D.Sc. and the University of London where he took an M.A. He studied further in Germany at the Universities of Heidelberg, Berlin, and Göttingen. In 1880-1882 Schurman taught English at Acadia College and moved to Dalhousie University, 1882-1886, also teaching literature and metaphysics. Returning to the United States, in 1886 he took a position at Cornell University and developed a close friendship with Henry W. Sage (1814-1897) who endowed a chair in Christian Ethics and Mental Philosophy which Schurman occupied. In 1890 Schurman was named dean of the Sage School of Philosophy which included many of his students in what would become known as the "Cornell School" of philosophy. Schurman was president of Cornell from 1892 to 1920 during which time he developed a prestigious university and pioneered women faculty appointments, racial equality in student life, and state support for certain programs. Even before his departure from

Cornell, he followed orthodox Republican politics and was rewarded with a string of diplomatic posts: chaiman of a **Philippines** Commission (1899-1900); minister to **Greece** and Montenegro (1912-1913); ambassador to **China** (1921-1925); and ambassador to **Germany** (1925-1930). The author of numerous books on foreign policy and philosophic subjects, Schurman's most important works were *Kantian Ethics and the Ethics of Evolution* (1881) and *Agnosticism and Religion* (1896).

SCOTCH BAPTISTS. Term applied in the Baptist heritage of Scotland to those churches in Scotland which were a native outgrowth of reactions to the Church of Scotland and its offspring. Also known as "Scots" Baptists, these churches are distinguished from the English Baptist churches of **Scotland**.

In the early 1760s various leaders of the Anti-Burgher section of the Session Church met to discuss articles of church government and polity. Among them were Robert Carmichael (?-1774) and **Archibald McLean** who had been associated for a time with the **Glasite** movement in Glasgow. They agreed that **baptism** was for believers only. Soon after Carmichael moved to Edinburgh to be the pastor of an independent church there. In 1765 Carmichael withdrew from the Independent church and formed a small congregation at the historic Mary Magdalene Chapel in the Cowgate. Carmichael applied to **John Gill** of London to be baptized and this occurred at the famous baptistery at the Barbicon on October 9, 1765, in the public company of about 600 people. The "mother church" of the Scotch Baptists was thus formed the following November at Edinburgh. After Carmichael's death in 1779, **Archibald McLean** became the principal figure in the evolution of the movement.

Among the doctrinal and polity standards which McLean had derived from the Glasites or achieved from his own **bible** study were strict communion, a plurality of **pastors**, a body of **deacons**, celebration of the **Lord's Supper** every Lord's Day, the Agape or **Love Feast**, public prayers, and contributions to the poor. Unanimity in decision-making and marriage only among Christians were also practiced. From the Glasites, the Scotch Baptists held to the absolute independence of each congregation.

As the movement spread throughout Scotland and into northern England, various splits occurred. In the 1790s the Scotch Baptists worked closely with the revivals begun by the **Haldane** brothers. James Haldane was baptized in 1808 and for a time the **Haldane Movement** moved upon Baptist principles. The Haldanes, however, were more tolerant on the question of baptism than were the Scotch Baptists and rifts occurred among the Haldane churches. Eventually some of the congregations permanently joined the Scotch Baptists, while others pursued an independent tradition, which would later be associated with the Campbellite Movement. See **Campbell, Alexander**.

In Canadian Baptist heritage the term "Scotch Baptist" has a slightly modified usage. As Haldanite Baptists emigrated to Upper and Lower **Canada** in the first two decades of the 19th century, some were referred to as "Scottish" Baptists and settled in the Ottawa Valley among the other Baptist churches. Some of these congregations evolved into the mainstream community, notably behind the leadership of men like **John Gilmour**. Others however, moved in a more Glasite direction and came under the influence of the Campbellite movement in the United States. Eventually these churches joined the Disciples of Christ denomination and were referred to at an interim stage as "Scotch Baptists." See also **Scotland**.

SCOTLAND. The Baptist movement in Scotland is the result of Baptist witness from England during the Commonwealth era (1648-1660) and indigenous growth. The earliest churches, composed of mostly English folk, were Leith (1652), Cupar (1652), and Perth (1653). These churches were formed from Baptists serving in English regiments during the Cromwell occupation. Indigenous Scottish Baptist life is dated from the Keiss church, founded in 1750 by Sir William Sinclair. Two streams of indigenous Scottish Baptists were prominent: the first, composed of dissenters from the Church of Scotland, Independents, Old Scots, **Glasites**, and Bereans (sometimes referred to as Scotch Baptists) and the second, those involved in the **Haldanite Movement**. The first Scottish Baptist Association dates from 1835; it was known as the Baptist Union of Scotland after 1843 until it lapsed in 1856. The current Baptist Union of Scotland dates from 1869 and includes ministerial funds, auxiliary associations, a women's organization, and district associations. Since 1908 the Union has been affiliated with the Baptist Union of Great Britain and Ireland. The doctrinal stance of the early Scottish Baptists was identical to that of the English Particular Baptists: in 1653 a Scottish version of the 1644 London Confession was produced. Since affiliation with the British **Baptist Union**, a common doctrinal understanding is assumed.

As of 1995 there were 172 churches with 15,781 members affiliated with the Baptist Union of Scotland. A theological college has operated at Glasgow since 1894. The Union publishes *The Scottish Baptist [Magazine] (1875-)*. The **Baptist Bible Fellowship** (BBF) opened a mission in Scotland in 1983.

SCREVEN, WILLIAM (1629-1713). English businessman and colonial American Baptist pastor, probably born in Somerset, England. Little is known of his background, except that it is assumed that one of the reasons he emigrated to the colonies was to escape religious difficulty. In the region of northern coastal Massachusetts (present-day southern Maine) Screven operated a trading business which eventually extended to southern Carolina colony. Convinced of a baptistic position sometime in 1681, Screven declined to have his child baptized in the Kittery Congregational Church. He travelled to Boston to confer with the Baptist Church there, and he was licensed to the **ministry** in January 1682. Returning to his home at Kittery, he formed a congregation and immediately drew the ire of authorities. Before the York County civil authorities, Screven maintained that infant **baptism** was an **ordinance** of the devil and he was sent to jail for his assertion. Upon release, he and his family and the friends who joined him in the congregation he had organized, ultimately about 1696 moved to the Cooper River near what became Charleston, South Carolina. There they joined a small, mostly General Baptist congregation, which had been constituted about a decade previously. Screven's descendants thus became the seed of the First Baptist Church of Charleston, and, by extension, the first Baptist congregation in what is now the southern United States.

SCRIPTURE, AUTHORITY OF. A basic Baptist tenet is a firm conviction that the final authority in determining faith and practice is Scripture. Baptists have universally described Scripture as the Word of God which is revealed to the Church in order that God's people may know God's will. Baptists also understand that within a body of believers, Scripture is a guide and comfort for new life in Christ. In the 17th century context, Baptists rejected the authority of ecclesiastical structures, especially the Church of England. Later, Baptists likewise moved away from the presbyterial system while empowering their own **associations** for specific tasks. More important were the canonical scriptures of the Old and New Testaments which were variously described as "sufficient," "infallible," "perfect," "divinely inspired," "without error," "the final authority." **Polity** manuals, theological treatises, and personal narratives all evince a Baptist understanding of Scripture as specifically relevant and applicable in people's lives as well as the corporate congregation. In each of the **confessions of faith**, countless Scripture references, notably 2 Timothy 3:15-17 and 2 Peter 1:19-20, are used to buttress theological assertions.

Baptist respect for the authority of Scripture led the denomination to take a premier role in the translation and distribution of Scriptures in the 19th century. Baptists helped to form the British and Foreign Bible Society in 1804 and the American and Foreign Bible Society in 1816. Baptist missionaries, such as like **William Carey**, **Adoniram Judson**, and **William Dean**, pioneered the translation of Scriptures in the missionary context. In a controversial movement in the American Bible Society, it was Baptists who started new **bible** associations to promote certain translations of the bible, notably the American Bible Union in 1850. Baptist scholars and educators also produced a number of bible commentaries and thematic studies of the bible through both denominational and other publishers.

In the later 19th century German higher criticism had influence in biblical studies and theology at key northern Baptist seminaries in the United States, notably Colgate, Rochester, Newton, Crozer, and the University of Chicago, and noticeably at smaller schools, including Southern Baptist Theological Seminary and Cobb Divinity School. At the University of Chicago, under the direction of **William Rainey Harper**, the critical approach was dominant. This caused a widespread reaction among churches over modernistic teachings which were perceived to reduce the authority of Scripture. The result was the birth of **fundamentalism**, which holds as its key doctrine an unassailably inerrant bible. New schools grew up to train leaders along these lines, for instance Northern Baptist Theological Seminary in Chicago, a response to the University of Chicago, and The Eastern Baptist Theological Seminary, a reaction to Crozer Theological Seminary. Eventually, this same phenomenon occurred in the Southern Baptist Convention, where Southern Baptist Theological Seminary and others were deemed to be "liberal" on the matter of Scriptural authority, and other institutions emerged to protect the authority of the bible. In Canada at McMaster University, the influx of critical thinking led to the establishment of the hyper-orthodox Toronto Baptist Seminary.

The overall Baptist community in North America has often become badly divided over the meaning and use of Scripture. Wide divergence exists in the denomination over the issue of authority, sometimes giving the impression that liberal thinkers are closer to mainstream Protestants and **evangelical**/fundamentalists are closer to independant, orthodox Presbyterian, and Brethren groups. See also **Bible**.

SEARS, BARNAS (1802-1880). American Baptist minister and educator, born at Sandisfield, Massachusetts. He was educated at Brown University and Newton Theological Institution. In 1828-1829 he was **pastor** at First Baptist, Hartford, Connecticut, but resigned for health reasons to take a faculty position teaching biblical theology at Hamilton Literary and

Theological Institution in Hamilton, New York. The leading member of the Hamilton faculty, he took a study leave to travel in Europe in 1833, making the acquaintance of numerous church leaders and theologians, including professors August Tholuck (1799-1877) and Wilhelm Gesenius (1786-1842) at Halle and Muller at Berlin. In 1834 he baptized **J. G. Oncken**, the Baptist apostle to Europe. Upon his return in 1835 he took the chair in Christian Theology at Newton Theological Institution, in 1839 becoming president of the seminary. He served as president of the Massachusetts Education Board, 1848-1855, during which time the "town system" was developed. Upon the resignation of **Francis Wayland**, Sears became president of Brown University in 1855, which he held concurrently with the professorship in Philosophy and Christian Evidences through the Civil War. In 1867 he accepted the secretaryship of the George Peabody Fund and in this role travelled widely in the southern states during Reconstruction. He advocated the development of public school systems in each state and took special interest in the creation of "normal" schools for teacher training. Sears was the author of a variety of books, including *Life of Luther* (1849) and *Objections to Public Schools Considered* (1875).

SECOND GREAT AWAKENINGS. Term applied to the series of religious renewals which occurred in the United States from about 1800 to 1835-1840. The initial phase erupted at Cane Ridge, Kentucky, in 1800 where outdoor camp meetings, primarily among the Presbyterians, produced general religious awakenings in the Appalachian Mountain region. Another phase took place at Yale College, New Haven, Connecticut, in the first decade of the new century where Timothy Dwight (1752-1817), a Congregationalist, spearheaded a renewal on that campus. Other manifestations included the ministry of Charles G. Finney (1792-1875), a Presbyterian, in upstate New York and throughout New England and the Western Reserve region in Ohio. Finney was particularly responsible for the "New Measures" a collection of behavior modifying strategies, such as the anxious bench, the altar call, protracted meetings, naming sinners, and seasons of prayer.

Baptists were caught up in the general religious enthusiasm in mostly indirect ways. Part of the Awakening was channeled through new voluntary societies for missions, education, and humanitarian concerns; Baptists followed the patterns set by others and created numbers of these societies (see **Voluntarism**). Some of the leaders in these awakenings were local church pastors, such as **William F. Broaddus** of Virginia, who in 1831-1833 adopted the "New Measures," preached widely in his **association**, and created a new congregation around the **revival** techniques. There were also Baptist evangelists who itinerated widely, preaching on ultraistic themes and claiming extraordinary results; these included **Jacob Knapp**. **Freewill Baptists** like **David Marks** were involved in the Second Great Awakenings as they planted new congregations throughout the United States and **Canada** and experimented with social and moral reform causes. See also **Revivals**.

SEEKERS. During the first half of the 17th century in English religious developments, a number of sects arose from a free interpretation of **Scripture** and in opposition to any form of establishment. Among these were Baptists, Quakers, **Ranters**, **Levellers**, **Familists**, and **Diggers**. The Seekers, whose name was loosely applied to people in search of the truth, questioned the value of the **sacraments**, churches, ministers, and organized worship. Many felt the end of the world was near and advocated radical social policies like poor relief, heavier taxation of the rich, identification of the saints with the poor, and abolition of ministers. William Erbury (1604-1654) was acclaimed the champion of the Seekers; he taught the universal redemption of mankind and that the fullness of the Godhead would be manifested in the saints. A number of disillusioned Baptists went over to the Seekers at least for a time, including **Roger Williams**. See also **Diggers**; **Levellers**; **Ranters**.

SEMPLE, ROBERT BAYLOR (1769-1831). American Baptist minister and historian, born at Rosemont, Virginia. He pursued a career in schoolteaching and studied law, before turning to **ministry** in 1789. He was ordained in 1790 and called to the Bruington, Virginia, Baptist Church which he served to his death. Semple was an advocate of missionary endeavor, education and associationalism. He was the first president of the Baptist General Association of Virginia in 1823 and president of the **General Baptist Missionary (Triennial) Convention** in 1820. A close friend of **Luther Rice**, Semple was a promoter of the national Baptist movement and adroitly maneuvered Virginia churches in that direction. His book, *The Rise and Progress of Baptists in Virginia* (1810), contains much primary source material and follows the pattern of historical writing set by **Morgan Edwards** and later by **David Benedict**. Brown University awarded Semple an honorary A.M. in 1814 and the doctor of divinity in 1824.

SENEGAL. In 1962 **Conservative Baptists** from the United States opened a mission at Thies, a coastal city, Diourbel, and Dakar. In 1969 the **Southern Baptists** appointed their first missionary to Senegal, Farrell

Runyan, who settled at Dakar. Work is much controlled by government restriction.

As of 1995 there were two congregations and about 100 members associated with the Mission Baptiste du Sénégal.

SEPARATE BAPTISTS. A movement of churches and ministers associated initially with the First **Great Awakening** in the American colonies, particularly the South. In New England the Separate movement was popularly known as **New Light Baptists**. As the revivalists itinerated in the New England and the Middle colonies, beginning in 1740, congregations emerged around tighter standards of church membership, the reassertion of sovereign grace, evidence of conversion, and **evangelism**. Some churches of a separate kind resulted from separating from older Congregational churches, while others sprang up around the **ministry** of younger preachers. By the late 1740s leaders like **Isaac Backus** were persuaded to adopt Baptist principles and many of the Separates became Separate Baptists, because they practiced believer's **baptism** and other Baptistic ideas. These churches stressed a pure church, they practiced the **associational principle**, held in priority the work of the Spirit, preaching, and evangelism. Most held to closed communion and high ethical expectations. The term "separate" came from their desire to be separate from churches and Christians who practiced open communion and more **liberal** standards of Christian faith and conduct.

Although the Separate Baptists initially had difficulties with Regular Baptist organizations, a learned ministry, and the **General Baptist** position, they gradually moved toward the mainstream and by 1787 in Virginia and 1801 in Kentucky, were assimilated into the Regular, Calvinistic family. Several of the New England Separates moved to the southern states, notably **John Leland** and **Shubael Stearns**, to carry the Separate emphases to that region. Among the leaders of the southern Separate Baptists were **James Ireland** and **John Taylor**, the latter eventually becoming antimissionary in his views. Those churches, particularly in Kentucky, that remained out of the Union of 1801 gradually evolved into the General Association of Separate Baptists in Christ (1912). See also **Great Awakening; New Light Baptists.**

SEPARATION OF CHURCH AND STATE. Part of the socio-political outlook of Baptists from their beginning was a doctrine of the separation of church and state. In some places, this has been more aggressively pursued than elsewhere.

In the first half of the 17th century, Baptists found themselves labelled "**Nonconformists**" in the context of a state and Established

Church, the Church of England. Under the policies of King James I (1603-1625), Charles I (1625-1649), Church of England Archbishop Laud, the Presbyterian Westminster Assembly, or the later Restoration monarchs Kings Charles II (1660-1685) and James II (1685-1689), from a Baptist perspective the interests of the state and the church were unhealthfully wed. To no one's surprise, therefore, Baptist writers came down on the "separateness" of the two spheres, the civil and the spiritual. **Roger Williams** was perhaps the first to develop the metaphor of a "wall of separation." By this he meant that there are two distinct spheres of influence, the civil and the spiritual, which should be maintained constitutionally and kept practically separate. In later English Baptist development, Baptists struggled to achieve toleration and advocated a completely **voluntary** system of church relationships. They contented themselves with influencing government policy through coalitions with other Nonconformists, notably the **Three Dissenting Denominations**, later the Dissenting Deputies, or their own elected members of Parliament and other government appointments.

An important contribution distantly related to the Baptist movement was made by **John Glas**, a Scotsman who favored an entirely voluntary system of church support and membership. While considered quite radical in his era, Glas's ideas influenced major Baptist thinkers as well as the Christian Church/Disciples of Christ, begun by **Alexander Campbell**. Outside the Baptist movement can be noted the work of Thomas Chalmers (1780-1847) in **Scotland**, who also made the case for dismantling established churches in Britain.

In the American colonies, a similar distrust of governments ensued with the colonial establishments, the Standing Order Congregationalists in New England and various shades of Anglicanism in the South. Taxation, licensing, and other attempts of colonial governments to intrude in personal and congregational religious experience forced Baptists to take the position that the state should not be allowed to interfere in the life and work of the church. **Isaac Backus** and **John Leland** were leading proponents of the separation ideal in the 18th century. Through the Massachusetts delegation to the Constitutional Convention, Backus proposed a dissolution of the principle of established churches supported by the states. Leland likewise influenced his friend James Madison (1751-1836), and perhaps Thomas Jefferson (1738-1826), to include in the Bill of Rights a clear guarantee that "Congress shall make no laws concerning an establishment of religion." The separation of church and state was thus guaranteed in the United States by constitutional amendment. Baptist groups, notably the **Baptist Joint Committee on Public Affairs**, are vigilant on government policies, lest the wall be breached.

Issues which cause debate in the United States are religious exercises in schools, government surveillance over unorthodox religious groups, Sunday "blue laws," the civic role of ecclesiastical persons, taxation of both personal income and church property, and the use of language about God in official national symbols. Most Baptists in the United States generally believe Christians have a responsibility under God to advocate Christian ideals and biblical faith in the making of public policy. This advocacy takes the form of supporting political candidates, campaigning for referenda issues, critique of public policy, and of course exercise of personal franchise. In the later decades of the 20th century, some **fundamentalistic** Baptists in the United States have held that there should be clear political advocacy and even political pressure groups and parties (i.e., the Moral Majority) dedicated to biblical ideals. See also **Religious Liberty** and **Voluntarism**.

SERBIA. The center of Baptist life in Serbia has been Novi Sad in the Vojvodina region, where Heinrich Meyer (1842-1919), a German Baptist missionary who had worked in **Hungary**, established the first church in 1875. In 1898 Peter Lehotsky (1873-1956) began a congregation in Belgrade, also in the German tradition. The Roumanian Baptists began an ethnic church at Straza in 1924 and a Slovakian ethnic minority church started at Backi Petrovac in 1897. As early as 1938 American Southern Baptists also commenced missionary work in Belgrade. A theological school started in Belgrade in 1940, closed during the war, reopened at Zagreb, Croatia, in 1954, moved to Daruvar in 1955, and finally settled in Novi Sad in 1957. Beginning in 1922 the Serbo-Croatian Conference included Germans, Slovaks, and Hungarians, and later this ethnic combination comprised the Baptist Union of Yugoslavia (officially recognized in 1926) until World War II.

Following the civil war of 1991 and more recently in 1995, Serbian Baptists have been constituted in two unions: roughly located among churches in the north is Savez Baptisticakih Crkava u Srbiji (Union of Baptist Churches in Serbia, offices in Belgrade), and Savez Evanvjeoskih Crkava Baptista (Union of Evangelical Christians-Baptists in Yugoslavia, offices in Vrnjacka Vanja), concentrated in the south. The northern union is multi-national, while the southern union is mostly Serbian.

Serbian Baptists in Belgrade helped to establish the Baptist churches in Macedonia, beginning in 1936. See **Macedonia**.

As of 1995 there were 51 churches with 1,619 members affiliated with the Savez Baptisickih Crkava u Srbiji. There is a theological school in Novi Sad.

SEVENTH DAY BAPTISTS (SDB). Seventh Day or sabbatarian Baptists first appeared in the mid-17th century English context of rapid **Nonconformist** development. British Baptist historian **William T. Whitley** and others believe that sabbatarians emerged from the biblical literalism associated with groups such as the **Fifth Monarchists**. Early sabbatarian writers include James Ockford, William Saller (fl. 1640-1680), and Thomas Tillam (fl. 1635-1670). Whatever their origin was, the first congregation can safely be identified as the Mill Yard Church (c. 1653). Both **General** and **Particular Baptists** crossed over to be involved as Seventh Day Baptists and the movement included a number of prominent people, such as **Francis Bampfield** and Dr. **Peter Chamberlen**. By 1730 the Seventh Day movement was essentially defunct in England, with only a few scattered congregations left by the 20th century. Among the reasons for the decline are reliance upon personal endowments rather than congregational stewardship, a lack of organized fellowship, employment of first day Baptist ministers, and crossover of Seventh Day Baptist members to first day congregations.

In the United States, however, there is an ongoing history for the group. In Newport, Rhode Island, in 1671 a schism grew up among the Regular Baptist churches over the sabbath, and a separate congregation was started by Seventh Day advocates. From this beginning a chain of churches in New Jersey, New York, Rhode Island, and the Upper Midwest evolved later to constitute a Yearly Meeting which became the Seventh Day Baptist General Conference, formed in 1802. Five associations were formed in 1835: Eastern, Central, Western, Northwestern, and Southeastern. In 1843 the Seventh Day Baptist Foreign Mission Society was founded and it maintained a field in **China** until 1950, when, due to closure of the field, missions were focused in **Burma**, **Poland**, **Malawi**, and **Mexico**. The Seventh Day Baptist Publication Society produced sabbatarian literature and the Education Society, originally located at Alfred, New York, supported candidates for the **ministry**. Centers of the movement include Alfred, New York, where there was a university related to the Seventh Day Baptists, and Salem, West Virginia, where a second school exists, Salem College. In 1965, six national conferences plus the General Conference of Seventh Day Baptists in the United States, formed the Seventh Day Baptist World Federation. The Federation provides increased communication, stimulates fellowship, and promotes evangelism and special projects.

American Seventh Day Baptists have a long ecumenical heritage, including membership for several years in the National Council of Churches (1905-1973) and the World Council of Churches (1948-1976); in 1963, merger with the American Baptist Convention was discussed, but later rejected in the 1970s. The denomination in the United States has also taken various moral positions on issues such as **peacemaking**, race relations, **separation of church and state**, and human right to life.

The Seventh Day Baptist national headquarters is in Janesville, Wisconsin (which includes the Historical Society), and the Conference publishes *The Sabbath Recorder* (1844-).

As of 1995 there were 68 churches and 5,000 members in the United States and **Canada**. See also **Solitary Brethren**.

SHAKESPEARE, JOHN HOWARD (1857-1928). English Baptist minister and denominational leader, born in Leicestershire. Shakespeare was educated at Regent's Park College and the University of London. In 1898 he became secretary of the **Baptist Union** (BU) and, in that role for the next three decades, he became the leading force of the ecclesiastical organization of British Baptists as a denomination. Shakespeare began the Twentieth Century and Sustentation Funds, superintended the building of Baptist Church House in London, and organized the Baptist **ministry** according to credentials with the Union. He also was instrumental in establishing the system of superintendency in 1916. Shakespeare was an advocate in 1905 of the **Baptist World Alliance** and later of a union of all the Free Churches in Great Britain. Shakespeare's published works give evidence of his ecumenical orientation: *Baptist and Congregational Pioneers* (1905), *The Free Churches and the National Life* (1910), and *The Churches at the Crossroads* (1918).

SHATTERED BAPTISTS. A term used by Quaker founder George Fox (1624-1691) to describe a community of Baptists he encountered in 1648 in Nottinghamshire. According to entries in Fox's *Journal* he was practicing his trade in Mansfield and he came in contact with Baptists in Nottingham who had lost their spiritual life and scattered. He referred to them as "shattered Baptists" and found two types: one group continued to meet on Sundays "to play at shovel-board and to be merry," the other was a group of **Separatists** whom Fox considered to be a "tender people." Significantly, **Elizabeth Hooten**, who later became a leading Quaker, was among the second group. Fox found many followers among the shattered Baptists and he organized some under the new name "Children of the Light." Among those who played games on Sundays, Rice Jones (fl. 1650-58) was a Nottingham Baptist leader who joined the Children of the Light for a time, but "returned out of the light to dark imaginations" thereafter. Jones became an adversary of Fox and in 1654 influenced many of the former Baptists among Fox's new group to rejoin Jones and later the **Ranter** movement, thus causing the first schism among the Quakers.

SHIELDS, THOMAS TODHUNTER (1873-1955). Canadian Baptist minister, born in Bristol, England. The Shields family emigrated to **Canada** in the 1880s where the father was a Primitive Methodist preacher who taught his children **theology** and biblical subjects. Thomas entered the **ministry** in the Baptist Convention of Ontario and Quebec and served several small congregations at Florence, Delhi, Dutton, and Hamilton (1894-1910) before accepting the call from the prestigious Jarvis Street Church in Toronto. From the beginning, Shields attacked what he perceived to be the evidences of liberal theology in the Convention, mostly centered on McMaster University. Between 1919 and 1921 he organized the Canadian wing of the **Baptist Bible Union** and became a symbol for emerging Canadian **fundamentalism**. In a major rift with the Convention in 1925, Shields left, forming a separate newspaper, *The Gospel Witness*, Toronto Baptist Seminary, and denominational organization, the Regular Baptist Missionary and Education Society. With **William Bell Riley** and **J. Frank Norris**, Shields built a North American fundamentalist empire; in 1927 he took control of Northern Baptist-related Des Moines (Iowa) University, hoping to operate it as a Baptist fundamentalist institution. This plan failed and for the remainder of his career he focused his efforts on his pulpit ministry and Toronto Baptist Seminary. Shields's publications include *The Plot That Failed* (1937) and *Russellism or Rutherfordism?* (1942).

SHOUTER BAPTISTS. A group of Baptists in **Trinidad** and **Tobago**, St. Vincent, and Jamaica whose forms of worship draw upon vivid African styles. Traced from Yoruba tribe slaves brought to the islands from Africa, the Shouters' worship involves handclapping, chanting, shouting, pouring of lotion, and bell-ringing. The handclapping and chanting are believed to be substitutes for drums and shac-shacs in the African custom. In the 19th century on several of the West Indies islands, Africans were persecuted for their often disruptive worship practices. They were called "Shakers" and they were frequently prohibited from worship by law, as in 1912 on St. Vincent. As a result, the Shakers held worship in secret and met in huts. In Trinidad and Tobago this same tradition was called "Shouter" or "Spiritual Baptists" and in 1917 their worship was outlawed. In 1951 the Ordinance banning the Shouters was repealed and the Shouters have come to associate with charismatic groups in the United States. The theological beliefs of the Shouters are similar to other

Baptists, with the addition of articles which define the connections between Yoruba dances and music and New Testament spirituality.

SHUCK, JEHU LEWIS (1812-1863). American, and later Southern, Baptist missionary, born in Alexandria, Virginia. He was educated at Virginia Baptist Seminary (later Richmond College) and was appointed with his wife, Henrietta Hall (1817-1844), by the **Baptist Board for Foreign Missions** (BBFM) for work with the Chinese. He was a protege of **William Dean**, first Baptist missionary to the Chinese and was sent initially to Macao near Canton. A misunderstanding over their financial support in the beginning of their mission soured the Shuck's relationship with the BBFM and nearly cost them their assignment. In 1842 they moved to **Hong Kong** when it was opened to the West. There Henrietta opened a school and Lewis preached at a local bazaar, with much success. In 1845 Shuck wrestled with his relationship to the Board and the news that a new Southern Baptist Board would be formed. He ultimately allied himself with the **Southern Baptist Convention** (SBC) and became its first missionary. His former colleagues, still under the patronage of the national board, shunned his decision. In 1852-1853 Shuck was accused of moral laxity and withdrew from the **China** field. He settled in California where he worked in the emigrant Chinese community and started a church among the English-speaking settlers in Oakland under the auspices of the Home Mission Board. In 1840 Shuck published *Portfolio Chinensis*, a collection of important Chinese state papers.

SIAM. See Thailand.

SIERRA LEONE. David George, the famous American and later Canadian **Black Baptist** missionary, established a Baptist presence at Freetown in 1792. Three years later the **Baptist Missionary Society** (BMS) from Great Britain established a work, but withdrew shortly afterward. George R. Thompson and J. J. Brown, who had been ordained in 1853 at Freetown by T. J. Bowen (1814-1875) of the Southern Baptists, came under support of the **Foreign Mission Board** in 1855, but the mission was hampered by shortage of funds. For many years Jamaican Baptists contributed generously to the small Baptist community in Sierra Leone. In 1964 the Nigerian Baptists entered the country and established a church at Bumbuna. This was followed by the European Baptist Missionary Society in 1966. In 1974 delegates of the Nigerian Mission, the European Mission, and the Bassa Baptist Church met in Mambolo to create the Baptist Convention of Sierra Leone. Finally, in 1984 U. S. Southern Baptists in their own right established a mission in Sierra Leone. The

Baptist Bible Fellowship (BBF) opened a mission in Sierra Leone in 1997.

As of 1995 there were 74 churches and 5,709 members affiliated with the Baptist Convention of Sierra Leone.

SIMMONS, WILLIAM J. (1849-1890). American Black Baptist minister and educator, born at Charleston, South Carolina. He was born into slavery but raised a free man in Pennsylvania and New Jersey. He served in the 41st U.S. Colored Troops during the Civil War and then turned to study for the Baptist ministry. Following education at Madison University and Howard University, he was a schoolteacher in Washington, D.C. and Ocala, Florida and a pastor in Lexington, Kentucky, 1879-1880. He took a faculty position at the Kentucky Normal and Theological Institute, a school sponsored by the **American Baptist Home Mission Society** (ABHMS). The ABHMS in 1887 appointed Simmons superintendent of their work in the South, which gave him the opportunity to travel extensively in the region. Sensing an opportunity, in 1886 he organized a meeting of Black leaders under the motto, "God, My Race and Denomination" to discuss possible organization; the result was the formation of the American National Baptist Convention with Simmons as the first president. During the remainder of his career, he advocated Negro progress, the liberation of Black women and he assailed White supremacy. In 1891, following his death, the Kentucky Normal Institute was renamed Simmons University.

SINGAPORE. The first Baptists in Singapore came through Malaya from Swatow, China, in 1905. The earliest congregation worshipped on an **ecumenical** basis until Lim Kian Tong, an educator from China, visited Singapore and urged the Baptists to constitute their own church. The first congregation was called the Overseas-Chinese (Swatow) Baptist Church of Singapore and it opened in 1937. Likewise in 1949 a church was organized among the Cantonese peoples living in Singapore. In 1951 U.S. **Southern Baptist** mission work began and the **Baptist Bible Fellowship** (BBF) opened a mission in 1970, the **Conservative Baptist** Foreign Mission Society (CBFMS) in 1983, and more recently the **Association of Baptists for World Evangelism** (ABWE) commenced a mission in 1992.

As of 1995 there were 30 churches and 5,937 members affiliated with the Singapore Baptist Convention.

SIX PRINCIPLE CALVINISTIC BAPTISTS. In (U.S.) colonial New England and the Middle colonies there were Calvinistic Baptists who followed the basic tenets of the Westminster Confession (1646), but who also practiced the "sixth principle," the **laying on of hands**. Among the churches who espoused this position were the Providence, Rhode Island, church after 1730, Wallingford, Connecticut, and perhaps North Kingston, Rhode Island. These congregations, recognizing the validity at least on a voluntary basis of the laying on of hands, attended the General Six Principle Baptist Association as fraternal delegates. In the Middle colonies, Welsh Baptist congregations and some English-speaking churches, like Great Valley in Pennsylvania, were Calvinistic but practiced imposition of hands at membership. See also **General Baptists; Five Principle Calvinistic Baptists**.

SLAVERY, AMONG BAPTISTS. Even with a demonstrated record on **religious liberty** and human rights from their origins in the 17th century, Baptists have from time to time countenanced economic systems which involve human servitude; Baptists have also been slaveholders. For instance, in **Jamaica William Knibb** reported that Baptists owned slaves. In the development of Baptist churches in the colonial southern United States, Baptist plantation owners employed field slaves and Baptist farmers and artisans employed household slaves and semi-skilled slaves. The segregation of slaves according to race is evident in Baptist churches, notably in Virginia and South Carolina where prominent pastors of White congregations like **Jeremiah B. Jeter** and **Richard Fuller** preached either to slaves in the balconies of their churches or to slave congregations in their cities and towns. Fuller later attempted to justify the slave system on biblical and humanitarian grounds in a famous written exchange with **Francis Wayland** of New England. Other southern slaveholders, like **William H. Brisbane**, manumitted their slaves and became ardent abolitionists. From at least 1755 at the plantation of William Byrd III (1728-1777) in Virginia a slave community was noticed in the greater Baptist tradition and the Baptist faith was attractive to freed slaves for its organizational simplicity and emphasis upon Christian experience. Former slaves achieved many results in the Baptist ministry or missionary service, notably **David George, Lott Carey, Richard H. Boyd**, and **William J. Simmons**. The slave experience in many emancipated Black leaders' experiences provided a rationale for the development of separate Black Baptist organizations and churches, in part to exercise authority and leadership within the Black community. See also **Antislavery, among Baptists**.

SLAVIC MISSIONARY SERVICES. Founded in 1933 in the Baptist tradition, Slavic Missionary Service engages in **bible** and literature distribution, broadcasting, and support of national workers, particularly in the Commonwealth of Independent States and **Ukraine**. Its headquarters are located in South River, New Jersey.

SLOVAK REPUBLIC. The first practitioners of believer's **baptism** were doubtless connected with the **Anabaptists**--**Balthasar Hubmaier** sought refuge in Slovakia in the 16ᵗʰ century. The modern Baptist movement was connected with Baptist missions in the Austro-Hungarian Empire and particularly with Bohemia, later the **Czech Republic**. The pioneer was August Meereis (b.1847), a **colporteur** of the British Bible Society working in eastern Bohemia. An early baptism took place in 1877 at Brandys, a place associated with Comenius. Meereis founded at Kezmarok-Vavrisovo a Slovak-German Baptist congregation in 1888. A second church was formed at Chvojnice in western Slovakia. From 1898 to 1901 the Slovak Baptist congregations were related to the Austro-Hungarian Baptist Union, with the Slovak churches gravitating to Vienna or Budapest for support.

　　　Work following World War I was characterized by missions from the **Northern Baptist Convention** (NBC) and the **Baptist Missionary Society** (BMS); in 1919 the churches in Slovakia entered a relationship with the Czechs called the Czechoslovak Baptist Union, which lasted until 1992 when the Slovak Republic emerged as an independent nation. In addition to the indigenous work, **Baptist Mid-Missions** from the United States established a mission in Kosice in 1946 and later one at Stitnik. In 1995 the **Association of Baptists for World Evangelism** (ABWE) commenced a mission in Slovakia.

　　　As of 1995 there were 15 churches and 1,984 members related to the Bratska Jednota Baptistov Rada V SR. Offices of the Union are located in Bratislava.

SLOVENIA. Prior to 1993 Baptist churches in Slovenia were part of the Savez Evandeoskih Hriscana-Baptista SR Jugoslavija (Baptist Union of Yugoslavia). That year with political independence, the Zveza Baptisticnih Cerkava v Republiki Sloveniji (Slovenian Baptist Union) was formed. In 1991 the **Conservative Baptist** Foreign Mission Society (CBFMS) opened a mission to Slovenia, focusing on refugee work and church planting in Ljubljana.

　　　As of 1995 there are six churches with 280 members affiliated with the Zveza Baptisticnih Cerkava v Republiki Sloveniji.

SMITH, ELIAS (1769-1846). American Baptist minister and editor, born at Lyme, Connecticut. He was raised in a **New Light** home and underwent a protracted conversion experience of his own. From 1787 to

1802 he itinerated as an **evangelist**, sometimes critical of the growing formalism among the Baptists. He was **pastor** at Woburn, Massachusetts, and later began to gather **independent** congregations among New England's working classes. The Baptists disfellowshipped Smith in 1804 and he bitterly attacked the Baptists as unscriptural and overly confessional. He referred to his church as a "Christian Church" and served at Portsmouth, New Hampshire (1802-1808). Beginning in 1808 he published a religious newspaper, *The Herald of Gospel Liberty*, said to be one of the oldest in the United States. After 1815 when he adopted **universalist** views, he won much acclaim among **Unitarians** and Universalists for his advocacy of **religious liberty**. His autobiography, *The Life, Conversion, Preaching, Travels and Sufferings of Elias Smith* (1816), was a vivid critical description of New England Baptists at the turn of the 19th century.

SMITH, GERALD BIRNEY (1868-1929). American Baptist minister, educator, and theologian, born at Middlefield, Massachusetts. He was educated at Brown University and Union Theological Seminary, and as an exceptional student, studied at the universities of Berlin, Marburg, and Paris. In 1900 he began a lifelong teaching career at the University of Chicago where he taught theology and ethics. Smith was greatly influenced by the work of German theologians Albert Ritschl (1822-1889) and Johann W. Hermann (1846-1922). He emphasized religious experience over biblical content as the basis for **theology**. One of the foremost members of the Chicago School with **Ernest D. Burton** and **Shailer Mathews**, Smith attempted to blend the results of scientific investigation with critical theology. In his need to move away from authoritarian religion, he came to advocate an empirical approach, and he refused to write a systematic theology, in view of changing contexts. His scholarship won international renown with such titles as *Practical Theology* (1903), *Social Idealism and the Changing Theology* (1913), and *The Principles of Christian Living: A Handbook of Christian Ethics* (1924). He was the editor of the *American Journal of Theology* (1909-1920) and the *Journal of Religion* (1921-1929).

SMITH, HEZEKIAH (1737-1805). American Baptist minister and chaplain, born at Hempstead, New York. Smith graduated from Hopewell Academy and the College of New Jersey, one of the first to be given a Baptist education in the colonies. In 1762 he began an itinerant ministry, keeping an extensive journal throughout the Revolutionary era. He settled in Haverhill, Massachusetts, where he gathered a church in 1764. During the Revolution, he identified with the Patriot cause and held the

Revolution to be an act for the salvation of America. In 1777 the Continental Congress appointed him a chaplain to the Army of the United States and he served with distinction in several campaigns. In later years as **pastor** at Haverhill, he was an advocate and founder of the Massachusetts Baptist Missionary Society. Smith published a tract on believer's **baptism** (1766), which became an important resource in the New England Baptist community.

SMYTH, JOHN (fl. 1586-1612). Separatist and later English Baptist minister, born possibly at Sturton. He graduated from Christ's College, Cambridge, about 1590, having studied under the Puritan scholar, Francis Johnson (1562-1618). Smyth was a fellow in Christ's College in 1594, after which he was ordained by the Bishop of Lincoln. In 1598 he was married, left Cambridge, and took a city lectureship in Lincoln, a popular outlet for ministers of Puritan sympathies. His sermons offended the wrong people and he practiced medicine for a time. About 1606 he left the Church of England and became a **Separatist** in Gainsborough where he served a congregation as **pastor**. At length the authorities bore down upon the congregation and Smyth and a prominent lay leader, **Thomas Helwys**, fled with much of the membership to Amsterdam. In Amsterdam Smyth wrote on the nature of the church and **ministry** and led his flock in close cooperation with the Mennonite congregation at the Singelkerk.

In 1609 Smyth and his congregation concluded that infant **baptism** was erroneous and Smyth baptized himself in order to begin a new gospel order of believers; this earned him the derisive title, "Se-baptist," meaning "self-baptizer." He then baptized Helwys and others, likely by pouring, in the Mennonite tradition. Feeling ostracized by the Christian community for his audacious act, Smyth opened negotiations with the Waterlander Mennonites and moved toward full inclusion in their fellowship. This in turn offended Helwys and a rift occurred between the two friends and within the congregation. Smyth apparently had adopted a more **Arminian** stance and took a radical stand on the matter of **religious liberty**. He wrote four important books and a significant **confession of faith,** which defined the earliest Baptists. He remains the parent of modern Baptists and the first Englishman to pen a case for full religious liberty. Smyth died in Amsterdam and was buried at the Nieuwkerk.

SOCIAL GOSPEL MOVEMENT. In the decades following the American Civil War (1861-1865), numerous writers addressed the social concerns raised by urbanization and industrialization. Among the leading voices was **Walter Rauschenbusch**, a Baptist of New York City and later

Rochester, New York, who wrote passionately in advocating a Christian response to these problems. He defined social Christianity in terms of the earthly Kingdom of God which should be the righteous rule of God in all human affairs. His theological treatises formed some of the most significant literature of the growing movement, which included social theorists, seminary professors, pastors, and denominational leaders. A new and broader doctrine of the church helped to redefine the mission of God's people: to witness in public affairs, advocate changes in the social and economic order according to the principles of Jesus, and seek justice on an international plane. Of particular interest to those in the social gospel movement were abusive labor practices involving women and children, the right of collective bargaining, improved urban housing, better treatment of immigrants, and an end to military action as a means of settling disputes. Among Baptists in the United States, the **Northern Baptist Convention** (NBC) pioneered the establishment of a Social Service Commission in 1910, headed by Samuel Zane Batten (1859-1925). **Thomas Clement Douglas** in western **Canada**, a distant disciple of the Rauschenbusch movement, applied the principles of the Social Gospel to Canadian welfare politics.

While the social gospel movement ushered in many useful innovations in understanding the task of the church, it also created much division. Frequently misunderstood as "socialism" it drew the wrath of ardent capitalists and individualists. **Fundamentalists** derided the social gospel as a modernist substitute for personal **evangelism** and the two were often seen as mutually exclusive. The major proponents of the social gospel prior to World War I tended to be associated with various new theological systems, including idealism, pragmatism, and modernism; the influence of German theologians, notably Albert Ritschl (1822-1889) was paramount. The Baptist educational centers of the movement were Rochester Theological Seminary, Crozer Theological Seminary, and the University of Chicago Divinity School.

"SOFT POLICY BAPTISTS." See **Baptist World Mission**.

SOLITARY BRETHREN. A colony of Baptistic Christians founded in 1721 by **Johann Conrad Beissel** at Mill Creek, Pennsylvania. Later, the colony was reconstituted at Ephrata near Lancaster, Pennsylvania. Beissel organized his followers around a celibate male order, the Brotherhood, and a virginal woman's order called the Sisterhood. Men and women were housed in separate monastic halls and practiced strict **discipline** and a type of mystical prayer life. Women were veiled in drab cloaks so as to obscure images of their humiliating sexuality and both sexes engaged in various crafts, including book making, learned from the eminent Christopher Sower (1693-1758), and illumination of manuscripts. The worship chapel was the largest in the colony in the early 18th century. Nightly the members of the order would process about the Ephrata grounds singing hymns led by Beissel. He required strict written confessions of spiritual accountability of all members. Sabbatarian and practicing believer's **baptism**, the group was also known as the **German Seventh Day Baptist Brethren** and derisively as "Beisseliener." The colony eventually declined with the death of Beissel in 1768. See also **German Baptist Brethren**.

SONSHIP CONTROVERSY. Within the Strict Baptist movement in Great Britain, beginning in the 1860s a rancorous debate opened over the nature of Jesus Christ as the Son of God. In 1861 **Joseph Philpot,** in his newspaper *The Gospel Herald*, called attention to what he felt was a pernicious error concerning the true sonship of Jesus. Philpot took the position that Jesus was eternally the Son of God and only as the Son of God could he be rightly a mediator between God and man. Others, following Charles W. Banks (1806-1886) held that rather than an eternal characteristic, the sonship of Jesus lies in His complexity and is the result of the incarnation, not as part of His absolutely divine nature. The limited view of the Sonship of Christ was first articulated at Zoar Chapel, Great Alie Street, in East London about 1859-1860. An editorial war ensued between the *Gospel Standard* Baptists and those who followed Banks in *The Earthen Vessel*, later called the *Gospel Herald* Baptists. See also **Strict Baptists**.

SOUTH AFRICA. It was William Miller (1779-1856) a Baptist emigrant from England who founded a congregation at Grahamstown in 1822-1823 that became the initial Baptist work in southern Africa. Another pioneer was Moses H. Bixby (1827-1901), a missionary of the **American Baptist Missionary Union** (ABMU), who stopped in Capetown en route to **Burma** and gathered the first Baptist congregation in that city.

In the late 1850s German settlers emigrated to South Africa and a number of German Baptists, influenced by **J. G. Oncken**, were among them. Small scattered congregations were founded, 1858-1861, and with the arrival in 1867 of Carl H. Gutsche (1845-1926), a protégé of Oncken, greater unity was achieved and an **association** of the German churches was formed in 1870. The Afrikaanse Baptiste Kerk began in 1886 in the Orange Free State at Sugarloaf (later Cornelia), comprised of Dutch-speaking Baptists.

In 1877 the Baptist Union of South Africa was formed, uniting many of the different cultural communities. In 1878 the **American Baptist Foreign Mission Society (ABFMS)** began a mission in Natal. The South African Baptist Missionary Society (1892) assumed evangelization and church development among Black communities. This work included Transkei, Natal, Transvaal, and the Orange Free State, among others. In 1927 the first Black church was founded, the Bantu Baptist Church, which became part of the Baptist Convention of South Africa (1966). Several of these congregations have subsequently left the Convention and joined the Baptist Union of Southern Africa.

In a collaborative arrangement Southern Baptists entered the homeland areas in 1977. That same year American Baptists signed a collaborative agreement with the **Baptist Missionary Society** (BMS) to conduct work in the country. The **Association of Baptists for World Evangelism** (ABWE) created a mission in South Africa in 1980, and the same year the **Baptist Bible Fellowship** (BBF) opened a mission in South Africa. In 1906, a Seventh Day Baptist church was established in South Africa.

As of 1995 there were 346 churches and 38,628 members in the Baptist Union of South(ern) Africa and 105 churches with 29,500 members affiliated with the Baptist Convention of South Africa. As the result of the demise of apartheid, in 1996 the Baptist Union of Transkei which had been formed in 1980 was dissolved. In 1951 the Baptist Theological College of Southern Africa opened, and there are presently schools located at Debenek, Johannesburg, Kempton Park, Menlo Park, and Randburg. The *South African Baptist* has been published since 1894 (later known as *Baptists Today*).

SOUTHERN BAPTIST CONVENTION (SBC). The largest organization of Baptists in the world, formed at Augusta, Georgia, on May 8, 1845. Symbolically, its "mother congregation" is First Baptist Charleston, South Carolina, the oldest in the American South, formed in 1681. Ostensibly, the reason for the separation from the **General Baptist Missionary** (Triennial) **Convention** was the slavery issue, whereby the northern-dominated mission societies declined to support slaveholding interests. In fact, a different **polity** and more unified theological tradition characterized the southern churches long before the schism.

In the original articles of incorporation, a unified body called the "Convention" superintended two boards, one for foreign missions, the second for domestic missions. In 1847 a Southern Baptist Publication Society was formed and endorsed by the Convention without being integral to it. Also related to the Convention was a Bible Board established in 1851 and an Indian Mission Board, which was later combined with the Domestic Mission Board in 1855. An initial attempt at a **Sunday School Board** in 1863 was aborted and the assets were turned over to the Domestic Board after a decade. The outbreak of the Civil War decimated the work of the Convention and its agencies, and following the war competition resumed with the northern Baptist societies.

During Reconstruction, numerous leaders held out the possibility that reunion with northern Baptists might take place. At the same time, however, signs revealed separation was permanent. In 1888 a Woman's Missionary Union auxiliary to the Southern Baptist Convention was formed. In 1898 a comity conference was held at **Fortress Monroe**, Virginia, where the northern Baptist societies agreed to separate territorial spheres of mission work. A third major event was the recreation in 1891 of a Sunday School Board, signalling final separation with the **American Baptist Publication Society**. The Southern Baptist Theological Seminary, reborn after the war, also did much to establish Southern Baptist leadership for the Convention.

In the first decades of the 20th century, Southern Baptist identity was greatly strengthened. New state conventions were formed across the southwestern states, new schools were formed in Texas and Louisiana, and a Laymen's Missionary Movement was begun in 1907. Denominational solidarity was further strengthened when the Relief and Annuity Board was made a part of the national Convention in 1918 and well in excess of $75 million were raised to commemorate the seventy-fifth anniversary of the SBC in 1920. That same year the membership of the Convention surpassed three million with over 27,000 churches.

In 1925 a confessional statement, the "**Baptist Faith and Message**," (based on the New Hampshire Baptist Confession of Faith of 1833) was adopted by the Convention, thus defining the theological stance as "progressive conservatism." The theological consensus achieved by **E. Y. Mullins** and others allowed for an unprecedented stewardship effort each year, known after 1925 as the Cooperative Program, because of its linkages of national boards, associations, state conventions, and local congregations.

Following World War II, Southern Baptists surged ahead in virtually every area of work. The **Foreign Mission Board** (FMB) expanded into every continent of the world, establishing national conventions, seminaries, and ties with the Convention. In North America the migration of southern Americans called for new southern-style churches outside the traditional South. Home missions were conducted in California, the Pacific Northwest, the Great Plains, the upper Middle Atlantic States, and New England. By the 1970s Southern Baptists entertained goals of a SBC congregation in every county in the United States. To provide leadership for the new congregations, two seminaries were expanded to six and a seminary extension department was established for the northern "territories." The new seminaries included Southeastern Baptist Theological Seminary in North Carolina, an outgrowth of Wake Forest College, New Orleans Baptist Theological Seminary, an upgrading of the Baptist Bible Institute, Midwestern Baptist Theological Seminary in Kansas City, Missouri, to offset the schism at American and Southern Baptist-related Central Baptist Seminary in Kansas, and Golden Gate Baptist Theological Seminary in Mill Valley, California, to establish a beachhead in the far west.

The last decades of the 20th century have witnessed growth, as in the "Bold Mission Thrust" campaign, whereby a combined effort by all Southern Baptists sought to present the gospel to every person in the period 1978 to A.D. 2000. However, severe tensions and schism erupted in the Convention over the ordination of women, tolerance for homosexuality, and perceived theological liberalism, offset on the conservative side by authoritarian pastoral and executive leadership. Resurgent **fundamentalism** has divided seminaries and universities from state conventions. A battle for the presidential control of the national Convention has led to a series of symbolically conservative elected officers, notably Charles Stanley (1932-) of Atlanta, Georgia, and Adrian Rogers (1931-) of Memphis, Tennessee, and a radical reorganization of the boards and agencies of the SBC.

In the 1980s two major voluntarist organizations have emerged to challenge the direction of the Convention, the Southern Baptist Alliance (1986), later the **Alliance of Baptists**, and the **Cooperative Baptist Fellowship** (1991). New educational ventures have also emerged in the moderate and progressive wings, notably new theological schools at Birmingham, Alabama; Richmond, Virginia; Macon, Georgia; Winston Salem, North Carolina; and the George W. Truett Seminary in Waco, Texas. Baylor and Furman Universities have also changed their charters to distance themselves from the fundamentalist directions of the national Convention.

As of 1995 the Southern Baptist Convention comprised 39 state conventions, 1,212 associations, 40,159 churches, and 15,474,611 members. Currently, there are 50 colleges or universities affiliated with the Southern Baptist Convention or its state organizations, six theological seminaries sponsored by the Convention, and five independent theological schools which are Southern Baptist in perspective and support. See also **Foreign** Mission Board; Southern Baptist Convention; **Sunday School Board.**

SOUTHWIDE BAPTIST FELLOWSHIP (SBF). A loosely connected coalition of fundamentalist Baptist churches in the American southeastern states. The Fellowship was organized in 1956 at Highland Park Baptist Church in Chattanooga, Tennessee. It began with 147 charter members, and accepts those who subscribe to its **fundamentalist**, premillennial doctrinal statement and pay two dollars per year. Among those active in the early years were **John R. Rice** and Lee Roberson (1909-), pastor of a 33,000 member church in Chattanooga. The Fellowship relates to Tennessee Temple Schools and Bob Jones University for religious education and **theological education**; the publication most closely associated with the churches is *The Sword of the Lord*, which Rice began in 1934. The SBF has a particular interest in contending with neo-evangelicalism, which many feel is infiltrating the ranks of historic fundamentalism.

SPAIN. Baptist work in Spain is traced to the evangelistic ministry of William Knapp, first an independent Baptist, then a missionary of the **American Baptist Missionary Union**. Knapp baptized numerous candidates and organized a church at Madrid in 1870. Later he began a church at Alicante, baptizing candidates in the Mediterranean Sea. Knapp was forced to leave the country in 1876. Later, in 1880 a Swedish Baptist Missionary, **Eric Lund**, began a literature and translation mission in Barcelona, and this was followed by the **Baptist General Conference of America** which sponsored a Spanish mission from 1914 to 1922 when it was transferred to the U.S. Southern Baptists. **Northern** and **Southern Baptists** in the United States agreed in 1920 (the **London Conference**) that the Spanish mission field should be administered by the **Southern Baptist Convention** (SBC). Spanish Baptists publish *El Eco de la Verdad* (*The Voice of the Truth*) (1892-). In addition to the indigenous work, the **Association of Baptists for World Evangelism** (ABWE) began a mission in 1968, the **Baptist Bible Fellowship** (BBF) opened a mission in Spain in 1970, **Baptist Mid-Missions** (BMM) from the United States established their work at Madrid in 1980, and the **Conservative Baptist** Foreign Mission Society (CBFMS) opened a mission to Spain in 1984.

As of 1995 there were 70 congregations and 8,092 members in the Unión Evangelica Bautista Española. There is a theological school located in Alcobenas.

SPANISH WORLD GOSPEL MISSION. Founded in 1959 by F. D. Toirac, a Cuban who served as a missionary to **Haiti**. The Mission is Baptistic in doctrine, in an independent Baptist tradition. It supports mission work in eight countries with about 20 missionaries. The headquarters are located in Winona Lake, Indiana, and it publishes *El Camino* (The Highway)..

SPILSBURY, JOHN (1593-1668). English Baptist minister, originally a cobbler at Aldersgate in London. Spilsbury was the first of many in the **"particular"** or Calvinistic Baptist tradition who influenced many churches with his view that Christ died for his elect only. He was pastor of the first Calvinistic congregation, located in London, where he remained from 1638 to 1656. Henry Cromwell (1628-1674) regarded Spilsbury highly and tried to induce him to go to **Ireland** to quiet the Baptists there. Instead, Spilsbury left the London church to serve at Wapping. He is remembered as the pioneer Particular Baptist, likely one of the principal authors of the first London Confession of Faith (1644). His publications include some of the earliest defenses of **baptism**: *A Treatise Concerning the Lawfull Subject of Baptisme; The Baptizing of Infants Confuted* (1643) and *Heart Bleedings for Professors Abominations* (1650).

SPURGEON, CHARLES HADDON (1834-1892). English Baptist minister, born at Kelvedon, Essex. Spurgeon lacked formal post-secondary education but was well read in the Puritan classics. He was converted at age 16 in a Methodist meeting and joined a Congregationalist church in Newmarket. Following his transfer to Baptist principles, at 20 he was called to serve John Rippon's church at Carter Lane. Following a move to New Park Street, Spurgeon developed a city-wide reputation as a great preacher and crowds thronged to hear him. Eventually the congregation erected the Metropolitan Tabernacle (at a cost of £30,000) where he was **pastor** until his death. At one service in the Crystal Palace, Spurgeon preached to over 23,000 people. He led his church to establish a Pastor's College (1856) and other **voluntary** enterprises, including Stockwell Orphanage in 1866. A strict Calvinist, Spurgeon was critical of modernistic tendencies in the **Baptist Union of Great Britain and Ireland** (BU). In the 1880s he wrote in his paper, *The Sword and Trowel*, of the Union's decline at "breakneck speed," which became known as the **"Downgrade Controversy."** This brought him into immediate and public controversy, particularly with **John Clifford**, a **General Baptist** who led the Union.

Spurgeon's sermons were widely published as well as hundreds of editions of devotional works. With **John Bunyan**, Spurgeon was one of the most widely published British Baptists of all time. Having attained an international reputation, Spurgeon ended his career alienated from the mainstream family of British Baptists. See also **Continental Baptists; Spurgeonic Baptists**.

SPURGEONIC BAPTISTS. A tradition of congregations and pastors in the Baptist family of Great Britain who associate themselves with **Charles Haddon Spurgeon** and his ministries. Beginning in the 1860s and reaching an apex in the **Downgrade Controversy** of the 1880s, a significant number of **Baptist Union of Great Britain and Ireland** (BU) congregations and some **Strict Baptists** identified with the Calvinistic and Puritan emphases of Mr. Spurgeon's theology. Many were subscribers to his paper, *The Sword and Trowel*, while others attended his ministerial meetings or supported one or more of his benevolent causes. Those men who attended or graduated from his Pastor's College, even after his death, were identifiably in the "Spurgeonic tradition."

SRI LANKA. Baptist mission entered Ceylon as an extension of the **Baptist Missionary Society** (BMS) mission in Bengal under **William Carey**. **James Chater** went to Colombo in 1812 and experienced meagre conversion results. At the ancient capital of Kandy there developed a strong center of Baptist work. A Baptist Union in Ceylon was founded in 1895. Other Baptist groups have entered the field in the 20th century: in 1989 the **Baptist Bible Fellowship** (BBF) opened a mission in Sri Lanka.

    As of 1995 there were 18 churches and 2,038 members associated with the Sri Lanka Baptist Sangamaya. There are two Baptist-related schools in Sri Lanka: Colombo and Pilimatalawa.

STAUGHTON, WILLIAM (1770-1829). English and American Baptist minister, born in Coventry. Baptized by **Samuel Pearce**, he was educated at Bristol Baptist College and was considered to succeed **John Ryland** at Northampton. An able preacher, he was present at the organizing meeting of the **Baptist Missionary Society** (BMS) at Kettering and held great promise as a leader in the denomination. His interest in emigration to America was strong and he left England for Georgetown, South Carolina, in 1793. Staughton served the church there until 1795 when he moved to the Baptist church in Bordentown, New Jersey, and then to Jacobstown and Burlington (New Jersey) where he remained until 1805. That year he became **pastor** at First Baptist, Philadelphia, which he served until 1811 when he formed a new congregation, the Sansom Street Baptist Church in Philadelphia. While at Sansom Street he built a new building, which was advanced architecturally for the era; he resigned in 1823 to become president of Columbian College (later George Washington University) in Washington, D.C.

Staughton had a lifelong interest in higher education: while in Bordentown he also served as principal of a seminary and in 1811 in Philadelphia he opened a theological school at his home, which became the first such school of the Baptists in the United States (see **Theological Education**). For six years he was the president of the Baptist attempt at a national university in Washington, and after a brief stay in Philadelphia, Staughton accepted the presidency of Georgetown College in Kentucky, the oldest Baptist institution west of the Appalachian mountains. While en route to take up his responsibilities, he died. He was the first secretary of the **Baptist Board of Foreign Missions** (BBFM) and, with **Luther Rice**, gave shape to the national organization of Baptists. In 1798 at an early age, Princeton College awarded him an honorary doctor of divinity degree. Staughton's published works include a number of sermons, *The Baptist Mission in India* (1811), *A Compendius System of Greek Grammar* (1813), and an edition of *The Works of Virgil* (1825).

STEADMAN, WILLIAM (1764-1837). English Baptist minister and denominational leader, born in Yorkshire. A graduate of Bristol Baptist College, he took the pastorate at Broughton, then moved to Bradford in 1805. There he became the president of the Baptist Academy and a founder of the Northern Education Society. For over 30 years Steadman managed the affairs of the academy, was **pastor** of a vital congregation, and busied himself in developing the Baptist denomination in the North. In 1809 he established the Baptist Itinerant Society to aid in establishing churches required by the growth of the Industrial Revolution; the academy specialized in a training pattern which emphasized the students' engagement in church planting and evangelism--"**evangelism** steadied by education." Steadman also helped to rally the churches of the North of England to the support of the **Baptist Missionary Society** (BMS) and the **Baptist Union** (BU), in whose interests he travelled widely. Steadman's published works include a dozen sermons on devotional and educational topics.

STEANE, EDWARD (1798-1882). English Baptist minister, born at Oxford, England. He studied at Bristol Baptist College and later at the University of Edinburgh, graduating in 1821. He became **pastor** at Camberwell in 1823 and served until 1853 when he became co-pastor with John Burnet. Although frequently ill, he served the Baptist denomination in a number of significant posts, including co-secretary of the **Baptist Union** (BU) with **John H. Hinton**, a member of the General Committee of the **Baptist Missionary Society** (BMS), editor of the *New Selection Hymnbook*, and one of the founders of the Bible Translation Society, formed in opposition to the British and Foreign Bible Society. Steane was a keen promoter of the formation of the Evangelical Alliance and was editor of its journal. In 1862, although removed from pastoral work, he retained the title in his congregation. Among his published works were *Christ, the First Fruits of the Resurrection* (1833), *The Religious Condition of Christendom* (1851), and *The Doctrine of Christ, Developed by the Apostles* (1872).

STEARNS, SHUBAEL (1706-1771). American Baptist minister, born at Boston, Massachusetts. The early life of Stearns is without detail, except that he was caught up in the **New Light** Congregationalist movement at the time when many were converting to Baptist principles. Baptized by Wait Palmer (fl. 1740-1780), the pastor of First Baptist Church, North Stonington, Connecticut, Stearns and his brother-in-law, **Daniel Marshall**, went South in 1754 and conducted itinerant **evangelism**. The result was the gathering of several churches in central North Carolina, which later became the Sandy Creek Association. Stearns considered himself a **Separate Baptist**, emphasizing believer's **baptism**, experiential conversion, and strict adherence to biblical lifestyle. **Morgan Edwards** reported in his travels that Stearns had collected a following of almost 600 people in Carolina colony.

STENNETT FAMILY. A family of Baptist ministers in England which enjoyed great distinction over four generations. Edward Stennett (d. 1705) was a clergyman during the Puritan Revolution who suffered great persecution, preaching at Abingdon, Wallingford, and Pinner's Hall, London. His persecution stemmed from participating in the Civil War on the side of Parliament and his violation of the **Clarendon Code** during the Restoration. Early in his life he developed sabbatarian tendencies and was instrumental in 1670 in establishing the first **Seventh Day Baptist** Church in the American colonies. Joseph (1663-1713), born at Abingdon, was a Seventh Day Baptist who preached at the Pinner's Hall Church on Saturdays and elsewhere among the **Particular Baptists** on Sundays. A poet and Hebrew scholar, he frequently defended Baptist beliefs and was well received by the Royal Family. He published five volumes of essays and sermons, as well as influencing positively the singing of contemporary hymns in the **Nonconformist** community.

Joseph's son, Joseph (1692-1758), was pastor of the Seventh Day Baptist Church at Mill Yard, Goodman's Fields, in London from 1720 to the 1750s. He also served first day congregations in Exeter and was **pastor** of the church at Little Wild Street in London, a Seventh Day minister in a Particular Baptist congregation. On behalf of the **Three**

Dissenting Denominations, he presented an address to King George II which pleased the King greatly on his return to England in 1745. He authored eight works and was given the doctor of divinity degree by the University of Edinburgh.

Joseph's son, Samuel Stennett (1727-1795), was born in Exeter. He was a language scholar and person of high social standing. He also served the Little Wild Street Church, following his father, for 47 years. The University of Aberdeen conferred upon him the doctor of divinity degree in 1763. Like his forbears, he enjoyed a wide political influence in addressing the concerns of **dissenters**. Samuel was also the author of scores of devotional and doctrinal works and numerous hymns, including "Majestic Sweetness Sits Enthroned" and "On Jordan's Stormy Banks," both favorites of generations of Baptists.

ST. HELENA AND ASCENSION ISLAND. Baptist life on St. Helena dates from the early 19th century when **Adoniram Judson** landed there in 1850 for a brief time. Baptist church development began in the 1880s as part of the care of Baptists in **South Africa**, largely influenced by the **Baptist Missionary Society** (BMS). As of 1995, there is a small Baptist community of one church with about 75 members on St. Helena.

STILLMAN, SAMUEL (1737-1807). American Baptist minister, born at Philadelphia, Pennsylvania. At an early age he moved to Charleston, South Carolina, and was tutored privately. Converted under the ministry of **Oliver Hart**, he also received his theological education under Hart as a personal mentor. In 1759 he was ordained an **evangelist** and assumed the pastorate at James Island, South Carolina. While on a tour of the Northeast, he received the A.M. degree from the College of Philadelphia and the next year an honorary degree from Harvard College. In 1761 he moved to the Baptist church at Bordentown, New Jersey, and in 1763 he became James Bound's (fl.1760) assistant at Second Baptist, Boston, Massachusetts. In 1765 he succeeded Jeremiah Condy (fl.1750-65) at First Baptist, Boston, where he remained until his death. For 42 years, Stillman was the leading Baptist minister in New England, if not the United States. He was a prime mover in the organization of the Massachusetts Baptist Missionary Society, the foremost preacher at **ordinations** and for election sermons in the region, and well respected among other denominations. Stillman's published works include over 30 sermons.

STINSON, BENONI (1798-1869). American Baptist minister, born at Montgomery County, Kentucky. In 1816 he experienced a call to **ministry** and served churches in the Wabash Association. He found the doctrinal standards of the Association rigidly Calvinistic and he formed a new congregation on the general atonement principle. At one point he considered joining the **Freewill Baptists,** but he disliked their connectionalism. By 1824 a following, called "Stinsonites," formed a new **association,** the Liberty Association of **General Baptists,** a forerunner of the **General Association of General Baptists** (GAGB). Stinson himself served the Liberty Baptist Church of Howell, Indiana, for 46 years (1823-1869).

STINTON, BENJAMIN (1677-1719). English Baptist minister and historian, born in London. He was educated in a grammar school and learned several languages, becoming a schoolteacher. In his early years he did translation work and wrote hymns. In 1704 he was persuaded to become the pastor at Horsley-down Baptist Church, which he served to his death. Stinton became a significant Baptist leader beyond the local church, serving as a delegate to the **Particular Baptist** Assembly in 1692, and organizing in 1713 a Baptist ministerium at the **Hanover Coffeehouse,** which became the denomination's link with the **Three Dissenting Denominations.** Stinton reached across theological lines to include General Baptists and he was respected among Congregational and Presbyterian **Nonconformists.** In 1717 he participated in a public debate with illustrious dissenters on a point of baptismal theology and he helped to found the Particular Baptist Fund in the same year. A collector of Baptist historical materials, Stinton was assigned the task of preparing a history of the Baptists which he diverted to a history of **baptism.** The task and his collected materials eventually devolved upon his son-in-law, **Thomas Crosby.** Stinton's records are the primary sources for the historical beginnings of the Particular Baptists. In 1730 Stinton published *A Short Catechism,* reprinted in several later editions.

STOW, BARON STEUBEN (1801-1869). American Baptist minister and denominational leader, born at Croydon, New Hampshire. He was among the first to register at Columbian College, the new Baptist university in the nation's capital, from which he graduated; the failure of the college, however, was a sore point to Stow and he blamed **Luther Rice** for its demise. This led ultimately to his service on a committee of investigation of Rice's conduct in 1826. Stow served churches in Portsmouth, New Hampshire, and Boston, Massachusetts, becoming an influential spokesman for New England-style organizations. In the Boston context, he supported revival meetings in 1838 and 1842, part of a city-wide awakening; his pastoral ministry include over 1,500 sermons and 25,000 miles of travel. Stowe was one of those asked to prepare a draft of a new organization for the **General Missionary Convention** in 1845 after the **Southern Baptist** delegates departed. His plan won, emphasizing the powers of the executive committee, and he was largely responsible for eliminating the debt of the old convention. Stow was a principal correspondence link with Baptists in Great Britain, each year composing data and opinion for their annual yearbook entries on American Baptists. His publications include *The Efficiency of Missions* (1838), *The Psalmist: A New Collection of Hymns for Use in Baptist Churches* (1843), and *The Missionary Enterprise* (1846).

STOWE, PHINEAS (1812-1868). American Baptist minister and missionary, born at Milford, Connecticut. He studied at New Hampton Literary and Theological Institute and served the South Danvers, Massachusetts, Baptist Church for two years, 1843-1845. Out of this **ministry** came a concern for seamen and at the Mariner's Exchange in Boston he formed a general purpose mission that focused on **evangelism**, personal care, education, and worship. This expanded into a Soldiers Home and ministries to prostitutes. His entire scheme was to become the Boston Baptist Bethel Society (1845), the term "Bethel" applying to the seamen's missions. Stowe's work in Boston became a model for other city missions in mid-19th century America. He was the author of *Ocean Melodies and Seamen's Companion* (1849).

STRATON, JOHN ROACH (1875-1929). Southern and American Baptist minister and educator, born at Evansville, Indiana. He attended Mercer University and studied for two years at Southern Baptist Theological Seminary. For short terms he taught oratory at Mercer and Baylor Universities, but turned to the pastoral **ministry**. He successively served churches at Louisville, Kentucky (1900-1903), Hubbard City, Texas (1903-1905), Chicago, Illinois (1905-1908), Baltimore, Maryland (1908-1913), Norfolk, Virginia (1914-1917), and New York City (1918-1929). Straton employed sensational methods (colorful language and name calling), and was considered one of the strictest **fundamentalists** of his era.

Straton's primary circle of influence was the Fundamentalist League of Greater New York City for Ministers and Laymen, which he founded in 1922. He was active in organizing fundamentalists in the **Northern Baptist Convention** (NBC), 1920-1926, ultimately withdrawing his church, Calvary Baptist in New York City, from the Convention in 1926. Confrontational in style, Straton began the first regular religious broadcast in New York City (WQAO) and held tent meetings about the region. He confronted prostitution districts in east coast cities, evolutionary teachings in Northern Baptist schools, and wealthy Baptist laymen like **John D. Rockefeller,** who supported what Straton termed "**liberal** causes" (see **Liberalism**). In 1928 he purchased a hotel in Ocean Grove, New Jersey, to operate a **bible** conference, but after only a short time it burned down, the result of arson. An opponent of the **social gospel**, the liquor traffic, and Alfred E. Smith (1873-1944) the Democratic candidate for president, Straton favored woman's suffrage as a vehicle to increase the political power of his fundamentalist agenda. His published works include *Ragtime Religion* (1899), *The Menace of Immorality in Church and State; Messages of Judgement* (1920), and *Fighting the Devil in Modern Babylon* (1929).

STRICT BAPTISTS (SB). A movement among English **Particular Baptists** of the late 18th and early 19th centuries which stressed **conservative**, high-Calvinistic doctrines and practice. In response to the perceived antinomianism and open communionism of the era and Baptist leaders such as **Robert Hall** and **Andrew Fuller**, certain Baptist ministers called for strict adherence to the faith. In the 1820s fellowship among churches and pastors was divided in the Norfolk and Suffolk Associations between supporters of George Wright (1789-1863), a strict Calvinist, and Cornelius Elvin (1797-1873), an open communionist. Another early leader was **William Gadsby**, who was followed by Joseph Tiptaft (1803-1864), Charles W. Banks (1806-1886), and **Joseph C. Philpot** in a strict, Calvinistic Baptist persuasion. Most of these pastors refused to accept "Fullerism" (see **Fuller, Andrew**) as a subtle concession to general atonement and, worse, perceived rising **universalism**, and they remained outside the regular associational life and membership in the **Baptist Union of Great Britain and Ireland**. Gadsby began publication of *The Gospel Standard, or Feeble Christian's Support* in 1835, which greatly united the emerging Strict Baptist churches. Those following the position of Gadsby came to be called "Gadsbyites."

Strict Baptists formed their own association in the Suffolk and Norfolk Strict Association (1829), the first such group to be called "Strict." In 1841 the Strict Communion Society was formed in London and evolved into the Baptist Evangelical Society, supporting missionary activity in **Germany** and **Denmark** and an educational institution, the Manchester Baptist College. In 1852 the London Strict Baptist Association was formed, becoming the Metropolitan Association of Strict Baptist Churches (1871) in the London region.

Schisms over the degree of hyper-Calvinism and Christological issues occurred with one branch following Philpot known as the *Gospel Standard* Strict Baptists a second branch which followed John Stevens of

London, dubbed the "Pre-existerians" because they held that Christ's human soul existed before the Incarnation, and a third branch which followed Banks and his paper, *The Earthen Vessel*, (later united with *The Gospel Herald*), which was open to discussion of doctrinal matters with other Baptists and considered by some open to error. Beginning in 1861 the *Gospel Standard* Strict Baptists engaged in a divisive disagreement with the *Earthen Vessel* Strict Baptists over the **Sonship Controversy**. At length defined as **Separatists** on doctrinal matters, the *Gospel Standard* Baptists in 1870 asserted a name for themselves, "The Living Family," in contrast with all other churches, which constituted the "Congregation of the Dead." In contrast, *The Earthen Vessel* Strict Baptists characterized themselves as "full, faithful, free grace, old-fashioned New Testament followers of Jesus." In more recent history, the generic term "Strict Baptist" has applied to at least three divisions, with the *Gospel Standard* group maintaining its sole claim to the historic Strict position. Certain segments of the Strict Baptists have had relations with the "Old School" or **Primitive Baptists** in the United States who share a similar doctrinal ethos. In the early years of the Strict Baptist movement the churches were characterized by plain dress, no instrumental music, and no ministerial titles such as "reverend." Strict Baptists commonly referred to Union Baptists as "amalgamated and aristocratic," meant in a pejorative sense.

In the later 20th century, one branch of the Strict Baptists, which includes many of the churches and four associations, has since 1961 taken the name "Grace Baptists," united by congregational freedom and several cooperative agencies. This contemporary movement supports the Grace Baptist Assembly (the annual gathering), Grace Baptist Mission (formerly the Strict Baptist Mission), four regional **associations**, a women's organization, a **Sunday School** association, a youth fellowship, a publishing house called Grace Publications Trust, and a monthly paper called *Grace*. Among their many objectives, the Grace associations seek to support the historic local churches against closure and dwindling resources. The "Gadsbyites", supporting the *Gospel Standard* publication constitute a separate group, and a third segment of Strict Baptists for many years rallied around the publication, *The Christian's Pathway*, published 1895-1969 at London. That branch continued energetically to promote the old theological distinctives. The terminology "Strict Baptist" remains in an historical society and a trust and pension fund.

As of 1995 there were 255 churches and approximately 25,000 members and adherents in the Strict Baptist connection. *Grace Magazine* (1970-), whose predecessors were the *Gospel Herald* (1833-1970) and the *Free Grace Record* (1920-1970), is published at Surrey and there is a Sovereign Grace Union in Swanwick.

STRONG, AUGUSTUS HOPKINS (1836-1921). American Baptist minister and educator, born at Rochester, New York. He was educated at Yale College and was one of the first graduates of Rochester Theological Seminary. For a time he followed the career of his father in newspaper writing, later turning to pastoral ministry at Haverhill, Massachusetts, and First Baptist, Cleveland, Ohio, from 1865-1872. At Cleveland he met **John D. Rockefeller** who almost persuaded Strong to head up a revised University of Chicago. Instead, Strong became the president of Rochester Theological Seminary and taught systematic theology there for 40 years. He became the leading American Baptist theologian of his era and his popular *Systematic Theology* (1907) was used by scores of Baptist professors and students as a statement of orthodox Baptist beliefs. Strong led Rochester Seminary into becoming a premier theological school of the Northern Baptists, attracting a distinguished faculty and a large endowment from donors such as Rockefeller and John Jay Jones (1831-1904). Strong's impressive list of publications includes *Philosophy and Religion* (1888), *The Great Poets and Their Theology* (1898), *Christ in Creation and Ethical Monism* (1899), and *A Tour of the Missions* (1918).

STUNDISM. A religious movement in Imperial **Russia** which led to the development of the Baptist movement in that country and **Ukraine**. The term seems to have appeared first in Odessa about 1867 to denote Christian believers who followed a pietistic lifestyle, including small group **bible study**, other pietistic practices of the early church, and a sober lifestyle. Its early leaders were Mikhail Ratushnyi (1830-1911) of Osnova and Ivan G. Riobashapka (1832-1902) of Liubomirka. About 1869 Efim Tsymbal (d.1880) led many Stundists to accept water **baptism** and in 1872 the movement split into two factions. The Novo-Stundists organized a congregation at Kosiakovko which became the first Baptist church in Ukraine. The term "Stundism" became synonymous with undesirable sectarianism and in 1894 Stundism broadly applied was outlawed by the Ministry of Internal Affairs of Russia.

ST. VINCENT. Baptist Mid-Missions (BMM) from the United States established a mission on the island in 1947 at Arnos Vale. The mission also serves churches on St. Lucia.

SUCCESSIONISM. Term applied to the attempt by some Baptist historians to trace the development of Baptists back through the ages in an unbroken line or "succession" to roots in the New Testament. In this tradition, each congregation grows out of another and is formed by the authority of another. Among those who espoused this position were **David Benedict**

(1813), G. H. Orchard (1838), **James R. Graves** (1855), **John T. Christian** (1896), W. B. Jarrel (1894), and D. B. Ray (1949). Refutation of the successionist theory began with **Henry C. Vedder** (1892), **William H. Whitsett** (1896), **Albert H. Newman** (1899), and most recently, W. Morgan Patterson (1969). While many still hold to the theory, it has for the most part been dismissed by serious historians. Many editions of the book *The Trail of Blood* (1931) by **J. M. Carroll** carry an illustrated historical successionist chart, and this has led to the popular epithet "Trail of Blood" applied to successionism. See also **Landmarkism; Local Church Protectionism.**

SUDAN. Baptist missionary work in Sudan has been minimal, due to governmental restrictions and the heavy Islamic population. In 1980 **Southern Baptists** began a medical and agricultural **mission** project growing from their work in Ethiopia, but this was withdrawn to Kenya in 1984. Several Baptist missions attempted church establishment and the result was scattered congregations which became part of the evangelical Christian community. As of 1995 it has been estimated there were about seven churches with 260 members of a baptistic type in Sudan.

SULLIVAN PRINCIPLES. In the 1970s and 1980s many North American Christians became sensitive to the racial segregation policy of the government of **South Africa,** known as "apartheid." Some organizations in the United States, notably the **American Baptist Churches in the U.S.A.,** took steps to influence the government of South Africa, and one strategy was the adoption of the "Sullivan Principles." Named for the Rev. Leon Sullivan (1922-), pastor of Zion Baptist Church in Philadelphia, Pennsylvania, the six principles involved non-segregation of races, fair employment practices, pay equity, training programs for Black employees, and appointment of more Black supervisors and managers in businesses. Underlying the principles were assumptions that economic pressure would eventuate in social changes. The American Baptist Churches General Board in June 1981 agreed to investigate banking and investment procedures and evaluate the ethical and moral bases of all involvements of companies representing the denomination's interests in South Africa, in addition to adopting the Sullivan Principles at the same time.

SUNDAY SCHOOL BOARD, SOUTHERN BAPTIST CONVENTION (BSSB). Several attempts were made to establish a publishing house and Sunday School organization from the beginning of the **Southern Baptist Convention** in 1845 through the 1870s. First was the Southern Baptist

Publication Society (1847-1863) which was charged with producing literature indigenous to the South. Next came the Bible Board (1851-1863), which circulated bibles across the South but soon came under **Landmarkist** influences. Third was the founding of the Southern Baptist Sunday School Union in 1857 which was decidedly under Landmark control and the result of efforts made by **James R. Graves.** These early organizations floundered due to competition or because of the Civil War. Following the war, several attempts were again made to create a southern publishing organization, notably with the inclusion of publication in the work of the Domestic and Indian Mission Board. Competition from the **American Baptist Publication Society**, however, again outdistanced the efforts of Southern Baptists.

It was in 1885 that **Isaac T. Tichenor** in the Home Mission Board called for a committee to provide **Sunday School** literature for the churches. Three years later the Sunday School Board was established by vote of the Convention. It began a denominational publishing business and aggressive outreach to the churches. Between 1901 and 1919 the Board developed a strategy to make the Sunday School a primary facilitator of **evangelism** and this emphasis marked its genius. In 1917 the Baptist Young People's Union came under the aegis of the Board. From 1935 through the 1950s the sales of the Board reached unprecedented levels and financially carried a good deal of the mission program of the Convention. In 1916 the BSSB was requested to develop an historical program for Southern Baptists and this eventually led to the development of the E. C. Dargan Library and to the establishment of the separate Historical Commission in 1951. Growth in Sunday Schools slowed in the 1960s and the Baptist Training Union program declined dramatically in the same era. To complicate matters further, controversy arose in the publishing house in the 1970s related to the Board, Broadman Press, over perceived **liberal** tendencies in producing **bible** commentaries. Change in leadership and a renewed emphasis upon biblically centered material, maintained the status of the Sunday School Board as the largest producer of Baptist-related educational materials in the world. Also related to the Board are regional Baptist Book Stores, the Baptist Conference Centers at Ridgecrest, North Carolina, and Glorietta, New Mexico, and the purchase of the Holman Bible Company. The world headquarters of the Sunday School Board are in Nashville, Tennessee. See also **American Baptist Publication Society**; **Sunday Schools**.

SUNDAY SCHOOLS. The idea of Sunday or sabbath school education emerged from a concern for the poorer and working-class children of England in the late 17th century. Charity schools were operated under the auspices of Christian leaders in the late 17th century. In the 1780s Robert Raikes (1735-1811) and **William Fox** pioneered a system of schools which held classes on the only free day of the week, Sunday. The purpose of Sunday Schools included inculcation of literacy, manners, and religious instruction.

Baptists were at the forefront of Sunday School development in the United States as well. In Philadelphia, Pennsylvania, the First Day Society was organized in 1791; the first Sunday School in New York was opened in 1803. Baptists became directly interested in the movement in 1826 when the **General Missionary Convention** urged American Baptists to develop Sunday Schools. In 1839 the Hudson River New York Baptist Association recommended the creation of an American Baptist Sunday School Union, based on the model of the New England Sabbath School Union, an ecumenical venture. This in turn led to the inclusion of the term "Sunday School" in the new charter of the **American Baptist Publication Society**, and it became the primary advocate of Sunday Schools among Baptists in the United States for the remainder of the 19th century. Southern Baptists, also sensing the importance of Sunday Schools, established in 1857 a Southern Baptist Sunday School Union, to be followed by a Board of Sunday Schools in 1863. What later became the Baptist **Sunday School Board** in 1891 became the largest producer in the world of program materials and literature for all ages. The Broadman Press was established by the Sunday School Board in honor of the first secretary, **John A. Broadus**, and the first president, Basil **Manly**, Jr. (1825-1892).

Among many Baptists, Sunday School is not only a forum for **evangelism** of children and youth but also a regular setting for Christian nurture and **bible** study for persons of all ages. Many Baptist groups administer "graded lesson plans" which correspond to school grades and have a regular development of bible content instruction. Others follow the Uniform lesson series, which follows a Protestant lectionary series of lessons. Typically the Sunday School meets either just prior to the morning worship service or during the last portion of the service.

SURINAME. In 1888 the initial Baptist presence was established in Suriname by a national of the country trained in England, Solomon Bromet. The congregation he commenced became an interdenominational work. Much later, **Southern Baptist** mission in Suriname began in 1971 at Paramaribo as an outgrowth of work in Trinidad. Baptist membership involves not only the Dutch community but also East Indian peoples living in Suriname. The United Baptist Church, a Baptist **association**, was formed around the main Baptist community.

As of 1995 there were approximately 15 churches with about 1,200 members affiliated with the United Baptist Church of Suriname.

SUTCLIF, JOHN (1752-1814). English Baptist minister, born at Hebden Bridge, England. Sutcliff was educated at Bristol Academy, and by **Dan Taylor** and **John Fawcett**. Sutcliff served briefly at the Baptist Church in Shrewsbury, and Cannon Street Baptist Church in Birmingham in 1774. He entered his long **ministry** at Olney in 1775. It was Sutclif who sent **William Carey** into the ministry and who was a prime mover in the establishment of the **Baptist Missionary Society** (BMS); he was present with Carey and Fuller and preached at the 1791 Northamptonshire Association meeting at Clipstone. Sutclif developed the idea of auxiliary societies in distant regions in support of the central society itself. He was a close confidant of **Andrew Fuller** and was remembered for his cautious attitudes. Among those who exerted theological influences on Sutclif was John Newton (1725-1807), who helped him to moderate his Calvinistic perspective. Sutcliff's publications include *First Principles of the Oracles of God* (1789), a widely used catechism for children.

SUTTON, AMOS (1802-1855). English Baptist missionary, born at Sevenoaks, Kent. He entered the New Connection of **General Baptists** and became in 1824 a missionary of the General Baptist Missionary Society to **India**. His appointment sent him to Calcutta, but he settled at Cuttack in Orissa State. Due to ill health in 1832 he travelled to the United States where he came in contact with the **Freewill Baptists** and he helped them form the Freewill Baptist Foreign Mission Society in 1832, becoming their first missionary. He returned to be pastor of the church at Cuttack in 1836-1847. Returning again to England in 1847-1850, he was **pastor** of the General Baptist church at Dover Street, Leicester, after which he went out a third time to Cuttack in Orissa. Sutton had a remarkably prolific publishing career, including a translation of the New Testament into Oriya (1845), *A Narrative of the Mission to Orissa* (1833), *Oriya Grammar* (1840), *Oriya Dictionary* (1843), and *Elements of Natural Philosophy* (1843).

SWAN, JABEZ SMITH (1800-1884). American Baptist evangelist, born at Stonington, Connecticut. Called to preach in 1822, he studied at Hamilton Literary and Theological Institution (later Madison University). He was ordained an evangelist in 1827, but settled at Norwich, New York, in 1830. Over the next 30 years, he moved from church to church and conducted several successful evangelistic and protracted revival meetings. His labors in **revival** were especially noteworthy in Preston,

New York (1837), Mystic Bridge and New London, Connecticut (1842-1843), Albany, New York (1848), and Providence, Rhode Island (1858), after which he served as pastor at Huntingdon Street, New London, Connecticut. For alternative years he was state Baptist evangelist in Connecticut and New York and one of the greatest exponents of the **Second Great Awakenings**. His biography, *The Evangelist* (1873), became a textbook of revival techniques.

SWAZILAND. Baptist witness in Swaziland began early in the 20th century with missionary efforts by the **Southern Baptists** and the **National Baptist Convention, U.S.A.**

As of 1995, there were 10 churches with 350 members in the Baptist community in Swaziland associated with the Southern Baptist Mission.

SWEDEN. Baptist life in Sweden is one of the oldest and strongest families in Europe. The first congregation dates from 1854 when two furriers started a work at Stockholm. **Anders Wiberg,** who had been baptized by **F. O. Nilsson,** became pastor of the church in 1856, and led in the dramatic development of the sect in Sweden. In 1857 a Union was formed and soon thereafter cordial relations were established with German leaders. A theological seminary named Betelseminariat was opened near Stockholm in 1866 and it did much to foster leadership for over a hundred churches. In 1889 the Swedish Union organized a missionary society which sponsored domestc missions and overseas efforts in **Spain**, **Russia,** Asia, and Africa. The Svenska Baptistsamfundet publishes *Vecko-posten* (Weekly Post) (1868-).

A major rift occurred among Swedish Baptists in 1892-1907 when a mission work was started at Örebro, an industrial town. The rift initially occurred over influences of the "New Movement," a type of Pentecostalism. Those associated with the mission under the leadership of John Ongman (1855-1931) were ardent supporters of **women** preachers, foreign **missions**, and **revivalism**. Ongman was independent in his attitude and started his own **theological school**. In the 1930s differences again arose over central organization, Pentecostal gifts, and **liberal** theology. In 1936 a formal split occurred as the Filadelfia Church in Örebro left the Union. Thus far, the Örebro Association has remained separate not only from the Baptist Union but also from the **Baptist World Alliance** (BWA). It publishes *Missions Banneret* (Banner of Missions) (1920-).

For all Baptists in Sweden an artistic treasure is the mural painting, "The Baptists," completed in 1886 by Baron Gustaf Cederstrom. It depicts an outdoor group baptismal scene on Lake Malaren near Uppsala.

Originally displayed in Paris as "Midsummer Night in Sweden," the painting reveals the painful personal transition from the established church to a **believer's church** relationship, as well as the stigma attached to Swedish dissenters in the 19th century. The painting is on display at Betelseminariat near Stockholm.

As of 1995 there were 295 churches and 19,315 members affiliated with the Baptist Union, 405 churches with 23,000 members affiliated with the Örebro Mission, 17 churches with 1,200 members affiliated with the Free Baptist Union, and 767 churches with 44,000 members in other Baptist communities. The **Baptist Bible Fellowship** (BBF) opened a mission in Sweden in 1985. Presently, there are two Baptist-related theological studies programs in Sweden: Betelseminariat and the Stockholm School of Theology.

SWITZERLAND. There are two classes of Baptists in Switzerland: those who are the result of **J. G. Oncken's mission** and those who practiced believer's baptism since the Reformation. Oncken visited Switzerland in 1847 and baptized several at Hochwart. By 1849 there was a church in Zurich, from which came congregations at St. Gall and Thurgau. A second group, the Wiedertaufer, began in Zurich and are not formally related to the mainstream Baptist movement. The Bund der Baptistgemeinden in der Schweiz was formed in 1923. From 1949 to 1996 the **Southern Baptist**-founded theological school at Rüschlikon (Zurich) was a center of European Baptist life and education. When the Swiss government immigration policies made it difficult and expensive to maintain the student body and faculty from outside Switzerland, the seminary relocated to Praque, the **Czech Republic**. The **Baptist Bible Fellowship** (BBF) opened a mission in Switzerland in 1987.

As of 1995 there were 17 churches and 1,355 members affiliated with the Bund der Baptistgemeinden in der Schweiz. The Bund publishes *Gemeindbote* (Church Notes) (1954-).

SWORD AND TROWEL BAPTISTS. See **Continental Baptists.**

SYRIA. In 1948 the first Baptist witness in Syria was undertaken by the American Evangelical Mission, which was reorganized in 1955 to become the Syrian Baptist Mission, Inc. In 1957 this work was assumed by **Evangelical Baptist Missions** (EBM).

T

TAIWAN. Baptist work in Taiwan results from the displacement of Baptist Missionaries from mainland **China** after the Communist revolution in 1949-1953. The **Southern Baptists** have built extensively in Taiwan, organizing the Chinese Baptist Convention in 1954. In addition to the larger Baptist work in Taiwan, the **Baptist Bible Fellowship** (BBF) began a mission there in 1946, the **Conservative Baptist Foreign Mission Society** (CBFMS) in 1952, and **Baptist Mid-Missions** (BMM) from the United States established its mission in 1972. At Hsilo is located the Taiwan Conservative Baptist Theological College, founded in 1957.

As of 1995 there were 152 churches and 17,162 members affiliated with the Chinese Baptist Convention. The Conservative Baptist Association in Taiwan includes about 25 churches with 1,691 members. There is a theological school located at Taipei related to the Southern Baptist mission work.

TAJIKISTAN. See **Middle or Central Asia.**

TANGANYIKA. See **Tanzania.**

TANZANIA. In 1964 the former states of Tanganyika and Zanzibar were united as Tanzania. Baptists entered Tanzania from **Nigeria** under the sponsorship of the Southern Baptist **Foreign Mission Board** (FMB). Work began in 1956 at Dar es Salaam and at Arusha a theological school opened in 1962. For a time Tanzania was part of the East Africa Baptist Mission; from the first **association** in 1960 has evolved the Baptist Convention of Tanzania (1971). The **Baptist Bible Fellowship** (BBF) opened a mission in Tanzania in 1988.

As of 1995 there were 1,400 churches and 96,258 members affiliated with the Baptist Convention of Tanzania.

TAYLOR, ADAM (1768-1833). English Baptist schoolmaster and historian, born at Halifax, England. The son of a coal miner and General Baptist minister, and the nephew of **Dan Taylor**, he was a schoolteacher in London for most of his career. He edited the *General Baptist Repository* (1810-1822) and wrote extensive biographies of his father and uncle. His *History of the English General Baptists* (1818) was the next attempt after **Thomas Crosby** to write the history of the denomination. He separated the General stream of Baptists from the **Particular** or Calvinistic Baptists, which Crosby had intermingled.

TAYLOR, DAN (1738-1813). English Baptist minister and denominational leader, born at Sour Milk Hall, Northowram. Taylor was the son of a miner. He was raised an Anglican and joined the Methodists in 1757. Taylor read theology and studied the **bible** as he itinerated and worked as a schoolteacher. He differed with Wesley on **discipline** and, after reading a history of **baptism**, converted to the Baptists, being baptized by a **General Baptist** in Nottinghamshire. For a time, Taylor joined the General Baptists but was critical of their spiritual laxity; in 1770 he formed the New Connexion of General Baptists, characterized by **evangelical** zeal and connectionalism. Taylor's leadership and **revivalistic** techniques lead to the establishment of numerous churches, a missionary society, **Sunday Schools** and various funds. Taylor continued fellowship with the Old General Baptists, reporting to their Assembly as the representative of the Leicestershire Association and pastor of Church Lane, Whitechapel. He also served as the principal of the General Baptist academy. Taylor's many published works include *Fundamentals of Religion in Faith and Practice* (1775), *A Humble Essay on Christian Baptism* (1776), *The Reality and Efficacy of Divine Grace* (1787), *An Antidote Against Deism* (1819), and *The Christian Religion: Its Leading Principles, Practical Requirements, and Experimental Enjoyments* (1844).

TAYLOR, JAMES BARRETT (1804-1871). Southern Baptist denominational leader, born in Lincolnshire, England. At an early age his parents emigrated to the United States, settling in New York City. After relocating to Christiansville, Virginia, he declared his call to **ministry** and studied under a local tutor. In 1826 he was commissioned a missionary by the Virginia General Association and during one of his tours he met **Jeremiah Jeter**, whose influence on Taylor's life was profound. He was offered the pastorate of Second Baptist Church in Richmond, which he served from 1826-1839. Following pastoral ministry he was chaplain to the University of Virginia, and was a principal founder of Virginia Baptist Seminary, later the University of Richmond. In 1846 when the **Southern Baptist Convention** formed its **Foreign Mission Board** (FMB), Taylor was chosen the first corresponding secretary. In that role for the remainder of his career through 1872, he built an overseas program for the Convention and personally supervised appointments and efforts to raise support. During the Civil War, he travelled throughout the South as a chaplain and sought to interpret the impact of the war on the overseas missionaries. During the period of Reconstruction he favored reconciliation with the Baptist churches of the North and he opened a significant correpondance with **Baron Stowe**, the secretary of the **American Baptist Missionary Union** (ABMU). Taylor's published works include *Lives of Virginia Baptist Ministers* (1837, 1859), *Memoir of Rev. Luther Rice* (1840), and *Restricted Communion; Or Baptism an Essential Prerequisite to the Lord's Supper* (1849).

TAYLOR, JOHN (1752-1835). American Baptist preacher and writer, born in Fauquier County, Virginia. He was not formally educated, baptized by **James Ireland**, a Virginia **Separate Baptist**, and became an itinerant frontier preacher. He first served churches in the Shenandoah Valley, later moving to Kentucky where he served eight churches in a decade. Taylor is best remembered for his book, *Thoughts on Missions* (1819), in which he was the fountainhead of the antimissionary movement. He denounced **Luther Rice** and opposed missionary **associations** and societies. Later in life Taylor is said to have regretted his earlier stances, but his book continued to be definitive of that movement. His other major work, *History of Ten Baptist Churches* (1823), is an important autobiographical account of frontier Baptist life.

TEMPERANCE, BAPTISTS AND. The temperance movement was a multiplicitous approach to public drunkenness and immoral behavior; the movement ranged from those who exercised restraint in social consumption of alcohol to total abstinance. Total abstainers have always been in the numerical minority even among most evangelical religious groups.

 For the most part, mainstream Baptists have reflected cultural patterns commensurate with their socio-economic status. The use of alcoholic beverages represents changing patterns in light of larger social trends. In the 17th century, English and North American Baptists doubtless drank wine at meals and on social occasions. This is attested to in the identification of Baptists in the working-class community and in the use of wine in the celebration of the **Lord's Supper**. Further, some Baptist laymen were involved in the production of beer, like **William Kiffin**. It is historically invalid to argue that these beverages were not commonly found in households and in social interaction, as with other **Nonconformist** groups. Less likely was serious consumption of spiritous liquors, largely because of price and availability. Baptist ministers and merchants are known to have imbibed brandy, scotch, and cordials on social and ecclesiastical occasions. Extant sermonic literature and associational records do not indicate widespread prohibitory injunctions before 1800.

 In the first two decades of the 19th century Christian moral behavior evolved to lifestyle expectations which cast a serious doubt on the consumption of alcohol. Many Christian churches fostered prejudices against alcohol based on its effect upon family and relationships when used to excess. As the Temperance crusade was launched, leadership came from **evangelical** denominations such as the Methodists, and to a lesser extent the Baptists. In England, for instance, in the 1830s Baptist ministers became involved in the moderation movement, notably James Jackson of Hebden Bridge in Yorkshire, who toured widely and founded numerous local temperance societies. By the 1840s Francis Beardsall (1799-1842) argued that only non-alcoholic wine should be used in the **ordinances** and Jabez Tunnicliff (1809-1866) founded at Leeds in 1847 the **Band of Hope** organization for children associated with the temperance cause. By the 1880s many associations had temperance chapters and the Baptist Total Abstinance Association was nationally organized in 1874, although its membership and resources were quite limited. Baptists in **Wales** have taken a dim view of intoxicating beverages; no less than **Christmas Evans** spoke at rallies in the 1830s on the subject of the drink and 19th century Welsh **associations** admonished members not to go to taverns on the sabbath. As late as 1905 British Baptist leader, **J. H. Shakespeare** delivered an address to the **Baptist World Alliance** (BWA) on the merits of temperance, indicating a continuing committment to the cause.

In the United States it was Lyman Beecher (1775-1863), a Congregationalist theologian, who led the crusade against drink, beginning in the 1820s. His six sermons on intemperance in 1825 catalyzed the evangelical moral crusade and were reprinted for many generations. At length many local societies were formed which called for making a pledge of abstinence. These efforts were only modestly successful among Baptists; however, a number of associations issued letters calling for temperance. In 1840 a new phase of the movement emerged in the Washingtonian societies, which pledged total abstinance. Baptists involved included evangelist **Jacob Knapp** and Virginia pastor **William F. Broaddus**. Many local churches joined the Sons of Temperance movement and some associations in Virginia required a "Test" to establish absolute abstinence from imbibing any intoxicating liquor.

By the 1860s, with the advent of the technology to produce unfermented grape juice commercially, Baptist ministers like Abraham Coles (1813-1891) took the position that the term translated "wine" in the New Testament meant unfermented wine. Although leading **bible** scholars took exception with this viewpoint, such as **Alvah Hovey** of Newton Theological Institution, most churches soon adopted grape juice in the **Lord's Supper** and a disinclination to admit to social uses of alcohol.

In the **social gospel** movement at the turn of the century, Northern Baptist leaders such as **Shailer Mathews** and Samuel Zane Batten (1859-1925) advocated temperance on a scientific platform. Southern Baptists were publicly and vehemently teetotal, partly in response to the fiery attacks on "demon rum" by **fundamentalists** like **J. Frank Norris**. Norris railed against those who failed to perceive the effects of drinking and preached a famous sermon on "Hebrew, Shebrew, the World is Going to Hell with Home Brew". (This was in contrast to the reputation of Southern Baptist Seminary **theologian James P. Boyce** who had a renowned winecellar and died of gout!) The ranks of those who called for closure of saloons and temperance for spiritual and medical reasons included nationally recognized leaders like George B. Cutten (1874-1962), president of Colgate University in 1942, and **Harry Emerson Fosdick**, who thought the merits of temperance outweighed the freedom to consume in an era of Prohibition.

Popularly speaking, during the 20th century, the majority of Baptists in the United States abstain from alcoholic consumption, but many are not openly critical of social drinking. Support for a temperance position is found in the words of a popular covenant (1836), "We will abstain from the use of intoxicating beverages." In Europe, social drinking is common among Baptists, in Latin America and eastern Europe alcoholic consumption can be associated with a more permissive lifestyle and the Roman Catholic tradition, thus it is not encouraged. In the missionary context, particularly where **Southern Baptists** and other **conservative** evangelical Baptists are located, abstinance is the norm both for the missionaries and usually the indigenous communities they serve.

THAILAND. Baptists began missionary work in Siam (Thailand) as an outgrowth of the **American Baptist** mission in Burma (**Myanmar**). In 1833 John Taylor Jones (1802-1851) established the first congregation at Bangkok; in 1835 **William Dean**, another American Baptist missionary, established the first Chinese Baptist Church in Bangkok. Although numerous missionaries were appointed to Siam, most left and went to one of the **China** fields. This caused the Siamese work to languish and American Baptists withdrew from the field in 1914.

The Chinese Baptist churches date their organization from William Dean in 1837 and formed many years later in 1959 the Pakh District Church of Christ. The Lahu Baptist Convention of the 18th District was organized in 1901; the Karen Baptists of the 19th District formed an association in 1954 and the Thailand Baptist Churches Association in the 16th District organized in 1989. With the closing of the Chinese field in 1949-1954, Siam became an important staging area for missions to China and, since the 1940s, American missionaries again have begun work permanently in Thailand. The Thailand Baptist Missionary Fellowship was formed in 1974 to coordinate the work of the American and Australian Baptists in the country; **Swedish Baptists** joined in 1976 and the **Baptist Missionary Society** (BMS) of Great Britain entered the arrangement in 1986. The **Baptist Bible Fellowship** (BBF) opened a mission in Thailand in 1983 and the **Association of Baptists for World Evangelism** (ABWE) began a mission to Thailand in 1992.

As of 1995 there were four major Baptist groups in Thailand: Karen Baptist Association with 82 churches and 16,229 members; Lahu Baptist Convention with 108 churches and 8,139 members; Pakh District Church of Christ in Thailand with 29 churches and 5,322 members; and Thailand Baptist Churches Association with 41 churches and 3,272 members. Presently, there is a theological school at Chiang Mai.

THEOLOGICAL EDUCATION. Theological education strictly speaking, applies to the training of ministers; among Baptists it has also applied to education for missionaries, educators, and lay training.

The first school for ministerial training was Bristol Academy in England. The roots of this school are found in the Edward Terrill Trust, established in 1679 to support the pastors of Broadmead Baptist Church, Bristol, in mentoring candidates for **ministry**. Bristol Baptist Academy was started in 1720, became a college in 1770, and affiliated with the University of Bristol in 1909. In 1787 the General Baptists founded Midlands College at Nottingham; in 1919 this school merged with Rawdon College.

Other schools in the British Baptist family were formed in the early 19th century. In the North, **William Steadman** pioneered the development in 1804 of an academy (which became Rawdon College) to train ministers for the churches of Lancashire and Yorkshire. Partly in response to the advance of the Baptists of the North, London Baptists founded the Theological College at Stepney in 1810, later to become Regent's Park College in Oxford. At Croydon, **C. H. Spurgeon** started the Pastor's College (later known as Spurgeon's College) in 1856. Closed communion Baptists in the North formed in 1866 a college at Bury, later the Manchester Baptist College, which in 1964 merged with Rawdon College to become the Northern Baptist College at Manchester. Related to Spurgeon's College was the establishment in 1892 of the Irish Baptist Theological College by Hugh D. Brown (1858-1918) at Belfast, later transferred to Dublin.

Baptist theological education in **Scotland** dates from the early 19th century. The **Haldanes** operated theological schools from 1797 to 1806, producing most of the domestic missionaries of that era. In 1820 **Robert Haldane** permanently established classes at Grantown-on-Spey. In 1837 the Baptist Academical Society for Scotland was formed and a year later Francis Johnstone (1810-1880) began the Baptist Theological Academy of Scotland, first at Cupar then at Edinburgh. In 1894 a second attempt to start a college was made with the establishment of the Baptist Theological College in Glasgow. It continues to the present.

In **Wales** there has been a significant interest in the training of ministers. An academy at Trosnant was started in 1734 by John Griffiths. The first college was opened at Abergavenny in 1807. Subsequently, colleges appeared at Pontypool (removed from Abergavenny in 1836), Haverfordwest (1839), and the Coleg Bartolomeus at Llangollan (1862); Pontypool College moved to Cardiff in 1893; the Baptist College at Haverfordwest moved to Aberystwyth in 1894 and closed in 1899. Following a major study in 1892, the number of colleges in Wales was reduced to two: Bangor in the North and, by 1899, Cardiff in the South.

In the extended British educational tradition are the Baptist schools in **Australia** and **New Zealand**. Australian Baptists maintain five colleges: Baptist Theological College of Victoria (Whitley College, 1891), Queensland Baptist Theological College (1904), Baptist Theological College of New South Wales (Morling College, 1916), Baptist Theological College of South Australia (Burleigh College, 1952), and Baptist Theological College of Western Australia (1963). Several of these colleges have some type of relationship with a local university. In New Zealand, there is one institution: the Baptist Theological College of New Zealand, at Auckland.

In North America, the first strategy of ministerial training involved being mentored by a senior **pastor**. This was popular in New England and the South, illustrated best in the life of **Samuel Stillman**, who was mentored by **Oliver Hart**. Later as the need grew, five basic institutional models of ministerial education have been employed. In 1764, Baptists of the **Philadelphia Baptist Association** led in establishing the College of Rhode Island, which offered a classical undergraduate university degree; this model was sufficient for several generations of select ministerial leadership, most of whom served eastern, urban congregations.

A second model was the school created by **William Staughton** in his home in Philadelphia in 1807, largely on the example of Bristol Baptist College in England, his alma mater. This model did not have a long history in the United States due to competition from leading schools in other denominations and the institutional progress of higher education. Staughton himself was persuaded to abandon the concept for the literary and theological school model (see below).

The third model was employed in the period 1830-1850, the manual labor "institute." Popular among many denominations, particularly in rural southern states, this concept involved students on an agricultural farm who attended lectures and enjoyed both practical and theoretical education. The cost of students was kept to a minimum, they being allowed to work for expenses, and it was generally considered to be a physically healthful approach to secondary and collegiate studies. Owing to the sponsorship of Baptist state organizations, theological subjects and religious exercises characterized instruction in the institutes. The manual labor model was used in Virginia (Richmond College, pre-1840), Indiana (Franklin College, 1837), North Carolina (Wake Forest College, 1834), Georgia (Mercer University, 1833), and South Carolina (Furman University, 1837). This model was quickly superceded by the L&T model, owing to the limit of students on a farm and the limitations of faculty, curriculum, and financial resources, which came mostly from urban areas.

A fourth major model was the literary and theological school (L&T) combination. Baptists in Maine followed this path first when they established Maine Literary and Theological Institution at Waterville in 1813. The idea called for a basic arts curriculum maintained in conjunction with a theological program taught by one or two professors. This was the model employed in Hamilton (New York) in 1819, Columbian (D.C.) in 1821, and in Granville Literary and Theological Institution, Ohio (1831), Michigan and Huron (1833), and Rock Springs, Illinois (1827). After a decade or so of the combined program, under pressure from the Andover model, most of the L&T schools placed their emphasis upon the arts curriculum and either closed the theological program (Colby, Columbian) or made it an independent department (Madison/Colgate).

The fifth model was the post-undergraduate theological seminary pioneered by Massachusetts Baptists at Newton Theological Institution, founded in 1825. Newton's curriculum was based on Andover Theological Seminary (Congregationalist) and rested on the assumption that candidates for the ministry would first complete a baccalaureate degree. Other institutions which followed this pattern include the transformed Theological Department of Madison University (later Colgate, 1835), Rochester Theological Seminary (1850), Southern Baptist Theological Seminary (1859), Crozer Theological Seminary (1867), Cobb Divinity School of Bates College (1870), and the Divinity School of the University of Chicago (1892).

In the 20th century, Baptist theological education in the United States has followed one of two streams: a denominational expansionary pattern or a pattern based on a theological **confession**. Those which were established to meet expanding needs of a particular group include North American Baptist Seminary (1851/1949), Bethel Theological Seminary (1871), Southwestern Baptist Theological Seminary (1909), Berkeley Baptist Divinity School (1912), Norwegian Baptist Theological Seminary (1913), New Orleans Baptist Theological Seminary (1947), Southeastern Baptist Theological Seminary (1950), Midwestern Baptist Theological Seminary (1959), and Golden Gate Baptist Theological Seminary (1954). Those for which a theological tradition was important are Northern Baptist Theological Seminary (1913), The Eastern Baptist Theological Seminary (1925), Western Conservative Baptist Seminary (1928), California Baptist Theological Seminary (1948), Denver Conservative Baptist Seminary (1953), Mid-America Baptist Theological Seminary (1972), Liberty Baptist Seminary (1973), and Beeson Divinity School (1988). Several factions in a more progressive theological tradition have established theological schools or faculties at Richmond, Virginia, Baylor University in Texas (1994), Mercer University in Georgia, and at Campbell University and Wake Forest University in North Carolina.

In **Canada** the literary and theological model was followed at Acadia University, New Brunswick Seminary (closed in 1872), and in the first generations at McMaster University. In 1957 McMaster shifted to an exclusively post-graduate model, as it recognized American theological school models; Acadia 10 years later made the same transition to a predominantly graduate-school level of instruction. The other Baptist theological schools, Carey Theological College, Edmonton Baptist Seminary (North American Baptist Conference), Canadian Southern Baptist Seminary, Heritage Baptist Seminary, and Associated Canadian Theological Schools (related to the Baptist General Conference, Fellowship Baptists, the Evangelical Free Church in Canada and Pentecostal Assemblies of Canada) all emphasize post-graduate level degrees, while some make provision for undergraduates.

Basically, the curriculum of most graduate Baptist theological schools includes instruction in biblical studies, theology, church history, sometimes ethics and sociology, practical areas such as preaching, counselling, religious education, and pastoral care. Attention is given to internships, usually referred to as field education.

Programs specifically designed for those in ministry other than pastors include religious education, music, and missions. Originally a project of the Women's Missionary Union, the **Carver** School of Missions and Social Work (1905) was merged with Southern Baptist Seminary in 1962.

Among several **conservative evangelical** and **fundamentalist** branches of the Baptist family, a **bible college** model is followed. The first of these was the **Freewill Baptist** Biblical School founded in 1840 at Whitestown, New York. A major impetus in the bible college tradition occurred in the establishment of Gordon Bible and Missionary Training School (1889). Later institutions include Baptist Bible College, Clark's Summit, Pennsylvania (1931), Baptist Bible College, Springfield, Missouri, Bible Baptist Seminary, Arlington, Texas, Faith Baptist Bible College, Ankeny, Iowa (1968), Grand Rapids Baptist Bible College and Theological Seminary, Grand Rapids, Michigan (1954), and the Baptist University of America, Doraville, Georgia (1975). Among Freewill Baptists in the southern United States, bible colleges characterized the training of ministers, particularly the Freewill Baptist Bible College (1942). The curricula of these schools follows an English Bible survey pattern, usually some form of **dispensationalist** theology, and practical courses such as **evangelism**, preaching, missions, and Christian education. Student involvement in church service and/or missions is usually expected.

Baptists in Europe also have an ancient tradition of theological education. The first seminary, Betelseminariet, opened at Stockholm, Sweden, in 1866. Later German Baptists, influenced by **J. G. Oncken**, started a seminary at Hamburg in 1880, which is now located at Elstal. National institutions at Tallinn, **Estonia**, Budapest, **Hungary**, and Warsaw, **Poland**, all emerged in the early mission advance of the Baptist movement in Europe. Small theological faculties exist at Tollose, **Denmark**, Stabekk, **Norway**, and Novi Sad, **Serbia**. **Southern Baptists** from the United States began in 1949 the Baptist Theological Seminary at Rüschlikon (later removed to Prague), **Switzerland**, to serve the international English-speaking needs of the entire European community. Following the political transition in the Soviet Union in 1991, Baptists opened a seminary at Odessa, **Ukraine**, in 1992 and in Moscow, **Russia,** in 1993.

In Asia primary theological colleges exist at Serampore, Andhra Pradesh, Jorhat, Ramapatnam, and Bangalore, **India**; **Hong Kong**; Manado, **Indonesia**; and Chiang Mai, **Thailand**. See also **Bible Colleges**; **Education**.

THEOLOGY AND THEOLOGIANS, BAPTIST. Contrary to popular opinion that Baptists have no particular theology, an identifiable set of theological traditions has emerged in the denominational family and there is a wide variety of theologians who work within a generally Baptistic perspective.

Sources of Baptist Theology. Essentially, there are three historic sources of Baptist theological understanding: **confessions of faith**, pastoral or popular theologians, and academic or systematic theologians. The confessions of faith, dating from the first decade of the 17th century and the beginnings of the Baptist movement, reflect consensus among pastors and laymen about theological beliefs on God, the church, the **bible**, the **ordinances**, Jesus Christ, salvation, humanity, and ethics, to mention the major categories of treatment. The purpose of confessions of faith was often to defend Baptists against false charges or to articulate one's theological position, a technique borrowed from the Reformers and more directly from the Puritans. Among the outstanding Baptist contributors to confessions are: **William Kiffin, Hanserd Knollys, Benjamin Keach, J. Newton Brown**, and **Herschel H. Hobbs**. The theological content of confessions of faith continues to be a resource of doctrinal understanding, particularly among **conservative evangelical** Baptist groups.

From the middle of the 17th century, pastors and leaders have been a source of theological statement for Baptists. Sermons and theological treatises published far beyond the original setting create a breadth of influence for such writers. English pastors such as **John Gill, Thomas Grantham, Robert Hall, Andrew Fuller, Charles H. Spurgeon**, and **Alexander Maclaren** typify this contribution, as do North Americans like **Thomas Baldwin, George Dana Boardman, Edward Judson, T. T. Shields, Harry Emerson Fosdick, Martin Luther King, Jr.**, and **Howard Thurman**.

Perhaps the most influential group of theologians, however, have been the academic or systematic theologians, in part because of their classroom and published authority, in part because of the reinforcement of their work in references and citations. Among the outstanding academic theologians have been in Britain: **Dan Taylor, Frederick W. Gotch, H. Wheeler Robinson, Ernest Payne**; in North America, **Francis Wayland, W. N. Clarke, A. H. Strong, E. Y. Mullins, D. C. Macintosh**, and the **Chicago School**.

The Evolving Content of Baptist Theology. In the 17th century, the earliest Baptist theologians reacted against the prevailing trends both of determinism of Calvinistic thought and high church sacramentalism. The **General Baptists** built their theology upon an openness on the issue of the application of Christ's redeeming work. They held a strong view of the authority of **Scripture**, doubtless derived from the Puritans and later Separatists. The **Particular Baptists,** in contrast, were consistent Calvinists who adopted most of the tenets of the Westminster Confession of Faith with its emphasis upon the nature of redemption of an elect body of the faithful. Holding also to a freedom of conscience, Particular Baptists sought to align themselves theologically with Presbyterians and Congregationalists in the greater Reformed Tradition. The most frequently articulated doctrines of the first and second generations of Baptist theologians were church, ordinances, and redemption, respectively. Both major divisions of the 17th century Baptist family developed a peculiar ecclesiology, holding the local congregation as the essence of the visible church, from which their understanding of the **sacraments**/ordinances, the **ministry**, and mission were derived.

The 18th century Baptist community on both sides of the Atlantic Ocean wrestled with the theological meaning and implications of **revivalism**. Many of the older tradition of strict Calvinists, including **John Gill** and **John Brine**, abhorred what they called "**Arminian**" or worse yet "Antinominan" thinking. They were both influenced by English high Calvinist theologians Richard Davis (1658-1714), Tobias Crisp (1600-1643), and Joseph Hussey (1660-1726). On the other hand by mid-century, younger thinkers such as **Andrew Fuller, John Collett Ryland, John Ryland, Jr.**, and **Robert Hall** of Arnesby argued for a loosening of determinism and a recognition of the church's responsibility to work for the conversion of sinners. John Ryland was an important bridge between the Old School and the new emphases, having been influenced by John Newton (1725-1807). Another key figure, **Dan Taylor**, was influenced by the Wesleys, and joined the "Arminianized" Baptists in England to revitalize the **General Baptist** movement. To add variety to the English Baptist scene, **William Vidler** and **Elhanan Winchester** sought an outer edge in **universalist** thought, while still claiming other Baptistic distinctives.

Early in the 19th century, the less compromising Calvinists gradually organized themselves in defense of a Puritan style of Calvinism, led by men like **Charles H. Spurgeon, Joseph C. Philpot**, and **William Gadsby**. In the United States, the **Primitive Baptists** and some **Old School** orders followed a Calvinistic tradition, without the leadership of an educated theologian. Outstanding pulpiteers like **Alexander Maclaren, Richard Fuller, John A. Broadus, A. J. Gordon, Russell H. Conwell, George W. Truett, E. Y. Mullins, W. J. Simmons**, and **Adam Clayton Powell, Sr.** helped to give shape to Baptistic theological discourse as warm-hearted religious experience.

Beginning in the mid-19th century, new patterns of Baptist theology emerged in Britain and the United States. Biblical scholars gradually informed their Baptist constituency of more critical questions impinging upon traditional views of the authority of the bible. Included in this group were **Frederick W. Gotch** and **S. H. Green** in Britain and **C. H. Toy** and **Nathaniel Schmidt** in the United States. Missionaries and theological professors like **John E. Clough** and **Shailer Mathews**, following the interaction with other Christian and non-Christian traditions, gave sanction in some circles to a more universal view of God and an evolutionary perspective on theological doctrine.

In response to these "modernistic" trends, some Baptists moved to defensive positions around classic doctrinal statements about the bible, **church**, Christian experience, and the finality of the work of Jesus Christ. Men such as **A. J. Gordon** and **Henry G. Weston** took an uncompromising stand on the issues. Some of the more **liberal** Baptists attempted to have editorial dialogue with the more **conservative** thinkers in an attempt to explain their new social science understandings of doctrine in traditional terms. Among this group were **William Newton Clarke, Harry Emerson Fosdick, George Burman Foster, Gerald B. Smith, Henry Clay Vedder**, and **Douglas Clyde Macintosh**. Clarke, Fosdick, and Foster emphasized experience in religious understanding, while Smith and Macintosh stressed an empirical basis for theology. These pioneers of the "New Theology" were met often with an uncompromising strident attack from traditionalist pulpit theologians, including **John Roach Straton, J. Frank Norris, J. C. Massee, T. T. Shields, W. B. Riley**, John R. Rice , and **G. B. Vick**.

In the 20th century, Baptist theology was predictably divided between those with a high view of the divine inspiration of **Scripture**, those who sought to reformulate theology in terms of social trends and scientific modernism, and those who ultimately took more radical approaches. As the century began, **A. H. Strong, Alvah Hovey, E. Y. Mullins,** and **W. T. Connor** ruled supreme in the theological schools, Strong evolving in view of scientific advances he needed to account for. That magisterial position of the "Baptist schoolmen" was broadened with Baptists who came to teach in other denominations' schools or ecumenical centers. A list of more contemporary Baptist theologians is characterized by great variety. They include Carl F.H. Henry (1913-), George Beasely-Murray (1916-), **Dale Moody**, Millard Erickson (1932-), Samuel Mikolaski (1923-), Clark Pinnock (1937-), James Leo Garrett (1925-), and James W. McClendon (1924-) who have each indirectly or explicitly reinforced traditional baptistic interpretation (with some interesting differentiating points).

At the same time Harvey Cox (1929-), William Hamilton (1924-), W. Kenneth Cauthen (1930-), **Howard Thurman**, Henry Mitchell (1919-), Michael Taylor (1937-), **Carlisle Marney,** and Thorwald Lorenzen (1936-), to name a few, have moved far afield of any traditional Baptist **evangelical** or strictly denominational agenda. Respectively, they have emphasized post-modern thought, radical theology, process theology, civil rights, environmental concerns, and human rights. Perhaps the widest departure from traditional Baptist thinking was that of William Hamilton, an advocate of the "Death of God" movement in radical theology.

New fields such as ethics, historical theology, biblical theology, philosophical theology, and pastoral theology have produced numerous Baptist writers and theologians in the broadest sense of the term, working out systems of theological reflection in their respective disciplines; these include Wayne Oates, Psychology (1917-); E. J. Carnell, Apologetics (1919-1967); Paul Simmons, Ethics (1936-); George Eldon Ladd, New Testament (1911-19); Frank Stagg, Biblical Theology (1911-); and John Jonsson, Missions (1925-). Many of those on both sides of the spectrum probably value their identity as "Baptist" theologians less than their conversancy with other evangelicals or social activists.

The Consensus of Baptist Thought. What characterizes historic Baptist theology? The majority of all Baptists emphasize Christian experience, the authority, if not plain interpretation, of Scripture, and the primacy of the local congregation in their determination and articulation of Christian doctrine. Whether **conservative** or **liberal** in outlook, Baptists of all kinds affirm liberty of conscience and freedom of expression as essential to their faith. **Separation of church and state** are widely held also, except among **fundamentalistic** Baptists in the United States where there is concern for influencing public policy with religious ideals and ethical standards. From these central theological tenets there is very wide differentiation on matters such as the sacraments/ordinances, the Kingdom of God, evangelization and missions, human rights, Christology and the Holy Spirit, and Last Things. Typically, most Baptists are biblicists, trinitarian, Christocentric, evangelical, experiential, and mildly Calvinistic and mildly sacramentarian in theological perspective. Their doctrine of the church is local in emphasis and one's freedom of personal religious opinion and expression is jealously guarded.

Baptist theology may be summarized as follows:

A Baptist Quadrilateral
Scripture

Freedom   CHRIST   Mission

Experience

THOMAS, JOHN (1760-1801). English Baptist surgeon and missionary, born at Fairford, England. He studied medicine and qualified as a surgeon in 1780. In 1783 he became a ship's surgeon, associated with the East India Company, and travelled to Calcutta, **India**. There he found no European Christians willing to worship with him and he advertised for those who would help to form a church. He returned to London in 1785 and became associated with the Baptist Church at Little Wild Street in London. When he returned to Calcutta in 1786 Thomas organized a congregation and recognized the great need for gospel work in Bengal. Returning again to Britain in 1792 he made the acquaintance of **William Carey** and convinced Carey and the newly formed Particular **Baptist Missionary Society** (BMS) to accept Bengal as their initial field. Thomas is thus rightly credited with focusing English Baptist missionary attention upon India. Thomas completed a Bengali translation of most of the New Testament, Psalms, and Prophets by 1795.

THOMAS, JOSHUA (1719-1797). Welsh Baptist minister and historian, born at Caio, Carmarthenshire, Wales. He was self-educated as a farmer who, at first, was encouraged by the Baptist church at Leominster to preach, and after several years of supply preaching in the vicinity of Hay-on-Wye in Brecknockshire, he was ordained in 1749. In 1754, Thomas was called to the pastorate at Leominster which he served for 43 years. In addition to being a model pastor, he collected historical materials on the Welsh Baptists and published eight historical works, two devotional tracts, and seven theological treatises. Among his most outstanding works were *Materials for a History of the Baptist Churches in the Principality* (1784), which is said to have been influenced by the work of **Morgan Edwards** in the United States, and *Ecclesiastical History of Wales* (1779). Thomas also supplied historical sketches for **John Rippon** and numerous obituary notices. He was recognized as a principal apologist for the Particular Baptist cause and the broader community of Baptists in Britain and America.

THREE DISSENTING DENOMINATIONS. Following the Act of Toleration, Baptists, like other English dissenters, began to expand their horizons and express their political opinions. The first concerns were for recognition of the church and **ministry** and later for benefits enjoyed by the Establishment. In 1714 **Benjamin Stinton** began to gather London ministers at a coffeehouse for discussion of common needs and goals. By 1723 this became what was later referred to as the Baptist Board. Beginning in 1727 similar Presbyterian and Congregational bodies joined with the Baptist Board to address common political concerns and provide an ongoing list of dissenting ministers and congregations. Meeting collectively at least annually, they came to be known as the Three Dissenting Denominations, later as the Dissenting Deputies.

THURMAN, HOWARD (1900-1981). American Black Baptist minister, born at Daytona Beach, Florida. He was educated at Morehouse College and Rochester Theological Seminary and served Mt. Zion Baptist Church in Oberlin, Ohio, 1926-1929. In 1929 he began a distinguished career in higher education, becoming professor of religion and director of religious life at Baptist-related Morehouse and Spelman Colleges in Atlanta, Georgia. In 1932 Mordecai Johnson (1890-1976) invited him to become Dean of the Chapel and Professor of Christian Theology at Howard University in Washington, D.C., where he served until 1944. Influenced by the thought of Mahatma Gandhi (1869-1948), Thurman and Alfred G. Fisk started the Church for the Fellowship of All Peoples in 1944 in San Francisco, California, which became a model of interracial and ecumenical cooperation. From 1953 to 1965 Thurman served as Dean of Marsh Chapel and Professor of Spiritual Resources and Disciplines at Boston University in Massachusetts. He was one of the best-known speakers and social prophets of his era and devoted his retirement years to the establishment of the Howard Thurman Educational Trust to encourage intercultural understanding and support for Black colleges. Among Thurman's many published works were *Jesus and the Disinherited* (1949), *The Creative Encounter* (1954), and *The Search for Common Ground* (1971).

TICHENOR, ISAAC TAYLOR (1825-1902). Southern Baptist minister and denominational leader, born in Spencer County, Kentucky. He was not formally educated and began to preach at an early age, earning the epithet, "boy orator of Kentucky." He served as a missionary for the American Indian Mission Association (1847), later becoming a pastor at Columbus, Mississippi (1848-1850), and First Baptist, Montgomery, Alabama (1852-1867). During the American Civil War, Tichenor served as a sharpshooter under General Braxton Bragg (1817-1896), at the same time serving as a missionary/chaplain. In 1867 he was president of the Montevallo Coal Mining Company in northern Alabama, which was responsible for discovering the vast coal reserves near what became Birmingham. For a time he was president of Auburn Agricultural and Mining College (1871), and in 1872 he was elected president of the Southern Baptist Home Mission Board, which he served for 17 years. In the latter post he completely reorganized Southern Baptist work, expanded it to the Caribbean, and offset the advance of the **American Baptist Home Mission Society** following the Civil War.

TIMPANY, AMERICUS VESPUCIUS (1840-1885). Canadian and American Baptist missionary, born at Vienna, Ontario. He was educated at Canadian Literary Institute and was influenced by **R. A. Fyfe.** As the Canadian churches had no overseas agency as yet, Timpany was appointed by the **American Baptist Missionary Union** (ABMU) to work in **India** in 1868. He began ministry with the Telugus and witnessed a large increase of converts from 1868-1872. He began the Ramapatam Theological Seminary in 1872 and organized the American Baptist Telugu Conference. While on furlough in 1876-1878, he and his wife Jane Bates toured **Canada** and raised support for the newly established Canadian Baptist Missionary Society and they began publication of *The Missionary Link*. Support for the Timpanys shifted to the Canadian society, and when they returned to India a new field was opened for Canadians at Cocanada. His duties included practicing medicine, translating Scripture, and working in the municipal government. Timpany's death caused quite a sensation among the Canadian churches and helped to solidify their efforts. Timpany published the extensive *Compendium of Theology* in Telugu (1877).

TOGO. The first Baptist church in Togo was organized at Lomé and it was initially related to the Baptist Convention of **Ghana**. In 1959 the **General Baptist** Missionary Society in the United States began a mission. In 1967 the Baptist Association of Togo was formed and this evolved into the Baptist Convention of Togo in 1988, jointly supported by the **Southern Baptists** and the **National Baptist Convention in the USA**. In 1973 the **Association of Baptists for World Evangelism** (ABWE) began a mission in Togo.

As of 1995 there were 225 churches and 11,900 members affiliated with the Association Baptiste Togolaise. Presently there is a Baptist-related theological school at Lomé.

TOLBERT, WILLIAM (1913-1980). Liberian Baptist political leader and minister. He was born at Bensonville, **Liberia,** and educated at Liberia College (later the University of Liberia). He entered public service in the Treasury Office and later served eight years in the Liberian House of Representatives. In 1951 he was elected vice president of Liberia, a post that included presidency of the country's Senate. He was re-elected to that office in 1953, 1955, 1959, and 1963. In 1971, on the death of President

Tubman, Tolbert became president of Liberia, to which post he was subsequently re-elected.

His involvement with the Baptist community was lifelong. In 1953 he became pastor of Zion Praise Baptist Church in Bensonville and in 1956 he founded Mount Sinai Baptist Church in the Tondee District, which he co-pastored with the Bensonville Church. In 1958-1965 he served as president of the Liberian Baptist Missionary and Education Convention, Inc. and vice president of the **Baptist World Alliance** (BWA) in 1960-1965. At the 11th Baptist World Congress meeting in Miami Beach, Florida, in 1965, Tolbert was elected president of the Alliance, which he served until 1970. Tolbert was assassinated in Liberia in 1980, becoming both a political and religious martyr.

TORBET, ROBERT GEORGE (1912-1995). American Baptist educator and historian, born at Spokane, Washington. He was educated at Wheaton College, The Eastern Baptist Theological Seminary, and the University of Pennsylvania, where he received the Ph.D. degree. He taught church history at Eastern Seminary from 1944-1952, after which he was a senior staff editor and later director of educational services at the American Baptist Board of Education and Publication. In 1958 Torbet became dean at Central Baptist Theological Seminary in Kansas City, Kansas, where he led in establishing its accreditation. His final post was as Associate General Secretary for **Ecumenical** Relations of the **American Baptist Convention** (ABC) from 1967-1977. In this role he was a leading force in the 1972 Lima meetings of the World Council of Churches' recognition of the place of believer's **baptism**. Torbet wrote major textbooks on the **Philadelphia Baptist Association** (1944), the *History of the Baptists* (1950), and the **American Baptist Foreign Mission Society** (1955). For the latter half of the 20th century, Torbet's Baptist history was the common textbook in the denomination.

TOY, CRAWFORD HOWELL (1836-1919). Southern Baptist minister and educator, born in Norfolk, Virginia. Educated at the University of Virginia and Southern Baptist Theological Seminary, he taught at Albemarle Female Institute and Richmond College. During the Civil War he was a Confederate chaplain and was captured at Gettysburg. While in prison he taught Italian and organized a Glee Club. Following the war, Toy returned to teaching languages and philosophy at the University of Alabama and Furman University. In 1869 he assumed the chair in Old Testament at Southern Baptist Seminary where he was highly regarded. In the 1870s, however, he opposed the **landmarkist** teachings of **James R. Graves**, and adopted German higher critical views of the **bible**. In

1879 Toy was forced to resign because of views of the bible which were held to be incompatible with the doctrinal statement of the seminary. Shortly thereafter, he went to Harvard College as the Hancock Professor of Semitics. The president of Harvard remarked of Toy's appointment that "Harvard Divinity Faculty now had an American heretic in its ranks." Toy built a strong reputation at Harvard in Semitic languages and Old Testament studies based on German documentary hypothesis theories. His great interest was in the application of comparative religions methodologies, which he pioneered among American theological educators. For a time he carried on a close relationship with **Charlotte Moon**, a missionary to **China**. Miss Moon, upon reading Toy's views, decided to end the romance. Toy published commentaries on Proverbs (1899) and Ezekiel (1899), plus *Judaism and Christianity* (1890) and *Introduction to the History of Religions* (1913).

TRAIL OF BLOOD. See **Successionism**.

TRASKITES. A 17th century English Non-conformist group which followed the teachings of John Traske (1585-1636). Originally a Puritan ordained by the Bishop of Salisbury, Traske became a popular preacher in Devon, Ely, and later London. Among his extraordinary views he adopted the teaching of the sabbath and became known as a religious radical. He drew a large following, known pejoratively as "Traskites," who spread through the country with Judaical teachings. Their doctrines and practices included observance of the old sabbath, differentiating meats, sinless perfectionism, the equation of the Old Testament priest Melchizedek as the Holy Spirit, and the keeping of the Feast of Passover. Traske himself categorized all men in one of three states: nature, repentance, and grace, the latter of which was the "Holy City of sinlessness." Some Traskites turned to Antinomianism and **Familism**; Traske himself was given a severe sentence in 1618 involving a fine, whipping, the pillory, and banishment from **ministry** for his Judaical teachings. In the late 1620s he joined the **Separatist** congregation in London, identified with **Henry Jacob** and **John Lathrop**. Although there is no evidence that Traske ever adopted baptistic views, his sabbatarian thought was a forerunner of that found in the **Seventh Day Baptist** movement associated with Mill Yard Church in the 1650s and his wife Dorothy (c.1585-1645) bridged the early development of sabbatarian thought with the development of later practicing congregations. Some Seventh Day Baptist historians claim Traske as their earliest exponent. See also **Seventh Day Baptists**.

TRIENNIAL CONVENTION. See **General Missionary Convention of the Baptist Denomination in the United States of America for Foreign Missions**.

TRINIDAD AND TOBAGO. Baptist history in Trinidad and Tobago began during the Napoleonic Wars as many freed slaves emigrated to the islands. Among these were Baptists who formed the first church in 1816. As the work grew, it caught the attention of the **Baptist Missionary Society** (BMS), which began support of a mission at Port of Spain in 1843. **E. B. Underhill**, secretary for the BMS, visited Trinidad in 1859 and noted the extraordinary overt, excited behavior in worship. This style of worship coalesced in the "Spiritual" or "**Shouter**" Baptists. In the 1890s the BMS gradually withdrew its missionaries in favor of an indigenous leadership; the Baptist Union of Trinidad was formed in 1854. Much fragmentation occurred within the Baptist community, such as in 1890 when the St. Paul's Independent Baptist Missionary Society was formed. This evolved into the Independent Order of Baptists (1900), the Independent Baptists Missionary Union (1944), The Independence Baptist Mission Churches, Inc. (1966), and finally a split in 1986 which generated the Independent International Baptist Church of Trinidad and Tobago, which has ties to the **Southern Baptist Convention** (SBC), the **National Baptist Convention U.S.A.** (NBCUSA), and the **National Baptist Convention of America** (NBCA). In more recent years the BMS has returned to support work in Trinidad (1946), and Southern Baptists launched a mission in 1970-76, but withdrew from direct cooperation with the Union, preferring the independent movement and an umbrella organization called the Caribbean Baptist Fellowship.

As of 1995 there were 23 churches and 3,000 members affiliated with the Baptist Union of Trinidad and Tobago, nine churches with 860 members affiliated with the Baptist Convention of Trinidad and Tobago, and 18 churches with 1,250 members affiliated with the Evangelical Baptist Association.

TRUETT, GEORGE WASHINGTON (1867-1944). Southern Baptist minister, born at Hayesville, North Carolina. Educated at Baylor University, he founded Hiawasee Academy in 1887 and returned in 1892 to Baylor as financial secretary to president **B. H. Carroll**. In 1897 he became pastor at Waco, Texas, and in 1897 at First Baptist Church in Dallas, Texas. Under Truett's **ministry**, which lasted for 47 years, the church became the center of Baptist life in the state and one of the largest congregations in the Baptist world. Truett is credited with great preaching, which increased the membership in Dallas tenfold while he was **pastor**. He was president of the **Southern Baptist Convention** (SBC) in 1927-1930 and of the **Baptist World Alliance** (BWA) in 1935-1940. The most memorable of Truett's sermons were published as *A Quest for Souls* (1917).

TUNKERS. See **Baptist (the Name); German Baptist Brethren**.

TUPPER, HENRY ALLEN (1828-1902). Southern Baptist minister and denominational leader, born in Charleston, South Carolina. He was educated at Madison University (later Colgate) and served pastorates at Graniteville and Washington, Georgia (1853-1872). During the American Civil War, Tupper served as a chaplain to the Confederate Ninth Georgia Volunteers Regiment, earning the nickname, "the Fighting Parson," although he never carried a weapon. In 1872 he was elected corresponding secretary of the Southern Baptist **Foreign Mission Board** (FMB).

A lifelong mission enthusiast, Tupper raised large sums of money while a **pastor** for the Southern Baptist foreign mission enterprise and was a natural choice to succeed **James B. Taylor**. He reorganized the Board into committees for various fields and expanded the outreach of Southern Baptists overseas in **Mexico, Brazil, Nigeria**, and **Japan**. At home he encouraged the establishment of support groups in each of the state conventions. One of his most outstanding achievements was the appointment of the first **women** missionaries; during his tenure the Woman's Missionary Union was organized in 1888. He also involved the Southern Board in the **ecumenical** Foreign Mission Conference of North America in 1892. The author of two books on the history of Southern Baptist foreign missions, Tupper ended his career as an instructor in biblical studies at Richmond College. Among Tupper's published works on missions was *A Decade of Foreign Missions 1880-1890* (1891).

TURKEY. Baptist work in Turkey is meagre, due to extreme government restrictions. **Southern Baptists** have one congregation at Ankara of approximately 100 members, and Canadian Baptists employ missionaries indirectly in Turkey.

TURKMENISTAN. The Baptist movement in the Asian republic of Turkmenistan is an outgrowth of Russian missionary endeavor, in large part since the downfall of the Soviet Union in 1992. Support for new church development is provided by the Euro-Asian Baptist Federation and the **European Baptist Federation**.

As of 1995 there were three churches with about 100 members in the Baptist community in Turkmenistan. See **Middle Asia.**

TURKS AND CAICOS ISLANDS. Baptist missions in these islands began with visits from **Jamaica**, the **Bahamas**, and **Trinidad and Tobago**. The Jamaican Baptist Union sent workers to Turks in 1849 and three historic congregations emerged from that effort. The Southern Baptist **Foreign Mission Board** (FMB) began work here in 1982 at the invitation of the Jamaica Baptist Union. Also, **fundamentalist** Baptists from the United States have a small missionary work in the islands.

As of 1995 there were about 750 members of about five congregations in Turks and Caicos Islands.

U

UGANDA. Baptist work in Uganda may be traced to 1956 when Southern Baptists began to plan for a mission in the country. However, before that happened, the **Conservative Baptist** Foreign Mission Society (CBFMS) began a mission in Uganda in 1961 with a center at Kampala. **Southern Baptists** officially began work at Kampala, Mbale, and Masindi. In 1970 the Baptist Convention of Uganda was organized; later during 1982 this became the Baptist Union of Uganda. During the civil unrest and war of 1979 and after, Conservative Baptist and Southern Baptist missionaries worked among the refugee communities.

As of 1995 there were 566 churches and 20,626 members affiliated with the Baptist Union of Uganda.

UKRAINE. The Baptist movement in Ukraine was introduced via **J. G. Oncken** about 1869. That year he participated in the ordination of a Mennonite, which led to the **baptism** of Ivan Riaboshapka (fl. 1870), a blacksmith in that same year. Baptist life in this region of the Russian Empire was closely allied with **Stundism**, an **evangelical**, pietistic sect. The growth of first Stundist, and later Baptist, congregations was remarkable, beginning with the church at Kosiakovko in 1875. After 1884, when the Russian Baptist Union was formed, steps toward more formal organization of Baptist churches and regional life took place in Ukraine. The Baptist church in the capital city, Kiev, was founded in 1886. At the signing of the Treaty of Brest-Litovsk in 1918, the Ukrainian congregations adopted a constitution for the All-Ukrainian Union of Baptists and commissioned a periodical. Growth was phenomenal and by 1921 there were 2,000 churches in Ukraine. In 1922-1925 Ukrainian leaders recognized that they were better served by the Russian Union and the All-Ukrainian Union of Associations became a department of the Russian Union, with offices in Kharkov. Fourteen territorial units, or raiony, were set up at that time. In 1929, growth was halted as Russian President Stalin closed all of the territorial unions, and the churches participated once again in the Russian Union and, after 1944, in the All Union Council of Evangelical Christians-Baptists. With the dismantling of the U.S.S.R. in 1991-1992, and the subsequent reorganization of the AUCECB in 1993, the main body of Baptists in Ukraine reorganized themselves in 1993 as Soyuz Yevangel'skikh Khristiyan-Baptistiv Ukraini (Union of Evangelical Christians-Baptists of Ukraine). The Union has published *Baptist Ukrainy* (Ukrainian Baptist) (1918-). In 1992 the **Conservative Baptist** Foreign Mission Society (CBFMS) began a mission in Ukraine, focused at Rovno and Donetsk. In 1993 a second group of Baptists in Ukraine emerged from what had been the illegal, unregistered, underground congregations for over two decades, Bratstvo Nzaleznykh Cerkov ta Misiy Evangelskikh Khristian-Baptistiv Ukrainy (Brotherhood of Independent Baptist Churches and Ministries of Ukraine). This group is headquartered at Kiev.

As of 1995 there were 69 churches and 7,050 members affiliated with Bratstvo Nezaleznykh Cerkov ta Misiy Evangelskikh Khristian-Baptistiv Ukrainy, and 1,540 churches with 116,034 members affiliated with the Soyuz Yevangel'skikh Khristiyan-Baptistiv Ukraini. There is a theological seminary located at Odessa.

UNDERHILL, EDWARD BEAN (1813-1901). English Baptist layman and denominational leader, born at Oxford. Not of robust health, he chose not to study for the **ministry**, received no university education, and entered business for over a decade. His marriage to the daughter of the Oxford University printer gave him the opportunity to observe scholarly publishing and the literature of the Oxford Movement. In 1843 he moved to a retreat in Gloucestershire and became a collector of books and wrote on the defenses of **evangelical** Christianity, also editing *The Baptist Record.* In 1849 Underhill became one of the two principal secretaries of the **Baptist Missionary Society** (BMS), his portfolio becoming the foreign fields. Between 1854-1857 he toured **India**, Ceylon and **China**, in 1859 the West Indies, and 1869 **Cameroon**, the first secretary to visit personally the fields. Underhill was first among historians of British Baptists in the mid-19th century, publishing notes on many original sources and organizing the **Hanserd Knollys** Society in 1845. He served as chair of the **Baptist Union of Great Britain and Ireland** (BU) from 1849-1876. In 1875 the University of Rochester (U.S.) conferred upon him the

LL.D. degree. Through his editorial labors with the **Hansard Knollys Society**, Underhill published numerous editions of Baptistiana, including *Struggles and Triumphs of Religious Liberty* (1851) and biographies of James Phillippo (1881), **Alfred Saker** (1884), and John Wenger (1886). His thorough account of *The Tragedy of Morant Bay* (1895) won him much international acclaim.

UNDERWOOD, ALFRED CLAIR (1885-1948). English Baptist missionary and historian, born at Leicester, England. He was educated at Oxford and London Universities and was appointed under the **Baptist Missionary Society** (BMS) in 1911 to teach church history at Serampore College in **India**. In 1920 he returned to England where he became president of Rawdon College and taught church history there. He retired from the presidency in 1940. Underwood wrote a history of Serampore College, but is best known for his *History of the English Baptists* (1947). His lesser-known works include *Conversion: Christian and Non-Christian, A Comparative and Psychological Study* (1925), and *Shintoism: The Indigenous Religion of Japan* (1934).

UNION BAPTISTS. See **Baptist Union of Great Britain and Ireland**.

UNITED ARAB EMIRATES. Baptist presence in this nation is small. As a result of **religious liberty** policies and the large numbers of expatriates and immigrant workers living in the U.A.E., Baptist witness has been conducted indirectly since 1993. Currently there are pastoral appointments serving in international congregations, which include Filipinos and Indian workers.

UNIVERSALISM, AMONG BAPTISTS. Universalism, or the belief in universal salvation for all people as the "elect," in contrast with the traditional Calvinistic position that only a few whom God ordains will be "elected," became a serious problem for Baptists on both sides of the Atlantic at the turn of the 19th century. In the United States, universalism, as well as unitarianism, was a noticeable position among **liberal** clergy in the Congregationalist churches, especially in eastern Massachusetts in reaction to the excesses of the **Great Awakening**. In 1770 John Murray (1741-1815), an English preacher, arrived in New Jersey and began circulating universalist teachings. Within 20 years, a significant number of congregations in New England adopted universalist theology and a national convention was held in Philadelphia in 1790. The most prominent Baptist to join the movement was **Elhanan Winchester**, who announced his profession to universal restoration and caused an uproar in the

Philadelphia Baptist Association and his church, First Baptist of Philadelphia. Winchester developed a universalist "confession of faith," which involved a belief in the revelation of the **bible**, the certainty of eventual salvation, and a moral imperative for good works. This became a standard for the development of universalism in England and the United States. Universalist thought proceeded in two basic directions: ultra-universalism, which rejected all future punishment (as advocated by Hosea Ballou), and restorationism, which held that limited punishment was part of the divine plan (as taught by **William Vidler**).

Generally, universalism was considered theologically conservative in contrast with unitarianism, in that it acknowledged the authority of the **bible** and the centrality of Jesus and his atonement. Universalist thinking was productive of schism among Baptists: William Vidler's announcement of universalist theology split his congregation at Battle and signalled the virtual collapse of the **General Baptist** movement in England, and Winchester's action sorely divided the most prestigious Baptist congregation in Philadelphia and drove the intellectual classes away from the Baptist movement. While the universalist position among Baptists waned by the 1830s, from time to time **evangelicals** have called attention to universalist tendencies in certain clergy, which is usually a sign of unacceptable **liberal** or heterodox thinking.

UPHAM, EDWARD (1710-1797). American Baptist minister, born at Malden, Massachusetts. He graduated from Harvard College, one of the best educated Baptist clergymen of his era. In 1738 he was called to be pastor at the Baptist Church in West Springfield, Massachusetts, which he served for 10 years. In 1748 he moved to the Baptist Church at Newport, Rhode Island, where he served until 1771. Upham's relocation to Newport was problematic, because his congregation at West Springfield refused to grant him a letter of dismission, and he was never **ordained**, or rather installed formally in Newport. In 1764 he was an advocate of the founding of the College of Rhode Island and served as one of its first trustees. When a vote on the relocation of the College was taken in 1770, Upham voted in favor of the Providence site and this stirred great opposition against him from organized labor in Newport. He was forced to resign and he returned to West Springfield, where for the next 20 years he led a campaign against the religious taxation of his members. Upham was theologically **Arminian**, in contrast with the prevailing Calvinism of his contemporaries, and he was often classed as an Old Light opponent of the **Great Awakening. Isaac Backus** considered Upham's doctrine of grace to be "unclear."

UPLAND BAPTISTS. A term used in early 19th-century Canadian Maritime Baptist life to designate those church members who professed to be convinced of the duty of believer's **baptism**, without actually ever being baptized. They practiced **mixed communion** with tolerant immersed believers, the latter expecting an eventual spiritual change toward believer's baptism. Many of the baptized persons were so fully convinced of the propriety of mixed communion over strict enforcement of believer's baptism that they appeared to sanction the neglect of Upland Baptists by admitting them to the same church privileges with themselves. Eventually, those advocating closed communion won the debate over church membership privileges and **associational** membership so that the Upland Baptists disappeared by 1800.

URUGUAY. In 1911 Argentine Baptists began mission work in Uruguay as part of the Mision Bautista del Rio Plata. Jaime and Lemuel Quarles opened a church at Montevideo in 1911. The Convención Bautista del Uruguay was organized in 1948, and in 1954 the Uruguayan Mission was separated from the Argentine work. A seminary, El Instituto Teologico Bautista, was opened at Montevideo in 1955. The **Baptist Bible Fellowship** (BBF) commenced a **mission** in 1958, and more recently in 1990 the **Association of Baptists for World Evangelism** (ABWE) began a mission in Uruguay. In 1995 the **Conservative Baptist** Foreign Mission Society (CBFMS) began a mission in Uruguay.

As of 1995 there were 57 churches and 4,500 members affiliated with the Convención Bautista del Uruguay.

UZBEKISTAN. See **Middle Asia**.

V

VALDER, HANS (1813-1899). Norwegian and American Baptist pastor and missionary, born at Ryfylke, **Norway**. Early in his life he was a schoolteacher and farmer. He emigrated to the United States in 1837 and helped to organize Norwegian settlements in Illinois. He converted from his Lutheran faith to that of a Baptist persuasion about 1841. In August 1844 Valder became the first ordained Norwegian Baptist in the world. Four years later, he became the first Scandinavian missionary of the **American Baptist Home Mission Society** (ABHMS), a role he held for two years. Valder became active in other **voluntary** associations and moved to Minnesota where he entered politics and eventually became a Methodist.

VARDAMAN, JEREMIAH (1775-1842). American Baptist minister and evangelist, born in Wythe County, Virginia. Lacking any formal education, he was a rugged frontiersman and travelled widely in the West, moving to Kentucky in 1779. His faith was quickened in 1792 under the **ministry** of a blind **evangelist**, Thomas Hansford, and Vardaman entered the full-time ministry himself. He served churches at Cedar Creek (1802-1810) and David's Fork (1810-1830), Kentucky, and organized other later leading congregations at Bardstown, Lexington, and Louisville, and at Nashville, Tennessee. He was the pioneer preacher in Missouri and helped to organize the Missouri Baptist Convention. It is believed Vardaman was instrumental in converting over 8,000 persons to the Christian faith.

VASSAR, MATTHEW (1792-1868). American Baptist industrialist and philanthropist, born at East Tuddingham, County of Norfolk, England. Emigrating to the United States in 1796, he later worked in the business of his father and also at a tannery in Newburgh, New York. In 1810 he returned to his father's brewery and ultimately assumed control of it, rebuilding after a fire, at Poughkeepsie, New York. Milo P. Jewett (1808-1882), a well-known educator, persuaded Vassar to endow a college for women and this he did in 1861. Vassar College was influenced also by the thought of Martin Brewer Anderson (1815-1890), president of the Baptist-related University of Rochester. While the college was listed among the Baptist-related schools for a time, Vassar was categorically opposed to any formal religious affiliation or doctrinal test, and it became essentially a non-sectarian, high calibre women's college. Mr. Vassar's religious beliefs are detailed in *The Autobiography and Letters of Matthew Vassar*, edited by Elizabeth Haight (1916).

VEDDER, HENRY CLAY (1853-1935). American Baptist minister and historian, born at DeRuyter, New York. He was educated at the University of Rochester (B.A., M.A.) and Rochester Theological Seminary. Following seminary he joined the staff of *The Examiner* in New York, which ultimately he edited, along with the *Baptist Quarterly Review* (1885-1892). In 1894 he went to Crozer Theological Seminary where he served as church history professor until 1926. Vedder began his career as a **conservative** thinker, but after about 1910 he advocated a "new" church history, by which he meant a greater appreciation for socialism, evolution, and pragmatism. Vedder desired a modification of Christianity to address the excesses of capitalism and, like those in the **Chicago School**, he embraced the theory of evolution as a tool for better understanding the Christian faith. He grew to become one of the chief targets for those in the early **fundamentalist** movement, publishing *The Fundamentals of Christianity* (1922). His historical works were groundbreaking and included *A History of Baptists in the Middle States* (1898), *Balthasar Hubmaier: The Leader of The Anabaptists* (1905), *A Short History of the Baptists* (1907), and *A Short History of Baptist Missions* (1927).

VENEZUELA. In 1925 the first Baptist missionaries entered Venezuela under the sponsorship of **Baptist Mid-Missions**; they established a mission at El Collao in 1927, with later stations at Tucupita, San Felix, and El Palmar. Following initial exploration in 1945 by **Southern Baptists** in Colombia, Julio Moros, who had begun a church at Barranquilla, started a congregation in Caracas in 1946. Three years later several of the early congregations affiliated with the Convención Colombo-Venezol and in 1951 a separate Convención Bautista Nacional was formed. The **Baptist Bible Fellowship** (BBF) opened a mission in Venezuela in 1966, and the **Conservative Baptist Foreign Mission Society** (CBFMS) began its mission in the country in 1986, centered in Caracas. In 1956 the Instituto Teológico opened at Los Teques.

As of 1995 there were 219 churches and 22,000 members affiliated with the Convención Bautista Nacional de Venezuela. The Convención publishes *Luminar Bautista (Baptist Light)* (1952-).

VICK, GEORGE BEAUCHAMP (1901-1975). American Independent Baptist minister and educator, born at Russellville, Kentucky. With no formal education, he worked on the Louisville and Nashville Railroad (1918-1920) and later the Fort Worth and Denver Railroad (1920-1924). While in Ft. Worth, he joined First Baptist Church and became interested in Sunday School **ministry** with **J. Frank Norris**. Beginning in 1932, he served Norris for six years and then went to work for Wade House as a song leader in his **revivals**. Later in this period, Vick worked for other travelling **evangelists**, including **Mordecai Ham**. In 1936 he again joined Norris as associate **pastor** in the Temple Baptist Church in Detroit, Michigan. Later as co-pastor in Detroit, he led in building a large congregation, averaging over 3,000 in **Sunday School**. In 1948 Norris invited Vick to become president of the Fundamental Bible Baptist Seminary in Texas, a school under Norris's control. At length he and Norris disagreed on administrative matters in 1950, and Vick separated from Norris's church and educational institutions and formed a movement with other sympathetic pastors, the **Baptist Bible Fellowship** (BBF). He was the founder of the Baptist Bible College in Springfield, Missouri

(1950-1975), and an ardent advocate of Baptist **fundamentalism**. A sample of Vick's writing is found in *Soul-Winning Sermons* (1958).

VIDLER, WILLIAM (1758-1816). English Baptist, and later Unitarian minister, born at Battle, England. Apprenticed as a bricklayer, he was raised in the Church of England but converted to an Independent. About 1816 he began to preach and joined the Baptists under Thomas Purdy at Rye. In 1780 he was baptized and ordained and started a congregation at Battle. To secure funds for a building, he travelled among the Baptists and other dissenters in 1791, and was drawn to **Arminian** Baptists and universalists. Under the influence of Richard Wright (1764-1836), a Unitarian preacher, Vidler professed **universalism** in 1792 and this split his church at Battle; he joined the recently emigrated American Universalist, **Elhanan Winchester**, at Artillery Lane in London in 1794 as an associate pastor and when Winchester returned to the United States, Vidler served both the London Church and his congregation at Battle 1794-1796. From 1796-1815 he served at Parliament Court as well as managing a bookseller's shop and publishing a periodical, *The Universal Theological Magazine*. In 1801 Vidler was admitted to the **General Baptist** Assembly, an action which offended the **evangelical** General Baptists and prompted the withdrawal of **Dan Taylor**. The next year Vidler announced his transition to unitarianism and he became active in the broader organization of English unitarianism, serving the Unitarian Fund and writing numerous tracts in defense of his position. He wrote a biography of Elhanan Winchester and, in a series of letters to **Andrew Fuller** in 1803, he defended universal restoration. Vidler's theological perspective is found in *God's Love to His Creatures Asserted and Vindicated* (1799) and *Letters to Mr. Fuller on the Universal Restoration* (1803).

VIETNAM. Baptist witness in Vietnam was late in commencement and followed American military presence. **Southern Baptists** began missionary work in Saigon in 1959, the first missionary being Herman Hayes (1928-1997). **Hong Kong** Baptists also sponsored a mission among the Chinese, beginning in 1968. The **Baptist Bible Fellowship** (BBF) opened a mission in Vietnam in 1971. Following the war's conclusion, Baptist witness ceased.

VOLUNTARISM. Term applied to the impulse among Christian individuals to engage in benevolent works and belong to various sorts of **associations** of a **missionary** or service character. In the Old and New Testaments there is abundant evidence of the voluntary impulse, for instance in the offerings brought before the Lord (Exodus 35:4-29) and in the way early disciples followed Jesus (Luke 5: 1-11). The gospel itself has been interpreted as an invitation which calls forth a voluntary response. In the early church, various acts of charity characterized the Christian movement; during the medieval period associations, orders, and itinerants went about conducting charitable and reforming ministries and missions.

It was during the Reformation that Protestant groups engaged in renewal movements which, though originally voluntary, became denominations. The Pietists, followed by Puritans and Anglicans, formed prayer groups, missions, funds, publishing concerns, and academies on the basis of voluntary associations. Thomas Chalmers (1780-1847), a Presbyterian leader of the Free Church movement in Scotland, advocated a voluntary system of Christian and humanitarian works. **Valentine Wightman**, a colonial American Baptist, made a case for the New Testament basis for a voluntary support of the **ministry**, which did much to establish the principle in New England. The later half of the 18th century saw English Baptists leading the voluntarist movement in forming associations for missions, education, and care of persons with special needs. During the 19th century the **evangelical** movement in the United States, Great Britain and western Europe forged most of its missionary work as voluntary associations. Entire segments of the Baptist denomination were constructed as voluntary associations, later to be restructured in bureaucratic patterns. The "society" model was especially popular among American Baptists and British Union Baptists. More recently, Black Baptists in the United States have followed a voluntary organizational pattern, as witnessed not only in their ecclesiastical bodies but also in their reform associations, such as the Montgomery Improvement Association and the Southern Christian Leadership Conference.

Voluntary organizations are usually characterized by volunteer personnel, support through voluntary donations, and democratic decision-making. Such associations have become a leading characteristic of American religious tradition, regardless of denomination. See also **Associations, Baptist**.

W

WALES. Baptist preaching in Wales was conducted by individuals early in the 17th century, the first churches possibly established in the Olchon

Valley in 1633. Yet other evidence suggests that early Baptist work was established at Llanfaches in 1639, at Llan-hir in 1646, and among soldiers in Cromwell's army preaching in Radnorshire and Breconshire in 1646-1648. Under the Act of 1650 for the Better Propagation of the Gospel, the first Baptist preachers of clear record entered Wales on preaching missions; they included **Vavasor Powell**, **John Myles**, Jenkin Jones, Thomas Evans, and William Thomas. The influence of John Myles was primary in creating Calvinistic, closed communion congregations. Myles was also instrumental in forming the first association among the churches he helped to found.

Welsh Baptists followed the English example of **voluntary** associations for mission and education, and cooperated with the English **Baptist Missionary Society** (BMS). English-speaking **associations** of Welsh Baptist churches were formed in Monmouthshire (1857), Glamorgan, and Carmarthenshire (1860) and an English Union in North Wales was established in 1879, which eventually affiliated with the Lancashire and Cheshire Association in 1912. Most of the English-language congregations also associated with the Welsh Baptist Union since 1866. Many of the congregations have belonged jointly to the Welsh Union and the Baptist Union of Great Britain and Ireland, though relations between the two bodies have not always been smooth. One of the characteristic features of Welsh Baptist life was the **Nonconformist** chapels built of fieldstone and simple interiors, notably at Rhydwilym (1701) and Hengoed (1710).

As of 1995 the Undeb Bedyddwyr Cymru includes 535 churches and 23,450 members. The periodical, *Seren Cymru* (Star of Wales), has been published since 1866, and there are two theological colleges, one at Cardiff, the other at Bangor (see **Theological Education**). The **Baptist Bible Fellowship** (BBF) opened a mission in Wales in 1982.

WALLER, JOHN (1741-1802). Southern Baptist preacher, born in Spotsylvania County, Virginia. Originally planning a career in the law, he unsuccessfully tried several vocations. In 1767 he was converted by the testimony of a Baptist minister, Lewis Craig, and Waller became a travelling **evangelist**. He was frequently imprisoned--once for a month and a half--and wrote denouncing his treatment. Called "fighting Jack Waller," he was a powerful advocate for **religious liberty** in Virginia, yet an erratic preacher among the Baptists. In the 1780s Waller adopted **Arminian** theology and a Wesleyan polity which caused other Baptists to avoid contact with him. He became a self-proclaimed Independent Baptist for a time until returning to Calvinistic views. His evangelistic **ministry**

produced 2,000 converts and he constituted 18 churches, mostly in the tidewater region.

WALLIN, BENJAMIN (1711-1782). English Baptist minister, born at Southwark, London. The son of Edward Wallin (1678-1733), a Baptist minister, Benjamin was crippled from birth. He was educated by a mentor, John Needham (d.1743), the Baptist pastor at Hitchin, Hertfordshire. Wallin became the pastor at Maze Pond Baptist Church, a 1691 break-off congregation from Horsely-down Church on the matter of not allowing singing in worship. He remained in this church for 27 years, one of the longest tenures in the century. One of Wallin's distinctives was that he may have enjoyed the longest **ordination** service ever conducted among English Baptists, four hours and 15 minutes in 1741. **John Gill** presided over the service, which involved 16 ministers. Wallin was both a scholarly and a devotional writer, among the leading hymnist-poets of the era. Among his published works were *The Folly of Neglecting Divine Institutions* (1758), *Lectures on Primitive Christianity* (1768), and *Scripture-Doctrine of Christ's Sonship* (1771).

WARD, JOHN (1679-1758). English Baptist layman and educator, born in London. Ward served in the Navy Office and then as a schoolmaster. In 1720 he became a professor of rhetoric at Gresham College, where he taught for the remainder of his career. An officer in the Royal Society, he was a founding trustee of the British Museum. Ward published several books and was awarded an honorary doctorate by the University of Edinburgh. He designed the fireworks display in 1748 to celebrate the Peace of Aix-la-Chapelle.

WARD, WILLIAM (1769-1823). English Baptist missionary, born at Derby. He served an apprenticeship as a printer and for a time was a newspaper editor. In 1796 he was converted and joined the Baptist church at Hull. Hearing of the **Baptist Missionary Society**'s (BMS) interest in a printer, he offered himself for service in **India**. He published a major work on the Hindus and became a valued companion in the "Serampore Trio" with **William Carey** and **Joshua Ward**. Ward was the first missionary to return from the East and he visited Holland and the United States, raising money for Serampore College, 1819-1821. He returned to India where he died. Ward's published works include *Farewell Letters to a Few Friends in Britain and America on Returning to Bengal in 1821* (1821) and *Brief Memoir of Krishna-Pal, the First Hindoo in Bengal Who Broke the Chain of Caste by Embracing the Gospel* (1822).

WASHINGTON, BOOKER TALIAFERRO (1856-1915). American Black Baptist leader and educator, born a slave on James Burroughs's plantation in Hale's Ford, Virginia. He was called "Booker" because of his studious habits. He studied at Hampton, Virginia, and later at Wayland Seminary in Washington, D.C. In his early career he pursued several trades, including masonry and teaching. In 1881 he was selected to head up a new Negro Normal School at Tuskeegee, Alabama, which evolved into Tuskeegee Institute. Upon the death of Frederick Douglass (1817-1893), Washington became the preeminent Black leader of the era, until the rise of the National Association for the Advancement of Colored People. He favored education and training as a means to improve the social status of Blacks, a position which W. E. B. Dubois (1868-1963) and others criticized because it denied the Negro of inherent civil rights. He was influenced early in his life by Baptists and was educated in a Baptist school, though his theology was said to be much inclined toward unitarianism. He was one of the most honored persons of his era, receiving a degree from Harvard in 1891. Washington was the author of *Up From Slavery* (1901) and *The Story of the Negro* (1909).

WAYLAND, FRANCIS (1796-1865). American Baptist minister and educator, born in New York City. He graduated from Union College (Albany, New York), then studied medicine, and finally turned to theological studies at Andover Theological Seminary. His first pastorate was First Baptist, Boston, which he served in 1821-1826 with some difficulty in pastoral work. He turned to teaching at Union College and after one year was elected president of Brown University. Wayland also taught moral philosophy at Brown and authored a popular textbook of the era. An influential denominational leader, it was Wayland who reshaped American Baptist **polity** along the lines of **voluntary** societies (see **Voluntarism**) rather than a strong national **convention**. President of the **General Missionary Convention** and chair of the **Baptist Board of Foreign Missions** (BBFM), Wayland was the most visible leader of Baptists in the North. During the 1840s he engaged in a series of debates on the subject of **slavery** with **Richard Fuller** of South Carolina; Wayland took the position that modern Christians must take a moral stand even on those issues which Christ recognized, but did not change. In the U.S. presidential campaign of 1860, Wayland was a prominent New England supporter of Abraham Lincoln (1809-1865). He was one of the most widely published writers of his era, including *The Elements of Moral Science* (1835), *The Elements of Political Economy* (1837), *Domestic Slavery Considered as a Scriptural Institution* (1845), *The Memoir of the Life and Labors of Adoniram Judson* (1853), *The Elements of Intellectual*

Philosophy (1854), and *Notes on the Principles and Practices of Baptist Churches* (1827). His sermon, *The Moral Dignity of the Missionary Enterprise* (1823), became a definitive tract in the American **evangelical** tradition.

WEBB, MARY (1779-1861). American Baptist missionary organizer, born at Boston, Massachusetts. From childhood she suffered from a crippling disease and was confined to a wheel chair. Influenced by her pastor, **Thomas Baldwin** at Second Baptist Church in Boston, she took an interest in **missions**. In 1800 she organized what became the first woman's missionary society in the United States, the Boston Female Society for Missionary Purposes. Originally an interdenominational society, Webb patterned her organization on the Massachusetts Baptist Missionary Society, which her pastor helped to found. In time the Society became exclusively Baptist and was a model for each state. Webb guided the Society into not only support of overseas missions but also direct involvement in work with widows, children, and Jewish persons.

WELCH, JAMES ELY (1789-1876). American Baptist missionary, born near Lexington, Kentucky. As a frontiersman, he lacked formal education, except study with **William Staughton** at his school in Philadelphia. Welch was appointed as one of the first domestic missionaries of the **Baptist Board of Foreign Missions** (BBFM) in 1817 to work with the Indian tribes in the Mississippi Valley. En route to their field at St. Louis, he and his wife organized a number of local missionary societies in the Ohio Valley. He started the first Baptist Church in St. Louis and a school, which became a model for later development. When his appointment with the Baptist Board expired, he worked for the American **Sunday School** Union. It was Welch's influence that caused the Baptists to conduct their Indian missions on or near tribal lands rather than in Caucasian settlements.

WELCOMING AND AFFIRMING BAPTISTS, ASSOCIATION OF. With changing attitudes toward various aspects of human sexuality, scattered Baptists in the gay, lesbian, and bisexual communities in the United States began in the 1980s to express their sexuality as church members and some as ordained clergy. This was initially met with strong antagonism mostly from the **evangelical** community, and distress among the leadership of the **American Baptist** regional and national organizations. The issue of homosexuality exploded in the American Baptist community in 1991 at the Charleston, West Virginia, Biennial Meeting where American Baptists Concerned (a support group for gays and lesbians) attempted to display its materials at the national gathering. Stiff opposition to their presence emerged and a Statement of Concern was adopted at that Biennial Meeting repudiating homosexual lifestyle, marriage, or **ordination**, and the establishment of gay churches or caucusses. The next formal step was taken at the American Baptist General Board Meeting in fall 1992 when that body voted "to affirm that the practice of homosexuality is incompatible with Christian teaching." A second resolution called for dialogue on issues of sexuality and acknowledged that there is a variety of understandings throughout the denomination about homosexuality, and a plea was also issued to respect the individual integrity of persons within the denomination as the issue of homosexuality was engaged.

At the Biennial Meeting in Charleston, a group of pastors agreed to form an association and in 1993 the Association of Welcoming and Affirming Baptists was formed to offer support for gay and lesbian people's membership and to provide a forum for better understanding of matters from sexuality to **disfellowshipping** churches in the denomination. As pastors and churches have announced their intention to join the Association, national gatherings have been held and a newsletter, *The Inspiriter* (1996-), has begun publication. As of 1995 there are about 50 congregations affiliated with the Association of Welcoming and Affirming Baptists.

WEST VIRGINIA FUNDAMENTAL BAPTIST MISSION. Among the hundreds of Baptist congregations in the state of West Virginia, many were sympathetic to the **fundamentalist** movement in the 1920s and 1930s. At Charleston, West Virginia, in January 1944 the West Virginia Fundamental Baptist Mission was founded for the purpose of organizing Baptist churches and supporting feeble congregations. The Mission was guided by the principles of local church autonomy and self-support of missions. In May 1950 the West Virginia Fundamental Baptist Mission merged its programs into the **Fellowship of Baptists for Home Missions**.

WESTERN BAPTIST MISSION. Pastors of the California State Association of Regular Baptists formed in 1942 the Pacific Home Mission of Regular Baptists, later known as the Western Baptist Mission. The objects of the domestic mission were to hold **bible** conferences, and **evangelistic** meetings, and also to assist needy churches in their building programs. The region of interest was the far western United States. In November 1949 the Western Baptist Mission merged its efforts with the **Fellowship of Baptists for Home Missions**.

WESTON, HENRY GRIGGS (1820-1909). American Baptist minister and educator, born at Lynn, Massachusetts. He was educated at Brown University and Newton Theological School. Owing to poor health, he served as a missionary pastor in Washington, Illinois, accepting the church at Peoria in 1846. In 1859 he became pastor of Oliver Street Baptist Church, New York City, where he served for nine years. In 1868 he was named president of Crozer Theological Seminary in Upland, Pennsylvania, where he served for 40 years, the longest tenure of an American Baptist seminary administrator. Weston built Crozer into a premier theological faculty and library, strongly related to the **Philadelphia Baptist Association** community. In scholarly terms, Weston specialized in the interpretation of the gospels and was a widely regarded teacher of the **bible**. He was a close friend of Dwight L. Moody (1837-1899), and served as an associate editor of the first edition of the *Scofield Reference Bible*, published in 1909. Weston was president of the **American Baptist Missionary Union** (ABMU) in 1872-1873 and editor of the *Baptist Quarterly* from 1869-1877. With **Augustus Hopkins Strong** at Rochester and **Alvah Hovey** at Newton, Weston was part of an educational triumvirate which built an outstanding network of theological schools for the Baptist community in the northern United States. Among Weston's published works were *Outline of Ecclesiology* (1895) and *Matthew: The Genesis of the New Testament: Its Purpose, Character, and Method* (1900).

WHITE, CHARLOTTE HAZEN ATLEE (fl. 1815-1830). American and English Baptist missionary, born in Pennsylvania. Following the organization of the Baptist **General Missionary Convention** in 1814, the **Baptist Board of Foreign Missions** (BBFM) appointed a printer to assist the **Judsons** in **Burma**. Mrs. Charlotte White, a widow, volunteered her services and her personal property to go to Burma to care for the women and children. Against stiff pressure within the Board and a restrictive definition of "**missionary**," the Board appointed her the first Baptist **woman missionary** from the United States. She arrived in India in 1816, met and married a widower named Joshua Rowe (1781-1823), who was under the appointment of the British **Baptist Missionary Society** (BMS), and she transferred to that Society. As a missionary spouse, Mrs. Rowe conducted work among Indian women at Digah and planned to start a system of schools. She also published a Hindustani spelling book for children. When Joshua died in 1823, however, Charlotte returned to the United States and taught English, music, and drawing in an academy in Loundesboro, Alabama.

WHITLEY, WILLIAM THEOPHILUS (1861-1947). English and Australian Baptist minister and historian, born at Islington, London. He was educated at King's College, Cambridge, taking degrees in the arts and law. Later he graduated from Rawdon College and served a church at Bridlington in 1888-1891. In 1891 he left for **Australia** where he became the first principal of Baptist College of Victoria in Melbourne. He earned a doctor of laws degree at Melbourne University and became a lecturer at Queen's College, University of Melbourne. In 1902 he returned to England and served congregations at Fishergate, Preston (1902-1917), and Droitwich (1917-1928). His literary contributions to Baptist historiography were enormous, producing editions of the *Works of John Smyth*, the *Minutes of the General Assembly of General Baptists*, and editing the *Transactions of the Baptist Historical Society*. He was a founder of that Society in 1908. One of Whitley's most important theses was the linkage between the New Model Army and the establishment of the first Baptist **associations**. The Baptist Theological College of Victoria in Melbourne was renamed Whitley College in 1965 in his honor.

WHITSETT, WILLIAM HETH (1841-1911). Southern Baptist minister and educator, born at Nashville, Tennessee. He was educated at Union University and served in the Confederate army before pastoral ministry at Mill Creek, Tennessee, and Albany, Georgia. In 1872 he became professor of ecclesiastical history at Southern Baptist Theological Seminary, distinguishing himself as a writer and researcher. Whitsett wrote in 1895 that he believed Baptists borrowed the practice of believer's **baptism** from the Dutch **Anabaptists**, and he questioned the **Landmarkist** and **successionist** positions that there was an unbroken line of Baptists from the New Testament. This controversy cost him the presidency of the Seminary, from which he had to resign in 1899. Thereafter he taught at Richmond College and helped lead a successful drive to establish the **Baptist World Alliance**. He also believed in the universal church and helped establish the notion that early Baptists were part of a larger movement of English religious life. Among Whitsett's published works were *Origins of the Disciples of Christ* (1887), *A Question in Baptist History: Whether the Anabaptists in England Practised Immersion Before the Year 1641?* (1896) and *Sidney Rigdon, Real Founder of Mormonism* (1918).

WIBERG, ANDERS (1816-1887). Swedish and American Baptist minister, born in Helsingland, Sweden. He was educated at the University of Uppsala and served for six years as a Lutheran pastor. He met **Julius Köbner** and **J. G. Oncken** and was drawn to the Baptist position. In 1852 he travelled to the United States to visit his exiled countryman, **F. O. Nilson**, who baptized him. Wiberg remained in the Midwest during 1853 as an itinerant minister in Iowa and Illinois. For two years in Philadelphia, he wrote tracts on Baptist doctrine for the **American Baptist Publication Society**. Returning to **Sweden** in 1855, he began an extensive work of church planting, **evangelism**, and education in conjunction with the Brothers **Palmquist** (**Gustaf**, Johannes, Per). Under this central administration, Wiberg superintended the growth of the Baptist Union to 125 churches by 1861. During this period Wiberg also served as a missionary of the ABPS and fostered the establishment of Betelseminariat, the first Swedish Baptist theological school. Wiberg's published work includes a classic study of **baptism**, *Christian Baptism Set Forth in the Words of the Bible* (1880?).

WIGHTMAN, VALENTINE (1681-1747). American Baptist minister, born at North Kingston, Rhode Island. Descendant of a line of Baptists who went back to the early 17th century, Wightman was ordained at North Kingston in the tradition of the **General Six Principle Baptists**. In 1705 he began preaching at Groton, Connecticut, and moved there two years later, without permission of the town selectmen. This caused a stir which eventuated in a celebrated legal proceeding and fines levied upon Wightman. After several appeals, Wightman paid the fines and was admitted to the town, thus establishing the first permanent Baptist congregation in the colony of Connecticut. Wightman served the Groton church until 1747 and was instrumental in starting churches in Waterford and Wallingford and in New York City.

Wightman continued to be a leader among the New England Baptists. In 1727 he participated in a debate with John Bulkley on matters ranging from the proper subjects of **baptism** to an exposition of **voluntarism** in the support of ministers. He was frequently involved in **ordination** proceedings, notably of Nicholas Eyres (1691-1759) in 1724 and Ephraim Bound (c. 1719-1765) in 1743. He contended for hymn singing in worship services and for the **laying on of hands** according to Six Principle practices. As the **Great Awakening** gained momentum in the 1740s, Wightman was a leader among **New Light Baptists**, along with **Ebenezer Moulton** and Thomas Green (1699-1773).

WILLIAMS, GEORGE WASHINGTON (1849-1891). American Black Baptist minister and political leader, born at Bedford Springs, Pennsylvania. During the Civil War, he enlisted in the Masasachusetts Regiment and served along the Texas-**Mexico** frontier with distinction. He was denied a promotion to the regular army because of color. Following military service, he entered Howard University in Washington, D.C. and also became its groundskeeper. He then graduated from Newton Theological Institution and was ordained to the Baptist **ministry**. He served 12th Street Baptist Church in Boston (1875) and Union Baptist Church, Cincinnati, Ohio (1875-1879), before entering politics. President Rutherford B. Hayes (1822-1893) appointed Williams a commissioner of internal revenue and he eventually won a seat in the Ohio legislature, 1879-1881. In 1885-1886 he served as U.S. minister to **Haiti** and then he worked for the Belgian government in the **Congo**. He was the author of *The History of the Negro Race in America* (1883), a classic text. He died at Blackpool, England.

WILLIAMS, ROGER (c.1603-1684). Anglican and Separatist minister and, for a time, American Baptist pioneer, born at London, England. He was educated at Cambridge University and served as a personal chaplain to Sir Edward Masham in 1627-1630. Dissatisfied with the state of the Church of England, he emigrated to Massachusetts and took the position of assistant pastor in the Congregationalist Church at Salem. He raised questions about the magistracy, treatment of Indian land claims, and religious freedom, and this brought him into adversarial relations with the authorities. He was banished in 1636 and he relocated to Narragansett Country (later Rhode Island), where he concluded a treaty with the Indians and organized a colony at Providence Plantations.

In 1638 Williams embraced the Baptist position and assisted in organizing the first Baptist church in America, at Providence. After only a few months in 1639, however, Williams evolved to a more radical position, generally referred to as a "Seeker," and there is no record of his being involved with Baptists thereafter. He wrote to John Winthrop, Jr. (1605-1676) in 1649 that he believed Baptist practice "came nearer the first practice of our great Founder Christ than other practices of religions doe, & yet I have no satisfaction neither in the authority by which **baptism** is done nor in the manner...." **Isaac Backus**, in the next century resurrected Williams from oblivion among Baptists and created in him a champion of **religious liberty** and pioneer status for Baptists in the United States, which his contemporaries little accorded him. Among Williams's published works were *A Key to the Language of America* (1643), *The Bloudy Tenent, of Persecution for Cause of Conscience, Discuss'd in a Conference Between Tryth and Peace* (1644), and *The Bloudy Tenent Yet More Bloody, By Mr. Cotton's Endeavour to Wash It White in the Blood of the Lambe* (1652), and *George Fox Digg'd Out of His Burrowes* (1676). See also **Roger Williams Fellowship**.

WINCHESTER, ELHANAN (1751-1797). American Baptist minister, born at Brookline, Massachusetts. Self-educated, he was an **evangelist** and then settled as pastor initially at Welsh Neck, South Carolina (1775-1779), and then at First Baptist, Philadelphia, in 1780. While pastor in Philadelphia, he adopted a **universalist** theology and was branded a heretic. Popular with a faction in the congregation, his emphases split the church and he took a group to meet at the University of Pennsylvania. At length he became a religious lecturer and travelled widely in Europe and the United States as a Universalist. In 1787 he settled in London, England, where he preached at Worship Street in the mornings, and Glass House Yard in the evenings. While in Great Britain he acquainted himself with several religious leaders, including John Wesley (1703-1791), who admired Winchester's **Arminian** theological tilt. He also lectured widely on prophetic themes. Apparently due to marital difficulties, he left England abruptly in 1794 and returned to the United States where he lectured in Massachusetts and Connecticut. Winchester continued to be a colorful figure, spontaneously ordaining a young **evangelist** Hosea Ballou (1771-1852) to the ministry at a service in 1794 and writing against the deistical tendencies of Thomas Paine (1737-1809). He was a forceful **antislavery** writer, beginning in 1774. Ironically for a radical thinker, he was also condemned for not adopting some of the new currents of thought. Among his important published works were *The Mystic's Plea for Universal Redemption as Held Forth* (1781), *The Universal Restoration Exhibited in a Series of Dialogues Between a Minister and His Friend* (1788), and *A Plain Political Catechism Intended for the Use of Schools in the United States of America* (1796).

WINEBRENNER, JOHN (1797-1860). American Reformed Church pastor and leader, born at Walkersville, Maryland. He was educated at Dickinson College and determined to enter the **ministry** of the German Reformed Church. He became a student of Samuel Helffenstein (1775-1866), a Reformed pastor in Philadelphia, Pennsylvania, and developed a pietistic and **revivalistic** theology. Winebrenner served churches in Harrisburg and Cumberland County, Pennsylvania. His extreme revivalistic style, similar to Charles Finney's (1792-1875) New Measures, led to his dismissal from his Reformed congregation in 1828. He continued to itinerate and preach on themes of renewal throughout central Pennsylvania and Maryland.

In 1830 he was rebaptized and he took on a reputation of developing Baptist leanings. He rallied his substantial following into a new organization which he called the "Church of God" based upon a New Testament apostolic plan. Winebrenner's baptistic **polity** and theology spread to the Ohio Valley. In 1845 he organized a general eldership for the Church of God. Derogatorily referred to as "Winebrennerians," the sect sought to be faithful to biblical literalism, restoration of the primitive order, and social reforms such as **antislavery**. Winebrenner himself remained aloof from the Baptist tradition, publishing a paper, *The Gospel Publisher*, and engaging in various forms of reform, including **peace** and **temperance**. His movement, the Church of God, was often included in 19th century listings of Baptistic groups, primarily because of their advocacy of believer's **baptism**.

WOELFKIN, CORNELIUS (1859-1928). American Baptist minister, born in New York City. He was educated at Colgate and Rochester Universities, after which he entered the pastoral **ministry**. He served several congregations: First Baptist, Hackensack, New Jersey (1887-1892), North Jersey City (1892-1894), and Green Avenue Baptist, New York City (1894-1905). From 1905-1912 he served as Wyckoff Professor of Homiletics at Rochester Theological Seminary. His first commitment was to the pastorate, however, and he returned to New York City in 1912 as pastor at Fifth Avenue Baptist Church in 1912-1928. While in that role, he was a distinguished president of the **American Baptist Foreign Mission Society** (ABFMS) in 1911. Woelfkin's chief monument was his substitute motion at the **Northern Baptist Convention** (NBC) annual meeting in 1922 to make the New Testament the sole rule of faith and practice, which ultimately outmaneuvered the **fundamentalist** faction led by **William Bell Riley**. **Harry Emerson Fosdick**, a close friend of Woelfkin, delivered the eulogy at his funeral. Woelfkin was well known for his sermon, *The Quest for Immortality* (1913), preached in the Brick Presbyterian Church in Rochester, New York.

WOMEN IN BAPTIST LIFE. From the earliest period of Baptist history in England, women have played a significant role in ministry and mission. Baptists have wrestled with biblical teaching on the appropriate roles for women in the church: a text which is perceived to limit the role of women is I Cor. 14:34-35; those which have been used to heighten the appreciation of women are Joel 2:28-29, John 8:36, and Galatians 3:28.

Women in the seventeenth century. Baptists were among the first of the **Nonconformist** community in 17th-century England to allow women to preach and engage in **ministry** within the congregations. Some historians believe that the openness to women in ministry was a trait of the Brownists during the Elizabethan era, which passed to the Baptist communities. Called "she-preachers" and "widows" (the latter in the biblical sense), women enjoyed many liberties not allowed elsewhere in the English Church and among **dissenters**. By the 1660s, however, the tide had changed and women were not as frequently found in congregational leadership roles. Doubtless this was the result of accommodation to the emerging mainstream Nonconformist consensus.

Among the early English **General Baptists, John Smyth** categorized women as part of the "private" sector of the congregation, in contrast with the "prophets." Smyth and **Thomas Helwys** allowed that women could serve as **deacons**; Helwys described the office of "widow," which he defined as women over 60 years old. There is scant mention of women in the **Particular Baptist** tradition. Thomas Edwards (1599-1647), Presbyterian author of *Gangrena*, railed against women preachers and such were known to be at Brasted, Westerham, and Bell Alley, London. (One of the problems noted of early General Baptist women preachers was long sermons; one woman was said to have preached for two hours.) A Mrs. Attaway among the General Baptists in the church at Coleman Street, London, was known as the "mistress of all the she-preachers." **Dorothy Hazzard** of Bristol, who discipled her husband, won acclaim for her leadership in the formation of Broadmead Church there.

Later in the 17th century there is evidence of separate women's organization within churches, as at **Benjamin Keach**'s church where there was a separate **prayer meeting**. Women writers such as Katherine Sutton and Jane Turner, a **Fifth Monarchist**, made contributions to the growing literature of **Nonconformity**. **Ann Dutton** wrote and spoke widely and was well known for her composition of hymns. For the most part, however, at the outset of a new century, women were seated separately from men and deprived of most leadership positions in British Baptist congregations.

In the American colonies there are isolated instances of women in significant leadership roles. As early as the 1640s **Deborah Moody** adopted Baptist principles in Massachusetts and encountered stiff opposition for her views. Rachel Scammon (fl.1720-30), also of Massachusetts, made several missionary forays into New Hampshire to distribute literature, which later led to the establishment of at least one congregation at Salem. In the southern colonies, there is scant evidence of women, such as Martha Stearns Marshall (fl.1750), being involved in revival meetings involving Baptists.

The role of women in Baptist life was greatly enhanced at the beginning of the 19th century. In Boston in 1800 **Mary Webb**, a crippled member of Second Baptist Church, organized the "mother society" of missionary support, from which both women's and broader missionary work among American Baptists stemmed. Later, with role models like the three wives of **Adoniram Judson**, women began to organize missionary groups and enjoy new roles outside the household circles. In Britain societies of benefit to women and administered by women were common by 1850. Notably, in 1890 British Baptist pastor **F. B. Meyer** helped to form a Baptist Sisterhood in London: the Baptist Deaconness Home and Mission became the Order of Baptist Deaconnesses, imitating Lutheran and Methodist experience. The **Baptist Missionary Society** (BMS) in 1854 approved the work of missionary spouses among women's exclusive communities (*zenanas*) in **India** and this led to the formation of the Ladies Association for the Support of Zenana Work in 1866, first woman's auxiliary to the BMS. The first official women missionaries in the British Baptist family were Emily Saker (1850-1932) and Carrie Comber (d. 1885), both commissioned in 1879 as single missionary workers in the zenana movement in **Cameroon**. By the conclusion of the century, in addition to the interdenominational organizations to which Baptist women contributed, there were 13 Baptist societies in the United States, two in Great Britain, and five major organizations in **Canada** focused on women's work.

Meanwhile the lot of women in local congregational leadership also evolved. In the British **Baptist Union** (BU), the first woman to serve as pastor of a congregation was Edith Gates (1883-1962), who began her long ministry at Little Tew and Cleveley in 1918. The first husband-wife combination ministry was that of Maria Living-Taylor, who served a series of churches with her husband beginning in 1922. Regent's Park College admitted a woman student, Violet Hedger (1900-1992), in 1923 and Bristol Baptist College registered its first woman candidate for ministry in 1937. Baptist laywomen in 1908 created the Baptist Women's Home Work Auxiliary, which evolved into the Baptist Women's League in 1910. Two women have served as presidents of the Baptist Union of Great Britain, Nell Alexander (d.1986) in 1978 and the Rev. Margaret Jarman (1932-) in 1987.

Baptist Women in North America. As with other denominations, North American Baptist women began to organize for missions. The first associations were prayer gatherings in homes. In 1800 one of these was made a formal society, the Boston Baptist Female Missionary Society, founded by **Mary Webb** in Second Baptist Church. This "mother society" became a model for Baptist women in the North and South. When the national **General Missionary Convention** and **Baptist Board for Foreign Missions** (BBFM) were formed in 1814, **Charlotte White** volunteered to go to Burma, prompting a debate over whether women should be allowed to serve as missionaries. In 1815 she was appointed and became the first single woman missionary in the denomination. Of course, each of the male missionaries appointed were married and a case has been made that their spouses constituted *de facto* missionaries from the beginning of overseas work.

The major role of women in the first half of the century continued to be in support of missions. In the Canadian Maritime Provinces, **Hannah Maria Norris Armstrong** organized numerous bands of missionary supporters in the early 1870s. At the same time, Baptist women in New England under the leadership of Mrs. Alvah Hovey formed the Woman's Baptist Foreign Mission Society (WABFMS) in 1871; simultaneously a western states society was formed in Chicago. Not only did these organizations bring women together in local congregations, they also increased the possibilities for women to engage directly in ministry as missionaries or administrators. In 1914, on the centennial anniversary of the recognition of **Ann Judson** in **Burma**, the two regional societies merged into the Woman's Baptist Foreign Mission Society. A similar story unfolded with women involved in domestic missions, the result becoming the Woman's American Baptist Home Mission Society (WABHMS), chartered in 1877 and made a national organization in 1909.

American Baptist women have been involved in some remarkable experiences. In the overseas context, Marilla Baker Ingalls (1828-1902) is an example. Appointed with her husband to the Arracan field of the **American Baptist Missionary Union** (ABMU), Lovell Baker died in 1858. The Board appointed Marilla to "independent work" due to her effectiveness as a teacher. Her tract distribution and outreach to Buddhists in particular, antagonized local gangs and Buddhist leaders. At one point a reward was placed upon her head for 10,000 rupees, but she was prevented from capture. It was said at her retirement that she influenced the conversion of 100 Buddhist priests to the Christian faith. Similarly, on the domestic front, a memorable set of events occurred in Kiowa Territory, Oklahoma, at the turn of the 20th century. **Isabel Crawford**, a missionary for the WABHMS, in 1905 supervised a celebration of the Lord's Supper at Saddle Mountain mission station in the absence of a local male pastor. She was judged to have acted contrary to Board policy, she was reprimanded, and subsequently she resigned from the Board. Her action and later protest raised the consciousness of women in the northern Baptist family in the United States during an era of increasing women's rights recognition.

The **Southern Baptists** of the United States have responded to direct leadership of women more slowly. There are no examples of women in pastoral roles in the 19th century; however, Harriet Baker (fl.1850) was appointed by the **Foreign Mission Board** (FMB) in 1851 to establish a school for female girls at Canton, **China**, thus becoming the first female appointment of Southern Baptists in missions. For many years after Baker's health failed, no further women were appointed. **Henry A. Tupper**, corresponding secretary of the FMB, changed profoundly this trend with the appointment of Lula Whilden (1846-1916) and Edmonia Moon (1851-1908) to China in 1873.

Southern Baptist women likewise organized themselves for missionary endeavor. In 1868 the first meeting of women in conjunction with the annual **Southern Baptist Convention** session was held in Baltimore and led by Ann Baker Graves, the mother of R. H. Graves, a prominent missionary. Ten years later, a Convention committee recommended establishing state committees of women, and in 1888 the national Woman's Missionary Union was founded under the aegis of Annie Armstrong (1850-1938).

Women among **Black Baptists** in the United States have also been organized. Prominent since the 19th century have been local church groups of "matrons" who serve in an auxiliary role in programs, missions, and education. Women have served in executive leadership in the denominational bodies and as missionaries.

Ordination of Women. **Ordination** of women has occurred in ever-increasing numbers since the latter half of the 19th century. A first step was taken in 1846 in the United States when Ruby Bixby was licensed to the ministry by the Honey Creek, Iowa, Freewill Baptist Quarterly Meeting. The first recorded ordination of a Baptist woman at the local church level (in contrast with denominational credentials) occurred among northern **Freewill Baptists** with A. Gerry in 1869; likewise among southern Freewill Baptists, in 1938 Lucy Wells, a member of the Eastern Conference, was ordained to the ministry by the denominational Examining Board. A Seventh Day Baptist woman, Experience P. F. Randolph (fl.1850-1890) was ordained between 1880 and 1885 at the Hornellsville, New York, **Seventh Day Baptist** Church. Susan Elizabeth Cilley Griffin (1851-1926) was the first woman to enjoy denomination-wide recognition for her ordination in the Elmira Heights (N.Y.) Baptist Church, ultimately related to the Northern Baptist Convention.

While more rarely, Southern Baptists in the United States have also ordained women, beginning with Addie Davis of Watts Street Baptist Church, Durham, North Carolina, on August 9, 1964. The second Southern Baptist ordination of a woman occurred in 1971 when Shirley Carter was ordained at Kathwood Baptist Church in Columbia, South Carolina. The following year, however, under pressure the church rescinded the ordination, the first such instance on record. Over the next 15 years, over 50 Southern Baptist women were ordained to the gospel ministry. One of the most celebrated occurrences surrounding the recognition of the ordination of women involved Nancy Hastings Sehested

(1951-). Ordained in 1981, Sehested was called in 1987 to be the senior minister at Prescott Memorial Baptist Church in Memphis, Tennessee. Once installed in that role, the church was **disfellowshipped** that year by the local Shelby County Baptist Association. In response to the growing frustration among women candidates for ministry and the need for mutual support, an alliance, the Southern Baptist Women in Ministry, was formed in 1983 as a support group for women in ministry of various kinds. As of 1995, there are 60 women pastors and 176 endorsed women chaplains relating to the Southern Baptist Home Mission Board.

Although the ordination of women in Black Baptist churches is rare, there are noteworthy exceptions. Jennie Johnson (1867-1967) was apparently the earliest Black woman to be ordained. She was a Canadian Free Baptist who, due to discrimination against women and Blacks, was actually ordained at Galesville, Michigan, on October 26, 1909. Her ordination was certified by the General Conference of Free Baptists. Similarly, Rosetta O'Neal (1937-) of Detroit, Michigan, was ordained in 1975 and, serving a congregation in Windsor, Ontario, has been president of the Baptist Convention of Ontario and Quebec, 1998-1999. Among Americans, Ella P. Mitchell (1917-) was ordained at Allen Temple Baptist Church in Oakland, California, in 1978 and Suzanne Johnson Cook (1957-) was ordained at Oliver Street Baptist Church in 1982, a dually aligned **American Baptist** congregation in New York City. The first duly elected woman executive (or regional) minister among Baptists was Kathryn Baker (1939-), ordained in 1976, who served the American Baptist Churches of the Niagara Frontier (New York), 1985-1993. In central Canada, Muriel Spurgeon Carder (1922-) was the first Baptist woman ordained in 1948, while Mae Benedict Field (1906-1998) was first among the western Canadian Baptists in 1959. Noteworthy among European Baptists was Birgit Carlson (1935-) who served as president of the Swedish Baptist Union, 1984-1995, the first female executive officer of a national organization of Baptists, and Ruth Lehotsky (1933-), the first woman theological school professor in eastern Europe. In the United States, Blanche Eliza Parks was appointed Dean of Women and Instructor in Methods of Missionary Service in 1925 at Berkeley Baptist Divinity School, as was Catherine H. Thompson, Instructor in Missions at The Eastern Baptist Theological Seminary the same year. Northern Baptist Theological Seminary appointed Ruthella Rodeaver in Christian Education in 1936. Later women appointments to previously all-male faculties were Martha Leypoldt in 1966 in Christian Education at Eastern Seminary, Phyllis Trible in Old Testament in 1971 at Andover Newton Theological School, and Beverly R. Gaventa in New Testament at Colgate Rochester Divinity School in 1976. In Canada, Lois A. Tupper (1911-) was appointed in 1968 as Professor of Christian Ministry at McMaster Divinity College, the first full-time female faculty member in any theological school.

WOMEN'S MISSIONARY ORGANIZATIONS, BAPTIST. Baptist women have long been active in support of missions, and the ensuing organizations which they have formed provide an important international chapter in Baptist history. The patterns for organized women's work were set in the British and American Baptist communities in the late 19th century. From that period, and as a result of missionary advance itself, most Baptist conventions and unions worldwide have a women's auxiliary or missionary support organization of the historic patterns.

Overseas missionary work. The first organization which Baptist women joined was undoubtedly the Boston Bethel Missionary Society, formed by **Mary Webb** in 1800. Chapters or missionary bands soon followed in support of America's first missionaries, the **Adoniram Judsons.** Doubtless there were women who joined the evangelical movements in the 1830s, such as those formed in the wake of David Abeel's (1804-1846) challenge toward organized women in London in 1834. The first strictly Baptist general women's organization in North America was the **Freewill Baptist** Female Missionary Society, formed in 1847 in New Hampshire. Later, in 1861 the Woman's Union Missionary Society of America for Heathen Lands was formed of numerous Baptist supporters. The popularity of this endeavor led to the organization of American Baptist women in 1870-1871. In Newton Center, Masachusetts, the Woman's Baptist Foreign Mission Society of the East was formed in April 1871, with the Woman's Baptist Foreign Mission Society of the West likewise formed the following May in Chicago. A third society was formed in the Far West in 1874, the Woman's Baptist Foreign Mission Society of the Pacific Coast. These organizations prepared candidates to serve in various fields approved by the **American Baptist Missionary Union** (ABMU), while also training a female administrative corps at home. Membership in these societies was kept at one dollar per year to include as many persons as possible. Women's work overseas through these three bodies came to include hospitals, schools, construction projects, and women's advocacy issues. In 1913 the societies from the east and west merged into the Woman's American Baptist Foreign Mission Society, which in 1955 was integrated into the **American Baptist Foreign Mission Society** (ABFMS), affiliated with the **American Baptist Convention** (ABC).

Other groups of Baptist women in the United States also organized in the period between 1880 and 1940. The largest of these was the

Women's Missionary Union (WMU) of the **Southern Baptist Convention**, founded in 1888, largely in response to a plea from missionary to China, **Charlotte Moon**. By 1915 the WMU recorded 250,000 members in over 13,000 affiliated local and state organizations. The Union has since 1887 superintended the annual Lottie Moon Christmas Offering, which accounts for a significant percentage of Southern Baptist missionary support. Likewise, the General Conference of the German Baptists in the United States in 1895 authorized the formation of a women's organization and this became a reality in 1907 with Der Allgemeine Schwesternbund Deutscher Baptisten von Nord Amerika (The General Women's Union of German Baptists of North America). This organization paralleled for a few years the development of a German Baptist deaconess movement, formed in Chicago in 1897. Following the pattern, in 1932 the Women's Commission of the **Baptist General Conference** (BGC) was organized in the Swedish Baptist community in North America.

Within the British Baptist Family, women's organization for support of overseas mission began in 1867 with the establishment of the Ladies Association for the Support of Zenana Work and Bible Women in India, as an auxiliary of the Baptist Missionary Society (BMS). Eventually this became a vehicle through which single female missionaries were appointed. In 1897 the Association became the Baptist Zenana Mission, which after recommendations from the Edinburgh 1910 Conference, was incorporated in 1914 as the Women's Missionary Association of the **Baptist Missionary Society**. By 1924 the Association became a department within the BMS structure.

Similarly, **voluntary** women's associations of local and regional kinds in support of the **Baptist Union** (BU) and the **Baptist Home Mission Society** (BHMS), became in 1908 the Baptist Women's Home Work Auxiliary, which in turn evolved into the Baptist Women's League in 1910. Eventually, a Women's Department of the BU was formed, and this coordinated with local church groups to coordinate fellowship among women. Desirous of greater integration in the life of the church as a whole, the formal organization and department evolved into the Baptist Women's Conference in the 1970s and the Baptist Women's Mission Network in the late 1980s. The organization disbanded in 1998.

Baptist women in **Canada** organized in the formative years 1880-1890. **Hannah Maria Norris** Armstrong in 1870 became the catalyst for organizing local societies in support of her plans to serve in **India**. In one summer she founded 32 societies in the Maritime Provinces. Ultimately, the result of this work was the formation of the United Baptist Woman's Missionary Union of the Maritime Provinces in 1884. Similar organizations emerged to serve the needs of central Canada, the Women's Baptist Foreign Mission Society of Ontario (West) in 1876 and the Women's Baptist Foreign Missionary Society of Eastern Canada in the same year. In 1953 the separate entities merged as the Baptist Women's Missionary Society of Ontario and Quebec. As part of the national movement among Canadian Baptists in the 1940s, there was for a time after 1940 a consultative body called the Dominion Committee of the Affiliated Baptist Women's Missionary Societies of Canada, which involved all of the organizations across the country.

Domestic Missionary Work and Support. As noted earlier, the first woman's organization in the Baptist community was the Boston Society formed by **Mary Webb**. This group actually provided more support for home and urban projects than for overseas work. Gradually, as women became interested in missionary work, primarily encouraged by the heroism of women like the Judson wives, local and state societies were formed in Ohio, Illinois, Connecticut, and Michigan, which forwarded contributions to the **American Baptist Home Mission Society** (ABHMS). Matching the development of the Women's foreign societies (see above), in 1877 a western woman's society (Chicago) was chartered and an eastern woman's society (Boston) was formed in 1878. These joined in 1910 as the Woman's American Baptist Home Mission Society (WABHMS). This organization, headquartered in Chicago, Illinois, trained and appointed women missionaries as teachers, nurses, friendship house workers, and urban workers in the United States and other fields of the American Baptist Home Mission Society (ABHMS). In 1955 The WABHMS was integrated with the ABHMS and the headquarters was moved to Valley Forge, Pennsylvania.

WORLD BAPTIST FELLOWSHIP (WBF). In 1933-1934 **J. Frank Norris** and a collection of **fundamentalist** Baptist pastors, including C. P. Stealey in Oklahoma and Robert White in Texas, founded the Premillennial Baptist Missionary Fellowship to enjoy "no officialism, but abounding fellowship." The purpose was to receive and distribute funds for acceptable missionaries, as advertised in *The Fundamentalist*. For its first five years, local pastors presided over its business. In 1938 Norris took personal control of the Fellowship and renamed it the World Fundamental Baptist Missionary Fellowship, with headquarters in Chicago. The creed of the group was in harmony with the former **Baptist Bible Union**, with a militant opposition to modernism, communism, and conventionism (the latter referring to the **Southern** and **Northern Baptist Conventions**). Norris boasted that 300 pastors supported the Fellowship as well as the related organizations, **China** Baptist Evangelization

Mission, the East China Mission, the French Bible Mission, and the San Antonio Spanish Mission. In 1950, a serious division occurred in the Fellowship which led to the formation of the **Baptist Bible Fellowship**. To distinguish the group from the splinter faction, Norris changed the name to World Baptist Fellowship.

The major asset of the WBF was the theological school, founded in 1939 as the Fundamental Baptist Bible Institute and renamed in 1944-1945 the Bible Baptist Seminary. Norris died in 1952, amidst concerns over financial management and authoritarian control, and the leadership of the WBF evolved to Louis Entzminger (1878-1956), at first Norris's lieutenant and later professor of English Bible. In recent years, the number of congregations has grown less dramatically than other fundamentalist groups, and the mission program is limited. The "Arlington Schools" in Ft. Worth, Texas, include a high school and **bible college**. About 1,000 churches cooperate in the fellowship; as a contemporary overseas mission agency, the Fellowship supports 135 missionaries in 25 countries, including South America, Europe, the Far East, and Central America. Since 1927 the WBF has published *The Fundamentalist* (formerly the *Fence Rail* 1917-1921 and the *Searchlight* 1921-1927).

WORLDWIDE NEW TESTAMENT BAPTIST MISSION. An independent, fundamentalist Baptist mission agency founded in 1971 by Bill Wingard (1934-), pastor of Calvary Baptist Church, New Bern, North Carolina. The purpose of the mission is to conduct evangelism and plant new churches on the New Testament model with strict adherence to a doctrinal position which emphasizes premillenial theology, the local church, and a separationist stance. As of 1998, there are about 60 missionary couples in 23 countries including Europe, Africa, Australia, Latin America, the Caribbean Islands, Micronesia, the United States and Canada. An executive board of 10 pastors drawn mostly from eastern North Carolina, operates the mission. Headquarters is located in New Bern, North Carolina.

WORSHIP IN BAPTIST TRADITION. Over the almost four centuries and the vast geo-cultural spread of Baptist principles, not to speak of the differentiation caused by local congregational styles, Baptist worship is highly variegated. Yet, some historical patterns do emerge.

From early English Baptist experience, the General Baptists seem to have followed principles first suggested by the Se-Baptist **John Smyth**. In a typical service the emphasis was upon spirituality in worship. **Scripture** was the ever-present resource for sermons, most often being understood in a literal sense. The dramas of the Old Testament were metaphorically applied to contemporary audiences and the didactic literature of the New Testament epistles form the most frequently quoted passages in Baptist sermons. The life of Christ for most Baptist sermons sets an ethical expectation and the birth and passion narrratives provide a rich theatre at the appropriate occasions of the year. The preaching of the word, in contrast with the **sacramental** traditions or those of a more mystical/illuminatory kind, tend to predominate in Baptist worship. It is taken for granted that one of the great assets of every believer-priest is the ability and insight to interpret Scripture for himself/herself, and therefore every Baptist has the potential to be a preacher as well as to offer to God individual sacrifices of person, prayer, and possessions. The typical 17th century Baptist worship service consisted of prayer, Scripture reading which was translated from the originals by the leader, exposition of the Scriptures, and prophesyings. There was no singing, except perhaps in the manner of some prophesying.

Singing became a controversial issue for English Baptists. While there was little doubt that recitation of psalms was an acceptable form of worship, any type of chanting (as in the Anglican or Catholic traditions) was unacceptable as was any musical form which was brought into the church from the external culture. Apparently during the Puritan Commonwealth years, Baptist soldiers practiced singing psalms. **Seventh Day Baptists** used **Lord's Supper** hymns at Colchester as early as 1657. Solo-singing was practiced in the 1660s as Katherine Sutton's published collection reveals, and it is obvious that **John Bunyan's** followers sung hymns. **Benjamin Keach** was among the first to advocate widespread use of singing and he published in 1691 the first Baptist hymnbook intended for congregational use, *Spiritual Melody*. **Joseph Stennett** (see **Stennett Family**) produced a collection of communion hymns in 1697 and hymns for **baptism** in 1712. A *Bristol Hymnbook* was produced in 1769 by Caleb Evans (1737-1791) and others for use in the West Country, which included material by other English writers.

The broad acceptability of Isaac Watts's (1674-1748) hymns pushed other Baptists to compose and publish hymns and psalm collections. From 1760-1800, Baptist enjoyed a "golden age of hymnody." In 1787 **John Rippon** published his *Selections* in which the tunes were identified for the first time. The **General Baptists** enjoyed wide use of *Barton Hymns* (1785), later preferring the *New Connexion Baptist Hymnal* (1879), which paralleled *Psalms and Hymns* among the **Particular Baptists** (1858). Reflecting the union of the two groups, the *Baptist Church Hymnal* of 1900 was published for a new century, to be succeeded by a Revised Edition in 1933 and a new *Baptist Church Hymnal* in 1954, which included the Baptist churches of **Australia, New Zealand** and **South Africa**. The contemporary *Baptist Church Hymnary*, which reflects an ecumenical interest, was first produced in 1962. Welsh folk tunes from the Old Country became popular across the Baptist family and are found in many Baptist hymnals and songbooks, for instance the popular tune "Cym Rhonda." Welsh singing festivals occur annually in Wales, Pennsylvania, and in eastern coastal U.S. ports since the 18th century.

As the Baptist community matured in the United States, the more urbane churches gravitated toward a group of popular composers and arrangers, such as Lowell Mason (1792-1872), Thomas Hastings (1784-1872), and William Bradbury (1816-1868). In the South and rural areas *The Sacred Harp* (1844) reflected Baptist folk culture. **William Howard Doane** edited the *Baptist Hymnal* (1883), which created a greater appreciation for liturgy and reflected the influence of the Oxford movement in Britain. Many Baptists joined with other evangelicals after the mid-19th century in using music first composed for **Sunday Schools** and camp meetings, in church worship experiences. By the mid-20th century, **Southern Baptists** led the denomination in producing new music and publishing song and hymnbooks for local churches and in the missionary contexts. Gradually, music among almost all Baptist groups became a vital expression of Christian experience and the typical worship service came to be punctuated with both choral and congregational singing. As several writers have shown, the hymnals which Baptists compiled and used in public services and private devotions, provided the worship resource found by Anglicans in the *Book of Common Prayer*. Like Methodists and other evangelical groups, many important themes and phrases indicative of popular Baptist Theology, are found in Baptist hymns and gospel songs.

Baptist worship in North America has moved in several streams over three centuries. In the **revivalistic** tradition there are groups which prefer a strictly **evangelistic** approach wherein the services are geared to evangelistic sermons leading to an invitation to accept Christ as Saviour or consecrate one's life to God. There is much uplifting and convictional singing, often supported by a choir. An outgrowth of the revivalist tradition is found among **fundamentalists** who stress dramatic preaching on doctrinal and ethical themes and invitations to join the church (following a weekly canvass of new member prospects), an act which is synonymous with adopting their views and lifestyle. While most of the typical fundamentalist Baptist service is given to preaching, there are choirs and the collection of an offering is emphasized to produce maximum response.

Yet other Baptists prefer a kind of didactic service of worship in which the focus is upon nurture, doctrinal emphases, and discipleship. Simple service of prayers, the collection of tithes and offerings, Scripture readings, and a 20 to 30-minute sermon, expository or thematic, illustrate this style. Such services close in hymns and prayers of service or dedication. The Liturical Renewal Movement had a deep impact upon many Baptist congregations in the 1960s in Britain and North America; it stressed a theological basis for worship, a prominent place for the **Lord's Supper** (called Eucharist after the sacramental tradition), and active involvement of laity in worship, through Scripture, choral work, ritual, and offering.

In the 1970s and 1980s in response to other denominations and traditions, Baptist congregations in **Canada** and the northern United States have absorbed elements of the charismatic and "praise and worship" traditions. These streams vary widely from singing adorational, repeating choruses often projected on an overhead screen or wall, or printed on songsheets or in published booklets, to healing services and ecstatic utterances and words of prophecy being delivered and interpreted. The use of musical instruments has in many churches shifted from organs and pianos to guitars, musical synthesizers, and electronic keyboards. Clapping of hands, bodily movement, unscripted utterances, and dancing can be evident in these services, which seem to be reactions against formalism and/or perceived lethargy in the traditional styles. Underlying this style is a sense of the presence of Christ in worship and the unity of soul, spirit, and body. A significant amount of time in these services is spent under the direction of a worship leader or team, after which a "teaching sermon" is given with ample time for overt behavioral responses.

Yet another continuing worship style is found typically in urban and upper middle-class Baptist congregations in the **Southern Baptist Convention**, many **American Baptist**, and Canadian Baptist churches. Modestly formal, the principal weekly worship service comprises a liturgy of a call to worship, hymns of adoration of God, consecration of self and dedication to God. Readings of Scripture from the Old and New Testaments, choral selections, a sermon which may draw upon a published lectionary, and a children's talk, round out what amounts to about one hour of worship on Sunday mornings. There may be a choral and ministerial procession and recession, though these are becoming more rare.

Black Baptist worship in North America can be a unique experience. Preaching is the primary focus of the worship service, supported by choirs and enthusiastic congregational singing of songs and hymns, which often reflect the African American experience, such as "Go Down, Moses," "We Are Climbing Jacob's Ladder," "Go Tell It On the Mountain," and "He's Got the Whole World in His Hands". Among many churches, the preacher is considered a mouthpiece of God and speaks with great authority and power. Metaphorical language can predominate and dramatic gestures and voice modulation accompany the delivery of the sermon. There may be several sermons in a morning worship service in the Black tradition.

Outside the Anglo-American patterns, there is diversification on familiar patterns. Across Europe, Baptists tend to be quietistic, placing much emphasis upon confessional preaching and ethics. Services run the familiar course of prayers, responses, and sermons. The celebration of the **ordinances/sacraments** is symbolic as a statement in contrast with Roman and Orthodox traditions. Choirs are a prominent feature of worship, especially in former Marxist countries, such as **Hungary**, **Poland**, and **Romania**; choral fests and travelling choirs have been an important social expression of the faith. Many services feature several sermons, not only from the pastors but also from deacons. African Baptists take delight in music and singing influenced by tribal idioms, and this constitutes a major part of worship which may last for several hours. In Latin America and the Caribbean, Baptist worship is vivid and charismatic, with an emphasis upon evangelistic preaching. For Asian Baptists, preaching has a didactic function, especially in view of the paucity in many locales of written Scriptures. The influence of missionaries, particularly American and British Baptists, has ensured that extemporaneous preaching is important, and singing of familiar hymns and gospel songs characteristic of the pietism and biblicism of historic Baptist tradition gives an international "sound" to Baptist worship.

In general, Baptist worship patterns reflect the overall culture and the particular social class and theological traditions of a congregation. It is not unusual to have "blended" worship of many styles in contemporary Baptist experience. See also **Prayer Meetings**.

Y

YEMEN. The history of Baptist presence in Yemen is a remarkable story. Based on the experience of the health care provided by the **Southern Baptist** (SBC) Hospital in Gaza, the Ministry of Health in Yemen in 1963 requested the Southern Baptists to begin a medical clinic in Yemen. In 1964 a clinic was opened at Taiz and a large hospital was subsequently begun at Jibla. Continuing Baptist presence in the country is related to medical and technical appointments.

YUGOSLAVIA. See **Bosnia; Croatia; Macedonia; Serbia; Slovenia.**

Z

ZAIRE. See **Congo, Democratic Republic of.**

ZAMBIA. Swedish Baptists were the first to plant a work in what was Northern Rhodesia in 1892. Results of the mission included a theological institute. The South African Missionary Society established its work in 1913 at Kafulafuta. In 1957 the **Reformed Baptists** of **Canada** started a work which was transferred to the Wesleyan Church in 1968. **Southern Baptists** entered Zambia in 1959 and in 1974 helped establish the Baptist Convention of Zambia. A theological school was established at Lusaka in 1967. The **Conservative Baptist** Foreign Mission Society (CBFMS) began a mission in Zambia in 1995.

As of 1995 there were 445 churches and 40,200 members affiliated with the Baptist Convention of Zambia.

ZIMBABWE. In 1913 the **Baptist Missionary Society** (BMS) established its first church at Gweru, which evolved into the Association of Baptist Churches of Rhodesia in 1950. That same year, **Southern Baptists** began a mission at Gatooma and this evolved into the Baptist Convention of Zimbabwe in 1981, composed mostly of indigenous churches.

As of 1995 there were 300 churches and 115,200 members affiliated with the Baptist Convention of Zimbabwe, 44 churches and 6,000 members affiliated with the United Baptist Churches of Zimbabwe, 35 churches and 3,027 members affiliated with the Baptist Union of Zimbabwe, and 20 churches with 1,867 members affiliated with the National Baptist Convention.

ZIONITIC BROTHERHOOD. A splinter group established in 1738 from the Ephrata Community formed by **Conrad Beissel.** Led by Gabriel Eckerling (also called Jotham) (?-1757), the movement consisted of a blend of Egyptian Freemasonry, Rosicrucianism, and baptistic practices. Eckerling became disenchanted with Beissel's leadership and established a mystical society at Coalico Creek in Lancaster County, Pennsylvania, where he became the first "Perfect Master," or Prior. Their goal was to obtain physical and moral regeneration by practicing high ethical standards and mystical exercises. A subgroup of the **German Baptist Brethren**, the Zionitische Bruderschaft became indistinguishable by the 19th century. Eckerling himself was captured by the French in western Pennsylvania/Virginia in 1757, and after being scalped and transported through Quebec to France, he died in a monastery.

Bibliography

The bibliography below is not intended to be exhaustive, but selective. Many classic entries are included; every effort has been made to include recent publications.

The bibliography is subdivided as follows:

General Reference

Anderson, Gerald, editor. *Biographical Dictionary of Christian Missions.* New York: Scribner's, 1997.

Brierley, Peter, editor. *World Churches Handbook.* London: Christian Research, 1997.

Burgess, G. A., and Ward, J. T. *Free Baptist Cyclopedia: Historical and Biographical.* Boston, MA: Free Baptist Cyclopedia, Inc, 1889.

Cathcart, William. *The Baptist Encyclopedia.* 2 vols. Philadelphia, PA: Louis H. Everts, 1883.

Goldman, Minton F. *Global Studies: Commonwealth of Independent States and Central/Eastern Europe.* Guilford, CT: Dushkin Publishing Group, 1992.

Siewert, John A., and Kenyon, John A. *Mission Handbook: A Guide to USA/Canada Christian Ministries Overseas.* Monrovia, CA: MARC, 1993.

Sprague, William B. *Annals of the American Baptist Pulpit.* New York: R. Carter, 1860.

Starr, Edward C. *A Baptist Bibliography.* 26 vols. Rochester, NY: American Baptist Historical Society, 1976.

Whitley, William T. *A Baptist Bibliography.* 2 vols. London: Carey Kingsgate Press, 1915-1922.

Wooley, Davis C., and May, Lynn E., Jr. *Encyclopedia of Southern Baptists.* 4 vols. Nashville, TN: Broadman Press, 1971-1982.

Primary Source Materials

Baker, Robert A., editor. *A Baptist Sourcebook, with Particular Reference to Southern Baptists.* Nashville, TN: Broadman Press, 1966.

Brackney, William H., editor. *Baptist Life and Thought.* Valley Forge, PA: Judson Press, 1998.

Hayden, Roger, editor. *The Records of a Church of Christ in Bristol 1640-1687.* Bristol: The Record Society, 1974.

Hobbs, Herschel H. *The Baptist Faith and Message.* Nashville, TN: Convention Press, 1971.

White, Barrington R., editor. *Associational Records of the Particular Baptists of England, Wales, and Ireland to 1660.* London: Baptist Historical Society, 1974.

Whitley, William T., editor. *Minutes of the General Assembly of General Baptist Churches in England, with Kindred Records.* 2 vols. London: Carey Kingsgate Press, 1909-1910.

Whitley, William T., editor. *The Works of John Smyth, Fellow of Christ's College, Cambridge 1594-98.* 2 vols. Cambridge: Cambridge University Press, 1915.

Backgrounds to Baptist History

Ball, Bryan W. *The Seventh-day Men: Sabbatarians and Sabbatarianism in England and Wales, 1600-1800.* Oxford: Clarendon Press, 1994.

Brachlow, Stephen. *The Communion of Saints: Radical Puritan and Separatist Ideology 1570-1625.* Oxford: Oxford University Press, 1988.

Burrage, Champlin. *The Early English Dissenters in Light of Historical Research.* 2 vols. Cambridge: Cambridge University Press, 1912.

Coggins, James R. *John Smyth's Congregation: English Separatism, Mennonite Influence, and the Elect Nation.* Scottdale, PA: Herald Press, 1991.

Edwards, Thomas. *Gangraena; or A Catalogue and Discovery of Many of the Errours, Heresies, Blasphemies, and Pernicious Practices of the Sectaries of This Time....* London: R. Smith, 1646.

Estep, William. *The Anabaptist Story.* Nashville, TN: Broadman Press, 1963.

George, Timothy. *John Robinson and the English Separatist Tradition.* Macon, GA: Mercer University Press, 1982.

Greaves, Richard L. *Saints and Rebels: Seven Nonconformists in Stuart England.* Macon, GA: Mercer University Press, 1985.

Hill, Christopher. *The World Turned Upside Down: Radical Ideas During the English Reformation.* London: Maurice Temple Smith, 1972.

Kliever, Lonnie D. "General Baptist Origins: The Question of Anabaptist Influence." *Mennonite Quarterly Review* 36:4 (October 1962): 291-321.

Krahn, Cornelius, *Dutch Anabaptism: Origin, Spread, Life and Thought (1450-1600).* The Hague: Martinus Nijhoff, 1968.

Littell, Franklin H. *The Anabaptist View of the Church: A Study in the Origins of Sectarian Protestantism.* Boston: Starr King Press, 1958.

Mosteller, James D. "Baptists and Anabaptists." *Chronicle* 20:1 (January 1957): 3-27; 20:3 (July 1957): 100-114.

Nuttall, Geoffrey. *The Beginnings of Nonconformity.* London: J. Clark, 1964.

Orchard, G. H. *A Concise History of Foreign Baptists.* Nashville, TN: Graves, Marks, 1855.

Payne, Ernest A. *The Anabaptists of the 16ᵗʰ Century*. London: Carey Kingsgate, 1949.

Sobel, Mechal. *Trabelin' On: The Slave Journey to an Afro-Baptist Faith*. Westport, CT: Greenwood Press, 1979.

Stassen, Glen H. "Anabaptist Influence in the Origin of the Particular Baptists." *Mennonite Quarterly Review* 36:4 (October 1962): 322-348.

Watts, Michael. *The Dissenters: From the Reformation to the French Revolution*. Oxford: Clarendon Press, 1978.

White, Barrington R. *The English Separatist Tradition*. Oxford: Oxford University Press, 1971.

Whitley, William T. "Continental Anabaptists and Early English Baptists." *Baptist Quarterly* 2 (1924-1925): 27.

Baptist History-General Studies

Anderson, Justo. *Historia de los Bautistas*. 3 vols. El Paso, TX: Casa Bautista de Publicaciones, 1990.

Armitage, Thomas. *A History of the Baptists, Traced by Their Vital Principles and Practices From the Time of Our Lord and Savior Jesus Christ to the Year 1886*. New York: Bryan Taylor, 1887.

Brackney, William H. *The Baptists*. Westport, CT: Greenwood Press, 1988.

McBeth, H. Leon. *The Baptist Heritage: Four Centuries of Baptist Witness*. Nashville, TN: Broadman Press, 1987.

Thompson, E. Wayne, and Cummins, Daniel L. *This Day In Baptist History: 366 Daily Devotions Drawn From the Baptist Heritage*. Greenville, SC: Bob Jones University Press, 1993.

Torbet, Robert G. *History of the Baptists*. Valley Forge, PA: Judson Press, 1963.

Wardin, Albert W., editor. *Baptists Around the World: A Comprehensive Handbook*. Nashville, TN: Broadman and Holman, 1995.

Baptists Groups - Geographical

Africa

Atanda, J. A. *Baptist Churches in Nigeria 1850-1950*. Ibadan: The Author, 1988.

Batts, H. J. *The Story of a Hundred Years 1820-1920; Being a History of the Baptist Church in South Africa*. Capetown: Miller, 1920.

Coger, Dalvan M. "An Early Missionary Enterprise: The Baptists at Fernando Po 1840-1860." *American Baptist Quarterly* 9:3 (September 1990): 158-166.

Hudson-Reed, Sydney. *History of the Baptist Union of South Africa.* Pietermaritzburg: South African Baptist Historical Society, 1977.

Jonnson, Jon N. "Baptists in Socio-Political Life in South Africa." *American Baptist Quarterly* (1985): 4.

Maddry, Charles. *Day Dawn in Yoruba Land.* Nashville, TN: Broadman Press, 1939.

Saunders, Davis L. "Baptists in East Africa: The Birth of Two Conventions." *Baptist History and Heritage* 6:4 (October 1971): 226-232.

Schneider, G. *A Graphic Portrayal of a Christian Mission at Work in the Cameroons.* Forest Park, IL: North American Baptist General Conference, 1957.

Stuart, Charles H. "The Lower Congo and the American Baptist Mission to 1910." Unpublished Ph.D. dissertation, Boston University, 1969.

Valcarcel, S. J. *A Short History of Baptists in Sierra Leone, 1792-1984.* Bad Homburg, Germany: European Baptist Mission, 1984.

Asia, Australia, and New Zealand

Bollen, J. P. *Australian Baptists--A Religious Minority.* London: Baptist Historical Society, 1975.

Brown, B. S. *Baptized Into One Body: A Short History of the Baptist Union of Australia.* Hawthorn: BUA, 1987.

Cho, Timothy H. "A History of the Korea Baptist Convention, 1889-1969." Unpublished Th. D. dissertation, Southern Baptist Theological Seminary, 1970.

Clough, John E. *From Darkness to Light: A Story of the Telugu Awakening.* Philadelphia: ABPS, 1892.

Dean, William. *China Mission; A History of Missions of All Denominations Among the Chinese, with Biographical Sketches of the Deceased.* New York: n.p., 1859.

Downs, Fred S. *The Mighty Works of God: A Brief History of the Council of Baptist Churches in Northeast India: The Mission Period 1836-1950.* Gauhati: Christian Literature Center, 1971.

Fenwick, Malcolm C. *The Church of Christ in Corea.* Seoul: Baptist Publications, 1967.

Gibson, Mary Ann. "Baptist Pioneers in Tasmania, Australia." *Chronicle* 11:3 (July 1948): 111-123.

Moore, Richard K. *Baptists of Western Australia: The First Ninety Years, 1895-1985.* Perth: Baptist Historical Society of Western Australia, 1991.

Prior, Alan C. *Some Fell on Good Ground: A History of the Beginnings and Development of the Baptist Church in New South Wales, Australia 1831-1965.* Sydney: The Baptist Union of New South Wales, 1966.

Puthenpurakal, Joseph. *Baptist Missions in Nagaland.* Calcutta, 1984.

Rogers, Lillie O., editor. *A History of Baptists in Malaysia & Singapore.* n.p., n.d.

Rubenstein, Murray. "American Evangelicalism in the Chinese Environment: Southern Baptist Missionaries in Taiwan, 1949-81." *American Baptist Quarterly* 2:3 (September 1983): 269-289.

Smith, Ebbie. "Baptist Advance in Indonesia" Unpublished M.A. thesis, Fuller Theological Seminary, 1970.

Tegenfeldt, Herman. *A Century of Growth: The Kachin Baptist Church of Burma.* Pasadena, CA: William Carey Library, 1974.

Tonson, Paul. *A Handful of Grain: The Centenary History of the Baptist Union of New Zealand.* 4 vols. Wellington: New Zealand Baptist Historical Society, 1982.

Wa, Maung Shwe. *Burma Baptist Chronicle.* Rangoon: Board of Publications, 1963.

Canada

Bentall, Shirley. *From Sea to Sea: The Canadian Baptist Federation 1944-1994.* Mississauga, ON: Canadian Baptist Federation, 1994.

Bill, I. E. *Fifty Years with The Baptist Ministers and Churches of the Maritime Provinces of Canada.* Saint John, NB: Barnes and Company, 1880.

Britten, Edward G. "A History of the Reformed Baptist Alliance of Canada." Unpublished B.D. thesis, Acadia University, 1964.

Ivison, Stuart, and Rosser, Fred. *The Baptists in Upper and Lower Canada before 1820.* Toronto, ON: University of Toronto Press, 1956.

Levy, George Edward. *The Baptists of the Maritime Provinces 1753-1946.* Saint John, NB: Barnes-Hopkins, 1946.

Lewis, James K. *The Religious Life of the Fugitive Slaves and the Rise of Coloured Baptist Churches 1820-1865 in What is Now Known as Ontario.* New York: Arno Press, 1980.

McCormick, Roland K. *Faith, Freedom, and Democracy: The Baptists in Atlantic Canada.* Moncton, NB: Four East Publishers, 1993.

McLaurin, C. C. *Pioneering in Western Canada: A Story of the Baptists.* Calgary, AB: Armac Press, 1939.

Renfree, Harry A. *Heritage and Horizon: The Baptist Story in Canada.* Mississauga, ON: Baptist Federation of Canada, 1988.

Saunders, Edward Manning. *History of the Baptists of the Maritime Provinces.* Halifax, NS: John Burgoyne, 1902.

Tarr, Leslie K. *This Dominion His Dominion: The Story of Evangelical Baptist Endeavour in Canada.* Willowdale, ON: Fellowship of Evangelical Baptist Churches in Canada, 1968.

Zeman, Jarold K. *Baptists in Canada: Search for Identity Amidst Diversity.* Burlington, ON: G. R. Welch, 1980.

Caribbean

Hackshaw, John W. *The Baptist Denomination.* Kingston, Jamaica: Amphy and Bashana Memorial Society, 1991.

Ramos, Tomas Rosario. *Historia de los Bautistas de Puerto Rico.* Santo Domingo: La Convencion 1979.

Russell, Horace O. *Foundations and Anticipation: The Jamaica Baptist Story: 1783-1892.* Columbus, OH: Brentwood Christian Press, 1993.

Sibley, Inez Knibb. *The Baptists of Jamaica 1793-1965.* Kingston: The Jamaica Baptist Union, 1965.

Symonette, Michael C. *Baptists in the Bahamas: An Historical Overview.* El Paso, TX: Baptist Spanish Publishing House, 1977.

Europe

Bednarczyk, Krzysztof. *Historia Zborow Baptystow w Polsce do 1939 roku.* Warszawa: Slowo Prawdy, 1997.

Bordeaux, Michael. *Religious Ferment in Russia: Protestant Opposition to Soviet Religious Policy.* London: Macmillan, 1968.

Eden, David. *Svenska baptisterna in Finland historia 1856-1931.*

Eidberg, Peder. *The People Called Baptist.* Stabekk: 1999.

Harrell, Norman L. "Beginnings of Baptist Work in Portugal 1808-1928." Unpublished M.A. thesis, Southern Baptist Theological Seminary, 1991.

History of the Evangelical Christian Baptists of the Soviet Union. Moscow: Union of Evangelical Christians-Baptists, 1989.

Hopper, John D. "Baptist Beginnings in Yugoslavia." *Baptist History and Heritage* 17:4 (October, 1982): 28-37.

Hylleberg, Bent, and Jorgensen, Bjarne M. *Et kirkesamfund bliver til.* Omslag, Denmark: Henning Aardestrup, 1989.

Lehman, Joseph. *Geschichte der deutschen Baptisten.* Hamburg: Oncken Verlag, 1896.

Novotny, Joseph. *The Baptist Romance in the Heart of Europe (Czechoslovakia): The Life and Times of Henry Novotny.* New York: John Felsburg, 1939.

Parker, G. Keith. *Baptists in Europe: History and Confessions of Faith.* Nashville, TN: Broadman Press, 1982.

Payne, Ernest A. *Out of Great Tribulation: Baptists in the USSR.* London: Baptist Union of Great Britain, 1974.

Rogaczewski, Jerzy P. "The Polish Baptist Identity in Historical Context." Unpublished M.Div. thesis, McMaster University, 1995.

Rousseau, Georges J. *Histoire des Eglises Baptistes.* Paris: Société de Publications Baptistes, 1951.

Sanfilippo, P. *L'Italia Battista.* Rome: Unione Cristiana Evangelica Battista d'Italia, 1959.

Steeves, Paul D. "The Russian Baptist Union 1917-1935: Evangelical Awakening in Russia." Unpublished Ph.D. dissertation, University of Kansas, 1976.

Sundquist, Alfons. "The Baptist Movement in Finland." *Chronicle* 11:1 (January 1948): 3-16.

Trutza, Peter. "A Short History of Roumanian Baptists." *Chronicle* 5:1 (January 1942): 9-21.

Vojta, Vaclav. *Czechoslovak Baptists.* Chicago, IL: Czechoslovak Baptist Convention of America, 1941.

Wardin, Albert. "The Baptists of Bulgaria." *Baptist Quarterly* 34:4 (October 1991): 148-159.

Great Britain and Ireland

Bassett, T. M. *The Welsh Baptists.* Swansea: Ilston House, 1977.

Bebbington, David. *Baptists in Scotland.* Glasgow: The Union, 1988.

Briggs, John H. Y. *The English Baptists of the Nineteenth Century.* Didcot: Baptist Historical Society, 1994.

Brown, Raymond. *The English Baptists of the Eighteenth Century.* London: The Baptist Historical Society, 1986.

Crosby, Thomas. *History of the Baptists.* 4 vols. London: The Editor, 1738-1740.

Evans, Benjamin. *Early English Baptists.* 2 vols. London: J. Heaton, 1862-1864.

Ivimey, Joseph. *History of the Baptists.* 4 vols. London: I. T. Hinton, 1811-1830.

Murray, Derek B. *The First Hundred Years: The Baptist Union of Scotland.* Glasgow: The Baptist Union of Scotland, 1969.

Paul, S. F. *Historical Sketch of the Gospel Standard Baptists.* London: Gospel Standard Publications, 1945.

Payne, Ernest A. *The Baptist Union: A Short History.* London: Carey Kingsgate Press, 1958.

Taylor, Adam. *History of the General Baptists.* 2 vols. London: T. Bore, 1818.

Thompson, Joshua. *Century of Grace: The Baptist Union of Ireland, A Short History 1895-1995.* Belfast: Baptist Union of Ireland 1995.

Underwood, A. C. *A History of the English Baptists.* London: Carey Kingsgate Press, 1947.

White, B. R. *The English Baptists of the Seventeenth Century.* Didcot: The Baptist Historical Society, 1996.

Whitley, William T. *A History of British Baptists.* London: Charles Griffin, 1923.

Latin America

Actas da Convecão Baptista Brasileira. 2 vols. Rio de Janeiro: Archivos de la Convencion, 1967.

Actas de la Union Bautista de Chile. 2 vols. Santiago: Archivo del Seminario, 1921, 1967.

Brackney, William H. *Bridging Cultures and Hemispheres: The Legacy of Archibald Reekie and Canadian Baptists in Bolivia.* Macon, GA: Smyth and Helwys, 1997.

Crabtree, A. R., and de Mesquita, Antonio N. *Historia dos Batistas do Brasil.* 2 vols. Rio de Janeiro: Cas Publicadora Batista, 1937-1940.

Loredo, Ignacio. *Un Hombre, Un Pueblo: Los bautistas argentinos a cien anos de la llegada de Pablo Besson.* Buenos Aires: Casa Bautista de Publicaciones, 1981.

Mesquita, Antonio Neves de. *Historia dos Batistas em Pernambuco.* Recife: Tipografia do CAB, 1930.

Nacho, Arturo. *Un Siglo de Evangelización, 100 Anos de la Obra Bautista en Bolivia.* Cochabamba, Bolivia: Comisión de Historia de la Union Bautista Boliviana, 1998.

Patterson, Frank W. *A Century of Baptist Work in Mexico.* El Paso, TX: Baptist Spanish Publishing House, 1979.

Pitts, William L. "Baptist Beginnings in Brazil." *Baptist History and Heritage* 17:4 (October 1982): 4-16.

Rodriquez, J.M. *Los Bautistas en las Republicas del Plata.* Buenos Aires: Junta Bautista de Publicaciones, 1930.

United States

Anderson, Donald E. *The 1960s in the Ministry of the Baptist General Conference*. Evanston, IL: Harvest Publications, 1961.

——. *The 1970s in the Ministry of the Baptist General Conference*. Arlington Heights, IL: Baptist General Conference, 1981.

Armstrong, O.K., and Armstrong, Marjorie. *The Indomitable Baptists: A Narration of their Role in Shaping American History*. New York: Doubleday, 1967.

Backlund, J. O. *Swedish Baptists in America*. Chicago, IL: Conference Press, 1933.

Backus, Isaac. *A History of New England with Particular Reference to the Denomination of Christians Called Baptists*. Newton, MA: Backus Historical Society, 1871.

Barnes, William W. *The Southern Baptist Convention 1845-1953*. Nashville, TN: Broadman Press, 1954.

Baxter, Norman A. *History of the Freewill Baptists: A Study in New England Separatism*. Rochester, NY: American Baptist Historical Society, 1957.

Benedict, David. *A General History of the Baptist Denomination in the United States and Other Parts of the World*. New York: Lewis Colby, 1848.

Bitting, W. C. *A Manual of the Northern Baptist Convention 1908-1918*. Philadelphia, PA: American Baptist Publication Society, 1918.

Bone, John S. *"The Better Maintainence of the Ministry": The First Seventy Five Years of the Ministers and Missionaries Benefit Board*. New York: Ministers and Missionaries Benefit Board, 1987.

Booth, William D. *The Progressive Story: New Baptist Roots*. Nashville, TN: PNBC, 1981.

Burkitt, Lemuel, and Read, Jesse. *A Concise History of the Kehukee Baptist Association From Its Original Rise Down to 1803*. Philadelphia, PA: Lippincott, Grambo and Co., 1850.

DiDomenica, Angelo. *Protestant Witness of a New American*. Philadelphia, PA: Judson Press, 1956.

Dodd, Damon C. *The Freewill Baptist Story*. Nashville, TN: National Association of Freewill Baptists, 1956.

Duggar, John W. *The Baptist Missionary Association of America*. Texarkana, TX: Baptist Publishing House, 1988.

Fisher, Miles Mark. *A Short History of the Baptist Denomination*. Nashville, TN: Sunday School Board, 1933.

Fitts, Leroy. *A History of Black Baptists*. Nashville, TN: Broadman, 1985.

Fletcher, Jesse C. *The Southern Baptist Convention: A Sesquicentennial History.* Nashville, TN: Broadman and Holman, 1994.

Goen, Clarence C. *Revivalism and Separatism in New England 1740-1800: Strict Congregationalists and Separate Baptists in the Great Awakening.* New Haven, CT: Yale University Press, 1962.

Glover, Conrad E., and Powers, Austin T. *The American Baptist Association 1924-1974.* Texarkana, TX: Bogard Press, 1979.

Hassell, Cushing B. *History of the Church of God, From the Creation to A.D. 1885, Including Especially the History of the Kehukee Primitive Baptist Association.* Middletown, NY: Gilbert Beebe's Sons, 1886.

Hubbard, Kenneth. "The Southwide Baptist Fellowship." Unpublished Th.D. dissertation, Southwestern Baptist Theological Seminary, 1968.

Jackson, Joseph H. *A Story of Christian Activism: The History of the National Baptist Convention, USA, Inc.* Nashville, TN: Townshend Press, 1980.

Jordan, Lewis G. *Negro Baptist History, USA.* Nashville, TN: Sunday School Publishing Board of the National Baptist Convention, 1930.

Lambert, B. C. *Rise of Antimission Baptists.* New York: Arno Press, 1980.

Latch, Ollie. *History of the General Baptists.* Poplar Bluff, MO: General Baptist Press, 1972.

Leonard, Bill J. *Dictionary of Baptists in America.* Downer's Grove, IL: Intervarsity Press, 1994.

——. *God's Last and Only Hope: The Fragmentation of the Southern Baptist Convention.* Grand Rapids, MI: Wm. B. Eerdmans, 1990.

McLoughlin, William G. *New England Dissent: Baptists and the Separation of Church and State 1630-1833.* 2 vols. Cambridge, MA: Harvard University Press, 1971.

Miller, Terry E. "Otter Creek Church, Indiana: Lonely Bastion of Daniel Parker's Two-Seedism." *Foundations* 18:4 (October 1975): 358-376.

Montgomery, D. B., editor. *General Baptist History.* Evansville, IN: Courier Co., 1882.

Newman, Albert H. *A History of Baptist Churches in the United States.* Philadelphia, PA: American Baptist Publication Society, 1898.

Olson, Adolf. *A Centenary History, As Related to the Baptist General Conference of America.* Chicago, IL: Baptist Conference Press, 1952.

Parry, Pam. *On Guard for Religious Liberty: Six Decades of the Baptist Joint Committee.* Macon, GA: Smyth and Helwys, 1996.

Pelt, Michael R. *A History of Original Free Will Baptists.* Mount Olive, NC: Mount Olive College Press, 1996.

Pelt, O. D., and Smith, R. L. *The Story of the National Baptists.* New York: Vantage Books, 1960.

Perrigan, Rufus. *History of Regular Baptists and their Ancestors and Assessors.* Hayes, VA: Privately Published,1961.

Pius, Nathaniel H. *An Outline of Baptist History.* Nashville, TN: National Baptist Publishing Board, 1911.

Rentz, James, editor. *What Hath God Wrought? Sixty Years of Christian Stewardship, 1901-1961.* Chicago, IL: Baptist Mission Union of America, 1961.

Rogers, Albert N. *Seventh Day Baptists in Europe and America.* 3 vols. Plainfield, NJ: Seventh Day Baptist Publishing House, 1972.

Rogers, John B. *The Rogerenes: Some Hitherto Unpublished Annals Belonging to the Colonial History of Connecticut.* Boston, MA: Stanhope Press, 1904.

Rosenburg, Ellen M. *The Southern Baptists: A Subculture in Transition.* Knoxville, TN: University of Tennessee Press, 1989.

Sachse, Julius F. *The German Sectarians of Pennsylvania, 1708-42; A Critical and Legendary History of the Ephrata Cloister and the Dunkers.* Philadelphia, PA: Stockhausen, 1899.

Sandford, Don A. *A Choosing People: The History of Seventh Day Baptists.* Nashville, TN: Broadman Press, 1992.

Stianson, Peter. *History of the Norwegian Baptists in America.* Philadelphia, PA: American Baptist Publication Society, 1939.

Sweet, William W. *Religion on the American Frontier: The Baptists.* New York: Henry Holt and Co., 1931.

Taylor, Wilburn S. "World Baptist Fellowship." *The Quarterly Review* 19:2 (April 1959): 35-39.

Torbet, Robert G. *Baptists North and South.* Valley Forge, PA: Judson Press, 1964.

Washington, James Melvin. *Frustrated Fellowship: The Black Baptist Quest for Social Power.* Macon, GA: Mercer University Press, 1985.

Wood, James E., editor. *Baptists and the American Experience.* Valley Forge, PA: Judson Press, 1976.

Woolley, Davis C., editor. *Baptist Advance: The Achievements of the Baptists of North America for a Century and a Half.* Nashville, TN: Broadman Press, 1964.

Woyke, Frank H. *Heritage and Ministry of the North American Baptist Conference.* Oakbrook Terrace, IL: North American Baptist Conference, 1979.

Baptist Missions

Adams, C. C., and Talley, Marshall A. *Negro Baptists and Foreign Missions*. Philadelphia, PA: Foreign Mission Board of the National Baptist Convention USA, Inc., 1944.

Allen, Catherine B. *A Century to Celebrate*. Birmingham, AL: Women's Missionary Union, 1987.

Anderson, Courtney. *To the Golden Shore: The Life of Adoniram Judson*. Boston, MA: Little, Brown, 1956.

Barnes, Lemuel C., editor. *Pioneers of Light: The First Century of the American Baptist Publication Society, 1824-1924*. Philadelphia, PA: American Baptist Publication Society, 1924.

Beers, G. Pitt. *Ministry to Turbulent America: A History of the American Baptist Home Mission Society, Covering Its Fifth Quarter Century, 1932-1957*. Philadelphia, PA: Judson Press, 1957.

Brumberg, Joan J. *Mission for Life: The Dramatic Story of the Family of Adoniram Judson*. New York: Free Press, 1980.

Cauthen, Baker J. *Advance: A History of Southern Baptist Foreign Missions*. Nashville, TN: Broadman Press, 1970.

Commons, Harold T. *Heritage and Harvest*. Cherry Hill, NJ: Association of Baptists for World Evangelism, 1981.

Cox, F. A. *History of the English Baptist Missionary Society from 1792 to 1842, to which is Added a Sketch of the General Baptist Mission*. London: T. Ward, 1842.

Estep, William R. *Whole Gospel, Whole World: The Foreign Mission Board of the Southern Baptist Convention 1845-1995*. Nashville, TN: Broadman and Holman, 1995.

Fellowship of Baptists for Home Missions. *Two Decades of Home Missions 1940-1960*. Elyria, OH: Fellowship of Baptists for Home Missions, 1960.

Finzel, Hans, editor. *Partners Together*. Wheaton, IL: Conservative Baptist Foreign Mission Society, 1993.

Freeman, Edward A. *The Epoch of Negro Baptists and the Foreign Mission Board, National Baptist Convention USA, Inc.* Kansas City, KS: Central Seminary Press, 1953.

Gammell, William. *A History of American Baptist Missions*. Boston, MA: Gould, Kendall, and Lincoln, 1849.

Harvey, William J. *Bridges of Faith Across the Seas*. Philadelphia, PA: National Baptist Convention, 1989.

Hervey, G. W. *The Story of Baptist Missions*. St Louis, MO: Barnes, 1886.

Hopewell, William J. *The Missionary Emphasis of the General Association of Regular Baptist Churches*. Chicago, IL: Regular Baptist Press, 1963.

Kverndal, Roald. *Seaman's Missions: Their Origin and Early Growth*. Pasadena, CA: William Carey Library, 1986.

Malcolm, Howard. *Travels in Southeastern Asia, Embracing Hindustan, Malaya, Siam, and China, with Notices of Numerous Missionary Stations*. Boston, MA: Gould, Kendall, and Lincoln, 1839.

Marshman, Joshua. *Brief Memoir Relative to the Operations of the Serampore Missionaries*. London: Parbury, Allen and Co., 1827.

McKivigan, John R. "The American Baptist Free Mission Society: Abolitionist Reaction to the 1845 Baptist Schism." *Foundations* 21:4 (October 1978): 340-355.

McLoughlin, William G. *Cherokees and Missionaries 1789-1839*. New Haven, CT: Yale University Press, 1984.

Means, Frank K. *Advance to Bold Mission Thrust: A History of Southern Baptist Foreign Missions, 1970-1980*. Richmond, VA: Foreign Mission Board of the Southern Baptist Convention, 1981.

Padelford, Frank W. *The Kingdom in the States: A Study of the Missionary Work of State Conventions*. Philadelphia, PA: Judson Press, 1928.

Potts, E. Daniel. *British Baptist Missionaries in India 1793-1837*. Cambridge: Cambridge University Press, 1967.

Puthenpurakal, Joseph. *Baptist Missions in Nagaland*. Calcutta: Baptist Press, 1984.

Rutledge, Arthur B. *Mission to America: A Century and a Quarter of Southern Baptist Home Missions*. Nashville, TN: Broadman Press, 1969.

Slaght, Lawrence T. *Multiplying the Witness: 150 Years of American Baptist Educational Ministries*. Valley Forge, PA: Judson Press, 1974.

Sparkes, Douglas C. *The Home Mission Story*. Didcot, England: Baptist Historical Society, 1995.

Stanley, Brian. *The History of the Baptist Missionary Society 1792-1992*. Edinburgh: T and T Clark, 1992.

Strong, Augustus H. *A Tour of the Missions: Observations and Conclusions*. Philadelphia, PA: Griffith and Rowland Press, 1918.

Strong, Polly. *Burning Wicks: The Story of Baptist Mid-Missions*. Cleveland, OH: Baptist Mid-Missions, 1984.

Talley, Marshall A. *Negro Baptists and Foreign Missions*. Philadelphia, PA: Foreign Mission Board of the National Baptist Convention, U.S.A., 1944.

Titterington, Sophie B. *A Century of Baptist Foreign Missions*. Philadelphia, PA: American Baptist Foreign Mission Society, 1891.

Torbet, Robert G. *Venture of Faith: The Story of the American Baptist Foreign Mission Society and the Woman's American Baptist Foreign Mission Society 1814-1954*. Philadelphia, PA: Judson Press, 1955.

Tupper, Henry A. *The Foreign Missions of the SBC*. Philadelphia, PA: American Baptist Publication Society, 1880.

Underhill, Edward B. *The Tragedy of Morant Bay: A Narrative of the Disturbances in the Island of Jamaica in 1865*. London: Alexander Shepheard, 1895.

Wayland, Francis. *The Moral Dignity of the Missionary Enterprise*. Boston, MA: James Loring, 1824.

White, Charles L. *A Century of Faith*. Philadelphia, PA: Judson Press, 1932.

Wright, Mary E. *The Missionary Work of the Southern Baptist Convention*. Philadelphia, PA: American Baptist Publication Society, 1902.

Baptist Theology and Beliefs

Aldwinckle, Russell. *More Than Man: A Study in Christology*. Grand Rapids, MI: Wm. B. Eerdmans, 1976.

Ashmore, William. *Outline of Theology for Chinese Students*. Yokohama: The Author, 1900?.

Boyce, James P. *Abstract of Systematic Theology*. Baltimore, MD: H. Wharton, 1887.

Bush, L. Russ, and Nettles, Tom J. *Baptists and the Bible: The Baptist Doctrines of Biblical Inspiration and Religious Authority in Historical Perspective*. Chicago, IL: Moody Press, 1980.

Butler, John J. *Natural and Revealed Theology*. Dover, NH: Freewill Baptist Printing Establishment, 1861.

Carey, William. *An Enquiry Into the Obligations of Christians to Use Means for the Conversion of the Heathen*. Leicester, England: Ann Ireland, 1792.

Cauthen, W. Kenneth. *The Rise of American Religious Liberalism*. New York: Harper and Row, 1962.

---*Systematic Theology: A Modern Protestant Approach*. Lewiston, NY: Edward Mellen Press, 1986.

Clarke, William N. *An Outline of Christian Theology*. New York: Charles Scribner's, 1909.

Connor, Walter T. *Christian Doctrine*. Nashville, TN: Broadman Press, 1937.

Cook, Henry. *What Baptists Stand For*. London: Carey Kingsgate Press, 1947.

Cox, Harvey. *Religion in the Secular City: Toward a Post-Modern Theology*. New York: Simon and Schuster, 1984.

Crabtree, Arthur B. *The Restored Relationship: A Study in Justification and Reconciliation*. Valley Forge, PA: Judson Press, 1963.

Dagg, J. L. *A Manual of Theology*. Charleston, SC: Southern Baptist Publication Society, 1857.

Dockery, David S., and George, Timothy, editors. *Baptist Theologians*. Nashville, TN: Broadman Press, 1990.

Erickson, Millard J. *Christian Theology*. Grand Rapids, MI: Baker Book House, 1983.

Foster, George B. *The Finality of the Christian Religion*. Chicago, IL: University of Chicago Press, 1906.

Fuller, Andrew. *The Gospel of Christ Worthy of All Acceptation*. Northampton: T. Dicey, 1785.

Garrett, James Leo. *Systematic Theology: Biblical, Historical, & Evangelical*. 2 vols. Grand Rapids, MI: Wm. B. Eerdmans, 1990.

Gill, John. A Complete Body of Doctrinal and Practical Divinity. London: The Author, 1769.

Grantham, Thomas. *Christianismus Primitivus*. London: Francis Smith, 1678.

Grenz, Stanley J. *Theology for the Community of God*. Nashville, TN: Broadman and Holman, 1994.

Hall, Robert. *Help to Zion's Travellers; Being An Attempt to Remove Various Stumblingblocks Out of the Way, Relating to Doctrinal, Experimental, and Practical Religion*. Alexandria, VA: John Par, 1814.

Hamilton, William. *The New Essence of Christianity*. New York: Association Press, 1966.

Helwys, Thomas. *A Short and Plaine Proofe by the Word and Workes of God that God's Decree is the Cause of Anye Mans Sinne or Condemnation; and that All Men are Redeemed by Christ; as also that no infants are Condemned*. London: n.p., 1611?.

Henry, Carl F. H. *God, Revelation, and Authority*. 6 vols. Waco, TX: Word Books, 1976-1983.

Hill, Christopher. *The English Bible and the Seventeenth Century Revolution*. London: Allen Lane, 1993.

Hovey, Alvah. *Christian Theology*. Newton Center, MA: Newton Theological Institution, 1896.

Jenkins, Charles A. *Baptist Doctrines*. St. Louis, MO: Chancy R. Barns, 1881.

Johnson, Elias H. *Outline of Systematic Theology*. Philadelphia, PA: American Baptist Publication Society, 1891.

Judson, Edward. *The Institutional Church: A Primer in Pastoral Theology*. New York: Lentilhon, 1899.

King, Martin Luther, Jr. *Strength to Love*. New York: Walker and Co., 1963.

Ladd, George E. *Theology of the New Testament*. Guildford: Lutterworth Press, 1975.

Lagergran, Carl G. *Bibelus grundlaror, systematisk teologi*. Minneapolis, MN: Veckobladets boktrycker, 1922.

Land, Richard D. "Doctrinal Controversies of English Particular Baptists (1644-1691), As Illustrated in the Career and Writings of Thomas Collier." Unpublished D.Phil thesis, University of Oxford, 1979.

Lewis, Gordon R., and Demarest, Bruce A. *Integrative Theology*. 3 vols. Grand Rapids, MI: Zondervan Publishers, 1987-1994.

Lumpkin, William L. *Baptist Confessions of Faith*. Valley Forge, PA: Judson Press, 1959.

Macintosh, Douglas C. *Theology as an Empirical Science*. New York: Macmillan, 1919.

Mathews, Shailer. *The Faith of Modernism*. New York: Macmillan, 1924.

McClendon, James W., Jr. *Systematic Theology: Ethics, Doctrine*. 2 vols. Nashville, TN: Abingdon Press, 1986, 1994.

McGlothlin, William J. *Baptist Confessions of Faith*. Philadelphia, PA: American Baptist Publication Society, 1910.

Moody, Dale. *The Word of Truth: A Summary of Christian Doctrine Based on Biblical Revelation*. Grand Rapids, MI: Wm. B. Eerdmans, 1981.

Mullins, Edgar Y. *The Christian Religion in Its Doctrinal Expression*. Philadelphia, PA: Judson Press, 1917.

Peden, Creighton, and Stone, Jerome A., editors. *The Chicago School of Theology-Pioneers in Religious Inquiry. 2 vols*. Lewiston, NY: Edwin Mellen Press, 1996.

Pendleton, James M. *Christian Doctrines: A Compendium of Theology*. Philadelphia, PA: American Baptist Publication Society, 1878.

Pepper, George D. B. *Outlines of Systematic Theology*. Philadelphia, PA: J. B. Rodgers, 1873.

Pinnock, Clark H. *The Scripture Principle*. New York: Harper and Row, 1984.

Rauschenbusch, Walter. *A Theology for the Social Gospel*. New York: Macmillan, 1917.

Robinson, Ezekiel G. *Christian Theology*. Rochester, NY: E. R. Andrews, 1894.

Smith, Gerald B. *Social Idealism and the Changing Theology*. New York: Macmillan, 1913.

Smyth, John. *Differences in the Churches of the Separation*. Amsterdam, 1608.

Strong, Augustus H. *Systematic Theology: A Compendium*. Philadelphia, PA: American Baptist Publication Society, 1907.

Taylor, Dan. *Fundamentals of Religion in Faith and Practice*. London: 1775.

Timpany, Americus V. *Compendium of Theology*. Madras: Foster, 1879.

Walton, Robert C. *The Gathered Community*. London: Carey Press, 1946.

Wayland, Francis. *Elements of Moral Science*. Boston, MA: Gould, Kendall and Lincoln, 1835.

Baptist Polity, Practice, and Worship

Aldwinckle, Russell F. *Of Water and the Spirit: A Baptist View of Church Membership*. Brantford, ON: Baptist Federation of Canada, 1964.

Ayer, William W. "The Independent Tabernacle Movement and the Organized Denominational Church." *Watchman-Examiner*, March 7, 1935: 242-243.

Baldwin, Thomas. *The Baptism of Believers Only, and the Particular Communion of the Baptist Churches, Explained and Vindicated in Three Parts*. Boston, MA: Manning and Loring, 1806.

Beasley-Murray, George R. *Baptism in the New Testament*. London: Macmillan, 1963.

Belzile, Michel. "Canadian Baptists at Worship." Unpublished D.Min. thesis, McMaster University, 1998.

Bogard, Ben M. *The Baptist Way Book: Manual Designed for Use in Baptist Churches*. Texarkana, TX: Baptist Sunday School Committee, 1927.

Briggs, John H. Y. "English Baptists and Their Hymnody: An Introduction." In *Baptist Faith and Witness*, edited by William H. Brackney and L.A. Cupit. McLean, VA: Samford University Press and Baptist World Alliance, 1995.

Buffington, W. L. "Clerical Titles Among Baptists." *Chronicle* (1942): 97.

Davies, Horton. *Worship and Theology in England: From Cranmer to Baxter and Fox, 1534-1690*. 2 vols. Princeton, NJ: Princeton University Press, 1970-1975.

Deweese, Charles W. *Baptist Church Covenants*. Nashville, TN: Broadman Press, 1990.

Dorgan, Howard. *Giving Glory to God in Appalachia: Worship Practices of Six Baptist Subdenominations.* Knoxville, TN: University of Tennessee Press, 1987.

Farnsley, Arthur E. *Southern Baptist Politics: Authority and Power in the Restructuring of an American Denomination.* University Park, PA: Pennsylvania State University Press, 1994.

Ford, Murray J. S., editor. *Canadian Baptist History and Polity: The McMaster Conference.* Brantford, ON: Hurley Publishing Co., 1982.

Graves, James R. *Old Landmarkism: What Is It?* Texarkana, AK: Baptist Sunday School Committee, 1880, 1928.

Griffiths, Benjamin. "Essay on the Association." In *Minutes of the Philadelphia Baptist Association A.D. 1707- A.D. 1807,* edited by Abraham D. Gillette. Philadelphia, PA: American Baptist Publication Society, 1851.

Hall, Robert, Jr. *On Terms of Communion, With a Particular View to the Case of the Baptists and the Paedobaptists.* Leicester, England: Thomas Combe, 1815.

Handy, Robert T. "American Baptist Polity: What's Happening and Why?" *Baptist History and Heritage* 14:3 (July 1979): 12-21.

Harkness, R. E. E. "Origin of the Prayer-Meeting Among English and American Baptists." *Chronicle* 1:4 (October 1938): 149-161.

Harrison, Paul M. *Authority and Power in the Free Church Tradition.* Princeton, NJ: Princeton University Press, 1959.

Hiscox, Edward T. *The Standard Manual for Baptist Churches.* Philadelphia, PA: American Baptist Publication Society, 1890.

Holmes, Elkanah. *A Church Covenant, Including a Summary of the Fundamental Doctrines of the Gospel.* Baltimore, MD: 1818.

Hudson, Winthrop S., editor. *Baptist Concepts of the Church.* Valley Forge, PA: Judson Press, 1959.

Jones, Samuel. *A Treatise on Church Discipline.* Philadelphia, PA: S. C. Ustick, 1798.

Lord, F. Townley. *Baptist World Fellowship: A Short History of the Baptist World Alliance.* Nashville, TN: Broadman Press, 1955.

Maring, Norman H. *A Baptist Manual of Polity and Practice.* Valley Forge, PA: Judson Press, 1993.

McNutt, William R. *Polity and Practice in Baptist Churches.* Philadelphia, PA: Judson Press, 1935.

Pendleton, James M. *Church Manual, Designed for the Use of Baptist Churches.* Philadelphia, PA: American Baptist Publication Society, 1867.

Robinson, H. Wheeler. *The Life and Faith of the Baptists.* London: Methuen, 1927.

Sacks, Francis. *The Philadelphia Tradition of Church and Church Authority: An Ecumenical Analysis and Theological Interpretation.* Lewiston, NY: Edwin Mellen Press, 1990.

Shurden, Walter. *Associationalism Among Baptists in America: 1707-1814.* New York: Arno Press, 1980.

Stoffer, Dale R., editor. *The Lord's Supper: Believers Church Perspectives.* Scottdale, PA: Herald Press, 1997.

Sullivan, James L. *Baptist Polity As I See It.* Nashville, TN: Broadman Press, 1983.

Torbet, Robert G. *The Baptist Ministry: Then and Now.* Philadelphia, PA: Judson Press, 1953.

---A Social History of The Philadelphia Baptist Association 1707-1940. Philadelphia, PA: Western Book Publishing Company, 1944.

Walker, Michael. *Baptists at the Table: The Theology of the Lord's Supper amongst English Baptists in the Nineteenth Century.* Didcot: Baptist Historical Society, 1992.

Wilkinson, William C. *The Baptist Principle, in Application to Baptism and the Lord's Supper.* Philadelphia, PA: American Baptist Publication Society, 1897.

Baptists and Other Christians

Boney, W. J., and Iglehart, Glenn A. *Baptists and Ecumenism.* Valley Forge, PA: Judson Press, 1980.

Brackney, William H., editor. *The Believers Church, A Voluntary Church.* Kitchener, ON: Pandora Press, 1998.

Champion, Leonard G. *Baptists and Unity.* London: A. R. Mowbray, 1962.

Estep, William R. *Baptists and Christian Unity.* Nashville, TN: Broadman Press, 1966.

Garrett, James L., editor. *Baptist Relations with Other Christians.* Valley Forge, PA: Judson Press, 1974.

---*Baptists and Roman Catholicism.* Nashville, TN: Broadman Press, 1965.

Gates, Erret. *The Early Relation and Separation of Baptists and Disciples.* Chicago, IL: R. R. Donnelly, 1904.

Gilmore, Alec. *Baptism and Christian Unity.* Valley Forge, PA: Judson Press, 1966.

Goadby, Joseph. *Baptists and Quakers in Northamptonshire, 1650-1700.* Northampton: No Publisher, 1882.

Hinson, E. Glenn. "Southern Baptists and Ecumenism: Some Contemporary Patterns." *Review and Expositor* (Summer 1969): 274.

Hughey, John D. "Baptists and the Ecumenical Movement." *Ecumenical Review* 10:4 (July 1958): 401-410.

Jackson, Joseph H. *Many But One: The Ecumenics of Charity.* New York: Sheed and Ward, 1964.

Payne, Ernest A. *The Fellowship of Believers.* London: Carey Kingsgate, 1954.

Pestana, Carla. *Quakers and Baptists in Colonial Massachusetts.* New York: Cambridge University Press, 1991.

Roberts-Thompson, E. *Baptists and Disciples of Christ.* London: Carey Kingsgate, 1951.

---*With Hands Outstretched: Baptists and the Ecumenical Movement.* London: Marshall, Morgan, and Scott, 1962.

Russell, David S. *Baptists and Some Contemporary Issues.* London: Baptist Union, 1968.

Stubblefield, Jerry M. "The Attitude and Relationship of the Southern Baptist Convention to Certain Other Baptist and Interdenominational Bodies." Unpublished Th.D dissertation, Southern Baptist Theological Seminary, 1967.

Swain, Anna C. "Baptists and Ecumenicity." *Chronicle* 18:2 (April 1955): 70-78.

Toews, Paul, editor. *Mennonites and Baptists: A Continuing Conversation.* Winnipeg, MB: Kindred Press, 1993.

Torbet, Robert G. *Ecumenism: Free Church Dilemma.* Valley Forge, PA: Judson Press, 1958.

Underwood, T. L. *Primitivism, Radicalism, and the Lamb's War: The Baptist-Quaker Conflict in Seventeenth Century England.* New York: Oxford University Press, 1997.

Themes in Baptist History

Ammerman, Nancy. *Baptist Battles: Social Change and Religious Conflict in the Southern Baptist Convention.* New Brunswick, NJ: Rutgers University Press, 1990.

Barnhart, Joe E. *The Southern Baptist Holy War.* Austin, TX: Texas Monthly Press, 1986.

Beale, David O. *SBC: House on the Sand.* Greenville, SC: Unusual Publications, 1985.

Boone, Isley. *Elements in Baptist Development: A Study of Denominational Contributions to National Life, Christian Ideals, and World Movements.* Boston, MA: Backus Historical Society, 1913.

Boylan, Anne M. *Sunday School: The Formation of an American Institution*. New Haven, CT: Yale University Press, 1988.

Brown, J. Newton. *Baptist Martyrs*. Philadelphia, PA: American Baptist Publication Society, 1854.

Brown, Louise F. *The Political Activities of the Baptists and Fifth Monarchy Men in England During the Interregnum*. Washington, DC: American Historical Association, 1912.

Carwardine, Richard. *Trans-Atlantic Revivalism: Popular Evagelicalism in Britain and America, 1790-1865*. Westport, CT: Greenwood Press, 1978.

Cothen, Grady. *What Happened to the Southern Baptist Convention?* Macon, GA: Mercer University Press, 1993.

Davis, Lawrence B. *Immigrants, Baptists, and the Protestant Mind in America*. Urbana, IL: University of Illinois Press, 1973.

Dekar, Paul R. *Baptist Peacemakers*. Macon, GA: Smyth and Helwys, 1993.

Dollar, George W. *A History of Fundamentalism in America*. Greenville, SC: Bob Jones University Press, 1973.

Eighmy, John Lee. *Churches in Cultural Captivity: A History of Social Attitudes of Southern Baptists*. Knoxville, TN: University of Tennessee Press, 1972.

Garrett, James Leo, Hinson, E. Glenn, and Tull, James E. *Are Southern Baptist Evangelicals?* Macon, GA: Mercer University Press, 1983.

Goodwin, Everett, editor. *Baptists in the Balance: The Tension Between Freedom and Responsibility*. Valley Forge, PA: Judson Press, 1997.

Heyrman. Christine L. *Southern Cross: The Beginnings of the Bible Belt*. New York: Alfred Knopf, 1997.

Hindmarsh, Bruce. *John Newton and the English Evangelical Tradition, Between the Conversions of Wesley and Whitefield*. Oxford: Clarendon Press, 1996.

Hudson, Winthrop S. *Baptists in Transition: Individualism and Christian Responsibility*. Valley Forge, PA: Judson Press, 1979.

Lappin, Maitland M. *Baptists in the Protestant Tradition*. Toronto, ON: Ryerson, 1947.

McLoughlin, William G. *Champions of the Cherokees: Evan and John B. Jones*. Princeton, NJ: Princeton University Press, 1990.

Moss, Lemuel. *The Baptists and the National Centenary: A Record of Christian Work: 1776-1876*. Philadelphia, PA: American Baptist Publication Society, 1876.

Newman, Albert H. *A Century of Baptist Achievement*. Philadelphia, PA: American Baptist Publication Society, 1901.

Patterson, W. Morgan. *Baptist Successionism.* Valley Forge, PA: Judson Press, 1969.

Peacock, James, and Tyson, Ruel W. *Pilgrims of Paradox: Calvinism and Experience Among the Primitive Baptists of Blue Ridge.* Washington, DC: Smithsonian Press, 1989.

Putnam, Mary G. *The Baptists and Slavery 1840-45.* Ann Arbor, MI: G. Wahr, 1913.

Shurden, Walter B. *Proclaiming the Baptist Vision: Religious Liberty.* Macon, GA: Smyth and Helwys, 1997.

---, editor, *The Struggle for the Soul of the SBC.* Macon, GA: Mercer University Press, 1993.

Stewart, Howard R. *Baptists and Local Autonomy.* Hicksville, NY: Exposition Press, 1974.

Storey, John W. *Texas Baptist Leadership and Social Christianity. 1900-1980.* College Station, TX: Texas A&M University, 1986.

Thompson, James J. *Tried As By Fire: Southern Baptists and the Religious Controversies of the 1920s.* Macon, GA: Mercer University Press, 1982.

Vedder, Henry C. *Baptists and the Liberty of Conscience.* Cincinnati, OH: J. Bauimes, 1884.

Women in Baptist Life

Bailey, Faith C., and Wenger, Margaret N. *Two Directions.* Rochester, NY: Baptist Missionary Training School, 1964.

Bellinger, Elizabeth, editor. *A Costly O : Sermons by Women of Steadfast Spirit.* Valley Forge, PA: Judson Press, 1994.

Briggs, John. "She-Preachers, Widows and Other Women: The Feminine Dimension in Baptist Life Since 1600." *Baptist Quarterly* 31:7 (July 1986): 337-352.

Brooks, Evelyn. "The Woman's Movement in the Black Baptist Church 1880-1920." Unpublished Ph.D. dissertation, University of Rochester, 1984.

Chatterjee, Sunil K. *Hannah Marshman: The First Woman Missionary In India.* Calcutta: The People's Little Press, 1987.

Daniel, Sadie I. *Women Builders.* Washington, DC: The Association Publishers, 1931.

Dowling, John, editor. *The Judson Offering, Intended as a Token of Christian Sympathy with the Living, and a Memento of Christian Affection for the Dead.* New York: L. Colby, 1846.

McBeth, H. Leon. *Women in Baptist Life*. Nashville, TN: Broadman Press, 1979.

Mitchell, Ella P. *Those Preachin' Women*. 3 vols. Valley Forge, PA: Judson Press, 1985, 1996.

Moore, Joanna P. *In Christ's Stead*. Chicago, IL: Woman's Baptist Home Mission Society, 1902.

Vail, Albert L. *Mary Webb and The Mother Society*. Philadelphia, PA: American Baptist Publication Society, 1914.

Van Brockhoven, Deborah B. *Abolitionists Were Female: Rhode Island Women and the Antislavery Network*. Urbana, IL: University of Illinois Press, 1999.

Vose, Heather M. "The Ministry of Women in the Baptist Churches of the U.S.S.R." In *Faith, Life and Witness*, edited by William H. Brackney. Birmingham, AL: Samford University Press, 1990.

Select Biographies

Abernathy, Ralph David. *And the Walls Came Tumbling Down*. New York: Harper and Row, 1989.

Allen, Catherine B. *The New Lottie Moon Story*. Nashville, TN: Broadman Press, 1980.

Babcock, Rufus, editor. *Memoirs of John Mason Peck, D.D.* Carbondale, IL: Southern Illinois University Press, 1965.

Balders, Gunter. *Theurer Bruder Oncken: Das Leben Johann Gerhard Onckens in Bildern und Dokumenten*. Kassel: Oncken Verlag, 1978.

Beck, James R. *Dorothy Carey: The Tragic and Untold Story of Mrs. William Carey*. Grand Rapids, MI: Baker Book House, 1992.

Benedict, David. *Fifty Years Among the Baptists*. New York: Sheldon, 1860.

Buckingham, William, and Ross, George W. *The Hon. Alexander Mackenzie: His Life and Times*. Toronto, ON: Rose Publishing Co., 1892.

Burgess, Walter H. *John Smyth the Se-Baptist, Thomas Helwys and the First Baptist Church in England*. London: James Clarke, 1911.

Burton, Joe W. *Road to Augusta: R.B.C. Howell and the Formation of the Southern Baptist Convention*. Nashville, TN: Broadman Press, 1976.

Byrt, G. W. *John Clifford: A Fighting Free Churchman*. London: Carey Kingsgate Press, 1947.

Camp, L. Raymond. *Roger Williams: God's Apostle of Advocacy: Biography and Rhetoric*. Lewiston, NY: Edwin Mellen Press, 1993.

Carey, John J. *Carlyle Marney: A Pilgrim's Progress*. Macon, GA: Mercer University Press, 1980.

Carlton, John W. *The World in His Heart: The Life and Legacy of Theodore F. Adams*. Nashville, TN: Broadman Press, 1985.

Carter, Joseph R. *The 'Acres of Diamond Man': A Memorial Archive of Russell H. Conwell*. 3 vols. Phildelphia, PA: Temple University, 1981.

Chaplin, Jeremiah. *Life of Henry Dunster: First President of Harvard College*. Boston, MA: J. R. Osgood, 1872.

Clark, Robert W. "The Contribution of Shailer Mathews to the Social Movement in American Protesrtantism." Unpublished Th.D dissertation, Southern Baptist Theological Seminary, 1959.

Cuthbert, James H. *Life of Richard Fuller D.D.* New York: Sheldon, 1879.

Davies, David. *Vavasor Powell: The Baptist Evangelist of Wales in the Seventeenth Century*. London: Alexander and Shepheard, 1896.

Davis, John W. "George Leile and Andrew Bryan, Pioneer Negro Baptist Preachers." *Journal of Negro History* 3:2 (April 1918): 119-127.

Day, Richard E. *Rhapsody in Black: The Life Story of John Jasper*. Philadelphia, PA: Judson Press, 1953.

Dill, Jacob S. *Isaac Taylor Tichenor, The Home Mission Statesman*. Nashville, TN: Sunday School Board, 1897.

Douglas, Crerar, editor. *Autobiography of Augustus Hopkins Strong*. Valley Forge, PA: Judson Press, 1981.

Elliott, David R., and Miller, Iris. *Bible Bill: A Biography of William Aberhart*. Edmonton, AB: Reidmore Books, 1987.

Elliott, Ralph H. *The Genesis Controversy and Continuity in Southern Baptist Chaos-A Eulogy for a Great Tradition*. Macon, GA: Mercer University Press, 1992.

Fletcher, Jesse. *Baker James Cauthen--A Man for All Nations*. Nashville, TN: Broadman Press, 1977.

Fosdick, Harry Emerson. *The Living of These Days: An Autobiography*. New York: Harper and Brothers, 1956.

Franklin, John Hope. *George Washington Williams: A Biography*. Chicago: University of Chicago Press, 1985.

Gano, John. *Biographical Memoirs of the Late John Gano of Frankfort, Kentucky, formerly of the City of New York*. New York: Southwick and Hardcastle, 1806.

Gaustad, Edwin S., editor. *Baptist Piety: The Last Will and Testament of Obadiah Holmes*. New York: Arno Press, 1980.

---*Liberty of Conscience: Roger Williams in America*. Grand Rapids, MI: Wm. B. Eerdmans, 1991.

Gayle, Clement. *George Leile: Pioneer Missionary to Jamaica.* Kingston: Baptist Union of Jamaica, 1982.

Gibson, Theo T. *Beyond the Granite Curtain: The Story of Alexander McDonald: Pioneer Baptist Missionary to the Canadian North-West.* Ancaster, ON: The Author, 1975.

---*Robert A. Fyfe: His Contemporaries and His Influence.* Burlington, ON: G. R. Welch, 1988.

Gilpin, W. Clark. *The Millennarian Piety of Roger Williams.* Chicago: University of Chicago Press, 1979.

Green, Bernard. *Tomorrow's Man: A Biography of James Henry Rushbrooke.* Didcot, England: The Baptist Historical Society, 1997.

Greene, Louise F. *The Writings of John Leland.* New York: Arno Press, 1969.

Guild, Reuben A. *Life, Times, and Correspondence of James Manning.* Boston, MA: Gould and Lincoln, 1864.

---*Chaplain Smith and the Baptists.* Philadelphia, PA: American Baptist Publication Society, 1885.

Hardin, Shields T. *The Colgate Story.* New York: Vantage Press, 1959.

Harlin, Louis R. *Booker T. Washington: The Making of a Black Leader 1856-1915.* 2 vols. New York: Oxford University Press, 1972, 1983.

Hatcher, *William E. Life of J.B. Jeter, D.D.* Baltimore, MD: H. M. Wharton, 1887.

Haykin, Michael A. G. *One Heart and One Soul: John Sutcliff of Olney, His Friends and His Times.* Durham: Evangelical Press, 1994.

Hines, Herbert W. *Clough: The Kingdom-Builder in South India.* Philadelphia, PA: Judson Press, 1929.

Hinton, John H. *Memoir of William Knibb, Missionary in Jamaica.* London: Houlston and Stoneman, 1847.

Hovey, George Rice. *Alvah Hovey: His Life and Letters.* Philadelphia, PA: Judson Press, 1928.

Hynes, W. *Shirley Jackson Case and the Chicago School: The Socio-Historical Method.* 1981.

James, Powhatan W. *George W. Truett: A Biography.* New York: The Macmillan Co., 1939.

Jeffrey, R. *Autobiography of Elder Jacob Knapp.* New York: Sheldon, 1868.

Jeter, Jeremiah Bell. *Recollections of a Long Life.* Richmond, VA: Religious Herald Publishing Co., 1880.

King, Martin Luther, Sr. *Daddy King: An Autobiography.* New York: William Morrow, 1980.

Kruppa, Patricia S. *Charles Haddon Spurgeon: A Preacher's Progress.* New York: Garland Press, 1982.

Lukey, Hans. *Gottfried Wilhelm Lehmann und die Entstehung einer deutschen Freikirche*. Kassel, Germany: Verlag Oncken, 1959.

Lynd, S. W. Lynd. *Memoir of the Rev. William Staughton D.D.* Boston, MA: Lincoln and Edmands, 1834.

Mallary, Charles D. *Memoirs of Elder Jesse Mercer*. New York: J. Gray, 1844.

Marchant, James. *Dr. John Clifford: Life, Letters, and Reminiscences*. London: Cassell and Co., 1924.

Marks, Marilla. *Memoirs of the Life of David Marks*. Dover, NH: Freewill Baptist Printing Establishment, 1846.

Marshman, John C. *The Life and Labors of Carey, Marshman & Ward, The Serampore Missionaries*. New York: U. D. Ward, 1867.

McDormand, Thomas B. *A Diversified Ministry: An Autobiography of Thomas B. McDormand*. Hantsport, NS: Lancelot Press, 1987.

Mellette, Peter. "Alexander Mackenzie, An Example of Christian Statesmanship." *Chronicle* 7:4 (October 1944): 171-181.

Mild, Warren P. *Howard Malcolm and the Great Mission Advance*. Valley Forge, PA: Board of International Ministries, 1988.

Miller, Robert M. *Harry Emerson Fosdick: Preacher, Pastor, Prophet*. New York: Oxford University Press, 1985.

Minus, Paul M. *Walter Rauschenbusch: American Reformer*. New York; Macmillan, 1988.

Murray, James O. *Francis Wayland*. Boston, MA: Houghton Mifflin, 1891.

Nelson, Wilbur. *The Hero of Aquidneck: A Life of John Clarke*. New York: Fleming H. Revell, 1983.

Oates, Stephen B. *Let The Trumpet Sound: The Life of Martin Luther King, Jr.* London: Search Press, 1982.

Owens, Loulie L. *Oliver Hart, 1723-1795: A Biography*. Greenville, SC: 1966.

Parker, F. Calvin. *Jonathan Goble of Japan: Marine, Missionary, Maverick*. Lanham, MD: University Press of America, 1990.

Perkin, J. R. C. *Morning in His Heart: A Biographical Sketch of Watson Kirkconnell 1895-1977*. Hantsport, NS: Lancelot Press, 1986.

Pipkin, H. Wayne, and Yoder, John H., editors. *Balthasar Hubmaier: Theologian of Anabaptism*. Scottdale, PA: Herald Press, 1989.

Powell, Adam Clayton, Jr. *Against the Tide*. New York: Arno Press, 1980.

Prestridge, J. N. *Modern Baptist Heroes and Martyrs*. Louisville, KY: World Press, 1911.

Reid, C. S. *Samuel Sharpe: From Slave to National Hero*. Montego Bay: The Bustamente Institute of Public Affairs, 1988.

Robertson, Archibald T. *Life and Letters of John Albert Broadus*. Philadelphia, PA: American Baptist Publication Society.

Rogers, James A. *Richard Furman: Life and Legacy*. Macon, GA: Mercer University Press, 1985.

Russell, C. Allyn. *Voices of American Fundamentalism; Seven Biographical Studies*. Philadelphia, PA: Westminster Press, 1976.

Saker, Emily H. *Alfred Saker, the Pioneer of the Cameroons*. London: Religious Tract Society, 1908.

Sears, Charles H. *Edward Judson: Interpreter of God*. Philadelphia, PA: American Baptist Publication Society, 1917.

Smith, Elias. *The Life, Conversion, Preaching, Travels and Suffering of Elias Smith*. Portsmouth, NH: Beck and Foster, 1816.

Smith, Luther E., Jr. *Howard Thurman: The Mystic as Prophet*. Lanham, MD: University Press of America, 1981.

Sorrill, Bobbie. *Annie Armstrong: Dreamer in Action*. Nashville, TN: Broadman Press, 1984.

Steadman, Thomas. *Memoir of the Rev. William Steadman D.D.* London: Thomas Ward, 1838.

Stearns, W. O. *William Newton Clarke: A Biography*. New York: Charles Scribner's, 1916.

Sweeny, Joseph R. "Elhanan Winchester and the Universal Baptists." Unpublished Ph.D. dissertation, University of Pennsylvania, 1969.

Tarr, Leslie K. *Shields of Canada: T. T. Shields (1873-1955)*. Grand Rapids, MI: Baker Book House, 1967.

Taylor, George B. *Life and Times of James B. Taylor*. Philadelphia, PA: Bible and Publication Society, 1872.

Thompson, Helen W. *Luther Rice: Believer in Tomorrow*. Nashville, TN: Broadman Press, 1967.

Thurman, Howard. *With Head and Heart: Autobiography of Howard Thurman*. New York: Harcourt, Brace, Jovanovich, 1979.

Tull, James E. *Shapers of Baptist Thought*. Valley Forge, PA: Judson Press, 1972.

Vick, Joyce. *From Victory to Victory: A Biography of Dr. G. B. Vick*. Akron, OH: n.p., n.d.

Wacker, Grant. *Augustus H. Strong and the Dilemma of Historical Consciousness*. Macon, GA: Mercer University Press, 1985.

Walden, Viola. *John R. Rice: The Captain of Our Team*. Murfreesboro, TN: Sword of the Lord Press, 1990.

Washington, James M., editor. *A Testament of Hope: The Essential Writings of Martin Luther King, Jr.* San Francisco, CA: Harper and Row, 1991?

West, W. M. S. *To Be A Pilgrim: A Memoir of Ernest A. Payne*. Guildford, England: Lutterworth Press, 1983.

Williams, A. D. *Benoni Stinson and the General Baptists*. Owensville, IN: General Baptist Press, 1880.

Wood, H. G. Terrot Reaveley Glover: A Biography. Cambridge: Cambridge University Press, 1953.

Woodson, Hortense. *Giant in the Land: A Biography of William Bullein Johnson, First President of the Southern Baptist Convention*. Nashville, TN: Broadman Press, 1950.

Libraries and Archival Repositories

American Baptist Historical Society. Rochester, New York and Valley Forge, Pennsylvania

Anabaptist and Baptist Collection, Baptist Theological Seminary. Prague, Czech Republic

Angus Library, Regent's Park College. Oxford, England

Atlantic Baptist Archives, Acadia University. Wolfville, Nova Scotia

Baptist Union of Sweden Archives, Betelseminariat. Stockholm, Sweden

Canadian Baptist Archives, McMaster University. Hamilton, Ontario

Dr. Williams' Library. Gordon Square, London, England

Franklin Trask Library, Andover Newton Theological School. Newton Centre, Massachusetts

Free Baptist Collection, Bates College. Lewiston, Maine

Freewill Baptist Collection, Mt. Olive College. Mt. Olive, North Carolina

Georgia Baptist Historical Collection. Mercer University, Macon, Georgia

German Union Archives, Theological Seminary. Elstal, Germany

Hungarian Baptist Archives, Baptista Teological Szeminarium. Budapest, Hungary

Irish Baptist Historical Society. Belfast, Northern Ireland

Italian Baptist Archives, Centro Filadelfia. Turin, Italy

John Hay Library, Brown University. Providence, Rhode Island

John Rylands Library of Manchester University. Manchester, England

North American Baptist Archives (German), North American Baptist Seminary. Sioux Falls, South Dakota.

Norwegian Baptist Archives, Theological Seminary. Stabbek, Norway

Polish Baptist Historical Archives, Church House, Warsaw, Poland

Swedish Baptist Archives, Betelseminariat. Stockholm, Sweden.

Scottish Baptist Archives, Baptist Theological College. Glasgow, Scotland

Southern Baptist Historical Collection. Nashville, Tennessee

Swedish Baptist Archives, Betelseminariat. Stockholm, Sweden

Swedish Baptist Collection, Bethel College. St. Paul, Minnesota

Virginia Baptist Historical Collection, University of Richmond. Richmond, Virginia

Welsh Baptist Historical Collection, Ilston House. Swansea, Wales

About the Author

William H. Brackney is principal of McMaster Divinity College and professor of historical theology at McMaster University in Hamilton, Ontario. He holds degrees from the University of Maryland (B.A., hons.), The Eastern Baptist Theological Seminary (M.A.R.), and Temple University (M.A., Ph.D.), and has taught religion and history at Houghton College, Colgate Rochester Divinity School, and The Eastern Baptist Theological Seminary. He has served as executive director and archivist for the American Baptist Historical Society and chair of the Division of Study and Research of the Baptist World Alliance. Previously he has published *Baptist Life and Thought* (1983, 1998), *The Baptists* (1988), and *Christian Voluntarism: Theology and Praxis* (1997).